Strategic Human Resource Management

Strategic Human Resource Management

Edited by Nina Clarke

Clanrye International
www.clanryeinternational.com

Clanrye International,
750 Third Avenue, 9th Floor,
New York, NY 10017, USA

ISBN: 978-1-64726-083-5

Cataloging-in-Publication Data

Strategic human resource management / edited by Nina Clarke.
p. cm.
Includes bibliographical references and index.
ISBN 978-1-64726-083-5
1. Personnel management. 2. Strategic planning. 3. Management. I. Clarke, Nina.
HF5549 .S77 2021
658.3--dc23

For information on all Clanrye International publications visit our website at www.clanryeinternational.com

Clanrye International

Contents

Preface

This book has been a concerted effort by a group of academicians, researchers and scientists, who have contributed their research works for the realization of the book. This book has materialized in the wake of emerging advancements and innovations in this field. Therefore, the need of the hour was to compile all the required researches and disseminate the knowledge to a broad spectrum of people comprising of students, researchers and specialists of the field.

The strategic approach to the effective management of people in a company or organization is known as human resource management, or HRM. This is usually done in order to enable the business gain a competitive advantage by maximizing the performance of the employees. The principle concerns of human resource management is the management of people within organizations while focusing on the systems and policies. There are several key roles within the organization which are performed by the HR department such as employee recruitment and performance appraisal. Reward management and overseeing employee benefits design are a few more areas which fall under this domain. This book discusses the fundamentals as well as modern approaches of human resource management in a strategic manner. It presents researches and studies performed by experts across the globe. Those in search of information to further their knowledge will be greatly assisted by this book.

At the end of the preface, I would like to thank the authors for their brilliant chapters and the publisher for guiding us all-through the making of the book till its final stage. Also, I would like to thank my family for providing the support and encouragement throughout my academic career and research projects.

Editor

1

Can transformational managers control turnover intention?

Author:
Massad A. Alatawi[1]

Affiliation:
[1]Department of Management, Taibah University, Saudi Arabia

Corresponding author:
Massad Alatawi,
matawi@taibahu.edu.sa

Orientation and research purpose: Employee turnover is a complex phenomenon that has negative consequences for organisations. The purpose of this study was to measure the correlation between transformational leadership style and turnover intention to control the employee turnover rate in organisations.

Research method: This study utilised a two-stage clustering method and web-based survey research with a correlational design to collect the data. A total of 356 responses were collected from 14 clusters in Southern California; however, the final selected data for analysis came from 210 subjects with a cluster-sampling design of (14 × 15).

Main findings and managerial implications: This study concluded that the transformational leadership style has a negative correlation with turnover intention. Managers who adopt this style of leadership can expect lower rates of turnover; thus, they can stay competitive in an unstable economy and achieve enhanced productivity, improved performance and reduction in expenses.

Introduction

Employee turnover is a complicated, continuous issue that affects the stability of the organisational climate, performance, productivity and the retention of the qualified employees. Abassi and Hollman (2000) represented employee turnover as the rotation of workers around the labour market; between organisations, jobs and occupations; and between the conditions of employment and unemployment. The expenses identified with employee turnover were evaluated to run from 25% to 500% of the annual compensation of a worker, with an average of $13 996 per worker. The high cost of employee turnover comprises human resources (HR) expenses such as recruiting, hiring and training costs and is connected with measures of productivity and performance of organisations (Ballinger, Craig, Cross & Gray, 2011; O'Connell & Mei-Chuan, 2007). Thus, controlling the employee turnover rate ought to be a priority amongst the most essential organisational goals.

Organisations must minimise expenses, maximise profits, expand productivity and deliberately plan to retain workers with the end goal to stay competitive in an unstable economy. Excessive employee turnover negatively influences organisations by delaying services and minimising profits as organisations attempt to recruit new workers as well as decreasing innovation as qualified workers leave. Most likely, excellent, talented workers are key employees. If they quit their jobs, then their organisations may not be able to finish key business transactions. To the contrary, employee turnover opens doors for newcomers who may carry with them experience, knowledge and innovation. Job changers may find a more advantageous workplace and better compensation (Fitz-Enz & Davison, 2001; Lee, Hsu & Lien, 2006; Mobley, 1982; Stovel & Bontis, 2002). Numerous determinants affect the choice of workers to stay in or quit their jobs; nonetheless, managerial style is known to significantly affect their decisions.

Managerial style alludes to a general form of leadership used by a manager: transformational, transactional or laissez-faire (Rensselaer Polytechnic Institute, 2000). It acts as a principal stimulus for turnover intention inside of organisations. The backgrounds and experiences of managers affect the workers' intention to quit their jobs. Managers with a narrow-minded vision encounter a high employee turnover rate. They may wind up with an untalented workforce because of the loss of talented employees. Workers who stay may be disappointed, unfaithful and perform their undertakings inadequately. They may convey less customised services to clients. At the point when conditions seem to be intolerable, they may consider options and look to change their employment (Abassi & Hollman, 2000; Lee et al., 2006; Mobley, 1982; Price, 2001; Stovel & Bontis, 2002). Employee turnover is a complex issue to examine.

Researchers examining employee turnover have experienced difficulty following the individuals who left their organisations; accordingly, this study measured the turnover intention rather than the actual turnover behaviour of employees. Turnover intention alludes to the extent to which employees plan to cease their membership with their organisations (Price, 2001). As it was stated earlier, turnover intention is a complex phenomenon that has negative consequences for organisations and needs close managerial attention. This study researched whether there was a connection between transformational leadership style and turnover intention to improve employee retention in Southern California. Subsequently, managers can adopt this managerial style with the aim to lower turnover rates amongst their workers, accordingly enhancing productivity, improving performance and reducing expenses. The purpose of this study was to measure the correlation between transformational leadership style and turnover intention to control the employee turnover rate in organisations.

Some studies (e.g. Griffith, 2004; Kleinman, 2004; Walumbwa & Lawler, 2003; Walumbwa, Wang, Lawler & Shi, 2004) have examined the relationship between transformational leadership style and turnover intention. Insufficient information is known about the impact of transformational leadership style on turnover intention (Griffith, 2004; Kleinman, 2004; Walumbwa & Lawler, 2003; Walumbwa et al., 2004). In one study, Griffith (2004) revealed that school principal transformational leadership has an indirect negative impact, through job satisfaction, on school staff turnover. In addition to the effect measured in schools, Walumbwa and Lawler (2003) and Walumbwa et al. (2004) stated that transformational leadership style is negatively related to turnover intention in other work settings. Dissimilarly, Kleinman (2004) showed that transformational leadership style is not significantly linked to staff nurse turnover. Certainly, previous studies are contradictory in their conclusions regarding the association of transformational leadership style with turnover intention.

Besides the attempt to remove the contradiction in previous research regarding the linkage between transformational leadership style and turnover intention, one of the significances of this study was its diverse sample of organisations, because occupational diversity would increase the probability of class diversity, as suggested by Price (2001). Another significance was its focus on only one causal factor of turnover intention, namely managerial style, as suggested by Ongori (2007).

Literature review

Managerial style – the characteristic decisions, relationships and behaviours of managers – has a considerable effect on the turnover intention of employees (Lee et al., 2006; Price, 2001; Stovel & Bontis, 2002). Dr Lindsay Ryan expressed that the primary reason labourers leave an occupation is that they have been assigned to work under ineffective supervisors (as cited in Lund, 2011). As indicated in an article in *Accountancy* ('Bad Month', 2009), more than half of employees in the banking industry quit their jobs because of ineffective administration, and around half would have been willing to take a pay cut to work with an effective manager. Changing the managerial style of insufficient managers could prompt better employee retention. Managers handle a scope of circumstances all through their day-to-day business schedules and perform numerous functions in their organisations. The basic functions of management include planning, organising, leading and controlling; in any case, these managerial functions no longer fit the 21st century. Employee retention is one of the top undertakings of managers and more essential today than at any other time (Daft, 2012; Lussier & Achua, 2012). Managers ought to change their managerial style throughout today's period of nanotechnology.

The current literature has demonstrated that transformational leadership style is an effective managerial style in all kinds of organisations. The most practiced managerial style by effective managers is transformational. Transformational leadership style is not reserved for exceptional individuals with certain leadership qualities and capacities; anybody can be a transformational leader through education, desire and practice. Organisations can benefit by offering transformational leadership training to their supervisors. The transformational leadership style is an approach that changes workers to fulfil more than what is expected of them and is concerned with vision, staff development, supportive leadership, empowerment, innovative thinking, leading by example and charisma (Avolio, 2011; Carless, Wearing & Mann, 2000; Lussier & Achua, 2012; Northouse, 2010). These seven variables compose the dimensions of the Global Transformational Leadership (GTL) scale, which was developed by Carless et al. (2000; Table 1).

Transformational managers provide employees with a vision, act as coaches, provide a supportive climate, listen for employees' needs, recognise employees' achievements and delegate work to employees. They offer meaning and challenge to employees' work, involve employees in decision-making, encourage teamwork, support autonomy and stimulate excellent task performance. They inspire innovation and promote problem-solving in new ways. They behave as

TABLE 1: Dimensions of Global Transformational Leadership.

Item	Dimension of GTL
1. Communicates a clear, positive vision of the future	Vision
2. Treats staff as individuals, and supports and encourages their development	Staff development
3. Gives encouragement and recognition to staff	Supportive leadership
4. Fosters trust, involvement and cooperation amongst team members	Empowerment
5. Encourages thinking about problems in new ways and questions assumptions	Innovative thinking
6. Is clear about his or her values and practices what he or she preaches	Lead by example
7. Instils pride and respect in others and inspires me by being highly competent	Charisma

Source: Carless, S.A., Wearing, A.J., & Mann, L. (2000). A short measure of transformational leadership. *Journal of Business and Psychology, 14*(3), 396. https://doi.org/10.1023/A:1022991115523

GTL, Global Transformational Leadership.

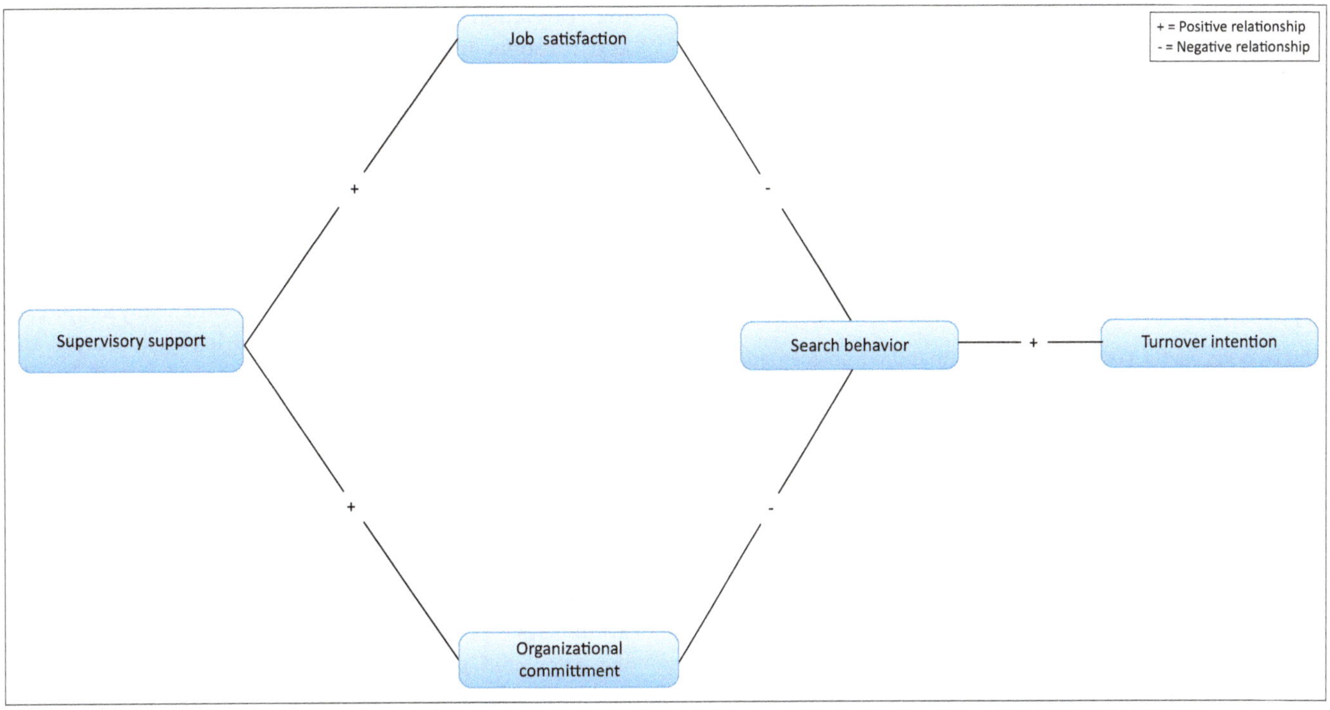

Source: Price, J.L. (2001). Reflections on the determinants of voluntary turnover. *International Journal of Manpower, 22*(7/8), 602. https://doi.org/10.1108/EUM0000000006233

FIGURE 1: A portion of the causal model of turnover.

models for employees and follow through with their promises. They demonstrate enthusiasm and can be trusted and respected to make good decisions for the organisation. One component that distinguishes transformational leadership style from other managerial styles is the inclusion of supportive leadership or supervisory support (Avolio, 2011; Carless et al., 2000; Northouse, 2010).

The causal model of turnover (Figure 1; introduced in 1981 by Price & Mueller) shows supervisory support as a determinant of turnover intention. Supervisory support, meaning help with job-related problems, decreases turnover by its positive influence on both job satisfaction and organisational commitment. Job satisfaction and organisational commitment reduce turnover intention, whereas search behaviour increases turnover intention. For the purpose of this study, transformational leadership style was considered as equivalent to supervisory support. It influences turnover intention through the intervening variables of job satisfaction, organisational commitment and search behaviour (see Figure 1). It decreases turnover intention indirectly by means of a positive influence on job satisfaction and organisational commitment (Price, 2001).

The current literature confirms that transformational leadership style correlates positively with job satisfaction and organisational commitment. In addition, it shows that turnover intention correlates negatively with job satisfaction and organisational commitment. Several studies have demonstrated that workers want to stay with transformational managers. Satisfied workers are less inclined to quit their jobs. Labourers who are supervised by transformational managers are willing to stay with and are loyal to their organisations, even under tough circumstances. Transformational managers encourage employees to overcome difficulties and to be effective in their work, resulting in a decrease in the turnover intention rate (Avolio, 2011; Hetland & Sandal, 2003; Judge & Piccolo, 2004; Kearney, 2008; Lee et al., 2006; Price, 2001; Walumbwa et al., 2004).

Method

Data and sample

This quantitative investigation of the anticipated relationship of a variable thought to be related to turnover intention used survey research with a correlational design and utilised a cluster-sampling method. The sample for this study comprised workers whose managers were members of the Professionals In Human Resources Association (PIHRA). PIHRA is an association that trains its members on perspectives of leadership and HR. It has roughly 3000 members who work in Southern California organisations from all ranges of industry inside of the most financially diverse territory in the nation (PIHRA, 2012). As proposed by Henderson and Sundaresan (1982) and the North Carolina Center for Public Health Preparedness (2012), this study used a two-stage cluster-sampling method. In the first stage, 150 managers (clusters) were chosen randomly, and the final response rate was 51%; however, just 14 clusters were utilised because of the research criteria.[1] In the second stage of cluster sampling, and particularly in December 2012, a total of 356 responses were collected from 14 clusters with a sample error of 5%. Nevertheless, the final selected data for analysis came

1. Some of PIHRA members (clusters) were students and self-employed individuals; thus, the criterion for selecting the managers (clusters) was that each one had to have at least seven employees, and the criterion for selecting the employees (units) was that all the employees had to work full time. Although it was very difficult to secure permission from managers to study their subordinates in many organisations, the desire was to secure a sample size of at least 210 subjects with a (30 × 7) design.

from 210 subjects with a cluster-sampling design of (14 × 15) because the process was controlled to limit over- or under-represented clusters. Therefore, the participants were thought to be representative of all workers in Southern California. Confidentiality was maintained by all means and especially by ensuring information that could be tracked to an individual participant was not included in any reports of this article.

Hypothesis

The hypothesis (H_1) of this study was that the transformational leadership style of PIHRA members is negatively correlated with turnover intention of their subordinates; that is to say that transformational leadership style is predictive of lower levels of turnover intention.

Variables and instrumentation

This study measured the transformational leadership style, the independent variable, through the 7-item GTL scale using a 5-point Likert scale ranging from *rarely or never* to *very frequently, if not always*. Summing the scores of each item and then dividing the sum by seven resulted in a final score for transformational leadership style. A higher score showed that a PIHRA member often demonstrated transformational leadership style. The item 'How often have you seriously considered quitting your present job?' developed by Spector (1985) measured turnover intention, the dependent variable, using a 5-point Likert scale ranging from *rarely or never* to *very frequently, if not always*. A lower score of this item showed that a subordinate of a PIHRA member intended to keep his or her job. To analyse data, the major statistical tests were correlation and regression analytical techniques.

Results

Table 2 shows the aftereffects of the Spearman rho correlation analysis, which demonstrated that there was a moderate, negative significant correlation between transformational leadership style utilised by PIHRA members and the levels of turnover intention amongst their subordinates (r_s = -0.41, p < 0.01). Higher transformational leadership style scores (M = 4.42) were connected with lower levels of turnover intention (M = 1.09). Further calculation concluded that 17% of the variance in the levels of turnover intention amongst PIHRA subordinates was explained by transformational leadership style utilised by PIHRA members.

Table 2 shows characteristics of the Spearman rho correlation coefficient, which is a descriptive measure of the correlation of the transformational leadership style and turnover intention. The t-test value is a measure of the hypothesis that the correlation between transformational leadership style and turnover intention found in the study sample exists in the population comprising subordinates of all PIHRA members. The hypothesis (H_1) was that the two variables are correlated; the null hypothesis (H_0) was that the two variables are not correlated. With 208 degrees of freedom [(n – 2) = (210 – 2) = 208], testing for significance at the 0.01 level, the critical values of ± 2.576 and a calculated t-test value of -6.40, the null hypothesis was rejected. The observed value of r_s is large enough to indicate a statistically significant correlation between transformational leadership style and turnover intention. This finding is corroborated by the calculated p-level of less than 0.01.

TABLE 2: Correlations between transformational leadership style and turnover intention.

Analysis	Score
Spearman's rho	-0.41
t-test value for hypothesis r = 0	-6.40
p-level	< 0.01

The outcomes of bivariate linear regression analyses are demonstrated in Table 3 and indicate that the transformational leadership style used by PIHRA members explained 17% of the variance (R^2 = 0.17, t = -9.45, p < 0.01) in the levels of turnover intention amongst their subordinates. As explained in the above paragraph, the t-value of less than -2.576 and the calculated p < 0.01 showed a regression model with statistically significant predictive power. The outcomes also suggested a regression model in which a one-percentage-point increase in transformational leadership style used by PIHRA members leads to a 0.32% reduction in turnover intention levels of their subordinates (b = -0.32, p < 0.01).

Discussion

This study revealed that the transformational leadership style of PIHRA members is negatively linked to turnover intention of their subordinates. This specific finding is not the same as that of Kleinman (2004), who found that transformational leadership style is not correlated with staff nurse turnover. Notwithstanding, this study's finding is in line with what Griffith (2004), Walumbwa and Lawler (2003) and Walumbwa et al. (2004) concluded about transformational leadership style and its negative correlation with turnover intention. This study's result removes the contradiction in previous research and creates a clearer context for the significance of transformational leadership style and its linkage to controlling employee turnover rate in organisations.

This study contributed that the transformational leadership style of PIHRA members is negatively correlated with turnover intention of their subordinates; that is to say that transformational leadership style is predictive of lower levels of turnover intention. The after-effect of this study can be generalised to most of the organisations in Southern California. This study adds insight to the body of knowledge concerning transformational leadership style and its significance to the retention of employees. It recognises the

TABLE 3: Linear regression of transformational leadership style and turnover intention.

Linear regression	Coefficients (b)	Standard error	t	p
Intercept	2.51	0.15	16.59	< 0.01
Transformational leadership style	-0.32	0.03	-9.45	< 0.01

negative relationship between transformational leadership style and turnover intention; hence, managers can apply transformational leadership as their managerial style with the expectation of a lower turnover rate. Consequently, they can stay competitive in an unstable economy and achieve enhanced productivity, improved performance and reduction in expenses.

This study revealed that supervisors with a transformational leadership style could be recruited. It found that the mean score of transformational leadership style was high (M = 4.42), showing that the participants' managers every now and again apply transformational leadership style in their organisations and that their enrolment in PIHRA has paid off. This outcome is in accordance with the current literature that shows transformational leadership is not reserved for individuals with exceptional attributes and capacities; rather, anyone can be transformational (Avolio, 2011; Carless et al., 2000; Lussier & Achua, 2012; Northouse, 2010). Managers can be transformational by (1) planning for the future, (2) coaching workers, (3) supporting workers to develop in their jobs and acknowledging their effort and achievement, (4) including employees in the decision-making process, (5) inspiring innovation, (6) being honest and following the rules and (7) acting as change specialists. Finally, they must practice regularly because mastering transformational leadership style takes time, exertion and commitment.

This study inferred that transformational leadership style is an effective managerial style. Managers should change their managerial style for the high-tech business world. They ought to enhance their transformational leadership abilities and skills. It is recommended that managers attend seminars, webinars or workshops, or join associations that teach and train their members on concepts of transformational leadership style. When recruiting new managers, HR managers ought to select transformational candidates keeping in mind the end goal to profit by enhancing the retention of employees. Organisations should train their current managers on transformational leadership style to improve the organisational climate. Business pioneers must be transformational; otherwise, the small-business labourers may leave, and as an outcome, the business may shut down.

The literature showed that a disagreeable managerial style is perhaps one of the reasons for the turnover intention phenomenon. However, if ineffective managers drive workers to intend to quit their jobs, it does not imply that effective managers drive workers to keep their jobs. Consequently, a suggested study would comprise experimental research to explore the cause–effect relationship of transformational leadership style and employee retention. The low mean score of intention to quit (M = 1.09) shows that the state of the economy (whilst conducting this research in 2012) may have impacted the members' choices about keeping their occupations and, consequently, may have affected the correlation measured between transformational leadership style and turnover intention. Further research is recommended to duplicate this study when the economy has recovered. Future studies concerning transformational leadership ought to utilise the GTL scale because it is reliable, valid, short and practical.

Finally, future research is suggested to replicate this study and look at a nondemocratic country to see if similar conclusions would be found about the relationship between transformational leadership style and turnover intention. This study has been carried out in the United States; therefore, it is reasonable to suppose that democratic, capitalistic countries are the areas to which the outcomes of this study apply. Yet, it would be interesting to see whether or not similar findings would be found in nondemocratic countries.

Conclusion

To conclude, this study made a contribution to the knowledge on the significance of transformational leadership style to the employee retention. It found a negative correlation between transformational leadership style and turnover intention. It found that a slight increase in transformational leadership style leads to a decrease in the levels of turnover intention among employees. Hiring or training transformational managers supports essentially control turnover. Managers should obtain transformational leadership behaviors and skills in order to reduce the turnover intention among their employees. Everyone can be transformational by practicing the behaviours and skills of this style.

Acknowledgements

The author thanks Dr Casey Goodall for comments that greatly improved the manuscript. Without Dr Goodall's thoughts and ideas, this manuscript would not appear in its great shape as it does.

Competing interests

The author declares that he has no financial or personal relationships that may have inappropriately influenced him in writing this article.

References

Abassi, S.M., & Hollman, K.W. (2000). Turnover: The real bottom line. *Public Personnel Management, 29*(3), 333–342. https://doi.org/10.1177/009102600002900303

Avolio, B.J. (2011). *Full range leadership development.* (2nd edn.). Thousand Oaks, CA: Sage.

Bad month: British managers. (2009). *Accountancy, 144*(1396), 12.

Ballinger, G., Craig, E., Cross, R., & Gray, P. (2011). A stitch in time saves nine: Leveraging networks to reduce the costs of turnover. *California Management Review, 53*(4), 111–133. https://doi.org/10.1525/cmr.2011.53.4.111

Carless, S.A., Wearing, A.J., & Mann, L. (2000). A short measure of transformational leadership. *Journal of Business and Psychology, 14*(3), 389–405. https://doi.org/10.1023/A:1022991115523

Daft, R.L. (2012). *Management.* (10th edn.). Mason, OH: South-Western.

Fitz-Enz, J., & Davison, B. (2001). *How to measure human resource management.* (3rd edn.). New York: McGraw-Hill.

Griffith, J. (2004). Relation of principal transformational leadership to school staff job satisfaction, staff turnover, and school performance. *Journal of Educational Administration, 42*(3), 333–356. https://doi.org/10.1108/09578230410534667

Henderson, R.H., & Sundaresan, T. (1982). Cluster sampling to assess immunization coverage: A review of experience with a simplified sampling method. *Bulletin of the World Health Organization, 60*(2), 253–260.

Hetland, H., & Sandal, G.M. (2003). Transformational leadership in Norway: Outcomes and personality correlates. *European Journal of Work & Organizational Psychology, 12*(2), 147. https://doi.org/10.1080/13594320344000057

Judge, T.A., & Piccolo, R.F. (2004). Transformational and transactional leadership: A meta-analytic test of their relative validity. *Journal of Applied Psychology, 89*(5), 755–768. https://doi.org/10.1037/0021-9010.89.5.755

Kearney, E. (2008). Age differences between leader and followers as a moderator of the relationship between transformational leadership and team performance. *Journal of Occupational & Organizational Psychology, 81*(4), 803–811. https://doi.org/10.1348/096317907X256717

Kleinman, C. (2004). The relationship between managerial leadership behaviors and staff nurse retention. *Hospital Topics, 82*(4), 2–9. https://doi.org/10.3200/HTPS.82.4.2-9

Lee, C., Hsu, M., & Lien, N. (2006). The impacts of benefit plans on employee turnover: A firm-level analysis approach on Taiwanese manufacturing industry. *International Journal of Human Resource Management, 17*(11), 1951–1975. https://doi.org/10.1080/09585190601000154

Lund, M. (2011, August). How bad managers lose good staff. *The Courier Mail (Brisbane)*, p. 4.

Lussier, R.N., & Achua, C.F. (2012). *Leadership: Theory, application, and skill development.* (5th edn.). Cincinnati, OH: South-Western College.

Mobley, W.H. (1982). *Employee turnover: Causes, consequences, and control.* Reading, MA: Addison-Wesley.

North Carolina Center for Public Health Preparedness. (2012). *Two-stage cluster sampling: General guidance for use in public health assessments.* Retrieved January 06, 2012, from http://cphp.sph.unc.edu/PHRST5/TwoStageSampling.pdf

Northouse, P.G. (2010). *Leadership theory and practice.* (5th edn.). Thousand Oaks, CA: Sage.

O'Connell, M., & Mei-Chuan, K. (2007). The cost of employee turnover. *Industrial Management, 49*(1), 14–19.

Ongori, H. (2007). A review of the literature on employee turnover. *African Journal of Business Management*, 49–54. Retrieved June 13, 2011, from http://www.academicjournals.org/AJBM/pdf/pdf2007/jun/ongori.pdf

Price, J.L. (2001). Reflections on the determinants of voluntary turnover. *International Journal of Manpower, 22*(7/8), 600–624. https://doi.org/10.1108/EUM0000000006233

Price, J.L., & Mueller, C.W. (1981). A causal model of turnover for nurses. *Academy of Management Journal, 24*(3), 543–565. https://doi.org/10.2307/255574

Professionals In Human Resources Association (PIHRA). (2012). *About PIHRA: Facts.* Retrieved January 05, 2012, from http://pihra.org/displaycommon.cfm?an=1&subarticlenbr=194

Rensselaer Polytechnic Institute. (2000, July 17). *Management styles.* Retrieved December 12, 2011, from http://www.rpi.edu/dept/advising/free_enterprise/business_structures/management_styles.htm

Spector, P.E. (1985). Measurement of human service staff satisfaction: Development of the job satisfaction survey. *American Journal of Community Psychology, 13*(6), 693–713. https://doi.org/10.1007/BF00929796

Stovel, M., & Bontis, N. (2002). Voluntary turnover: Knowledge management friend or foe? *Journal of Intellectual Capital, 3*(3), 303–322. https://doi.org/10.1108/14691930210435633

Walumbwa, F.O., & Lawler, J.J. (2003). Building effective organizations: Transformational leadership, collectivist orientation, work-related attitudes, and withdrawal behaviors in three emerging economies. *International Journal of Human Resource Management, 14*(7), 1083–1101. https://doi.org/10.1080/0958519032000114219

Walumbwa, F.O., Wang, P., Lawler, J.J., & Shi, K. (2004). The role of collective efficacy in the relations between transformational leadership and work outcomes. *Journal of Occupational & Organizational Psychology, 77*(4), 515–530. https://doi.org/10.1348/0963179042596441

2

Factors influencing the intention to use social media for work-related purposes at a South African higher education institution

Authors:
Liezel Cilliers[1]
Willie T. Chinyamurindi[2]
Kim Viljoen[2]

Affiliations:
[1]Department of Information Systems, University of Fort Hare, South Africa

[2]Department of Business Management, University of Fort Hare, South Africa

Corresponding author:
Liezel Cilliers,
lcilliers@ufh.ac.za

Orientation: The rapid development of information communication technology (ICT) has changed much of contemporary society. ICT's influence extends to the working context with ramifications not only for employees but also for the entire organisation.

Research purpose: The primary purpose of this research was to investigate the behavioural intention of a sample of employees at a traditional higher education institution to make use of social media within the workplace.

Motivation for the study: Social media has become a common tool within society for communication and networking purposes. An understanding of the factors that influence behavioural intention to use social media within the workplace can assist the organisation to better manage social media usage within the workplace.

Research design, approach and method: The research adopted the positivism paradigm with a quantitative research approach. The data were analysed making use of exploratory factor analysis and multiple regression analysis. A traditional higher education institution was chosen as the research site for the study, relying on a convenience sample (n = 134) and data gathered using the work-related social media scale and behavioural intention to use scale.

Main findings: Although most employees make use of social media for problem-solving and communication purposes already in the workplace, organisations should allow their employees to help manage their reputation on social media.

Practical and managerial implications: An understanding of the factors that influence behavioural intention to use social media within the workplace can serve as a useful precursor for both employee and organisational-specific interventions. This study has specific relevance to the use of ICT platforms, such as social media, in traditional higher education institutions in South Africa. The study's results are therefore useful to both employees as end-users and managers as drivers of such interventions in the workplace.

Contribution: This study is one of the first within a South African work context to investigate social media usage in a traditional higher education institution and proposes a workplace social media usage framework (WSMUF) that helps not only employees but also the entire organisation to predict intention to use social media in the workplace.

Introduction

The rapid development of information and communication technologies (ICT) has changed how the workplace functions. Social media is seen as a powerful tool that can be used for a variety of purposes within the workplace, resulting in organisations dedicating a separate budget for this activity (Hysa, Mularczyk & Zdonek, 2015; Nielsen, 2013). More and more organisations are including social media in their marketing activities, market research, customer service, recruitment and promotion strategies (Gerber, 2016; Okazaki & Taylor, 2013). In accordance with this trend, Chinyamurindi and Louw (2010) argue that more research should be conducted that focuses on technology within the South African context.

Social media is defined as 'a group of Internet-based applications that build on the ideological and technological foundations of Web 2.0, and that allow for the creation and exchange of user-generated content' (Kaplan & Haenlein, 2010, p. 60). The decision to include social media in the organisation's business strategies is motivated by several factors. These include the convenience of using social media services, greater awareness of the benefits that may be gained through social media tools and access to potential recruits with the possibility of disseminating information to a wider audience (Palonka & Porebska-Miac, 2014). For the customer, social media provides an online communication platform to discuss their favourite brands or raise concerns about the organisation (Stefko, Bacik & Fedorko, 2014).

In South Africa, nearly 30 million South Africans have access to social media networks through their mobile phones. Examples of social media networks include Facebook, Twitter, LinkedIn, Instagram, Google + and YouTube. BusinessTech (2015) reported that the most popular social media site in South Africa is Facebook with an estimated 12 million users. This popularity, as framed in the literature, could be because of a number of reasons. Firstly, Facebook has transformed the workplace in that it is social in nature and allows participants to send, receive and process information freely for use by others (Aula, 2010). Furthermore, Facebook allows for open participation and the assimilation of information across different communication channels (Gerber, 2016). It also provides a communication channel for employees to discuss work-related issues away from management oversight and to share personal and work information. This, however, means that the organisation (unlike with conventional media) is no longer able to control the information that is put in the public domain about their products or services (Aula, 2010).

Secondly, Facebook is commonly referred to as *grassroots technology*, which means that the employees were using the technology before the organisation implemented a social media strategy. This means that employees are familiar with the technology and are more likely to adopt it for business purposes. Thus, many social media tools, such as Facebook, can be used both at work and at home, obscuring the boundary between these two contexts. For example, employees can upload information on their personal page that could be inconsistent with or may harm the organisation's image or brand (Dreher, 2014). In a study, 60% of management believed that they had a right to know what their employees post, but despite this acknowledgement, only 17% of these organisations had implemented a programme to monitor and mitigate risks related to social networks (Lanham, 2010). These characteristics provide an interesting question concerning the factors that will determine how employees in traditional higher education institutions decide to make use of social media to perform their duties.

Employee social media usage can be considered a strong indicator of the technology's success and will ultimately determine the acceptance, implementation and strategic benefit of social media in the workplace (Ajzen, 1991; Ali-Hassan, Nevo & Wadec, 2015). Organisations are also interested in their employees' social media usage to derive benefits from and assess the business value of the technology. Behavioural intention occurs when the employee decides to use the different features of the information technology artefact (in this case Facebook) to accomplish a task that is associated with a predefined organisational goal (Ajzen, 1991).

Researchers have previously studied the use of social media in the workplace, with most of these studies focusing on a specific discipline or field, for example, corporate, public sector, academia or the health care sector (Gholami-Kordkheili, Wild & Strech, 2013; Guy, 2012; Magro, 2012; Wu, Sun & Tan, 2013). These studies focused almost exclusively on the externally focused usage of social media technologies such as advertising, communication and marketing of organisations in developed countries. The internal usage of social media, in comparison, has not been investigated as thoroughly (Ouirdi, Ouirdi, Segers & Henderickx, 2015). In addition, very few studies have been conducted in developing countries.

Academia has traditionally used social media to improve collaboration and communication with students to improve teaching and learning (external usage of social media; Cilliers, 2016). Social media technologies have been recognised as a viable supplement to the traditional learning environment. However, in line with the international trend, not many studies have focused on the internal usage of social media among academic employees in developing countries such as South Africa.

Research purpose and objectives

Research into the use of social media in the workplace is growing both locally and internationally (Hysa et al., 2015; Palonka & Porebska-Miac, 2014). Nevertheless, there is a need for further research in South Africa on the factors that will determine the behavioural intention to use social media in the workplace. Although it is acknowledged that social media is often used in the higher education context to improve teaching and learning or for external purposes such as marketing the institution, there is very little information available about how employees in higher education institutions decide to make use of social media to perform their duties, for example, internal usage (Birch & Irvine, 2009; Chen & Bryer, 2012; Cilliers, 2016). The purpose of this study was to identify employees' behavioural intention to make use of social media in the workplace at a South African traditional higher education institution. The overall research question that guided this study was: 'What factors influence the behavioural intent of employees in the South African higher education sector to make use of social media for work purposes?'

Literature review

Theoretical development

This research draws on the theoretical underpinnings of the technology acceptance model (TAM) (Venkatesh, Morris, Davis & Davis, 2003), which posits that attitude towards social media usage reflects the potential to not only use but also adopt the technology. This view within a South African setting has been supported by a number of studies (e.g. Chinyamurindi & Louw, 2010; Chinyamurindi & Shava, 2015; Shava, Chinyamurindi & Somdyala, 2016) leading to the TAM, specifically behavioural intention to use, being theorised to be a useful predictor of behaviours, such as intention, when deciding to adopt technology (Agundo-Peregrina, Hernández-García & Pascual-Miguel, 2014; Venkatesh et al., 2003).

Social media usage and behavioural intention to use

The TAM was developed by Davis in 1986 and is one of the most cited theoretical frameworks in the Information Systems field. It is used to examine the perceived usefulness and perceived ease of use that will ultimately determine the employee's intention to make use of social media and can, therefore, be used to predict and validate factors that will influence technology adoption, acceptance and use (Cilliers & Flowerday, 2012). Within an organisational setting, an employee's intention to make use of social media platforms, such as Facebook, can improve co-worker and supervisor support and create a platform to highlight job-related demands as it provides direct communication in the quickest possible time (Lilley, Grodzinsky & Gumbus, 2012; Ouirdi et al., 2015). Furthermore, the intention to make use of social media in the assimilation of new, young employees was found to increase morale and the employees' feelings of cultural belonging, whereas the use of an internal social networking improved employee engagement and job performance (Ouirdi et al., 2015). Landers and Callan (2014) proposed a Work-related Social Media Questionnaire (WSMQ) that could be used to determine the beneficial and harmful social media-related work behaviours that are applicable across various industries and jobs. The positive work-related social media behaviours were identified as reputation management, extra-office communication, and task-related and intra-office communication, whereas the negative behaviours included offending others and behaviours that can damage reputation and relationship or waste time.

Fusch (2011) divides social media tools into three important categories for the user: communication, sharing and collaboration. Facebook, the social media site chosen for this study, provides employees with the opportunity to conduct activities in all three groups. Employees can further communicate with each other by posting on other employees' Facebook sites, they can share information or documents, and groups of employees can open a Facebook page with the aim to collaborate on a specific topic (Guy, 2012). For these reasons, Facebook is one of the most popular social media platforms in South Africa with some estimates being at 12 million users (BusinessTech, 2015).

Within the organisational setting, some concerns exist around social media usage. For instance, concerns are raised around the type of content that can be posted on platforms such as Facebook, which speaks to the usefulness of the technology (Hysa et al., 2015; Palonka & Porebska-Miac, 2014). Other researchers caution that Facebook can have a negative influence on both employee and workplace productivity, or ease of use, resulting in social media platforms being blocked during working hours (Hysa et al., 2015). Shullich (2011) cautions that the increased use of social media in the workplace can be a source of malware (Trojans, viruses and spyware) that can compromise the data security and integrity of the organisation. To safeguard against such threats, Dreher (2014) advises organisations to pay attention to issues through the implementation of policy governing social media usage in organisations. Such policy should be accompanied by both punitive and corrective measures when violations occur (Hysa et al., 2015). In addition, Gerber (2016) argues for a greater presence of the ICT department in supporting all business functions, given that social media usage may transcend across business functions.

A review of the extant literature positions the need for this study on three fronts. Firstly, there is a growing body of empirical work paying attention to the role of ICTs within the South African workplace (e.g. Chinyamurindi & Louw, 2010; De Wet, Koekemoer & Nel, 2016; Erasmus, Rothmann & Van Eeden, 2015). However, within this growing body of work, scant attention is given to social media usage within the workplace. Secondly, no proposed framework(s) appear to have emerged based on the findings of the growing body of empirical work within a South African context in relation to social media usage. Thirdly, calls exist for studies that investigate work-related social media usage in various national, cultural, social and economic contexts (Landers & Callan, 2014). As its contribution, this study seeks to fill these identified research gaps through assessing the following four hypotheses:

- **Hypothesis 1 (H1):** A significantly positive relationship exists between university employees' problem-solving methods and intention to use social media.
- **Hypothesis 2 (H2):** A significantly positive relationship exists between university employees' (intra and extra) communication methods and intention to use social media.
- **Hypothesis 3 (H3):** A significantly positive relationship exists between university employees' reputational management methods and intention to use social media.
- **Hypothesis 4 (H4):** A significantly positive relationship exists between university employees' task accomplishment and intention to use social media.

Research method

Research approach

Saunders, Lewis and Thornhill (2009) consider a research paradigm as a means to study social phenomena from which certain understandings can be achieved. This study made use of a positivistic paradigm with a descriptive research design and a quantitative approach. Such a philosophy and approach has been used in previous studies especially within a South African context following the same research lines (Chinyamurindi & Louw, 2010; Chinyamurindi & Shava, 2015; Cilliers, 2016; Shava et al., 2016). Positivism assumes that social reality is singular, objective and is not affected by the researcher's attempts to investigate it (Collis & Hussey, 2009).

Quantitative research is deductive as it is concerned with testing theories; generating models, theories and hypotheses; developing instruments and methods for measurements; experimental controls; and collection of empirical data (Kuhn, 1961). For the purpose of this study, a quantitative survey method was used to gather data, whereas a convenience sampling method was used to identify the study participants. A survey method was considered appropriate as large quantities of raw data could be accumulated in a short period of time, thus facilitating advanced statistical analyses. A key component of analysis of the data collected for this study included factor analysis. The purpose of factor analysis in social research is to summarise the data through the identification of latent relationships within the data.

Research instrument

The WSMQ was used as the data collection tool in this study. The WSMQ is a tool used to measure how employees use social media within the workplace for reasons related either positively or negatively to their work performance. The instrument used consists of three sections and 27 items overall. Section A (6 questions) solicited demographic information from respondents (gender, ethnic group, age, level of education, employment status and level of computer knowledge). Section B (18 questions) measured the positive work-related social media actions on a 5-point Likert scale (1 = strongly disagree to 5 = strongly agree). The final section (Section C) of the instrument consisted of the dependent variable comprising three items and measuring behavioural intention to use social media in the workplace as identified in previous studies (Ajzen, 2006; Ong & Lai, 2006). The scale measures intent, prediction and planning, which represent three progressive levels of seriousness about the intention to use social media in the workplace. The scale was found to have sufficient ratings of reliability above the recommended threshold of 0.7 suggested by Nunnally (1978).

A pilot study was used to pre-test the original WSMQ questionnaire among a sample of 20 respondents (10 academics and 10 administrators) that was not included in the subsequent main study. Suggestions and amendments from this process were used to refine the research instrument of the main study. These included aspects of simplicity and clarity of questions and a suggestion to include a detailed definition of what is meant by social media in the workplace in the accompanying instructions. Further, two lecturers in the human resources management and Information Systems fields were consulted to review a copy of the questionnaire before it was used for data collection. The pilot study provided for the face and content validity of the questionnaire.

Research respondents

Data were collected from university staff (n = 202) at one campus of a traditional university. All respondents were affiliated with the university either as an academic or administrative staff member. Respondents were informed of their rights that participating in the study was voluntary and that they could withdraw at any time. If respondents were in agreement to this, an ethical consent form was signed before completion of the questionnaire. A total of 200 questionnaires were randomly distributed to academics and administrators at a university event (over a period of 1 week). A total of 134 questionnaires were returned, yielding a response rate of 67%, which was deemed acceptable. Table 1 provides a summary of the descriptive statistics of the respondents who took part in the study.

The results in Table 1 show a dominance of black female respondents with the majority being aged between 30 and 50 years. The majority of the respondents had obtained a post Grade 12 qualification. The respondents indicated that they had 'a good' knowledge of computers. All of these results are regarded as representative of the gender, age, qualifications and computer knowledge of the work population at a traditional university (Higher Education South Africa, 2015).

Descriptive statistics

In examining the descriptive statements related to the WSMQ as displayed in Table 2, it is evident that more participants viewed the statements positively as opposed to negatively, with some having higher means than others. Statements 9 and 11 pertaining to employees contacting co-workers via social media and employees posting on their organisations' social media pages appear to have higher means than statements such as WSMQ4 and 6 which relate to contacting clients or customers via social media. Because of the fact that

TABLE 1: Descriptive statistics of respondents.

Demographic	n	%
Gender		
Male	50	37.3
Female	84	62.7
Ethnicity		
Black African	111	82.8
Mixed race	19	14.2
White	4	3.0
Age		
20–30 years	11	8.2
31–40 years	65	48.5
41–50 years	51	38.1
Above 50 years	7	5.2
Educational qualifications		
Matric	4	3.0
Certificate	2	1.5
Diploma or degree	78	58.2
Postgraduate studies	50	37.3
Position in university		
Academic	58	43.3
Administrator	76	56.7
Computer knowledge		
Great	39	29.1
Good	93	69.4
Average	2	1.5

n = 134.

TABLE 2: Descriptive statistics for Work-related Social Media Questionnaire results.

Number	Question	Minimum	Maximum	Mean	Standard deviation
WSMQ1	I have found tutorials and lessons on social media to help me learn how to perform my job better.	2	5	3.57	0.594
WSMQ2	I have used social media to learn how to perform better at my job.	2	5	3.39	0.612
WSMQ3	I communicate with existing customers or clients via social media.	1	5	3.42	0.739
WSMQ4	I maintain contact with existing customers or clients using social media.	1	5	3.33	0.646
WSMQ5	I reach out to potential new customers and clients using social media.	2	5	3.49	0.622
WSMQ6	I've identified potential customers and clients by searching social media.	2	5	3.38	0.611
WSMQ7	I request help from people on social media when I am having trouble solving a problem at work.	2	5	3.48	0.646
WSMQ8	When I can't solve a problem at work, I ask for help on social media.	2	5	3.42	0.579
WSMQ9	I use social media to contact my co-workers when I am unable to reach them by other means.	2	5	3.62	0.647
WSMQ10	Through social media, I maintain contact with other people in my organisation.	2	5	3.42	0.579
WSMQ11	I post on my organisation's social media site or group page.	2	5	3.60	0.639
WSMQ12	I use my organisation's official social media presence to network.	2	5	3.46	0.609
WSMQ13	I have found pictures, videos, or other content on social media of a co-worker that may harm his or her reputation and warned him or her about them.	2	5	3.54	0.596
WSMQ14	I have told my co-worker about slander others have posted on social media about him or her.	2	5	3.47	0.622
WSMQ15	When someone posts something negative about our organisation or its employees on social media, I try to do something about it.	2	5	3.47	0.645
WSMQ16	If I find something on social media that will harm the reputation of my co-workers or our organisation, I let people know.	2	5	3.45	0.583
WSMQ17	I have taken advantage of the technical features of social media (like file sharing or scheduling functions) to accomplish work tasks.	2	5	3.47	0.584
WSMQ18	I have used software features of social media to accomplish a work task faster or more easily.	2	5	3.47	0.622

this study takes place in a university setting, these findings would be consistent with the nature of the organisation, involving administrators and academics who do not generally contact students via social media.

Reliability and validity testing

The researchers adhered to issues of reliability and validity while collecting, analysing and interpreting the data. The statistical analyses were carried out with SPSS V24. The Cronbach's alpha coefficient (α) was used to test for internal consistency of the measuring instrument (Pallant, 2010). A high Cronbach's alpha coefficient suggests that the scale used is reliable. Values of 0.70 and above represent a good level of reliability, whereas values between 0.50 and 0.69 are considered to indicate an acceptable level of reliability (Pallant, 2010). The Cronbach's alphas were calculated for Sections B and C of the questionnaire and found to be acceptable in both cases. Table 3 provides the results of the empirical reliability testing for the scales used in this research. Both the Cronbach's alpha coefficient for the positive workplace social media scale and behavioural intention to use scale indicated adequate levels of reliability.

An exploratory factor analysis (EFA) was used to identify and validate the sub-constructs contained in the 18-item WSMQ. Prior to performing the principal components analysis, the suitability of data for factor analysis was assessed. Inspection of the correlation matrix revealed the presence of many coefficients of 0.4 and above. The Kaiser–Meyer–Olkin (KMO) measure was 0.686, exceeding the recommended value of 0.6, and the Bartlett's Test of Sphericity reached statistical significance, supporting the factorability of the correlations matrix (Kaiser, 1970, 1974). Thus, the EFA was conducted for the purpose of determining validity of the constructs and their associated items. Principal components analysis revealed the presence of three components that collectively accounted for 55.98% of the variance in the data. The principal components analysis conducted utilised Equamax with Kaiser normalisation as the rotation method. The rotated solution revealed three components (problem-solving, communication and reputation management) with a number of items loading on each of the components, as is evident in Table 4. The three factors were assessed and named according to the components of the workplace social media usage framework (WSMUF). These factors include problem-solving, communication with peers and clients, and

TABLE 3: Cronbach's alpha coefficients for the scales comprising the measuring instrument.

Scale	Items	Cronbach's alpha
Positive work-related social media scale	18	0.704
Behavioural intention to use social media scale	3	0.698

TABLE 4: Exploratory factor analysis results.

Item	Problem-solving	Communication	Reputation management
WSMQ6	0.682	-	-
WSMQ8	0.777	-	-
WSMQ10	0.749	-	-
WSMQ12	0.731	-	-
WSMQ5	-	0.766	-
WSMQ7	-	0.820	-
WSMQ9	-	0.697	-
WSMQ11	-	0.724	-
WSMQ15	-	-	0.758
WSMQ16	-	-	-0.707
WSMQ17	-	-	0.502

reputation management. It is important to note that the sub-construct of job performance was eliminated from the study at this point because of the fact that the measurement instrument appeared not to capture the essence of the construct adequately, and therefore, it could not be operationalised properly.

To conclude the issue of validity and reliability of the measurement instruments, it is important to note that retests of reliability were conducted based on the factors derived from the EFA. Adequate Cronbach's alphas for the three factors were achieved. Further to the retest of reliability, it is necessary to address the issue of the credibility of the scale used to measure the dependent variable: behavioural intention to use. The dependent variable scale was tested for both reliability and validity, and the following results were derived: The Cronbach's alpha score recorded was 0.698, indicating the scale was moderately reliable, and the factor loadings to establish unidimensionality of the scale ranged from 0.724 to 0.874, indicating the scale was measuring a singular construct.

Correlation and multiple regression results

In order to derive results to the hypotheses posed, a correlation analysis was first conducted to determine the significance of individual relationships. The correlation analysis was followed by a multiple regression analysis (MRA) which provided further insights into the strengths and directions of the hypothesised relationships. As previously indicated, Hypothesis 4 was eliminated from the analysis; therefore, Hypotheses 1 to 3 were tested. The results of the correlations achieved between the constructs are provided in Table 5.

Table 5 indicates that Pearson's correlation coefficient was used to depict the level of correlation achieved between the variables under study. A *p*-value of less than 0.05 was selected to indicate statistical significance. Based on this explanation, it can be concluded from Table 5 that the only significant and positively highly correlated relationship evident between the dependent variables (behavioural intention to use) and the independent variables (problem-solving, communication and reputation management) is the one that exists between behavioural intention to use and reputation management. To further contextualise the various relationships and to understand the possible influence the independent variables have on the dependent variables, an MRA was conducted. The various summarised outputs generated from the MRA are presented in Table 6.

Ethical considerations

Ethical approval was obtained from the University Ethics Committee.

Discussion

Outline of the findings

The purpose of this study was to identify the behavioural intention of a sample of employees at a traditional higher education institution to make use of social media within the workplace. The MRA indicates that the independent variables explain 41.90% of the behavioural intention to use the construct. Table 6 confirms the findings of the correlation analysis presented in Table 5. The only significantly positive relation evident is the one between behavioural intention to use and reputation management ($b = 0.650$; $p < 0.005$) which, therefore, supports Hypothesis 3. These results indicate that employees are actively concerned with maintaining their organisations and co-workers' reputations on social media and will actively pursue behaviour that results in reputation management. The findings, however, also reveal that there is no statistically significant relationship, negative or positive, between the other two independent variables (problem-solving or communication) and the dependent variable (behavioural intent), respectively. Based on these findings, no support can be found for Hypotheses 1, 2 or 4. These findings imply that employees do not actively intend to use social media to assist them with task accomplishment, such as

TABLE 6: Influence of independent variables on behavioural intention to use social media.

Independent variables	Beta	*t*	Significance (*p*)
Problem-solving	-0.050	-0.737	0.463
Communication	-0.117	-1.736	0.085
Reputation management	0.650	9.615	0.000*

Dependent variable behavioural intention to use – $R^2 = 0.419$.
*, $p < 0.005$.

TABLE 5: Test of correlation between constructs.

Construct	Description	Behavioural intention to use	Problem-solving	Communication	Reputation management
Behavioural intention to use	Pearson's correlation	1	-0.009	-0.044	0.635**
	Sig. (2-tailed)	-	0.921	0.612	0.000
	N	134	133	134	134
Problem-solving	Pearson's correlation	-0.009	1	-0.053	0.053
	Sig. (2-tailed)	0.921	-	0.547	0.542
	N	133	133	133	133
Communication	Pearson's correlation	-0.044	-0.053	1	0.109
	Sig. (2-tailed)	0.612	0.547	-	0.211
	N	134	133	134	134
Reputation management	Pearson's correlation	0.635**	0.053	0.109	1
	Sig. (2-tailed)	0.000	0.542	0.211	-
	N	134	133	134	134

**, Correlation is significant at the 0.01 level (2-tailed).

problem-solving and communication at work, and there could be various reasons for this, for example, restricted access to Facebook. However, the findings should be contrasted with the descriptive findings reported in Table 3 which indicate that employees are already using social media for communication and problem-solving in a work environment. In considering the items used to measure the constructs of problem-solving and communication, it is possible that employees use social media as a 'last resort' when they are unable to contact a colleague or need some form of assistance and have not been able to obtain it from another channel in the organisation. Thus, although employees are using social media to assist them in the workplace, they perhaps do not consider these to be legitimate 'work tools', thus explaining the lack of relationship between problem-solving, communication and behavioural intent to use social media in the workplace. The main findings of this research indicate that the behavioural intent to use social media in the academic workplace is predicated by only one factor: reputation management.

Thus, one of the contributions of this study, given the scant empirical focus on studies on social media usage in the South African workplace, is the knowledge that although academic staff does make use of social media in the workplace for communication and problem-solving, only reputational management of the institution is pursued actively. This extends understanding to the growing body of empirical work in South Africa focusing on the role of ICTs in South Africa (De Wet et al., 2016; Erasmus et al., 2015) and uniquely with social media usage. Practically, organisations can emphasise the communication capability as argued by the WSMUF to improve not only communication processes but also channels through which information is shared. Furthermore, the WSMUF can be a useful basis through which interventions that follow responsible social media usage can be based on. For instance, through the factor associated with reputation management, employees can be made aware of the positives and negatives of social media on not only employee reputations but also organisational reputations. A platform such as social media should not be seen as entirely counterproductive to ideals of improving organisational productivity but one that can improve such.

Relating main findings to the literature

Social media has been identified in literature as being used by organisations for marketing activities, market research, customer service, recruitment and promotion strategies (Gerber, 2016). These strategies have an external focus. Very little has been written about the internal usage and behavioural intent to make use of social media among employees. Facebook, in particular, has allowed for open participation and the assimilation of information across a variety of different communication channels (Stefko et al., 2014). The WSMUF supports this notion as communication and problem-solving among employees in the workplace were identified as two factors that will predict behavioural intent to use social media in the workplace. The third factor, reputation management, is the most important predictor of behavioural intent to use social media in the workplace. Organisations recognise that brand management becomes more difficult if employees are allowed to post information that may be incongruent with the organisation's image, as they no longer control the information that is put in the public domain about their products or services (Aula, 2010). The employees believe that managing the reputation of their organisation and fellow employees is one of the key tasks when they engage in social media in the workplace. This means that the organisation could use their employees to manage their brand on social media.

Limitations of the study

Although the study was a useful precursor to understanding the factors that influence behavioural intention to use social media, some limitations can be flagged. Firstly, the findings of the study are only generalisable to the entire population of employees working in universities that fit the same profile as those respondents sampled or any other South African university. Secondly, the study made use of a sample consisting of both an academic and administrative function. The findings of this work should be viewed with caution especially given the skewed sample. The purpose of this work was to access a sample most accessible to the researchers, hence adoption of a convenience sampling approach. Finally, a further shortcoming of this research is its reliance on retrospective data that include how employees use social media. The reliability of such data is questionable as in some cases employees may forget events and experiences.

Suggestions for future research

Future research could qualitatively explore the factors in the WSMUF as proposed in this study. This could take the form of exploring the tensions and relatedness (if any) that may exist between the factors in the WSMUF. Future research could also test the WSMUF in other contexts of interest, such as the science, technology, engineering and mathematics (STEM) sector, argued by Chinyamurindi and Louw (2010) to be key Human Resource Management clusters of the South African economy. Although the scale for measuring work-related social media usage is relatively new (Landers & Callan, 2014), given the diversity that exists in the South African context, future research could test this against such.

Conclusion

Social media is transforming the workplace in South Africa. The study set out to determine what factors will influence the behavioural intention of employees at a traditional higher education institution to make use of social media in the workplace. The main activities identified through the WSMUF that will contribute to this intention are communication among colleagues, problem-solving and reputation management. The WSMUF for the first time provides a tool for South African organisations to manage their employees' behavioural intent to make use of social media in the workplace to stay competitive in the social networking age.

Acknowledgements

Competing interests

The authors declare that they have no financial or personal relationships that may have inappropriately influenced them in writing this article.

Authors' contributions

L.C. was responsible for conceptualisation and literature review and K.V. was the statistician. W.T.C. was responsible for conceptualisation and data collection.

References

Agundo-Peregrina, Á.F., Hernández-García, A., & Pascual-Miguel, F.J. (2014). Behavioral intention, use behavior and the acceptance of electronic learning systems: Differences between higher education and lifelong learning. *Computers in Human Behavior, 34*, 301–314. https://doi.org/10.1016/j.chb.2013.10.035

Ajzen, I. (1991). The theory of planned behaviour. *Organizational Behavior and Human Decision Processes, 50*, 179–211. https://doi.org/10.1016/0749-5978(91)90020-T

Ajzen, I. (2006). *Constructing a TPB questionnaire: Conceptual and methodological considerations*. World Wide Web. Retrieved April 15, 2016, from http://www.people.umass.edu/aizen/pdf/tpb.measurement.pdf

Ali-Hassan, H., Nevo, D., & Wadec, M. (2015). Linking dimensions of social media use to job performance: The role of social capital. *Journal of Strategic Information Systems, 24*, 65–89. https://doi.org/10.1016/j.jsis.2015.03.001

Aula, P. (2010). Social media, reputation risk and ambient publicity management. *Strategy & Leadership, 38*(6), 43–49. https://doi.org/10.1108/10878571011088069

Birch, A., & Irvine, V. (2009). Preservice teachers' acceptance of ICT integration in the classroom: Applying the UTAUT model. *Educational Media International, 46*(4), 295–315. https://doi.org/10.1080/09523980903387506

BusinessTech. (2015). *Facebook reveals user numbers for South Africa*. Retrieved April 16, 2016, from http://www.businesstech.co.za/news/internet/98085/facebook-reveals-user-numbers-for-south-africa/15

Chen, B., & Bryer, T. (2012). Investigating instructional strategies for using social media in formal and informal learning. *The International Review of Research in Open and Distance Learning, 13*(1), 87–104. https://doi.org/10.19173/irrodl.v13i1.1027

Chinyamurindi, W., & Shava, H. (2015). An investigation into e-learning acceptance and gender amongst final year students. *South African Journal of Information Management, 17*(1), 1–9. https://doi.org/10.4102/sajim.v17i1.635

Chinyamurindi, W.T., & Louw, G.J. (2010). Gender differences in technology acceptance in selected South African companies: Implications for electronic learning. *South African Journal of Human Resources Management, 8*(1), 1–7. https://doi.org/10.4102/sajhrm.v8i1.204

Cilliers, L. (2016). Wiki acceptance by university students to improve collaboration in higher education. *Innovations in Education and Teaching International*, 1–9. https://doi.org/10.1080/14703297.2016.1180255

Cilliers, L., & Flowerday, S. (2012). *Technology acceptance of Telemedicine in the Eastern Cape Department of Health*. Presented at IST-Africa 2012, Dar Es Salaam, Tanzania.

Collis, J., & Hussey, R. (2009). *Business research: A practical guide for undergraduate and postgraduate students*. New York: Palgrave.

De Wet, W., Koekemoer, E., & Nel, J.A. (2016). Exploring the impact of information and communication technology on employees' work and personal lives. *South African Journal of Industrial Psychology, 42*(1), 1–11. https://doi.org/10.4102/sajip.v42i1.1330

Dreher, S. (2014). Social media and the world of work. *Corporate Communications: An International Journal, 19*(4), 334–356. https://doi.org/10.1108/CCIJ-10-2013-0087

Erasmus, E., Rothmann, S., & Van Eeden, C. (2015). A structural model of technology acceptance. *South African Journal of Industrial Psychology, 41*(1), 1–12. https://doi.org/10.4102/sajip.v41i1.1222

Fusch, D. (2011). Social media and student learning: Moving the needle on engagement. *Academic Impressions*, 15.

Gerber, P. (2016). Achieving IT Governance of social media at strategic and operational levels. *International Business and Economics Research Journal, 15*(4), 1–16. https://doi.org/10.19030/iber.v15i4.9753

Gholami-Kordkheili, F., Wild, V., & Strech, D. (2013). The impact of social media on medical professionalism: A systematic qualitative review of challenges and opportunities. *Journal of Medical Internet Research, 15*(8), e.184. https://doi.org/10.2196/jmir.2708

Guy, R. (2012). The use of social media for academic practice: A review of literature. *Kentucky Journal of Higher Education Policy and Practice, 1*(2), 7.

Higher Education South Africa. (2015). Strategic framework for HESA. *Insight*, 1–15.

Hysa, B., Mularczyk, A., & Zdonek, I. (2015). Social media: The challenges and the future direction of the recruitment process in HRM area. *Studia Ekonomiczne, 234*, 54–69.

Kaiser, H. (1970). A second generation Little Jiffy. *Psychometrika, 35*, 401–415. https://doi.org/10.1007/BF02291817

Kaiser, H. (1974). An index of factorial simplicity. *Psychometrika, 39*, 31–36. https://doi.org/10.1007/BF02291575

Kaplan, A., & Haenlein, M. (2010). Users of the world, unite! The challenges and opportunities of social media. *Business Horizons, 53*, 59–68. https://doi.org/10.1016/j.bushor.2009.09.003

Kuhn, T.S. (1961). The function of measurement in modern physical science. *Isis, 52*, 161–193. https://doi.org/10.1086/349468

Landers, R.N., & Callan, R.C. (2014). Validation of the beneficial and harmful work-related social media behavioral taxonomies: Development of the Work-related Social Media Questionnaire (WSMQ). *Social Science Computer Review, 32*, 628–646. https://doi.org/10.1177/0894439314524891

Lanham, J. (2010). *Social media in the workplace*. New York: Employment Law.

Lilley, S., Grodzinsky, F., & Gumbus, A. (2012). Revealing the commercialized and compliant Facebook user. *Journal of Information, Communication and Ethics in Society, 10*(2), 82–92. https://doi.org/10.1108/14779961211226994

Magro, M. (2012). A review of social media use in e-government. *Administrative Sciences, 2*(2), 148–161. https://doi.org/10.3390/admsci2020148

Nielsen. (2013). *Paid social media advertising: Industry update and best practices*. Retrieved April 06, 2016, from http://www.nielsen.com/content/dam/corporate/us/en/reports-downloads/2013%20Reports/Nielsen-Paid-Social-Media-Adv-Report-2013.pdf

Nunnally, J.C. (1978). *Psychometric theory*. New York: McGraw-Hill.

Okazaki, S., & Taylor, C. (2013). Social media and international advertising: Theoretical challenges and future directions. *International Marketing Review, 30*(1), 56–71. https://doi.org/10.1108/02651331311298573

Ong, C.S., & Lai, J.Y. (2006). Gender differences in perceptions and relationships among dominants of e-learning acceptance. *Computers in Human Behavior, 22*(5), 816–829. https://doi.org/10.1016/j.chb.2004.03.006

Ouirdi, A., Ouirdi, M., Segers, J., & Henderickx, E. (2015). Employees' use of social media technologies: A methodological and thematic review. *Behavior & Information Technologies, 34*(5), 454–464. https://doi.org/10.1080/0144929X.2015.1004647

Pallant, J. (2010). *SPSS survival manual*. Berkshire: McGraw Hill.

Palonka, J., & Porebska-Miac, T. (2014). *Social recruitment*. Rzeszów, Poland: Oficyna Wydawnicza PTZ.

Saunders, M., Lewis, P., & Thornhill, A. (2009). *Research methods for business students*. London: Pearson Education Limited.

Shava, H., Chinyamurindi, W.T., & Somdyala, A. (2016). An investigation into the usage of mobile phones among technical and vocational educational and training students in South Africa. *South African Journal of Information Management, 18*(1), 1–8. https://doi.org/10.4102/sajim.v18i1.716

Shullich, R. (2011). *Risk assessment of social media*. Retrieved April 07, 2016, from http://www.sans.org/reading-room/whitepapers/privacy/risk-assessment-social-media-33940

Stefko, R., Bacik, R., & Fedorko, I. (2014). Facebook content analysis of banks operating on Slovak Market. *Polish Journal of Management Studies, 10*(1), 145–152.

Venkatesh, V., Morris, M., Davis G.B., & Davis, F. (2003). User acceptance of information technology: Toward a unified view. *MIS Quarterly, 27*, 425–427.

Wu, J., Sun, H., & Tan, Y. (2013). Social media research: A review. *Journal of Systems Science and Systems Engineering, 22*(3), 257–282. https://doi.org/10.1007/s11518-013-5225-6

3

Current collective engagement stakeholder strategies for South African labour relations

Authors:
Popi C. Madlala[1]
Cookie M. Govender[1]

Affiliations:
[1]Department of Industrial Psychology and People Management, University of Johannesburg, South Africa

Corresponding author:
Popi Madlala,
pcmadlala@gmail.com

Orientation: Collective engagement stakeholder strategies are significant for the creation of harmony in the workplace. It is a known fact that the South African (SA) labour environment has been dominated by industrial action before and after the 1994 democratic transition. To be precise, the statistics reveals that industrial action has increased and become more destructive post-1994.

Purpose: The purpose of this article was to present the current collective engagement stakeholder strategies for South African labour relations.

Motivation for the study: The SA mining sector has seen more violent strikes, with a higher number of deaths, injuries, criminal activities, arrests, dismissals and job losses in recent years. This article captures the current mining stakeholder strategies shaping the existing labour relations environment.

Research approach, design and method: This is a theoretical article highlighting the recent literature on collective engagement in the mining sector in South Africa.

Main findings: This article presents the current labour relations incidents, reflecting the need for more effective collective engagement and stakeholder management strategies.

Practical and managerial implications: The current labour relations context has prompted key stakeholders at the National Economic Development and Labour Council (NEDLAC) to look specifically at promoting employment, labour market stability, the right to strike, minimising violence through collective bargaining and highlighting the role of the state, reducing vulnerability through social protection and increasing the minimum wage.

Contribution or value add: This article adds theoretically to the existing body of knowledge regarding collective engagement and stakeholder strategies in the SA mining sector.

Introduction and background to the problem

The status of South African (SA) collective engagement has failed to transform to the desirable level since the democratisation of the labour relations environment, with the promulgation of the *Labour Relations Act* (No. 66 of 1995) (OECD, 2000). Chinguno (2013) argued that democracy and violence should have an inverse relationship. However, in South Africa, violence remains a significant phenomenon despite the transition to democracy, both in the labour relations environment and in society as a whole. This demonstrates the lack of a collaborative collective engagement strategy.

According to Nwankwo (2016), collective engagement refers to the negotiation, administration and interpretation of a written agreement between two parties that covers a specific period of time. The International Labour Organization (ILO) has defined collective engagement as negotiations on working conditions and terms of employment between an employer, or a group of employers, and one or more employee organisations, with a view to reaching an agreement. The terms of that agreement serve as a contract, defining the rights and obligations of each party (Nwankwo, 2016). Most importantly, the collective agreement must shape the labour relations landscape in a more positive way.

Although the current collective engagement framework is deemed to be comprehensive and sufficient, the evidence collected by various analysts (as would be presented in the discussions that follow) suggests that there is a need to overhaul the current stakeholder collective engagement strategies (Coleman, 2013; Congress of South African Trade Unions [COSATU], 2012; Hartford, 2012). The current collective engagement in the mining environment, especially in the decentralised environment, leaves much to be desired and suggests that there is room for further strategic improvements at all levels of the bargaining process.

This theoretical article presents the current collective engagement strategies for labour relations by current stakeholders and adds value by contributing to the theoretical knowledge regarding collective engagement strategies in the mining sector in SA. It also adds value in a practical way by contributing to the debate on what strategies union and employer managers and leaders should utilise to create harmonious labour relations in the mining sector.

Current collective engagement stakeholder strategies

The current collective engagement strategies are presented under the subheadings of collective engagement framework in SA, an overview of the current SA collective engagement strategy and external factors impacting SA collective engagement strategies.

Collective engagement framework in South Africa

According to Sachs (2013), the labour law regime provides for unionisation that requires workers to organise for the purpose of collective engagement. Sachs suggests that the process of collective engagement has also been captured by political influences, where public policies and financial regulations are designed to facilitate political organising by the poor and middle classes, through collective engagement. Collective engagement practices and strategies in the SA mining sector were in the spotlight even before the shocking killings of mineworkers in Marikana in 2012. The statutory collective engagement framework is provided by the *Labour Relations Act* (LRA), as presented in Table 1, and describes the functions and powers of key stakeholders as governed by statutory legislation in SA (Coleman, 2013).

The workplace collective engagement framework, as provided for by legislated guidance on collective agreements, is outlined in Table 2. The table describes the stakeholder platforms, the functions and the powers of each.

It is expected that with such a well-designed framework, the SA mines should be able to contain unnecessary tensions that lead to unwanted conflict. The government has accepted that the industrial action experiences at the Marikana Platinum Mine in 2012 prompted the SA Government to reinforce social discourse and collective engagement. According to the Department of Labour (DoL), it was noted that the relapse of industrial disputes is a symptom of the failure of social discourse in the working environment, and persistent inequality is because of the ineffectiveness of policy implementation strategy in the SA labour market (DoL, 2012). The other reality is the absence of effective collective engagement strategies from the key collective engagement

TABLE 1: Levels of statutory bargaining in South Africa.

Governed by statute	Functions and powers	Registration
Bargaining councils	• Make and enforce collective agreements. • Prevent and resolve labour disputes. • Establish and manage a dispute resolution fund. • Promote and establish training and education schemes. • Establish and manage schemes or funds to benefit its parties or members. • Make and submit proposals on policies and laws that affect a sector or area.	• May be formed by one or more registered trade union/s and one or more registered employers' organisation/s, given that these parties are 'sufficiently representative'. • NEDLAC is assigned the task of determining their scope and area of justification.
Statutory councils	• Resolve labour disputes. • Promote and manage education and training schemes. • Form and manage schemes or funds for the benefit of its parties and members. • Make collective agreements. • May perform any other bargaining council functions.	• May be formed by a registered trade union or employers' organisation that does not boast sufficient membership to meet the representation requirement to form a bargaining council. Registration is thus unilateral.

Source: Adapted from the Organization for Economic Co-operation and Development (OECD). (2000). *Tackling inequalities in Brazil, China, India and South Africa. The role of labour market and social policies*. Paris: OECD; and Coleman, N. (2013). Towards new collective bargaining, wage and social protection strategies in South Africa – Learning from the Brazilian experience. Global Labour University, Working Paper No. 17. Retrieved November 17, 2013, from http://www.global-labour-university.org

NEDLAC, National Economic Development and Labour Council.

TABLE 2: Current levels of workplace collective engagement in South Africa.

Outside of statute	Functions and powers	Description
Plant or firm-level bargaining	• Bargain over issues otherwise covered by Bargaining or Statutory Councils.	• Collective bargaining between an individual employer and the trade union(s) representing the employees of that particular employer.
Workplace forums	• Promote the workers' interests by consulting and making joint decisions. Employers must provide relevant information to workplace forums. • A workplace forum has the right to be consulted by the employer on: ▪ restructuring existing and new work methods ▪ partial or total plant closure ▪ mergers and ownership transfers ▪ retrenching workers ▪ job grading ▪ criteria for merits and bonuses ▪ education and training ▪ product development plans ▪ export promotions ▪ health and safety measures.	• Workplace forums may be formed when there are more than 100 people by applying to the Commission for Conciliation, Mediation and Arbitration (CCMA).

Source: Adapted from the Organization for Economic Co-operation and Development (OECD). (2000). *Tackling inequalities in Brazil, China, India and South Africa. The role of labour market and social policies*. Paris: OECD; and Coleman, N. (2013). Towards new collective bargaining, wage and social protection strategies in South Africa – Learning from the Brazilian experience. Global Labour University, Working Paper No. 17. Retrieved November 17, 2013, from http://www.global-labour-university.org

stakeholder representatives to eradicate the existing collective engagement challenges.

The Minister of Labour indicated that the one thing that needed to be dealt with regarding the Marikana incident was the re-establishment of the bargaining system in the platinum mines (DoL, 2012). The minister suggested a multi-pronged approach in the collective engagement system and suggested ensuring that all relevant stakeholders be included in the dialogue (DoL, 2012). This paper seeks to locate the reasons for the failures in the collective engagement system, and thereafter to make recommendations that will contribute to the current debate on the subject.

Hartford (2012) argued that the most noticeable feature of the events preceding the mining strike upsurge is the lack of any form of analysis of the economic- and social-democratic drivers. Hartford suggested that the lack of analysis led to the collapse of established collective bargaining institutions, agreements and norms in the labour relations process. Hartford's viewpoint recommended a review of the collective engagement framework to explore strategies that will ensure the harmonisation of the labour relations climate in the SA mining environment.

The Farlam Commission of Inquiry report of 2015 underlined the fact that the processes of collective bargaining are embedded in the SA Constitution and in a set of sophisticated enactments, central to which is the LRA (Farlam, Hemraj & Tokota 2015). The labour relations dispensation is, at its core, a framework for officially organised union and employer entities, functioning within a bargaining environment that not only normalises their interface but also provides for the possibility of resorting to lawful strike or lockout measures (Farlam et al., 2015).

The intention of the LRA in establishing the bargaining councils is to centralise the collective engagement process to be sector specific (South African Government, 2015). Centralised collective engagement assists in creating consistent patterns of employment conditions within the same sector. The gold and coal sectors have a centralised collective engagement system, and history reveals that the mines in these sectors have competitive employment conditions. As much as the legislation's intentions to regulate collective engagement are good, the negative connotation is that it acts as a deterrent for inclusive collective engagement. The legislation excludes smaller trade unions in crucial stages of collective engagement and where it matters most. For example, in collective bargaining, only significantly recognised trade unions are given a passport to collective engagement. Kruger and Tshoose (2013) cited legislation as one of the hindrances, as it shuts the minority out of the collective engagement process, especially when dealing with crucial employee socio-economic issues. They argued that Section 23 of the LRA specifically excludes the minority, as it allows for the collective agreement with a significantly representative trade union to be imposed on all minority trade unions (Kruger & Tshoose, 2013). This exclusion amounts to exclusion based on freedom of association, as the interests represented by smaller trade unions may be ignored.

The weaknesses and shortcomings in the labour legislation are that it does not provide for employee participation in decision-making in the mining sector (Kruger & Tshoose, 2013; Lester, 2014). The argument is that workplace forums can contribute significantly to creating worker participation in the collective engagement process; however, the current labour legislation dispensation leaves the establishment of the workplace forum to the trade unions rather than the employer. Labour analysts suggested a review of the legislation in order to ensure broader participation in the collective engagement process (Lester, 2014).

Harvey (2013) argued that the current institutional labour relations policy framework perpetuates trade union rivalry to value violence over cooperation, amongst other causes. The argument is that the clear existence of a policy dilemma in the labour relations landscape within SA's mining industry warrants strategic redesign to avert the damaging effects of mutual inconstancy. A possible means of attaining the focal goal would be to mandate the legislator to remove bargaining rights from any union guilty of endorsing illegal or violent strike action (Harvey, 2013). According to Coleman (2013), the following recommendations are to be noted: the overhaul of the collective engagement system, an integrated proposal connecting the transformation of collective bargaining to a wage and income strategy and the transformation of social protection. According to the suggestion, the recommendation is for wages, social protection and collective bargaining to be brought together into one coherent package.

From the above discussion, it is clear that the current collective engagement framework in SA, especially in the mining industry, needs to be overhauled. This can be achieved through peaceful negotiation, engagement, win-win intentions and a powerful collective engagement strategy. The objective of this article is to review the current stakeholder collective engagement strategies and deduce the intention of leaders, managers and unions in bringing about a peaceful labour relations environment in the mining sector of SA.

Overview of the current South African collective engagement strategy

The Farlam Commission of Inquiry report identified inconsistent engagement strategies that contributed significantly to the instability in the collective engagement processes (Farlam et al., 2015). For instance, the National Union of Mineworkers (NUM) was involved in a collective engagement process with Implats on the Rock Drill Operators (RDOs) conditions of employment, which lifted the Implats RDOs above the industry norm. National Union of Mineworkers should have been aware of what the consequences of its achievement at Implats would be on its constituencies in surrounding mines. Furthermore, the union failed to negotiate similar conditions successfully for its members at the Lonmin mine. In recent times, after the Marikana debacle, similar to RDO, demands have been made and realised in other mines in SA (Farlam et al., 2015).

Collective engagement strategies of trade unions and employers shape the pay equity effects of a minimum wage policy (Grimshaw, Bosch & Rubery, 2014). This was further supported by the outcome of the study conducted by Karen Roberts in 2015, which recorded the results as showing a difference between collaboratively and competitively bargained contracts in two areas, namely, direct responses to a changing national minimum wage and responses to the absence or weakness of a national minimum wage (Roberts, 2015). The Marikana debacle raises the debate about the best-fit strategy between decentralised and centralised collective bargaining, wherein the question that arises is: Of decentralisation and centralisation, which is the better strategy? Currently, the platinum mining sector practices decentralised collective bargaining, unlike the gold and coal sectors. Some have argued that the platinum sector was sufficiently similar to that of the gold mining sector to warrant centralised bargaining, notwithstanding the general problems associated with the practice (Chinguno, 2015; Lester, 2014).

Dawkins (2014) concluded that substantive operational indicators of collective engagement are lacking in the literature to guide collective engagement stakeholders on effective strategies for managing collective engagement. Earlier, Coleman (2013) postulated that the labour movements, and labour in general, are faced with the need to introduce new quality strategies to advance the wages and social protection of workers in the labour market. COSATU (2012) suggested that a more offensive strategic perspective to substantially restructure the current collective engagement architecture is required to confront the failures of the current SA national collective engagement system, which has failed to meet its objectives. New public policies and regulatory frameworks ought to be proposed to promote the consolidation of centralised engagement, a developmental engagement framework which increases wage equity, and the alignment of centralised bargaining with industrial and economic development strategies (COSATU, 2012).

A paper on new collective bargaining, learnt from experiences in Brazil, was presented by COSATU in 2012, which suggested that to achieve the new way of collective bargaining, some shortcomings from the existing system needed to be identified. The identified gaps, included, among others the need to develop new strategies to advance the position of workers in the labour market qualitatively. The COSATU paper identified that the key stakeholders have not succeeded in fundamentally changing the apartheid wage structure, with the partial exception of the public service and local government, and some pockets of the manufacturing sector, such as metal and engineering, and less so in the mining sector. There is a lack of centralisation of collective engagement in the platinum mining sector that has created severe inequalities amongst mining operations in this sector. The current gains achieved through the collective engagement process are deemed to be less efficient in real terms or sometimes reflect no change in real wages and lifestyle. There is therefore the danger that current strategies are in critical respects reinforcing the cheap labour structure of apartheid. The paper highlighted that there is widespread poverty amongst workers which remains a serious problem in SA. This is attributed to the high levels of unemployment and lack of social protection, leading to a greater dependency on low wages.

Having realised these challenges and the need to review the national collective engagement strategy in SA, COSATU proposed the following strategic intent: the need to campaign for the adoption of a national minimum wage; the need for the development of federation-style collective bargaining strategies, especially to reconfigure the pay structure; the need for the introduction of legislated mandatory centralised bargaining; the need to campaign for universal income support to cover all adults; the package of labour market and social protection measures should form the basis of a national agreement through the National Growth Plan (NGP), which is connected to an overhaul of the SA macro-economic policies; and, where employment is threatened in crisis-hit industries, a package of rescue measures needs to be devised and implemented by the parties, together with the government (COSATU, 2012).

An analysis of the Marikana Commission of Enquiry report identified eight emerging conditions lacking in the strategies of collective engagement stakeholders (South African Board of People Practices [SABPP], 2015). The first omission is that it is not easy to build a relationship of trust through collective engagement with employees as long as employees' living conditions are unpleasant and outside the mine premises. The second omission is that collective engagement failed to adequately match investment in employee housing to the cycles of platinum prices. The third omission is that there was a failure of the parties to engage thoroughly, separately and collectively on matters. The fourth omission is that most of the time, compromises and consensus are only considered during the dispute phase of the collective engagement process and when emotions are out of control. The fifth omission is that the failure to continue engaging during a dispute fuels the destructive nature of a strike. The sixth omission is the use or intervention of non-collective engagement agents during a dispute or strike situation, which causes havoc and raises emotions. The seventh omission is the lack of a communication strategy or contingency plan to deal with a strike situation that threatens to be disastrous. Lastly, there is a failure to listen to minority parties during a strike situation that can extend the size of the strike, as those unions or employees not involved in a dispute may be prevented from continuing with regular work. This results in forcing non-striking employees to continue working as normal during a volatile strike, putting the lives of innocent people at risk. Management needs to assess the risks and institute action that will protect non-striking employees (SABPP, 2015).

The SABPP picked up lessons from the Marikana debacle and suggested the following strategies as the way forward for collective engagement in the workplace. The first suggestion is the creation of a climate of trust, cooperation and stability within an organisation. The second suggestion is achieving a harmonious and productive working environment which enables the organisation to compete effectively in its marketplace. The third suggestion is to establish a framework for conflict resolution. The fourth suggestion is to establish a framework for collective bargaining, where relevant. The fifth suggestion is ensuring capacity building and compliance to relevant labour legislation and codes of good practice as per the ILO and DoL standards. The sixth suggestion is that management must at all times give honest information about its financial circumstances and ensure that employees understand the information. The seventh suggestion is that commitments made to any plan or agreement must be adhered to, or stakeholders must be involved in any proposed changes to those commitments. The eighth suggestion is that information on any change in the employment relations climate, which may occur from many different causes, should be gathered and carefully evaluated. Lastly, all stakeholders should be involved sooner rather than later in the resolution of disputes (SABPP, 2015).

As a major labour movement in the country, COSATU has accepted that the status of collective engagement requires a major strategic overhaul (Coleman, 2013). COSATU has acknowledged that the labour markets are facing significant challenges, which include the following: collective bargaining institutions becoming fragmented and constantly being destabilised, no coherent wage policy in the country to address poverty and inequality amongst workers and no consistent framework to link labour market strategies and institutions to a broader economic development strategy (Coleman, 2013).

There are a number of interventions that can restore the SA mining industry to a good, healthy state, specifically if jointly driven by stakeholders (government, labour movements and employers) who have the will to modernise and transform the industry. Hartford (2012) endorsed the following essential interventions: transforming and investing in the migrant labour system to modernise labour migrancy through a new migratory labour model founded on human dignity and the promotion of the mining industry as an employment attractor; short work cycles and continuous operations; significant pay rewards in a flatter remuneration structure on re organised work processes; modern, adequate living quarters for migrants underpinned by an efficient migrant commuter transport network (flight, rail or road); restoring migrant nuclear families to good health and banking facilities to facilitating maximum remittances to rural areas; overhauling stakeholder relationships and transforming or enabling the front-line managers to understand freedom of association, worker democracy, positively managing people, problem resolution capacity, union rights, levels of bargaining and recognition procedures; ensuring constituency-based union accountability and democracy; deepening freedom of association and democratic processes for union accountability in bargaining units, rights of shop stewards and threshold representation levels; rapidly transforming line management function to create language synergy and strong interpersonal problem-solving skills; restoring line function to be accountable for people problem resolution and employee communication, and measuring and rewarding line management for effective people problem resolution and effective communication.

Elgoibar, Munduate and Euwema (2016) highlight trust as a deterrent and argue that a good trust relationship is critical in the management of inevitable tensions and conflicts of interest related to change, and in the process of repairing broken relationships between management and employees, and their representatives. At Marikana, the employees did not trust either NUM or management, and for this reason wanted to engage on their own with the company representatives; thus, they felt excluded by both parties. As an alternative, the RDOs turned to the Association of Mineworkers and Construction Union (AMCU) for assistance with their bargaining issues, and soon most other job category employees also diverted to AMCU.

Webster (2013) cited that the engaging parties' ability to compromise is a possible limitation to harmonious collective engagement. Furthermore, the inability of the social partners to implement a delicate concession seems to be hampered by the complex legacy of SA's apartheid past. With the above discussion in mind, one wonders whether a collective engagement framework, as outlined in Tables 1 and 2, is considered by stakeholders in the mining sector when attempting to create sustainable harmonious policies, strategies, procedures and practices. It is evident from the literature review that there is an empirical research gap in stakeholder strategies for managing collective engagement in SA mines.

Whether the proposed collective engagement strategy changes will overhaul the mining industry remains to be tested in practice. It seems that the current intentions and strategies of the current collective engagement stakeholders in SA may not be geared towards co-creating harmonious working environments in the country because of internal and external factors.

External factors impacting South African collective engagement strategies

External circumstances can impact internal employment relations processes. Hence, the collective engagement stakeholder representatives must continually scan and evaluate the external environment. The lack of attention paid to the conditions under which employees live, and attempting to improve socio-economic conditions of employees, means that leaders and managers are less likely to pay attention to radical elements from inside or outside. The external factors impacting the SA collective engagement strategies are presented under the subheadings of legacy and socio-political factors and global labour market influences.

Legacy issues and socio-political factors

Benjamin (2005) argued that attempts were made in the early post-apartheid period to forge a more social, democratic and coordinated variety of capitalism; however, this floundered as the government adopted neoliberal macro-economic policies against the wishes of organised labour. Hence, black economic empowerment policies further undermined an already racially fraught business sector. Di Paola and Pons-Vignon (2013) concur with Coleman (2013) to confirm the reports produced by the International Monetary Fund (IMF), which state that the SA Government has yielded to feared warnings of populism in the labour market. They argued that market flexibility has been destroyed by rigid rules established for overprotected workers who are poorly skilled or over-unionised. This is a deadly mix that results in high unemployment and poverty.

The shift in the political environment of the country, meanwhile, has had a more fundamental transformative impact, shaking the institutional underpinnings of collective bargaining in the mining sector (Szabó, 2013). The SA mining industry is challenged by the need to address a number of legacy issues that promote a undesirable review of the industry and perpetuate discontent, leading to potential policy change (Humby, 2016). Humby suggested that the past is unlikely to be addressed through a uniform process and that the industry would do better to be more attentive to the remedial theories, limitations and opportunities inherent in multiple forms of engagement, as these manifest in flashpoints of conflict that invoke legacy issues. Szabó (2013) suggested that the economic crisis has affected collective bargaining through two channels: direct economic challenges and political change. SA's economic challenges have led to the polarisation of the labour force in the private sector and further sternness in the public sector.

A study conducted by Price, Bailey and Pyman in 2014 concluded that an environment in which unions are not forced to fight to represent members can be conducive to collaborative employment relations, particularly in industries where the parties do not adopt an adversarial stance (Price et al., 2014). Bluestone and Kochan (2014) agreed that the continuing fiscal crisis facing the commonwealth countries and its municipalities can provide the motivation for forging a fundamental change in public sector labour relations. This could not only lead to a more efficient and effective government service but could also play a critical role in improving public services and closing the achievement gap.

The dominance of competitiveness is a central frame reference in the wage policies of different trade unions (Cruces, Trillo & Leonardi, 2015). This competitiveness has a negative impact on economic growth and social cohesion. Seldén (2014) concluded that competing discourses co-existed with regard to the measures to be taken, displaying important and historically rooted differences between trade unions regarding the context, scope and objectives of transnational collective action. A good stakeholder collective engagement strategy should, therefore, be able to fit within the environmental factors (past, present and future) that have an influence on the labour market and that have an impact on collective engagement processes.

Global labour market influences

Multinational firms pay above-industry average wages compared to local firms in the country in which they operate, thus impinging on competitors, and on employment policies of the labour market in general (Driffield, 2013). Multinational firms have bargaining power weakness when compared to local firms; first, because of their positions in global structures, and second, because of their desire to buy industrial peace which they can afford because of high volumes of productivity and profitability (Driffield, 2013). Most of the mining companies in SA are part of the global companies; hence, they pay higher averages in comparison with local companies in other sectors. The local mining companies are forced to compete with these global companies, putting strain on their financial outlook and causing them to fail in sustaining their businesses.

The labour market firms influence economic growth and impact the supply of key skilled workers to new and expanding firms, and the shedding of workers from declining and failing firms (Henrekson, 2014). Growth-favouring labour market institutions include the following as part of the payment package: portable pension plans and other job tenure rights, health insurance untied to the current employer, individualised wage-setting and public income insurance systems that encourage mobility and risk-taking. Blanton, Blanton and Peksen (2015) stated that organised labour has consistently been critical of International Financial Institutions (IFI) policy prescriptions attached to loans, as such policies harm workers' interests. On the contrary, these financial institutions refute the organised labour claims, arguing to the contrary that they work with relevant labour organisations and that many of their arrangements call for compliance with core labour standards (Blanton et al., 2015). It seems that very little research has been devoted to whether IFI programmes affect labour laws and the actual labour practices of recipient countries. It also seems that international financial institutes undermine collective labour rights and that policy reforms are necessary.

Discussion

In this article, the current literature has been reviewed according to the current collective engagement stakeholder strategies to establish their effectiveness and relevance. The conclusion is that most of the research conducted has been focused on collective engagement failures and that there is a need to pay more attention to future collective engagement strategies that will contribute positively to a harmonious labour relations environment. Figure 1 outlines the analysis of the current collective engagement stakeholder strategies and the gaps that need to be addressed.

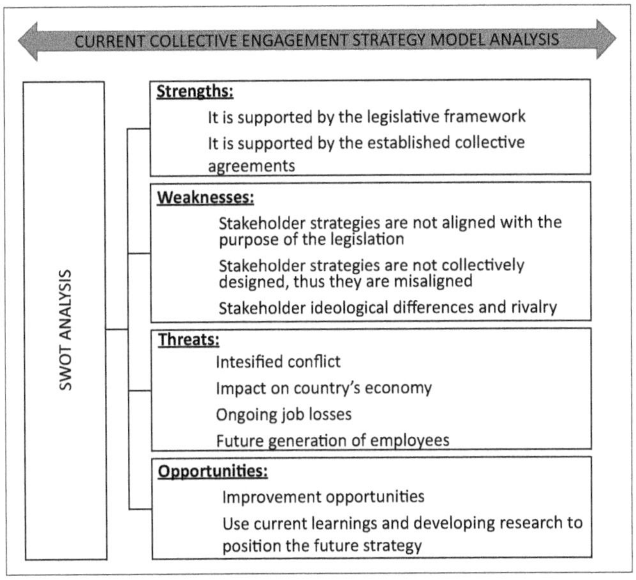

FIGURE 1: Current collective engagement strategy analysis.

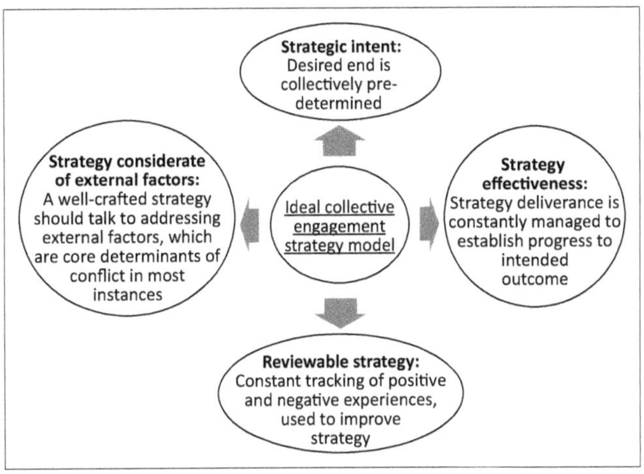

FIGURE 2: Proposed collective engagement strategic model.

Cognisance was taken of the evolving labour relations environment and the fact that there is a need for a constant review of labour strategies to sustain labour peace, meaning that empirical research in this area should be continuous. Based on the literature discussion, it is suggested that an effective stakeholder strategy should reflect the following: there should be strategic intent; there should be a clear analysis of past and current strategy impact to the labour relations environment to establish the future strategy; the strategy should be measurable; the strategy should be amenable to change where the new developments in the labour market dictate as much; the strategy should address not only wages and terms of employment but must also take cognisance of socio-economic and political factors that have a direct or indirect impact; and there should be a collective establishment of the strategy that is aligned with other similar business sectors.

The review of the current labour relations challenges and weaknesses, together with the analytical suggestions, resulted in a proposed strategic model for harmonious collective engagement in SA. Figure 2 proposes what a possible future labour relations strategic model should consider with regard to strategic intent, strategy effectiveness, reviewable strategy and impact of external factors.

Figure 2 suggests a collaborative approach in the development of strategies, either at plant or central bargaining levels or at policy formulating levels. Collective engagement stakeholder representatives should be able to predetermine critical matters of interest for any intended collective engagement and jointly adopt appropriate collective engagement strategies that are relevant for the purpose. A clear engagement agenda should be jointly generated and agreed upon, and should be measured as to whether it is responding positively, efficiently and effectively to matters of importance, both internally and externally.

Conclusion

This theoretical article presented an overview of the current stakeholder strategies for collective engagement for harmonious labour relations in the SA mining sector. The introduction and background presented the unstable and violent collective engagement processes in the employment relations environment in SA. The existing collective engagement strategies were identified and presented. A discussion of the suggestions and recommendations for harmonious labour relations in the SA mining sector resulted in a strengths, weaknesses, opportunities and threats (SWOT) analysis and a proposed collective engagement strategic model.

Although the current collective engagement framework in SA is sound and stable, the stakeholder's ability to create harmonious strategies supporting the framework is found to be lacking. Ideally, the country, and specifically the mining sector, should have a set of standards prescribing best practices for peaceful negotiations and resolutions of employer–employee–union conflicts.

Acknowledgements

The University of Johannesburg has funded this study.

Competing interests

The authors declare that they have no financial or personal relationships that may have inappropriately influenced them in writing this article.

Authors' contributions

P.C.M. is a student who conducted the research study into the collective engagement and stakeholder strategy for harmonious labour relations in a mining organisation, submitted in fulfilment of the requirements for the Master of Philosophy in Employment Relations degree. C.M.G. is a senior lecturer who supervised the study conducted and co-authored the production of this article.

References

Benjamin, P. (2005). *A review of labour markets in South Africa: Labour market regulation: International and South African perspectives*. Human Science Research Council. Retrieved n.d., from http://www.repository.hsrc.ac.za

Blanton, R.G., Blanton, S.L., & Peksen, D. (2015). The impact of IMF and World Bank programs on labor rights. *Political Research Quarterly, 68*(2), 324–336. https://doi.org/10.1177/1065912915578462

Bluestone, B., & Kochan, T.A. (2014). *Toward a new grand bargain: Collaborative approaches to labor-management reform in Massachusetts*. Report. Boston, MA: The Boston Foundation.

Chinguno, C. (2013). *Marikana and the post-apartheid workplace order*. Society, Work and Development Institute (SWOP), Working Paper No. 1. Braamfontein: University of the Witwatersrand.

Chinguno, C. (2015). The unmaking and remaking of industrial relations: The case of Impala Platinum and the 2012–2013 platinum strike wave. *Review of African Political Economy, 42*(146), 577–590. https://doi.org/10.1080/03056244.2015.1087396

Coleman, N. (2013). Towards new collective bargaining, wage and social protection strategies in South Africa – Learning from the Brazilian experience. Global Labour University, Working Paper No. 17. Retrieved November 17, 2013, from http://www.global-labour-university.org

COSATU. (2012). *Concept paper: Towards new collective bargaining, wage and social protection strategies – Learning from the Brazilian experience*. Input to COSATU CEC. Retrieved May 28, 2012, from http://www.cosatu.org.za/docs/discussion/2012/cec_conceptpaper.pdf

Cruces, J., Álvarez, I., Trillo, F., & Leonardi, S. (2015). Impact of the euro crisis on wages and collective bargaining in southern Europe – a comparison of Italy, Portugal and Spain. In G. van Gyes & T. Schulten (eds.), *Wage bargaining under the new European economic governance: Alternative strategies for inclusive growth*, (pp. 93–137). Brussels: European Trade Union Institute.

Dawkins, C.E. (2014). The principle of good faith: Toward substantive stakeholder engagement. *Journal of Business Ethics, 121*(2), 283–295. https://doi.org/10.1007/s10551-013-1697-z

Di Paola, M., & Pons-Vignon, N. (2013). Labour market restructuring in South Africa: Low wages, high insecurity. *Review of African Political Economy, 40*(138), 628–638. https://doi.org/10.1080/03056244.2013.858432

DoL. (2012). *Annual industrial action report*. Pretoria: Government Printers.

Driffield, N. (2013). *Global competition and the labour market*. Routledge. Retrieved May 13, 2013, from http://www.routledge.com

Elgoibar, P., Munduate, L., & Euwema, M. (2016). *Building Trust and Constructive Conflict Management in Organizations: Industrial Relations & Conflict Management*. Cham: Springer.

Farlam, I.G., Hemraj, P.D., & Tokota, B.R. (2015). *Marikana commission of inquiry: Report on matters of public, national and international concern arising out of the tragic incidents at the Lonmin mine in Marikana, in the North West Province*. Retrieved March 13, 2015, from http://www.lonmin-farlam.com

Grimshaw, D., Bosch, G., & Rubery, J. (2014). Minimum wages and collective bargaining: What types of pay bargaining can foster positive pay equity outcomes? *British Journal of Industrial Relations, 52*(3), 470–498. https://doi.org/10.1111/bjir.12021

Hartford, G. (2012). The mining industry strike wave: What are the causes and what are the solutions? *GroundUp*. Retrieved October 10, 2012, from http://groundup.org.za/content/mining-industry-strike-wave-what-are-causes-and-what-are-solutions#sthash.blKcK2zl.dpuf

Harvey, R. (2013). *Releasing the prisoners from their dilemma: How to resolve labour tensions in South Africa's mining sector*. Cape Town: SAIIA. (n.d.). Retrieved from https://www.africaportal.org/documents/11211/saia_spb_81_harvey_20131231.pdf

Henrekson, M. (2014). How labor market institutions affect job creation and productivity growth. *IZA World of Labor*. https://doi.org/10.15185/izawol.38

Humby, T.L. (2016). Redressing mining legacies: The case of the South African mining industry. *Journal of Business Ethics, 135*(4), 653–664. https://doi.org/10.1007/s10551-014-2380-8

Kruger, J., & Tshoose, C.I. (2013). The impact of the Labour Relations Act on minority trade unions: A South African perspective. *PER: Potchefstroomse Elektroniese Regsblad, 16*(4), 1–45.

Lester, D.B. (2014). *Employee participation in decision making in the mining sector*. Doctoral dissertation. Cape Town: University of the Western Cape.

Nwankwo, N.U. (2016). *The role of collective bargaining on management and labour relations: A case study of First Aluminium Company Limited and West African Glass Industry Limited Port Harcourt*. Doctoral dissertation. Enugu: University of Nigeria.

Organization for Economic Co-operation and Development (OECD). (2000). *Tackling inequalities in Brazil, China, India and South Africa: The role of labour market and social policies*. Paris: OECD.

Price, R., Bailey, J., & Pyman, A. (2014). Varieties of collaboration: The case of an Australian retail union. *The International Journal of Human Resource Management, 25*(6), 748–761. https://doi.org/10.1080/09585192.2012.743477

Roberts, K. (2015). *Does collaborative bargaining make a difference in nursing agreements?* East Lansing, MI: Michigan State University.

SABPP. (2015). *Where did it all go wrong? Findings of the Farlam Commission Report – How Lonmin Employment Relations Management practice compared to the SABPP HR Management Standard on ERM*. Parktown: SABPP.

Sachs, B.I. (2013). The unbundled union: Politics without collective bargaining. *Yale Law Journal, 123*(1), 148–207. Retrieved October 08, 2013, from https://ssrn.com/abstract=2337561

Seldén, K.L. (2014). Laval and trade union cooperation: Views on the mobilizing potential of the case. *International Journal of Comparative Labour Law and Industrial Relations, 30*(1), 87–104.

South African Government. (2015). *Labour Relations Act, no. 66, of 1995, amended in 1996, 1998, 2002, 2015*. Pretoria: Government Printers.

Szabó, I. (2013). Between polarization and statism – effects of the crisis on collective bargaining processes and outcomes in Hungary. *Transfer: European Review of Labour and Research, 19*(2), 205–215.

Webster, E. (2013). The promise and the possibility: South Africa's contested industrial relations path. *Transformation: Critical Perspectives on Southern Africa, 81*(1), 208–235. https://doi.org/10.1353/trn.2013.0000

4

Electronic human resource management: Enhancing or entrancing?

Authors:
Paul Poisat[1]
Michelle R. Mey[2]

Affiliations:
[1]Graduate School, Nelson Mandela Metropolitan University, South Africa

[2]School of Industrial Psychology and Human Resources, Nelson Mandela Metropolitan University, South Africa

Corresponding author:
Michelle Mey,
michelle.mey@nmmu.ac.za

Orientation: This article provides an investigation into the current level of development of the body of knowledge related to electronic human resource management (e-HRM) by means of a qualitative content analysis. Several aspects of e-HRM, namely definitions of e-HRM, the theoretical perspectives around e-HRM, the role of e-HRM, the various types of e-HRM and the requirements for successful e-HRM, are examined.

Research purpose: The purpose of the article was to determine the status of e-HRM and examine the studies that report on the link between e-HRM and organisational productivity.

Motivation for the study: e-HRM has the capacity to improve organisational efficiency and leverage the role of human resources (HR) as a strategic business partner.

Main findings: The notion that the implementation of e-HRM will lead to improved organisational productivity is commonly assumed; however, empirical evidence in this regard was found to be limited.

Practical/managerial implications: From the results of this investigation it is evident that more research is required to gain a greater understanding of the influence of e-HRM on organisational productivity, as well as to develop measures for assessing this influence.

Contribution: This article proposes additional areas to research and measure when investigating the effectiveness of e-HRM. It provides a different lens from which to view e-HRM assessment whilst keeping it within recognised HR measurement parameters (the HR value chain). In addition, it not only provides areas for measuring e-HRM's influence but also provides important clues as to how the measurements may be approached.

Introduction

In recent years, the use of technology in facilitating the human resource management (HRM) function has increased significantly. A number of business objectives have been raised in support of the introduction of electronic human resource management (e-HRM) in the 21st century. These have included cost savings and increased efficiency, the facilitation of strategic aims, and improvements in client services, all of which are clearly beneficial from an organisational perspective (Marler, 2009; Ruël, Bondarouk & Looise, 2004). However, before organisations expend resources on e-HRM systems, it is important to determine whether e-HRM is indeed supporting the attainment of business objectives. In this regard, it is important to consider the role played by e-HRM, the factors that influence the successful implementation of e-HRM systems, and the link between e-HRM and organisational productivity. This article aims to explore these considerations as well as provide an overview of the current body of knowledge related to e-HRM.

In this study, 100 articles, journals and other research products were examined of which 67 were included in the final analysis. These research products were chosen based on their relevance in exploring the following areas: definitions of e-HRM, various types of e-HRM, theoretical perspectives on e-HRM, e-HRM's effect on productivity and other key issues surrounding e-HRM.

Purpose of the study

The objective of this qualitative content analysis is, firstly, to provide a theoretical overview of the current understanding of the nature and relevance of e-HRM, secondly, to identify the major contemporary areas of e-HRM research and, thirdly, to examine the link between e-HRM and organisational productivity. The findings of this analysis are offered in an attempt to stimulate the thinking of e-HRM researchers in terms of applying their efforts to exploring the influence of e-HRM from a more strategic perspective, in particular in researching the influence of e-HRM on organisational productivity and developing reliable measures in this regard. In the following section, a definition of e-HRM is provided.

Current theoretical perspectives

Defining electronic human resource management

Bondarouk and Ruël (2009, p. 506) argued that e-HRM definitions have 'flourished, with little consistency or agreement in sight'. The authors further argue the importance of understanding how researchers define e-HRM. They assert that minor differences in terminology may result in consequent studies assuming multiple directions, or in a range of user 'subsets' within the e-HRM target population. Since early works on the intersection between web-based technologies and HRM, a number of definitions have been proposed regarding this phenomenon. e-HRM has been referred to as HR Information System (HRIS), virtual HR(M), web-based HRM and intranet-based HRM, although the literature strikes a distinction between these various electronic and web-based phenomena.

To gain a clear understanding of what comprises HRIS is important. HRIS was initially defined as comprising a 'specialised information system within the traditional functional areas of the organisation, designed to support the planning, administration, decision-making, and control activities of human resource management' (DeSanctis, 1986, p. 16). In later years, HRIS was described as a system used to acquire, store, manipulate, analyse, retrieve and distribute pertinent information about the human resources of an organisation (Haines & Petit, 1997). Despite the term HRIS still being in use today, there is an assumed difference between the early information systems for HRM (HRIS) and the information technologies required for current e-HRM applications.

Magnitude and reach appears to be a prominent difference between an HRIS and e-HRM. Some definitions of e-HRM in existing literature focus on a network structure as a central defining feature. For example, Strohmeier (2007, p. 20) defined e-HRM as the 'planning, implementation and application of information technology for both networking and supporting of at least two individual or collective actors in their shared performing of HR activities'. Lepak and Snell (1998, p. 216) used the term 'virtual HR' to encompass a 'network-based structure built on partnerships and mediated by information technologies to help the organisation acquire, develop, and deploy intellectual capital'.

E-HRM is thus regarded as a way of implementing HR strategies, policies and practices in organisations through a conscious and directed support of and/or with the full use of web technology-based channels (Ruël et al.'s, 2004). e-HRM provides multiple functions to its users including managing employee information for various purposes and supporting many HR activities such as recruitment and selection, performance management, compensation and benefits, training and development, health and safety, employee relations, retention, and policies on work-life balance (Ensher, Nielson & Grant-Vallone, 2002; Olivas-Lujan, Ramirez & Zapata-Cantu, 2007). Thite and Kavanagh (2009) divided HRM activities into three categories: (1) transactional activities, involving day-to-day transactions and recordkeeping, (2) traditional HRM activities, such as recruitment, selection, planning, training, compensation and performance management and (3) transformational activities which add value to the organisation, such as organisational development, talent management and learning. As technology has become increasingly incorporated into HR systems large proportions of transactional activities are now delivered electronically. In the following section the differences between computerised human resource information system/human resource information systems (CHRIS/HRIS) and e-HRM are explored in an attempt to ascertain the pertinence of a technology driven and web-based interface aimed at multiple users in driving HRM effectiveness and efficiency.

The difference between computerised human resource information system/human resource information systems and electronic human resource management

Kettley and Reilly (2003) identified a CHRIS as comprising a fully integrated, organisation-wide network of HR-related data, information, services, databases, tools and transactions. This system forms an integral part of e-HRM and relates to the application of conventional, web and voice technologies to improve HR administration, transactions and process performance. Existing literature fails to provide a consistent definition of e-HRM and the term is often interchangeably used with HRIS, human resource management systems (HRMSs), HR software, web-based HR, HR Self-Service, business to employee (B2E) and other terms.

Walker (2001) defined HRIS as involving a systematic procedure for collecting, storing, maintaining, retrieving, and validating data about an organisation's human resources, personnel activities, and organisational unit characteristics. In understanding what constitutes e-HRM it is important to consider the following. An integrated HRIS, as well as appropriate technology, is required in order for e-HRM to be effectively implemented and thus allow for the acquisition, storage, analysis and flow of human resource information throughout the organisation (Van Heerden, Poisat & Mey, 2012). HRIS must, through an effective e-HRM platform, assist both human resource and line managers in decision-making that is linked to the achievement of strategic business objectives through systematically generating accurate, timely and relevant information (Van Heerden et al., 2012).

There are several fundamental differences between HRIS and e-HRM. In essence, HRIS are directed towards the HR department itself as users of these systems are mainly HR staff (Ruël et al., 2004). These systems increase HR departmental efficiency which then purportedly extends to the achievement of business objective (Ruël et al., 2004). e-HRM is not the sole domain of HR staff. It extends to employees and managers within the broader organisational context through HR services which are offered via an intranet and/or the Internet (Ruël et al., 2004). The switch from the automation of HR services per se, towards broader technological support and the provision of information on HR data and services to multiple users is regarded as the major difference between HRIS and e-HRM (Ruël et al., 2004). In other words, e-HRM is a way of implementing HR strategies, policies, and practices in organisations through a conscious and directed support of and/or with the full use of web-technology-based channels (Ruël et al., 2004). In determining the position and relevance of e-HRM from an organisational perspective it is important to consider e-HRM in the context of business appropriate theoretical perspectives. This contextualisation is provided in the following section.

Theoretical perspectives related to electronic human resource management

Four major theoretical frameworks or perspectives on e-HRM are identifiable in the literature: contingency theory, resource-based view theory, transaction cost theory and new institutional theory. Firstly, according to Lawrence and Lorsch's (1967) *contingency theory*, organisations are largely influenced by the environment in which they operate and thus organisational success is dependent on the extent to which the organisation adapts internal structuring to account for the limitations imposed by the environment (Lawrence & Lorsch, 1967). There must be a fit between micro and macro environmental factors and suitable organisational structures in place to achieve desired outcomes (Ruël & Van Der Kaap, 2012). Secondly, the *resource-based theory* states that the most valuable element of organisational competitive advantage is the human resources of the firm which, in terms of this theory, is regarded as valuable, unique, inimitable, and not easily substitutable (Barney, 1991). e-HRM functions such as e-recruiting and e-learning can be viewed as tools which enable organisations to ensure this competitive advantage. Thirdly, *transaction cost theory* identifies cost effectiveness as the best explanation for institutional arrangements. Saving costs becomes the driving force behind organisations' complex, partially outsourced, partially decentralised and partially delegated e-HRM systems (Lepak & Snell, 1998). Fourthly, *institutional theory* has been used to clarify HRM practices and influence in the e-HRM field (Heikkilä, 2013). Institutionalism promotes a critical view on the factual consequences of organisational actions as well as offering explanations of the relation between institutional context and configurations of e-HRM (Strohmeier, 2007).

In further exploring the position and relevance of e-HRM in enhancing organisational efficiencies and effectiveness the following section explores the role of e-HRM as determined through the literature review.

The role of electronic human resource management

E-HRM is regarded as having three over-arching goals, namely (1) reducing cost, (2) improving HR services and (3) improving strategic orientation (Bondarouk, Ruël & Van der Heijden, 2009; Brockbank, 1997; Lepak & Snell, 1998; Stanton & Coovert, 2004). These goals are subject to external factors, such as the impact of globalisation, and lack a clear definition in the practice of e-HRM. From the literature review, it seems apparent that e-HRM is regarded as being mostly concerned with cost reduction and efficiency increases in the provision of HR services, rather than on improving the strategic orientation of HRM (Gardner, Lepak & Bartol, 2003; Parry & Tyson, 2011; Ruël et al., 2004; Ruta, 2005). It is argued that increasing the use of e-HRM allows HR professionals to improve their performance through participating more as internal consultants and focusing less on transactional and administrative duties, thereby providing value to the organisation and improving the standing of HRM in the organisation (Hussain, Wallace & Cornelius, 2007; Lawler & Mohrman, 2003). To this end, e-HRM is regarded as a medium which provides executive reports and summaries to help HR professionals and management in making strategic decisions (Broderick & Boudreau, 1992).

In understanding the contribution afforded to organisations in adopting a true e-HRM system, in other words one which is distinguishable from an HRIS and supported by the necessary technology and web-enabled platform, the following section explores the differing forms of and related HRM functions associated with e-HRM. These considerations are deemed important in determining the benefits of associating HRM functions with e-HRM from a broad-based HRM value chain perspective.

Types of electronic human resource management

Lepak and Snell (1998) identified three types of e-HRM: operational e-HRM, relational e-HRM and transformational e-HRM.

Firstly, *operational e-HRM* consists of the basic administrative activities of the HR department such as payroll, personnel data management, departmental record maintenance and others which make up the bulk of the workload of the HR Department. A number of authors have supported the cost-reducing benefits and increase in efficiency created by e-HRM in this regard (Marler, 2009; Ruël et al., 2004). This is achieved through minimising HR staff bonded to these activities, increasing processing speed and reducing the amount of administrative work, thus freeing time for other activities (Ruël et al., 2004; Ruta, 2005; Strohmeier, 2007).

Secondly, *relational e-HRM* comprises those HR activities that support a mutual relationship between the HR department and other departments, both within the organisation and externally. These types of e-HRM activities include functions such as e-recruitment, e-learning and e-performance management. Relational e-HRM may provide employees and managers with remote access to HR information, thus increasing their ability to connect with other internal and external stakeholders, as well as providing individuals with the tools to perform HR activities themselves. This again lessens the involvement of HR staff, allowing them to refocus their priorities.

Thirdly, *transformational e-HRM* focuses on the strategic activities of HRM, such organisational change processes, strategic re-orientation, strategic competence management and strategic knowledge management. By improving the strategic orientation of HRM, e-HRM has the capacity to transform the HR function (Ruël et al., 2004). A strategic HR function links HRM activities to the strategic management process and strategic objectives of the business. This leads to an integrated set of policies and practices developed to execute the company's implicit or explicit business strategy through the management of the firm's human capital (Martin-Alcazar, Romero-Fernandez & Sanchez-Gardey, 2005; Wright & McMahan, 1992). A pivotal goal of e-HRM is thus to contribute to the strategic alignment of the HRM function. In this regard, e-HRM systems provide managers with accurate and reliable data about their employees which may prove crucial in business decisions (Ghazzawi, Al-khoury & Saman, 2014). This is perhaps the least considered and explored role of e-HRM, as may be evidenced by subsequent considerations in this review.

The success of e-HRM in enhancing the HRM value chain for the HRM department, line managers and other users or stakeholders of e-HRM is dependent on a number of requirements. These are outlined in the following section.

Key requirements for electronic human resource management success

The literature investigated revealed that a number of key issues need to be addressed in order to successfully implement e-HRM. These are discussed below.

Human resources skills

Changes to service delivery, and hence the HR role, cannot be achieved without the development of new skills within an organisation's HR team. Practitioners must possess consultancy, strategic thinking, analytical, advanced communication, negotiation, process engineering, project management and business writing skills (Parry & Tyson, 2011). If these skills do not already exist within the HR function then organisations will be unable to meet the required improvements in service delivery needed to take on the challenges associated with e-HRM and even consider moving the mode of HRM service delivery to a more strategic role (Parry & Tyson, 2011; Wright & Snell, 1998).

Training in electronic human resource management use

Providing sufficient training for users of the e-HRM system has a great influence on the outcomes of e-HRM use. Organisations that fail to do so report that systems do not provide the desired efficiency savings as users frequently have to contact HR to obtain support (Parry & Tyson, 2011). A recommendation provided in this regard is to allow HRM staff more time to practise on the system so that they require less support once the system is live (Panayotopoulou, Vakola, & Galanaki, 2007; Parry & Tyson, 2011). In some cases, employees are not aware of the full functionality of the system and are therefore not able to take full advantage of this (Parry & Tyson, 2011).

Engagement with electronic human resource management

It is important for both managers and employees to engage with a new e-HRM system for it to be accepted and used within the organisation. Difficulties in encouraging managers and employees to make use of e-HRM systems have been experienced as managers have complained that using e-HRM is not a good use of their time and some still resort to using traditional offline systems (Parry & Tyson, 2011). This example emphasises the importance of encouraging people to change their mindset in regard to the value of adopting e-HRM to avoid delays and reaping the associated benefits (Parry & Tyson, 2011). The role of skills development, training and a relatable e-HRM system are highlighted as important in this regard.

The adoption of e-HRM may also be influenced by cultural factors, as the national culture in which a company is situated may in turn impact the culture of the organisation (Bondarouk, Schilling & Ruël, 2016). For example, a culture that relies on face-to-face relationships and personal connections may find e-HRM practices less personal and thus more difficult to adopt and engage with (Bondarouk et al., 2016).

Engagement with e-HRM is also influenced by the web of delivery channels which have evolved over time. This has influenced perceptions of a more advanced e-HRM. HR-shared service centres serve as one example hereof (Farndale, Paauwe & Hoeksema, 2009). Face-to-face HRM services are seen as becoming obsolete, with organisations preferring modern, well-designed and technically well-functioning IT-based e-HRM platforms. The inflexibility, rigidity, innovative incapacity, and inferior efficiency and effectiveness of traditional two-level HRM functions developed around the HR department and middle managers are becoming obsolete.

Design of the electronic human resource management system

The design of the e-HRM system may affect the outcomes of the introduction of that system (and therefore the realisation of goals). A system that is not user-friendly or intuitive increases the amount of administration necessary for managers rather than reducing it (Parry & Tyson, 2011). A further important consideration in terms of design is that of imitation. e-HRM is not exempt from the impact of imitation through the diffusion of technological innovations across economies, sectors and organisations (Ciborra, 2002). Adopting the same or a similar e-HRM application without considering organisational uniqueness may destroy the competitive advantage which may be associated therewith.

Familiarity with technology

Organisational culture which readily accepts the use of technology will find it easier to introduce e-HRM systems and to realise the benefits of said systems. User acceptance is of great importance in determining the success or failure of e-HRM systems. The technology acceptance model (TAM) is the most widely applied model of user acceptance and subsequent usage of information systems (Huang & Martin-Taylor, 2013). This model emphasises two main constructs: perceived usefulness and perceived ease of use (Huang & Martin-Taylor, 2013). Perceived usefulness is the belief that using a system will enhance job performance and perceived ease of use is the belief that using a system will require minimum effort (Huang & Martin-Taylor, 2013).

Conceptualising relationships between electronic human resource management and human capital development

At a strategic level, the relationship between e-HRM and human capital development needs to be clear for all users of e-HRM platforms. Global talent search and retention is believed to be facilitated by e-HRM. HR portals, explored by Shilakes and Tylman (1998) and Bondarouk and Ruël (2009), are considered a method of insuring informed business decisions, which are made based on personalised information from organisations, as well as the practice of monitoring, collecting and developing organisation-wide knowledge resources. This is particularly important in the alignment between HR portal configuration and HR strategy on the creation of intellectual capital (Bondarouk & Ruël, 2009). Frequently and easily accessed HR portals lead to the alignment of the HR portal configuration, with the HR strategy which allows for the ability to leverage intellectual capital creation and development. HR professionals become accountable for e-HRM (HR portal) design and choices regarding its applications (Bondarouk & Ruël, 2009).

Measurement of value creation for diverse groups of users

A core concern in the development and implementation of e-HRM is on how value creation is measured for diverse groups of users (Bondarouk & Ruël, 2009). E-HRM users have become increasingly comfortable with the use of e-sources in finding reliable and high-quality information and learning how to work with applications and software that they are not traditionally familiar with (Bondarouk & Ruël, 2009; Martin, Reddington & Alexander, 2008). Therefore, for current and new e-HRM applications to be constructive, their use and value must be acknowledged by their users. Different user groups will have different views on the relevance of e-HRM (Bondarouk & Ruël, 2009). Limited value exists in the simple division of users into management, employees and HR professional groupings as multiple subgroupings can be identified within these groups. All of these groups and subgroups have unique needs that must be met.

Following the above exposition of the nature, role and importance of e-HRM, including information on the drivers for the successful implementation of e-HRM, it becomes important to consider the influence of e-HRM on productivity (Parry, 2011).

Electronic human resource management and productivity

Watson (2002) identified four factors which provide evidence of the value of e-HR: productivity improvements, cost reductions, return on investment and better employee communications. Several pieces of existing literature and case studies hint at increased productivity as a result of e-HRM. This is seen as being achieved through a reduction in HR staff, cost savings and less administrative burden due to automation (Hawking, Stein & Foster, 2004; Ruël et al., 2004 as cited in Strohmeier, 2007). However, it is not possible to directly translate the time saved by e-HRM into financial benefits (Dias, 2001). E-HRM can help achieve relational goals, namely, the provision of high-quality services to the internal customers of the organisation, through increasing the timeliness and improving the client-service orientation of HR professionals (Snell, Pedigo & Krawiec, 1995 as cited in Lepak & Snell, 1998).

According to Walker (2001), improving the level of service, reducing costs and allowing more time for higher value tasks are of great importance for the success of technology in the HR domain. It is expected that the HR function provides strategic direction to human capital management in an organisation and becomes a strategic partner in the achievement of organisational objectives (Hawking et al., 2004; Lepak, Bartol & Erhardt, 2005). Thus investments in technology are aimed at bringing about efficiency in operational tasks (Bell, Lee & Yeung, 2006; Lawler & Mohrman, 2003). It is believed that e-HRM can promote the quality of HR functions as well as help managers to supervise employees efficiently and effectively (Yusoff, Ramayah & Haslindar, 2010). In relation to the role of e-HRM and organisational productivity, it is argued that e-HRM helps to achieve the aim of globalisation of organisations, which has led to the development of terms like global HRIS, global information system (GIS) and international human resource management (IHRM; Akmanligil & Palvia, 2004; Ruël et al., 2004). Many unknown and complex challenges are created by globalisation. E-HRM provides considerable benefits in alleviating these challenges (Akmanligil & Palvia, 2004). Employees are able to work remotely, thanks to technological advancement, with HR staff able to carry out tasks from any location (Van Heerden, 2011). This increases flexibility and produces better results amongst staff.

Problem statement and research objectives

The purpose of this study was to investigate the current level of development of the body of knowledge related to e-HRM, specifically in relation to the influence of e-HRM on organisational productivity, more particularly in South Africa. The research methodology associated with this study is provided in the following section.

Research design

As stated, the purpose of this review was to determine the status of e-HRM and examine the studies that report on the link between e-HRM and organisational productivity. The study aimed to determine the existence of South African research in this regard. Because of the extremely limited research encountered in South Africa, it was decided to expand this study to a search for relevant international studies. Although this study focuses mainly on research produced after 2000, some earlier seminal works, such as that of Lepak and Snell (1998), were used.

Research approach

A qualitative content analysis, taking the form of a systematic review of existing literature, was conducted. A content analysis followed by a thematic analysis of key themes that emanated from the literature. To this end, 100 articles, journals and research products were sourced using EBSCOhost, JSTOR and Google Scholar, and examined for relevance. Keywords and phrases used in the search included HRM, e-HRM and productivity, e-HRM in South Africa, and CHRIS/HRIS. Of the articles examined, only 67 were found to be relevant and included in the final review. These studies were categorised into research areas, some of the findings of which are presented in the literature discussed above and further highlighted in the following section.

Results

For the purposes of this study, a review of current literature on the nature and extent of e-HRM was conducted. It was initially envisaged that this study would be limited to a South African context. However, a paucity of studies in this regard led to a more general analysis of these considerations. In an attempt to stimulate both local and international research, Table 1 outlines the major e-HRM research areas explored through the survey of existing literature. The table

TABLE 1: Research areas to date.

Research area	Authors
Value creation • HR service delivery • People efficiency or effectiveness • Training, recruitment and benefits • Redeployment into strategic roles • Supporting strategic tasks • Extra time available	Ruël and Van Der Kaap (2012); Bissola and Imperatori (2013); Ruta (2005); Burbach and Dundon (2005); Hussain et al. (2007); Lawler and Mohrman (2003)
Cost reduction • Outsourcing or automating • Reduced administrative workload • Reduced turnover or reduced staffing • Performance improvement • Streamline processes • Online HR activities • Effectiveness	Marler (2009); Strohmeier (2007); Lepak and Snell (1998); Marchington and Wilkinson (2005); Findikli and Bayarcelick (2015); Heikkilä (2013); Dias (2001); Akmanligil and Palvia (2004); Brockbank (1997); Stanton and Coovert (2004); Bondarouk et al. (2009)
e-HRM tools • Administrative structures • Intranet, extranet, HR portals • Simple management reporting • HRIS/CHRIS • Diagnostic tools • Employee and managerial self-services • IT/ICT	Sanayei and Mirzaei (2008); Burbach and Dundon (2005); Kettley and Reilly (2003); Findikli and Bayarcelick (2015); DeSanctis (1986); Haines and Petit (1997); Strohmeier (2007); Lepak and Snell (1998); Walker (2001); Hopkins and Markham (2003); Andersen (2008); Broderick and Boudreau (1992); Parry and Tyson (2011); Farndale et al. (2009)
e-HRM issues • Changed role of HRM • Acceptance issues • Employee readiness issues • Reduced headcount • Telecommunication issues or illiteracy	Hooi (2006); Parry and Tyson (2011); Ruël et al. (2004); Martin-Alcazar et al. (2005); Wright and McMahan (1992); Findikli and Bayarcelick (2015); Hawking et al. (2004); Gardner et al. (2003); Ruta (2005); Broderick and Boudreau (1992); Hendrickson (2003)
Organisational success • Rapid development of electronic HR systems • Skills • Expertise • Strategic learning • Openness to innovation • Casual mapping	Yusliza and Ramayah (2011); Lepak and Snell (1998); Van Heerden, Poisat and Mey (2012); Ruël et al. (2004); Lawrence and Lorsch's (1967); Parry and Tyson, (2011); Bowman and Ambrosini (2000)
HR and organisational effectiveness • User involvement • Training and education • Employee self-services • Increased performance • Effective use of human capital • Becoming a strategic business partner • Evaluation of effectiveness • Supportive learning • Facilitating organisational development and change • Enhanced job performance	Zafar (2010); Bondarouk et al. (2009); Ruël et al. (2004); Shrivastava and Shaw (2003); Ball (2001); Bowman and Ambrosini (2000); Marler (2009); Strohmeier (2007); Van Heerden, Poisat and Mey (2012); Ruta (2005); Martin-Alcazar et al. (2005); Wright and McMahan (1992); Marchington and Wilkinson (2005); Benson, Johnson and Kuchinke (2002); Heikkilä (2013); Lawler and Mohrman (2003); Bell, Lee and Yeung (2006); Bowman and Ambrosini (2000)
Positive effect on HR department or organisation • Operational performance • Shared services for HR domain • Create competitive advantage • Align the function with business strategy	Ruël and Van Der Kaap (2012); Findikli and Bayarcelick (2015); Heikkilä (2013); Ensher, Nielson and Grant-Vallone (2002); Olivas-Lujan Ramirez and Zapata-Cantu (2007); Hopkins and Markham (2003); Ruta (2005); Akmanligil and Palvia (2004); Van Heerden (2011); Strohmeier (2007); Parry and Tyson (2011)
Productivity	Watson (2002); Walker (2001)

also indicates the corresponding authors considered for each area. This approach is deemed appropriate in light of the fact that e-HRM is not a country or continent 'bound' phenomenon, and supports the notion of globalised HRM practices.

Table 1 reflects that the majority of e-HRM research has focused on the tools and effectiveness of e-HRM. However, most of the studies in question have been of a theoretical nature and empirical evidence in this regard is limited. In particular, no studies were found that empirically linked an increase in organisational productivity to the implementation of e-HRM. Authors such as Watson (2002) and Walker (2001) hint at this improvement in productivity but do not provide empirical proof.

Lee, as cited in Boninelli and Meyer (2011), asserts that the core mandate of HRM is to have a positive impact on organisational outcomes. To this end, he described the linkages between HR and desired outcomes in terms of the HR value chain. The value chain is broadly constituted of the following elements:

- What HR believes and understands (philosophy, values, culture and strategy).
- What HR does (programmes, operating procedures and interactions).
- What happens with people (KSAs, attitudes, and motivation and health).
- HR-related resources (HRISs, facilities, communication and other systems).
- What the people achieve in the organisation (productivity, customer and external stakeholder reactions).
- What the company achieves in the market or society (financial, environmental and societal).
- The moderating effect of environmental context (political, economic, sociocultural and technological).

Utilising the HR value chain typology as proposed by Lee (2011) to view the content of the e-HRM research areas as indicated in Table 1 reflects that much of the research focuses on 'what HR does'; 'what happens with (HR) people'; 'HR related resources' and 'what (HR) people achieve in the company'. These focus areas suggest that e-HRM is evaluated and researched largely in terms of the benefits and value addition that it creates for the HR department and supports the contention of Gardner et al. (2003), amongst others, that e-HRM is mostly concerned with cost reduction and efficiency as opposed to improving the strategic orientation of HRM. Dias (2001) asserts that it is not possible to directly translate the time saved by e-HRM into financial benefits.

Discussion

From the analysis conducted, it would thus appear that a direct line of sight has not been drawn between the implementation of e-HRM and organisational success based on empirical evidence, more particularly when it comes to determining the influence thereof on productivity. The diversity of organisations and their contexts and the multitude of e-HRM platforms and applications should be considered in this regard (Shenet al. 2009). What seems apparent is that the influence of e-HRM on organisational productivity needs to be determined through qualitative and quantitative research.

In this study, an attempt was made to determine the current status of e-HRM and the body of knowledge which exists in this regard. To this end, a quantitative content analysis was undertaken which formed the backdrop to this study. It further allowed for a delineation of current research areas. It was initially planned that this study be conducted within the South African context. However, because of limited research encountered, it was deemed appropriate to extend the study to include international studies.

It is argued that e-HRM can increase the efficiency of HR activities, improve HR service delivery and transform the role of the HR function into one that is more strategic (Hendrickson, 2003; Martin et al., 2008; Ruël et al., 2004). This implies that the use of e-HRM may allow the HR function to increase its value and contribute to the competitive advantage of the firm. The increasing deployment of HR technology and systems could be an additional source of organisational value as these assets have lower barriers to imitability than factors such as know-how (Dierickx & Cool, 1989; Rumelt, 1982).

The suggestion that e-HRM can improve the efficiency of HR activities through reducing costs and increasing the speed of HRM processes can be found in many pieces of existing literature. Lepak and Snell (1998) and Hendrickson (2003) both suggested that e-HRM leads to the streamlining of HR transactional processes and thus increases efficiency. One of the main goals of e-HRM is to produce efficiency gains or cost reductions by reducing headcount in HR departments and removing administration (Ensher et al. 2002; Lengnick-Hall & Moritz, 2003; Martin et al., 2008; Ruël et al., 2004). E-HRM can thus be used as an alternative to having people perform administrative or transactional tasks manually and also deliver these tasks more efficiently. Sophisticated e-HRM systems may be used to offer manager and employee self-service options to further reduce administrative tasks.

Conclusion

It is clear that some aspects of e-HRM are more commonly researched than others. The findings of this analysis appeared to suggest that much of the research focused on the relevance and value of e-HRM for the HR department and personnel. More research is required to gain a greater understanding of this field and prove the assumption that the implementation of e-HRM will lead to strategic advantages, including improved productivity. This implies a focus in terms of Lee's HRM value chain on 'what the company achieves in the market/society'. This would entail empirical studies focused on establishing reliable and valid measures to demonstrate the link between e-HRM and reduced costs, increased revenue or profit, return on investment, economic value addition, shared earnings, reduction in pollution levels, poverty alleviation, amongst others. In addition, it is further proposed that future research should focus on assessing the relevance of, and value creation associated with, e-HRM for diverse groups of users, including operational employees and line management. This would imply that an HRM value chain focuses on 'what happens with the people' and 'what the people achieve in the company'. Research in these areas would also necessitate independent research by organisations as to the appropriateness of the assessment criteria (metrics) which are used to determine success in these areas (Lee as cited in Boninelli & Meyer, 2011).

Acknowledgements

Competing interests

The authors declare that they have no financial or personal relationships that may have inappropriately influenced them in writing this article.

Authors' contributions

M.R.M. and P.P. were jointly responsible for collecting the data. Both the authors were responsible for the writing and editing of the article.

References

Akmanligil, M., & Palvia, P. (2004). Strategies for global information systems development. *Information and Management, 42*(1), 45–59. https://doi.org/10.1016/j.im.2004.01.001

Andersen, P.A. (2008). *Nonverbal communication: Forms and functions*. Long Grove, IL: Waveland Press.

Ball, K.S. (2001). The use of human resource information systems: A survey. *Personnel Review, 30*(5/6), 677–693. https://doi.org/10.1108/EUM0000000005979

Barney, J.B. (1991). Firm resources and sustained competitive advantage. *Journal of Management, 17*(1), 99–120. https://doi.org/10.1177/014920639101700108

Bell, B.S., Lee, S., & Yeung, S.K. (2006). The impact of e-HR on professional competence in HRM: Implications for the development of HR professionals. *Human Resource Management, 45*, 295–308. https://doi.org/10.1002/hrm.20113

Benson, A.D., Johnson, S.D., & Kuchinke, K.P. (2002). The use of technology in the digital workplace: A framework for human resource development. *Advances in Developing Human Resources, 4*(4), 392–404. https://doi.org/10.1177/15 2342202237518

Bissola, R., & Imperatori, B. (2013). Facing e-HRM: The consequences on employee attitude towards the organisation and the HR department in Italian SMEs. *European Journal of International Management, 7*(4), 450–468. https://doi.org/10.1504/EJIM.2013.055282

Bondarouk, T., & Ruël, H. (2009). Electronic human resource management: Challenges in the digital era. *The International Journal of Human Resource Management, 20*, 505–514. https://doi.org/10.1080/09585190802707235

Bondarouk, T., Ruël, H., & Van der Heijden, B. (2009). E-HRM effectiveness in a public sector organization: A multi-stakeholder perspective. *International Journal of Human Resource Management, 20*(3), 578–590. https://doi.org/10.1080/09585 190802707359

Bondarouk, T., Schilling, D., & Ruël, H. (2016). E-HRM adoption in emerging economies: The case of subsidiaries of multinational corporations in Indonesia. *Canadian Journal of Administrative Sciences/Revue Canadienne des Sciences de l'Administration, 33*(2), 124–137. https://doi.org/10.1002/cjas.1376

Boninelli, I., & Meyer, T. (2011). *Human capital trends: Building a sustainable organisation*. Montreal, South Africa: Knowres Publishing.

Bowman, C., & Ambrosini, V. (2000). Value creation versus value capture: Towards a coherent definition of value in strategy. *British Journal of Management, 11*, 1–15. https://doi.org/10.1111/1467-8551.00147

Brockbank, W. (1997). HR's future on the way to a presence. *Human Resource Management, 36*(1), 65–69. https://.org/10.1002/(SICI)1099050X(199721)36: 1%253C65::AIDHRM11%253E3.0.CO;2-D

Broderick, R., & Boudreau, J.W. (1992). Human resource management, information technology, and the competitive edge. *Academy of Management Executive, 6*(2), 7–17. https://doi.org/10.5465/AME.1992.4274391

Burbach, R., & Dundon, T. (2005). The strategic potential of human resource information systems: Evidence from the Republic of Ireland. *International Employment Relations Review, 11*(1/2), 97–117.

Ciborra, C. (2002). *The labyrinths of information*. New York: Oxford University Press.

DeSanctis, G. (1986). Human resource information systems: A current assessment. *MIS Quarterly, 10*, 15–27. https://doi.org/10.2307/248875

Dias, C. (2001). Corporate portals: A literature review of a new concept in information management. *International Journal of Information Management, 21*, 269–287. https://doi.org/10.1016/S0268-4012(01)00021-4

Dierickx, I., & Cool, K. (1989). Asset stock accumulation and sustainability of competitive advantage. *Management Science, 35*(12), 1504–1511. https://doi.org/10.1287/mnsc.35.12.1504

Ensher, E.A., Nielson, T.R., & Grant-Vallone, E. (2002). Tales from the hiring line: Effects of the internet and technology on HR processes. *Organizational Dynamics, 31*(3), 224–244. https://doi.org/10.1016/S0090-2616(02)00111-0

Farndale, E., Paauwe, J., & Hoeksema, L. (2009). In-sourcing HR: Shared service centres in the Netherlands. *International Journal of Human Resource Management, 20*(3), 544–561. https://doi.org/10.1080/09585190802707300

Findikli, M.A., & Bayarçelik, E.B. (2015). Exploring the outcomes of electronic human resource management. *Procedia – Social and Behavioral Sciences, 207*, 424–431. https://doi.org/10.1016/j.sbspro.2015.10.112

Gardner, S., Lepak, D., & Bartol, K. (2003). Virtual HR: The impact of information technology on the human resource professional. *Journal of Vocational Behavior, 63*, 159–179. https://doi.org/10.1016/S0001-8791(03)00039-3

Ghazzawi, K., Al-khoury, P., & Saman, J. (2014). The effect of implementing technology in HRM on the level of employee motivation. *Human Resource Management Research, 4*(2), 33–39. https://doi.org/10.5923/j.hrmr.20140402.04

Haines, V., & Petit, A. (1997). Conditions for successful human resource information systems. *Human Resource Management, 36*(2), 261–275. https://doi.org/10.1002/(SICI)1099-050X(199722)36:2<261::AID-HRM7>3.0.CO;2-V

Hawking, P., Stein, A., & Foster, S. (2004). E-HR and employee self-service: A case study of a Victorian public sector organization. *Issues in Informing Science and Information Technology, 1*, 1017–1026.

Heikkilä, J.P. (2013). *Perspectives on e-HRM in the multinational setting*. Uva.Fi, *173*. Retrieved June 30, 2016, from http://www.uva.fi/materiaali/pdf/isbn_978-952-476-472-8.pdf

Hendrickson, A. (2003). Human resource information systems: Backbone technology for contemporary human resources. *Journal of Labor Research, 24*(3), 381–394. https://doi.org/10.1007/s12122-003-1002-5

Hooi, L.W. (2006). Implementing e-HRM: The readiness of small and medium sized manufacturing companies in Malaysia. *Asia Pacific Business Review, 12*(4), 465–485. https://doi.org/10.1080/13602380600570874

Hopkins, B., & Markham, J. (2003). *E-HR: Using intranets to improve the effectiveness of your people*. Hampshire: Gower Publishing Limited.

Huang, J., & Martin-Taylor, M. (2013). Turnaround user acceptance in the context of HR self-service technology adoption: An action research approach. *The International Journal of Human Resource Management, 24*(3), 621–642. https://doi.org/10.1080/09585192.2012.677460

Hussain, Z., Wallace, J., & Cornelius, N.E. (2007). The use and impact of human resource information systems on human resource management professionals. *Information and Management, 44*(1), 74–89. https://doi.org/10.1016/j.im.2006.10.006

Kettley, P., & Reilly, P. (2003). *E-HR: An introduction (Report No 398)*. Brighton: Institute of Employment Studies.

Lawler, E.E. & Mohrman, S. (2003). HR as a strategic partner – What does it take to make it happen? *Human Resource Planning, 26*(3), 15–29.

Lawrence, P.R., & Lorsch, J.W. (1967). Differentiation and integration in complex organizations. *Administrative Science Quarterly, 12*(1), 1–47. https://doi.org/10.2307/2391211

Lee, G. (2011). *HR metrics*. 1st ed. Randburg, South Africa: Knowres Publishing.

Lengnick-Hall, M., & Moritz, S. (2003). The impact of e-HR on the human resource management function. *Journal of Labor Research, 24*(3) 365–379. https://doi.org/10.1007/s12122-003-1001-6

Lepak, D.P., Bartol, K.M., & Ernhardt, N.L. (2005). A contingency framework for delivering HR practices. *Human Resources Management Review, 15*, 139–159. https://doi.org/10.1016/j.hrmr.2005.06.001

Lepak, D.P., & Snell, S.A. (1998). Virtual HR: Strategic human resource management in the 21st century. *Human Resource Management Review, 8*, 215–234. https://doi.org/10.1016/S1053-4822(98)90003-1

Marchington, M., & Wilkinson, A. (2005). *Human resource management at work: People management and development*. (3rd edn.). London: Chartered Institute of Personnel & Development (CIPD) Publishing.

Marler, J. (2009). Making human resources strategic by going to the Net: Reality or myth? *International Journal of Human Resource Management, 20*(3), 515–527. https://doi.org/10.1080/09585190802707276

Martin-Alcazar, F., Romero-Fernandez, P.M., & Sanchez-Gardey, G. (2005). Strategic human resource management: Integrating the universalistic, contingent, configurational and contextual perspectives. *The International Journal of Human Resource Management, 16*(5), 633–659. https://doi.org/10.1080/09585190500 082519

Martin, G., Reddington, M., & Alexander, H. (2008). *Technology, outsourcing and transforming HR*. Oxford: Elsevier.

Olivas-Lujan, M.R., Ramirez, J., & Zapata-Cantu, L. (2007). E-HRM in Mexico: Adapting innovations for global competitiveness. *International Journal of Manpower, 28*(5), 418–434. https://doi.org/10.1108/01437720710778402

Panayotopoulou, L., Vakola, M., & Galanaki, E. (2007). E-HR adoption and the role of HRM: Evidence from Greece. *Personnel Review, 36*(2), 277–294. https://doi.org/10.1108/00483480710726145

Parry, E. (2011). An examination of e-HRM as a means to increase the value of the HR function. *The International Journal of Human Resource Management, 22*(5), 1146–1162. https://doi.org/10.1080/09585192.2011.556791

Parry, E., & Tyson, S. (2011). Desired goals and actual outcomes of e-HRM. *Human Resource Management Journal, 21*, 335–354. https://doi.org/10.1111/j.1748-8583.2010.00149.x

Ruël, H., Bondarouk, T., & Looise, J. (2004). E-HRM: Innovation or irritation. An explorative empirical study in five large companies on web-based HRM. *Management Revue, 15*(3), 364–381.

Ruël, H., & Van Der Kaap, H. (2012). E-HRM usage and value creation. Does a facilitating context matter? *Zeitschriftfür Personal Forschung, 26*(3), 260–281.

Rumelt, R.P. (1982). Diversification strategy and profitability. *Strategic Management Journal, 3*, 359–369. https://doi.org/10.1002/smj.4250030407

Ruta, C. (2005). The application of change management theory to HR portal implementation in subsidiaries of multinational corporations. *Human Resource Management, 44*(1), 35–53. https://doi.org/10.1002/hrm.20039

Sanayei, A., & Mirzaei, A. (2008). Designing a model for evaluating. The effectiveness of e-HRM (case study: Iranian organizations). *International Journal of Information Science and Technology* 3(9), 79–98.

Shen, J., Chanda, A., D'netto, B., & Monga, M. (2009). Managing diversity through human resource management: An international perspective and conceptual framework. *The International Journal of Human Resource Management, 20*(2), 235–251. https://doi.org/10.1080/09585190802670516

Shilakes, C.C., & Tylman, J. (1998). *Enterprise information portals.* New York: Merrill Lynch.

Shrivastava, S., & Shaw, J.B. (2003). Liberating HR through technology. *Human Resource Management, 42*(3), 201–222. https://doi.org/10.1002/hrm.10081

Snell, S.A., Pedigo, P.R., & Krawiec, G.M. (1995). Managing the impact of information technology on human resource management. In G.R. Ferris, S.D. Rosen, & D.T. Barnum (Eds.), *Handbook of Human Resource Management* (pp. 159–174). Oxford: Blackwell Publishers.

Stanton, J.M., & Coovert, M.D. (2004). Turbulent waters: The intersection of information technology and human resources. *Human Resource Management, 43*(2), 121–126. https://doi.org/10.1002/hrm.20010

Strohmeier, S. (2007). Research in e-HRM: Review and implications. *Human Resource Management Review, 17*, 19–37. https://doi.org/10.1016/j.hrmr.2006.11.002

Thite, M., & Kavanagh, M.J. (2009). *Human resource information systems: Basics, applications and directions* (pp. 3–24). Thousand Oaks, CA: Sage.

Van Heerden, J. (2011). *The impact of the implementation of e-HRM on the human resource management function.* MBA, Faculty of Business and Economic Sciences, Port Elizabeth: Nelson Mandela Metropolitan University.

Van Heerden, J.M., Poisat, P., & Mey, M.R. (2012). *The impact of the implementation on e-HRM on the human resource function.* Paper presented at 6th International Business Conference. Business Schools Partners Network, Mombassa, Kenya.

Walker, A.J. (2001). *Web-based human resources: The technologies and trends that are transforming HR*. New York: McGraw-Hill.

Watson, W. (2002). *The net effect: E-HR and the Internet 2000.* Retrieved July 13, 2016, from http://wsu.worldcat.org/title/net-effect-ehr-and-the-internet-2000-survey-report/oclc/729765551?referer=di&ht=edition

Wright, P.M., & McMahan, G.C. (1992). Theoretical perspectives for strategic human resource management. *Journal of Management, 18*(2), 295.

Wright, P.M., & Snell, S.A. (1998). Toward a unifying framework for exploring fit and flexibility in strategic human resource management. *Academy of Management Review, 23*(4), 756–772. https://doi.org/10.1177/014920639201800205

Yusliza, M.Y., & Ramayah, T. (2011). Explaining the intention to use electronic HRM among HR professionals: Results from a pilot study. *Australian Journal of Basic and Applied Sciences, 5*(8), 489–497.

Yusoff, Y.M., Ramayah, T., & Haslindar, I. (2010). E-HRM: A proposed model based on technology acceptance model. *African Journal of Business Management, 4*(13), 3039–3045.

Zafar, J. (2010). The role of information technology in the personnel department: HRM in the knowledge economy. *Canadian Social Science, 6*(5), 54–59.

5

The role of psychological capital in the relationship between authentic leadership and work engagement

Authors:
Marieta du Plessis[1]
Adre B. Boshoff[1]

Affiliations:
[1]Department of Industrial Psychology, University of the Western Cape, South Africa

Corresponding author:
Marieta du Plessis,
mduplessis@uwc.ac.za

Orientation: The focus on positive psychology in the workplace includes interest in engagement of employees and the conditions and/or characteristics that explain variance in engagement levels.

Research purpose: Psychological capital (PsyCap) can be used as a substitute or enhancer for leadership in the development of work engagement in cases where the individual has a high level of PsyCap.

Motivation for the study: With work engagement becoming increasingly critical to the competitiveness of today's organisations, there is a need to better understand the role of leadership and psychological strengths that support work engagement among employees.

Research approach/design and method: In the quantitative study (on the responses of 647 managers from a national private healthcare organisation), the mediating and moderating role of psychological capital (PsyCap) on the relationship between authentic leadership and work engagement was tested.

Main findings: Psychological capital partially mediated the relationship between authentic leadership and work engagement. Similarly, PsyCap was also a moderator of the relationship, although the main effects remained significant.

Practical/managerial implications: Organisations and leaders should focus on developing a high level of PsyCap within their followers in order to retain high levels of work engagement.

Contribution/value-add: The role of PsyCap in the leadership–engagement relationship indicates that individuals can draw from their PsyCap to improve work engagement.

Introduction

The number of studies on engagement of employees has increased rapidly over the past two decades (Bakker & Albrecht, 2018). From a workplace perspective, engagement of employees is a desirable characteristic of the workforce in the creation of peak performance (Bakker, Demerouti, & Sanz-Vergal, 2014). Even though the engagement of more than a million employees has been studied (Bargagliotti, 2012), it is anticipated that employee engagement will remain an important concern for countries and organisations who seek to increase labour productivity (Gallup, 2013). Not only does engagement enhance important organisational outcomes, it also has positive effects on the psychological well-being of employees (Robertson & Cooper, 2009). Thus, from a psychological perspective, the growth and interest in the field of Positive Psychology, with its focus on happiness, human strengths and optimal functioning (Seligman & Csikszentmihalyi, 2000), gave impetus to the interest in engagement. Seligman (2011) proposed that engagement is regarded as one of the routes to happiness as well as one of the dimensions of human flourishing.

Leaders play an important role in creating a climate of engagement within the organisation (Kahn & Heaphy, 2014). When leaders support, encourage and develop their employees, employees are more likely to have a high level of engagement (Harter & Adkins, 2015). Harter and Adkins (2015) proposed that up to 70% of the variance in engagement scores can be ascribed to leader behaviours. Against the background of positive organisational behaviour, Luthans and Avolio (2003) conceptualised a positive form of leadership, which is termed 'authentic leadership'. Authentic leaders have a well-developed capacity to process information about themselves (including their values, beliefs, goals and feelings); they have clarity regarding their personal identity and have an ability to adjust their leadership behaviours to the needs and preferences of their followers, while still acting in accordance to their personal identity (Chan, Hannah, & Gardner, 2005).

An important part of authentic leadership includes the personal identification of the employee with the leader. Through this identification, authentic leaders influence the thinking and behaviour of members of the organisation (Sparrowe, 2005). The positive modelling of authentic leaders fosters internalised regulation processes among followers, which contribute to greater levels of well-being and engagement (Deci, Connell, & Ryan, 1989). Avolio and Gardner (2005) state that these exchanges would possibly assist individuals to find meaning and purpose in their jobs and craft jobs that best suit their strengths, and the leader would also encourage individuals to persist in their work-related efforts. These actions may result in enhancing employees' vigour, dedication and absorption in their work. Leaders furthermore have an influence on their followers' positive psychological states and psychological capital (PsyCap) by increasing followers' self-confidence and creating hope, optimism and resilience (Ilies, Morgeson, & Nahrgang, 2005; Mäkikangas, Feldt, Kinnunen, & Mauno, 2013).

Avolio and Mhatre (2012) suggest that, although research on authentic leadership continues to grow, researchers should also explore a broader range of mediating and moderating mechanisms in an attempt to explain the authentic leadership construct and its relationship with other organisational variables. For instance, Hsieh and Wang (2015) reported that employee trust mediates the relationship between authentic leadership and work engagement. It should be considered that not all employees' needs are the same and that employees also have psychological capacities that could influence how they interpret and integrate their leader's supportive behaviours into their work behaviours. Followers who are led by authentic leaders feel more efficacy and take greater ownership of their work, as well as being more resilient and hopeful (Rego, Sousa, Marques, & Pina e Cunha, 2012). Similarly, employees who have more personal resources (including self-efficacy, optimism and resilience) have higher levels of work engagement (Mäkikangas et al., 2013). However, authors have suggested that specific leadership styles may be more effective for some followers than for others (Conger & Kanungo, 1998; Pillai & Meindl, 1998), and hence the followers' characteristics would act as a moderator of the influence of the leader. It may be valuable to explore the role of PsyCap because of its predictive properties in explaining peak performance.

Purpose

PsyCap could intervene in the relationship between broad contextual and leadership factors, such as authentic leadership (Avey, Wernsing, & Luthans, 2008), and individual outcomes, such as organisational citizenship behaviour and work performance (Luthans, Norman, Avolio & Avey, 2008; Norman, Avey, Nimnicht, & Pigeon, 2010). As PsyCap seems to be instrumental in facilitating the impact of a positive organisational context on various desirable outcomes (Youssef & Luthans, 2012), it was proposed that PsyCap mediates the relationship between authentic leadership and work engagement. It was further proposed that PsyCap could be a mechanism through which individuals adapt their responses to attain higher levels of work engagement. High PsyCap levels offer employees cognitive (i.e. efficacy), motivational (i.e. hope) and other positive psychological strengths (such as resilience and optimism) (Sweetman, Luthans, Avey & Luthans, 2011), which may assist them in immersing themselves fully in their work apart from the influence of leadership support. Thus, the moderating effect of PsyCap on the relationship between authentic leadership and work engagement was studied.

Literature review

Authentic leadership

Luthans and Avolio (2003) conceptualised a positive form of leadership, which is termed 'authentic leadership'. Authentic leadership draws from both positive psychological capacities of the leader and a highly developed organisational context. These factors, in turn, result in greater self-awareness and self-regulated positive behaviours on the part of the leader. Authentic leadership comprises self-awareness, relational transparency, internalised moral perspective and balanced processing (Avolio & Mhatre, 2012). Self-awareness is defined as an individual's accurate knowledge of his or her own strengths and weaknesses and the way one makes sense of the world. Relational transparency involves appropriate self-disclosure and a genuine presentation of oneself to other people. Balanced processing includes the collection and use of objective, relevant information and balancing this with beliefs that are held, even if the objective information challenges prior beliefs. An internalised moral perspective would influence an individual to act with self-determination and self-regulation, rather than acting in accordance with situational demands (Avolio, Walumbwa, & Weber, 2009).

The theory of authentic leadership emphasises positive and developmental interactions between leaders and followers (Woolley, Caza, & Levy, 2011). Avolio, Gardner, Walumbwa, Luthans and May (2004) proposed a theoretical framework that links authentic leadership to the attitudes and behaviours of followers. According to Avolio et al. (2004), authentic leaders influence their followers' attitudes and behaviours by creating a sense of personal and social identification and setting high moral values and standards. For instance, authentic leaders would use role modelling to display high moral standards to their followers in order for the followers' values and beliefs to become more similar to those of the leaders (Gardner, Avolio, Luthans, May, & Walumbwa, 2005). Another example would be the leader's concern regarding a follower's transparent and genuine discussion of his or her own vulnerabilities, thereby emphasising the constant focus on growth and development of the follower as well as the leader (Avolio et al., 2004).

Followers' personal and social identification with authentic leaders has been shown to lead to higher levels of hope (Snyder, Irving, & Anderson, 1991) and trust (Avolio et al., 2004; Chan et al., 2005; Gardner et al., 2005). Hsieh and Wang (2015) reported that employee trust mediates the relationship between the leader's level of authentic leadership and follower work engagement. Furthermore, positive emotions

(Avolio et al., 2004; Chan et al., 2005) and positive states (Luthans, Youssef, & Avolio, 2007), including higher levels of PsyCap (Munyaka, Boshoff, Pietersen, & Snelgar, 2017), have also resulted from identification of followers with leaders.

Jensen and Luthans (2006) reported that employee perceptions of authentic leadership were the strongest predictor of employee job satisfaction, organisational commitment and work happiness. Further empirical research has demonstrated a positive relationship between the frequency with which authentic leadership is exhibited and the job performance of followers (Peterson, Walumbwa, Avolio, & Fredrickson, 2010, cited in Cameron & Spreitzer, 2012).

Authentic leadership was found to play an important role in the PsyCap development of the follower (Luthans, Avolio, Avey & Norman, 2007; Woolley et al., 2011). It has also been empirically established that PsyCap and a positive organisational context are antecedents of authentic leadership development (Petersen, 2015). Hence, it becomes clear that authentic leadership theory ascribes an important role to the PsyCap of leaders and followers.

Psychological capital

Bearing in mind the criteria for constructs to be included in PsyCap (Luthans, 2002), the positive constructs of efficacy, hope, optimism and resilience met the inclusion criteria (Luthans, Youssef, & Avolio, 2007). These writers termed the combination of these positive constructs as PsyCap. PsyCap is defined as follows:

> An individual's positive psychological state of development that is characterised by: (1) having confidence (self-efficacy) to take on and put in the necessary effort to succeed at challenging tasks; (2) making a positive attribution (optimism) about succeeding now and in the future; (3) persevering toward goals, and, when necessary, redirecting paths to goals (hope) in order to succeed; and (4) when beset by problems and adversity, sustaining and bouncing back and even beyond (resilience) to attain success. (p. 3)

Apart from the importance of each of the four constructs, the synergistic phenomenon of overall PsyCap has been shown to have a higher correlation with performance outcomes than any of the four individual constructs (Luthans, Avolio, et al., 2007). This finding is consistent with Hobfall's (2002) psychological resource theory, which suggests that some constructs are best understood as indicators of broader underlying factors as they may interact synergistically to produce differentiated behaviours over time and different contexts. As a result, PsyCap is classified as a second-order (or higher-order) construct that includes the first-order factors of efficacy, hope, resilience and optimism but also the synergy and shared variance between these four dimensions (Avey, Reichard, Luthans, & Mhatre, 2011; Luthans & Youssef-Morgan, 2017).

A meta-analysis of PsyCap revealed that a number of studies have tested the relationship between PsyCap and various employee attitudes, behaviours and performance (Avey et al., 2011). These writers argue that individuals who possess a high level of PsyCap are likely to be energised and produce effort that leads to higher levels of performance over extended periods of time. PsyCap has been positively correlated to employee performance and satisfaction (Luthans, Avolio et al., 2007), as well as organisational commitment and psychological well-being at work (Avey et al., 2011). Self-efficacy, hope, resilience and optimism, as well as overall PsyCap, have also been shown to have positive relationships with work engagement (Simons & Buitendach, 2013). PsyCap has also been found to mediate the relationship between a supportive organisational climate and performance (Luthans et al., 2008). Furthermore, Huang and Luthans (2014) reported that PsyCap mediated the relationship between learning goal orientation and creativity.

Luthans, Luthans and Luthans (2004) reported that, as with human and social capital, PsyCap may be developed and used in the workplace. PsyCap capacities are psychological states, as opposed to fixed traits, and are therefore open to development through methods such as role modelling, social persuasion, mastery experiences or performance attainments (Luthans et al., 2004). By utilising these development techniques, leaders may have a significant role to play in the development of the PsyCap of their employees.

Work engagement

Schaufeli and Bakker (2003) explain work engagement as a positively satisfying, work-related state of mind that is exemplified by vigour, absorption and dedication. Bakker and Demerouti (2008) state that vigour is characterised by high energy levels and mental resilience while working, whereas absorption signifies being fully concentrated during one's work, with time passing quickly and difficulty being experienced in separating oneself from work. Dedication encompasses being involved in one's work and experiencing significance, enthusiasm, inspiration, pride and challenge.

In further exploring the work engagement construct, it is important to stress that employees' psychological presence in their roles is still at the core of the work engagement construct. Work engagement is believed to be rooted in the theory of authenticity. Authenticity is based on the belief that there can be value in displaying one's whole self that can be utilised to the benefit of work (Rothbard & Patil, 2012). Authentic leadership helps followers to satisfy their own needs, develop themselves and set goals that are in concordance with their own values and beliefs (Gardner et al., 2005).

Studies have demonstrated a positive relationship between work engagement and performance (Cameron & Spreitzer, 2012). Work engagement has been linked to increased organisational citizenship behaviours (Rich, LePine, & Crawford, 2010), enhanced overall performance, high levels of job satisfaction and reduced levels of turnover intention (Bakker & Demerouti, 2008).

With regard to the antecedents of work engagement, studies have shown that personal resources such as self-efficacy, optimism (Xanthopoulou, Bakker, Demerouti, & Schaufeli, 2007) and resilience (Bakker, 2009) are important antecedents of work engagement. These personal resources assist engaged employees to control and impact their work environment in a positive manner (Alesandri, Consiglio, Luthans, & Borgogni, 2018; Luthans et al., 2008). Self-efficacy, optimism and resilience are described as dimensions of PsyCap, and hence it can be deducted that PsyCap could also be an antecedent of work engagement. The proposed link was tested in an empirical study by Simons and Buitendach (2013), who confirmed the relationship between dimensions of PsyCap and work engagement. Authentic leadership has also been shown to significantly predict work engagement (Penger & Černe, 2014). Moreover, Giallonardo, Wong and Iwasiw (2010) found higher levels of work engagement when employees perceived authentic leadership behaviour in their leader.

Low levels of engagement have been found in many countries (Robertson & Cooper, 2010), including South Africa (Rothmann, 2017). Maslach, Schaufeli and Leiter (2001) theorised that the impact of the changing world of work is demonstrated in the expectations imposed on employees. These expectations include expending more time and effort and possessing greater skills and flexibility, while the organisation, on the other hand, is offering less in terms of career opportunities, employment and job security. There is also a general lack of supportive leadership behaviours to assist employees to deal with the job demands they face.

Dissatisfied employees are not committed to an organisation and they are also frequently absent from work in an attempt to cope with or escape from the high work demands (Rothmann, 2017). Organisations with a disengaged workforce may experience severe financial constraints and also lack the competitive edge to survive in the market. It is therefore important for management to focus on ways in which to enhance those aspects of the job that will make employees feel energetic, dedicated and engaged in their work (Mostert & Rathbone, 2001). For the purpose of the present study, the possible influence of PsyCap on the hypothetical relationship between authentic leadership and work engagement was explored.

Method

The research design was quantitative in nature and a survey was used to collect the empirical data. A composite questionnaire containing the Utrecht Work Engagement Scale (UWES) (Schaufeli & Bakker, 2003), PsyCap questionnaire (PCQ) (Luthans et al., 2007) and the Authentic Leadership Questionnaire (ALQ) (Walumbwa, Avolio, Gardner, Wernsing, & Peterson, 2008) was electronically completed by 647 managers from a national organisation in the healthcare industry in South Africa.

Research procedure

The sample for the study was selected through purposive sampling. The requirements that were set for participation in the study were access to a computer and the Internet, and acceptable English literacy, as the questions required respondents to be able to differentiate between fine nuances of behaviour described in words. Employees from all branches of the organisation were included. Eight hundred and fifty-five members of the organisation met these characteristics and were invited to respond to the survey. After the process of data gathering, 670 responses were recorded. However some of these responses were incomplete and had to be excluded from the sample. Therefore, the survey response rate of usable responses was calculated as 76% ($n = 647$).

Participants

The sample consisted mostly of female (77% of the sample) and Afrikaans-speaking (66%) respondents. Further to this, the largest proportion of the sample was managers (81%). The respondents' ages ranged from 25 to 63, with an average age of 45 years ($SD = 8.08$). Although some respondents were quite new to the organisation, the mean tenure of the respondents were 11 years ($SD = 6.197$). The mean reporting period to current manager of 4 years ($SD = 4.046$) also indicates a fairly stable workforce at the managerial level.

Measurement instruments

The Utrecht Work Engagement Scale (UWES) items are scored on a seven-point Likert scale (0 = 'never' to 6 = 'always'). Previous South African studies reported scores from the UWES to have good internal consistency reliability ranging from 0.78 for vigour and 0.89 for dedication to 0.78 for absorption (Storm & Rothmann, 2003). Using the UWES as unidimensional, Laba and Geldenhuys (2016) reported a Cronbach's alpha reliability of 0.90. The internal reliability of scores from the unidimensional UWES in the present study sample was 0.92.

The PCQ consists of 24 items to measure the four dimensions, namely self-efficacy, hope, resilience and optimism. It is scored on a six point Likert scale, ranging from 1 ('strongly disagree') to 6 ('strongly agree'). Scores from the PCQ had evidence of adequate reliability ranging from 0.67 to 0.90 (Görgens-Ekermans & Herbert, 2013; Simons & Buitendach, 2013). The internal reliability of scores from the PCQ in the present sample was 0.89.

The ALQ comprises 16 items to measure four subscales of authentic leadership, namely self-awareness, relational transparency, balanced processing and internalised moral perspective (Luthans & Avolio, 2003). It is scored on a five-point Likert scale with the item responses ranging from 0 ('not at all') to 4 ('frequently'). A previous South African study using a healthcare industry sample reported reliability coefficients of 0.93 for scores from the ALQ (Stander, De Beer, & Stander, 2015). The internal reliability of scores from the ALQ in the present study was 0.95.

Data analysis procedure

Descriptive and inferential statistics were used to analyse the data, which include Pearson correlation analysis and multiple regression analysis (which was also used for mediation and moderation analysis). SPSS version 24 was employed for the analysis, and the PROCESS macro (Hayes, 2013) was utilised for the mediation and moderation analysis.

Ethical consideration

Ethical clearance was received from the University of the Western Cape ethics committee (reference number 13/5/36). The information page and informed consent contained in the electronic questionnaire utilised for the data collection at the participating organisation assisted to ensure ethical practice. Firstly, it provided an explanation of the nature and rationale for the research. Secondly, it informed participants that their participation in the research study was voluntary and that they could withdraw from the study at any time prior to submission of their responses. Participants were also informed that their non-participation or withdrawal from the research would not be known to anybody other than themselves and therefore there would be no consequences should they decide not to participate. Thirdly, the information page explained that the responses would be kept anonymous and that it would not be possible, in any way, to trace the responses back to individuals. If the participants wanted to discuss any aspect related to the research, the contact details of both the researcher and the research supervisor were given.

Results

The relationships between authentic leadership, psychological capital and work engagement

Authentic leadership and PsyCap respectively correlated 0.314 and 0.578 with work engagement. All correlations were significant at the 0.01 level. The Cronbach's alpha reliability analysis also indicated acceptable reliability, ranging from 0.89 for the PCQ24 to 0.95 for the ALQ. The results are displayed in Table 1.

When comparing the mean item score of the research sample with the norm scales provided in the UWES-17 manual, the healthcare industry sample can be described as – on average – having a high level of work engagement. A mean of 4.67–5.53 indicates that respondents feel engaged in their work 'often' to 'very often' or 'once a week' to 'a few times a week'. Similarly, the sample tended to have high levels of PsyCap and scored their leaders as having high levels of authentic leadership.

The mediating role of psychological capital

Multiple regression analyses were conducted to assess each component of the mediation model. The independent variable for the analyses was authentic leadership (X), the dependent variable was work engagement (Y) and PsyCap was the proposed mediator (M). Firstly, it was found that authentic leadership was positively associated with work engagement ($\beta = 0.12$, t [2, 647] = 3.410, $p = 0.0007$). It was also found that authentic leadership was positively related to PsyCap ($\beta = 0.20$, t [2, 647] = 7.91, $p = 0.000$). Lastly, results indicated that the mediator, PsyCap, was positively associated with work engagement ($\beta = 0.80$, t [2, 647] = 15.00, $p = 0.0000$). Because all three of the relationships were significant, mediation analyses were carried out using the bootstrapping method with bias-corrected confidence estimates (Hayes, 2013). The 95% confidence interval (CI) of the indirect effects was obtained with 5000 bootstrap resamples. Results of the mediation analysis confirmed the mediating role of PsyCap in the relation between authentic leadership and work engagement ($\beta = 0.16$; $CI = 0.12–0.21$). As the relationship between authentic leadership and work engagement remained significant ($\beta = 0.12$, t [2, 647] = 3.42, $p = 0.0007$) when controlling for PsyCap, partial mediation of PsyCap is suggested. Figure 1 provides a display of the results.

The moderating role of psychological capital

The PROCESS macro was applied to determine the potential moderating effect of a third variable on the relationship between authentic leadership and work engagement (X and Y). Mean centring was done for all the variables in an effort to reduce multicollinearity. In order to confirm whether the third variable has a moderation effect on the relationship between the two variables (X and Y), it must be proven that the nature of this relationship changes as the values of the moderating variable (M) changes, according to Hayes (2013). The variables explained a combined 35.6% (F [3, 643] = 118.63, $p < 0.001$, $R^2 = 0.3563$) of the variance in work engagement. The detailed results are displayed in Table 2.

From Table 2 it can be seen that both predictors remained statistically significant, with authentic leadership $b = 0.12$,

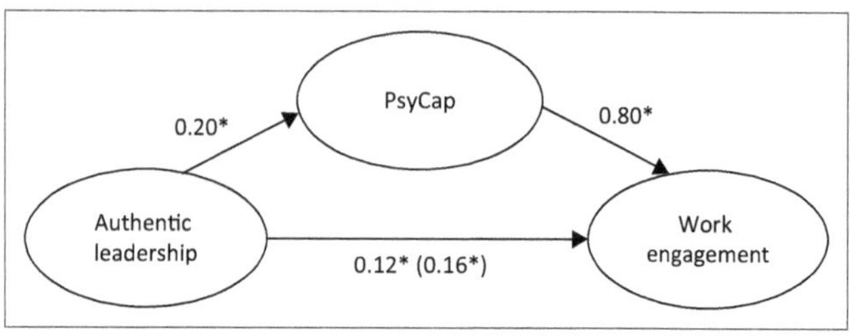

*, $p < 0.001$.

FIGURE 1: Indirect effect of authentic leadership on work engagement through psychological capital. PsyCap, psychological capital.

TABLE 1: Descriptive statistics and correlations between the variables (N = 647).

Variable	M	SD	α	1	2	3
1. Authentic leadership	2.80	0.84	0.95	–	–	–
2. Psychological capital	4.95	0.51	0.89	0.335*	–	–
3. Work engagement	4.88	0.77	0.92	0.314*	0.578*	–

M, mean; SD, standard deviation; α, Cronbach's alpha.

*, $p < 0.01$.

TABLE 2: Moderation analysis with psychological capital as moderator (N = 647) and work engagement as dependent variable.

Independent variables	β	SE	t	p	LLCI	ULCI
Constant	0.0185	0.0254	0.7285	0.4666	−0.0314	0.0685
PsyCap (centred)	0.7791	0.0513	15.1756	0.0000	0.6783	0.8799
Authentic leadership (centred)	0.1236	0.0306	4.0360	0.0001	0.0635	0.1838
Interaction term (PsyCap * AL)	−0.1289	0.0521	−2.4748	0.0136	−0.2312	−0.0266

β, standardised regression coefficient; SE, standard error; LLCI, lower level confidence interval; ULCI, upper level confidence interval; AL, authentic leadership; PsyCap, psychological capital.
*, PsyCap is multiplied with authentic leadership (AL) to compute the interaction term.

TABLE 3: Conditional effects of authentic leadership on work engagement at different levels of psychological capital.

Variable	Effect (b)	SE	t	p	LLCI	ULCI
Low PsyCap	0.1894	0.0404	4.6889	0.000	0.1101	0.2688
Average (M) PsyCap	0.1236	0.0306	4.0361	0.0001	0.0635	0.1838
High PsyCap	0.0578	0.0407	1.4195	0.1562	−0.0222	0.1378

Effect (b), unstandardised simple slope; SE, standard error; t, t-statistic; p, p-value; LLCI, lower level confidence interval; ULCI, upper level confidence interval; M, mean; PsyCap, psychological capital.

t (643) = 4.04, p = 0.00 and PsyCap b = 0.78, t (643) = 15.18, p = 0.00. In other words, for every one unit increase in authentic leadership, there is a 0.12 increase in work engagement. Similarly, for every one unit increase in PsyCap there is a 0.78 increase in work engagement. The interaction variable (i.e. PsyCap * authentic leadership is also statistically significant at the $p > 0.05$ level (b = -0.13, t [643] = -2.47, p = 0.01).

In order to create a better understanding of the moderating effect of PsyCap on the relationship between authentic leadership and work engagement, simple slopes for different levels of PsyCap were investigated. The different PsyCap levels present the mean and plus or minus one standard deviation from the mean. For ease of reference, these categories will be called 'low PsyCap' (mean minus one SD), 'average PsyCap' (mean) and 'high PsyCap' (mean plus one SD). These slopes are presented in Table 3.

From the analysis of the conditional effects of authentic leadership on work engagement at low, average and high levels of PsyCap, it becomes apparent that the effect of PsyCap on the relationship between authentic leadership and work engagement is statistically significant for the low PsyCap (b = 0.19, t [643] = 4.69, p = 0.00) and average PsyCap (b = 0.12, t [643] = 4.04, p = 0.00) groups. However, there is no statistically significant relationship between authentic leadership and work engagement for the high PsyCap group (b = 0.06, t [643] = 1.42, p = 0.16). In other words, every unit of authentic leadership provides an increase of 0.19 in work engagement for those with low PsyCap levels and an increase of 0.12 for those with average PsyCap levels. It therefore seems that the impact of authentic leadership on work engagement decreases as the level of PsyCap increase.

Discussion

Although no other studies have reported on the mediating role of PsyCap between authentic leadership and work engagement, PsyCap has been found to mediate the relationship between authentic leadership and performance (Wang, Sui, Luthans, Wang, & Wu, 2014). Avey et al. (2008) stated that employees with higher levels of PsyCap tend to proactively facilitate positive changes in the organisation. Therefore, it seems that PsyCap is important in facilitating the impact of a positive organisational context on desired workplace outcomes.

Authentic leadership does have a direct influence on work engagement. However, this influence is increased as a result of the mediating role of PsyCap. In practical terms this means that an individual's perception of the authentic leadership behaviours of their leader will influence their level of work engagement. If this individual also has high levels of PsyCap, they may interpret their leader's behaviour more positively. Therefore, there will be an increased influence of such leadership behaviour on their work engagement.

Considering the results of the moderating effect of PsyCap on the relationship between authentic leadership and work engagement found in the present sample, it becomes evident that as the PsyCap levels of respondents increase, the influence of the leader's behaviour on the respondent's level of work engagement becomes less important. Wang et al. (2014) found that a higher level of performance was achieved when a lack of PsyCap was complemented with high levels of authentic leadership. Similar to the findings of the present study, Wang et al. (2014) conclude that the impact or need for authentic leadership is decreased when the employee already has a high level of PsyCap. Wang et al. (2014) stated that PsyCap may have a complementary role to leadership rather than a supplementary role. The supplementary role is the more common approach to leadership where a leader's influence is enhanced by followers' characteristics. Complementary congruity theory (Kiesler, 1983) suggests that leaders and followers coordinate their actions by one party acting dominant and the other then being expected to be submissive (and thus, the leader might not always be the dominant party). Following the thinking of complementary congruity and the classical substitutes for leadership theory, Wang et al. (2014) speculates that follower PsyCap could be viewed as a substitute for authentic leadership.

Practical implications

The results of the present study indicate that PsyCap explains the biggest unique proportion of the variance in work engagement. Hence, for organisations trying to improve the levels of employee work engagement and decrease dependence on leadership intervention, PsyCap development may prove useful. Specifically, individuals with a high level of PsyCap rely on their own PsyCap rather than the authentic behaviours of their leaders in order to improve their work engagement. Therefore, human resource professionals could provide PsyCap training and micro-interventions that could impact the level of work engagement in a positive manner. Development activities such as the Psychological Capital Intervention (Luthans et al., 2007; Luthans & Youssef-Morgan, 2017) could be used as short training sessions. The content could include activities such as goal-setting, generating pathways and options to attain the set goals, considering possible obstacles to attainment of the goal, sharing the goal with other participants and being encouraged through their feedback, and reflection on past successes and stressors to build resilience. Individual coaching and mentoring would also be a viable method to develop PsyCap (Luthans et al., 2007). Novel techniques such as video games and gamification techniques also show promise for the development of PsyCap (Luthans & Youssef-Morgan, 2017).

Limitations and recommendations

With regard to methodological choices for future research, it is suggested that longitudinal studies should be conducted to determine the relationships between the variables over time. One of the characteristics of PsyCap and work engagement is that both are state-like in nature. Even though both variables have been shown to be stable over a period of time, longitudinal research is needed to determine whether there is also stability in the relationships between the variables. Allesandri et al. (2018) reported that more than two waves of data may be needed to improve the helpfulness of the findings.

Furthermore, hierarchical levels of analysis can also be utilised. This could include studying the leadership impact on work engagement by utilising nested models that would measure the impact of a specific leader's behaviour on the work engagement of employees. Moreover, studying the psychometric variables at the group and organisational levels can also offer valuable insights to understanding positive employee behaviour in the workplace.

In addition, the definition of authentic leadership (Luthans & Avolio, 2003) indicates that authentic leadership draws from a highly developed organisational context. This context includes the organisation's vision, strategy and culture, which act as antecedents of authentic leadership development on organisations. In the case where the organisational culture is negative, with abusive leadership and dominant organisational politics, authentic leadership is unlikely to develop and thrive (Luthans & Youssef-Morgan, 2017). Thus, the influence of the organisational context should be considered in future studies on authentic leadership.

Conclusion

In the present study, the role of PsyCap in the relationship between authentic leadership and work engagement was explored. PsyCap explained a large proportion of the variance in work engagement for all employees. For individuals with high levels of PsyCap, the authentic leadership behaviours they perceived in their leader did not have a significant influence on their levels of work engagement. Thus, the development of hope, efficacy, resilience and optimism in employees may be a viable option to improve levels of employee work engagement.

Acknowledgements

This work is based on research supported in part by the National Research Foundation (NRF) of South Africa. Any opinions, findings and conclusions or recommendations expressed in this material are those of the authors and the NRF does not accept any liability in this regard. This work is based on the PhD work of the first author: Du Plessis (2014). The authors also acknowledge the research organisation for their support in facilitating the data collection.

Competing interests

The authors declare that they have no financial or personal relationships that may have inappropriately influenced them in writing this article.

Authors' contributions

M.D.P. was responsible for all writing, data gathering and data analysis. A.B.B. was the supervisor of this PhD research study and reviewed the draft and final version of the manuscript.

References

Alessandri, G., Consiglio, C., Luthans, F., & Borgogni, L. (2018). Testing a dynamic model of the impact of psychological capital on work engagement and job performance. *Career Development International, 23*(1), 33–47. https://doi.org/10.1108/CDI-11-2016-0210

Avey, J. B., Reichard, R. J., Luthans, F., & Mhatre, K. H. (2011). Meta-analysis of the impact of positive psychological capital on employee attitudes, behaviors and performance. *Human Resource Development Quarterly, 22*(2), 127–152. https://doi.org/10.1002/hrdq.20070

Avey, J. B., Wernsing, T. S., & Luthans, F. (2008). Can positive employees help positive organizational change? Impact of psychological capital and emotions on relevant attitudes and behaviors. *The Journal of Applied Behavioral Science, 44*(1), 48–70. https://doi.org/10.1177/0021886307311470

Avolio, B. J., & Gardner, W. L. (2005). Authentic leadership development: Getting to the root of positive forms of leadership. *Leadership Quarterly, 16*, 315–338. https://doi.org/10.1016/j.leaqua.2005.03.001

Avolio, B. J., Gardner, W. L., Walumbwa, F. O., Luthans, F., & May, D. R. (2004). Unlocking the mask: A look at the process by which authentic leaders impact follower attitudes and behaviors. *The Leadership Quarterly, 15*, 801–823. https://doi.org/10.1016/j.leaqua.2004.09.003

Avolio, B. J., & Mhatre, K. H. (2012). Advances in theory and research on authentic leadership. In K. S. Cameron, & G. M. Spreitzer (Eds.), *The Oxford handbook of positive organizational scholarship* (pp. 773–783). New York: Oxford University Press.

Avolio, B. J., Walumbwa, F. O., & Weber, T. J. (2009). Leadership: Current theories, research and future directions. *Annual Review of Psychology, 60*, 421–449. https://doi.org/10.1146/annurev.psych.60.110707.163621

Bakker, A. B. (2009). Building engagement in the workplace. In R. J. Burke & C. L. Cooper (Eds.), *The peak performing organization* (pp. 50–72). Oxon, UK: Routledge.

Bakker, A. B., & Albrecht, S. (2018). Work engagement: Current trends. *Career Development International, 23*(1), 4–11. https://doi.org/10.1108/CDI-11-2017-0207

Bakker, A. B., & Demerouti, E. (2008). Towards a model of work engagement. *Career Development International, 12*, 209–223. https://doi.org/10.1108/13620430810870476

Bakker, A. B., Demerouti, E., & Sanz-Vergel, A. I. (2014). Burnout and work engagement: The JD–R approach. *Annual Review of Organizational Psychology and Organizational of Behaviour, 1*(1), 389–411. https://doi.org/10.1146/annurev-orgpsych-031413-091235

Bargagliotti, L. (2012). Work engagement in nursing: A concept analysis. *Journal of Advanced Nursing, 68*(6), 1414–1428. https://doi.org/10.1111/j.1365-2648.2011.05859.x

Cameron, K. S., & Spreitzer, G. M. (2012). Introduction: What is positive about positive organizational scholarship? In K. S. Cameron, & G. M. Spreitzer (Eds.), *The Oxford handbook of positive organizational scholarship* (pp. 1–14). New York: Oxford University Press.

Chan, A. Y. L. H., Hannah, S. T., & Gardner, W. L. (2005). Veritable authentic leadership: Emergence, functioning, and impacts. In W. L. Gardner, B. J. Avolio, & F. O. Walumbwa (Eds.), *Authentic leadership theory and practice: Origins, effects, and development* (Vol. 3, pp. 3–41). New York: Elsevier.

Conger, J. A., & Kanungo, R. N. (1998). *Charismatic leadership in organizations*. Thousand Oaks, CA: Sage.

Deci, E. L., Connell, J. P., & Ryan, R. M. (1989). Self-determination in a work organization. *Journal of Applied Psychology, 74*(4), 580. https://doi.org/10.1037/0021-9010.74.4.580

Du Plessis, M. (2014). The relationship between authentic leadership, psychological capital, followership and work engagement. Unpublished PhD dissertation, University of the Western Cape. Retrieved from http://etd.uwc.ac.za/bitstream/handle/11394/3903/Du%20Plessis_PHD_2014.pdf?sequence=1&isAllowed=y

Gallup. (2013). *State of the global workplace: Employee engagement insights for business leaders worldwide*. Washington, DC: Gallup.

Gardner, W. L., Avolio, B. J., Luthans, F., May, D. R., & Walumbwa, F. (2005). 'Can you see the real me?' A self-based model of authentic leader and follower development. *The Leadership Quarterly, 16*, 343–372. https://doi.org/10.1016/j.leaqua.2005.03.003

Giallonardo, L. M., Wong, C. A., & Iwasiw, C. L. (2010). Authentic leadership of preceptors: Predictor of new graduate nurses' work engagement and job satisfaction. *Journal of nursing management, 18*(8), 993–1003. https://doi.org/10.1111/j.1365-2834.2010.01126.x

Görgens-Ekermans, G., & Herbert, M. (2013). Psychological capital: Internal and external validity of the Psychological Capital Questionnaire (PCQ-24) on a South African sample. *SA Journal of Industrial Psychology, 39*(2), 12. https://doi.org/10.4102/sajip.v39i2.1131

Harter, J., & Adkins, A. (2015). What great managers do to engage employees. *Harvard Business Review.* Retrieved from: https://hbr.org/2015/04/what-great-managers-do-to-engageemployees

Hayes, A. F. (2013). *Introduction to mediation, moderation, and conditional process analysis: A regression-based approach*. New York: Guilford Press.

Hobfoll, S. E. (2002). Social and psychological resources and adaptation. *Review of General Psychology, 6*(4), 307–324. https://doi.org/10.1037/1089-2680.6.4.307

Hsieh, C-C., & Wang, D-S. (2015). Does supervisor-perceived authentic leadership influence employee work engagement through employee-perceived authentic leadership and employee trust? *The International Journal of Human Resource Management, 26*(18), 2329–2348. https://doi.org/10.1080/09585192.2015.1025234

Huang, L., & Luthans, F. (2014). Towards better understanding of the learning goal orientation-creativity relationship: The role of positive psychological capital. *Applied Psychology, 64*(2), 444–472. https://doi.org/10.1111/apps.12028

Ilies, R., Morgeson, F. P., & Nahrgang, J. D. (2005). Authentic leadership and eudaemonic well-being: Understanding leader–follower outcomes. *The Leadership Quarterly, 16*, 373–394. https://doi.org/10.1016/j.leaqua.2005.03.002

Jensen, S. M., & Luthans, F. (2006). Entrepreneurs as authentic leaders: Impact on employees' attitudes. *Leadership and Organizational Development Journal, 27*(7), 646–666. https://doi.org/10.1108/01437730610709273

Kahn, W. A., & Heaphy, E. D. (2014). Relational context of personal engagement at work. In C. Truss, R. Delbridge, E. Soane, K. Alfes, & A. Shantz (Eds.), *Employee engagement in theory and practice* (pp. 163–179). London, UK: Routledge.

Kiesler, D. J. (1983). The 1982 interpersonal circle: A taxonomy for complementarity in human transactions. *Psychological Review, 90*(3), 185. https://doi.org/10.1037/0033-295X.90.3.185

Laba, K., & Geldenhuys, M. (2016). Psychological availability and work engagement: The moderating role of sex and race. *Journal of Psychology in Africa*, 26(2), 107–112. https://doi.org/10.1080/14330237.2016.1163888

Luthans, F. (2002). Positive organizational behavior: Developing and managing psychological strengths. *Academy of Management Executive, 16*, 57–75.

Luthans, F., & Avolio, B. J. (2003). Authentic leadership: A positive developmental approach. In K. S. Cameron, J. E. Dutton, & R. E. Quinn (Eds.), *Positive organizational scholarship: Foundations of a new discipline* (pp. 241–258). San Francisco, CA: Berrett-Koehler.

Luthans, F., Avolio, B. J., Avey, J. B., & Norman, S. M. (2007). Positive psychological capital: Measurement and relationship with performance and satisfaction. *Personnel Psychology, 60*, 541–572. https://doi.org/10.5465/ame.2002.6640181

Luthans, F., Luthans, K. W., & Luthans, B. C. (2004). Positive psychological capital: Beyond human and social capital. *Business Horizons, 47*(1), 45–50. https://doi.org/10.1016/j.bushor.2003.11.007

Luthans, F., Norman, S. M., Avolio, B. J., & Avey, J. B. (2008). The mediating role of psychological capital in the supportive organizational climate-employee performance relationship. *Journal of Organizational Behavior, 29*(2), 219–238. https://doi.org/10.1002/job.507

Luthans, F., Youssef, C. M., & Avolio, B. J. (2007). *Psychological capital: Developing the human capital edge.* Oxford, England: Oxford University Press.

Luthans, F., & Youssef-Morgan, C. M. (2017). Psychological Capital: An evidence-Based positive approach. *Annual Review of Organizational Psychology and Organizational Behavior, 4*, 339–366. https://doi.org/10.1146/annurev-orgpsych-032516-113324

Mäkikangas, A., Feldt, T., Kinnunen, U., & Mauno, S. (2013). Does personality matter? Research on individual differences in occupational well-being, In A. B. Bakker, (Ed.), *Advances in positive organizational psychology* (Vol. 1, pp. 107–143). Bingley: Emerald.

Maslach, C., Schaufeli, W. B., & Leiter, M. P. (2001). Job burnout. *Annual Review of Psychology, 52*, 397–422. https://doi.org/10.1146/annurev.psych.52.1.397

Mostert, K., & Rathbone, A. D. (2001). Work characteristics, work-home interaction and engagement of employees in the mining industry. *Management Dynamics, 16*(2), 36–52.

Munyaka, S. A., Boshoff, A. B., Pietersen, J., & Snelgar, R. (2017). The relationships between authentic leadership, psychological capital, psychological climate, team commitment and intention to quit. *SA Journal of Industrial Psychology/SA Tydskrif vir Bedryfsielkunde, 43*, a1430. https://doi.org/10.4102/sajip.v43i0.1430

Norman, S. M., Avey, J. B., Nimnicht, J. L., & Pigeon, N. G. (2010). The interactive effects of psychological capital and organizational identity on employee organizational citizenship and deviance behaviours. *Journal of Leadership and Organization Studies, 17*(4), 380–391. https://doi.org/10.1177/1548051809353764

Penger, S., & Černe, M. (2014). Authentic leadership, employees' job satisfaction, and work engagement: A hierarchical linear modelling approach. *Economic Research, 27*(1), 508–526. https://doi.org/10.1080/1331677X.2014.974340

Petersen, K. (2015). *Authentic leadership and unit outcomes: Additive and interactive contributions of climate and psychological capital*. PhD Thesis, Bellevue University of Bellevue, NE.

Pillai, R., & Meindl, J. R. (1998). Context and charisma: A 'meso' level examination of the relationship of organic structure, collectivism, and crisis to charismatic leadership. *Journal of Management, 24*, 643–671.

Rego, A., Sousa, F., Marques, C., & Pina e Cunha, M. (2012). Authentic leadership promoting employees' psychological capital and creativity. *Journal of Business Research, 65*(3), 429–437. https://doi.org/10.1016/j.jbusres.2011.10.003

Rich, B. L., LePine, J. A., & Crawford, E. R. (2010). Job engagement: Antecedents and effects on job performance. *Academy of Management Journal, 53*(3), 617–635. https://doi.org/10.5465/amj.2010.51468988

Robertson, I. T., & Cooper, C. L. (2010). Full engagement: The integration of employee engagement and psychological well-being. *Leadership & Organization Development Journal, 31*(4), 324–336. https://doi.org/10.1108/01437731011043348

Rothbard, N. P., & Patil, S. V. (2012). Being there: Work engagement and Positive Organizational Scholarship. In K. S. Cameron, & G. M. Spreitzer (Eds.), *The Oxford handbook of positive organizational scholarship* (pp. 56–69). New York: Oxford University Press.

Rothmann, S. (2017). Employee engagement. In L. G. Oades, M. Steger, A. Delle-Fave, & J. Passmore (Eds.), *The Wiley-Blackwell handbook of the psychology of positivity and strengths-based approaches at work*, (pp. 317–341). Wiley: Chichester.

Schaufeli, W. B., & Bakker, A. B. (2003). *UWES Utrecht Work Engagement Scale: Preliminary manual (Version 1).* Utrecht University: Occupational Health Psychology Unit.

Seligman, M. E. P. (2011). *Flourish: A new understanding of happiness and well-being – and how to achieve them.* London, UK: Nicolas Brealey.

Seligman, M. E. P., & Csikszentmihalyi, M. (2000). Positive psychology: An introduction. *American Psychologist, 55*, 5–14. https://doi.org/10.1037/0003-066X.55.1.5

Simons, J. C., & Buitendach, J. H. (2013). Psychological capital, work engagement and organisational commitment amongst call centre employees in South Africa. *SA Journal of Industrial Psychology, 39*(2), 12. https://doi.org/10.4102/sajip.v39i2.1071

Snyder, C. R., Irving, L. M., & Anderson, J. R. (1991). Hope and health. *Handbook of Social and Clinical Psychology: The Health Perspective, 162*, 285–305.

Sparrowe, R. T. (2005). Authentic leadership and the narrative self. *The Leadership Quarterly, 16*(3), 419–439. https://doi.org/10.1016/j.leaqua.2005.03.004

Stander, F. W., De Beer, L. T., & Stander, M. (2015). Authentic leadership as a source of optimism, trust in the organisation and work engagement in the public health care sector. *SA Journal of Human Resource Management, 13*(1), 12. https://doi.org/10.4102/sajhrm.v13i1.675

Storm, K., & Rothmann, S. (2003). A psychometric analysis of the Utrecht Work Engagement Scale in the South African police service. *SA Journal of Industrial Psychology, 29*(4), 62–70. https://doi.org/10.4102/sajip.v29i4.129

Sweetman, D., Luthans, F., Avey, J. B., & Luthans, B. C. (2011). Relationship between positive psychological capital and creative performance. *Canadian Journal of Administrative Sciences/Revue Canadienne des Sciences de l'Administration, 28*(1), 4–13. https://doi.org/10.1002/cjas.175

Walumbwa, F. O., Avolio, B. J., Gardner, W. L., Wernsing, T. S., & Peterson, S. J. (2008). Authentic leadership: Development and validation of a theory-based measure. *Journal of Management, 34*, 89–126. https://doi.org/10.1177/0149206307308913

6

Do talent management strategies influence the psychological contract within a diverse environment?

Authors:
Paul Poisat[1]
Michelle R. Mey[2]
Gary Sharp[3]

Affiliations:
[1]Graduate School of Business, Nelson Mandela University, South Africa

[2]School of Industrial Psychology and Human Resource Management, Nelson Mandela University, South Africa

[3]Department of Statistics, Nelson Mandela University, South Africa

Corresponding author:
Michelle Mey,
michelle.mey@mandela.ac.za

Orientation: Even though globalisation has resulted in a more diverse workforce and working environment, talent management strategies have not evolved catering for the diversity experienced in organisations. It is assumed that talent management strategies developed on Western principles can be applied effectively to employees in emerging markets. However, the success of these strategies in creating a high-performance work culture is widely questioned.

Research purpose: This study aims to empirically determine the relationship between talent management strategies on the psychological contract, and whether this relationship influences employee retention within diverse working environments, which includes generational cohorts, gender and ethnicity.

Motivation for the study: As talent management strategies impact differently on the psychological contract of individuals across the generations, gender and ethnicity, it therefore implies that a fit for purpose talent management strategy must consider these variables. The reason for this study was to determine the influence of talent management strategies on the psychological contract and ultimately retention within the diverse environment of different generations, genders and ethnicity.

Research approach/design and method: A structured, closed-ended Likert-type validated questionnaire was distributed to employed persons of differing ethnicity, gender and generations and emanating from various professions within the private and public sector (n = 711). A quantitative survey design was used.

Main findings: A significant relationship between the work environment and the psychological contract on retention exists. On the contrary, no significant differences exist between growth and development and financial security. Unlike other research conducted on generational cohorts, this study revealed a strong correlation between talent management strategies and generational cohort preferences.

Practical/managerial implications: Talent management strategies need to be flexible and inclusive in terms of generational differences, including but not limited to ethnicity and gender. Human resource practitioners are made aware that the work environment impacts most significantly on the psychological contract and ultimately on retention.

Contribution/value-add: This study subscribes to the international literature and provides empirical evidence that demonstrates the importance of generational cohorts, gender and ethnicity when executing talent management strategies. This study empirically provides the basis for human resource (HR) practitioners to develop a customised generational talent management strategy to retain high performing individuals.

Introduction

Highly skilled employees are a scarce resource, particularly in developed countries. This is partly because of the ageing profile of Western and European workforces, as well as the consistent negative population growth in many established economies. In an increasingly globalised business world, multinational organisations must look to emerging markets to attract and retain talented individuals. This requires a fit for purpose talent management approach to attract, engage and retain employees in emerging markets as traditional approaches are based on Western principles and practices (Bluen, 2013). The Global Talent Competitiveness Index 2018 found that South Africa's ability to retain talent is poor as indicated by a ranking of 97 out of 119 countries (Knowledge Resources, 2018). An ageing workforce, coupled with diversity and generational considerations, requires that organisations reconsider their talent management strategies so as to address the varied expectations of employees pertaining to the work environment, financial security and growth and development (Knowledge Resources, 2017a; Thomsons Online Benefits, 2017).

Multiple authors have emphasised the universal need for talent management (Bluen, 2013; Böhmer & Schinnenburg, 2016; Hafez, AbouelNeel & Elsaid, 2017). In addition to being ranked 63rd overall on the Global Talent Competitiveness Index 2018, a lack of capacity, the risk of employee non-performance and the extremely high costs associated with replacing staff are just a few of the reasons why talent management remains an increasingly important organisational consideration. Despite these realities, many organisations have failed to adapt to the challenges associated with increased globalisation and the resulting war for talent (Bluen, 2013; Knowledge Resources, 2017; Thunnissen, Boselie, & Fruytier, 2013). Boudreau and Ramstad (2005) emphasise the significance of having a talent management focus in the organisation, whereas Lewis and Heckman (2006) point out the lack of research-based findings to acknowledge and understand the importance of talent management.

In addition, the importance of a psychological contract and its influence on retention needs to be considered. This is highlighted by Sonnenberg, Koene and Paauwe (2011) who support this and provide evidence that the more talent management practices an organisation employs, the higher employees perceived their psychological contract fulfilment, which results in higher levels of commitment and well-being and lower levels of intention to quit.

This article investigates the relationship between talent management strategies, the psychological contract and employee retention within the context of the various generational cohorts, gender and ethnicity. As such, this article contributes to the international literature by providing empirical evidence that a more specific and customised talent management approach is necessary while considering generational cohorts, gender and ethnicity.

Talent management defined

Although talent management is an integral part of organisational success, the concept itself lacks theoretical frameworks. Even though Collings and Mellahi (2009) are of the opinion that there is a lack of consistent definitions, they propose that talent management is seen as activities and practices that identify critical positions and develop high performers as well as establish 'differentiated human resource architecture to facilitate filling of these positions'. Typically, there are three mainstream interpretations of talent management. Talent management may firstly be described as a new term for common human resource practices; secondly, as an allusion of succession planning practices; and lastly, as referring to the general management of talented employees (Al Ariss, Cascio, & Paauwe, 2014).

There is no one-size-fits-all solution to talent management. Generalisations made in terms of talent management strategies are complicated by diversity considerations, including the range of generations employed. Talent management strategies must be adjusted to accommodate the different values, characteristics, attitudes towards work and general world view of the different generational cohorts working together (Bluen, 2013; Festing & Schäfer, 2014; Knowledge Resources, 2017b). Given the broad definitions of talent management, our approach is to view talent management strategies to include HR practices and policies pertaining to the work environment, financial security and growth and development. The operationalisation of these variables will follow.

Operationalisation of variables

An organisation is only as good as its people, and talent management should thus form the foundation on which organisations are built (Grobler et al., 2017). Figure 1 presents a conceptual model for this study. The model highlights talent management strategies relating to the working environment, financial stability, and growth and development as the independent variable, and retention as the dependent variable. Diversity considerations, including generational cohorts, gender and ethnicity, are presented as variables which were controlled for in this study, as they may or may not have affected the strength of the relationship between talent management and retention. The model further suggests that both organisational considerations (talent management strategies) and individual considerations (diversity issues) play a role in determining the nature of the psychological contract, which in itself may influence the dependent variable of retention.

Work environment

The work environment is vital to employee satisfaction. For the purpose of this study, work environment includes the conditions wherein an employee operates, their roles and responsibilities, whether sufficient authority is given to employees to make and implement decisions about their work and the nature of working relationships. One such working relationship is that between management and employees. This relationship needs to be one of trust, mutual respect and belief in employee capabilities. Changing ways of working necessitated by the knowledge-intensive nature of work as well as the continuously developing possibilities provided by information and communication technology have also inevitably changed the working environment.

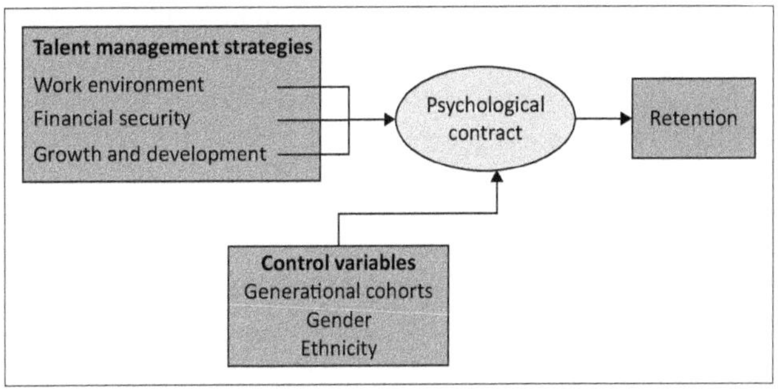

FIGURE 1: Conceptual model for the study.

Several authors such as Bosch-Sijtsema, Fruchter, Vartiainen and Ruohomäki (2011); Gorgievski, Bakker and Schaufeli (2010); Peters, Poutsma, Van der Heijden, Bakker and Bruijn (2014) and Van der Voordt (2004) have explored these changing working practices. Flexible and mobile work practices have increased in popularity as they provide employees with more autonomy in deciding when, where and how their work gets done. Flexibility in work practices is especially important for females and ultimately leads to employee retention (Du Plessis & Barkhuizen, 2015). There are also the preferences that the different generational cohorts bring to the work environment. Gursoy, Maier and Chi (2008) found that Baby Boomers have a high respect for authority and hierarchy in the workplace. Conversely, Generation Xers are seen as being more self-reliant, independent and sceptical of authority (Crumpacker & Crumpacker, 2007). Millennials prefer more flexibility and time off work that will suit their lifestyle (Roy, 2008). These characteristics will, in turn, affect the preferred work environment of the different generations.

Financial security

Financial security as a variable is complex and comprises of financial and non-financial rewards (Bussin & Van Rooy, 2014). Financial security is the individual's peace of mind that their income is sufficient to cover their expenses. Research in the South African context with regard to financial security and generational cohorts is inconclusive as the different generations place value on different aspects of financial security (Bussin & Van Rooy, 2014; Masibigiri & Nienaber, 2011; Moore & Bussin, 2012). For the purpose of this study, factors contributing to financial security include work–life balance, recognition and achievements which, in turn, lead to job security.

Growth and development

The characteristics of a generation do not apply unilaterally to each member of a generational cohort as each individual is unique. Consideration must be given to the changing needs of employees which include freedom and flexibility in their job, opportunities to grow personally and professionally, as well as to experience fun at work. In this study, gender as a variable was controlled for as Clarke (2011) argues that development programmes should be specific to gender as this allows for discussion of challenges pertaining to that gender. D'Amato and Herzfeldt (2008) found that employees who have a higher organisational commitment and greater orientation are more likely to stay for the next 3 years. This finding highlights the importance of providing learning opportunities within the organisation to retain talent across generations.

Psychological contract

In his seminal work, Rousseau (1990) defines a psychological contract as the individual's beliefs in terms of reciprocal obligations between employees and employers. The contract emerges when a contribution is made, and thus, an obligation is created to provide future benefits or fulfilment of needs. This expected reciprocal obligation has an impact on employee performance beyond the levels expected in their formal contract (Ye, Cardon, & Rivera, 2012). Differences in the interpretation of what constitutes a psychological contract between parties may be a challenge because of the contract being of an unwritten nature and may cause problems within the organisation (Ye et al., 2012). The employee evaluates these individual perceptions by comparing organisational experiences such as talent management practices to their own psychological contracts (Festing & Schäfer, 2014).

When employers live up to the expectations of employees in terms of the psychological contract, employees are more likely to experience job satisfaction, demonstrate organisational commitment and eagerness to develop and learn within the organisation, and display willingness to contribute to organisational goals (Festing & Schäfer, 2014). However, if they fail to meet employee expectations, they may be met with negative reactions such as reduced loyalty, reduced job performance and commitment, and the intention to quit (Festing & Schäfer, 2014).

Crampton and Hodge (2007) postulate that generations develop different characteristics and work-related values and attitudes based on shared experiences in the formative years which contribute to shaping their lives. Research by Schambach (2001) suggests that the psychological contract may be perceived stronger by younger employees, as they feel the obligation of the reciprocal relationship more so than older employees, who have paid their dues to the organisation. A study on basic human value differences between generational cohorts indicated differences between Millennials and Generation Xers on 'openness to change' and 'self-enhancement' (Lyons, Duxbury, & Higgins, 2007). Younger generations, early in their careers, may be prone to accept higher levels of risk (Johnson & Lopes, 2008). The requirements of the psychological contract differ between individuals (Farndale, Pai, Sparrow, & Scullion, 2014). This will result in different generations having varying needs and expectations in terms of the psychological contract (D'Amato & Herzfeldt, 2008; Festing & Schäfer, 2014).

The above discussion leads to the formulation of the following hypothesis:

> **H1**: Talent management strategies with a positive influence on the psychological contract enhance retention.

Retention

Research results claim that 65% of black employees have changed jobs at least once within three years (Zulu & Parumasur, 2009). Therefore, it is critical that organisations explore strategies aimed at enhancing employee retention. These include maintaining a work-life balance, and ways to increase job satisfaction and organisational commitment (Ilies, Wilson, & Wagner, 2009; Qu & Zhao, 2012). These strategies, however, need to be flexible when dealing with different generational groups. Baby Boomers seek power, influence and authority over others, seek out status symbols, seniority and experience, and value opportunities to mentor others (Close, 2015). Generation Xers value control over their lives and place an immense value on work-life balance (Close, 2015). Millennials desire career progression and advancement, and want opportunities for on-the-job education (Close, 2015). Millennials are attracted to work that is challenging, meaningful and flexible and offers career mobility (Close, 2015).

The above leads to the formulation of the following hypothesis:

> **H2**: The more positively talent management strategies are experienced by the generational cohorts, the more positive the employees' experience of the psychological contract will be and, in turn, retention will be enhanced.

Generational cohorts

Generational differences may also influence the preferred methods of communication within the organisation. Baby Boomers prefer to communicate face to face during meetings rather than over the phone (Simons, 2009). Wagner (2007), however, found that Generation X and Millennials generally prefer email and text messages. This may cause intergenerational issues as using communications methods that are unfamiliar or undesirable to one group may cause discomfort and conflict.

Baby Boomers are seen as being willing to sacrifice their personal and professional lives to achieve success and financial security (Glass, 2007), whereas Generation Xers focus on balancing their personal and professional lives, resulting in the reputation of being the generation that 'work to live not live to work' (Simons, 2009). Atkinson (2008) found that although Millennials see money as important, they are more motivated to maintain a good work-life balance. Millennials want strong workplace relationships, a sense of purpose and a feeling that they are making a difference. Not meeting these needs may decrease job satisfaction which may negatively impact on job security, resulting in the departure of highly qualified personnel, and the costs associated with employee turnover and weaker growth prospects (Cheese, Thomas, & Craig, 2008 as quoted in Kilfman, 2009).

Baby Boomers tend to be more established in their careers than Millennials and will thus not place the same value on opportunities for learning and development (Close, 2015). This is largely because of Millennials generally being in the early stages of their career and desiring on-the-job training (Carlson, 2015). Even though it is generally accepted that Baby Boomers may have more knowledge and experience within the organisation, it will still be expected that they should be challenged to develop new skills and refresh old ones.

Three main generations are identified in today's workforce, namely Baby Boomers (born between 1945 and 1965), Generation X (1966–1977) and Millennials (1978–1990) (Bussin & Van Rooy, 2014). Although the exact dates that must be met to fall into one of these categories vary and some overlap exists, these generational cohorts show distinct characteristics which play a role in terms of how they perform in the workforce.

Cohort theory argues that growing up around the same time and experiencing events such as natural disasters, politics, economic conditions and pop culture at about the same point in their development lead individuals within a particular generational cohort to develop similar values, attitudes, opinions, employment expectations and life experiences (CIPD, 2009; D'Amato & Herzfeldt, 2008; Festing & Schäfer, 2014; Leuty & Hansen, 2011; Macky, Gardner, & Forsyth, 2008; Mayhew, 2014).

The above leads to the formulation of the following hypothesis:

> **H3**: The influence of talent management strategies on the psychological contract is perceived differently between the different generational cohorts.

Ethnicity

South Africa has a wide range of cultural and racial diversity, as well as a history of discrimination against individuals on this basis. Issues around marginalisation and exclusion are still prominent in the South African context. Typically, South African organisations comprise of a multitude of cultures and must therefore develop talent management strategies that take all of these cultural differences into account. This is confirmed by The Economist Intelligence Unit (2010) report and Knowledge Resources (2017b), which highlight some of these challenges such as cultural conflict between employees (50%), problems understanding the local culture (47%) and variations in working styles and norms of behaviour in the office (42%). Statistics of South Africa reveals that the blacks comprise of 75% of the South African total employed population (Knowledge Resources, 2018). The above leads to the question as to how the nature of the psychological contract is perceived by different ethnic groups.

The above leads to the formulation of the following hypothesis:

> **H4**: The influence of talent management strategies on the psychological contract is perceived differently among ethnic groups.

Research methodology

A quantitative approach was selected for this study as it is appropriate in studies that emphasise quantification in the collection and analysis of data, and which adopt a deductive approach placing emphasis on the testing of theories (Bryman & Bell, 2014).

Development of the measuring instrument

A structured, closed-ended, five-point Likert-type questionnaire comprising 33 items was used to collect the data. The independent variable, talent management (TM) strategies, varies vastly among organisations based on size, type of industry and geographical location (Lewis & Heckman, 2006). In order to derive a standardised measure of TM, employees' perceptions of TM strategies were assessed based on the motivational aspects derived from the job characteristics approach first developed by Campion in 1988. Twenty items, derived from the motivational scale developed by Campion and McClelland (1991) were clustered into three subsections comprising work environment (WE), financial security (FS), and growth and development (GD). Coefficient alpha values for this study ranged from 0.793 (WE), 0.807 (FS) and 0.844 (GD) and compared favourably to Campion and McClelland's (1991) alpha values ranging from 0.81 to 0.94 (see Table 3).

Meyer and Allen's (1997) scale measuring employees' emotional attachment to, identification with, and involvement in the organisation served as proxy for measuring employees' psychological contract (PC). The moderating variable, psychological contract, comprised eight statements. The coefficient alpha for this study was 0.847 (PC) and it was compared favourably to the study of Meyer and Allen's (1997) validated scale ranging from 0.77 to 0.88.

Retention, the dependent variable, was measured using Lee, Mitchell, Sablynski, Burton and Holtom's (2004) five-item intention to quit scale. The coefficient alpha for this scale was 0.859 (see Table 2). Literature indicates that behavioural intention is generally a good predictor of future behaviour (Armitage & Connor, 2001). Furthermore, Griffeth, Hom and Gaertner (2000) have shown that turnover intention is a strong predictor of actual turnover. In addition, generational cohort, gender and ethnicity were controlled for in this study in order to determine their impact on the psychological contract and retention.

Study population

The target population of this study was employees across the various generational cohorts in South Africa within the private and/or public sector and at all organisational levels including managerial, non-managerial and support and/or administrative employees, and comprising different gender and ethnic groupings. For the purpose of this study, the generational cohorts referred to include Baby Boomers, Generation X and Millennials as represented by the age categories presented in the discussion (refer to Table 1).

Data collection

The respondents were identified by means of the snowball convenience sampling technique. The questionnaire link was emailed to potential respondents, and a total of 711 useable questionnaires were returned.

TABLE 1: Demographic profile of respondents.

Profile	Category	No. of respondents	Count	Percentage
Gender	Female	711	319	44.8
	Male	-	392	55.2
Age profile	Baby Boomers	711	155	21.8
	Gen X	-	281	39.5
	Millennials	-	275	38.7
Ethnicity	African	711	288	40.5
	Mixed race and Asian	-	207	29.1
	White	-	216	30.4
Employment	Full-time	711	643	90.4
	Part-time	-	68	9.6
Employment sector	Private	711	450	63.3
	Public	-	230	32.3
	NGO	-	17	2.4
	Other	-	14	2.0

NGO, non-governmental organisations.

Statistical analysis

Structural equation modelling (SEM) was used to analyse the conceptual framework presented in Figure 2. The variables referred to in this study, work environment (WE), financial security (FS), growth and development (GD), psychological contract (PC) and retention (R), have been theoretically explored and operationalised using validated questionnaires. These variables were confirmed using exploratory factor analysis (EFA). Prior to the analyses being performed, the appropriateness of the data was assessed using Bartlett's Test of Sphericity and the Keiser–Meyer–Olkin measures of sampling adequacy (MSA), and ensuring an adequate sample size. Once deemed adequate, the analysis was performed. The SEM analysis was performed using a two-tiered model-building approach. The confirmatory factor models were analysed to ensure suitable model fit prior to testing the structural models (Hair, Anderson, Tatham, & Black, 1998). Each model was assessed using several goodness-of-fit indices. Once an appropriate model fit was obtained, the path estimates were interpreted and conclusions drawn (Byrne, 2010).

Analysis of data

The data were captured, cleaned and the biographical information analysed (Table 1). Of the 711 responses obtained, 44.8% were female and 55.2% male. The respondents were fairly evenly spread among the three generational age profiles: Baby Boomers (21.8%), Generation X (39.5%) and Millennials (38.7%). The African ethnic group had the greatest frequency at 40.5%. This was followed by the white ethnic group at 30.4% and the mixed race and Asian ethnic group at 29.1%.

The Bartlett's Test of Sphericity and Kaiser–Meyer–Olkin MSA were calculated. The MSA value calculated was 0.915, significantly higher than the minimum required value of 0.50 (Hair, Black, Babin, & Anderson, 2014). The Bartlett's Test of Sphericity was found to be significant. This along with a sample size of 711 deemed the data appropriate for EFA.

The EFA was performed and the results were consistent with the theoretical variables. Within this study, the

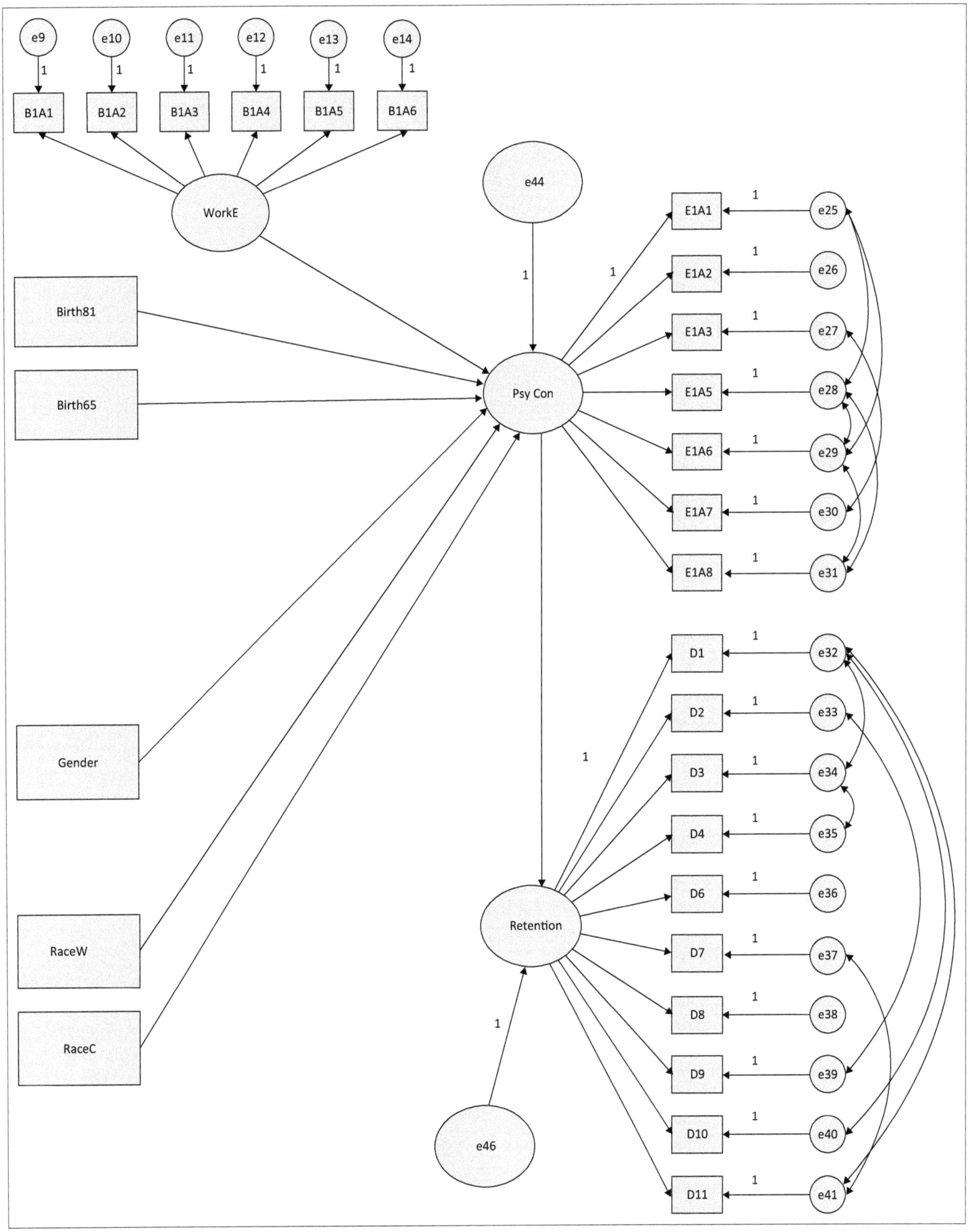

FIGURE 2: Final structural equation modelling model.

measurement model comprises of 33 items that explain the five constructs (WE, FS, GD, PC and R). Factor loadings of 0.45 were considered significant, which falls above the recommendation of 0.40 for sample sizes greater than 350 respondents (Hair, Black, Babin, & Anderson, 2006). Several items did not load adequately and were therefore removed from the analysis. The EFA results provided evidence of the construct and discriminant validity of the measurement

TABLE 2: Factor loadings of the variables.

Factor	Item indicator	Standardised loading	Average variance extracted	Cronbach's alpha
Attraction work environment (WE)	B1A3	0.723	-	0.793
	B1A2	0.647	-	-
	B1A1	0.637	-	-
	B1A6	0.595	-	-
	B1A5	0.589	-	-
	B1A4	0.564	-	-
Attraction financial stability (FS)	B1A15	0.841	-	0.807
	B1A9	0.800	-	-
	B1A13	0.761	-	-
	B1A10	0.581	-	-
	B1A14	0.463	-	-
Attraction growth and development (GD)	B1A16	0.814	-	0.844
	B1A17	0.796	-	-
	B1A20	0.680	-	-
	B1A18	0.674	-	-
	B1A7	0.605	-	-
Psychological contract (PC)	E1A1	-0.715	-	0.847
	E1A2	-0.694	-	-
	E1A3	-0.691	-	-
	E1A5	0.723	-	-
	E1A6	0.727	-	-
	E1A7	-0.746	-	-
	E1A8	0.745	-	-
Retention	D1	0.709	-	0.859

TABLE 3: Regression weights.

Regression	Estimate	SE	CR	*p*
Psychological contract ← Work environment	0.156	0.087	1.785	0.074
Psychological contract ← Gender	-0.176	0.086	-2.052	0.040
Psychological contract ← Race – White	0.555	0.093	5.943	-
Psychological contract ← Race – Mixed race	0.031	0.094	0.33	0.741
Psychological contract ← Birth65	-0.09	0.087	-1.031	0.302
Psychological contract ← Birth81	-0.495	0.088	-5.611	-
Retention ← Psychological contract	0.832	0.045	18.339	-

SE, standard error; CR, capability ratio.

instrument. The internal reliability was assessed using Cronbach alphas and factor loadings, as seen in Table 2. A value of 0.70 or higher is considered reliable (Nunnally & Bernstein, 1994).

As each construct had a Cronbach's alpha value of greater than 0.70, they were all deemed reliable. These constructs were then used in the SEM analysis. Each confirmatory factor model was analysed and assessed. The structural model based on the conceptual model in Figure 1 was analysed. The variables gender, generational cohort and ethnicity were then added to the structural model. The constructs GD and FS were removed from the analysis as the relationships between these constructs and PC were insignificant (Byrne, 2010). The resulting model can be found in Figure 2.

The model fit was assessed for the model in Figure 2 and indicates an average fit upon review of the indices. The CMIN/df value, also called chi-square to df ratio, indicating an adequate model fit, of this sample size, is a value less than 5. The CMIN/df from the model indicates an appropriate model fit with a value of 4.935. The root mean square error of approximation (RMSEA) value of 0.074 indicates a good model fit falling below the recommended value of 0.08. The goodness-of-fit index (GFI) and comparative fit index (CFI) values were 0.863 and 0.841, respectively, which are both close to the recommended value of 0.90 (Iacobucci, 2009). Therefore, the overall model fit indicates an average fit.

The unstandardised regression weights were then reviewed (Table 3). From the results, the relationship between WE and PC was significant at a 10% level, indicating a positive relationship. The relationship between gender and PC was significant at a 5% level, representing a negative relationship. The relationships of the mixed race ethnic grouping with PC, and Baby Boomers with PC, were found to be insignificant. The relationship between the white ethnic grouping and PC indicated a significant positive relationship, whereas the relationship between Millennials and PC indicated a significant negative relationship. This indicates that the white ethnic grouping tends to favour a higher level of PC, whereas the Millennials respondents did not favour a higher level of PC. The relationship between PC and retention indicated a significant positive relationship. This indicates that as the level of PC increases this leads to an increase in the level of retention.

From the results, it can be concluded that WE, white ethnic grouping and retention had a significant positive relationship with PC, whereas gender and Millennials had a significant negative relationship with PC.

Discussion and recommendations

Strong support was found for H1 with the goodness-of-fit indices providing satisfactory measures for the structural model depicted in Figure 2. The structural model affirms that talent management strategies with a positive influence on the psychological contract enhance retention. This finding adds to psychological contract theory by isolating talent management strategies (TMS), more specifically WE, as having the most significant impact on psychological contract fulfilment within the context of gender, ethnic and generational cohorts. Our results show and affirm differences in perception among generational cohorts, thereby adding to the limited empirical evidence supporting generational differences. Understanding the nexus between the causal dynamics of TMS, its relationship to the psychological contract and the resultant impact on retention is fundamental to good management practice and creating an enabling work environment.

Millennials' perception of the influence of TMS on the psychological contract showed a significantly negative relationship (-0.495, p = 0.000). Considering that overall results confirmed a statistically positive relationship between TMS and the PC, it is significant to note that Millennials (38.7% of the sample) perceived the influence to be negative. This finding supports earlier research outlining that work-related attitudes are influenced more by generational experience (Twenge, Campbell, & Hoffman, 2010). No significant statistical relationships were found for either Baby Boomers or Generation Xers. Therefore, H2 cannot be supported; however, Millennials' strong negative experience of TMS on the PC provides strong evidence of their dissatisfaction with TMS. Dissatisfaction with TMS may be as a result of the high premium they place on training, development and career mobility and also account for the difficulty experienced by organisations in retaining Millennial employees. The regression results for older generational cohorts (Baby Boomers and Generation X) were not significant and may be attributed to employees in these life stages being more settled in their careers and thus less likely to change jobs (Festing & Schäfer, 2014). Nevertheless, findings amplify the need for TMS to be diversified in accordance with employees' life stages. TMS should include flexibility in working conditions (hours, off-site work), types of contracts (flexible work arrangements, gig-employees), remuneration and use of multimedia communication and be cognisant of the work–life balance of employees. Gender also showed a negative relationship with psychological contract (-0.176, $p = 0.04$), therefore reinforcing the need for a diversified, flexible TMS and supporting the notion that one size does indeed not fit all.

The findings support H3 that TMS influence employees' perceived psychological contract, with WE indicating a significant positive relationship with the psychological contract (0.156, $p = 0.074$) and is consistent with earlier research (Guest & Conway, 2001; Sonnenberg et al., 2011). Based on the findings, WE takes precedence over financial security as well as growth and development that showed no significant relationship in influencing employees' psychological contracts. The conditions under which employees operate inclusive of roles and responsibilities, authority to implement decisions, feeling valued, participating in decision-making by offering ideas, and sharing information all contribute in creating an environment that positively influences employees' psychological contract. It is proffered that managers and HR practitioners carefully consider adopting strategies that create an inclusive climate conducive to participative decision-making based on openly sharing information within departmental and/or sectoral divisions. In addition, when allocating responsibility, the necessary authority should be clearly outlined and leadership should recognise employees for meeting agreed objectives.

Regression figures indicate that a strong positive relationship (0.555, $p = 0.000$) exists for the white ethnic grouping's perception of the influence of TMS on the psychological contract. Conversely, no meaningful statistical relationships were found for any of the other ethnic groups. This variance in statistical findings among ethnic groups, axiomatically support H4 indicating that the influence of TMS on the psychological contract is perceived differently among ethnic groups. Consequently, it requires HR practitioners to vary and adjust their TMS in accordance with the preferences which may be expressed by different ethnic groupings. As such, constructs measuring cultural norms and customs will assist HR practitioners in mapping cross-cultural TMS. In addition to recognising the differences among generational cohorts, multinational global organisations operating in emerging markets have to provide locally relevant TMS. Strategies, other than those applied in developed (Western) economies and cognisant of the local culture, should be pursued. Our study showed that WE has a significant positive relationship with the PC but not so for the mixed race ethnic group and Baby Boomers. Therefore, HR practitioners and managers must understand the necessity of varying their leadership style, types of communication, level of inclusivity, types of rewards, involvement in decision-making and exercise of authority, which provide an enabling WE inclusive of ethnic and generational cohorts. Failing to adjust the work environment in line with cross-cultural demands may not create an environment conducive for the younger generation to contribute their creativity and productivity (Leung, Maddux, Galinsky & Chiu, 2008). Moreover, the work environment may not engage the younger generation and add to lower levels of performance and impact upon retention (De Meuse & Mlodzik, 2010). Specific acculturated strategies fall outside the ambit of this article; thus, further research is needed in understanding and translating local culture into TMS that stimulates a positive WE.

This article has sought to show that a relationship exists among TMS, the psychological contract, retention within the rich tapestry of generational cohorts, and gender and ethnic groupings. Sufficient statistical support for the aforementioned thesis has been provided against the back drop of generational cohort, gender and ethnic contextual complexities. Recommendations call for a cross-cultural and diversified talent management strategy that is flexible, inclusive, and sensitive to ethnic (cultural), gender and generational cohorts. The results of this study provide a basis for HR practitioners from which to develop a customised talent management strategy that is nuanced for the different generations, cultures and genders. More specifically, HRM practitioners should formulate specific inclusive WE strategies while considering industry specific needs.

Limitations and implications for future research

A limitation of the research was that the sample size was relatively small and that a larger sample would have allowed the authors to make more meaningful inferences on the data obtained.

The provision of development opportunities is likely to increase the organisational commitment of younger generations and to attract talented employees. Future research could investigate the developmental opportunities and corresponding perception of cohorts in emerging markets. Further enquiry is necessary into the cross-cultural dimensions of generational and ethnic cohorts that impact an enabling environment supporting creativity and engagement. Our research indicated that gender had a strong negative relationship between work environment and the psychological contract. As such, we believe further research is necessary to determine specific work environment requirements within a cross-cultural frame for female employees.

Conclusion

Retention of key employees is critical to the long-term success of an organisation. Retaining talented employees plays a vital role in customer satisfaction, product sales, satisfied co-workers and effective succession planning. To achieve the benefits of a competitive advantage and long-term success, talent management must become a critical strategic imperative. For this to be achieved, a clear and compelling strategy must be developed to attract, engage and retain staff across the different generations. By becoming more aware of the needs and preferences of their diverse workforce, organisations can develop suitable TMS. It is also important to determine whether strategies can be uniformly applied across the board or whether different strategies are required for various generations of employees comprising different gender and ethnic groupings.

Acknowledgements

Competing interests

The authors declare that they have no financial or personal relationships that may have inappropriately influenced them in writing this article.

Authors' contributions

P.P. was the project leader and was responsible for the design of questionnaire and compilation of literature. M.R.M. was responsible for the design of questionnaire and compilation of literature. G.S. was responsible for the data analysis.

References

Al Ariss, A. A., Cascio, W. F., & Paauwe, J. (2014). Talent management: Current theories and future research directions. *Journal of World Business, 49*, 173–179. https://doi.org/10.1016/j.jwb.2013.11.001

Atkinson, P. (2008). Millennials: Researching the application of demographics to build customer relationships and HR strategy. *Management Services, 52*(1), 6–11. Retrieved from http://connection.ebscohost.com/c/articles/31726638/millennials-researching-application-demographics-build-customer-relationships-hr-strategy

Armitage, C. J., & Conner, M. (2001), Efficacy of the theory of planned behaviour: A meta-analytic review. *British Journal of Social Psychology, 40*, 471–499. https://doi.org/10.1348/014466601164939

Bluen, S. (2013). *Talent management in emerging markets*. Randburg, South Africa: Knowledge Resources Publishing.

Bosch-Sijtsema, P. M., Fruchter, R., Vartiainen, M., & Ruohomäki, V. (2011). A framework to analyze knowledge work in distributed teams. *Group & Organization Management, 36*(3), 275–307. https://doi.org/10.1177/1059601111403625

Böhmer, N., & Schinnenburg, H. (2016). How gender and career concepts impact Global Talent Management. *Employee Relations, 38*(1), 73–93.

Boudreau, J. W., & Ramstad, P. M. (2005). Talentship and the new paradigm for human resource management: From professional practices to strategic talent decision science. *People and Strategy, 28*(2), 17.

Bryman, A., & Bell, E. (2014). *Research methodology*. Cape Town, South Africa: Oxford University Press.

Byrne, B. M. (2010). *Structural equation modelling with AMOS: Basic concepts, applications and programming*. New York: Routledge.

Bussin, M., & Van Rooy, D. J. (2014). Total rewards strategy for a multi-generational workforce in a financial institution. *SA Journal of Human Resource Management, 12*(1), 1–11. https://doi.org/10.4102/sajhrm.v12i1.606

Campion, M. A., & McClelland, C. L. (1991). Interdisciplinary examination of the costs and benefits of enlarged jobs: A job design quasi-experiment. *Journal of Applied Psychology, 76920*, 186–198. https://doi.org/10.1037/0021-9010.76.2.186

Carlson, C. (2015). *Traditionalists, baby boomers, Generation X, Generation Y (and Generation Z) working together. What matters and how they learn*, pp. 1–13. New York: Executive Office – United Nations Joint Staff Pension Fund.

Cheese, P., Thomas, R. J., & Craig, E. (2008). *Talent powered organization. Strategies for globalization, talent management and high performance*. London, UK: Kogan Page Limited.

CIPD. (2009). *Employer branding: Maintaining momentum in a recession: Chartered Institute of Personnel and Development (CIPD) guide*. London: CIPD.

Clarke, M. (2011). Advancing women's careers through leadership development programs. *Employee Relations, 33*(5), 498–515. https://doi.org/10.1108/01425451111153871

Close, D. (2015). *Generational motivation and preference for reward and recognition in a South African facilities management firm*. Retrieved from http://uir.unisa.ac.za/bitstream/handle/10500/18558/dissertation_close_ds.pdf

Collings, D. G., & Mellahi, K. (2009). Strategic talent management: A review and research agenda. *Human Resource Management Review, 19*(4), 304–313. https://doi.org/10.1016/j.hrmr.2009.04.001

Crampton, S. M., & Hodge, J. W. (2007). Generations in the workplace: Understanding age diversity. *Business Review, 9*(1), 16–22. Retrieved from https://www.researchgate.net/publication/291087554_Generations_in_the_workplace_Understanding_age_diversity

Crumpacker, M., & Crumpacker, J. M. (2007). Succession planning and generational stereotypes: Should HR consider age-based values and attitudes a relevant factor or a passing fad? *Public Personnel Management, 36*(4), 349–369. Retrieved from http://journals.sagepub.com/doi/pdf/10.1177/009102600703600405

D'Amato, A., & Herzfeldt, R. (2008). Learning orientation, organizational commitment and talent retention across generations. *Journal of Managerial Psychology, 23*(8), 929–953. https://doi.org/10.1108/02683940810904402

De Meuse, K. P., & Mlodzik, K. J. (2010). A second look at generational differences in the workforce: Implications for HR and talent management. *People & Strategy, 33*(2), 50–58.

Du Plessis, Y., & Barkhuizen, N. (2015). Exploring the career path barriers of women professional engineers in a South African context. *South African Journal of Labour Relations, 39*(1), 38–57.

Farndale, E., Pai, A., Sparrow, P., & Scullion, H. (2014). Balancing individual and organizational goals in global talent management: A mutual-benefits perspective. *Journal of World Business, 49*, 204–214. https://doi.org/10.1016/j.jwb.2013.11.004

Festing, M., & Schäfer, L. (2014). Generational challenges to talent management: A framework for talent retention based on the psychological-contract perspective. *Journal of World Business, 49*, 262–271. https://doi.org/10.1016/j.jwb.2013.11.010

Glass, A. (2007). Understanding generational differences for competitive success. *Industrial & Commercial Training, 39*(2), 98–103. https://doi.org/10.1108/00197850710732424

Gorgievski, M. J., Bakker, A. B., & Schaufeli, W. B. (2010). Work engagement and Workaholism: Comparing the self-employed and salaried employees. *The Journal of Positive Psychology, 5*(1), 83–96. https://doi.org/10.1080/17439760903509606

Griffeth, R. W., Hom, P. W., & Gaertner, S. (2000). A meta-analysis of antecedents and correlates of employee turnover: Update, moderator tests, and research implications for the next millennium. *Journal of Management, 26*, 463–488. https://doi.org/10.1177/014920630002600305

Grobler, P., Bothma, R., Brewster, C., Carey, L., Holland, P., & Warnich, S. (2017). *Contemporary issues in human resource management* (4th edn.). Cape Town: Oxford University Press.

Guest, D., & Conway, N. (2001). *Public and private sector perspectives on the psychological contract: Results of the 2001 CIPD survey*. Wimbledon, London: Chartered Institute of Personnel and Development.

Gursoy, D., Maier, T. A., & Chi, C. G. (2008). Generational differences: An examination of work values and generational gaps in the hospitality workforce. *International Journal of Hospitality Management, 27*(3), 448–458. https://doi.org/10.1016/j.ijhm.2007.11.002

Hafez, E., AbouelNeel, R., & Elsaid, E. (2017). An exploratory study on how talent management affects employee retention and job satisfaction for personnel administration in Ain Shams University Egypt. *Journal of Management and Strategy, 8*(4), 1. https://doi.org/10.5430/jms.v8n4p1

Hair, J. F., Jr., Anderson, R. E., Tatham, R. L., & Black, W. C. (1998). *Multivariate data analysis*. Upper Saddle River, NJ: Prentice Hall.

Hair, J. F., Black, W. C., Babin, B. J., & Anderson, R. E. (2006). *Multivariate data analysis*. Upper Saddle River, NJ: Prentice Hall.

Hair, J. F., Black, W. C., Babin, B. J., & Anderson, R. E. (2014). *Multivariate data analysis*. New Jersey, United States: Pearson Education Limited.

Iacobucci, D. (2009). Structural equations modeling: Fit Indices, sample size, and advanced topics. *Journal of Consumer Psychology, 20*, 90–98. https://doi.org/10.1016/j.jcps.2009.09.003

Ilies, R., Wilson, K. S., & Wagner, D. T. (2009). The spillover of daily job satisfaction on the employees' family lives: The facilitating role of work–family integration. *Academy of Management Journal, 52*(1), 87–102. https://doi.org/10.5465/AMJ.2009.36431938

Johnson, J. A., & Lopes, J. (2008), The intergenerational workforce revisited. *Organizational Development Journal, 26*, 31–37.

Kilfman, S. (2009). *Talent management in a multigenerational workforce. (2018)*. Masters, Tilburg University.

Knowledge Resources. (2017a). *Human Capital and Labour Report: South Africa*. South Africa.

Knowledge Resources. (2017b). *On the Rise: Africa's Talent Mobility in the 21st Century Report*. South Africa.

Knowledge Resources. (2018). *Human Capital and Labour Report: South Africa*. Randburg, South Africa: KR Publishing (PTY) LTD.

Lee, T. W., Mitchell, T. R., Sablynski, C. J., Burton, J. P., & Holtom, B. C. (2004). The effects of job embeddedness on organisational citizenship, job performance, volitional absences and voluntary turnover. *The Academy of Management Journal, 47*(5), 711–722. Retrieved from http://www.jstor.org/stable/20159613

Leung, A. K. Y., Maddux, W. W., Galinsky, A. D., & Chiu, C. Y. (2008). Multicultural experience enhances creativity: The when and how. *American Psychologist, 63*(3), 169. https://doi.org/10.1037/0003-066X.63.3.169

Leuty, M. E., & Hansen, J. I. C. (2011). Evidence of construct validity for work values. *Journal of Vocational Behavior, 79*(2), 379–390. https://doi.org/10.1016/j.jvb.2011.04.008

Lewis, R. E., & Heckman, R. J. (2006). Talent management: A critical review. *Human Resource Management Review, 16*, 139–154. https://doi.org/10.1016/j.hrmr.2006.03.001

Lyons, S. T., Duxbury, L., & Higgins, C. (2007). An empirical assessment of generational differences in basic human values. *Psychological reports, 101*(2), 339–352. https://doi.org/10.2466/pr0.101.2.339-352

Macky, K., Gardner, D., & Forsyth, S. (2008). Generational differences at work: Introduction and overview. *Journal of Managerial Psychology, 23*(8), 857–861. https://doi.org/10.1108/02683940810904358

Masibigiri, V., & Nienaber, H. (2011). Factors affecting the retention of Generation X public servants: An exploratory study. *SA Journal of Human Resource Management, 9*(1), 1–11. https://doi.org/10.4102/sajhrm.v27i4.318

Mayhew, D. R. (2014). *Placing parties in American politics: Organization, electoral settings, and government activity in the twentieth century*. Princeton, NJ: Princeton University Press.

Meyer, J. P., & Allen, N. J. (1997). *Commitment in the workplace*. Thousand Oakes, CA: Sage.

Moore, A., & Bussin, M. (2012). Reward preferences for generations in selected Information and Communication Technology companies. *SA Journal of Human Resource Management, 10*(1), 1–9. https://doi.org/10.4102/sajhrm.v10i1.325

Nunnally, J. C., & Bernstein, I. H. (1994). *Psychometric theory*. New York, NY: McGraw-Hill.

Peters, P., Poutsma, E., Van der Heijden, B. I., Bakker, A. B., & Bruijn, T. D. (2014). Enjoying new ways to work: An HRM-process approach to study flow. *Human Resource Management, 53*(2), 271–290. https://doi.org/10.1002/hrm.21588

Qu, H., & Zhao, X. (2012). Employees' work–family conflict moderating life and job satisfaction. *Journal of Business Research, 65*(1), 22–28. https://doi.org/10.1016/j.jbusres.2011.07.010

Rousseau, D. M. (1990). New hire perceptions of their own and their employer's obligations: A study of psychological contracts. *Journal of Organizational Behavior, 11*(5), 389–400. https://doi.org/10.1002/job.4030110506

Roy, J. G. (2008). Ten tips for retaining the next generation. *Utility Automation and Engineering T&D, 13*(2), 8. Retrieved from http://connection.ebscohost.com/c/articles/35636085/ten-tips-retaining-next-generation

Schambach, T. (2001). Age, motivation, and participation in professional development. *Journal of Computer Information Systems, 41*(4), 57–64.

Simons, A. (2009). Changing workplace demographics: T + B + Y + X = opportunity. *CPA Practice Management Forum, May*, 15–23.

Sonnenberg, M., Koene, B., & Paauwe, J. (2011). Balancing HRM: The psychological contract of employees: A multi-level study. *Personnel Review, 40*(6), 664–683. https://doi.org/10.1108/00483481111169625

The Economist Intelligence Unit. (2010). *The Economist Intelligence Unit*. Retrieved from http://www.eiu.com/home.aspx

Thunnissen, M., Boselie, P., & Fruytier, B., 2013. Talent management and the relevance of context: Towards a pluralistic approach. *Human Resource Management Review, 23*, 326–336. https://doi.org/10.1016/j.hrmr.2013.05.004

Thomsons Online Benefits. (2017). *Expectations vs reality: The widening gap in global benefits*. Retrieved from https://www.thomsons.com/resources/whitepapers/the-widening-gap-between-expectations-and-reality/

Twenge, J. M., Campbell, S. M., Hoffman, B. J., & Lance, C. E. (2010). Generational differences in work values: Leisure and extrinsic values increasing, social and intrinsic values decreasing. *Journal of Management, 36*(5), 1117–1142. https://doi.org/10.1177/0149206309352246

Van Der Voordt, T. J. (2004). Productivity and employee satisfaction in flexible workplaces. *Journal of Corporate Real Estate, 6*(2), 133–148. https://doi.org/10.1108/14630010410812306

Wagner, K. L. (2007). Filling the gap: The generation gap in the workplace creates challenges for managers wanting to build a team. *Journal of Property Management, 72*(5), 29–36.

Ye, J., Cardon, M. S., & Rivera, E. (2012). A mutuality perspective of psychological contracts regarding career development and job security. *Journal of Business Research, 65*, 294–301. https://doi.org/10.1016/j.jbusres.2011.03.006

Zulu, P. S., & Parumasur, S. B. (2009). Employee perceptions of the management of cultural diversity and workplace transformation. *SA Journal of Industrial Psychology, 35*(1), 49–57. https://doi.org/10.4102/sajip.v35i1.426

7

Maternity and paternity leave and career progression of black African women in dual-career couples

Authors:
Lucky L. Motaung[1]
Mark H.R. Bussin[1]
Renjini M. Joseph[1]

Affiliations:
[1]Department of Industrial Psychology and People Management, University of Johannesburg, South Africa

Corresponding author:
Mark Bussin,
drbussin@mweb.co.za

Orientation: The study focused on examining the perceptions of dual-career couples at a state-owned company about the influence of taking maternity and paternity leave on the career progression of black African women in middle management and leadership occupations.

Research purpose: The primary purpose of the study was to identify core barriers in relation to maternity and paternity leave that contribute negatively in the career progression of black African women in dual-career couples.

Motivation for the study: To obtain insight into the underrepresentation and progression of black African women within dual-career couples, in middle management and leadership occupations.

Research design, approach and method: This study was qualitative, comprising a sample of 10 black African women and 10 black African men, with data collected through in-depth semi-structured interviews. Thematic analysis was utilised to analyse the interview dialogues.

Main findings: The findings established that taking maternity leave has a negative influence on the career progression of black African women in dual-career couples at the state-owned company. The participants further confirmed that involuntary time off work and productiveness were principal influencing barriers of taking maternity leave, leading to other undesirable consequences, such as unproductiveness and reliability.

Practical and managerial implications: The state-owned company should review its current talent management and recruitment and selection policies, in order to positively contribute to increasing the representation and facilitating career progression of black African women within dual-career couples, in middle management and leadership occupations.

Contributions or value-add: Insights were provided on the influences of taking maternity and paternity leave in the underrepresentation and progression of black African women within dual-career couples, in middle management and leadership occupations.

Introduction

Family and organisational support are two primary elements that play a pivotal role in the career progression of women into leadership and top management roles, especially those who are part of a dual-career couple (DCC) (Smit, 2006). Many current work practices do not facilitate gender equality (Smit, 2006), which is one of the values upheld by the South African Constitution and the *Employment Equity Act* (*Labour Relations Act*, RSA, 1998b; RSA Constitution, 1996). In relation to this article, there exists a challenge in the underrepresentation of black African women in middle management and leadership occupations, as well as their slow progression to such positions.

Focus of the study

The study focused on examining how taking maternity leave (ML) and paternity leave (PL) influences the career progression of black African women in DCCs, in middle management and leadership occupations. The study was conducted in a state-owned company (SOC), as SOCs are some of the primary custodians in promoting equal employment opportunities as per the *Employment Equity Act* (EEA, 1998a). SOCs are legal entities that undertake commercial activities on behalf of an owner government. The legal status of an SOC varies from being part of the government to being stock companies with the state as a majority stakeholder (*Public Finance Management Act* 1, 1999).

The primary purpose of the study was to identify core barriers in relation to ML and PL that contribute negatively to the career progression of black African women in DCCs. The study also enabled the researcher to determine how black African women manage tension between their work and family roles and the impact this may have on their career goals and success. It could be argued that if a woman successfully manages family responsibilities with sufficient and relevant support, her career could positively progress, as she will have a fair opportunity to pursue her career goals (Nath, 2000). The study provided a broad examination of how taking ML and PL may influence the career progression of black African women as part of a DCC in middle management and leadership occupations at an SOC, by examining both internal and external factors.

Background to the study

For the purposes of this study, the term black African women refers to only black South African women, excluding women of mixed race and those of Indian background. The below extract provides an indication on how black African women are bound, to a certain extent, by culturally inherent practices that define them, and their place in society and within the family unit:

> The vital life goal of Black African women is to be oriented within their culture. This means to be rooted in the knowledge and practice of the culture of one's peoples, to extract lessons from it and to use it in emancipatory, transformative and enriching ways. Being a Black African women begins with and is rooted in African tradition and culture. (Karenga & Tembo, 2012, p. 40)

Traditionally, men were expected to fulfil the role of sole earner in the household. Women were then expected to assume economic dependency and the role of motherhood, with no aspiration for career acknowledgement and fulfilment (Bosch, De Bruin, De Bruin & Kgaladi, 2012). Bosch et al. (2012) also indicated that, from an early age, black African girls are culturally indoctrinated to grow up into childbearing and motherhood roles, whereby they do not see themselves as equal to men in any aspects of their being.

Such socialisation can bring about many consequences that could eventually influence young black African women when they are mature and are required to make life-enhancing decisions that affect their future and growth. Such influence could bring about thinking among black African women that they would never be equal to men, be it socially or economically. For many years, the majority of black African women have been inactive in the employment arena, with most of those that are employed not being as career-orientated as men. This is a result of the historical role that was imposed on them (Greenhaus, Callanan & Godshalk, 2010). Although more black African women are now employed, there exist some consequences of the socialisation of black African women.

Herman (2016) and Mumma (2001) describe a DCC as a household where both the woman and the man earn an income and both spouses are dedicated to their professional occupations in which they pose specialist content knowledge in their field. Being a spouse in a DCC can be a challenging role, which entails time and devotion (Greenhaus & Powell, 2006; Ilies, Keeney & Scott, 2011).

Hall (2002) defined a career as a lifetime development of employment-related engagements and deeds that embrace both objective and independent elements. Career success may have different meanings for men and women from the beginning of their careers to maturity. Rajadhyaksha and Bhatnagar (2000) argued that the significant difference between the male and female definitions of career success is that women aspire to achieve importance in what they deliver, when compared to men, who aspire for seniority in their occupations.

Research objective and problem

The primary aim of the study was to examine how taking ML and PL influences the career progression of black African women as part of DCCs at an SOC. The research problem was that we did not adequately understand the impact that taking ML and PL had on the career progression of black African women as part of DCCs at the SOC, within middle management and leadership occupations.

Trends from literature

Motherhood has developed from the standard care-giving role towards a role of rising importance regarding attaining individual aspirations within the context of life, as well as a career (Moore, 2013). The current minimal participation of men as caregivers in the form of formalised PL puts more pressure on women in balancing their careers and care-giving roles (Moore, 2013).

The fertility rate of black African women in 2010, with an average of 2.3 children, shows a clear obligation that is still being experienced by black African women in their quest to balance career goals and childbearing responsibilities (Smit, 2006). The fertility rate of black African women dropped from 6.8 in the 1950s, to 5.8 in the 1970s, to the current rate of 2.3, which suggests that black African women are now minimising and delaying childbearing in an attempt to focus more on their career goals and progress and to minimise their time off work because of ML (Moore, 2013). Among other reasons, this delay could also be because of financial constraints resulting from the high unemployment rate among black African women (Stats SA, 2015). Nonetheless, it is imperative to take note that having children, although fewer than before, is still a vital part of black African women's identity, even though it may influence their career progression and success (Moore, 2013).

While care-giving behaviours have been mostly related to feminine values and characteristics (Mainiero & Sullivan, 2005), recent studies indicate that, to a large extent, men are also developing increased self-consciousness regarding care roles (Harrington, Van Deusen & Mazar, 2012). Men not only aspire to be economically supportive but also seek to be psychologically and physically supportive within their households (Harrington et al., 2012). In Ireland, where PL is policy, working fathers who have utilised PL mentioned that it has enabled them to be good fathers to their children and to feel more psychologically attached to their family units (Pesonen, 2015). This indicates the essential support PL can provide to the DCC family unit and broader socio-economic context if properly and legislatively formalised.

Value-add of the study

Through this study, it has been established that taking ML and PL has a direct and indirect influence on the perceived career progression of black African women in DCCs at a specific SOC, in middle management and leadership occupations. In the acknowledgement of this influence, the study also contributed to the limited theory and knowledge on the topic and field of study within the context of South Africa (SA). Furthermore, the study identified a relationship between the black African women and black African men in their experiences and understandings of the influence of ML on the career progression of black African women in DCCs at an SOC, with a 90% support of such an influence across all the participants. The identification of this relation proved to be quite essential and added value to the overall study in indicating certain commonalities regarding how black African women and black African men perceive one another within the workplace and family environment.

The following section reviews relevant current literature on ML and PL and the career progression of black African women. The research design is then presented followed by a report on the data gathered. The article is concluded after a detailed discussion on the main findings, limitations of the study and recommendations for future research.

Literature review

Black African women in the South African labour market

The isolation of women in the notion of working-class encounters in SA must ideally be studied within the framework of the colonial and apartheid constructions of African women (Tshoaedi, 2012). Overall, women in the SA labour market have been secluded and discriminated against for a number of years, whereby for a majority of them, their contributions, if any, were only restricted to unskilled roles (Floro & Komatsu, 2011; Gurjao, 2006). Despite the effects of colonialism and apartheid, numerous positive strides have been made in the liberation and upliftment of women and black African women in the SA labour market (EEA, 1998a).

Some of these developments lie in the establishment of legislation and policies that promote the participation of women in the labour market, such as the *LRA* of 1995, the *EEA*, the *Skills Development Act* of 1998. These legislative policies have played a great role in promoting the equality journey of women in the SA labour market (EEA, 1998a).

In spite of some of the accomplishments of women in SA, a lot still has to be overcome both socially and economically to see more meaningful change for women in SA. It has been argued that notwithstanding the nuanced gender equality rights and complemented legislation on paper, women still encompass the majority of the underprivileged and marginalised in SA (Sadie, 2015). This marginalisation transpires in that 'patriarchal' power still underlies the economic relegation of women (Bentley, 2004). The overarching dilemma in this negative phenomenon is that some of these equality policies tend to only look promising on paper, but most of the time their practical implementation lacks impact (Sadie, 2015). It can be argued that out of all the races of women in SA, black African women have been by far the worst affected and discriminated against in many possible ways (Flood, Hoosain & Primo, 1997).

Historically, black African women who were privileged enough to have been employed were customarily employed as domestic workers mainly. In 1998, an estimated total average of more than 80% of all domestic workers was black African women. While also concurrently acting as heads of their families in certain instances, black African women were greatly disadvantaged, as they also often received far lower incomes than black African men (Forger et al., 2001; Ministry for Welfare & Population Development, 1998).

During black African women's career progression prior to 1994, black African women were subjected to a conceptual acknowledgement called 'double jeopardy' or 'double discrimination' (De Vries, 1991; Davidson, 1997; Sewpaul, 1994; Talley-Poss, 1995). Black African women in SA were being oppressed, both for being 'black' and also for being women (Commission of Gender Equality, 2001). These were some of the unfortunate realities that black African women were faced with in their daily lives within the SA labour market and broader socio-economic landscape, in addition to their struggle for equality and liberation. There may be undesirable effects of such 'double discrimination' that could have hindered their confidence, self-esteem and courage. It can be contended that these effects may still be indoctrinated in some of their social behaviours, which could take years to totally eradicate within their psychological system and general outlook on life.

Attainments and challenges in maternity leave

Maternity leave refers to granting women time off work before and after childbirth and, in some cases, for adoption of a child (*Basic Conditions of Employment Act* [BCEA], 1997; Smit, 2006). This time off provides some degree of job and social security to women during the process of childbirth and early childcare (BCEA, 1997).

In the SA context, ML is a legislative entitlement under the BCEA, which stipulates that ML can be taken for a period of up to four consecutive months (BCEA, 1997). Employers have their own policies on remunerating employees, but if an employer does not provide financial ML benefits, a female employee can claim benefits for 17 weeks from the Unemployment Insurance Fund (UIF). Givati and Troiano (2012) argue that the provision of paid ML is an inadequate answer to the numerous impediments of maternity discrimination, disparity in the workplace and lack of representation of women in managerial and leadership occupations. Paid ML may be regarded as only a small advance in the journey towards eradicating all forms of discrimination against women in our labour markets.

It is also quite cognisant to appreciate the efforts by some countries including SA and many European countries in making paid ML a reality, whereas women in other countries like United States are not privileged to this right (LRA, 1995; OECD, 1995). Contemporary research has revealed that the main impact of paid ML could merely just be a gesture to the acknowledgement of equality and inclusion, supplementary to it being a definite diagnosis for it (Givati & Troiano, 2012).

Attainments and challenges in paternity leave

Paternity leave refers to the short-term leave available to fathers in the period subsequent to the delivery or adoption of a child, affording men the opportunity to devote additional time to their families, while maintaining job security (Evans, 2007; Haas, 2003). It is important to acknowledge that PL is not legally enforced within the SA labour environment and that it is only utilised as a benefit within the family responsibility leave category for fathers, limited only to 3 days per annum in some organisations (BCEA, 1997; Mokomane, 2009; Morrell & Richter, 2006).

Most southern African countries compare poorly to European Union countries when comparing PL policies and legislation. Slovenia offers PL of 90 days, Finland 7–21 days and Denmark 14 days (Lammi-Taskula, 2008; quoted in Smit, 2006). Moss (2012) highlights PL as a compensated father's privilege as opposed to a duty, to a few days absence, engaged concurrently with the mother after childbirth. As much as PL may be an entitlement, it is important to take cognisance that PL is not considered a right to men, but only a privileged entitlement to a few (Mokomane, 2009; Morrell & Richter, 2006).

There is little knowledge documented regarding the understanding and involvement of black African men as fathers within the context of PL (Wall, 2014). The uniqueness regarding black African men is to be seen in their embedded culture and traditional conceptions in terms of a woman's role in the family unit as 'housewife and child bearer' (Santho, 1995). It is also important to acknowledge that this cultural stigma is slowly fading away among black African men who are fathers, as many men seem to appreciate the value of PL recently (Wall, 2014).

Motherhood and marriage within the labour markets

Hardill (2002) mentions that although there is autonomous decision making regarding compensated employment, the obligations of social reproduction still exclusively remain a women's responsibility. This highlights the over-encompassing challenge of women having to maintain a peculiar balance between their ever-conflicting roles, as childbearer and as full-time employee (Atkinson & Hall, 2009). Empirical evidence indicates that, even within DCC households, gender disparities in decision making and time allocation still remains an incitement, with some degree of disagreement and compromise extremely persistent (Wheatly, 2013).

The interchange to parenthood may seem to be a seamless family portrayal, but may also have the potential of negatively impacting the work domain (Wheatly, 2013). Salmera-Aro, Nurmi, Saisto and Halmesmaki (2000) argue in congruence of this imbalanced development in a study of pregnant parents. The study indicated that the conversion to parenthood not only affects individual goals in the domestic domain but also hinders achievement objectives within the employment domain as well. They further indicated that during pregnancy, women tend to prioritise family-associated objectives more and employment achievement aspirations less, whereas there was no subsequent impact on the employment achievement goals among men (Salmera-Aro et al., 2000).

Representation of black African women in management positions and their progression to leadership roles in the South African labour market

Table 1 indicates the high labour force population of black African women within the SA labour market across all groups of women. Even though black African women represent the majority of women within the labour market at 73.5% in 2015, it must be noted that most of them only occupy semi-skilled to low-skilled jobs. Out of their overall 73.5% labour force composition, 39.0% occupy semi-skilled occupations and 43.4% occupy low-skilled occupations, leaving only 17.6% occupying skilled jobs within which middle management and leadership roles would fall.

Table 1 further highlights that white and Indian/Asian women workforce groups dominate employment in skilled occupations as compared to black African women and women of mixed race, despite black African women being the dominant group within the woman workforce. Black African women remain highly underrepresented and disadvantaged within skilled, professional and managerial occupations at only 17.6% – the lowest of all the women groups. This negative gap that exists to date between black

TABLE 1: Employment by occupation, population group and sex, Q3: 2015.

Women	Skilled	Semi-skilled	Low-skilled
White	57.8	41.4	0.8
Asian/Indian	48.0	47.9	4.1
Mixed race	20.7	46.6	32.7
Black African	17.6	39.0	43.4

Source: Statistics South Africa (Stat SA). (2015). *Quarterly Labour Force Survey – Quarter3*. Statistics South Africa. Retrieved September 17, 2015, from http://www.statssa.gov.za

Note: 'Skilled' includes manager, professional and technician occupations; 'Semi-skilled' includes clerk, sales and services, skilled agriculture, craft and related trade and plant and machine operator occupations; 'Low-skilled' includes elementary and domestic worker occupations.

African women and other women groups within the skilled, professional and managerial occupations are not representative of the demographics of SA. This gap becomes more prominent in an era where, to a certain extent, black African women pose more or less similar offerings in terms of education, knowledge, skills and capabilities, as women of other race groups, but still remain the most disadvantaged. This underrepresentation and slow progression of black African women in skilled, professional and managerial occupations support the literature in indicating that they are the most disadvantaged group among women in SA (Forger et al., 2001; Ministry for Welfare & Population Development, 1998).

Research design

Research approach

This study was qualitative, whereby in-depth, semi-structured interviews were utilised in examining the influence of ML and PL on the career progression of black African women who are part of DCCs at an SOC, in middle management and leadership occupations. A qualitative design enriched the context of the study in comprehending real-life social experiences that black African women encounter in their daily working lives. The qualitative approach allows little or no disruption and manipulation of their existing working social life cohesion (Holiday, 2007; Holloway & Wheeler, 2010).

Research strategy

An interpretivist theoretical approach was adopted in the study. The ontological stance of the researcher in the study was that there is no one realism. Based on the researcher's view, reality is subjective, socially accumulated and founded on the insights and experiences of the researcher and the participants (Creswell, 2007; Crotty, 1998). The epistemology was that of a naturalistic inquiry (Lincoln & Cuba, 1985). According to Blumer (1969, pp. 46–48), 'a naturalistic inquiry refers to a special form of inquiry that respects the natural integrity of the empirical problem under study'. In the appreciation of this natural reliability, the problem must be deliberated in its normal enduring atmosphere, in the absence of any possible predetermined elements to it (Blumer, 1969).

Research method

Research setting

The study was conducted at an SOC in SA, as SOCs are considered to be one of the primary custodians in promoting employment equity in the best interest of the country's transformation policies. This SOC operates within the research and development and energy sectors. Its primary activities include research and development, engineering and manufacturing.

Entrée and establishing researcher roles

A researcher normally gains admission to an organisational setting by obtaining the consent of the persons in charge. Permission to conduct the study at this SOC was granted by the Group Executive: Corporate Services. The researcher's role in this study was primarily that of an insider researcher; with consideration that the researcher is male, not yet married, not part of a DCC and not yet a father. This to a certain extent enhanced the researcher's lack of bias. The role was furthermore limited to that of a Human Resource (HR) business partner aspiring to add value and novel knowledge to the field of study (Schurink, 2005).

Population and sampling

The population of the study comprised black African women and black African men, who work at the SOC in middle and leadership occupations and who are part of a DCC. The sample consisted of 20 participants. Non-random convenience purposive sampling was utilised. The selection of the participants in qualitative studies largely emanates from the target population of the research setting, which materialises in a convenience purposive sample of individuals. These individuals would have had exposure to some of the problem statement elements (Ryan, Coughlin & Cronin, 2007). As a result, their insights would greatly contribute towards the achievement of the study's objectives (Quick & Hall, 2015).

The sample comprised 10 black African women and 10 black African men – whereby all 20 participants were permanent black African employees of the SOC, who had functional backgrounds in finance, human resources, science and engineering, research and development, training and development and corporate business management. Furthermore, the primary participants were black African women within the various levels of the organisational hierarchy, with a majority of them in middle management and leadership positions. Middle-level to leadership management–level positions were selected as they are the roles that are being researched. These positions are being studied as they are deemed to be career phases, which are both demanding and arduous in terms of leadership and achievement.

Furthermore, the sample selection criterion was that the black African women and black African men participating in the study must be married and part of a DCC and also have a minimum of one child in their individual family unit. Participants who had a minimum of one child offered an opportunity to examine the complexity involved in balancing domestic and employment roles as well as how ML and PL are utilised. This also highlighted the intricacy that transpires within the fundamentals of child-caring responsibilities.

Data collection methods

Semi-structured, in-depth, face-to-face interviews were utilised as the primary data collection mechanism for this study. In-depth interviewing, also called 'conversational interviewing' is a common technique utilised by qualitative researchers (Schurink, 1998). According to Schurink (1998), in-depth interviewing entails one or more face-to-face dialogues between an interviewer and an interviewee.

Recording of data

When recording data during qualitative research, researchers must pledge to keep their data physically well organised, develop a plan about how they foresee doing it and ensure that they adhere to their scheme or plan. Researchers must also create a back-up system. It is important to keep hard copies of all recorded data in a manual filing system, to ensure that valuable data are not lost in case of any unforeseen circumstances. Many different types of documents are used by researchers to enrich their data, and these need to be stored safely (Bogdan & Biklen, 1992).

In this study, all the interviews were recorded by means of a digital dictaphone, accompanied by representative field notes. The researcher transcribed the data from the interviews to enhance confidentiality and anonymity of the participants (Nath, 2000). These measures ensured meticulousness in reflecting the participants' actual words, tone of voice and any other substantial information, which aided in understanding and analysing the responses of the participants. All the data were digitally stored on a laptop and backed up on two external hard drives for safeguarding (Schurink, 2004).

Data analysis

Thematic analysis was utilised to analyse the interview dialogues in the data analysis of this research. Thematic analysis can be stated to be a qualitative statistical methodology of factor analysis or exploration gathering, dually aiming to define a complex data set in relation to a number of scopes or groupings (Barker & Pistrang, 2012). This entailed methodically classifying and consolidating understandings into patterns of meaning (themes) from the data.

Furthermore, the purpose of utilising thematic analysis was to realise and make sense of shared significances and experiences (Braun & Clarke, 2012). It is mostly used to analyse interview data, whereby the researcher analyses the material inductively. Themes are derived from the data, rather than being established beforehand (Barker & Pistrang, 2012).

Soundness of the study

The soundness of the study was determined by its credibility, transparency and transferability. Credibility can be established by whether the data dialogued with the participants relates to the conclusions of the research inquiry (Esterberg, 2002). Transferability is the capability to use a similar research method and process in other but similar circumstances and obtain comparable outcomes (Barker & Pistrang, 2012).

Elliott, Fischer and Rennie (1999); Mays and Pope (2000) provide the below recommendations regarding trustworthiness, which were followed in the study:

1. Foundation (providing some of the raw data upon basing findings);
2. Transparency (revealing own preferences and prospects);
3. Consistency (themes correspond with data outline); and
4. Credibility checks (engaging other sources). (Barker & Pistrang, 2012, n.p.)

In the quest to attain sound validity and credibility in qualitative research, a researcher's insider involvement has to be proclaimed throughout a qualitative study, irrespective of the picture this may depict (Miles & Huberman, 1994). The involvement of the researcher has been clarified in this study.

In the endeavour to enrich credibility, comprehensive details pertaining to data gathering, analysis and interpretation of a study should be provided. Beck (2009), Patton (2014) and Shenton (2004) indicate that this practice accords replication of the research enhancing transparency, credibility and soundness of a study, highlighting the undesirable or different themes that materialised throughout the research project. In this study, field notes, taped dialogue recordings, original interview questionnaires, data and analyses were some of the key measures in supporting and apprehending the soundness of the study.

Ethical considerations

The researcher adhered to research ethics throughout this study. The primary objective and value of ethics is striving to protect the dignity, well-being, rights and interests of the participants involved in a research study at all times, regardless of any possible setbacks it may convey to a study (Quick & Hall, 2015). Firstly, the participants were informed of the objectives of the research as well as their right to voluntary participation. The researcher also signed a declaration of confidentiality with the participants regarding the information obtained during the interviews. Participants also signed consent forms for their participation in the research and with regard to the recording of the interviews. The overall findings of the study will be shared with those participants who have requested to be informed once the study is completed, as a measure of enhancing transparency in the study.

Research findings

The primary purpose of the study was to examine the influence of ML and PL on the career progression of black African women as part of DCCs at an SOC, in order to obtain more insight on the underrepresentation and slow progression of black African women in middle management and leadership roles. As a result, eight key themes, described below, were identified during the interview process.

Theme 1: Commitment and motivation

The initial theme that came about was that of commitment and motivation. Lack of commitment and motivation was a challenge or barrier, in that its absence within black African women represented a hindering element that led to a complacent focus in black African women's career aspirations, affecting and delaying any proactive efforts of a positive career progression.

The participant responses in the study supported the above discussion and interpretation, whereby black African women indicated that a lack of commitment and motivation towards their careers was a self-imposed challenge. In comparison to men, the attitudes of women tend to be an important barrier in women's careers, if they are not being truly committed and motivated. Male participants in the study shared the same implication regarding black African women and women in general as not being committed and motivated to their careers, resulting in them not progressing as ideally as they had hoped. Based on the response summary of the participants, 70% of the black African women supported this theme and 80% of black African men were also in support of the theme, signifying its importance.

Theme 2: Patriarchal dominance and power

The second theme that came about in the study was patriarchal dominance and supremacy. This theme primarily indicated that apart from women being a great barrier in their career progression in terms of lacking commitment and motivation, men transpired to be an important barrier in their career progression, through a societal system that advantages and privileges men. Johnson (2005) describes patriarchy as a societal system that operates by essentially constructing privileges for men and concomitantly repressing women, which we all form a part of in one way or another.

Within the study, both male and female participants acknowledged patriarchal dominance and supremacy in their society as a barrier in the career progression of women in DCCs at the SOC, and more specifically for black African women. The participants' supporting responses indicated that the labour market is greatly male dominated and predominantly white male dominated, especially within the middle management to leadership positions.

Theme 3: Internal family support

The third theme that came about in the study was internal family support. As indicated in the literature, internal support is one of the most essential support elements for the career progression of black African women in DCCs, bearing in mind that black African women are still responsible for most of the household and childrearing burdens (Hall & MacDermid, 2009; OECD, 2013). Besides the substantiating grounds for PL in terms of internal family support, 80% black African women participants indicated that emotional support was by far the most essential form of internal family support. Black African women also indicated that they admire emotional support more than any other benefits that can be derived from either PL or any other form or structure of internal family support. The participants further ascribed internal family support towards establishing and having a strong internal support structure at home.

Theme 4: Organisational and managerial support

Organisational and managerial support was the fourth theme that came about in the study. As depicted in the literature, April, Dreyer and Blass (2007) argued that, based on the situation-centred theory, employment and its environment can also become obstacles to the professional advancement of women.

The participants' responses supported the above interpretation in that they further acknowledged time off and availability as another deficient organisational support mechanism that also greatly influenced the career progression of black African women and women in general in DCCs at an SOC. This came about on a number of substantiating grounds, whereby 85% of the participants maintained that involuntary time off work and unavailability resulting from taking ML were the dominating and limiting factors in the career progression of black African women in DCCs.

Theme 5: Culture and upbringing

The fifth theme that came about in the study was culture and upbringing. Traditionally, men were expected to fulfil the role of sole earner in the household, while women were expected to assume economic dependency and the role of motherhood, with no aspiration for career acknowledgement and fulfilment (Bosch et al., 2012).

A certain number of black African women participants further portrayed a customary undesirable behaviour of perceiving the motherhood burden solely on themselves. Black African women seem to not realise that times and customary tradition have evolved and that men are equally accountable for actively taking part in fatherhood and household responsibilities (Harrington et al., 2012). As such, women tend to sell themselves short, by upholding certain customary practices that disadvantage them in the long run, even though times and culture have evolved to an extent that they are not compelled to do so.

Theme 6: Training and development

Training, development and mentoring came about as the sixth theme of the study. Both spouses in DCCs work vastly in experienced managerial, professional and leadership roles. As a result, it becomes quite apparent that education, training and even mentoring stand to be essential elements in both spouses gaining entry into these occupations and more importantly, in maintaining these roles and their work–life balance. In the absence of education, training and mentoring, they would most likely not have the necessary knowledge in being competent and excelling within their professional occupations (Hakim, 2002).

In the study, 65% of the participants supported and greatly acknowledged the impact of training, development as well as mentoring on the career progression of black African women in DCCs at an SOC. The sustenance came from both black

African women and black African men participants underpinning the essentiality of this theme in the careers of black African women in DCCs. The participants' responses further specified the importance of career guidance at an early stage, as an important component in ensuring that black African women make the right career choices systematically and early within their career journeys. None of the black African women participants indicated having been mentored in any way thus far in their career journey, except for receiving some form of support from a manager.

Theme 7: Socio-economic support

The seventh theme that came about in the study was socio-economic support. The absence of a fundamental socio-economic support system that solemnly prioritises the participation and advancement of black African women in the labour market is considered a barrier to the career progression of black African woman. Within the study, 55% of the participants' responses supported the above argument, whereby there was vast acknowledgement of black African women being the most undermined and underrepresented group of women in the labour market. The participants' responses further indicated a need for legislated PL. They also argued that although legislative bodies had the authority of implementing such legislated PL, they were not prioritising it on their agenda.

Theme 8: Fairly progressed but not ideal careers for black African women

The last and eighth theme that came about in the study was 'fairly progressed but not ideal' careers for black African women. This theme supported and reinforced all the previous themes generated and identified in the study, portraying a comprehensive overall story about the research data. All the identified themes in the study comprehended this unified and overarching theme of fairly progressed but not ideal careers for black African women. As a result, 80% of black African women participants indicated that their careers had progressed fairly, but acknowledged that they were not in their ideal career phase. Of the black African men participants, 60% also acknowledged that their spouses' careers had progressed, but not ideally as they had hoped. Only 20% of black African men admitted to their spouses' careers having progressed well, attributing such success to the support they had provided throughout their spouses' career.

Discussion

The primary aim of the study was to examine how taking ML and PL influences the career progression of black African women as part of DCCs at an SOC. The main and key finding of this study was that it was established that taking ML and PL had a direct and indirect influence on the career progression of black African women in DCCs at this SOC, in middle management and leadership occupations. Of the participants, 90% agreed that taking ML has a negative influence on the career progression of black African women in DCCs at the SOC, in middle management and leadership occupations. There were a number of direct and indirect influencing reasons for this influence, but the most predominant reasons emanated as a result of taking ML and PL, and their underlying components, as indicated below.

Of the black African women participants, 80% indicated that their careers had progressed fairly, but acknowledged that they were not at their ideal career phase because of taking ML and other family-related commitments. Furthermore, 85% of the participants confirmed involuntary time off work and productiveness as principal influencing barriers of taking ML in the career progression of black African women in DCCs at the SOC, leading to other undesirable consequences, which can further impede on the career progression of black African women, such as unproductiveness, unreliability and stunted growth opportunities.

Of the black African men participants, 60% acknowledged that their spouses' careers had progressed, but not as ideally as they had hoped because of taking ML and other family-related commitments. Only 20% of black African men admitted to their spouses' careers having progressed well, attributing success to the support they had provided throughout their spouses' careers. Of the participants, including both black African women and black African men, 95% agreed that taking PL has a positive influence on the career progression of black African women in DCCs at an SOC.

Practical implications

The low representation of black African women in DCCs at the SOC in middle management and leadership occupations depicts the influence that taking ML can have on their career progression. Current talent management and recruitment and selection policies engaged by management require to be reviewed in contributing positively to the career progression of black African women.

Limitations to the study

The most dominant limitations was that the study was only limited to one specific SOC, and therefore, does not represent the current status of other SOCs within the SA labour market. The private sector and other spheres of the government sector were not included as part of the research setting, omitting an untapped school of knowledge within the research topic. The sample of the study was limited to black African women and black African men within DCCs at this SOC, possibly leaving some untapped experiences of other black African women and women in general within their career progression journey. Furthermore, there was limited literature about African DCCs in general and about the relationship between ML and PL and the career progression of black African women in particular.

Recommendations for future research

Future research could be carried out on the same topic covering a broader sample of black African women and across the entire SA labour market in order to confirm the findings and durability of the current study. Furthermore, a quantitative approach covering a larger population could be adopted. Extended research could also look into other challenges and barriers, besides taking ML and PL, which play a role in the career progression of black African women within the SA labour market, specifically within the private sector or within SOCs.

Conclusion

The study established that there are direct and indirect influences that taking ML and PL have on the career progression of black African women at an SOC, in middle management and leadership occupations. In acknowledgement of this influence, the literature determined that in their quest for career progression, a majority of black African women still occupy unskilled occupations, highlighting their struggle in progressing into middle management and leadership occupations (QLFS, Q3, 2015). This highlighted the challenges of black African women especially those in DCCs, in their attempts to achieve their ideal career progression goals and objectives. The study further indicated that legislation still fails black African women, resulting in discrimination and stereotypes that still persist and remain a prevalent barrier. However, the study ascended two unfamiliar barriers; firstly that some black African women lack dedication to their careers and secondly, that their male counterparts are afforded privileges and advantages as a result of patriarchal dominance in the society, which further suppresses women in their career growth.

Acknowledgements

Competing interests

The authors declare that they have no financial or personal relationships which may have inappropriately influenced them in writing this article.

Authors' contributions

The study was conducted by L.L.M. as part of his Masters in Human Resource Management research project in 2016. M.H.R.B. was L.L.M.'s supervisor and edited the work for publication. R.M.J. was L.L.M.'s co-supervisor and also assisted in editing the work for publication.

References

April, K., Dreyer, S., & Blass, E. (2007). Gender impediments to the SA executive boardroom. *SA Journal of Labour Relations, 31*(2), 51–67.

Atkinson, C., & Hall, L. (2009). The role of gender in varying forms of flexible working. *Gender, Work & Organization, 16*(6), 650–666. https://doi.org/10.1111/j.1468-0432.2009.00456.x

Barker, C., & Pistrang, N. (2012). Varieties of qualitative research: A pragmatic approach to selecting methods. In H. Cooper (Ed.), *APA handbook of research methods in psychology*: *Research designs* (Vol. 2., pp. 5–18). Los Angeles, CA: Sage.

Beck, C.T. (2009). Critiquing qualitative research. *AORN Journal, 90*(4), 543–554. https://doi.org/10.1016/j.aorn.2008.12.023

Bentley, K. (2004). Women's human rights and the feminisation of poverty in South Africa. *Review of African Political Economy, 31*(100), 247–261. https://doi.org/10.1080/0305624042000262275

Blumer, H. (1969). *Symbolic interactionism: Perspective and method*. Englewood Cliffs, NJ: Prentice Hall.

Bogdan, R.C., & Biklen, S.K. (1992). *Qualitative research for education: An introduction to theory and methods.* 2nd ed. Boston, MA: Allyn & Bacon.

Bosch, A., De Bruin, G.P., De Bruin, K., & Kgaladi, B. (2012). Life role salience among black African dual-career couples in the South African context. *The International Journal of Human Resources Management, 23*(14), 2835–2853. https://doi.org/10.1080/09585192.2012.671506

Braun, V., & Clarke, V. (2012). *Thematic analysis*. In H. Cooper (Ed.), *APA handbook of research methods in psychology*. Research designs, 2, (pp. 57–70). Los Angeles, CA: Sage.

Creswell, J. (2007). *Qualitative inquiry and research design: Choosing among five approaches*. London: Sage.

Crotty, M. (1998). *The foundations of social research: Meaning and perspective in the research process*. London: Sage.

Davidson, M. (1997). *The black and ethnic minority women manager cracking the concrete ceiling*. London: Paul Chapman.

De Vries, L. (1991). A study of the extent of discrimination against women in the workplace and the problems they encounter in the developing of an integrated management team. MBA Sociology. Stellenbosch: University of Stellenbosch.

Elliott, R., Fischer, C.T., & Rennie, D.L. (1999). Evolving guidelines for publication of qualitative research studies in psychology and related fields. *British Journal of Clinical Psychology, 38*, 215–229. https://doi.org/10.1348/014466599162782

Esterberg, K.G. (2002). *Qualitative methods in social research*. Boston, MA: McGraw-Hill.

Evans. P.M. (2007). Comparative perspectives on changes to Canada's paid parental leave: Implications for class and gender. *International Journal of Social Welfare, 16*, 119–128. https://doi.org/10.1111/j.1468-2397.2006.00450.x

Flood, T., Hoosain, M., & Primo, N. (1997). *Beyond inequalities: Women in South Africa*. Cape Town: Southern African Research and Documentation Centre.

Floro, M.S., & Komatsu, H. (2011). Gender and work in South Africa: What can time use data reveal? *Feminist Economics, 2*(1), 1–37. https://doi.org/10.1080/13545701.2011.622722

Forger, H., Dimant, T., Corrigan, T., Mophuthing, T., Spratt, J., Pienaar, D., et al. (2001). *South Africa Survey 2000/01*. Johannesburg: South African Institute of Race Relations.

Givati, Y., & Troiano, U. (2012). Theory of mandated benefits and evidence from maternity leave policies. *The Journal of Law and Economics, 55*(2), 339–364. https://doi.org/10.1086/663632

Greenhaus, J.H., Callanan, G.A., & Godshalk, V.M. (2010). *Career management* (4th ed.). New York: Sage.

Greenhaus, J.H., & Powell, G. (2006). When work and family are allies: A theory of work-family enrichment. *Academy of Management Review, 31*, 72–92. https://doi.org/10.5465/AMR.2006.19379625

Gurjao, S. (2006). *Inclusivity: The changing role of women in the construction workforce*. London: The Chartered Institute of Building (CIOB).

Haas, L. (2003). Parental leave and gender equality: Lessons from the European Union. *Review of Policy Research, 20*, 89–114. https://doi.org/10.1111/1541-1338.00006

Hakim, C. (2002). Lifestyle preferences as determinants of women's differentiated labor market careers. *Work and Occupations, 29*(4), 428–459. https://doi.org/10.1177/0730888402029004003

Hall, D.T. (2002). *Careers in and out of organizations*. Thousand Oaks, CA: Sage.

Hall, S., & MacDermid, S. (2009). A typology of dual earner marriages based on work and family arrangements. *Journal of Family and Economic, 30*(3), 215–225. https://doi.org/10.1007/s10834-009-9156-9

Hardill, I. (2002), *Gender, migration and the dual career household*. International Studies of Women and Place series. London: Routledge.

Harrington, B., Van Deusen, F., & Mazar, I. (2012). *The new dad: Right at home*. Boston, MA: Boston College Centre for Work & Family.

Hermann, K.M. (2016). Dual-career couples. In W.K. Killam, S. Degges-White, R.E. Michel, W.K. Killam, S. Degges-White & R.E. Michel (Eds.), *Career counseling interventions: Practice with diverse clients*, (pp. 35–43). New York: Springer Publishing Co.

Holiday, A. (2007). *Doing and writing qualitative research: Approaching qualitative research*. London: Sage.

Holloway, I., & Wheeler, S. (2010). *Qualitative research in nursing and healthcare*. West Sussex: Wiley-Blackwell.

Ilies, R., Keeney, J., & Scott, B. A. (2011). Work-family interpersonal capitalization: Sharing positive work events at home. *Organizational Behaviour and Human Decision Processes, 114*, 115–126. Industry Statistics, Pretoria.

Johnson, A.G. (2005). *The gender knot: Unraveling our patriarchal legacy*. Philadelphia, PA: Temple University Press.

Karenga, T., & Tembo, C. (2012). Kawaida womanism: African ways of being woman in the world. *Western Journal of Black Studies, 36*(1), 33–47.

Lincoln, Y.S., & Cuba, E.G. (1985). *Naturalistic enquiry*. Beverly Hills, CA: Sage.

Mainiero, L.A., & Sullivan, S.E. (2005). Kaleidoscope careers: An alternative explanation for the 'opt-out' revolution. *Academy of Management Executive, 19*, 106–123. https://doi.org/10.5465/AME.2005.15841962

Mays, N., & Pope, C. (2000). Assessing quality in qualitative research. *British Medical Journal, 320*, 50–52. https://doi.org/10.1136/bmj.320.7226.50

Miles, M.B., & Huberman, M. (1994). *Qualitative data analysis: An expanded sourcebook*. London: Sage.

Mokomane, Z. (2009). Work-family conflict and gender equality in South Africa. Unpublished paper presented at the 26 IUSSP International Population Conference, Held in Marrakech, Morocco, 27 September–02 October.

Moore, E. (2013). Transmission and change in South African motherhood: Black mothers in three-generational Cape Town families. *Journal of Southern African Studies, 39*(1), 151–170. https://doi.org/10.1080/03057070.2013.764713

Morrell, R., & Richter, L. (2006). *Men and fatherhood on South Africa*. Cape Town: HSRC Press.

Moss, P. (2012). International review of leave policies and related research 2012. Retrieved n.d., from http://www.leavenetwork.org/fileadmin/Leavenetwork/Annual_reviews/2012

Mumma, J. (2001). Relocation issues in today's workforce. *Employment Relations Today, 28*(1), 55–65. https://doi.org/10.1002/ert.1005.abs

Nath, D. (2000). Gently shattering the glass ceiling: Experiences of Indian women managers. *Women in Management Review, 15*(1), 44–52. https://doi.org/10.1108/09649420010310191

OECD. (1995). Long-term leave for parents in OECD countries. In OECD, *Employment Outlook*, (pp. 171–202). Paris: OECD.

OECD. (2013). *Employment outlook 2013*. Paris: OECD Publishing.

Patton, M.Q. (2014). *Qualitative evaluation and research methods*. Saint Paul, MN: Sage.

Pesonen, A. (2015). Encouraging work-family balance to correct gender imbalance: A comparison of the family and medical leave act and the Iceland Act on maternity/paternity and parental leave. *Journal of International Studies, 15*(1), 157–196.

Quick, J., & Hall. S. (2015). Spotlight on research. *Part Two: Qualitative Research, 25*(7–8), 125–133.

Rajadhyaksha, U., & Bhatnagar, D. (2000). Life role salience: A study of dual-career couples in the Indian context. *Human Relations, 53*(4), 491–493. https://doi.org/10.1177/0018726700534002

Ryan, F., Coughlin, M., & Cronin, P. (2007). Step by step guide to critiquing research Part 2: Qualitative research. *British Journal of Nursing, 16*(12), 738–744. https://doi.org/10.12968/bjon.2007.16.12.23726

Sadie, J. (2015). Gender policy and legislation during the first 20 years of democracy. *Strategic review for Southern Africa, 36*(2), 111–125.

Salmera-Aro, K., Nurmi, J.E., Saisto, T., & Halmesmäki, E. (2000). Women's and men's personal goals during the transition to parenthood. *Journal of Family Psychology, 14*, 171–186. https://doi.org/10.1037/0893-3200.14.2.171

Santho, S. (1995). *The elimination of gender inequality in the public service with specific reference to the Free State provincial administration*. MPA Economic and Administrative Science. Bloemfontein: University of the Orange Free State.

Schurink, E.M. (1998). Data analysis in qualitative research. In A. de Vos (Ed.), *Research at grass roots: A primer for the caring professions*. Pretoria: Van Schaik Publishers.

Schurink, W.J. (2004). Qualitative research introducing key features of an interpretative approach to social science research: Lecture Eleven B, Grounded Theory. Doctoral Programme in Leadership in Performance and Change (pp. 1–23). Johannesburg: University of Johannesburg.

Schurink, W.J. (2005). *Qualitative research design: Part 1 lecture notes to D- and M-students from the leadership in performance and change programme*. Johannesburg: University of Johannesburg,

Sewpaul, V. (1994). The position of black women in South African society: A feminist perspective. *Social Work, 30*(4), 346–354.

Shenton, A.K. (2004). Strategies for ensuring trustworthiness in qualitative research projects. *Education for Information, 22*, 63–75. https://doi.org/10.3233/EFI-2004-22201

Smit, R. (2006). Family related policies in Southern African countries: Are working parents reaping any benefits? *Journal of Comparative Family Studies, 1*(1), 15–36.

South Africa. (1995). *Labour Relations Act, Act 66 of 1995*. Pretoria: Government Printer.

South Africa. (1996). *Constitution of the Republic of South Africa, Act 108 of 1996*. Pretoria: Government Printer.

South Africa. (1997). *Basic Conditions of Employment Act, Act 75 of 1997*. Pretoria: Government Printer.

South Africa. (1998a). *Employment Equity Act, Act 55 of 1998*. Pretoria: Government Printer.

South Africa. (1998b). *Labour Relations Amendment Act, Act 127 of 1998*. Pretoria: Government Printer.

South Africa. (1998c). *Skills Development Act, Act 97 of 1998*. Pretoria: Government Printer.

South Africa. (1999). *Public Finance Management Act, 1*. Government Gazette No. 33059. Pretoria: Government Printer.

South Africa. (2001). *Commission on Gender Equality Act, Act 39 of 1996*. Pretoria: Government Printer.

South Africa. Ministry for Welfare and Population Development. (1998). *White Paper on Population Policy*. Retrieved June 21, 2015, from http://www.gov.za/whitepaper

Statistics South Africa (Stat SA). (2015). *Quarterly Labour Force Survey – Quarter3*. Statistics South Africa. Retrieved September 17, 2015, from http://www.statssa.gov.za

Talley-Ross, N. (1995). *Jagged edges: Black professional women in white male worlds*. New York: Peter Lang.

Tshoaedi, M. (2012). Women in the forefront of workplace struggles in South Africa: From invisibility to mobilization. *Labour, Capital and Society, 45*(2), 58–83.

Wall, K. (2014). Fathers on leave alone: Does it make a difference to their lives. *Fathering*. Men's Studies Press, *12*(2), 196–210.

Wheatly, D. (2013). Location, vocation, location? Spatial entrapment among women in dual-career households. *Gender, Work & Organization, 20*(6), 720–736.

8

Exploring workplace diversity and organisational effectiveness: A South African exploratory case study

Authors:
J. Veli Mazibuko[1]
Krishna K. Govender[2]

Affiliations:
[1]Department of Business Administration and Management, Regenesys Business School, South Africa

[2]School of Management, IT and Governance, University of KwaZulu-Natal, South Africa

Corresponding author:
Krishna Govender,
govenderkrishna@gmail.com

Orientation: Transformation and managing diversity are organisational imperatives, especially in South Africa. Thus, it is important for international companies with major operations in South Africa (SA) to embrace the benefits of managing a divergent workforce and translate this for organisational benefits.

Research purpose: The article explores the perceptions of management and staff on diversity and its value to the organisation, by empirically evaluating the relationship with organisational effectiveness and performance through the development and testing of five hypotheses.

Motivation for the study: Legislation has made it mandatory for transformation of the South African workplace and ensuring that diversity is embraced. However, not all companies have fully understood the benefits of recruiting and managing diverse teams for the benefit of the organisation.

Research approach, design and method: Both quantitative and qualitative approaches were used, whereby a survey was conducted among 227 employees using the Towers Watson Employment Employee Insight Survey (EIS). Inferential statistical techniques were used to test relationships among related variables postulated through five hypotheses.

Main findings: It was ascertained that understanding and managing diversity has played a pivotal role in the (research) organisation's performance and effectiveness over the past 5 years. More specifically, diversity management created room for appreciation, innovation and creativity that gave the organisations an edge to tackle diverse markets.

Practical/managerial applications: South Africa has a diverse population, and when individuals join an organisation, they bring a unique set of characteristics referred to as personalities, which, through the socialisation process, get assimilated into teams' norms and values, and the culture of the organisation. Managing diversity in the workplace is part of employee retention and attraction, with the intention to energise workplace productivity, thus increasing the organisation's competitive edge.

Contributions or value add: The positive impact engendered by diverse recruitment and retention is also supported by employee engagement, which presupposes employee ownership of change, by making it happen, and it is driven by employees that offer solutions to problems, by helping one another and who are proud of being part of the organisation. Its impact in the bigger scheme of events is to drive business performance, growth, cost management, and ability to attract, retain and engage top talent by establishing a winning and inclusive culture.

Introduction

When individuals join an organisation, they bring a unique set of characteristics referred to as personalities, and through the socialisation process, they get assimilated into their teams' norms and values, and eventually, the culture of the organisation. Ferreira and Coetzee (2010) posit that managing diversity in the workplace is part of employee retention and attraction, with the intention to energise workplace productivity, thus increasing the organisation's competitive edge. The positive impact engendered by diverse recruitment and retention is also supported by employee engagement (Neault & Mondair, 2011). Employee engagement presupposes employee ownership of change, by making it happen, and it is driven by employees that offer solutions to problems, by helping one another and who are proud of being part of the organisation. Its impact in the bigger scheme of events is to drive business performance, growth, cost management, and ability to attract, retain and engage top talent by establishing a winning and inclusive culture.

Although there is much debate on the definition of diversity, Esty, Schorr-Hirsh and Griffin (1995), cited in Green, Lopez, Wysocki and Kepner (2002), define diversity as 'acknowledging, understanding, accepting, valuing, and celebrating differences among people with respect'. McEnrue (1993) posits that diversity management is an organisational imperative and competitive necessity that contributes to its strategic intent. Daniel (1994) argues that the lack of diversity is the businesses' downfall, and the understanding and appreciation of diversity is beyond mere compliance. It has to transcend legislation by being an organisational imperative that truly recognises the value individuals add to an organisation without being stigmatised or dubbed affirmative action appointees.

The argument for diversity is complex, and it is not just about comparing and pitting people or groups against one another, but recognition and appreciation of the uniqueness and contribution to the team and organisation. Kamps and Engelbrecht (2011) assert that discrimination as part of the political legacy in South Africa (SA) has created serious challenges for workplace diversity. If organisations could determine requirements that reinforce diversity, they are better placed to improve cohesion, interaction and team work.

Diversity is also confused with employment equity and affirmative action, although the aforementioned programmes should be viewed as 'tools' to engineer and drive diversity (Mason, Williams & Cranner, 2009). A number of workplaces still battle to meet employment equity targets, with specific reference to gender and the disabled. It is at the core of this challenge that society and organisations must ensure that people managers leverage the untapped resources that contribute to the diverse workforces (Rogatschnig, 2011).

Although most studies focus on diversity management, there is a gap in establishing the empirical link between diversity, diversity management and organisational effectiveness that translates into business performance. Kochan et al. (2003) capture the essence of this 'gap' which raises ambiguity on whether diversity is good or bad for business. The closest body of knowledge and research that explores this link in the South African context is within the financial service sector (Carelse, 2013). The aforementioned asserted that successful implementation of diversity management brings about positive employee attitude and creates a competitive organisation. Leonard and Grobbler (2006), as cited in Booysen and Nkomo (2014), posit that implementation of Employment Equity (in SA) has been reduced to legal compliance, instead of substantial compliance, and affirmative action is perceived as reverse discrimination, thus creating resistance to the process, as well as casting doubt around affirmative action appointees with an outlook of incompetence, lack of skill, ability and qualifications (Booysen & Nkomo, 2014).

In light of the above, this article will attempt to fill this 'void' by investigating whether an organisation that embraces diversity is more effective and whether performance is in any way impacted on by their diversity.

Literature review

The end of apartheid has brought a resurgence of research into racial identities, attitudes and behaviour in SA (Seekings, 2008), and the legacy of systematic racial ordering and discrimination under apartheid is that SA remains deeply racialised, in cultural and social terms, as well as unequal in terms of distribution of income and positions held in organisations.

South Africans have also experienced major changes in the landscape of employment relations in organisations over the past two decades (Booysen, 2007), and although numerous legislations have been put in place to achieve greater social justice, progress in redressing unfair discrimination in the workplace has been slow and uneven.

Coupled with the above challenges that define the South African workplace, managing diversity, multiculturalism, affirmative action and equal employment opportunity are words in 'common currency in a newly democratic South Africa, as they are in most democratic countries of the world' (Human, 1996).

The largest field-based research project was undertaken by Diversity Research Network under the auspices of BOLD (Business Opportunities for Leadership Diversity) (Kochan et al., 2003). BOLD recommended the promotion and development of a culture that is geared to value and appreciate diversity. There are striking similarities between the aforementioned research that was conducted in the USA with the current South African study. In SA, legislations like the *Employment Equity Act* of 1998, *Promotion of Equality and Prevention of Unfair Discrimination Act* of 2000, and *Black Economic Empowerment Act* of 2003 were enacted to transform workplaces and provide access to equal opportunities. The essence of the abovementioned legislations was to eliminate exclusion in the workplace, of persons based on race, gender and sex.

South Africa has experienced radical political transformation over the past 12 years that is epitomised by shifts in the dominance, status and power bases of different population groups (Booysen, 2007). This transformation has in turn resulted in identity crises with the unbundling of former social identification and socialisation to refined and redefined self-concepts. The most salient identity groups in SA are race, gender, ethnicity and language (Booysen & Nkomo, 2014). Tensions and conflicts are prevalent between diverse groups in the South African workplace, and this is no different from the international norm; but the most pressing conflict in the South African workplace is based on changes and conflicts associated with race and gender (Booysen & Nkomo, 2014); thus, legislations have had to be enacted to fast track transformation with a view to engender equality.

Although some researchers (Jackson, May & Whitney, 1995) assert that there is no verified literature that confirms that diverse groups necessarily perform better, others (Hofstede, 1994, cited by Schultz, Bagraim, Potgieter, Viegde & Werner, 2003) have linked diversity to creative problem-solving and productivity. Moreover, Simons and Rowland (2011) argue that functional diversity and non-functional diversity are critical to diversity management, and Bunderson and Sutcliffe (2002) posit that functional diversity improves organisational effectiveness and creative thinking.

Although the Corporate Research Forum (CRF) (2011) focuses on the problem-solving aspects of diversity and the diversity paradox which argues that diversity engenders conflict, it also recognises that conflict and contradictions result in innovation and well-thought through solutions to a problem. Conflict in this instance is seen as a catalyst to debate, discussions, engagement and innovation that fosters continuous improvement and business performance. According to Tatli and Ozbilging (2012), organisational commitment to diversity is determined by a business case, and diversity management enables performance improvements. Knouse and Dansby (1999) argue that organisational diversity fosters synergy, networks and multi-tasking, and organisations that manage diversity properly are successful in the accomplishment of their objectives. Organisations are motivated by a number of factors to implement diversity management, and it is consideration of this motivation, and a shift from the bottom line to the triple bottom line, that has engendered significant in-roads and influences the way the organisation approaches diversity (Brabet, 2011; Guillaume, Dawson, Woods, Sacramento & West, 2013; Jonsen, Tatli, Özbilgin & Bell, 2013; Klarsfeld, Ng & Tatli, 2012).

Research on whether diversity leads to better performance (or not) has produced contradictory results, and in some instances, no clear conclusions have been forthcoming. Some researchers (Weiliang, Mun, Chern, Fong & Yuan, 2012) posit that organisations that embrace strong gender diversity have demonstrated superior performance, and companies with diverse teams have shown exceptional performance. However, the aforementioned researchers have also clarified that the performance depends on whether the climate in the organisation fosters trust and mutual support.

Konrad (2003) presented three primary arguments in making a business case for diversity. Firstly, organisations compete for the best talent that makes it necessary for them to cast their net wide when they recruit, hence the quest for diversity. Secondly, diversity prepares the organisation to deal with diverse markets so as to increase its market share. Thirdly, diversity becomes the foundation for creative thinking by producing various ideas, opinions and solutions to a problem, which makes the team flexible and competitive. The fact that markets are diverse, affirming and accepting differences is 'socially acceptable' by embracing diversity that reflects the markets. The aforementioned view is aligned with the CRF (2011) report that alludes to an effective way of creating an inclusive culture and valuing diversity.

Schreuder and Coetzee (2011) posit that the 21st century workplace has been evolutionary instead of revolutionary, and within the South African context, 'affirmative action (AA)' and 'employment equity (EE)' have become significant tools to address the inequalities of the past. Madihlaba's (2011) assertion of 'legal compliance versus substantive compliance' or ethical imperative necessitates attention. There is need to refocus this perception to benefit the organisation and avoid unnecessary lawsuits as a result of perceived discrimination or citation of reverse discrimination.

Muhtar Kent, President of Coca-Cola, posits that everything that is done at Coca-Cola in terms of diversity is based on the simple, powerful and global premise, namely that Coca-Cola's diversity should be as inclusive as the brand itself (Kent, 2012). This is aligned to the global mission, which is to mirror the diversity of the marketplace that the company serves, by being the market leaders in diversity, inclusion and fairness in every aspect of the business, from the workplace, marketplace, supplier engagement and the community. Thus, diversity at Coca-Cola is integral to how the company operates and how they perceive the future.

Ssegawa (2011) explains that Coca-Cola South Africa's talent strategy is also aligned with the Company's Vision 2020, which recognises that the world is changing very fast. Coca-Cola (SA's) strategy for delivering great results is built on the strong foundation of a 'total rewards' platform, which involves competitive pay, the opportunity to grow and thrive, and a work environment that promises sustainability, diversity, wellness and the observance of human rights. The Coca-Cola Code of Conduct is a set of policies, principles and values that each and every new employee gets inducted into, with continuous annual refresher training to embed the following: treat colleagues fairly, honestly and with respect; respect and promote diversity in the workplace; health and safety in the workplace; and respect for colleagues and human rights. According to Ssegawa (2011), Coca-Cola SA actively seeks to create and inspire people to be their best.

This study on which the article has been developed tracks the evolution of diversity over the past 5 years, so as to determine what is the level of diversity in the organisation and what significance (if any) does diversity hold for the organisation and its employees. More specifically, the impact of diversity on performance as posited by Guillaume et al. (2013) is investigated. Moreover, the fact that the company was dominated by white male and male in general motivated the context of the study.

Velaquez (2013) posits that diversity is loaded with all kinds of myths, misconceptions and baggage that have presented management challenges, which among others, the Coca-Cola Company is striving to address, namely different culture and history that have to be tailored to suit the conditions of the country, region and geographic location; work–life balance to suit the needs of the various employees in its employ, especially women and the previously marginalised or disadvantaged; high cost of diversity with programmes undertaken to ensure accommodation of the diverse workforce; and lawsuits as a result of reported discriminatory cases.

It is against the above background that this article seeks to understand the research organisation's approach to diversity, and to ascertain whether diversity is a strategic tool to enhance organisational performance. In order to explore the aforementioned, the following hypotheses were formulated with respect to the research organisation:

- **Hypothesis 1 (H1):** Managing and valuing diversity enhances performance.
- **Hypothesis 2 (H2):** Diversity influences organisational effectiveness.
- **Hypothesis 3 (H3):** Performance is the outcome of diversity.
- **Hypothesis 4 (H4):** Diversity influences and drives transformation.
- **Hypothesis 5 (H5):** Diversity influences organisational effectiveness that translates into performance improvement.

Research methodology

A quantitative approach was used, aimed at determining the employees' perception of diversity, its relevance to them as employees and whether it adds value to their performance. The population (539) comprised all employees of the organisation in SA, and the probability sample of 300 was randomly selected after the population was stratified on the basis of occupational level, race, gender and tenure, with only those who were more than 5 years in the organisation being included. Questionnaires were hand delivered to employees across all occupational levels, from top management or directors to semi-skilled employees who were employed in the organisation for 5 years and longer. In terms of race, the sample was dominated by Africans (239), followed by 49 white people, 7 Indians and 5 mixed race.[1,2]

Data collection and analysis

The survey questionnaire mirrored the Employee Insight Survey (EIS) (2014) questionnaire used by Towers Watson to determine causality between diversity, organisational effectiveness and business performance. It comprised 25 Likert scaled questions designed to determine employees' perceptions of diversity, value of diversity, belief in the goals and objectives of the organisation, pride in the organisation as the best place to work, by being enabled, energised and engaged. Diversity in this instance is the independent variable on which performance and effectiveness are dependent. A 5-point scale was used where 5 = strongly agree, 4 = agree, 3 = not sure, 2 = disagree and 1 = strongly disagree. The questionnaire, though adapted for the South African context, is valid and reliable, because it has been consistently used in the research organisation in the past 5 years, and has yielded consistent results. The performance results of the organisation for the last 5 years, Broad-Based Black Economic Empowerment (BBBEE) Certificates and EE reports were also analysed to establish the link between diversity in the workplace, organisational effectiveness and business performance. The equity reports that were a mandatory annual submission to the Department of Labour were also scrutinised to authenticate the complexion of the organisation, based on gender and demographics (designated groups), in alignment with the actual statistics generated from the survey. This was also supported by analysis of the BBBEE certificates to determine the level of transformation that covers a host of elements like ownership, procurement and corporate social investment, that is, matched to diversity.

The data were analysed using the SPSS programme to calculate percentages and conduct correlation and analysis of variance (ANOVA) tests.

Findings

A total of 227 questionnaires were completed and returned, comprising 82 from semi-skilled, 74 unskilled, 48 skilled, and 15 middle and 8 senior managers. There was male dominance at the unskilled staff level, whereas gender representation at other levels was more balanced. Table 1 indicates dominant response by Africans, followed by white people, which indicates that the organisation still lacks adequate Indian and mixed race representation in the workforce. Among the 173 African employees, the majority (74) were either unskilled or semi-skilled (67), and among the 42 white employees, the majority (23) were either skilled professionals or semi-skilled.

The reliability of the five dimensions in the survey were examined using the Cronbach's alpha coefficient statistics. Although only two dimensions produced alpha coefficients that exceeded 0.7, namely knowledge sharing and the impact of diversity on organisational effectiveness, and the other individual scores ranged between 0.45 and 0.56; the overall reliability of the instrument was 0.85, which according to Cronbach and Meehl (1955) is an acceptable score.

With regard to 'the value of diversity', Table 2 indicates that the majority (60%) of the respondents 'strongly agree' that they are treated with dignity and respect. The results also confirm the respondents' appreciation of the company's recruitment of a diverse workforce. Furthermore, the vast majority (71%) of the respondents confirm that diversity enhances innovation and productivity, and 56% 'strongly disagree' that diversity creates confusion and conflict in the workplace.

It is evident from Table 3 that the corrected model is significant and shows that managing and valuing diversity enhances performance. The results of the ANOVA test showed that diverse workforce [$F(4.174) = 13.10, p < 0.001$], individual differences [$F(4.174) = 7.16, p < 0.001$] and confusion conflict [$F(4.174) = 5.52, p < 0.001$] are significantly related with

1. In the South African context, black people comprise Africans, Indians and mixed race.

2. There are 56.5 million people in SA (Stats SA, 2017): 79.4% Africans, 9.2% white people, 8.8% mixed race and 2.6% Indians.

TABLE 1: Racial profile of respondents by occupational level.

Occupational level	Racial group				Total
	Africans	Mixed race	Indian	White people	
Top management	0	0	0	0	0
Senior management	4	0	1	3	8
Middle management	9	1	1	4	15
Skilled professionals	19	4	2	23	48
Semi-skilled	67	0	3	12	82
Unskilled	74	0	0	0	74
Total	**173**	**5**	**7**	**42**	**227**

TABLE 2: Employee's perceptions of the value of diversity.

Question	SD	DS	Do not know	AS	SA
I am treated with dignity and respect at work	27	12	31	20	137
The company recruits employees from all walks of life and has a diverse workforce	25	5	20	9	168
Individual differences are valued and appreciated by the organisation	37	9	29	5	147
A diverse workforce creates confusion and conflict in the workplace	126	20	18	11	52
A diverse workforce creates innovation and workplace productivity	18	8	23	17	161

SD, strongly disagree; DS, disagree somewhat; AS, agree somewhat; SA, strongly agree.

TABLE 3: Statistical results on diverse workforce, innovation and productivity.

Source	Type III sum of squares	*df*	Mean square	*F*	Sig.
Corrected model	307.45[a]	52	5.91	20.50	0.00
Intercept	552.01	1	552.01	1914.10	0.00
Dignity respect	0.97	4	0.24	0.84	0.50
Diverse workforce	15.11	4	3.78	13.10	0.00*
Individual differences	8.26	4	2.06	7.16	0.00*
Confusion conflict	6.37	4	1.59	5.52	0.00*
Dignity respect * diverse workforce	0.00	0	-	-	-
Dignity respect * individual differences	0.45	6	0.08	0.26	0.95
Dignity respect * confusion conflict	0.67	3	0.22	0.77	0.51
Diverse workforce * individual differences	0.00	0	-	-	-
Diverse workforce * confusion conflict	0.11	2	0.05	0.18	0.83
Individual differences * confusion conflict	0.26	1	0.26	0.89	0.35
Dignity respect * diverse workforce * individual differences	0.00	0	-	-	-
Dignity respect * diverse workforce * confusion conflict	0.00	0	-	-	-
Dignity respect * individual differences * confusion conflict	0.00	0	-	-	-
Diverse workforce * individual differences * confusion conflict	0.00	0	-	-	-
Dignity respect * diverse workforce * individual differences * confusion conflict	0.00	0	-	-	-
Error	50.18	174	0.29	-	-
Total	4554.00	227	-	-	-
Corrected total	**357.63**	**226**	-	-	-

[a], R squared = 0.86 (Adjusted R squared = 0.82).
*, Significant at level of significance of 0.05.

performance in terms of innovation and workplace productivity. These were the only p-values less than the level of significance of 0.05; thus, H1 is supported.

Table 4 reflects that the corrected model is not significant, which implies that diversity in terms of success attributes diversity [$F(4.174) = 0.20$, $p = 0.94$], innovative solution [$F(4.174) = 1.35$, $p = 0.25$] and diverse customer need [$F(4.174) = 0.43$, $p = 0.79$] is not related with the performance of an organisation in terms of the organisation's strategic priorities. The reason for this conclusion is because the p-values were greater than the level of significance of 0.05. Based on the aforementioned, H2 is not supported by the findings of this study.

According to Table 5, the corrected model is significant, which implies that leadership diversity strongly influences organisational performance and/or effectiveness. Specifically, the results of the ANOVA test show that diverse programmes [$F(4.174) = 11.33$, $p < 0.001$] and sexism or discrimination [$F(4.174) = 2.61$, $p = 0.04$] are significantly related with performance in terms of 'proud to be part of their organisation and recommend it as the best place to work'. All the p-values were less than the level of significance of 0.05. Hence, it may be concluded that H3 is supported in this study.

Table 6, which represents the influence of diversity on transformation, indicates that 75% of the respondents 'strongly agree' that AA is a positive measure that supports

TABLE 4: The influence of diversity on organisational effectiveness.

Source	Type III sum of squares	*df*	Mean square	*F*	Sig.
Corrected model	140.03[a]	25	5.60	3.85	0.00
Intercept	431.91	1	431.91	296.47	0.00
Success attribute diversity	1.17	4	0.29	0.20	0.94
Innovative solution	7.85	4	1.96	1.35	0.25
Diverse customer need	2.50	4	0.62	0.43	0.79
Success attribute diversity * innovative solution	15.01	2	7.50	5.15	0.01
Success attribute diversity * diverse customer need	2.98	1	2.98	2.04	0.15
Innovative solution * diverse customer need	1.14	1	1.14	0.78	0.38
Success attribute diversity * innovative solution * Diverse customer need	0.00	0	-	-	-
Error	292.82	201	1.46	-	-
Total	4417.00	227	-	-	-
Corrected total	**432.86**	**226**	-	-	-

[a], R squared = 0.32 (Adjusted R squared = 0.24).

TABLE 5: The influence of leadership diversity on performance and effectiveness.

Source	Type III sum of squares	*df*	Mean square	*F*	Sig.
Corrected model	68.94[a]	14	4.92	4.89	0.00
Intercept	619.80	1	619.80	614.94	0.00
Diversity programmes	45.67	4	11.42	11.33	0.00*
Sexism or discrimination	10.51	4	2.63	2.61	0.04*
Diversity programmes * sexism or discrimination	13.30	6	2.22	2.20	0.04
Error	213.68	212	1.01	-	-
Total	4830.00	227	-	-	-
Corrected total	**282.62**	**226**	-	-	-

Dependent variable: 17. I am proud to be part of my organisation and recommend it as the best place to work.

[a], R squared = 0.24 (Adjusted R squared = 0.19).

*, Significant at level of significance of 0.05.

TABLE 6: Influence of diversity on transformation.

Question	SD	DS	Do not know	AS	SA
Affirmative action is a positive measure to support diversity in the company	29	8	12	8	170
Affirmative action is reverse discrimination	102	1	21	6	97
The company is gender balanced and supports women leadership at work	21	7	14	23	162
Employment equity is good and ethical, and my company is beyond compliance	21	6	42	11	147
The company supports transformation and is compliant	25	8	40	7	144

SD, strongly disagree; DS, disagree somewhat; AS, agree somewhat; SA, strongly agree.

diversity. AA as reverse discrimination is not differentiated by respondents who strongly agree and strongly disagree and is almost balanced at 43% and 45%, respectively. The vast majority (71%) of the respondents 'strongly agree' that the company is gender balanced and supports women leadership at work. The confirmation of AA as a positive measure in line with gender balance, transformation and equity supports the dominant view in the organisation on the influence diversity plays in transformation.

Table 7, which represents the univariate statistical analysis for determining the influence of diversity in driving transformation, reveals that the corrected model is significant, which shows that diversity influences and drives transformation. Specifically, the results of the ANOVA test showed that AA positive [$F(4.174) = 7.83$, $p < 0.001$], AA discrimination [$F(3.174) = 23.15$, $p < 0.001$] and women leadership [$F(4.174) = 4.07$, $p < 0.001$] are significantly related with driving transformation. The p-values were less than the level of significance of 0.05. Given the above, H4 is supported, and it is concluded that diversity influences transformation.

With respect to the drivers of organisational outcomes that determine the relationship between diversity, organisational effectiveness and performance, it became evident that 84% of the respondents are in favour of the promotion of diversity as the key driver of organisational outcomes. The majority (62%) of the male respondents are in support of promoting diversity, compared with 37% of the female respondents. The vast majority (76%) of the African employees' respondents supported the view that diversity is a motivational aspect of performance.

Table 8 reflects that promoting diversity is significantly related with performance improvement in terms of knowledge to drive transformation [$X^2(1) = 13.10$, $p < 0.001$], increased previously disadvantaged individuals (PDIs) at senior management level [$X^2(1) = 37.35$, $p < 0.001$], and cultural diversity and gender sensitive [$X^2(1) = 19.34$, $p < 0.001$]. It is therefore concluded that there is a relationship between diversity and organisational effectiveness, which translates into performance improvement; thus, H5 is supported.

It was also ascertained that 64% of the respondents 'strongly agreed' that the organisation allows for knowledge sharing

TABLE 7: Statistical test results for diversity influence on transformation.

Source	Type III sum of squares	*df*	Mean square	*F*	Sig.
Corrected model	358.64[a]	36	9.96	22.83	0.00
Intercept	256.76	1	256.76	588.34	0.00
Affirmative action positive	13.68	4	3.42	7.83	0.00*
Affirmative action discrimination	30.32	3	10.11	23.15	0.00*
Women leadership	7.10	4	1.78	4.07	0.00*
Beyond compliance	3.88	4	0.97	2.22	0.07
Affirmative action positive * affirmative action discrimination	0.00	0	-	-	-
Affirmative action positive * women leadership	5.12	1	5.12	11.73	0.00
Affirmative action positive * beyond compliance	0.44	2	0.22	0.51	0.60
Affirmative action discrimination * women leadership	0.00	0	-	-	-
Affirmative action discrimination * beyond compliance	6.49	1	6.49	14.86	0.00
Women leadership * beyond compliance	6.22	2	3.11	7.13	0.00
Affirmative action positive * affirmative action discrimination * women leadership	0.00	0	-	-	-
Affirmative action positive * affirmative action discrimination * beyond compliance	0.00	0	-	-	-
Affirmative action positive * women leadership * beyond compliance	0.00	0	-	-	-
Affirmative action discrimination * women leadership * beyond compliance	0.00	0	-	-	-
Affirmative action positive * affirmative action discrimination * women leadership * beyond compliance	0.00	0	-	-	-
Error	81.61	187	0.44	-	-
Total	4129.00	224	-	-	-
Corrected total	**440.25**	**223**	-	-	-

Dependent variable: 10. The company supports transformation and is compliant.

a, R squared = 0.82 (Adjusted R squared = 0.78).

*, Significant at level of significance of 0.05.

TABLE 8: The relationship between diversity, organisational effectiveness and business performance.

Independent variable	Value	*df*	Asymp. Sig. (two-sided)
Developing skills	2.62	1	0.11
Knowledge to drive transformation	10.47	1	0.00*
Increased PDI's at senior management level	37.35	1	0.00*
Cultural diversity and gender sensitive	19.34	1	0.00*
Increased emphasis to legislative compliance	1.17	1	0.28

Dependent variable: 1. Promoting diversity.

PDI, previously disadvantaged individuals.

*, Significant at level of significance of 0.05.

among employees; the vast majority (71%) of the respondents 'strongly agreed' that they share knowledge and views with their peers.

Discussion of the findings

It is evident that with respect to the research organisation, managing and valuing diversity enhances performance, which findings are in line with Roberge, Lewicki, Heitapelto and Abdyldaeva (2011) and Carelse (2013). The policies, procedures, systems and values that include teamwork are among the initiatives that received emphasis in the organisation, clearly demonstrating employee awareness of the importance of diversity. The aforementioned finding is similar to Bulbulia's (2003:n.p.) argument that 'the goal of managing diversity should be to maximise employee potential unhindered by group identities by ensuring a conducive workplace where similarities and differences are appreciated'. Ely and Thomas (2001) suggest that depending on the work group's diversity perspective, members of culturally diverse groups can relate to each other, such that the members feel valued and respected and this has been the key in the research organisation. Rosado (2006) argues in favour of total quality diversity as a holistic diversity management programme that assures unity in diversity, and the research organisation truly represents this.

Although Page (2011) argues in favour of diversity and different levels of experience for performance improvement, he also pointed out that diversity in terms of 'success attribute', innovative solutions and diverse customer need is not related with the productivity of an organisation. In line with the aforementioned, Kochan et al. (2003) posited that diversity does not necessarily engender productivity. The results of this study therefore confirm the mixed results presented by Bowers, Pharmer and Salas (2000) and Webber and Donahue (2001), namely, that diversity does not necessarily improve performance, and it points to the so-called double-edged sword effect of diversity (Milliken & Martins, 1996).

Although it became evident that the success of the (research) organisation in the last 5 years can be ascribed to diversity with innovative solutions, it is, however, important to note that the 'innovative solution' is linked to aspects like capability building through the Competency Acquisition and Management Development programmes. The results are similar to Horwitz and Horwitz's (2007) findings that positive teams' impact performance on task-related diversity versus bio-demographic diversity.

In line with previous studies (Chin, 2013), it was ascertained that leadership diversity strongly influences organisational performance and/or effectiveness. The leadership role is assumed to clear up the ambiguity of contrasting theories on whether diversity influences performance, which performance in turn results in the realisation of strategic organisational objectives. Ssegawa (2011:n.p.) posits that the organisation must 'get ready for tomorrow today' by attracting, developing and engaging highly talented and diverse workforce to drive cross-pollination of innovative ideas, and this was evident in the organisation where this study was conducted.

The findings in this study are consistent with what is reflected in the BBBEE certification of the research organisation, which reflect its ratings as rising from level 4 in 2010 to level 2 at the time of research. This reflects not just management evolution, but shareholder engagement of 'Broad-Based' partners that control 70% of the shareholding, and 5% ownership by employees on Share Appreciation Rights Scheme. The impact of this transformation is reflected in initiatives which the organisation undertook to involve women entrepreneurs and the footprint it established in its corporate social investment in ensuring that it achieves more than the triple bottom line. Swanepoel, Erasmus and Schenk (2008) argue that the platform set by the *BBBEE Act* challenges organisations to empower more and more black people through affirmative action. With respect to the research organisation, women were recruited or promoted into leadership roles beyond the 25% compliance through focused recruitment.

Ferreira and Coetzee (2010) posit that managing diversity in the workplace is part of employee retention and attraction with the intention to energise workplace productivity, thus increasing the organisation's competitive edge. It was determined that in the last 3 years, the research organisation showed growth in production volume from 38 to 45 million cases, which at some stage in 2010 was at a staggering 20 million cases per annum. The aforementioned achievement is supposedly linked to the diverse talent and innovation in the organisation because DeVeale and Manea (2007) assert that a diverse workforce leverages on the differences among the teams by strengthening their communication networks and eliminating the barriers that hinder their creative function.

With respect to employee engagement, the survey revealed a change from 52% to 84% in 2015, indicating increased employee commitment and participation. The fact that innovation is encouraged among team members and different opinions are openly discussed creates a platform to innovate through debate and discussions, so as to find well-thought through solutions to problems. This is key to effectiveness and performance that are linked to individual capacity to perform, spanning through to the team/department and organisation performance.

Conclusion and recommendations

The conclusions with respect to the decisions on the hypotheses are summarised in Table 9.

From the findings reported above as well as the summary decisions on the hypotheses, it may be concluded that organisations in SA are challenged by the legacy of apartheid that still subtly divide organisations through 'covert' racism, prejudice and stereotyping. Hence, there is need to acknowledge, understand, accept, value and celebrate differences among people as part of the organisational policy. Diversity awareness training programmes should form part of the organisation's induction, so as to ensure that dignity, respect and valuing differences are understood by all employees and form part of the organisation's DNA.

It is management's responsibility to attract, retain and engage talent by establishing a winning and inclusive culture. Commitment to diversity promotes the right behaviour that employees will emulate, thus mitigating the negative impact diversity would have in the workplace. Organisational diversity training and development programmes must engender a culture that creates smooth assimilation of employees. Line managers should be trained in team development and conflict management to reinforce an inclusive culture that the organisation enshrines, so as to extract maximum benefit from diverse teams.

For organisations that are market driven, their strategy to serve the customer should mirror the diverse markets the company serves. An effective diversity management programme should not happen by default but by design, with clearly set objectives that do not look at transformation as 'compliance' but as an organisational imperative and an integral part of its policy and procedures.

Because employee engagement engenders participation and involvement that translates into effectiveness, there is need to constantly 'test the organisational temperature' as part of the key performance indicator of the organisation's health. It is recommended that engagement forms part of the organisational, functional and team performance metrics and key performance indicators.

TABLE 9: Decisions on the hypotheses and conclusions.

Hypotheses	Decision	Conclusion
H1: Managing and valuing diversity enhances performance.	Accepted	Managing and valuing diversity enhances performance.
H2: Diversity influences organisational effectiveness.	Rejected	Diversity in terms of success attribute diversity, innovative solution, and diverse customer need are not related with the performance of an organisation in terms of the organisation's strategic priorities.
H3: Performance is the outcome of diversity.	Accepted	Leadership diversity strongly influences organisational performance and/or effectiveness.
H4: Diversity influences and drives transformation.	Accepted	Diversity influences and drives transformation.
H5: Diversity influences organisational effectiveness which translates into performance improvement.	Accepted	Promoting diversity is significantly related with performance improvement in terms of knowledge to drive transformation.

Limitations of the study and future research

The study was limited to only one Fast Moving Consumer Goods (FMCG) company in SA. Future research could be conducted in other multi-nationals with critical mass in SA, so as to be able to compare the findings and determine success stories. The racial composition of the sample (minority Indian and mixed race participants) may not have been truly representative of the South African rainbow nation. Thus, a more diverse organisation study would be beneficial.

The causal link between diversity, engagement, effectiveness and performance should be explored using inferential statistical techniques. Because diversity management energises workplace productivity and increases the company's competitive edge, it would be critical to determine whether workplace diversity and employee engagement produce similar results. It would also be important to investigate the link between engagement, diversity, effectiveness and performance, in lieu of the fact that it commits employees by fostering growth for both the individual and the organisation.

Acknowledgements

Competing interests

The authors declare that they have no financial or personal relationships that may have inappropriately influenced them in writing this article.

Authors' contributions

J.V.M. conducted the research towards his MBA dissertation, under guidance of K.K.G. The article was developed and written entirely by K.K.G.

References

Booysen, L.A.E. (2007). Societal power shifts and changing social identities in South Africa: Workplace implications for management. *South African Journal of Economics and Management Sciences, 10*(1), 1–20. https://doi.org/10.4102/sajems.v10i1.533

Booysen, L.A.E., & Nkomo, S.M. (2014). New developments in employment equity and diversity management in South Africa. In L.A.E. Booysen, A. Klarsfeld, E. Ng, and A. Tatli (Eds.), *International handbook on diversity management at work: Country perspectives on diversity and equal treatment*, Vol. 2 (pp. 131–182). Cheltenham: Edward Elgar Publishing.

Bowers, C.A., Pharmer, J.A., & Salas, E. (2000). When member homogeneity is needed in work teams: A meta-analysis. *Small Group Research, 31*, 305–327. https://doi.org/10.1177/104649640003100303

Brabet, J. (2011). Corporate social responsibility and its models in a contested field. *Responsible Organization Review (ROR) 6*(2), 38–50. https://doi.org/10.3917/ror.062.0038

Bulbulia, S. (2003). *Diversity: Too hot to handle*. Retrieved November 29, 2015, from http://www.biz-communication.com/Article/196/18/2501.html

Bunderson, J.S., & Sutcliffe, K.M. (2002). Comparing alternative conceptualizations of functional diversity in management teams. *The Academy of Management Journal, 45*(5), 875–893. https://doi.org/10.2307/3069319

Carelse, K. (2013). *Employee perceptions towards workplace diversity in a financial institution operating in the Western Cape*. Faculty of Economics and Management Sciences, University of Western Cape, Cape Town.

Chin, J.L. (2013). Diversity leadership: Influence of ethnicity, gender and minority status. *Open Journal of Leadership, 2*, 1–10. https://doi.org/10.4236/ojl.2013.21001

Corporate Research Forum Report. (2011). *Diversity and business performance*. Retrieved November 30, 2015, from http://www.crforum.co.uk/research-and-resources/diversity-and-business-performance-2

Cronbach, L.J., & Meehl, P.E. (1955). Construct validity on psychological test. *Psychological Bulletin, 52*, 281–302. https://doi.org/10.1037/h0040957

Daniel, C. (1994). *How societies change*. Thousand Oaks, CA: Pine Forge.

DeVeale, C., & Manea, L. (2007). Companies embrace power of diversity. *Canadian HR Reporter, 20*(22), 14–15.

Ely, R., & Thomas, D.A. (2001). Making differences matter: A new paradigm for managing diversity. *Administrative Science Quarterly, 46*(2), 229–273. https://doi.org/10.2307/2667087

Employee Insight Survey (EIS). (2014). Diversity councils and business resource groups. Retrieved September 23, 2015, from http://www.coca-colacompany.com/our-company/diversity/diversity-councils-andbusiness-resource-groups

Ferreira, N., & Coetzee, M. (2010). Psychological career resources and organisational commitment: Exploring socio-demographic differences. *South African Journal of Labour Relations, 34*(2), 25–41.

Green, K.A., Lopez, M., Wysocki, A., & Kepner, K. (2002). *Diversity in the workplace: Benefits, challenges, and the required managerial tools*. Gainesville, FL: Department of Food and Resource Economics, Institute of Food and Agricultural Sciences, University of Florida. Retrieved November 29, 2015, from http://edis.ifas.ufl.edu

Guillaume, Y.R., Dawson, J.F., Woods, S.A., Sacramento, C.A., & West, M.A. (2013). Getting diversity at work to work: What we know and what we still don't know. *Journal of Occupational and Organizational Psychology, 86*(2), 123–141. https://doi.org/10.1111/joop.12009

Horwitz, S., & Horwitz, I. (2007). The effects of team diversity on team outcomes: A meta-analytic review of team demography. *Journal of Management, 33*(6), 987–1015. https://doi.org/10.1177/0149206307308587

Human, L. (1996). Managing workforce diversity: A critique and example from South Africa. *International Journal of Manpower, 17*(4/5), 46–64. https://doi.org/10.1108/01437729610127659

Jackson, S.E., May, K.A., & Whitney, K. (1995). *Dynamics of diversity in decision making teams*. In R.A. Guzzo & E. Salas (Eds.), *Team effectiveness and decision making in organizations*, (pp. 89–131). San Francisco, CA: Jossey-Bass.

Jonsen, K., Tatli, A., Özbilgin, M.F., & Bell, M.P. (2013). The tragedy of the uncommons: Reframing workforce diversity. *Human Relations, 66*(2), 271–294. https://doi.org/10.1177/0018726712466575

Kamps, J.M., & Engelbrecht, A.S. (2011). The influence of emotional intelligence on diversity complexity cognition and the attitude towards diversity. *South African Journal Business Management, 42*(3), 37–48.

Kent, M. (2012). *Diversity: The Coca-Cola Company*. Retrieved September 23, 2015, from http://www.coca-colacompany.com/our-company/diversity

Klarsfeld, A., Ng, E., & Tatli, A. (2012). Social regulation and diversity management: A comparative study of France, Canada and the UK. *European Journal of Industrial Relations, 18*(4), 309–327. https://doi.org/10.1177/0959680112461091

Knouse, B.S., & Dansby, R.M. (1999). Percentage of work-group diversity and work-group effectiveness. *Journal of Psychology, 133*(5), 486–494. https://doi.org/10.1080/00223989909599757

Kochan, T., Bezrukova, K., Ely, R., Jackson, S., Joshi, A., Jehn, K., et al., (2003). The effects of diversity on business performance: Report of the Diversity Research Network. *Human Resource Management, 42*(1), 3–21. https://doi.org/10.1002/hrm.10061

Konrad, A. (2003). Defining the domain of workplace diversity scholarship. *Group and Organization Management, 28*(1), 4–17. https://doi.org/10.1177/1059601102250013

Madihlaba, J. (2011). *Variables influencing management of diversity in the South African Public Sector*. Johannesburg: University of Johannesburg.

Mason, G., Williams, G., & Cranmer, S. (2009). Employability skills initiatives in higher education: What effects do they have on graduate Labour market outcomes? *Education Economics, 17*(1), 1–30. https://doi.org/10.1080/09645290802028315

McEnrue, M.P. (1993). Managing diversity: Los Angeles before and after the riots. *Organizational Dynamics, 21*(3), 18–29. https://doi.org/10.1016/0090-2616(93)90068-C

Milliken, F.J., & Martins, L.L. (1996). Searching for common threads: Understanding the multiple effects of diversity in organizational groups. *The Academy of Management Review, 21*(2), 102–133.

Neault, R.A., & Mondair, S. (2011). Supporting workplace diversity: Emerging roles for employment counsellors. *Journal of Employment and Counselling, 48*(1), 72–80. https://doi.org/10.1002/j.2161-1920.2011.tb00116.x

Page, S.E. (2011). *Diversity and complexity*. Princeton, NJ: Princeton University Press.

Roberge, M., Lewicki, R., Heitapelto, A., & Abdyldaeva, A. (2011). From theory to practice: Recommending supportive diversity practices. *Journal of Diversity Management, 6*(1), 1–20. https://doi.org/10.19030/jdm.v6i2.5481

Rogatschnig, M. (2011). *Debunking diversity management. Challenges go beyond narrow definitions*. Cape Town: Connemara.

Rosado, C. (2006). *What do we mean by 'Managing Diversity'?* Hyderabad, India: ICAFAI University.

Schreuder, A., & Coetzee, M. (2011). *Careers: An organisational perspective*. Claremont: Juta and Co. Ltd.

Seekings, J. (2008). The continuing salience of race: Discrimination and diversity in South Africa. *Journal of Contemporary African Studies, 26*(1), 1–25. https://doi.org/10.1080/02589000701782612

Schultz, H., Bagraim, J., Potgieter, T., Viegde, C., & Werner, A. (2003). *Organisational behavior*. Pretoria: Van Schaik.

Simons, S.M., & Rowland, K.N. (2011). Diversity and its impact on organizational performance: The influence of diversity constructions on expectations and outcomes. *Journal of Technology Management and Innovation, 6*(3), 172–174. https://doi.org/10.4067/S0718-27242011000300013

Ssegawa, D. (2011). *Workplace culture*. Retrieved July 15, 2013, from http://www.coca-colacompany.com/our-company/diversity/workplace-culture

Swanepoel, B.J., Erasmus, B.J., & Schenk, H.W. (2008). *South African human resources management. Theory and Practice*. Cape Town: Juta and Co. Ltd.

Tatli, A., & Özbilgin, M.F. (2012). An emic approach to intersectional study of diversity at work: A Bourdieuan framing. *International Journal of Management Reviews, 14*(2), 180–200. https://doi.org/10.1111/j.1468-2370.2011.00326.x

Velaquez, M. (2013). *The Coca-Cola series*. Retrieved September 25, 2015, from http://www.diversitydtg.com/article/best-practices-inclusive-strategies/the-coca-colaseries-three-articles

Webber, S.S., & Donahue, L.M. (2001). Impact of highly and less job-related diversity on work group cohesion and performance: A meta-analysis. *Journal of Management, 27*(2), 141–162. https://doi.org/10.1177/014920630102700202

Weiliang, E.C., Mun, L.K., Chern, T.S., Fong, T.S., & Yuan, Y.P. (2012). *The effects of workforce diversity towards the employee's performance in an organization*. Faculty of Business and Finance. Malaysia: University Tunku.

9

Investigating the relationship between work values and work ethics: A South African perspective

Authors:
Petronella Jonck[1]
Freda van der Walt[2]
Nthombi Sobayeni[2]

Affiliations:
[1]Research and Innovation Unit, National School of Government, South Africa

[2]Faculty of Management Sciences, Central University of Technology, South Africa

Corresponding author:
Freda van der Walt,
fvdwalt@cut.ac.za

Orientation: As a result of the proliferation of unethical behaviour in the workplace, the study of work ethics has received new impetus.

Research purpose: The research study sought to determine the relationship between work ethics and work values, with the objective of determining whether work ethics statistically significantly predict work values.

Motivation for the study: As work ethics (i.e. behavioural intent) are a determinant of work values (i.e. overt behaviour), researchers are investigating their potential in preventing unethical behaviour.

Research design, approach and method: A descriptive quantitative research design was employed in the study. A survey was conducted using the Multidimensional Work Ethic Profile and the Values Scale, which in previous studies have produced acceptable Cronbach's alpha coefficients. Data were collected from 301 respondents in one geographical area in South Africa.

Main findings: Work values did not appear to be highly esteemed by respondents, as only 6 of the 22 dimensions had a positive score. However, all seven dimensions of work ethics had positive scores. A negative correlation was found between work ethics and work values. In addition, work ethics predicted 9% of the variance in work values, providing sufficient evidence to accept the postulated research hypothesis.

Practical implications: The findings of the study could be used by human resource managers to promote ethical behaviour, by focusing not only on work ethics but also on the relationship between work ethics and work values.

Contribution: The study provides evidence of a relationship between work ethics and work behaviours, such as work values, within the South African context, and it thus addresses a research gap in this area.

Introduction

Unethical behaviour is a worldwide phenomenon, within increasingly unethical societies. Within these societies, individuals are required to make decisions on many different matters on a daily basis, where it is not always easy to distinguish a good decision from a bad decision. Vyas-Doorgapersad (2007) argues that developing countries, such as South Africa, are more susceptible to unethical behaviour because of widespread poverty, relatively low public-sector compensation, a lack of risk mechanisms (e.g. insurance and a well-developed market), opportunities created by complex, poorly defined, continually changing, and inadequate rules and regulations, a lack of properly established laws and principles, a lack of institutions to enforce a code of conduct and an absence of watchdog agencies. Unethical behaviour in South Africa, mainly in the form of corruption through bribery, has reached crisis proportions (Patel, 2013) and, as such, on a daily basis, citizens are confronted with media reports of corruption, fraudulent activities and bribery, among other things.

A study by Boshoff and Van Zyl (2011) reports that South Africa has the highest rate of white-collar crime in the world, and that South African organisations had an average loss of income of R7.4 million due to fraud for the period 2006/2007. The Global Economic Crime Survey 2016 reports that 69% of South African organisations have experienced economic crime, and that 15% have been asked to pay a bribe (PwC, 2016). In response to recent ethics scandals, organisations are emphasising ethics awareness, or work ethics (Quesenberry, Woodburne & Yang, 2013). However, even if an organisation has a code of ethics, ethical leadership and internal support for ethical management, this would not necessarily produce ethical behaviour (Van Vuuren, 2002). The reason for this is that while work ethics as a construct refer to attitudes and beliefs regarding what is ethical and what is unethical behaviour, presence or absence of work ethics does not necessarily lead to ethical or unethical behaviour (Miller, Woehr & Hudspeth, 2002; Ravangard et al., 2014). However, previous research studies have confirmed that behavioural intent predicts actual behaviour (Kurland, 1995). Studies have also confirmed that an individual's personal values are a significant predictor of ethical behaviour (Quick & Nelson, 2011). In addition, personal values are associated with and influence decision-making behaviour, and, consequently, ethical behaviour (Ivaniš & Šturlić, 2016).

Purpose

Previous research studies have not established a consistent causal relationship between work ethics and work behaviours, such as work values (Mann, Taber & Haywood, 2013). As such, there is a paucity of research studies that have investigated the relationship between work ethics and work values, particularly in the South African context. Given that to date no study within the South African context has been identified that has studied the aforementioned relationship, the primary objective of this study was to investigate the relationship between work ethics and work values in a South African sample. In addition, it was hypothesised that a proportion of the variance in work values can be explained by work ethics. The secondary objective was to establish which work values and which dimensions of work ethics are important in the South African work environment.

Literature review

Work ethics

The origin and make-up of the construct of ethics has been the subject of debate for millennia, and myriad philosophers has offered opinions on the topic. Although not all scholars agree, it seems reasonable to conclude that the concept of ethics is derived from the Greek word *ethos*, which originally referred to customs, habitual conduct, usages and character (Melden, 1967). The concept of ethics refers to the pattern, norm, or code of conduct adopted by a group of people, although the group will not necessarily obey this code of conduct (Jones, Sontag, Beckner & Fogelin, 1977). Thus, as deviant workplace behaviour refers to violation of the norms of an organisation, one can argue that unethical behaviour equates to deviant behaviour. However, Rogojan (2009) maintains that deviant work behaviour and unethical behaviour do not necessarily constitute the same thing, as unethical behaviour is judged as wrongdoing when societal guidelines determine the morality of behaviour, not organisational norms. For the purposes of this study, however, unethical behaviour will be regarded as behaviour that is both unethical and deviant.

The construct of work ethics has its origins in the writings of the twentieth-century scholar Max Weber, which saw the conception of the construct of the Protestant work ethic (PWE) (Van Ness, Melinsky, Buff & Seifert, 2010). The PWE, in its original manifestation, was based on four principal beliefs, namely (1) working hard is honourable and a calling from God, (2) economic success is a sign of God's grace, (3) an individual is responsible for controlling their own actions and (4) an individual should avoid any wasteful materialism that could result from hard work (Cokley et al., 2007, p. 76). The PWE has a strong religious undertone, and some may argue that it is not relevant in contemporary workplaces. However, as South Africa is still a very religious society, with people generally having strong religious convictions (Van der Walt & De Klerk, 2015), it seems appropriate to use the PWE as the theoretical underpinning to investigate work ethics for a South African sample.

Work ethics can be defined as a productive orientation that values work as compulsory and a worthwhile life interest in order to achieve certain objectives (Bergh & Theron, 2009). Miller et al. (2002), as well as Ravangard et al. (2014), have asserted that work ethics consists of attitudes and beliefs regarding work behaviour, and that they are a multidimensional construct that is reflected in decision-making and behaviour. Thus, the work ethics of employees may be regarded as the overall framework from which values emanate, where work values, in turn, potentially influence the behaviour of individuals at work. Within the context of Max Weber's original PWE theory, Miller et al. (2002) developed the Multidimensional Work Ethic Profile (MWEP) to measure seven dimensions of the construct of work ethics, namely self-reliance, morality or ethics, leisure, hard work, centrality of work, wasted time and delay of gratification (Miller et al., 2002). Self-reliance refers to striving for independence in one's everyday work (Miller et al., 2002), or depending on oneself, and not relying on others (Dwyer, 2012) (also see Van der Walt, Jonck & Sobayeni, 2016). Morality and ethics, as measured by the MWEP, is regarded as one dimension of work ethics, and it refers to 'beliefs pertaining to a just and moral existence' (Miller et al., 2002, p. 11). However, morality and ethics are often considered as separate constructs, where morality refers to customs or manners that are usually applied to one's behaviour, and ethics relates to an individual's character (Chidi, Ogunyomi & Badejo, 2012). Nevertheless, these two concepts are often used interchangeably to refer to the way individuals behave in the work context, or the way they are expected to behave (Van Ness et al., 2010) (also see Van der Walt et al., 2016).

Leisure refers to pro-leisure attitudes and a belief in the importance of non-work activities, such as spending time relaxing (Miller et al., 2002) or indulging in personally meaningful and pleasurable activities (Chun, Lee, Kim & Heo, 2012) (also see Van der Walt et al., 2016). Hard work may be understood as a belief in the virtue of hard work (Miller et al., 2002), or the belief that one can become a better person and achieve objectives through commitment to the value and importance of work (Van Ness et al., 2010) (also see Van der Walt et al., 2016). Centrality of work refers to a belief in work for work's sake (Miller et al., 2002), the degree of importance that working has in the life of an individual at any given point in time, or the meaning of work (Schreuder & Coetzee, 2011) (also see Van der Walt et al., 2016). Wasted time relates to attitudes and beliefs that reflect an active and productive use of time (Miller et al., 2002), that is, not wasting time on activities that will not result in production of valuable goods or services (Horman & Kenley, 2005). Van Ness et al. (2010) explain that wasted time in the context of work ethics can be conceived of as part of a continuum, where high commitment to time management occupies one end of the continuum, and low commitment to time management occupies the other end of the continuum. Delay of gratification relates to a future orientation and postponement of rewards (Miller et al., 2002), in other words, sacrificing short-term rewards to achieve long-term objectives (Abd-El-Fattah & AL-Nabhani, 2012) (also see Van der Walt et al., 2016). As the aforementioned dimensions of work ethics were measured, the PWE theory represents the theoretical underpinning of the study. It should be noted, however, that Stones and Philbrick (2001) cautioned that there is a paucity of systematic exploration of the PWE theory in the African context.

Work values

The literature on work values is characterised by a plethora of definitions (Steyn & Kotze, 2004). Wils, Saba, Waxin and Labelle (2011) attribute this lack of synthesis to incomplete and inconsistent theorisation regarding the mentioned construct. As such, Wong and Yuen (2015, p. 31), citing Ros, Schwartz and Surikiss (1999), indicated that 'work values' is a term used to describe feelings, attitudes and beliefs held in regard to employment in general, and specifically various types of occupations, in addition to particular attributes, such as prestige, remuneration, job security and the work environment. Hattrup, Mueller and Joens (2007, p. 481) defined work values as beliefs about the desirability of specific outcomes related to employment. Consistent with these definitions, Ho (2006, p. 11) and Uçanok (2008, p. 157) defined work values as the goals that employees attempt to achieve through working. Wils et al. (2011), based on research conducted by various authors, stated that work values are desirable and trans-situational goals that represent a frame of reference for employees at work. Pek, Lim and Yee's (2008, p. 147) definition of work values is more comprehensive, and it states that work values consist of individual preferences for the type of work or work environment, views about the importance of the prerequisites in a work situation, and the guiding principles for job-related decision-making, action and overt behaviour.

Notwithstanding the fact, mentioned above, that Wils et al. (2011) have attributed incomplete theorisation to work values, Cogin (2012) used congruence theory as theoretical underpinning to investigate work values. Congruence theory posits that work values have a significant influence on organisational functioning, in that misalignment of the needs, demands, goals and objectives of various components within the organisation can impede organisational functioning (Cogin, 2012). However, previous research regarding work values has mostly focused on determining the dimensionality of these values, and identifying the factors that influence, or the factors that are influenced by, work values (Ueda & Ohzono, 2013). As such, Nord, Brief, Atieh and Doherty (1990), cited in Uçanok (2008, p. 158), suggested a two-dimensional classification for work values, namely intrinsic and extrinsic work values. Intrinsic work values include values such as self-actualisation, personal growth and development, the opportunity to be creative, and use of initiative (Steyn & Kotze, 2004). Hirschi (2010) indicated that extrinsic work values refer to high income, job security, fast and easy entry to the job, leisure time besides work, and prestigious work. Thus, intrinsic work values refer to the work that an employee does, while extrinsic work values are regarded as the outcome or consequence of employment (Twenge, Campbell, Hoffman & Lance, 2010). Various scholars (i.e. Hirschi, 2010; Liu & Lei, 2012; Twenge et al., 2010) have supported this dichotomous classification of work values into intrinsic and extrinsic work values.

Elizur, cited in Uçanok (2008, p. 158), developed a trichotomous classification for work values, and labelled the three categories 'instrumental values' (e.g. work conditions and benefits), 'cognitive values' (e.g. interests and achievement) and 'affective values' (e.g. relations with others). Although the terminology used for the three categories of work values posited differs among researchers, it seems that most researchers use the labels 'intrinsic values', 'extrinsic, or materialistic, values' and 'social values' to refer to the three types of work values (Sergio, Dungca & Ormita, 2015). Ros et al. (1999) identified four dimensions of work values, namely extrinsic, intrinsic, social and power values. Power values can be defined as how much authority, influence, and prestige an employee has over others (Liu & Lei, 2012, p. 50). Salamzadeh, Nejati and Salamzadeh (2014) proposed five dimensions of work values, including self-development, contribution to society, job satisfaction, interpersonal harmony, and work-life balance. O'Connor and Kinnane (1961), cited in Liu and Lei (2012, p. 51), considered a six-dimensional classification for work values, and proposed the following classifications: security-economic-material values, social-artistic values, work conditions and associates, heuristic-creative values, achievement-prestige values and independence-variety values.

In light of the above discussion relating to the classification of work values, the lack of synthesis that was attributed by Wils et al. (2011) is clearly evident. Hence, it is essential that further research be conducted regarding work values, specifically with the aim of developing appropriate theories (Ueda & Ohzono, 2013).

The relationship between the constructs of work values and work ethics

An individual's values predict attitudinal and behavioural outcomes (Rohan, 2000, cited in Montgomery, 2011) and are also regarded as a significant predictor of ethical behaviour (Quick & Nelson, 2011). It has also been established that personal values are associated with and influence decision-making behaviour and, consequently, ethical behaviour (Ivaniš & Šturlić, 2016). Although it has previously been established that personal values predict attitudinal and behavioural outcomes (Rohan, 2000, cited in Montgomery, 2011) and ethical behaviour (Ivaniš & Šturlić, 2016; Quick & Nelson, 2011), the current study will investigate whether work ethics predict work values. While work values are associated with work and work-related activities, work ethics, as such, refers to attitudes and beliefs, as opposed to behaviour (Miller et al., 2002; Ravangard et al., 2014). Previous research has found that attitude is the most influential factor in behavioural intent (Jafarkarimi, Saadatdoost, Sim & Hee, 2016). This finding is consistent with the theory of reasoned action, which posits that attitude towards behaviour, together with subjective norms regarding behaviour, determines behavioural intent. Thus, employees' work ethics may be regarded as the overall framework from which work values emanate, where work values, in turn, influence individuals' behavioural intent, and potentially their behaviour at work.

Schwartz and Bilsky (1990) suggest that work ethics, specifically the PWE, are correlated with components of value systems. Quesenberry et al. (2013), Richards, Gilbert and Harris (2002), and Wittmer (2000) found that work ethics (i.e. ethical perception and intention to do the ethical thing) correlated with work values. Mann et al. (2013) indicated that research findings to date have found small but significant correlations between espousal of a work ethic and willingness to work hard, regardless of external reward (Tang, 1990), which indicates presence of intrinsic work values.

Method

A fundamental part of the research project is the research methodology employed. The methodology used in this study will be explicated in the following subsections.

Research approach

The authors used a quantitative research approach within a positivistic research orientation to achieve the research objective. More specifically, a descriptive quantitative research design was employed, so as to describe the relationship between work values and work ethics as accurately as possible at a particular point in time (Salkind, 2012). Because of the synchronic nature of this research, it could also be characterised as having employed a cross-sectional research design (Leedy & Ormrod, 2013). Wagner, Kawulich and Garner (2012) asserted that descriptive research provides a detailed picture of a relationship. The sampling design used in the research was a non-probability sampling design.

Measures

Participants

The final sample consisted of 301 respondents. Individuals were the unit of analysis, and the population parameter was working-age individuals who were either working or who had work experience, but currently unemployed. The population consisted of organisations in different sectors but situated in the same geographical area within South Africa. A convenience sampling method was employed to generate the sample, in that readily accessible potential respondents were requested to participate in the research project (Jordan, Werner & Venter, 2015). Hence, caution is advised when generalising the findings to the larger population, due to the fact that a non-random sampling technique was employed, which would adversely affect the external validity of the study (Wagner et al., 2012).

Of the 540 questionnaires distributed, 301 were completed and returned, which translates to a response rate of 55.7%. The self-administered questionnaire was distributed (to be returned anonymously) by the researcher. Where possible, the researcher personally collected the questionnaires, which were placed in a sealed envelope, on a pre-arranged day and time. Respondents were given 14 days to complete the questionnaire at their own convenience.

Measuring instrument

Two unabridged questionnaires were administered, accompanied by a self-constructed biographical questionnaire.

Biographical questionnaire: The biographical questionnaire was designed by the researchers in a way that it would solicit relevant demographic information from the participants in terms of their age, sex, race, employment tenure, generational cohort and highest academic qualification.

The Values Scale: When it was first developed, the aim of the Values Scale (VS) was to understand the needs that respondents experience, and to assess the relative importance of the work role as a means of needs satisfaction, given the context of other life roles (Langley, Du Toit & Herbst, 1992). Thus, the aim of the VS is to determine the value of certain work-related aspects to individual respondents. The VS (Langley et al., 1992) comprises 110 items in a Likert-scale format, with response categories ranging from 1 ('of little importance') to 4 ('very important'). The VS measures 22 aspects relating to work, namely ability utilisation, achievement, advancement, aesthetics, altruism, authority, autonomy, creativity, cultural identity, economic rewards, economic security, own lifestyle, personal development, physical activities, physical prowess, prestige, risk, social interaction, social relationships, spirituality, variety and agreeable working conditions. A sample item is 'I find pleasure in the beauty of my work', which is an example from the aesthetics dimension. Another example is 'I make my own decisions at work', which represents the autonomy dimension of work values. Within a South African context, Boonzaier (2008) and Langley et al. (1992) reported acceptable Cronbach's alpha coefficients. Langley et al. (1992) reported an inter-item correlation coefficient of 0.7.

The Multidimensional Work Ethic Profile: The 65-item MWEP was developed by Miller et al. (2002, p. 1), and it 'measures seven conceptually and empirically distinct dimensions of the work ethic construct'. Items for each subscale include the following: 'To be truly successful, a person should be self-reliant' (self-reliance), 'One should always take responsibility for one's actions' (morality or ethics), 'Life would be more meaningful if we had more leisure time' (leisure), 'Nothing is impossible if you work hard enough' (hard work), 'I feel uneasy when there is little work for me to do' (centrality of work), 'It is important to stay busy at work and not waste time' (wasted time), and 'If I want to buy something, I always wait until I can afford it' (delay of gratification). The questionnaire followed a Likert-type format, with response categories ranging from 'strongly agree' to 'strongly disagree'. The instruction to participants was to provide responses based on their opinion or belief about each item. The MWEP has previously been subjected to psychometric validation (Van Ness et al., 2010). Miller et al. (2002) reported the following Cronbach's alpha values: 0.89 (self-reliance), 0.80 (morality or ethics), 0.85 (leisure), 0.83 (hard work), 0.81 (centrality of work), 0.80 (wasted time) and 0.76 (delay of gratification).

Reliability and validity of the study: Cronbach's alpha coefficients were used to calculate the inter-item consistency of the two measuring instruments (the results are depicted in Table 1). From these results, it can be concluded that the scores obtained from the two instruments used were very reliable, as scores of 0.95 and 0.94 were obtained for the VS and the MWEP, respectively. More specifically, the reliability values for the various dimensions of the VS were as follows: $\alpha = 0.64$ (ability utilisation), $\alpha = 0.66$ (achievement), $\alpha = 0.61$ (advancement), $\alpha = 0.63$ (aesthetics), $\alpha = 0.75$ (altruism), $\alpha = 0.63$ (authority), $\alpha = 0.62$ (autonomy), $\alpha = 0.69$ (creativity), $\alpha = 0.72$ (cultural identity), $\alpha = 0.73$ (economic reward), $\alpha = 0.69$ (economic security), $\alpha = 0.64$ (own lifestyle), $\alpha = 0.60$ (personal development), $\alpha = 0.73$ (physical activities), $\alpha = 0.76$ (physical prowess), $\alpha = 0.68$ (prestige), $\alpha = 0.67$ (risk), $\alpha = 0.65$ (social interaction), $\alpha = 0.66$ (social relations), $\alpha = 0.65$ (spirituality), $\alpha = 0.70$ (variety) and $\alpha = 0.55$ (agreeable working conditions). The reliability values for each sub-construct of the MWEP were as follows: $\alpha = 0.66$ (self-reliance), $\alpha = 0.87$ (leisure), $\alpha = 0.75$ (hard work), $\alpha = 0.78$ (centrality of work), $\alpha = 0.77$ (wasted time) and $\alpha = 0.71$ (delay of gratification).

Validity refers to the degree to which a measuring instrument determines what it is supposed to determine, by gathering relevant data on the constructs under investigation (Jordan et al., 2015). In this research, the relevant constructs are work ethics and work values. Two types of validity were pursued, namely content validity and face validity, particularly considering that previous research findings have confirmed the psychometric properties of the unabridged questionnaires.

TABLE 1: Cronbach's alpha coefficients for the scales.

Scale	Number of items	Cronbach's alpha
VS (Work values)	110	0.95
MWEP (Work ethics)	65	0.94

VS, Values Scale; MWEP, Multidimensional Work Ethic Profile.

To ensure face validity of the questionnaires, they were distributed to two experts in the field of human resource management, who also confirmed the content validity of the instruments. A pilot study with ten respondents from the target population was conducted to further ensure the face validity of the questionnaires. The aim was to check for any ambiguous, biased or leading questions, and to determine the minimum time required to complete the questionnaire. No changes to the measuring instrument were indicated by the pilot study participants. In addition, a statistician reviewed the questionnaire in terms of its format and layout, and the suitability of the items for statistical analysis.

Factor analysis results to determine the construct validity of the VS indicated that the data were factorable, as the Kaiser–Meyer–Olkin (KMO) test for sampling adequacy returned a value of 0.824, and Bartlett's test of sphericity returned a statistically significant value, on the 99th percentile (X^2 = 15 701.176; df = 5995; p = 0.000**). An exploratory factor analysis with oblique (oblimin) rotation was employed, and it was determined that 30 components had an eigenvalue exceeding 1, accounting for 68.160% of the total variance. However, an inspection of the scree plot indicated a clear break after the fourth factor. It was thus decided to retain four components for purposes of further investigation in a Monte Carlo parallel analysis. Results obtained from the analysis indicated that four components had eigenvalues exceeding the corresponding criterion value for a randomly generated data matrix of the same size (110 variables × 301). The aforementioned results lend support to the notion that the subscales can be used as unidimensional factors.

In the same way, a factor analysis was performed to determine the construct validity of the MWEP. The results indicated that the data were factorable, with a KMO of 0.830, and a Bartlett's test of sphericity value that was statistically significant, on the 99th percentile (X^2 = 7442.558; df = 2080; p = 0.000**). The exploratory factor analysis with oblique rotation indicated that 19 components had an eigenvalue exceeding 1, accounting for 65.662% of the total variance. The scree plot, however, indicated the presence of seven factors, while the Monte Carlo parallel analysis results indicated that eight components had eigenvalues exceeding the corresponding criterion value for a randomly generated data matrix of the same size (65 variables × 301). The results should be interpreted in the light of the fact that the MWEP measures seven conceptually and empirically distinct dimensions of the work ethic construct (Miller et al., 2002) with one general dimension that all the items load onto.

Analysis

Data were analysed using Statistical Package for the Social Sciences (SPSS) version 20. First, Cronbach's alpha coefficients were computed for the VS and the MWEP. Descriptive statistics included frequency distributions, measures of central tendency and measures of dispersion. Inferential statistics included a Pearson product-moment correlation, to ascertain the relationship between the constructs, and a multiple regression analysis, to assess whether work values predicted work ethics.

Ethical considerations: Prior to data collection, ethical clearance was obtained from the research faculty committee of the institution concerned. Permission was also granted by the organisations at which the respondents were employed at the time of data gathering. Lastly, participant signed consent was obtained before commencing with data collection. Standard ethical guidelines were adhered to.

Results

The descriptive statistics and the inferential statistics results are reported separately in this section.

Demographic characteristics

The sample group consisted of mostly African (91.4%) female (62.5%) respondents between the ages of 18 and 23 years (51.5%). Respondents with 1 year or less of service made up 44.2% of the sample, and those with a Grade 12 qualification made up 62.8% of the sample. Table 2 depicts the demographic profile of the sample.

Prevalence of work values and work ethics

The findings of the study, as illustrated in Table 3, reveal that respondents did not esteem work values highly.

The mean scores of the following dimensions of work values were above the median, and were thus positive: authority (M = 14.23; SD = 2.780), creativity (M = 16.07; SD = 2.541), economic security (M = 17.02; SD = 2.408), prestige (M = 16.12; SD = 2.894), risk (M = 12.11; SD = 3.377), social relationships (M = 13.20; SD = 3.116). However, the mean scores of the following work value subscales were below the median, and these dimensions of work values were thus not highly valued by the respondents: ability (M = 17.73; SD = 2.228), achievement (M = 17.41; SD = 2.251), advancement (M = 17.47; SD = 2.235), aesthetics (M = 15.75; SD = 2.805), altruism (M = 16.48; SD = 2.723), autonomy (M = 14.46; SD = 3.019), cultural identity (M = 14.83; SD = 3.282), economic rewards (M = 16.87; SD = 2.856), own lifestyle (M = 15.31; SD = 2.873), personal development (M = 17.40; SD = 2.173), physical activities (M = 14.86; SD = 3.111), physical prowess (M = 12.71; SD = 3.526), social interaction (M = 14.66; SD = 2.825), spirituality (M = 15.81; SD = 2.645), variety (M = 14.79; SD = 2.967) and working conditions (M = 15.52; SD = 2.669). From the above findings, it would appear that respondents indicated the above values as 'very important', except for the values of cultural identity, risk, social interaction, social relationships, and variety, which were perceived as 'important'. As far as the mean scores for the dimensions of work ethics are concerned, respondents scored positively on all the dimensions, namely self-reliance (M = 20.50; SD = 5.283), morality or ethics (M = 23.21; SD = 4.363), leisure (M = 28.20; SD = 8.110), hard work (M = 16.10; SD = 5.183), centrality of work (M = 20.94; SD = 5.980), wasted time (M = 15.60; SD = 4.663), and delay of gratification (M = 14.82; SD = 4.514).

TABLE 2: Demographic profile of the sample group.

Category	Variable	*n*	%
Sex	Male	112	37.2
	Female	188	62.5
Population group	African	275	91.4
	White	17	5.6
	Coloured	7	2.3
	Indian/Asian	1	0.3
Age	13–23 years	155	51.5
	24–43 years	112	37.2
	44–63 years	34	11.3
Years of service	0–1 years	133	44.2
	2–5 years	114	37.9
	6–10 years	24	8.0
	11–15 years	8	2.7
	15+ years	17	5.6
Highest academic qualification	Below Grade 12	10	3.3
	Grade 12	189	62.8
	National diploma	70	23.3
	Honours/bachelor's degree	23	7.6
	Master's degree	7	2.3
	Doctorate	1	0.3

Pearson correlation analysis

To investigate the intercorrelations between the various work values and work ethics subscales, a Pearson product-moment correlation was calculated, to identify significant relationships between the subscales of work values and those of work ethics. It should be noted that normality was assumed. Due to the high number of variables involved in the research, 29 altogether, results will only be discussed, and not illustrated. Most of the correlations were significant and negative on either the 99th or the 95th percentile, for example, the work ethics dimension of self-reliance had weak intercorrelations (according to guidelines as given in Pallant [2011, p. 134], who indicated that an *r*-value of between 0.10 and 0.29 can be considered as weak) with ability utilisation ($p \leq 0.037$*; $r = -0.120$), achievement ($p \leq 0.039$*; $r = -0.119$), aesthetics ($p \leq 0.004$**; $r = -0.168$), authority ($p \leq 0.017$*; $r = -0.138$), autonomy ($p \leq 0.000$**; $r = -0.207$), cultural identity ($p \leq 0.003$**; $r = -0.172$), economic security ($p \leq 0.003$**; $r = -0.170$), own lifestyle ($p \leq 0.000$**; $r = -0.205$) and working conditions ($p \leq 0.006$**; $r = -0.157$), to mention a few. As far as the dimensions of work ethics are concerned, morality/ethics had weak intercorrelations with, among others, aesthetics ($p \leq 0.006$**; $r = -0.157$), own lifestyle ($p \leq 0.006$; $r = -0.158$), physical prowess ($p \leq 0.009$**; $r = -0.151$), risk ($p \leq 0.000$**; $r = -0.240$), social interaction ($p \leq 0.001$**; $r = -0.183$), social relationships ($p \leq 0.000$**; $r = -0.230$) and spirituality ($p \leq 0.002$**; $r = -0.179$). The work ethics dimension of leisure had weak intercorrelations with autonomy ($p \leq 0.000$**; $r = -0.237$), cultural identity ($p \leq 0.000$**; $r = -0.201$), own lifestyle ($p \leq 0.000$**; $r = -0.209$), risk ($p \leq 0.000$**; $r = -0.219$), and social relationships ($p \leq 0.000$**; $r = -0.280$). Similarly, the work ethics dimension of hard work correlated weakly with ability utilisation ($p \leq 0.000$**; $r = -0.267$), achievement ($p \leq 0.000$**; $r = -0.266$), advancement ($p \leq 0.000$**; $r = -0.263$),

TABLE 3: Measures of central tendency and dispersion – work values and work ethics.

Factor	Item	Mean	SD	60%	Min	Median (50%)	Max
Work values	Ability utilisation	17.73	2.228	19	5	18	20
	Achievement	17.41	2.251	18	5	18	20
	Advancement	17.47	2.235	18	5	18	20
	Aesthetics	15.75	2.805	17	6	16	20
	Altruism	16.48	2.723	17	6	17	20
	Authority	14.23	2.780	15	6	14	20
	Autonomy	14.46	3.019	15	7	15	20
	Creativity	16.07	2.541	17	7	16	20
	Cultural identity	14.83	3.282	16	5	15	20
	Economic rewards	16.87	2.856	18	6	17	20
	Economic security	17.02	2.408	18	5	17	20
	Own lifestyle	15.31	2.873	16	8	16	20
	Personal development	17.40	2.173	18	8	18	20
	Physical activities	14.86	3.111	16	5	15	20
	Physical prowess	12.71	3.526	14	5	13	20
	Prestige	16.12	2.894	17	5	16	20
	Risk	12.11	3.377	13	5	12	20
	Social interaction	14.66	2.825	15	6	15	20
	Social relationships	13.20	3.116	14	6	13	20
	Spirituality	15.81	2.645	17	6	16	20
	Variety	14.79	2.967	16	6	15	20
	Working conditions	15.52	2.669	16	5	16	20
Work ethics	Self-reliance	20.50	5.283	21	10	20	44
	Morality/ethics	23.21	4.363	24	10	23	41
	Leisure	28.20	8.110	30	10	28	49
	Hard work	16.10	5.183	17	9	15	45
	Centrality of work	20.94	5.980	22	10	20	45
	Wasted time	15.60	4.663	16.20	6	15	37
	Delay of gratification	14.82	4.514	15	6	14	35

creativity ($p \leq 0.000$**; r = -0.202), economic security ($p \leq 0.000$**; r = -0.225), personal development ($p \leq 0.000$**; r = -0.234), prestige ($p \leq 0.000$**; r = -0.209), spirituality ($p \leq 0.000$**; r = -0.234) and variety ($p \leq 0.000$**; r = -0.212). The dimension of centrality of work correlated weakly with aesthetics ($p \leq 0.000$**; r = -0.208), altruism ($p \leq 0.000$**; r = -0.291), physical activities ($p \leq 0.000$**; r = -0.246), physical prowess ($p \leq 0.000$**; r = -0.215), and spirituality ($p \leq 0.000$; r = -0.283). The dimension of wasted time correlated weakly with altruism ($p \leq 0.000$**; r = -0.243), physical activities ($p \leq 0.000$**; r = -0.218) and spirituality ($p \leq 0.000$**; r = -0.252), to mention a few. Lastly, the dimension of delay of gratification correlated weakly with aesthetics ($p \leq 0.000$**; r = -0.213), altruism ($p \leq 0.000$**; r = -0.219), physical prowess ($p \leq 0.000$**; r = -0.239), risk ($p \leq 0.000$**; r = -0.222) and spirituality ($p \leq 0.000$**; r = -0.256).

Because of the large amount of information, the data were reduced by categorising the 22 work values into four categories (Ros et al. [1999] recommend that data be reduced when there is a large amount of information), on the basis of the factor analysis results reported on in the methodology section. The factor analysis results indicated the presence of four factors. The four dimensions of work values were extrinsic, intrinsic, social and power values. The category of intrinsic work values consisted of ability utilisation, achievement, creativity, own lifestyle, personal development, spirituality and variety. The extrinsic work values category included advancement, aesthetics, economic rewards, economic security, physical activities, physical prowess, risk and agreeable working conditions. The social work values category consisted of altruism, cultural identity, social interaction and social relationships. Lastly, the power work values category included authority, autonomy and prestige. The reliability for the total scale was 0.88, while the reliability for the four dimensions of work values was as follows: α = 0.86 (intrinsic work values), α = 0.78 (extrinsic work values), α = 0.70 (social work values), and α = 0.66 (power work values).

The results of the Pearson product-moment correlations for the four dimensions of work values and the seven work ethics subscales are depicted in Table 4.

As can be seen from Table 4, most of the work ethics dimensions exhibited medium to strong correlations with each other, with the exception of the dimension of leisure. Leisure did not correlate with hard work, centrality of work and wasted time. These results can be expected. The four dimensions of work values displayed strong positive relationships with each other. For example, extrinsic and intrinsic work values were found to intercorrelate, with an r-value of 0.735, which indicates a strong positive relationship (Pallant, 2011), and the relationship was statistically significant, on the 99th percentile. There was also a strong positive correlation between power work values and intrinsic work values (r = 0.703; $p \leq 0.000$**). It is interesting to note that the four dimensions of work values correlated negatively

TABLE 4: Pearson product-moment correlations between measures of work values and work ethics.

Subscale	1	2	3	4	5	6	7	8	9	10	11
Self-reliance (1)	-	-	-	-	-	-	-	-	-	-	-
Morality/ethics (2)	r = 0.453 p = 0.000**	-	-	-	-	-	-	-	-	-	-
Leisure (3)	r = 0.364 p = 0.000**	r = 0.347 p = 0.000**	-	-	-	-	-	-	-	-	-
Hard work (4)	r = 0.492 p = 0.000**	r = 0.368 p = 0.000**	r = 0.023 p = 0.692	-	-	-	-	-	-	-	-
Centrality of work (5)	r = 0.304 p = 0.000**	r = 0.331 p = 0.000**	r = −0.109 p = 0.059	r = 0.431 p = 0.000**	-	-	-	-	-	-	-
Wasted time (6)	r = 0.345 p = 0.000**	r = 0.368 p = 0.000**	r = −0.077 p = 0.186	r = 0.511 p = 0.000**	r = 0.691 p = 0.000**	-	-	-	-	-	-
Delay of gratification (7)	r = 0.375 p = 0.000**	r = 0.395 p = 0.000**	r = 0.124 p = 0.031*	r = 0.504 p = 0.031*	r = 0.513 p = 0.000**	r = 0.593 p = 0.000**	-	-	-	-	-
Intrinsic work values (8)	r = −0.164 p = 0.004**	r = −0.159 p = 0.006**	r = −0.124 p = 0.524	r = −0.299 p = 0.000**	r = −0.152 p = 0.008**	r = −0.156 p = 0.007**	r = −0.180 p = 0.002**	-	-	-	-
Extrinsic work values (9)	r = −0.181 p = 0.002**	r = −0.156 p = 0.007**	r = −0.138 p = 0.017*	r = −0.210 p = 0.000**	r = −0.245 p = 0.000**	r = −0.182 p = 0.002**	r = −0.242 p = 0.000**	r = 0.73 p = 0.000**	-	-	-
Social work values (10)	r = −0.119 p = 0.038*	r = −0.219 p = 0.000**	r = −0.195 p = 0.001**	r = −0.158 p = 0.006**	r = −0.197 p = 0.001**	r = −0.150 p = 0.009**	r = −0.224 p = 0.000**	r = 0.633 p = 0.000**	r = 0.648 p = 0.000**	-	-
Power work values (11)	r = −0.200 p = 0.000**	r = −0.132 p = 0.022*	r = −0.185 p = 0.001**	r = −0.177 p = 0.002**	r = −0.054 p = 0.351	r = −0.039 p = 0.503	r = −0.116 p = 0.044*	r = 0.703 p = 0.000**	r = 0.666 p = 0.000**	r = 0.540 p = 0.000**	-

*$p \leq 0.05$; **$p \leq 0.01$ (two-tailed).

with the seven dimensions of work ethics. This means that if work values increase, there is a decrease in work ethics, and vice versa. The correlations were mostly weak. For example, there was a weak negative relationship between power work values and self-reliance, as is evident from the *r*-value of -0.200. However, the relationship was statistically significant, on the 99th percentile.

Multiple regression analysis

Multiple regression analysis was conducted to investigate the multivariate relationship between the independent variable of work ethics and the dependent variables of intrinsic work values, extrinsic work values, social work values, and power work values. It was hypothesised that work ethics statistically significantly predict the various work values, as stated above. The results of the multiple regression analysis are presented in Table 5.

The results presented in Table 5 indicate that work ethics predicted 5.7% of the variance in intrinsic work values, as is evident from the multiple R^2-value of 0.057 (β = -0.239; p = 0.000**). In addition, work ethics was responsible for 8.7% of the variance in extrinsic work values (multiple R^2 = 0.087; β = -0.296; p = 0.000**), 7.9% of the variance in social work values (multiple R^2 = 0.079; β = -0.280; p = 0.000*), and 4.3% of the variance in power work values (multiple R^2 = 0.043; β = -0.207; p = 0.000*). The relationship was statistically significant, as the *p*-values were all less than 0.01, which indicates statistical significance, on the 99th percentile. The negative coefficient implied that positive work ethics will most probably result in negative work values in an organisation. The results provide support for the assumption that there is a significant relationship between work ethics and work values in respondents included in the sample.

Discussion

Outline of results

The findings suggest that not all the work values that were measured were highly regarded by respondents. This is evident from the fact that respondents had positive scores on only 6 of the 22 work values measured, namely authority, creativity, economic security, prestige, risk and social relationships. It is somewhat unusual for employees to value both authority and social relationships, because authority is positively related to Machiavellianism, which is regarded as an antisocial interpersonal style associated with strategic manipulation (Niemi & Young, 2013). Palmer (1983) offers a similar argument, when she states that authority is associated with power (i.e. the capacity to control the behaviour of others), which impedes helping or caring relationships. Furthermore, while people often gain power through traits and actions such as empathy, collaboration, openness, fairness, and sharing, once they wield power, they are more likely to engage in rude, selfish, and unethical behaviour (Keltner, 2016).

In terms of work ethics, respondents had positive scores on all seven dimensions of work ethics that were measured, namely self-reliance, morality/ethics, leisure, hard work, centrality of work, wasted time and delay of gratification. This shows that the PWE is still relevant. Having said this though, the majority of the sample was African (91.4%), and African values include being a good member of the community, living and enjoying life, belonging to a group, group recognition, accountability towards the community and 'ubuntu' (the belief that a person is only a person through their relations with other people) (Du Plessis & Rousseau, 2005). In contrast with traditional African values, European (or Western) values focus more on individualism, materialism, achievement, success, self-reliance, self-interest,

TABLE 5: Multiple regression analysis results.

Dependent variable	Item	Unstandardised regression coefficient	Beta (ß)	Std error of coefficient	t (301)	p	Value
Intrinsic work values	Intercept	132.012	-	4.176	31.609	0.000**	-
	Work ethics	-0.126	-0.239	0.030	-4.254	0.000**	-
	Multiple R	-	-	-	-	-	0.239
	Multiple R^2	-	-	-	-	-	0.057
	Adjusted R^2	-	-	-	-	-	0.054
	F-value	-	-	-	-	-	18.10
	p-value	-	-	-	-	-	0.000**
	Std error of estimate	-	-	-	-	-	12.527
Extrinsic work values	Intercept	146.336	-	4.555	3.129	0.000**	-
	Work ethics	-0.172	-0.296	0.032	-5.354	0.000**	-
	Multiple R	-	-	-	-	-	0.296
	Multiple R^2	-	-	-	-	-	0.087
	Adjusted R^2	-	-	-	-	-	0.084
	F-value	-	-	-	-	-	28.668
	p-value	-	-	-	-	-	0.000**
	Std error of estimate	-	-	-	-	-	13.661
Social work values	Intercept	146.336	-	2.760	26.416	0.000**	-
	Work ethics	-0.172	-0.296	0.020	-5.053	0.000**	-
	Multiple R	-	-	-	-	-	0.280
	Multiple R^2	-	-	-	-	-	0.079
	Adjusted R^2	-	-	-	-	-	0.076
	F-value	-	-	-	-	-	25.531
	p-value	-	-	-	-	-	0.000**
	Std error of estimate	-	-	-	-	-	8.278
Power work values	Intercept	52.723	-	2.193	24.040	0.000**	-
	Work ethics	-0.057	-0.207	0.015	-3.666	0.000**	-
	Multiple R	-	-	-	-	-	0.207
	Multiple R^2	-	-	-	-	-	0.043
	Adjusted R^2	-	-	-	-	-	0.040
	F-value	-	-	-	-	-	13.441
	p-value	-	-	-	-	-	0.000**
	Std error of estimate	-	-	-	-	-	6.578

$n = 301$; $^{**}p \leq 0.01$.

self-confidence, self-esteem and self-fulfilment, which have a PWE undertone (Du Plessis & Rousseau, 2005). One may argue that Africans have had to conform to and adopt Western values, which are subscribed to in many South African organisations, to be recognised and rewarded in these workplaces, and that this may consequently influence their ethical behaviour.

In terms of the specific dimensions of work values that were measured, valuing delay of gratification may show that individuals are becoming increasingly concerned about the future, as a result of the global and national economic decline. Showing high regard for self-reliance and hard work in a capitalist country, such as South Africa, is not surprising, as capitalism promotes and rewards individualism. Despite centrality of work and hard work being held in high regard by the sample, leisure and wasted time were also regarded as important. This shows that although the sample values work and working hard, they also enjoy spending time on personal activities that are meaningful, pleasurable and relaxing.

The positive scores on morality or ethics are surprising, but pleasing if one considers that ethics and morality are essential to make ethical decisions and uphold moral behaviour in the workplace (Bowden & Smythe, 2008; Bowen, 2005). Furthermore, it would seem that ethics and morality are particularly important in a country such as South Africa, where societal and business leaders are increasingly encountering unethical behaviour. Therefore, creating strong ethical organisational cultures is necessary to support ethical behaviour. In addition, employees need to be coached by mentors in morality and/or ethics, so as to create a common understanding thereof. In a study by McManus and Subramaniam (2009), it was found that unethical behaviour is affected by mentoring support and the perceived standard of ethical conduct by peers. Similarly, new employees entering the workplace need to be coached during induction programmes, so as to preserve strong ethical organisational cultures, which are embraced by all organisational members.

The initial correlation coefficient indicated various intercorrelations ranging from strong (e.g. between achievement and ability utilisation – $r = 0.73$; $p \leq 0.000$) to weak (e.g. between economic rewards and altruism – $r = 0.217$; $p \leq 0.000$). To reduce the large amount of data, the 22 work values were categorised into four overarching values, namely extrinsic, intrinsic, social and power work values. A second Pearson product-moment correlation revealed a weak negative correlation between the four work values and the seven dimensions of work ethics. Despite the weakness of the relationship, the p-value did indicate statistical significance. The aforementioned finding confirms

Schwartz and Bilsky's (1990) finding that there is a correlation between work ethics and work values. Similarly, Quesenberry et al. (2013), Richards et al. (2002), and Wittmer (2000) found that work ethics (i.e. ethical perception, and intention to do the ethical thing) correlated with work values (i.e. overt behaviour), while Tang (1990), as cited in Mann et al. (2013), reported a small but significant correlation between work ethics and intrinsic work values. However, the direction of the relationship was not mentioned.

The results from the regression analysis confirm negative statistically significant relationships between work ethics and the four dimension of work values. It should, however, also be noted that the respondents did not place a high value on the work values measured, which may have influenced the results. As far as could be established, this finding has not been reported before. Based on the results discussed, the formulated hypothesis, namely that work ethics statistically significantly predict work values, is accepted.

Practical implications

In order to preserve strong ethical organisational cultures, which are embraced by all organisational members, new employees entering the workplace need to be coached during induction programmes. Moreover, to avoid current employees from engaging in unethical behaviour when appointed in positions of power, it is important to create greater self-awareness, through reflection and engaging in spiritual practices, to develop mindfulness (Keltner, 2016). Furthermore, South African organisations need to consider whether current human resource practices and interventions are still relevant and supportive of the personal values that are subscribed to by the majority of the population. The results also imply that human resource specialists need to consider creative initiatives that will advance the work-life balance of employees.

Limitations and recommendations

The following caveats are made. First, the study was cross-sectional, and data were collected at a specific point in time. In addition, the study was localised, and a non-probability sampling technique was used to generate the sample. As a result, the external validity of the research may be compromised. Caution is advised when generalising the findings to a larger population. Because the research was only conducted in one geographical area in South Africa, it is recommended that the study be replicated nationally.

Conclusion

As a result of the proliferation of unethical behaviour, and the concomitant decline in work ethics, there is renewed interest in work ethics. However, the contemporary construct of work ethics is based on outdated theories and measuring instruments, which may not be relevant in the current workforce, which is characterised by continual change. In addition, the PWE may not be relevant to the African context. Furthermore, studying behavioural intent (i.e. work ethics) in isolation from overt behaviour (i.e. work values) may not result in the envisioned change. Based on the results, and particularly as the respondents did not score high on the measured work values, it is recommended that future research should focus not only on work ethics but also on the relationship between work ethics and work values. Thus, it could be concluded that respondents may have the intention to exhibit ethical behaviour, but that this behavioural intent does not seem to find expression in overt behaviour. Therefore, it is important to continue research regarding ethical behavioural intent, since behavioural intent predicts actual behaviour. Future research studies could focus on the relationship between cognitive moral development and behavioural control of employees, and the various individual characteristics and situational factors that may possibly influence this relationship.

Acknowledgements

This article was language-edited by a freelance language editor, Anthony Sparg. He has edited several academic journal articles and master's theses in the discipline of human resource management. He has an MA cum laude in African Languages (isiXhosa), an MA cum laude in Linguistics and a Higher Diploma in Education.

Competing interests

The authors declare that they have no financial or personal relationships that may have inappropriately influenced them in writing this article.

Authors' contributions

P.J., F.v.d.W. and N.S. were equally responsible for the research project, all contributing towards the literature review, data analysis and data interpretation.

References

Abd-El-Fattah, S.M., & AL-Nabhani, H.Z. (2012). From self-theories of intelligence to academic delay of gratification: The mediating role of achievement goals. *Australian Journal of Educational and Developmental Psychology, 12*, 93–107.

Bergh, Z., & Theron, A. (2009). *Psychology in the work context*. (4th edn.). Cape Town: Oxford University Press.

Boonzaier, A. (2008). *The influence of transactional, transformational leadership on leader-follower value congruence and leadership success*. Unpublished master's thesis, University of Stellenbosch, Stellenbosch.

Boshoff, E., & Van Zyl, E.S. (2011). The relationship between locus of control and ethical behaviour among employees in the financial sector. *Koers, 76*(2), 283–303. https://doi.org/10.4102/koers.v76i2.17

Bowden, P., & Smythe, V. (2008). Theories on teaching & training in ethics. *EJBO – Electronic Journal of Business Ethics and Organization Studies, 13*(2), 19–26.

Bowen, S.A. (2005). A practical model for ethical decision making in issues management and public relations. *Journal of Public Relations Research, 17*(3), 191–216. https://doi.org/10.1207/s1532754xjprr1703_1

Chidi, O.C., Ogunyomi, O.P., & Badejo, A.E. (2012). Promoting ethical human resource management practices in work organisations in Nigeria: Roles of HR professionals. *International Journal of Human Resource Studies, 2*(2), 116–131.

Chun, S., Lee, Y., Kim, B., & Heo, J. (2012). The impact of leisure participation and leisure satisfaction on stress-related growth. *Leisure Sciences, 34*(5), 436–449. https://doi.org/10.1080/01490400.2012.714704

Cogin, J. (2012). Are generational differences in work values fact or fiction? Multi-country evidence and implications. *The International Journal of Human Resource Management, 23*(11), 2268–2294. https://doi.org/10.1080/09585192.2011.610967

Cokley, K., Komarraju, M., Pickett, R., Shen, F., Patel, N., Belur, V. et al., (2007). Ethnic differences in endorsement of the Protestant work ethic: The role of ethnic identity and perceptions of social class. *The Journal of Social Psychology, 147*(1), 75–89. https://doi.org/10.3200/SOCP.147.1.75-89

Du Plessis, P.J., & Rousseau, G.G. (2005). *Buyer behaviour: A multi-cultural approach*. (3rd edn.). Oxford: Oxford University Press.

Dwyer, T. (2012). *Legal and ethical issues in the media*. Basingstoke, UK: Palgrave Macmillan.

Hattrup, K., Mueller, K., & Joens, I. (2007). The effects of nations and organizations on work value importance: A cross-cultural investigation. *Applied Psychology: An International Review, 56*(3), 479–499. https://doi.org/10.1111/j.1464-0597.2007.00268.x

Hirschi, A. (2010). Positive adolescent career development: The role of intrinsic and extrinsic work values. *Career Development Quarterly, 58*(3), 276–287. https://doi.org/10.1002/j.2161-0045.2010.tb00193.x

Ho, C.-C. (2006). *A study of the relationships between work values, job involvement and organisational commitment among Taiwanese nurses*. Unpublished doctoral thesis, Queensland University of Technology, Australia.

Horman, M.J., & Kenley, R. (2005). Quantifying levels of wasted time in construction with meta-analysis. *Journal of Construction Engineering and Management, 131*(1), 52–61. https://doi.org/10.1061/(ASCE)0733-9364(2005)131:1(52)

Ivaniš, M., & Šturlić, R.M. (2016). Influence of managers personal values and ethical behaviour on business success of hotel entrepreneurs. In *Tourism & Hospitality Industry Conference Proceedings*, 28–29 April 2016 (pp. 80–94). Opatija, Croatia.

Jafarkarimi, H., Saadatdoost, R., Sim, A.T.H., & Hee, J.M. (2016). Behavioral intention in social networking sites ethical dilemmas: An extended model based on theory of planned behavior. *Computers in Human Behavior, 62*, 545–561. https://doi.org/10.1016/j.chb.2016.04.024

Jones, W.T., Sontag, F., Beckner, M.O., & Fogelin, R.J. (1977). *Approaches to ethics*. (3rd edn.). New York: McGraw-Hill.

Jordan, P.J., Werner, A., & Venter, D. (2015). Achieving excellence in private intensive care units: The effect of transformational leadership and organisational culture on organisational change outcomes. *South African Journal of Human Resource Management, 13*(1), Art. #707, 1–10. https://doi.org/10.4102/sajhrm.v13i1.707

Keltner, D. (2016, October 1). Managing yourself: Don't let power corrupt you. *Harvard Business Review*, 1 October, pp. 112–115.

Kurland, N.B. (1995). Ethical intentions and the theories of reasoned action and planned behavior. *Journal of Applied Social Psychology, 25*(4), 297–313. https://doi.org/10.1111/j.1559-1816.1995.tb02393.x

Langley, R., Du Toit, R., & Herbst, D.L. (1992). *Manual for the Values Scale (VS)*. Pretoria: Human Sciences Research Council.

Leedy, P.D., & Ormrod, J.E. (2013). *Practical research: Planning and design*. (10th edn.). Upper Saddle River, NJ: Pearson Education.

Liu, Y., & Lei, Y. (2012). The connotation of work values: A preliminary review. *Asian Social Science, 8*(1), 47–53.

Mann, M.J., Taber, T.D., & Haywood, K.J. (2013). Work ethics revisited: Identification and operationalising new dimensions of work ethic a century after Weber. *Journal of Business Discipline, 11*(1), 65–101.

McManus, L., & Subramaniam, N. (2009). Ethical evaluations and behavioural intentions of early career accountants: The impact of mentors, peers and individual attributes. *Accounting & Finance, 49*(3), 619–643. https://doi.org/10.1111/j.1467-629X.2009.00301.x

Melden, A.I. (1967). *Ethical theories: A book of readings*. Englewood Cliffs, NJ: Prentice-Hall.

Miller, M.J., Woehr, D.J., & Hudspeth, N. (2002). The meaning and measurement of work ethic: Construction and initial validation of a multidimensional inventory. *Journal of Vocational Behavior, 60*(3), 451–489. https://doi.org/10.1006/jvbe.2001.1838

Montgomery, W. (2011). *Human value structure and emotions*. Dissertation. Göteborg, Sweden: Department of Psychology, University of Gothenburg.

Niemi, L., & Young, L. (2013). Caring across boundaries versus keeping boundaries intact: Links between moral values and interpersonal orientations. *PLoS One, 8*(12), 1–12. https://doi.org/10.1371/journal.pone.0081605

Nord, W.R., Brief, A.P., Atieh, J.M., & Doherty, E.M. (1990). Studying meanings of work: The case of work values. In A. Brief & W. Nord (Eds.), *Meanings of occupational work: A collection of essays*. Lexington, KY: Lexington Books.

O'connor, J.P., & Kinnane, J.F. (1961). A factor analysis of work values. *Journal of Counseling Psychology, 8*(3), 263–267. https://doi.org/10.1037/h0047440

Pallant, J. (2011). *SPSS survival manual: A step by step guide to data analysis using SPSS*. (4th edn.). Canberra, Australia: Allen & Unwin.

Palmer, S.E. (1983). Authority: An essential part of practice. *Social Work: A Journal of the National Association of Social Workers, 28*(2), 120–125.

Patel, K. (2013, December 05). Analysis: Perceptions and reality of corruption in South Africa. *Daily Maverick*. Retrieved August 13, 2014, from http://www.dailymaverick.co.za/article/2013-12-05-analysis-perceptions-and-reality-of-corruption-in-south-africa/#.U-tpt-OSySo

Pek, C.-K., Lim, Y.-M., & Yee, A.-P. (2008). Work values of baby-boomers and generation X of the Chinese community in Malaysia. *International Journal of Business and Management, 3*(10), 147–153.

PwC. (2016). *Global Economic Crime Survey 2016*. (5th South African edn.). Retrieved October 15, 2016, from http://www.pwc.co.za/en/assets/pdf/south-african-crime-survey-2016.pdf

Quesenberry, L., Woodburne, P.R., & Yang, C. (2013). Assessment of ethical reasoning at a public university. *Journal of Business Disciplines, 11*(1), 1–36.

Quick, J.C., & Nelson, D.L. (2011). *Principles of organizational behavior: Realities and challenges*. (7th edn.). Mason, OH: South-Western.

Ravangard, R., Sajjadnia, Z., Jafari, A., Shahsavan, N., Bahmaie, J., & Bahadori, M. (2014). The association between work ethics and attitudes towards organizational changes among the administrative, financial and support employees of general teaching hospitals. *Journal of Medical Ethics and History of Medicine, 7*(12), 1–9.

Richards, C.H., Gilbert, J., & Harris, J.R. (2002). Assessing ethics education needs in the MBA program. *Teaching Business Ethics, 6*(4), 447–476. https://doi.org/10.1023/A:1021183009537

Rogojan, P.T. (2009). *Deviant workplace behavior in organizations: Antecedents, influences and remedies*. Master's dissertation, University Wien, Austria.

Rohan, M.J. (2000). A rose by any name? The values construct. *Personality and Social Psychology Review, 4*, 255–277.

Ros, M., Schwartz, S.H., & Surkiss, S. (1999). Basic individual values, work values, and the meaning of work. *Applied Psychology: An International Review, 48*(1), 49–71. https://doi.org/10.1111/j.1464-0597.1999.tb00048.x

Salamzadeh, Y., Nejati, M., & Salamzadeh, A. (2014). Agility path through work values in knowledge-based organizations: A study of virtual universities. *Innovar, 24*(53), 177–186. https://doi.org/10.15446/innovar.v24n53.43942

Salkind, N.J. (Ed.). (2012). *Exploring research*. (8th edn.). New York: Pearson.

Schreuder, A.M.G., & Coetzee, M. (2011). *Careers: An organisational perspective*. (4th edn.). Cape Town: Juta.

Schwartz, S.H., & Bilsky, W. (1990). Toward a theory of the universal content and structure of values: Extensions and cross-cultural replications. *Journal of Personality and Social Psychology, 58*(5), 878–891. https://doi.org/10.1037/0022-3514.58.5.878

Sergio, R.P., Dungca, A.L., & Ormita, L.A.G-L. (2015). The demographic variables and emotional intelligence as correlates of work values: A cross-cultural examination towards organizational change. *Journal of Economics, Business and Management, 3*(2), 167–175. https://doi.org/10.7763/JOEBM.2015.V3.175

Steyn, C., & Kotze, H. (2004). Work value change in South Africa between 1995 and 2001: Race, gender and occupations compared. *South African Journal of Labour Relations, 28*(1), 4–33.

Stones, C.R., & Philbrick, J.L. (2001). Work attitudes among a sample of Black South African students. *The Journal of Social Psychology, 132*(2), 281–284. https://doi.org/10.1080/00224545.1992.9922984

Tang, T.L.-P. (1990). Factors affecting intrinsic motivation among university students in Taiwan. *The Journal of Social Psychology, 130*(2), 219–230. https://doi.org/10.1080/00224545.1990.9924572

Twenge, J.M., Campbell, S.M., Hoffman, B.J., & Lance, C.E. (2010). Generational differences in work values: Leisure and extrinsic values increasing, social and intrinsic values decreasing. *Journal of Management, 36*(5), 1117–1142. https://doi.org/10.1177/0149206309352246

Uçanok, B. (2008). The effects of work values, work-value congruence and work centrality on organizational citizenship behavior. *International Journal of Behavioral, Cognitive, Educational and Psychological Sciences, 1*(1), 1–14.

Ueda, Y., & Ohzono, Y. (2013). Differences in work values by gender, marital status, and generation: An analysis of data collected from "Working Persons Survey, 2010." *International Journal of Human Resource Studies, 3*(2), 28–41. https://doi.org/10.5296/ijhrs.v3i2.3131

Van der Walt, F., & De Klerk, J.J. (2015). The experience of spirituality in a multicultural and diverse environment. *Journal of Asian and African Studies, 14*(4), 253–288. https://doi.org/10.1163/15692108-12341346

Van der Walt, F., Jonck P., & Sobayeni, N.C. (2016). Work ethics of different generational cohorts in South Africa. *African Journal of Business Ethics, 10*(1), 52–66.

Van Ness, R.K., Melinsky, K., Buff, C.L., & Seifert, C.F. (2010). Work ethic: Do new employees mean new work values? *Journal of Managerial Issues, 22*(1), 10–34.

Van Vuuren, L.J. (2002). Institutionalising business ethics: A multi-level ethics strategy. *Management Dynamics, 2*(2), 21–27.

Vyas-Doorgapersad, S. 2007. Corruption in the public sector: A comparative analysis. *Journal of Public Administration, 42*(5), 285–299.

Wagner, C., Kawulich, B., & Garner, M. (Eds.). (2012). *Doing social research: A global context*. Maidenhead, UK: McGraw-Hill Higher Education.

Wils, T., Saba, T., Waxin, M.-F., & Labelle, C. (2011). Intergenerational and intercultural differences in work values in Quebec and the United Arab Emirates. *Industrial Relations, 66*(3), 445–469. https://doi.org/10.7202/1006347ar

Wittmer, D.P. (2000). Ethical sensitivity in management decisions: Developing and testing a perceptual measure among management and professional student groups. *Teaching Business Ethics, 4*(2), 181–205. https://doi.org/10.1023/A:1009866315139

Wong, S.-W., & Yuen, M. (2015). Super's work value inventory: Issues of subtest internal consistency using a Chinese university student sample in Hong Kong. *Journal of Employment Counseling, 52*(1), 29–35. https://doi.org/10.1002/j.2161-1920.2015.00054.x

10

The mediation role of motivation between leadership and public sector performance

Authors:
Dzivhuluwani Mavhungu[1]
Mark H.R. Bussin[1]

Affiliations:
[1]Department of Industrial Psychology and People Management, University of Johannesburg, South Africa

Corresponding author:
Mark Bussin,
drbussin@mweb.co.za

Orientation: As a result of poor performance in 2013, five departments in the Limpopo province were placed under administration in terms of Section 100 (1) (b) of the Constitution of the Republic of South Africa.

Research purpose: The main purpose of this study was to investigate the importance of the individual level of performance when diagnosing performance issues in the public sector by focusing on the mediatory role of motivation in the relationship between leadership and public sector performance.

Motivation for the study: The diagnosis conducted focused more on the analysis of administrative and operational systems. The solutions were based on normalising financial statements and systems to improve performance.

Research design, approach and method: The study took a positivist approach as the philosophy of the study. Using quantitative methods, a cross-sectional survey was used to collect data from 65 employees working in one of the departments that were affected by the intervention.

Main findings: The study confirmed the existence of a relationship between leadership and performance in the public sector. It was also found that Public Sector Motivation plays a mediatory role between Perceived Leadership Styles and Individual Job Performance.

Practical/managerial implications: The findings imply that it is important that the Limpopo Provincial Government makes an effort to employ and retain employees who are readily showing high levels of Public Sector Motivation.

Contribution or value additions: The study focused on an overlooked area in the study of performance in the public sector. The study was able to produce a tool that should be able to provide information to assist managers to make better performance improvement strategy decisions.

Introduction

Key focus of the study

There has been notable increase in the academic interest in Public Service Motivation in the last 12 years (Bozeman & Su, 2014; Van der Wal, 2014). Public Sector Motivation (PSM) has been generally defined by Paarlberg and Lavigna (2010) as:

> the beliefs, values, and attitudes that go beyond self-interest and organisational interest to energise employees to do good for others and to contribute to the well-being of organisations and society. (p. 710)

Scholars such as Moynihan and Pandey (2010) have linked general motivational levels that were a result of supportive and constructive leadership styles to superior organisational performance.

The individual and team performance of public sector employees, especially those who interact with the recipients of public sector services, is crucial as their level of performance is usually perceived as that of the entire public sector. In this regard, it also becomes crucially important that public sector policies and strategies be established and implemented to maximise public sector employee performance for the purpose of improving public service delivery.

Therefore, a public sector–based study covering three variables that contribute to organisational performance in the public sector; Perceived Leadership Styles, PSM and Individual Job Performance was deemed necessary for the purpose of improving the performance of individuals, teams and, consequently, the public sector output to society.

Background to the study

In 2013, five departments in the province were placed under administration in terms of Section 100 (1) (b) of The Constitution of the Republic of South Africa. This intervention was the result of poor performance in the financial administration and management functions within these departments.

The Section 100 (1) (b) national government intervention led to the conclusion that there were performance issues in the Limpopo province, specifically in the departments that were directly affected by administrative issues. The main problem lay in the diagnosis of performance problems and the solutions that were recommended based on the findings of the diagnostic investigations.

Neglecting the individual level of performance improvement, the diagnosis and both short-term recovery plans and long-term turn-around strategies prioritised the group processes and organisational levels of performance improvement.

The diagnosis process flows from the organisational to the individual performance improvement context (Ulrich, Brockbank, Johnson & Younger, 2009). It was found necessary, as suggested in Ulrich et al. (2009), to diagnose and improve performance at individual level by focusing on two psychological aspects that drive individuals' performance: their perceptions of their supervisors (Moynihan, Pandey, & Wright, 2011) and individual motivation levels (Hasnain, Manning & Pierskalla, 2014).

Trends from the research literature

In recent literature, performance has been explained as having a relationship with both leadership (Jacobsen & Andersen, 2014) and motivation (Belle, 2012). Experimental studies were also able to demonstrate the positive effect of Perceived Leadership Styles on employee motivation (Belle, 2013; Frey, Homberg & Osterloh, 2013; Hasnain et al., 2014; Paarlberg & Lavigna, 2010; Wright, Moynihan & Pandey, 2012).

However, public- and private-sector employees do not respond to the same motivation orientations (Frey et al., 2013). Public sector employees are intrinsically motivated, while private-sector employees are extrinsically motivated (Ritz, 2009). Thus, as noted, the dimensions of PSM possess elements that are similar to those of intrinsic motivation.

Research objectives

Voids and conflicts

The purpose of this section is to discuss voids and conflicts found in empirical and literature findings as per the three variables of the study.

Leadership and performance

In addition to the necessity to address the gap of a clear definition of public sector leadership concept, scholars also need to focus on engaging in comparative studies that compare public sector specific leadership dimensions in different countries that have different cultures and values (Tummers & Knies, 2014). This is important as the value of organisational support and Perceived Leadership Styles may differ from one country to another.

In a study of the effects of leadership styles and performance, Obiwuru, Okwu, Akpa and Nwankwere (2011) found a significant positive relationship between transactional leadership style and performance. The transactional leadership style was first defined in Burns (1978) as a style of leadership where the leader uses tangible rewards that are valued by followers to motivate them to achieve goals desired by the leader and subsequently by the organisation.

The transformational leadership style had a positive impact on performance, its effect was insignificant. The transformational leadership style is heavily based on trust between leaders and followers, which instils confidence that either party in the relationship knows and will do what is necessary to achieve success as defined by both parties (Schaubroek, Lam & Peng, 2011). Arham (2014) found contradictory results to those of Obiwuru et al. (2011), showing that transformational leadership style resulted in a more significant impact on performance than the transactional leadership style.

However, Bro et al. (2014) adopt an alternative stance to either of the authors just mentioned in that transactional and transformational leadership styles complement rather than oppose each other. When implemented simultaneously, the two leadership styles are capable of achieving higher performance than when one style is used and the other ignored.

Motivation and performance

In terms of PSM and context, Bozeman and Su (2014) share similar sentiments to those of Tummers and Knies (2014). Bozeman suggests environmental aspects such as individual attitudes and organisational socialisation should be considered when studying PSM. Furthermore, there is a need for experimental studies to reach heights that empirical studies in the field could not (Belle, 2012; Bozeman & Su, 2014).

Belle (2012) undertook an experimental study that measured the relationship between PSM and Individual Job Performance. The findings of Belle (2012) were that PSM which positively affected the Individual Job Performance of subordinates is manifested in their persistence, output, vigilance and productivity. Belle (2012) also reported that public sector employees are also likely to perform better at their job if their purpose is awakened by direct contact with the people that they serve.

However, contrary to the latter findings of Belle (2012), in their study of police, municipality, school, hospital and prison employees, Van Loon, Vandenabeele and Leisink (2015) established that higher PSM amongst employees whose jobs impacted directly on the society resulted in higher job burnout and lower and lower job satisfaction, especially in cases where they could not do much to impact or improve the situations of those that they serve.

Research problem and objectives

In light of the above voids and conflicts in the literature, the research problem and objectives are discussed below.

Research problem

It was believed that the general diagnosis of performance problems in the Limpopo province overlooked the individual level of performance improvement. It was therefore necessary to conduct a further diagnosis that focused specifically on the people factor of performance improvement in order to avoid future performance relapses.

Perceptions and motivation of employees are created by the leadership behaviours of their supervisors (Moynihan et al., 2011). Hence, it was proposed that at the individual level of performance, a diagnosis should be conducted by means of analysing the leadership styles of supervisors as perceived by their subordinates and, most importantly, the mediatory role played by the subordinate's levels of PSM in the relationship between Perceived Leadership Styles and Individual Job Performance in the public sector.

Objectives of the study

The objectives of the study were twofold. Each is briefly discussed below.

Theoretical objectives

The first objective was to find theoretical grounds to justify the relationship between the three broad variables of the study: leadership (independent variable), performance (dependent variable), and motivation (confounding variable) of the study. The aim was to test and have in place a theoretical model that diagnosed public sector performance issues at individual level.

Practical objectives

The primary objective was to bring about practical solutions to improve performance in the public sector by focusing on improving performance at the individual level of the performance improvement context. The purpose of the study was to be achieved when the study was able to provide people professionals in the field of performance management with a practical tool, in a form of a model and a set of questionnaires, which could be used to detect public sector performance issues at the individual level of the performance improvement context.

The potential value-add of the study

The potential value-add of the study was twofold. Each is discussed below.

Theoretical contribution

As mentioned by Hartog, Boselie and Paauwe (2004), the significance of Individual Job Performance for organisational success is in most cases assumed, rather than tested. Given that the majority of studies in the field of leadership, motivation and performance were conducted in American and European environments, the current study proposed to investigate the associations and relationships between the three variables of the current study using locally collected data that are influenced by the South African public sector environment.

The current study proposed a research agenda that was more specific regarding the factors that affect Individual Job Performance. The confirmed relationships between variables could then be used to solve practical performance issues in the South African public sector, especially at the individual level of performance.

Practical contribution

One of the most prominent challenges of performance improvement at individual level has been to establish how leaders and managers can manipulate employee motivation in order to foster greater organisational performance (Paarlberg & Lavigna, 2010). The current study therefore proposed a value-add in terms of practical solutions that would provide people management professionals and line-managers responsible for performance management with a framework that could be used to detect or diagnose Individual Job Performance issues at the individual level of performance.

In the sections below, the following three sections will be discussed; research design, results, and discussion. Firstly, the research design section will discuss the research approach, method, participants, procedure, measuring instruments, and statistical analysis of the study. Secondly, the results section will cover the descriptive statistics of the scales used in the study and inferential statistics relating to the hypotheses of the study. Thirdly, the discussion section will provide an overview of the study's main objectives and contributions, summary of literature and empirical findings, conclusions and recommendations, and limitations and of the study and suggestions for future research.

Synthesis and critical evaluation of literature

Leadership

In recent literature, leadership has been defined as a skill used by trusted leaders (Schaubroek et al., 2011), to influence followers within a specific context to achieve predetermined organisational goals by using transactional and transformational styles that depend on role expectations of leaders, followers and peers (Arham, 2014).

Leadership that is good, effective and efficient can have a positive impact on and improve organisational performance (Arham, 2014). Therefore, studying various leaders clears the path that leads to the understanding of the success of organisations, be these in the public or private sector. In a study of teacher performance in Danish schools, Jacobsen and Andersen (2014) reported a weak correlation between intended and perceived transformational and transactional leadership styles. However, the perceived transactional and transformational leadership styles were found to be related to performance.

Previous empirical and theoretical research has demonstrated that transactional and transformational leadership styles have an impact on employee motivation (Belle 2013; Hasnain et al., 2014). Motivation is accordingly discussed below.

Motivation

The quest to understand human motivation was initiated thousands of years ago by Greek philosophers who argued that the concept of motivation (Kanfer, 1990), which cannot be observed directly, was a driving force behind all human behaviours (Steers, Mowday & Shapiro, 2004).

Motivation levels of employees have been said to be the bridge through which leaders can influence the performance of individuals and subsequently of the organisation as a whole (Aslayed, Motaghi & Osman, 2012). Several studies have also explored the relationship and identified a link between the motivation levels of employees and their performance (Hasnain et al., 2014; Moynihan & Pandey, 2010).

However, a study that compared PSM research in Europe, the United States, and non-Western countries showed that theoretical and methodological approaches that are used in Western countries are at times not suited for non-Western contexts (Van der Wal, 2014).

The mediating role of Public Sector Motivation between Perceived Leadership Styles and Individual Job Performance

A number of previous empirical studies have demonstrated the relationship between PSM and both Perceived Leadership Styles (Belle, 2013; Frey et al., 2013; Hasnain et al., 2014; Houston, 2009; Paarlberg & Lavigna, 2010; Wright et al., 2012), as well as Individual Job Performance (Belle, 2012; Van Loon et al., 2015) in the public sector. However, there is not enough literature, to the researcher's knowledge, that investigated the PSM as a confounding variable in the relationship between the variables of Perceived Leadership Styles and Individual Job Performance.

Although previous studies have explored the relationship between PSM and the variables of Perceived Leadership Styles and Individual Job Performance, separately, Belle (2013) reported that PSM influenced the relationship between Perceived Leadership Styles and Individual Job Performance in the public sector.

Stating hypotheses

Hypothesis 1

Belle (2013), Frey et al. (2013), Hasnain et al. (2014), Paarlberg and Lavigna (2010), and Wright et al. (2012) have demonstrated, through experimental research, the positive effect of Perceived Leadership Styles on employee motivation. Thus the first hypothesis proposed was as follows:

- **Null Hypothesis 1:** There is no positive linear association between Perceived Leadership Styles and Public Sector Motivation.

Hypothesis 2

The second hypothesis was inspired by Belle (2012) who is convinced, based on experimental research findings, that the relationship between Public Service Motivation and employee performance is directly proportional. Therefore, the second hypothesis is summarised below:

- **Null Hypothesis 2:** There is no positive linear association between Public Sector Motivation and Individual Job Performance.

Hypothesis 3

In empirical studies conducted mainly in Western countries, Bro et al. (2014) and Jacobsen and Andersen (2014) found a relationship between leadership and public sector employee performance. Accordingly, this motivated the third hypothesis provided below:

- **Null Hypothesis 3:** There is no positive linear association between Perceived Leadership Styles and Individual Job Performance.

Hypothesis 4

The fourth hypothesis was proposed as a result of the empirical findings by Obiwuru et al. (2011) who are of the belief that transactional leadership behaviour leads to better performance in the public sector. The hypothesis is stated as follows:

- **Null Hypothesis 4:** Subordinates who perceive their supervisor's leadership style as dominantly transactional, have higher Individual Job Performance ratings compared to subordinates who perceive their supervisor's leadership styles as dominantly transformational.

Hypothesis 5

Based on the empirical findings of Arham (2014), who argues that transformational leadership behaviour is a reliable predictor of public sector performance, the fifth hypothesis reads as follows:

- **Null Hypothesis 5:** Subordinates who perceive their supervisors' leadership style as dominantly transformational show higher Individual Job Performance ratings compared to subordinates who perceive their supervisor's leadership style as dominantly transactional.

The research design is discussed below.

Research design

Research approach

The study took a positivist approach to be the philosophy of the study. The positivists approach is known to be objective in nature. With the objective nature of its premise, the positivist approach is aligned to quantitative methods (Collis & Hussey, 2014), which made it more suitable for the current study.

The premise of the positivist approach made it suitable for the study given that the ultimate methodological objective of the study was to use objectives-aligned statistical methods to test existing theory and hypotheses on the catalytic role of Public Service Motivation in the relationship between Perceived Leadership Styles and Individual Job Performance in the public sector.

Research method

With the assumption made in the research approach section above, quantitative methods were selected to also allow for the generalisation of findings to the population from which the sample under study was sourced, that is, the generalisation of findings from the sample to the population of the five Limpopo province departments which were placed under administration.

In addition to their explainable accurate and precise prediction of cause and effect between dependent and independent variables under study, quantitative methods are widely primarily hailed for their reliability and validity in measurement. Numerical data associated with the quantitative method can be obtained quickly, thus saving time and resources (Choy, 2014). Numerical data associated with the current study were obtained quickly by sending out short questionnaires that participants could complete in little time.

The premise of the positivist approach made it suitable for the study as this approach offered the opportunity to use statistical methods such as Spearman's correlation, partial correlation, and linear regression, to test existing theory and hypotheses on the mediatory role of PSM in the relationship between Perceived Leadership Styles and Individual Job Performance in the public sector.

Research participants

The population for the research was located in one of the 13 departments of the Limpopo Provincial Government of South Africa. The target organisation, as mentioned, was one of the five Limpopo province departments which were placed under administration in terms of Section 100 (1) (b) by the Cabinet of South Africa, making it a desirable location for the study.

Random sampling was adopted as the sampling design for the study. With the researcher using this design, all the members of the population had an equal opportunity of participating in the study (Collis & Hussey, 2014). With a sampling frame of 198 employees undertaking production and craft jobs, the targeted minimum sample size, as suggested by Collis and Hussey (2014), was 132 participants. The total sample size for the study was 65. The profile of the sample in terms of age, gender and years working in the public service is illustrated in frequency tables briefly discussed below. Firstly, the sample was classified in terms of the age of participants.

In Table 1, the largest number of participants, at 44.60%, were between the ages of 20 and 30. Forty per cent of participants were between the ages of 31 and 40, while 9.20% were between the ages of 41 and 50. Lastly, only 6.20% of the participants were of age 51 and above.

Secondly, the gender of the participants was also important for the study, thus being recorded in Table 2.

Table 2 shows the frequencies of participants' gender. The majority of participants were females at 50.80%, while the male gender represented 49.20% of the participants.

Thirdly, the participants were profiled in terms of their years of employment in the public sector.

Table 3 shows the profile of the participants in terms of their number of years in public sector employment. 73.80% of participants had worked for a period of 1–10 years in the public sector, while 21.50% had done so for 11–20 years. Only 3.10% of the participants had worked for this sector for 21–31 years, while a mere 1.50% had worked for 31 years and longer in it.

Measuring instruments

In addition to the collection of biographical data, two self-reporting instruments were used to collect data on Perceived Leadership Styles and Public Service Motivation. Each of these is briefly discussed below.

TABLE 1: Frequencies of participants' age.

Valid	Frequency	Per cent	Valid per cent	Cumulative per cent
20–30	29	44.60	44.60	44.60
31–40	26	40.00	40.00	84.60
41–50	6	9.20	9.20	93.80
51 and above	4	6.20	6.20	100.00
Total	**65**	**100.00**	**100.00**	-

TABLE 2: Frequencies of participants' gender.

Valid	Frequency	Per cent	Valid per cent	Cumulative per cent
Male	32	49.20	49.20	49.20
Female	33	50.80	50.80	100.00
Total	**65**	**100.00**	**100.00**	-

TABLE 3: Frequencies of participants' years of public service.

Valid	Frequency	Per cent	Valid per cent	Cumulative per cent
1–10	48	73.80	73.80	73.80
11–20	14	21.50	21.50	95.40
21–30	2	3.10	3.10	98.50
31 and above	1	1.50	1.50	100.00
Total	**65**	**100.00**	**100.00**	-

Leadership

To measure the Perceived Leadership Styles, the Multi-factor Leadership Questionnaire (MLQ) Form (5x-Short) was used. The MLQ (5x-Short), consisting of 45 items, was originally developed by Bass and Avollio (1995). With Cronbach's alpha values ranging between 0.89 and 0.95, the questionnaire was also employed in recent studies (Belle, 2013; Park & Rainey, 2007). The questionnaire was rated according to a 5-point Likert-scale ranging from 0 (not at all) to 4 (frequently if not always).

Motivation

For the purpose of the current study, the original PSM scale, which has been employed in similar recent studies (Belle, 2013; Moynihan & Pandey, 2010) with an overall Cronbach's alpha of 0.90, was used. The Cronbach's alpha for the four independent dimensions ranged between 0.69 and 0.74 (Perry, 1996). The 5-point Likert-scale ranged from 0 (not at all) to 4 (frequently if not always).

Research procedure

The study was conducted in one organisation, the Limpopo Provincial Treasury. Two instruments were combined into one questionnaire of two pages in length. Data were collected in two rounds. In the first round, the questionnaire was distributed to the entire sampling frame of 292 using the internal e-mailing system. For the second round, the hard copies of the questionnaire were printed and distributed to participants during arranged one-on-one meetings to improve the response rate. The completed copies of the questionnaires were collected and safely stored.

Statistical analysis

The Statistical Package for the Social Sciences (IBM SPSS Statistics 22) in consultation with the STATKON office at the University of Johannesburg, was employed to analyse the data from both the first and second rounds of data collection. The software was used so as to maximise accuracy and reliability of findings. It was utilised to generate the following groups of statistics.

Inferential statistics

Factor analysis

Factor analysis was made use of as a technique to reduce the number of items in the questionnaire, thus reducing the data to be collected for the study. Factor analysis summarises a large number of variables into smaller factors that are manageable (Pallant, 2013). Factor analysis was run to generate factor loadings that determined the correlations between the factors of each of the three variables, which were measured on rating scales.

Scale validity and reliability

Two of the variables of the study, Perceived Leadership Styles and PSM, were explanatory. Explanatory variables are abstract and contain hypothetical constructs that are not directly observable, thus providing ground for the necessity of validity and reliability tests (Collis & Hussey, 2014).

Validity testing was conducted to determine whether the instruments used in the study measured what they were intended to (Collis & Hussey, 2014). The said instruments were validated by previous extensive research conducted by Bass and Avolio (1995) and Perry (1996) and, as noted, measured Perceived Leadership Styles and PSM, respectively.

For the current study, Cronbach's alpha coefficients were generated to determine the internal reliability and inter-item correlations of each of the two multiple-item scales used in the study, the MLQ (5x-short) and PSM scale.

Descriptive statistics

Descriptive statistics allow for the measuring of central tendency, dispersion of data, and examination of frequency distributions (Collis & Hussey, 2014). For the purpose of the current study, descriptive statistics were generated to allow for the summarising of data into frequency tables of the biographical data collected.

Spearman's correlation

To measure the linear association between variables, the Spearman's correlation was utilised. This required the availability of non-parametric data for two variables collected using an interval, ratio or ordinal scale (Collis & Hussey, 2014). For the purpose of the current study, this technique was applied to measure the association between the independent variable of Perceived Leadership Styles and the dependent variable of Individual Job Performance.

Linear regression

Provided that there is a linear relationship between two variables under study, linear regression is employed to measure the extent to which the independent variable can predict the outcome of the dependent variable (Collis & Hussey, 2014). For the purpose of the current study, linear regression was generated to measure the ability of Perceived Leadership Styles and to predict the outcome of Individual Job Performance.

Partial correlation

The generation of partial correlation is necessary if there is a confounding variable that is suspected to be influencing the two variables that are of main interest. The variable can be statistically removed in order to determine the relationship between the two variables of interest with accuracy (Pallant, 2013). In the current study, PSM was identified and used as a confounding variable.

This variable was suspected to influence the relationship between Perceived Leadership Styles and Individual Job Performance. Thus, partial correlation was generated to control the impact of PSM on the relationship between Perceived Leadership Styles and Individual Job Performance.

Results

Descriptive and reliability statistics of scales

The results of the reliability tests for the two instruments used in the current study are discussed below.

Public Sector Motivation Scale

The reliability statistics of the Public Service Motivation Scale are shown in Table 4.

In the current study, as evident in Table 4, the overall Cronbach's alpha coefficient of the PSM scale with a total of 14 items and 4 dimensions is 0.46. The Cronbach's alpha coefficient failed to meet the minimum value of 0.70 for internal consistency as recommended by Pallant (2013).

Indeed, only one dimension of the scale met the conditions that are required for good internal consistency. The self-sacrifice dimension had a Cronbach's alpha coefficient of 0.71, while the other remaining three dimensions had coefficients that ranged from -0.23 to 0.63. The negative Cronbach's alpha value indicates a weak negative inter-item correlation between the items of the attraction to public policy variable. To address the weak internal consistency, the reliability analysis was rerun using the reverse-coding method.

However, even with the reverse-coding of the variable, the Cronbach's alpha value stayed the same at -0.23. For this reason, the attraction to public policy construct and its two items were discarded. The three constructs of self-sacrifice, compassion and commitment to public interest were retained.

Multi-factor Leadership Questionnaire

The reliability statistics of the MLQ are depicted in Table 5.

Table 5 illustrates the reliability statistics of the MLQ that consisted of a total of 22 items and 7 dimensions. The overall Cronbach's alpha coefficient was 0.73 which, according to Collis and Hussey (2014), means that the scale can produce reliable findings that are accurate and precise.

Three individual dimensions had a coefficient value of more than 0.8, exceeding the Cronbach's alpha coefficient recommended by Collis and Hussey (2014). The remaining individual four dimensions recorded coefficient values that ranged between 0.61 and 0.69, which is slightly lower than the minimum recommended Cronbach's alpha coefficient of 0.70 as recommended by Pallant (2013).

Inferential statistics

The purpose of this section is to test hypotheses using the correlation analysis method. The overall results of this analysis are found in Table 6.

The testing of hypotheses of the study is based on the correlation analysis results in Table 6. The subsections below highlight these results.

Hypothesis 1

Hypothesis 1 was tested using the correlation analysis of the association between Perceived Leadership Styles and PSM. The results are depicted in Table 7.

The results in Table 7 are based on Perceived Leadership Styles as an independent variable and PSM as a dependent variable. For a sample size of 65 participants, the results showed a correlation coefficient of 0.02 and a p-value of 0.89.

The findings of $r = 0.02$, $n = 65$, $p < 0.01$ indicate that there is a low positive correlation between Perceived Leadership Styles and PSM. However, the p-value of 0.89 indicates that the results are insignificant at the 1% level. Therefore, the researcher fails to reject the null hypothesis at $p \leq 0.01$ because of the results being insignificant at 1% significance level.

TABLE 4: Reliability statistics of the Public Sector Motivation scale.

Scale	Number of items	Cronbach's alpha
Self-sacrifice	3	0.71
Compassion	3	0.55
Commitment to public interest	3	0.63
Attraction to public policy	2	-0.23
Total	**14**	**0.46**

TABLE 5: Reliability statistics of the Multi-factor Leadership Questionnaire.

Scale	Number of items	Cronbach's alpha
Idealised influence	4	0.81
Individualised consideration	4	0.87
Inspirational motivation	2	0.61
Intellectual stimulation	4	0.67
Laissez–Faire leadership	2	0.83
Management by exception (active)	2	0.69
Management by exception (passive)	4	0.66
Total	**22**	**0.73**

TABLE 6: The overall correlation analysis of the three variables in the study.

Spearman's rho	Coefficient	Performance	Leadership	Motivation
Performance	Correlation coefficient	1.00	-0.040	0.14
	Sig. (2-tailed)	-	0.759	0.25
	N	65.00	65.000	65.00
Leadership	Correlation coefficient	-0.04	1.000	0.02
	Sig. (2-tailed)	0.76	-	0.89
	N	65.00	65.000	65.00
Motivation	Correlation coefficient	0.14	0.020	1.00
	Sig. (2-tailed)	0.25	0.890	-
	N	65.00	65.000	65.00

TABLE 7: Correlation analysis between Perceived Leadership Styles and Public Sector Motivation.

Spearman's rho	Coefficient	Motivation
Leadership	Correlation coefficient	0.02
	Sig. (2-tailed)	0.89
	N	65.00

Hypothesis 2

Hypothesis 2 was tested using the correlation analysis of the association between PSM and Individual Job Performance. The results of the analysis are reported in Table 8.

The results in Table 8 are based on PSM as an independent variable and individual performance as a dependent one. The results indicate a correlation coefficient of 0.14 and a *p*-value of 0.25.

The $r = 0.14$, $n = 65$, $p < 0.01$, indicate that there is a low positive correlation between Perceived Leadership Styles and PSM. However, the *p*-value of 0.25 means that one must fail to reject the null hypothesis at $p \leq 0.01$ as the results are insignificant at 1% significance level.

Hypothesis 3

Correlation analysis was used to test hypothesis 3 on the association between Perceived Leadership Styles and Individual Job Performance. The results are presented in Table 9.

The results depicted in Table 9 are based on leadership as an independent variable and individual performance as a dependent one for a sample size of 65 participants. The results yield a correlation coefficient of -0.04 and a *p*-value of 0.76.

The $r = -0.04$, $n = 65$, $p < 0.01$ means that there is a low negative correlation between Perceived Leadership Styles and Individual Job Performance. However, the *p*-value of 0.76 indicates that the results are insignificant at the 1% level. For this reason, the researcher fails to reject the null hypothesis at $p \leq 0.01$.

Hypothesis 4

Hypothesis 4 was tested using the correlation analysis of the association between transactional leadership and Individual Job Performance. Such leadership, as mentioned, is divided into three dimensions: management by passive exception (MEP), management by active exception (MEA), and contingent reward (Moynihan et al., 2011). For the purposes of the current study, only the dimensions MEP and MEA were combined to make up transactional leadership as shown in Table 10.

TABLE 8: Correlation analysis between Public Sector Motivation and Individual Job Performance.

Spearman's rho	Coefficient	Performance
Motivation	Correlation coefficient	0.14
	Sig. (2-tailed)	0.25
	N	65.00

TABLE 9: Correlation analysis between Perceived Leadership Styles and Individual Job Performance.

Spearman's rho	Coefficient	Performance
Leadership	Correlation coefficient	-0.04
	Sig. (2-tailed)	0.76
	N	65.00

The results of the analysis in Table 10 are such that transactional leadership is the independent variable and Individual Job Performance the dependent one. The correlation coefficient of transactional leadership is a combination of the correlation coefficients of MEP ($r = -0.03$, $p = 0.80$) and MEA ($r = -0.13$, $p = 0.31$). Thus, for a sample size of 65 participants, transactional leadership shows a correlation coefficient value of -0.22 and a *p*-value of 0.56.

The results of $r = -0.22$, $n = 65$, $p < 0.01$ indicate that there is a low negative correlation between the transactional leadership style and Individual Job Performance. The *p*-value of 0.56 indicates that the results are insignificant at the 1% level. Thus, the researcher fails to reject the null hypothesis at $p \leq 0.01$.

Hypothesis 5

Correlation analysis was again used to test hypothesis 5. The focus was to analyse the association between transformational leadership and Individual Job Performance. It has been pointed out that transformational leadership comprises four dimensions: inspirational motivation (IM), individualised consideration (IC), idealised influence (II), and intellectual stimulation (IS). The results of the analysis are provided in Table 11.

TABLE 10: Correlation analysis between transactional leadership and Individual Job Performance.

Spearman's rho	Coefficient	Performance
MEP	Correlation coefficient	-0.03
	Sig. (2-tailed)	0.80
	N	65.00
MEA	Correlation coefficient	-0.13
	Sig. (2-tailed)	0.31
	N	65.00
Transactional Leadership	Correlation coefficient	-0.22
	Sig. (2-tailed)	0.56
	N	65.00

MEP, management by passive exception; MEA, management by active exception.

TABLE 11: Correlation analysis between transformational leadership and Individual Job Performance.

Spearman's rho	Coefficient	Performance
II	Correlation coefficient	-0.10
	Sig. (2-tailed)	0.44
	N	65.00
IS	Correlation coefficient	-0.14
	Sig. (2-tailed)	0.28
	N	65.00
IM	Correlation coefficient	-0.04
	Sig. (2-tailed)	0.74
	N	65.00
IC	Correlation coefficient	-0.03
	Sig. (2-tailed)	0.81
	N	65.00
Transformational Leadership	Correlation coefficient	-0.08
	Sig. (2-tailed)	0.57
	N	65.00

II, idealised influence; IS, intellectual stimulation; IM, inspirational motivation; IC, individualised consideration.

The results in Table 11 are based on transformational leadership as an independent variable and Individual Job Performance as a dependent one. The transformational leadership correlation coefficient is a total combination of the correlation coefficients of II (r = -0.10, p = 0.44), IS (r = -0.14, p = 0.28), IM (r = -0.04, p = 0.74), IC (r = -0.03, p = 0.81). Thus, the results of transformational leadership are as follows: r = -0.08, p = 0.57, n = 65.

The r = -0.08, n = 65, $p < 0.01$ indicates a perceived low negative correlation between transformational leadership and Individual Job Performance. However, the p-value of 0.57 indicates that the results are insignificant at the 1% level. The p-value leads to the rejection of the null hypothesis at $p \leq 0.01$.

Discussion

The main objectives of the study

The objectives of the study were grouped into three categories: theoretical, methodological and practical.

Firstly, given that the majority of theory in the literature related to the problem statement of the current study stemmed mostly from Western countries, the main theoretical objective was to produce findings that would allow for the generation of theory which explained the relationship of the variables of the current study in a South African context.

Lastly, the practical objective was to produce findings that could be used on a daily basis by managers who sought to enhance the performance of the organisation through improving the Individual Job Performance of their subordinates.

The main contributions of the study

Theory

It will be recalled that the theoretical objective of the study was to investigate the theoretical relationship between Perceived Leadership Styles, PSM, and Individual Job Performance. The study was able to explore the relationship between Perceived Leadership Styles and PSM, and Individual Job Performance in the public sector. However, there was not enough previous literature that explicitly investigated PSM as a confounding variable in the relationship between Perceived Leadership Styles and Individual Job Performance in the public sector.

Therefore, the current study added value to theory in that its investigation focused on an overlooked area in the study of performance in the public sector, that is, the role of PSM as a confounding variable in the relationship between Perceived Leadership Styles and Individual Job Performance in the public sector.

Practice

The practical objective of the study was to contribute to public sector performance improvement by producing a framework that could be used to detect performance problems at the individual level.

The current study was able to meet the objective as it managed to produce a single questionnaire that could be used to measure how the Perceived Leadership Styles of supervisors may affect the Individual Job Performance of subordinates while taking into account the subordinate's PSM levels. The current study has added a practical value in that it was able to produce a tool that should be able to provide information to assist people professionals in the field of performance in the public sector to make better performance improvement strategy decisions.

Summary of results

The study consisted of five hypotheses which were informed by previous literature and empirical findings. The hypotheses and findings were as follows:

- **Null Hypothesis 1:** There is no positive linear association between Perceived Leadership Styles and Public Sector Motivation.
  - A low positive correlation was found between Perceived Leadership Styles and Public Service Motivation.
- **Null Hypothesis 2:** There is no positive linear association between Public Sector Motivation and Individual Job Performance.
  - The results showed that there was a low positive correlation between PSM and Individual Job Performance.
- **Null Hypothesis 3:** There is a no positive linear association between Perceived Leadership Styles and Individual Job Performance.
  - It was established that there was a low negative correlation between Perceived Leadership Styles and Individual Job Performance.
- **Null Hypothesis 4:** Subordinates who perceive their supervisor's leadership style as dominantly transactional, have higher Individual Job Performance ratings compared to subordinates who perceive their supervisor's leadership styles as dominantly transformational.
  - The results demonstrated a low negative correlation between transactional leadership style and Individual Job Performance.
- **Null Hypothesis 5:** Subordinates who perceive their supervisors' leadership style as dominantly transformational show higher Individual Job Performance ratings compared subordinates who perceive their supervisor's leadership style as dominantly transactional.
  - A low negative correlation was found between transformational leadership style and Individual Job Performance.

However, because of p values that were greater than 0.01, the five hypotheses were rejected at $p \leq 0.01$, and all the findings were insignificant at the 1% significance level.

Conclusion and recommendations

Perceived Leadership Styles versus Individual Job Performance

Both the literature review and empirical findings indicate that a correlational relationship exists between Perceived Leadership Styles and Individual Job Performance. However, the findings from the literature review show a positive correlation between the two variables while the empirical findings of the current study yield a negative correlation. Based on the findings from the literature review, it is concluded that employees who rate the leadership styles of their supervisors positively tend to exhibit high Individual Job Performance.

Therefore, it is recommended that to avoid future performance difficulties, the Limpopo Provincial Government should focus on the development of leadership competencies of managers and supervisors within their departments. Through customised Management Development Programmes, managers and supervisors must be made aware of the impact of their leadership styles on the performance of their subordinates.

Transactional and transformational leadership styles versus Individual Job Performance

Similar to the correlational findings of the relationship between Perceived Leadership Styles and Individual Job Performance, the breaking down of the Perceived Leadership Styles variable into transactional and transformational leadership styles in the current study pointed to conflicting findings from the literature review and the empirical research.

By means of establishing positive correlation coefficients, the reviewed literature indicated that the transformational leadership style had more impact, compared to the transactional leadership style, on Individual Job Performance. However, by means of determining a negative correlation coefficient, the empirical findings of the current study revealed that a transactional leadership style, as opposed to a transformational leadership style, had more impact on Individual Job Performance.

Based on both the literature and empirical findings, it is concluded that both transactional and transformational leadership styles have a role to play in inspiring greater Individual Job Performance. Thus, it is recommended that the Management Development Programmes which should be implemented to prevent future performance issues in the Limpopo Provincial Government should emphasise the importance of both transactional and transformational leadership styles.

Public Sector Motivation versus Individual Job Performance

The findings from the literature review indicated that high levels of PSM had a negative impact on Individual Job Performance. Because of undesirable working conditions and lack of resources, public sector employees with high levels of PSM are most likely to experience high stress levels, which then affect the execution of their tasks; thus, they perform poorly in their jobs. However, the empirical findings of the current study produced results that were opposite to those in the reviewed literature, in other words that PSM was positively correlated to Individual Job Performance.

Based on both the literature review and the empirical findings, it is concluded that PSM plays an important role in determining Individual Job Performance in the public sector. Therefore, it is recommended that the Limpopo Provincial Government should minimise the demotivation of public service employees by improving working conditions and the availability of resources, to allow public sector employees to be motivated to do their work more effectively.

Perceived Leadership Styles versus Public Sector Motivation

Both literature review and empirical findings are in line regarding the relationship between Perceived Leadership Styles and PSM. Both sets of findings showed a positive correlation between these variables.

Guided by both sets, it is concluded that high levels of PSM are likely to be witnessed in subordinates who perceive the leadership style of their supervisors positively. Therefore, it is recommended that the Limpopo Provincial Government should focus on developing leadership competencies of managers and supervisors within their departments for the purpose of evoking PSM in their subordinates. The existence and importance of PSM should be embedded in the recommended Management Development programme for managers and supervisors.

The mediatory role of Public Sector Motivation in the relationship between Perceived Leadership Styles and Individual Job Performance

Although previous studies have explored the relationship between PSM and the variables of Perceived Leadership Styles and Individual Job Performance, separately, Belle (2013) reported that PSM influenced the relationship between Perceived Leadership Styles and Individual Job Performance in the public sector. The empirical findings of the current study confirmed the findings in literature by demonstrating that PSM was indeed a confounding variable in the relationship between Perceived Leadership Styles and Individual Job Performance.

Based on both the empirical and literature review findings, it is concluded that PSM plays a mediatory role between Perceived Leadership Styles and Individual Job Performance. Therefore, it is important that the Limpopo Provincial Government makes an effort to employ and retain employees who are readily showing high levels of PSM. It is recommended that the Limpopo Provincial Government uses the Public Service Motivation Scale as an assessment to assist in the selection of new employees and retaining existing ones.

Limitations of the study

Both literature review and empirical findings of the study had contextual and applicability limits. The literature review findings, as acknowledged, were based on environmental contexts that were different from the local South African context, therefore making the applicability of such findings in the local context questionable. The majority of the empirical findings were insignificant at 1% significance level, consequently limiting the applicability of the findings in practice.

Suggestions for future research

The literature review findings reveal that more research is needed into the impact of PSM as a confounding variable in the relationship between Perceived Leadership Styles and Individual Job Performance, specifically in the public sectors of African countries. From an empirical finding's perspective, future research should ensure that the collected data are gathered from sample sizes that are congruent with the population under study. Larger samples will assist in boosting the significance and generalisability of findings. Future studies should also employ electronic means of collecting data to access larger numbers of participants.

Most importantly, future studies should use data collection instruments that are language-adapted to minimise any ambiguity of items and maximise the common understanding of such items by the targeted samples. The adaptation could also assist in maximising the questionnaire response rate of the studies.

Acknowledgements

Competing interests

The authors declare that they have no financial or personal relationships that may have inappropriately influenced them in writing this article.

Authors' contributions

The study was conducted by D.M. as part of his Master's thesis at the University of Johannesburg. M.H.R.B. was the supervisor and co-wrote the article.

References

Arham, A.F. (2014). Leadership and performance: The case of Malaysian SMEs in the service sector. *International Journal of Asian Social Science, 4*(3), 343–355.

Aslayed, A.K., Motaghi, M.H., & Osman, I.B. (2012). The use of the Multifactor Leadership Questionnaire and Communication Satisfaction Questionnaire in Palestine: A research note. *International Journal of Scientific and Research Publications, 2*(11), 1–9.

Bass, B.M., & Avolio, B.J. (1995). *MLQ Multi-leadership questionnaire*. Redwood City, CA: Mind Garden.

Belle, N. (2012). Experimental evidence on the relationship between Public Service Motivation and job performance. *Public Administration Review, 73*(1), 143–153. https://doi.org/10.1111/j.1540-6210.2012.02621.x

Belle, N. (2013). Leading to make a difference: A field experiment on the performance effects of transformational leadership, perceived social impact, and Public Service Motivation. *Journal of Public Administration Research and Theory Advance Access, 1*(1), 1–28.

Bozeman, B., & Su, X. (2014). Public Service Motivation concepts and theory: A critique. *Public Administration Review, 1*(1), 1–11.

Bro, L.L., Andersen, L.B., Bollingtoft, A., Eriksen, T., Holten, A., Jacobsen, C.B., et al. (2014). *Leadership training, leadership strategies and organisational performance: Designing an experiment to test the causal effect of leadership on performance*. Ottawa: Paper presented on the IRPSM conference.

Burns, J.M. (1978). *Leadership*. New York: Harper & Row.

Choy, L.T. (2014). The strengths and weaknesses of research methodology: Comparison and complimentary between qualitative and quantitative approaches. *Journal of Humanities and Social Science, 19*(04), 99–104.

Collis, J. & Hussey, R. (2014). Business research: A practical guide for undergraduate & postgraduate students. New York: Palgrave McMillan. https://doi.org/10.1007/978-1-137-03748-0

Frey, B.S., Homberg, F., & Osterloh, M. (2013). Organisational control systems and pay-for-performance in the public service. *Organisations Studies, 34*(7), 949–972. https://doi.org/10.1177/0170840613483655

Hartog, D.N., Boselie, P., & Paauwe, J. (2004). Performance management: A model and research agenda. *Journal of Economic Literature*, 1–21. Retrieved May 20, 2015, from http://www.scribd.com/doc/2530136/Hartog-D-N-Boselie-P-Paauwe-J-2004-Performance-management-A-model-and-research-agenda

Hasnain, Z., Manning, N., & Pierskalla, J.H. (2014). The promise of performance pay? Reasons for caution in policy prescriptions in the Core Civil Service. *International Bank for Reconstruction and Development, 29*, 1–30. https://doi.org/10.1093/wbro/lku001

Houston, D.J. (2009). Motivating knights or knaves? Moving beyond performance-related pay for the public sector. *Public Administration Review, 69*(1), 43–57.

Jacobsen, C.B., & Andersen, L.B. (2014). *Is leadership in the eye of the beholder? A study of intended and perceived leadership strategies and organisational performance*. Copenhagen: The Rockwool Foundation Research Unit.

Kanfer, R. (1990). *Motivation theory and industrial and organisational psychology*. Palp Alto: Consulting Psychologists Press.

Moynihan, D.P., & Pandey, S.K. (2010). The big question for performance management: Why do managers use performance information? *Journal of Public Administration Research and Theory, 20*, 849–866. https://doi.org/10.1093/jopart/muq004

Moynihan, D.P., Pandey, S.K., & Wright, B.E. (2011). Setting the table: How transformational leadership fosters performance information use. *Journal of Public Administration Research and Theory, 22*, 143–164. https://doi.org/10.1093/jopart/mur024

Obiwuru, T.C., Okwu, A.T., Akpa, V.O., & Nwankwere, I.A. (2011). Effects of leadership style on organisational performance. *Journal of Business and Management Research, 1*(7), 100–111.

Paarlberg, L.E., & Lavigna, B. (2010). Transformational leadership and public service motivation: Driving individual and organisational performance. *Public Administration Review, 70*(5), 710–716. https://doi.org/10.1111/j.1540-6210.2010.02199.x

Pallant, J. (2013). *SPSS Survival Manual: A step by step guide to data analysis using IBM SPSS*. Crows Nest: Allen & Unwin.

Park, S.M. & Rainey, H.G. (2007). Antecedents, mediators, and consequences of affective, normative, and continuance commitment: Empirical tests of commitment effects in federal agencies. *Review of Public Personnel Administration, 27*(3), 197–226. https://doi.org/10.1177/0734371X06296866

Perry, J.L. (1996). Measuring public service motivation: An assessment of construct reliability and validity. *The Journal of Public Administration Research and Theory, 6*(1), 5–22. https://doi.org/10.1093/oxfordjournals.jpart.a024303

Ritz, A. (2009). Public service motivation and organisational performance in Swiss federal government. *International Review of Administrative Sciences, 75*(1), 53–78. https://doi.org/10.1177/0020852308099506

Schaubroek, J., Lam, S.S.K., & Peng, A.C. (2011). Cognition-based and affect-based trust as mediators of leader behaviour influences on team performance. *Journal of Applied Psychology, 96*(4), 863–871. https://doi.org/10.1037/a0022625

Steers, R.M., Mowday, R.T., & Shapiro, D.L. (2004). Introduction to special topic forum: The future of work motivation theory. *Academy of Management Review, 29*(3), 379–387. https://doi.org/10.2307/20159049

Tummers, L., & Knies, E. (2014). The public leadership questionnaire: The development and validation of five dimensions of public leadership behaviours. *Conference proceedings of the IRSPM Conference held in Ottowa. Conducted by Panel "New Directions in Public Leadership, Innovation and Change Research"*, Canada, Ottowa.

Ulrich, D., Brockbank, W., Johnson, D., & Younger (2009). *Human Resource Competencies: Rising to meet the business challenge*. The RPL white paper series. Retrieved March 30, 2016, from http://www.hrnorge.no/wpcontent/uploads/2013/07/HumanResourceCompetenciesRisingtomeetthebusinesschallenge.pdf

Van der Wal, Z. (2014). "All quiet on the non-Western front?" A systematic literature review of Public Service Motivation scholarship in non-Western contexts. *Asia Pacific Journal of Public Administration, 1*(1), 1–19.

Van Loon, N., Vandenabeele, W., & Leisink, P.L.M. (2015). On the bright and dark side of Public Service Motivation: Investigating the relationship between PSM and employee wellbeing from an institutional perspective. *Public Money and Management, 1*(1), 1–30.

Wright, B.E., Moynihan, D.P., & Pandey, S.K. (2012). Pulling the levers: Transformational leadership, public service motivation, and mission valence. *Public Administration Review, 72*(2), 206–215. https://doi.org/10.1111/j.1540-6210.2011.02496.x

11

The impact of team dialogue sessions on employee engagement in an information and communication technology company

Authors:
Michael A.W. Seymour[1]
Dirk J. Geldenhuys[1]

Affiliations:
[1]Department of Industrial and Organisational Psychology, University of South Africa, South Africa

Corresponding author:
Dirk Geldenhuys,
geldedj@unisa.ac.za

Orientation: Engaged employees are regarded as extremely valuable in today's unstable economic environment. However, despite spending large amounts of money on the improvement of employee engagement, the effect thereof is seldom determined. This study was about determining the impact of team dialogue sessions on the enhancement of employee engagement in a large information and communication technology company over a 2-year period.

Research purpose: This study focused on determining the improvement of employee engagement through an organisation development intervention. The intervention was based on a social constructionist perspective, namely, team dialoguing, and was facilitated over a period of two years.

Motivation for the study: Although the matter regarding the improvement of employee engagement seems to be extensively discussed in the literature, research on the use of interventions to enhance employee engagement is to a large extent still lacking. Based on a theoretical integration, it was argued that team dialoguing could improve employee engagement.

Research design, approach and method: This was a quantitative study, employing a quasi-experimental design. An experimental group was exposed to an organisation development intervention of team dialogues over a 2-year period and then compared to a control group that had not been exposed to the intervention.

Main findings: Although with a small effect size, it was discovered that facilitating team dialogue sessions had a positive impact on employee engagement, more specifically on the exercise of discretionary effort, intention to remain, rational commitment, communication and supervisory support as dimensions.

Practical and managerial implications: The practical implication of this study is that the engagement of employees can be enhanced by involving the direct supervisor and his or her team in dialoguing sessions.

Contribution or value-add: The study contributed to the literature on employee engagement by reporting on the implementation of an intervention over a period of two years to enhance employee engagement.

Introduction

This study concerns the impact of team dialogue on employee engagement. The importance of employee engagement is not disputed in the literature, especially in publications in journals referring to its benefits and overall contribution to organisational effectiveness (Markos & Sridevi, 2010). For instance, according to Dick (2007), engaged employees are more motivated, responsive to change and more willing to perform different demanding work activities. Furthermore, Robinson, Perryman and Hayday (2004) state that engaged employees are more productive, make more money for the company and create emotional engagement by loyal customers. They contribute to good organisational climate where people are productive, ethical and accountable. They remain with the organisation for a longer period and are more committed to quality and growth than non-engaged and actively disengaged employees. Recently, Gupta and Sharma (2016) emphasised the crucial role of employee engagement in the volatile economic world. For instance, they referred to research findings indicating that employee engagement was found to be a significant predictor of productivity, retention, customer satisfaction and, also shareholder return.

The manager plays a crucial role in representing the organisation for the employee [Bakker, 2017; Corporate Leadership Council (CLC), 2004]. Dick (2007), for example, referred to the research findings indicating that where employees trusted their managers, liked their leadership styles and perceived them as competent, they aligned with the company's values and were honoured to be a member of the company.

Although the matter regarding the improvement of employee engagement seems to be extensively discussed in the literature, research on the use of interventions to enhance employee engagement is largely still lacking (Van der Colff & Rothmann, 2009). This is especially true for applying interventions that are based on social constructionism, such as team dialogue sessions (Geldenhuys, 2015). The rationale in this article is that organisation development (OD) interventions that are based on social constructionism, more specifically team dialogue sessions, can be used to enhance employee engagement. Camargo-Borges and Rasera (2013) indicated that social constructionism, with its focus on concepts such as dialogue, imagination, co-creation and meaning-making, introduced new ways of working with teams in organisations by studying and analysing the interconnectedness of, and mutual influence between, team members. These authors are therefor of the opinion that social constructionism offers new opportunities for organisational interventions that may be used by managers, consultants and group leaders alike.

Research objective

The purpose of this study was to determine the impact of dialogue sessions on employee engagement in work teams over a 2-year period.

The theoretical framework that follows served as the basis for the study, the research design, the reporting of the results and the discussion thereof.

Employee engagement

The study of employee engagement has led to the development of four main research directions (Simpson, 2009). Firstly, employee engagement is regarded as personal engagement, a concept introduced by Kahn (1990). Kahn reasoned that engagement is a multidimensional construct where employees can be emotionally engaged (psychological safety), physically engaged (psychologically availability) and cognitively connected with their work roles (psychological meaningfulness), with cognitive and emotional engagement as the two major dimensions. Kahn (1990, p. 694) subsequently defines employee engagement as 'the harnessing of organisation members' selves to their work roles; in engagement, people employ and express themselves physically, cognitively and emotionally during role performances'. It is therefore the result of being psychologically present when occupying and performing an organisational role. Workers are likely to be more engaged in situations that allow them to experience more psychological meaningfulness and psychological safety, as well as when the workers are more psychologically available (Kahn, 1990). In a field study conducted by May, Gilson and Harter (2004), who furthered the work of Kahn, support was found for the relationship between engagement and all three psychological conditions.

Secondly, employee engagement is regarded as the positive antithesis of burnout. This line of reasoning was developed by Maslach, Schaufeli and Leiter (2001) and Leiter and Maslach (2004). Maslach et al. (2001, p. 417) defined employee engagement as 'a persistent, positive affective-motivational state of fulfilment'. According to Maslach et al., employee engagement is characterised by the direct opposites of the three burnout dimensions (exhaustion, cynicism and inefficacy), namely energy, involvement and efficacy.

Thirdly, the study of employee engagement is based on the conceptualisation of Schaufeli and Bakker (2004), who preferred to use the term 'work engagement'. Engagement is regarded as a positive, fulfilling, work-related state of mind characterised by vigour, dedication and absorption (Schaufeli, Salanova, González-Romá, & Bakker, 2002). Vigour refers to high levels of energy, mental resilience and a willingness to put effort into one's work. Dedication is associated with enthusiasm, inspiration, pride, challenge and a sense of significance; and absorption refers to a state where time passes quickly and where the employees find it difficult to detach themselves from work (Schaufeli et al., 2002).

Schaufeli et al. (2002) reasoned that vigour is the opposite of emotional exhaustion, dedication is the opposite of cynicism and absorption is a third component of work engagement. Furthermore, Schaufeli and Bakker (2004) reasoned that both engagement and burnout can be integrated into a comprehensive and overarching framework, which they coined as the job demands resources model (JDR model). According to the JDR Model, work engagement is a function of the demands of the job and resources provided by the organisation. Engagement is at its highest when employees experience interesting job demands but simultaneously have access to sufficient job resources (Bakker, 2017).

Finally, the concept as developed by Harter, Hayes and Schmidt (2002) entails job satisfaction, involvement and enthusiasm, a set of motivating resources, such as recognition and support from managers and colleagues, performance feedback, and opportunities for learning and development. This concept was measured using the Gallup Work Audit.

According to Erikson (2004), employee engagement is not only about job satisfaction but also involves aspects such as commitment, loyalty and pride in the organisation, a willingness to advocate for the organisation and a sense of personal responsibility. Employee engagement therefore entails discretionary effort where employees decide whether to do their very best and put in extra effort, or just do the bare minimum of what is expected of them.

Therefore, it seems that there is no consensus on conceptualising employee engagement and hence the dimensions thereof (Bakker, 2011; Gupta & Sharma, 2016). For the purpose of this study, employee engagement refers to the degree to which employees demonstrate discretionary effort (willingness to go 'above and beyond' the call of duty), as well as their intention to remain employed in that organisation (CLC, 2004). Employee engagement includes the extent to which an employee displays rational commitment, that is, the degree to which employees are of the opinion that managers, teams and their organisation have their interests at heart. It also includes emotional commitment, that is, the degree to which employees believe in, value and enjoy their jobs. Highly engaged employees are more likely to remain with their current organisation, to be productive and to engage more positively with customers than employees with lower engagement levels.

From the above discussion on the perspectives on employee engagement, the following dimensions of employee engagement have been identified for the purpose of this study.

Discretionary effort: Referring to doing one's very best and putting in extra effort that promotes the effectiveness of the organisation without explicitly being rewarded for their efforts by the formal system (Erikson, 2004; Kahn, 1990; Organ, 1997).

Turnover intention: Tett and Meyer (1993, p. 262) defined turnover intention as the 'conscious and deliberate willingness to leave the organisation'. It has also been described as 'the last in a sequence of withdrawal cognitions, a set to which thinking of quitting and intent to search for alternative employment also belong' (Tett & Meyer, 1993, p. 262). Withdrawal behaviour is the primary way in which employees deal with issues in the employment relationship (Lo & Aryee, 2003).

Emotional commitment: Kahn (1990) suggests that engagement relates to the emotional engagement (psychological safety) of employees. Rothbard (2001) considers engagement to have a dimension of psychological presence 'absorption', while Schaufeli (2013) and Bakker (2004) consider employee engagement to be a positive and rewarding state of mind. Psychological safety is defined as 'feeling able to show and employ one's self without fear of negative consequences to self-image, status, or career' (Kahn, 1990, p. 703). In addition, employee engagement involves the active use of 'emotions and behaviours' (May et al., 2004, p. 12).

Rational commitment: Saks (2006) states that engagement has cognitive behavioural components associated with individual role performance, while Kahn (1990, p. 694) maintains that 'people employ and express themselves cognitively in role performances'. May et al. (2004, p. 12) agree with Kahn (1990) and introduce 'psychological meaningfulness', 'the value of a work goal or purpose' and 'a primary motive to seek meaning in their work'. Rothbard (2001, p. 656), on the other hand, refers to 'cognitive availability and the amount of time one spends thinking about a role'.

Communication: Two-way, open communication forms a fundamental part of employee engagement (Erikson, 2004).

Perceived supervisory support: The crucial role played by supervisors in employee engagement is emphasised by Dick (2007), referring to research findings indicating that where employees trusted their supervisors, liked their management styles and were of the view that they were competent, they shared the company's values and were proud to be employed by the company.

Perceived team support: May et al. (2004) also found that co-worker relations were positive predictors of employee engagement.

For the purpose of this study and based on the work conducted by the CLC (2004), discretionary effort and turnover intention are regarded as the main constructs of employee engagement.

Team dialogue

The word 'dialogue' has two Greek roots: *dia* (meaning 'through' or 'with each other') and *logos* (meaning 'the word') (Isaacs, 1994). Dialogue is 'the art of thinking together' and is 'a sustained collective inquiry' into everyday experience, and what we take for granted (Isaacs, 1994, p. 353). According to Ellinor and Gerard (1998), dialogue entails:

> [s]eeing the whole rather than breaking it into parts; seeing connections rather than distinctions; inquiring into assumptions rather than justifying or defending them; learning through inquiry and disclosure rather than persuading, selling or telling; and creating shared meanings rather than gaining agreement on one meaning. (p. 21)

Dialoguing is based on social constructionism as ontological and epistemological underpinning and explores the manner in which knowledge is embedded in cultural values and practices. Meanings are socially constructed through the coordination of people in their various encounters (Camargo-Borges & Rasera, 2013).

There is a difference between dialoguing and debating, discussing or persuasion. In a debate, there is normally a clash of opinions and positions where the most rational argument is regarded as superior. Persuasion, however, takes a milder approach, with the aim of finding convincing ways to influence people to make a choice. Dialogue, in contrast, constructs a space for conversation that welcomes participants to invite a multiplicity of voices. It is a process that is intimately connected with the co-creation of new realities (Gergen, McNamee, & Barrett, 2002). It is not focused on finding the 'right way' or 'the only way' of doing things, but on finding ways to generate and create opportunities for people to feel connected and willing to participate.

Furthermore, dialogue is also different from consensus building (Isaacs, 1994). While consensus building often seeks to limit options and find strategies that are acceptable to most people, dialogue seeks to surface fundamental assumptions and an understanding of why they arise. Dialogues allow, through sharing, to externalise what is on a person's mind and eventually change the underlying patterns of meaning (Herrera, 2015). The goal of dialogue is not to eliminate differences but to create a space where the differences can co-exist and be studied, not be ignored or put aside to arrive at something all parties can agree on.

Dialoguing requires the identification of socially constructed realities or assumptions by means of listening, inquiring and reflecting (Duffy & Wong, 2016; Gerard & Teurfs, 1995); bringing similarities and differences into the open for discussion, common understanding and modification (Lau & Shani, 1992, p. 99); and by respecting other perspectives by suspending judgement (Gerard & Teurfs, 1995).

Applied to organisations, Duffy and Wong (2016) stated that dialogue is fundamental to organisational learning, for without dialogue individuals and groups cannot exchange ideas effectively, nor can they develop shared understanding. For the Greeks, *dialogos* meant a free flowing of meaning through a group, allowing the group to discover insights not attainable individually (Senge, 1990).

Theoretical integration

Based on the literature, it seems that the dimensions of employee engagement that are related to teamwork can be mostly influenced by team dialogue sessions. For instance, Erikson (2004) indicates eight factors that consistently surface as drivers of employee engagement; of these, teamwork, involvement and belonging, open two-way communication, trust and confidence in leadership are directly linked to the team.

Also, according to Maslach et al. (2001), a breakdown of community among team members will weaken their commitment to each other. Without a sense of community, a work team lacks the synergies required for an integrated work group. Moreover, a poor sense of community directly affects productivity and creates a vulnerability to conflict between the group members. Unresolved conflict drains the team members emotionally and thereby influences their emotional commitment (Maslach et al., 2001).

Furthermore, of the six drivers of employee engagement identified by Saks (2006), perceived supervisor and organisational support are particularly important in the team context. When employees feel that they are allowed to reveal their true selves without fearing negative consequences, they gain a sense of psychological safety; this stems from the amount of support that they perceive to be provided by their manager, their work colleagues and the organisation (Kahn, 1990; May et al., 2004; Schaufeli & Bakker, 2004). This view is supported by Robinson et al. (2004), who reasoned that employees are more engaged in circumstances where there is a good relationship with clear communication from their manager, when they have a clear path set for focusing on what they do best and have strong relationships with and feel a strong commitment to their co-workers, thus enabling them to take risks and stretch for excellence.

May et al. (2004) describe employee engagement in terms of psychological meaningfulness, psychological safety and psychological availability. The workplace dimension related to psychological safety includes supervisory relations, co-worker relations, work role insecurities and behavioural norms, which are directly applicable to the team context.

In teams, effective dialogue directly influences the functioning of a team, the communication within a team, the relationships between the team members in a team and the relationship team members have with their supervisor. As stated by Lau and Shani (1992):

> One of the basic and most persistent problems of organisational life is that different people see situations, issues, or goals differently, depending on their particular perspectives, experiences, backgrounds, and biases – yet everyone typically assumes that everyone else sees things as they do. (p. 99)

According to Schein (1993, p. 44), 'dialogue aims to build a group that can think generatively, creatively, and most importantly, together', and reasoned that dialogue is revealed when the way in which someone interprets a concept is recognised as being different from one's own; that is, there is a willingness to accept differences in the way that people reason and act under conditions of high uncertainty and high task interdependence can lead to greater levels of understanding of alternative ways of thinking and dedication to a particular worldview.

Robinson et al. (2004) agree that employees are more engaged in circumstances where there is clear communication from their manager. The following noted by Lau and Shani (1992):

> Communication dialoguing is one way to overcome contradictory expectations by bringing similarities and differences in perspective out into the open. They can then be discussed, modified by other data or new interpretations, and shared ... Such exchange is the foundation for understanding, trust, and thus effective working relations, and successful managers and employees use it frequently. (p. 98)

Research design

Research approach

This was a quantitative study, using a non-equivalent quasi-experimental design (Cooper & Schindler, 2011). As volunteers were recruited for the experimental group and non-volunteers were used for the control group, the self-selected experimental group design was used as variation of the design (Cooper & Schindler, 2011). The membership of the experimental group was exposed to the team dialogue intervention over a period of 2 years and compared to a control group that had not been exposed to the dialogue intervention.

The team dialogue intervention was conducted with work teams, including their direct supervisors. All the sessions were facilitated by a human resource (HR) specialist facilitator who was responsible for creating a relational space where dialogue was encouraged. Such dialogue had to be characterised by openness and curiosity, in which conversations could be brought together or coordinated, based on multiple realities, representing various stakeholders with different stories and experiences, bases of power and belief systems. In exploring ways of creating a context that invites dialoguing, the emphasis was on the relational processes between the team members and not on the team members as entities themselves (Geldenhuys, 2015).

The facilitator also had to ensure that the dialogue sessions adhered to the nature of dialoguing such as thinking together, suspending judgement, identifying assumptions, listening, inquiring and reflecting and, finally, collaborative learning. The content of the dialogue sessions not only had to focus on the vision and mission of the company, as well as the core values, but also had to include dialogue on team functioning, communication, team relationships, perceived team support and relationships between team members and their supervisors.

The team dialogue sessions were conducted on a monthly basis and lasted for approximately two hours. During the session, the facilitator took notes, which the team could refer to in the following session.

Research method

Research participants

The population for this study comprised all the 23 000 individual full-time employees of an information and communication technology (ICT) organisation. The sample for this study numbered 660 employees who participated in the employee engagement surveys conducted before and after participating in team dialogue sessions over this period, which was the experimental group. The control group consisted of 660 randomly selected individual full-time employees who participated in both the employee engagement surveys conducted, but did not participate in the organisation intervention of team dialogue sessions.

The demographic characteristics of the experimental group and the control group are compared in Figure 1. As displayed

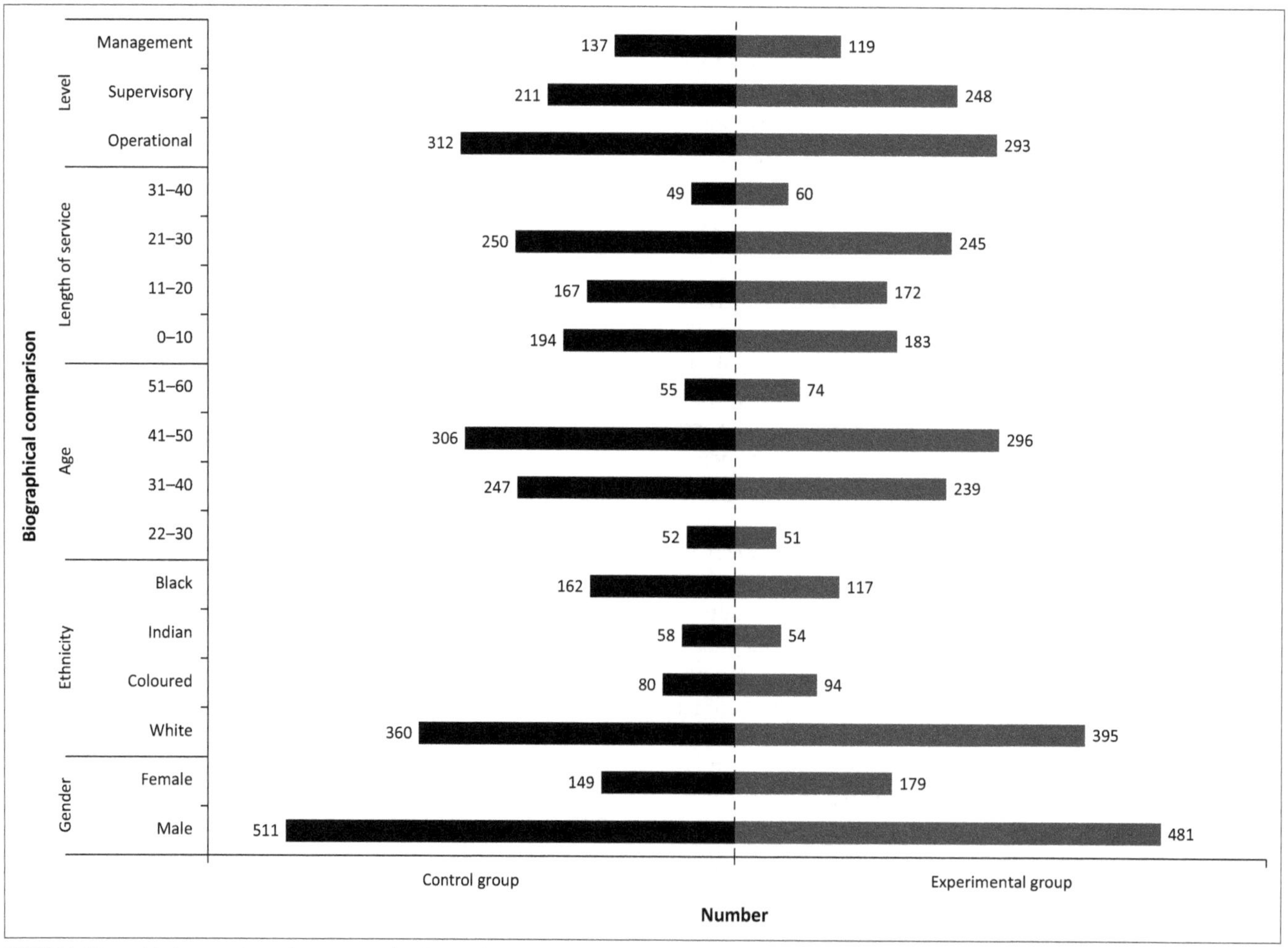

FIGURE 1: Biographical comparison of experimental and control groups.

in Figure 1, the demographic distribution characteristics of the experimental group and the control group are largely similar. This implies that the differences between the experimental group and the control group can be measured accurately to determine the influence of team dialogue sessions on employee engagement. This also means that the research can reliably use non-parametric tests for comparing the control group and the experimental group.

Measuring instrument

The employee engagement scale, developed by the CLC, was used as measuring instrument for this study. To validate this survey, several studies of employee engagement were conducted, using this survey questionnaire with more than 50 000 employees across the world. Overall, Cronbach's alpha of over 0.70 (CLC, 2004) was reported. The reason for selecting this scale was not only its reliability and validity but also its capability to measure the dimensions as conceptualised for the purpose of this study that might be influenced by team dialogues, namely, emotional commitment and rational commitment, communication, perceived team support and perceived supervisory support, as well as turnover intention and discretionary effort. Respondents had to rate items on a five-point Likert scale, ranging from 1 (strongly disagree) to 5 (strongly agree). The scale for some of the items ranged from 1 (very poor) to 5 (excellent). Provision was also made for 'unable to rate' (0). Examples of the questions asked are presented below:

- *Discretionary effort*: I am willing to work many additional hours over the next year if it helps achieve its goals.
- *Turnover intention*: I actively search for job opportunities at other companies.
- *Rational commitment*: All in all, it I would say 'it is worth it' for my family, my career and for me personally to work here.
- *Emotional commitment*: Working with ITC has a great deal of personal meaning to me.
- *Communication*: Overall how would you rate ITC's employee communications?
- *Perceived supervisory support*: Providing the right amount of supervision and guidance.
- *Perceived team support*: Being in a section/team you have a strong personal attachment to.

Research procedure

The institution through which the research was conducted provided ethical clearance for the study. Permission was also obtained from the company and voluntary participation of all participants and confidentiality of all information were assured. A personal invitation was sent out by an e-mail to the entire population, with the Universal Resource Locator (URL) address of the online survey attached. When administering the four employee engagement surveys, a census-based approach was used with the intention of surveying all employees in the heterogenic population (everybody in the target population had an equal opportunity to participate in the survey). These surveys were conducted over a period of 1 month, 2 years apart, before and after the intervention. It should be noted that participation in the intervention was also on a volunteering basis according to the best ethical practice in organisation development (OD) as stipulated in the 'Ethical guidelines for an OD/Human Systems Development (HSD) Professional' as developed by the Human Systems Development Consortium (Cummings & Worley, 2015, pp. 70–73).

Statistical analysis

Data captured from the online web-based surveys were analysed, using version 23 of the IBM Statistical Package for the Social Sciences (SPSS). It was decided to make use of non-parametric tests for the analysis of the data as non-parametric tests are less demanding to use, do not specify stringent assumptions such as normally distributed populations or equality of variance (Easton & McColl, 2004) but still achieve an efficiency as high as 95% (Cooper & Schindler, 2011).

Furthermore, the Kolmogorov–Smirnov test was applied to measure the differences in the means between the experimental group and the control group (Easton & McColl, 2004). This test is often used in organisational studies and is recommended for independent related samples with ordinal data (Brewerton & Millward, 2001; Cooper & Schindler, 2011).

Hypotheses

The following hypotheses were formulated:

- $\mathbf{H_0}$: Team dialogues have no influence on employee engagement.
- $\mathbf{H_1}$: Team dialogues have a significant influence on employee engagement.

Results

Instrument reliability

The overall Cronbach's alpha coefficient score of 0.778 that was yielded by the measuring instrument as a whole can be regarded as acceptable (Pallant, 2007). The Cronbach's alpha coefficients for the individual dimensions are presented in Table 1.

All Cronbach's alpha scores (ranging from 0.744 to 0.832) are indicative of the acceptable reliability of the measuring instrument (Pallant, 2007).

Descriptive statistics

The means and standard deviations of the experimental group and the control group, both before and after the intervention, are presented in Table 2.

As shown in Table 2, the experiment had a mean of 3.40 before the intervention, with a mean of 3.51 after the intervention, indicating an improvement after the intervention. Furthermore, the control group is lower on employee engagement than the experimental group, both before and after the intervention. A possible explanation for this is that the experimental group volunteered for the intervention and could therefore be positively biased towards the dialogue sessions. According to Sidebottom (2015), some people do not prefer a face-to-face communication. Those employees who do not favour face-to-face communication probably do not volunteer to be part of the intervention.

Non-parametric paired sampling test

To determine if the two samples may reasonably be assumed to originate from the same distribution, the Kolmogorov–Smirnov test was used. The results are presented in Table 3.

Non-parametric independent sampling test

The Wilcoxon signed-rank test was used to measure the differences in the means between the experimental group and the control group (Easton & McColl, 2004). The results are presented in Table 4.

The negative rank score in Table 4, for both the experimental group and the control group, indicates a significant difference between before the intervention and two years thereafter, and an improvement in the employee engagement rating. The negative rank score for the experimental group ($Z = -3.942, p < 0.001, \eta^2 = 0.024$) indicates a higher score than that of the control group ($Z = -3.927, p < 0.001, \eta^2 = 0.024$), and the degree of the difference between before and after the intervention for the experimental group is also larger. This indicates that the improvement in the employee engagement rating was larger for the experimental group between the two tests in comparison with the control group. However, it should be noted that the effect size is relatively small ($\eta^2 = 0.024$) for both the experimental and the control groups (Hattie, 2009).

Dimension differences between the experimental group and the control group

The differences in the scores for the dimensions of employee engagement are presented in Table 5.

The differences in the scores of the dimensions of discretionary effort, turnover intention, rational commitment, emotional commitment, communication, perceived supervisor support and perceived team support are presented in Table 6.

The extent of the differences between the experimental group and the control group regarding discretionary effort, turnover intention, rational commitment, emotional commitment, communication, perceived supervisor support and perceived team support are presented in Table 7 and Figure 2.

Between the two years, the experimental group indicated a greater improvement regarding discretionary effort, turnover intention, rational commitment, communication and perceived supervisor support.

The control group, on the other hand, indicated a greater improvement between the two years regarding emotional commitment and perceived team support. Turnover intention deteriorated for the control group. The extent of the differences between the improvement in the experimental group and control group between the two years are presented in Table 7 and Figure 2.

TABLE 1: Cronbach's alpha coefficient scores.

Factor	Cronbach's alpha coefficient
Employee engagement	0.832
Discretionary effort	0.754
Turnover intention	0.770
Rational commitment	0.746
Emotional commitment	0.744
Communication	0.749
Perceived supervisory support	0.753
Perceived team support	0.749

TABLE 2: Descriptive statistics.

Sample group	N	Mean	Std. deviation	Minimum	Maximum
Experimental before	660	3.40	0.76	1	5
Experimental after	660	3.51	0.74	1	5
Control after	660	1.75	1.21	1	4
Control before	660	1.88	1.19	1	4
Total group	**1320**	**1.50**	**0.500**	**1**	**2**

TABLE 3: Hypothesis test summary.

Number	Null hypothesis	Test	Sig.	Decision
1	Distribution of the experimental group before the intervention with a mean of 3.40 and a standard deviation of 0.76	One-sample Kolmogorov–Smirnov test	< 0.001	Reject the null hypothesis
2	Distribution of the experimental group after two years with a mean of 3.51 and a standard deviation of 0.74	One-sample Kolmogorov–Smirnov test	< 0.001	Reject the null hypothesis

Sig., significance.

TABLE 4: Wilcoxon ranks table.

Group	Timing	Ranks	N	Mean rank	Sum of ranks	Z	P	Effect size η^2
Experimental	After intervention Before intervention	Negative ranks	106	134.38	14244.00	-3.943	< 0.001	0.024
		Positive ranks	168	139.47	23431.00	-	-	-
		Ties	386	-	-	-	-	-
		Total	660	-	-	-	-	-
Control	After intervention Before intervention	Negative ranks	103	129.04	13291.00	-3.927	< 0.001	0.024
		Positive ranks	163	136.32	22220.00	-	-	-
		Ties	394	-	-	-	-	-
		Total	660	-	-	-	-	-

TABLE 5: Experimental group comparison between the two years.

Factor	Before	After	% Improvement
Discretionary effort	525	601	11.5
Turnover intention	304	289	-2.3
Rational commitment	386	430	6.7
Emotional commitment	387	399	1.8
Communication	104	139	5.3
Perceived supervisor support	268	281	2.0
Perceived team support	256	259	0.5

TABLE 6: Control group comparison between the two years.

Factor	Before	After	% Improvement
Discretionary effort	544	591	7.1
Turnover intention	281	332	7.7
Rational commitment	406	438	4.8
Emotional commitment	379	417	5.8
Communication	119	141	3.3
Perceived supervisor support	278	281	0.5
Perceived team support	234	265	4.7

TABLE 7: Extent of differences between the experimental group and the control group over two years.

Factor	Experimental group (%)	Control group (%)	% Difference
Discretionary effort	11.5	7.1	4.4
Turnover intention	-2.3	7.7	-10.0
Rational commitment	6.7	4.8	1.8
Emotional commitment	1.8	5.8	-3.9
Communication	5.3	3.3	2.0
Perceived supervisor support	2.0	0.5	1.5
Perceived team support	0.5	4.7	-4.2

Discussion

This study investigated the influence that team dialogue intervention sessions over a period of 2 years, had on employee engagement.

Overall, it can be concluded that dialogue as a team intervention that was conducted over a period of two years positively influenced the employee engagement of the team. The results should however be viewed with caution as the practical significance of the influence was relatively small.

Based on the results it could be argued that the dialogue sessions offered the teams a relative sense of psychological safety and availability, two important dimensions of employee engagement (May et al., 2004). Psychological safety is experienced when employees are prepared to share their true feelings without fearing negative consequences; this, for instance, relates to the amount of support that they perceive to be provided by their manager and the organisation (Kahn, 1990; May et al., 2004; Schaufeli & Bakker, 2004).

Furthermore, through dialogue, the team members probably developed skills to think creatively together, to understand alternative ways of thinking and a willingness to accept differences (Schein, 1993). According to Bakker (2011), stimulating personal growth, learning and development

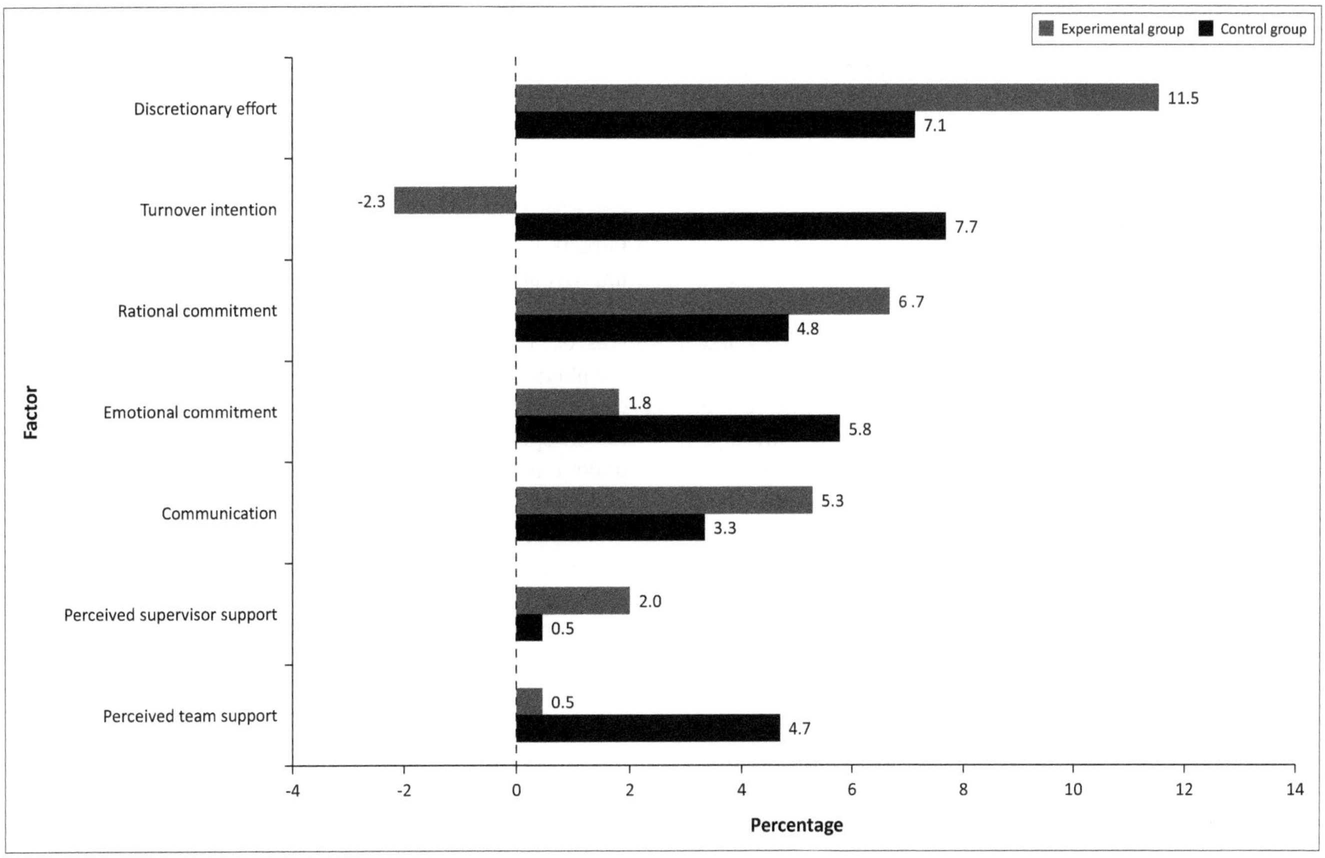

FIGURE 2: Extent of differences between experimental group and control group over two years.

is regarded as job resources that serve as a driver for employee engagement.

Dimensions

Discretionary effort

Regarding the different dimensions, improvement in discretionary effort was rated higher by the respondents who participated in the team dialogue sessions in comparison with non-participants. Employee engagement concerns discretionary effort, where employees decide on whether to do their utmost best and put in extra effort or to do just the bare minimum of what is expected (Erikson, 2004). This result is in support of Gupta and Sharma (2016) who reasoned that engagement is a two-way process in which management puts in extra effort to engage employees and, in return, employees give the discretionary effort that motivates them to contribute to the success of the organisation and simultaneously enhance their own sense of well-being.

Intention to leave

Regarding intention to leave the organisation, the results indicated that employees who participated in the team dialogues were more inclined to stay with the organisation than those who did not participate. As dialogues create opportunities for conversation that welcomes participants to be involved in co-creating the future (Gergen et al., 2002), the dialogues could have increased the employees sense of belonging. A greater sense of belonging may lead to a decrease in withdrawal behaviour by employees. Withdrawal behaviour is one of the main ways in which employees deal with issues in the employment relationship (Lo & Aryee, 2003). Engaging in dialoguing sessions therefore probably provided the participants with resources for connecting them with each other, including the supervisor, who represents the organisation.

Rational commitment

The improvement on rational commitment was also rated higher by members of the experimental group in comparison with the control group. Rational commitment relates to the extent to which employees believe that managers, teams and organisations are acting in their financial, developmental or professional self-interest (CLC, 2004). It would appear that the success of the team dialogue session is linked to the extent that team members were willing to create shared meaning, rather than gaining agreement on one meaning; they were accordingly more able to learn from each other and to 'criss-cross' their views with each other, thus enhancing their understanding of the types of issues that impede their ability to perform (Jabri, 2004).

Emotional commitment

The dimension of emotional commitment indicated a greater improvement in the control group than the experimental group. From the results, it can be concluded that there is a possibility that the team dialogue sessions were, from an emotional commitment perspective, viewed less positively by the experimental group than the control group. Kahn (1990) suggests that engagement relates to the emotional engagement (psychological safety) of employees. This finding could be explained in the sense that members experienced less safety when others were allowed to offer viewpoints different to their own. It could also be interpreted as supporting the notion that a team's creation of shared meaning could influence the emotional commitment of individual team members and that, where a shared understanding is created, it would in turn improve rational commitment (Jabri, 2004).

Communication

The communication dimension indicated a larger improvement in the experimental group in comparison with the control group. This result corresponds with the expectation that team dialogue will improve communication among the team members. Differences and similarities in perspectives can be dealt with by allowing these differences and similarities to be shared in the open and to be modified by other data or new perspectives (Lau & Shani, 1992). 'Such exchange is the foundation for understanding, trust, and thus effective working relations, and successful managers and employees use it frequently' (Lau & Shani, 1992, p. 99).

Schein (1993) considers dialogue as a basic process for building common understanding, in that it allows one to see the hidden meanings of words, first by revealing these hidden meanings in our own communication. Schein (1993, p. 44) stated that 'dialogue aims to build a group that can think generatively, creatively, and most importantly, together'.

Perceived supervisory support

Perceived supervisory supports indicated greater improvement in the experimental group, with an improvement of 2%, compared to the control group where the improvement was 0.5%. The direct supervisors of the teams were also members of the dialogue sessions. It therefore seems that the direct dialogues through which team members, together with their supervisors, could engage in open, non-judgmental dialoguing could have created the perception that their supervisors supported them. This result is in line with research conducted by Benkoff (Dick, 2007), indicating that where employees trusted their supervisors and liked their management style, the employees shared the company's values and were proud to be employed by the company. Similarly, May et al. (2004) concluded that relationship with supervisor was a positive predictor of employee engagement.

Perceived team support

Other than expected, the improvement in perceived team support was higher for the control group in comparison with the experimental group. However, it could be reasoned that the dialogue sessions impacted prevalent group dynamics where the team could have been a closed knit unit before the intervention, characterised by group thinking, not allowing for differences to be expressed. This is supported by May et al. (2004), indicating that co-worker norms and self-consciousness are negative predictors of employee engagement. Lau and Shani (1992) stated:

> One of the basic and most persistent problems of organisational life is that different people see situations, issues, or goals differently, depending on their particular perspectives, experiences, backgrounds, and biases – yet everyone typically assumes that everyone else sees things as they do. (p. 99)

Conclusion

In conclusion, the evidence presented by this study suggests that team dialogues, although with a small practical significance, have a positive impact in terms of improving employee engagement levels within an organisation, more specifically, on the major dimensions of discretionary effort, turnover intention, rational commitment, communication and perceived supervisory support. It is therefore, argued that dialogue sessions as applied from a social constructionist perspective could be considered a long-term intervention to enhance employee engagement.

Limitations

The score before the intervention was lower for the control group than for the experimental group. As the experimental group volunteered to be part of the intervention, these participants could have been positively biased towards the dialogue sessions. This could have influenced the impact of the intervention in both directions. For instance, employees who were not positive before the intervention, and therefore did not participate, could have found the intervention more valuable in comparison with those who did participate (because of high expectations).

A further possible limitation of this study is that both the experimental group and the control group were drawn from the same ICT sector population. Therefore, any generalisation to populations outside the ICT sector should be made with caution.

Implications and recommendations

When practised successfully, dialogue may have an influence on the level of employee engagement, as it allows groups to move beyond any one individual's understanding to gain new insights and to create ideas in ways that could not be achieved individually (Hale, 1998). Because of its centrality to team effectiveness and team learning, dialogue and the open healthy communication that allows it to occur can be considered a 'core competency' that should be aspired by the managers striving to maximise their potential (Hale, 1998).

A unique relationship develops among team members who regularly enter into dialogue, as they develop a deep trust that cannot help but carry over to discussions taking place in the team. They develop a richer understanding of the uniqueness of each person's point of view and experience how larger understandings emerge by holding one's own point of view 'gently'. Part of the vision of dialogue is the assumption of a 'larger pool of meaning' accessible only to a group. This idea, while may appear radical at first, has deep intuitive appeal for managers who have long cultivated the subtle aspects of collective inquiry (Senge, 1990).

Acknowledgements

Competing interest

The authors declare that they have no financial or personal relationship(s) that may have inappropriately influenced them in writing this article.

Authors' contributions

Both authors contributed equally to the writing of this article.

References

Bakker, A.B. (2011). An evidence-based model of work engagement. *Current Directions in Psychological Science, 20*, 265–269. https://doi.org/10.1177/0963721411414534

Bakker, A.B. (2017). Strategic and proactive approaches to work engagement. *Organizational Dynamics, 46*, 67–75. https://doi.org/10.1016/j.orgdyn.2017.04.002

Brewerton, P., & Millward, L. (2001). *Organizational research methods.* London: Sage.

Camargo-Borges, C., & Rasera, E.F. (2013). Social constructionism in the context of organization development: Dialogue, imagination, and co-creation as resources of change. *SAGE Open, 3*(2), 1–7. https://doi.org/10.1177/2158244013487540

Cummings, T.G., & Worley, C.G. (2015). *Organization development and change* (10th ed.). Stamford, CT: Cengage Learning.

Cooper, D.R., & Schindler, P.S. (2011). *Business research methods* (11th ed.). Singapore: McGraw-Hill.

Corporate Leadership Council (CLC). (2004). *Employee engagement survey.* London: Research Corporate Executive Board.

Dick, G. (2007). The progress of female police officers? An empirical analysis of organisational commitment and tenure explanations in two UK police forces. *International Journal of Public Sector Management, 20*(2), 81–100. https://doi.org/10.1108/09513550710731463

Duffy, G.L., & Wong, A.K. (2016). Complementary strengths. *The Journal for Quality and Participation, 39*(2), 20–22.

Easton, V.J., & McColl, J.H. (2004). *Steps statistics glossary*. The University of Glasgow. Retrieved from http://www.stats.gla.ac.uk/steps/glossary/nonparametric.html

Ellinor, L., & Gerard, G. (1998). *Dialogue: Rediscover the transforming power of conversation.* New York: Wiley.

Erikson, B. (2004). Nature times nurture: How organizations can optimize their people's contribution. *Journal of Organizational Excellence, 24*(1), 21–30. https://doi.org/10.1002/npr.20034

Geldenhuys, D.J. (2015). Relational constructionism and relational practices as a paradigm for organisational psychology in the South African context. *SA Journal of Industrial Psychology/SA Tydskrif vir Bedryfsielkunde, 41*(1), Art. #1225, 1–10. https://doi.org/10.4102/sajip.v41i1.1225

Gerard, G., & Teurfs, L. (1995). Dialogue and organizational transformation. In K. Gozdz (Ed.), *Community building: Renewing spirit and learning in business* (pp. 143–153). San Francisco, CA: New Leaders Press.

Gergen, K.J., McNamee, S., & Barrett, F.J. (2002). Realizing transformative dialogue. In N.C. Roberts (Ed.), *The transformative power of dialogue* (pp. 77–105). Oxford, UK: Elsevier Science.

Gupta, N., & Sharma, V. (2016). Exploring employee engagement – A way to better business performance. *Global Business Review, 17*(3), 45–63. https://doi.org/10.1177/0972150916631082

Hale, J.P. (1998). *The theory and practice of dialogue in organisational settings.* CCO Research Paper. Retrieved from http://www.workteams.unt.edu/literature/paper-jhale.html

Harter, J.K., Hayes, T.L., & Schmidt, F.L. (2002). Business-unit-level relationship between employee satisfaction, employee engagement, and business outcomes: A meta-analysis. *Journal of Applied Psychology, 87*(2), 268–279. https://doi.org/10.1037/0021-9010.87.2.268

Hattie, J. (2009). *Visible learning.* London: Routledge.

Herrera, D. (2015). The record company as a learning structure: Identifying performance and learning inhibitors. *Journal of the Music and Entertainment Industry Educators Association, 15*(1), 121–146. https://doi.org/10.25101/15.6

Isaacs, W.S. (1994). *Team learning. The fifth discipline fieldbook: Strategies and tools for building a learning organization.* New York: Doubleday.

Jabri, M. (2004). Team feedback based on dialogue implications for change management. *Journal of Management Development, 23*(2), 141–151. https://doi.org/10.1108/02621710410517238

Kahn, W.A. (1990). Psychological conditions of personal engagement and disengagement at work. *Academy of Management Journal, 33,* 692–724. https://doi.org/10.2307/256287

Lau, J.B., & Shani, A.B. (1992). *Behaviour in organisations. An experiential approach* (5th ed.). Boston, MA: Irwin.

Leiter, M.P., & Maslach, C. (2004). Areas of worklife: A structured approach to organizational predictors of job burnout. In P. Perrewé & D.C. Ganster (Ed.), *Research in occupational stress and wellbeing* (Vol. 3, pp. 91–134). Oxford, UK: Elsevier.

Lo, S., & Aryee, S. (2003). Psychological contract breach in a Chinese context: An integrative approach. *Journal Management Studies, 40,* 1005–1020. https://doi.org/10.1111/1467-6486.00368

Markos, S., & Sridevi, M.S. (2010). Employee engagement: The key to improving performance. *International Journal of Business and Management, 5*(12), 89–96.

Maslach, C., Schaufeli, W.B., & Leiter, M.P. (2001). Job burnout. *Annual Review of Psychology, 52,* 397–422. https://doi.org/10.1146/annurev.psych.52.1.397

May, D.R., Gilson, R.L., & Harter, L.M. (2004). The psychological conditions of meaningfulness, safety and availability and the engagement of the human spirit at work. *Journal of Occupational and Organizational Psychology, 77,* 11–37. https://doi.org/10.1348/096317904322915892

Organ, D. (1997). Organizational citizenship behaviour: It's construct clean-up time. *Human Performance, 10*(2), 85–97. https://doi.org/10.1207/s15327043hup1002_2

Pallant, J. (2007). *SPSS survival manual: A step by step guide to data analysis using SPSS for windows* (3rd ed.). England: McGraw Hill Open University Press Milton Keynes, UK.

Robinson, D., Perryman, S., & Hayday, S. (2004). *The drivers of employee engagement, IES report 408.* Retrieved from http://www.employment-studies.co.uk/summary/summary.php?id=408

Rothbard, N.P., (2001). Enriching or depleting? The dynamics of engagement in work and family roles. *Administrative Science Quarterly, 46,* 655–684. https://doi.org/10.2307/3094827

Saks, A.M. (2006). Antecedents and consequences of employee engagement. *Journal of Managerial Psychology, 21*(7), 600–619. https://doi.org/10.1108/02683940610690169

Schaufeli, W.B. (2013). What is engagement? In C. Truss, K. Alfes, R. Delbridge, A. Shantz, & E. Soane (Eds.), *Employee engagement in theory and practice.* London: Routledge, 1–2 http://www.wilmarschaufeli.nl/publications/Schaufeli/414.pdf

Schaufeli, W.B., & Bakker, A.B. (2004). Job demands, job resources and their relationship with burnout and engagement: A multi-sample study. *Journal of Organizational Behavior, 25*(3), 293–315. https://doi.org/10.1002/job.248

Schaufeli, W.B., Salanova, M., González-Romá, V., & Bakker, A.B., (2002). The measurement of engagement and burnout: A confirmative analytic approach. *Journal of Happiness Studies, 3,* 71–92. https://doi.org/10.1023/A:1015630930326

Schein, E. (1993). On dialogue, culture and organizational learning. *Organizational Dynamics, 21,* 40–51. https://doi.org/10.1016/0090-2616(93)90052-3

Senge, P.M. (1990). *The fifth discipline: The art and practice of the learning organisation.* New York: Currency-Doubleday.

Sidebottom, J. (2015). Six ways to develop high-performance teams. *Consulting – Specifying Engineer.* Retrieved from https://0-search.proquest.com.oasis.unisa.ac.za/docview/1738105364?accountid=14648

Simpson, M.R. (2009). Engagement at work: A review of the literature. *International Journal of Nursing Studies, 46*(7), 1012–1024. https://doi.org/10.1016/j.ijnurstu.2008.05.003

Tett, R.P., & Meyer, J.P. (1993). Job satisfaction, organisational commitment, turnover intention and turnover: Path analysis based on meta-analytic findings. *Personnel Psychology, 46*(2), 259–293. https://doi.org/10.1111/j.1744-6570.199 3.tb00874.x

Van der Colff, J.J., & Rothmann, S. (2009). Occupational stress, sense of coherence, coping, burnout and work engagement of registered nurses in South Africa. *SA Journal of Industrial Psychology, 35*(1), 1–10. Retrieved from http://www.scielo.org.za/scielo.php?script=sci_arttext&pid=S2071-07632009000100001&lng=en&tlng=pt

12

The relationship between transformational leadership and leadership effectiveness in Kenyan indigenous banks

Authors:
Lynette Louw[1]
Samuel M. Muriithi[1]
Sarah Radloff[2]

Affiliations:
[1]Department of Management, Rhodes University, South Africa

[2]Department of Statistics, Rhodes University, South Africa

Corresponding author:
Lynette Louw,
l.louw@ru.ac.za

Orientation: Effective leadership is critical to the survival and growth of organisations. For such leadership to be realised, organisational leaders need to be competent in transformational leadership, which is described as a situation in which the leader and followers empower and shape each other's behaviour to attain a desired goal.

Research purpose: The purpose of this study is to empirically test the relationship between transformational leadership competency and leadership effectiveness in Kenyan indigenous banks.

Motivation for this study: In spite of the fact that indigenous banks have been performing better recently, their overall poor performance is cause for concern. This study was motivated by a desire to establish the extent to which the recent improvement is attributable to transformational leadership competency and effectiveness. It is also anticipated that this investigation can highlight aspects of leadership which require more attention in order to sustain improved performance.

Research design, approach and method: The study utilised a survey method to collect both quantitative and qualitative data while probability and non-probability techniques were used to sample target population. With 494 respondents targeted in the study, 257 responses were received and analysed. Data analysis was performed using structural equation modelling with Cronbach's alpha, confirmatory factor analysis and goodness-of-fit indices for analysis and for testing relationships.

Main findings: The overall findings confirm that a strong relationship exists between transformational leadership competencies and leadership effectiveness among the leaders of the indigenous banks in Kenya.

Practical/managerial implication: Based on the findings of this study, Kenyan indigenous banks are able to identify specific and essential transformational leadership competencies and leadership effectiveness attributes.

Contribution: The study has identified that transformational leadership abilities of inspirational motivation, intellectual stimulation, individualised consideration and idealised influence, together with the leadership effectiveness indicators of cross-cultural competency, influence, follow commitment, versatility and group organisation are essential for the effectiveness of Kenyan banks.

Introduction

The banking industry is a leading agency of commerce in industrial development (Nagar, Masih & Badugu, 2011). However, various banking practices and behaviours have been associated with major financial crises worldwide (Brunnermerier, 2009). The last six decades in particular have seen a number of international financial crises blamed on banking industry conduct, leading to poor performance by most world economies (Grant Thornton, 2013).

Banking sectors in Africa have seen slow growth, with many communities yet to profit from the numerous financial benefits that can arise from banking practices. It is notable that the banking industry in Africa is highly concentrated in the cities, with marginal distribution in the rural areas. The industry is also characterised by small markets, weak creditors, low income, low deposit levels, low intermediaries, lack of entry barriers, foreign bank dominancy and poor legal frameworks (Mlachila, Park & Yaraba, 2013). These characteristics have resulted in Africa being the lowest financial performer compared with the rest of the world.

Like many African countries characterised by poor performance, Kenya has undergone several decades of financial crisis, especially between 1970 and 2005. During this period, more than 20 banks and other financial institutions went bankrupt or were put under receivership (Mwangi, 2012; Sokpor, 2006). The banks that failed were all locally and privately owned (also known as indigenous banks). It has been asserted that these bank failures were attributable to factors such as ineffective leadership (Mwangi, 2012; Njuguna, 2013), which is largely associated with the type of leadership exercised and the competencies of leaders. Kenyan bank failures have also been associated with deregulation, non-performing loans, lack of internal control mechanisms and liquidity problems, all of which relate to leadership incompetency (Ambutsi, 2005; Waweru & Kalani, 2009). Leadership competency denotes the knowledge, skills, expertise, beliefs, value motives and personal behaviour characteristics that distinguish a leader (Pagon, Banutai & Bizjak, 2008). According to Al-Zoubi (2012), it is the leaders' competencies which enable them to integrate and perform set tasks while at the same time ensuring that effectiveness is attained. Burns (1978) describes transformational leadership as a situation whereby leaders and followers empower each other, resulting in higher levels of morality, motivation and leadership effectiveness. Scholars such as Tang, Yin and Nelson (2010) stress that transformational leadership competency forms the basis of leadership effectiveness. Such leadership effectiveness denotes the leader's ability to exercise personal influence, skills, knowledge and abilities to accomplish expected goals or objectives (Cooper, Fenimore & Nirenberg, 2012). Johnson, Lenartowicz and Apud (2006) state that there is a lack of adequate research on the main determinants of leadership effectiveness. This lack of research provides a further rationale for this study which also aimed to better understand the leadership effectiveness attributes that would contribute towards the improvement of the Kenyan indigenous banks' performance.

Problem definition

As in other parts of the world, the negative performance of the banking sector in Kenya for several decades has largely been attributed to ineffective leadership (Mwangi, 2012). To be effective, leaders in banking require appropriate leadership competencies in strategic thinking, technical ability and interpersonal skills; should have integrity and honesty, and team-building abilities and emotional intelligence (Amos, 2012; Barnes, 2013; Hogan & Warrenfeltz, 2003; PricewaterhouseCoopers, 2011). However, it is transformational leadership that is considered critical to leadership effectiveness. A study by Northouse (2013) analysing 39 studies in transformational literature found that transformational leaders were more effective and produced better results in their organisations. This sentiment is supported by Weese (1994, p. 188) who emphasises that transformational leaders 'have a positive impact on employee satisfaction, productivity and organisational effectiveness'. Before 2005, the Kenyan indigenous banks were said to lack the appropriate competencies to steer their banks to great heights (Sokpor, 2006). This drawback was demonstrated in the poor performance of Kenyan indigenous banks, leading to vast financial losses by their stakeholders and customers. Despite the past performance of these banks, in recent years, the indigenous banks have performed better with many of them recording encouraging results (Mwangi, 2012). However, considering their poor performance in the past, this study was motivated by a desire to establish the extent to which the recent improvement is attributable to transformational leadership competency and effectiveness. It is also anticipated that this investigation can highlight aspects of leadership which require more attention in order to sustain improved performance.

In the Kenyan context, although many studies exist on the banking industry, there is no specific study focusing on leadership in the banks, especially transformational leadership (Hedley, White, Roche & Banerjea, 2006; PWC, 2007). Bearing in mind the importance of transformational leadership in the quest to attain bank leadership effectiveness, it became critical to conduct a study on the relationship between transformational leadership and leadership effectiveness among Kenyan indigenous banks, a sector considered instrumental to the country's economic development.

Research objectives

This study investigates the relationship between transformational leadership competency (independent variable) and leadership effectiveness (dependent variable) in the current Kenyan indigenous banking industry. As such, the relevant research question is whether the transformational leadership competencies of the leadership in the Kenyan indigenous banks are positively correlated to their leadership effectiveness and could be associated with the current positive performance of the sector. Two further objectives for this study are:

- To determine whether there is a positive correlation between transformational leadership competency and its sub-variables, namely, *inspirational motivation*, *intellectual stimulation*, *individualised consideration*, *idealised influence (attributes)* and *idealised influence (behaviour)*.
- To determine whether there is a positive correlation between leadership effectiveness and its sub-variables, namely, *cross-cultural competence*, *influence*, *follower commitment*, *versatility* and *group organisation*.

Literature review and hypothesis development

Contextualising transformational leadership

The term 'transformation' was first associated with Downton (1973), and was popularised by Burns (1978) through his research on leadership. Later, the concept of transformational leadership became the focus of research as an important leadership style in both business and non-business contexts (Bass & Avolio, 1990; Bass, Waldman & Avolio, 1978).

For most researchers and scholars, transformational leadership refers to a leadership style in which the leader and followers empower each other in terms of a higher level of morality and motivation (Burns, 1978). Bass (1985) observes that transformational leadership enables leaders to exceed their expected performance. This results in enhancement of followers' levels of trust, admiration and loyalty. It is a style that enables both the leader and followers to engage in mutually trusting commitment that generates above-normal results.

While some consider transformational leadership synonymous with transactional leadership, there are in fact significant differences between the two. Transactional leadership focuses on efficiency and making sure strategies are implemented at the middle and lower management levels, while transformational leadership focuses on effectiveness through creation of a harmonious working relationship between leaders and followers (Edward & Gill, 2012). It has been argued that leaders need to develop transformational leadership behaviour and competencies to be effective and competitive (Amos, 2012). Others have asserted that both transactional and transformational leadership competencies are required to ensure leaders' effectiveness irrespective of the level in the organisation (Bass & Avolio, 1995). Various studies have found that transactional and transformational leadership contribute to subordinate satisfaction, performance, inspiration and positive attitude among organisational membership (Avolio, Howell & Sosik, 1999).

Despite support for both types of leadership competencies, transformational leadership is considered to be more critical. For instance, Walumbwa, Avolio and Zhu (2008) note that there are numerous research focusing on effective transformational leaders and their relationship with followers. Bass and Avolio (1995) contend that using transformational leadership is the ideal way to help deal with contemporary business world challenges. Similarly, Shadraconis (2013) argues that the transformational style is effective during times of crisis as it gives organisational leaders the platform to exercise their authority and respond accordingly. This suggests that transformational leadership is appropriate to addressing the Kenyan indigenous bank challenges and could be associated with the positive performance of the industry in the recent past.

Conceptualising transformational leadership competence

Transformational leadership is understood to positively affect the productivity of followers or employees, and of the overall effectiveness of the organisation (Tuuk, 2012), owing to the competencies associated with this leadership style. To measure transformational leadership, scholars and researchers have over the years developed different attributes, referred to in this study as transformational leadership sub-variables (Bass, 1990; Bass & Avolio, 1994; Hall, Johnson, Wysocki & Kepner, 2012; Hayward, 2005; Hebert, 2011). Bass and Avolio (1990, 1994) single out four main sub-variables associated with transformational leadership, namely, inspirational motivation, intellectual stimulation, individualised consideration and idealised influence attributes (commonly known as the Four I's). However, a more recent study by Hayward (2005) identified an additional sub-competency of idealised influence behaviour, which is included in this study as the fifth sub-competency, making a contribution to the theoretical conceptualisation of transformational leadership. The five sub-variables are discussed below.

Inspirational motivation denotes a leader's ability to inspire and mentor others (Bass & Avolio, 1994), a task achieved through good communication skills and mentoring, visioning, corrective action and risk-taking. Furthermore, the leader is a hard worker with confidence that inspires optimism among employees, especially during crises (Hebert, 2011). These leaders also encourage individual championship and team spirit in order to attain set goals and realise high performance in terms of revenues and growth (Hall et al., 2012).

Intellectual stimulation emphasises a leader's ability to be creative and innovative (Bass & Avolio, 1994; Hall et al., 2012) in encouraging their followers to be creative by providing a conducive environment to test and develop new ideas (Bass, 1990). In a business context, this enables employees to courageously think independently of ways to improve their performance and creative ability, thereby providing solutions to critical organisational problems and challenges (Bass, 1990; Hebert, 2011).

In terms of individual consideration, the leader is said to have the ability to assess, diagnose and evaluate employees' individual needs rather than treating them as a group (Bass & Avolio, 1994). This approach ensures that the needs of individuals are identified, addressed and mentorship provided to equip employees with skills to deal with challenging opportunities or positions (Bass, 1990; Hall et al., 2012).

Idealised influence competencies relate to a leader's ability to capture and communicate a vision and mission, successfully showing respect, building confidence and trust among followers or employees while at the same time encouraging them to pursue individual or collective goals (Bass, 1995). The leader also exhibits role model behaviour and is inspirational, considerate and able to stimulate self and others in terms of creativity and innovativeness (Hall et al., 2012; Hebert, 2011).

Idealised influence behaviour focuses on the leader's ability not only to have a vision and mission for the organisation and its members but also to demonstrate the appropriate behaviour desired for effective performance (Hayward, 2005).

Conceptualising leadership effectiveness

The term 'effectiveness' refers to the ability to realise set goals or objectives (Yukl, 2010). In relation to leadership, effectiveness denotes a leader's ability to steer an organisation towards attaining set goals (Green, 2010; Yukl, 2010). Though essential to organisational performance, defining leadership effectiveness remains controversial with little agreement on the common definition both in the past and among contemporary scholars and researchers (Arnold, Cooper & Robertson, 1998). In this regard, Stogdill (1974), Bass (1981) and Bass (1990) catalogued and interpreted about 5000 studies where they found great differences in definition. Emphasising these differences, Burns (1978) notes that leadership effectiveness 'is one of the most observed and least understood phenomena on earth'. For example, Norma (1997) and Yukl (1994) defined leadership effectiveness as a process whereby one person influenced other people's behaviour with an aim to achieve set goals. Such a leader must also win the followers' attention and commitment in order to realise set goals. For most scholars, however, leadership effectiveness is demonstrating appropriate skills, abilities, beliefs and behaviour (Green, 2010; Yukl, 2010) to achieve a desired goal. For this study, leadership effectiveness implies the leader's ability to exercise personal influence, skills and abilities to accomplish expected goals or objectives (Cooper et al., 2012).

To measure leadership effectiveness, scholars and researchers have developed many different attributes, referred to in this study as leadership effectiveness sub-variables (Epitropaki & Martin, 2005; Green, 2010). Some of these attributes include ability to inspire a shared vision, foster unity, exercise power effectively, empower others, establish appropriate learning environment, satisfy job-related needs of employees, group organisation, follower satisfaction, follower commitment, level of impact, cross-cultural competence and versatility (Green, 2010; National Centre for Research in Vocation Education, 1994; Yukl, 2010). Further research identified five sub-variables as most appropriate measures of leadership effectiveness, namely, cross-cultural competence, influence, follower commitment, versatility and group organisation (Green, 2010). The current study used the latter five sub-variables to measure leadership effectiveness in the indigenous banking industry. The five sub-variables are discussed below.

Cross-cultural competence denotes the leader's ability to work with and attain results from followers coming from different cultures (Green, 2010). Several studies highlight the role of cross-cultural competence in shaping the leader's behaviour and the increasing demand to have leaders who are able to manage diversity in the workplace (Earley & Ang, 2003; Johnson et al., 2006). For instance, Yukl (2010) emphasises the importance of recognising the role of cultural competency and diversity management as influencing the leader's behaviour. However, Johnson et al. (2006) recognise that there is insufficient research on cross-cultural competence particularly in international business arenas and therefore wanting its inclusion in this study.

Influence implies the leader's ability to impact on the behaviour of others to achieve the desired results (Green, 2010). To be effective, a leader's influence must make a positive impression, not only on those supervised directly but also on the whole organisation. In applying influence, leaders should show understanding and appreciation of followers in order to gain their commitment and attention.

Follower commitment refers to organisational members' commitment and dedication to a common goal and objective (Green, 2010). Follower commitment is a key determinant of a leader's effectiveness, and it enables attainment of set goals and objectives in unison (Yukl, 2010). A leader who emphasises and supports follower commitment, results in an enthusiastic workforce full of commitment and confidence in the leader and the leadership style, leading to positive and satisfactory performance.

Versatility indicates the leader's ability to work with others and obtain desired results. The concept is used in the context of obtaining results from others, especially different line managers and across departments (Green, 2010). Versatility is based on the increasing demand to have leaders manage people outside their traditional organisational structures or levels.

Group organisation refers to the way a group is organised to ensure it works effectively to achieve set goals (Yukl, 2010). Employees are greatly influenced by group organisation (Epitropaki & Martin, 2005). According to prevailing literature, there is a need to have a positive leader–subordinate relationship, if effective work is to be realised, a goal which is achievable through group organisation. Similarly, the effectiveness of a leader is determined by understanding and being involved in group organisation. However, this can only be realised if the leaders and subordinates build strong mutual trust and respect, and work as a group (Epitropaki & Martin, 2005). Yukl (2010) comments that subordinates must be satisfied with the leader if their group is to perform effectively. With increased emphasis on attaining leadership effectiveness in organisations, group organisation has become central to leadership success.

Theoretical overview and hypotheses development

As previously mentioned, transformational leadership is a style where both leaders and followers accept, consult and work together to achieve a common goal (Burns, 1978). According to the prevailing literature, transformational leadership results in understanding and change of attitude, beliefs and heart in order to realise set goals in a mutually acceptable and satisfying manner (Bass, 1985). Both literature and empirical evidence identify transformational leadership competencies mandatory for leaders to perform effectively, namely, *inspirational motivation, intellectual stimulation, individualised consideration, idealised influence (attributes) and idealised influence (behaviours)* as derived from Avolio and Bass (2004), Hall et al. (2012) and Hayward (2005). Several studies support transformational leadership competencies as key ingredients in ensuring leadership effectiveness (such as Avolio, Howell & Sosik, 1999; Barling, Slater & Kelloway, 2000; Edward & Gill, 2012). To demonstrate the importance of transformational leadership competency in relation to leadership effectiveness, over 500 doctoral studies have been done since 1995 (Bass & Avolio, 2004). From a majority of the studies, it is hypothesised that a strong relationship exists between transformational leadership competencies and leadership effectiveness (Avolio & Bass, 2004; Edward & Gill, 2012; Howell & Hall-Marenda, 1999). Based on the theoretical review, the current study hypothesises an existence of a relationship between transformational leadership competency and leadership effectiveness within the indigenous banking sector in Kenya.

In order to achieve the purpose of this study, the hypothesised relationship between transformational leadership (independent variable) and leadership effectiveness (dependent variable) is depicted in Figure 1.

The following hypothesis is formulated and tested to establish the existence or lack of a correlation between transformational leadership and leadership effectiveness:

- **Hypothesis 1 (H¹):** There is a positive correlation between transformational leadership and leadership effectiveness.

Research design methodology

This study used a positivist approach which is most suited to the quantitative nature of the data gathered to establish the relationship between transformational leadership competencies and leadership effectiveness.

Sampling and response rate

The population in this study consisted of 30 Kenyan indigenous banks and their employees. In order to participate in the study, respective market share was used to rank the banks ranging from the largest to the smallest. A sample of 15 (50%) banks was selected based on the size of their market share, with 13 of them finally participating in the study. Non-probability sampling to purposely select managers or supervisors and simple random techniques to select non-managers were used, with a total of 494 participants. While 273 questionnaires were received back, only 257 were found to be usable for statistical analysis, a response of 55.3%.

Measuring instruments

The self-administered measuring instrument consisted of a cover letter and four sections. Section 1 of the questionnaire had 20 statements containing information on Kenyan indigenous banking, bank existence, leadership competencies and growth. Section 2 on transformational leadership competency and Section 3 on leadership effectiveness had 25 statements, respectively. The measuring statements in

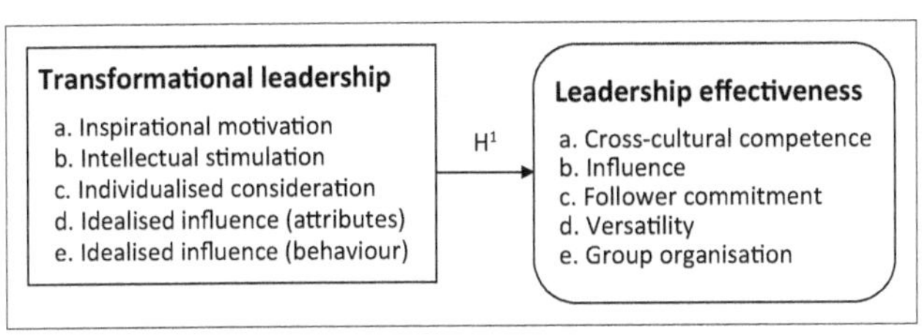

FIGURE 1: Proposed hypothesised framework of the relationship between transformational leadership and leadership effectiveness.

Sections 2 and 3 were made up of a multi-item labelled five-point Likert-type scale. As such, respondents indicated their level of agreement with given statements, where 1 = strongly disagree and 5 = strongly agree. Section 4 focused on demographic information, ranging from sex, age, education level, work position to bank rating.

Research procedure in data collection

Prior to collecting the data, the researcher sought the permissions from the target banks for the study to be conducted. Furthermore a permit was attained from the National Council for Science and Technology (NCST), a government body responsible for research conducted in Kenya. In addition the study abided by the required research ethics standards requirements at Rhodes University. The questionnaire distributed was accompanied by a cover letter explaining the purpose of the research, importance of voluntary participation and confidentiality and the need for participants' consent before participation. Through the use of research assistants, some of the questionnaires were physically distributed and collected while others were administered and completed electronically as preferred by some respondents. The actual data collection took place over a period of 4 months.

Data analysis

To ensure the desired results were attained, structural equation modelling (SEM) was used for data analysis. Specifically, the software program AMOS (IBM SPSS Statistics, Version 21, 2013) was used for the SEM. The analysis included Cronbach's alpha (CA) and confirmatory factor analysis (CFA) to assess the discriminant reliability, validity of the measuring instrument and goodness-of-fit indices. From a SEM perspective, a response of 257 is sufficient for analysis. According to literature, an acceptable range for analysis is between 200 and 400 responses (Farrington, 2009). However, responses of between 150 and 200 have been used for analysis (Loehlin, 1992). There are other studies that have similarly argued that a sample of between 100 and 200 is appropriate (Hair, Anderson, Tatham & Black, 1998). This means that the response rate used for this study is within the accepted parameters.

Results

The descriptive statistics shows that the majority of the respondents from the current study are women (52.1%) while men account for 47.9%. The findings further indicate that most of the respondents (63.8%) were aged between 25 and 40 years, placing most of the respondents as young employees. Similarly, over half of the respondents (54.4%) were university graduates. A majority (84%) worked in the banking industry for a period ranging from 1 to 10 years, of which 52.1% had worked at the bank for a period of between 1 and 5 years. Another finding indicates that more than half (64.2%) of the respondents reported that their banks had experienced financial crisis.

Discriminant validity and reliability results

In order to perform discriminant validity and reliability tests, both CFA and CA were conducted. First, CFA was conducted to establish the unique factors in the data and assess the discriminant validity of the scales measuring the independent and dependent variables. The validity of the *transformational leadership* competency, independent variable, termed a construct, was made up of five sub-constructs, namely, *inspirational motivation, intellectual stimulation, individualised consideration, idealised influence (attributes) and idealised influence (behaviour)*. In this study, all factor analysis scores were acceptable at 0.3 (Hair, Black, Babin, Anderson & Tatham, 2006). All the transformational leadership sub-constructs were accepted after the measuring items loaded as expected and were therefore analysed further. The following CFA scores for the leadership competency sub-construct measuring scales were attained, namely, *inspirational motivation* (0.654), *intellectual stimulation* (0.545), *individualised consideration* (0.730), *idealised influence attributes* (0.700) *and idealised influence behaviour* (0.599). The five factors, previously referred to as sub-constructs, explain 69.3% of the variance in the data.

Similarly, the five sub-constructs of the dependent variable, *leadership effectiveness* (*cross-cultural competence, influence, follower commitment, versatility* and *group organisation*) were used in the CFA test. The result was that three of the sub-constructs loaded successfully with CFA scores of *influence* (0.759), *follower commitment* (0.752) and *versatility* (0.738). Two factors (*group organisation* and *cross-cultural competence*) failed to load at the minimum factor analysis score of 0.3. The three factors that loaded successfully explain 48.6% of the variance in the data.

The CA's assessment was done to establish the reliability of the scales of the measuring instrument. The independent variable (*transformational leadership competency*) and dependent variable (*leadership effectiveness*) constructs gave CA scores of 0.953 and 0.914, respectively. The scores were considered very reliable compared to the minimum acceptable score of 0.7 (Nunnally, 1978). For all factors, coefficients of greater than 0.7 (Nunnally, 1978, p. 226) were returned. Sufficient evidence of validity and reliability for the scales measuring the independent and dependent variables is thus provided. The specific scores for *transformational leadership* sub-constructs were: *individualised consideration* (0.892), *idealised influence behaviour* (0.844), *inspirational motivation* (0.868) *intellectual simulation* (0.869) and *idealised influence attributes* (0.849). The CA scores are in agreement with similar studies, thereby making the measuring instrument and data reliable (Hayward, 2005).

Similarly, the result for the sub-constructs for *leadership effectiveness* that were retained for further analysis in this study had the following scores: *influence* (0.759), *follower commitment* (0.752) and *versatility* (0.738). The results indicated that the items used to measure *leadership effectiveness* construct were reliable with all the scores being greater than 0.7. The findings also agree with similar studies (Green, 2010).

The results of structural equation modelling

The results of both the CFA and CA indicate that all of the sub-constructs (independent variable) were accepted for analysis. Two sub-constructs from the dependent variable (*cross-cultural competencies* and *group organisation*) failed to load as expected and were consequently dropped from further analysis. The changes in the number of sub-constructs required for further analysis led to the modification of the proposed theoretical framework, henceforth referred to as a model (see Figure 2).

To determine the goodness-of-fit for the model and to test the hypotheses, SEM was used. Similarly, in order to validate and test the hypotheses and sub-constructs, SEM was conducted for *transformational leadership* and *leadership effectiveness* constructs. Because of space constraints, the structural relationship models have not been included in this article. Instead, the structural and measurement model for *transformational leadership* and its sub-constructs is shown in Table 1.

Goodness-of-fit

A goodness-of-fit test is usually conducted in order to measure the fitness of the actual or observed input correlation or covariance in relation to the prediction made by a theoretical model (Hair et al., 1998). In this study, the goodness-of-fit was determined using four measures, namely, normed Chi-square (the ratio of Chi-square to degrees of freedom [χ^2/df], the root mean square error of approximation [RMSEA], the goodness-of-fit index [GFI] and the comparative fit index [CFI]). The criteria used to measure goodness-of-fit indices are shown in Table 2.

Based on the criteria set in Table 2, the results of the goodness-of-fit indices for transformational leadership are represented in Table 3.

As shown in Table 3, the results show that the Normed Chi-square or CMID/DF value is 3.599 and falls between 2.0 and 5.0, indicating a good fit (Hooper et al., 2008; Tabachnick & Fidel, 2007). The RMSEA value is 0.101, which is above the maximum acceptance fit value of 0.08 and is therefore a poor fit and unacceptable (Grimm & Yarnold, 2000). The GFI value of 0.813 is less than 0.90. However, according to Hu and

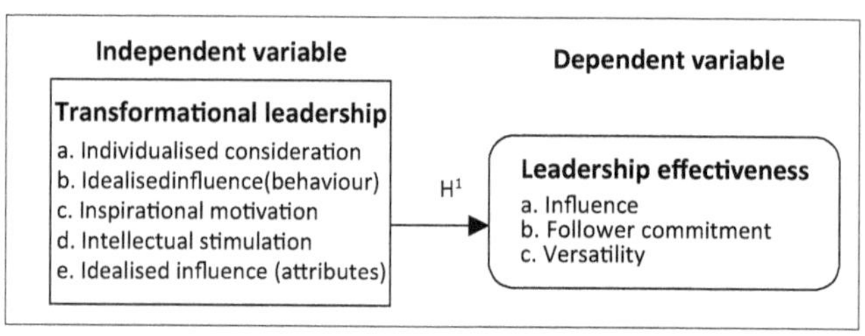

FIGURE 2: The revised hypothesised mode of the relationship between transformational leadership and leadership effectiveness.

Bentler (1999), a value of 0.813 is still within acceptable fit. The final measure, CFI, has a value of 0.861 and is between 0.8 and 0.9, indicating a good fit (Byrne, 1998; Hooper et al., 2008). The CFI result value of 0.861 can therefore be termed as a good fit. With three of the tests (CMIN/DF, GFI and CFI) indicating good fits, there is a goodness-of-fit between the sub-model and approximation of the data.

In terms of the relationship between the *transformational leadership competency* construct and its sub-constructs, SEM analysis was used to establish if a relationship existed as shown in Table 4.

Table 4 demonstrates the existence of a positive correlation ($p < 0.001$) between all the sub-constructs and *transformational leadership* construct. The results indicated that all the transformational leadership sub-constructs are significant ($p < 0.001$) to *transformational leadership competency*.

The findings further showed that *intellectual stimulation* sub-construct (estimate = 0.663; $p < 0.001$) had greater influence on *transformational leadership*. This is followed by *individualised consideration* (estimate = 0.616; $p < 0.001$), *idealised influence* (attributes) (estimate = 0.570; $p < 0.001$), *idealised influence* (behaviour) (estimate = 0.488; $p < 0.001$) and *inspirational motivation* (estimate = 0.465; $p < 0.001$), respectively.

The relationship between the *leadership effectiveness* construct and its sub-constructs was also examined (see Table 5) rather than including the structural model of structural relationships in this article.

Based on the criteria indicated in Table 2, the results of the goodness-of-fit indices for leadership effectiveness are represented in Table 6.

The results of goodness-of-fit shown in Table 6 indicated a CMIN/DF value of 2.671, signifying a good fit between data and the sub-model. The RMSEA on the other hand had a value of 0.081, indicating a poor goodness-of-fit (MacCullum et al., 1996). Similarly, the GFI value of 0.924 (Ghazali et al., 2013) and the CFI value of 0.921 indicate a very good fit (Hair et al., 2006). With three of the tests (CMIN/DF, GFI and CFI) indicating good fits, there is a goodness-of-fit between the sub-model and approximation of the data.

The relationship between the *leadership effectiveness* construct and its sub-constructs (*influence, follower commitment* and *versatility*) was analysed and confirmed by SEM. The findings showing the parameters and the p-values are presented in Table 7.

From Table 7, it is clear that there is a positive correlation ($p < 0.001$) between the *leadership effectiveness* construct and its sub-constructs. Based on importance, the *influence* sub-construct had the greatest impact (estimate = 0.717; $p < 0.001$), followed by *follower commitment* (estimate = 0.664; $p < 0.001$) and finally *versatility* sub-construct (estimate = 0.483; $p < 0.001$).

TABLE 1: Definition of structural constructs and measurements for the transformational leadership model and its sub-constructs.

Model	Construct	Sub-constructs	Measured or observed sub-constructs
Transformational leadership structural model	Transformational leadership	Idealised influence (attributes), Idealised influence (behaviour), Inspirational motivation, Intellectual stimulation, Individualised consideration	-
Transformational leadership measurement model	-	Idealised influence (attributes)	Att1, Att2, Att3
	-	Idealised influence (behaviour)	Beh1, Beh2, Beh3, Beh4
	-	Inspirational motivation	Ins1, Ins2, Ins3, Ins4, Ins5
	-	Intellectual stimulation	Sti1, Sti2, Sti3, Sti4
	-	Individualised consideration	Con1, Con2, Con3, Con4, Con5

TABLE 2: Criteria for goodness-of-fit indices.

Goodness-of-fit measure	Types of test	Criteria
Normed Chi-square (χ^2/degree of freedom)	Absolute fit and model parsimony	0.00 to < 1.90 indicates a very good fit (Politis, 2003; Ullman, 2001)
		2.00–5.00 indicates a good fit
		5.0 indicates acceptable fit
		> 5.00 indicates poor fit (Hooper, Coughlan & Mullen, 2008)
The root mean square error of approximation (RMSEA)	Absolute fit	0.00 to < 0.05 indicates a very good fit (Adendorff, 2004)
		0.051 to < 0.060 indicates a good fit (Grimm & Yarnold, 2000; Hair et al., 1998; Hu & Bentler, 1999)
		0.061–0.08 indicates an acceptable or reasonable fit (Hu & Bentler, 1999)
		> 0.08 indicates a poor fit (MacCullum, Browne & Sugawara, 1996)
The goodness-of-fit index (GFI)	Absolute fit	0.91–0.95 is considered a very good fit (Ghazali, Ahmad, Uli, Suandi & Hassan, 2013)
		0.90–0.84 indicates good fit (Keskin, 2014)
		0.85 to ≤ 0.89 indicates acceptable fit (Keskin, 2014)
		0.0–0.84, with higher values indicating better model fit (Hu & Bentler, 1999)
Comparative fit index (CFI)	Incremental fit	0.90 to ≤ 0.95 indicates a very good fit (Hair et al., 2006)
		Between 0.50 and 0.89 indicates good fit (Byrne, 1998; Hooper et al., 2008; Hu & Bentler, 1999)
		Between 0.3 and 0.5 is an acceptable fit (Fan, Thompson & Wang, 1999)
		0 ≥ indicates poor fit (Li, 2007)

Source: Muriithi, S.M. (2015). *Relationship between leadership and organisational effectiveness among indigenous banks in Kenya.* Unpublished PhD thesis, Rhodes University, Grahamstown, South Africa

Note: Please see the full reference list of the article, Louw, L. Muriithi, S.M., & Radloff, S. (2017). The relationship between transformational leadership and leadership effectiveness in Kenyan indigenous banks. *SA Journal of Human Resource Management/SA Tydskrif vir Menslikehulpbronbestuur, 15*(0), a935. https://doi.org/10.4102/sajhrm.v15i0.935, for more information.

TABLE 3: Goodness-of-fit indices for the structural model transformational leadership.

Goodness-of-fit measure	Criteria
Sample size	257
Normed Chi-square (χ^2/degree of freedom)	3.599
The root mean square error of approximation (RMSEA)	0.101
Goodness-of-fit index (GFI)	0.813
Comparative fit index (CFI)	0.861

TABLE 4: Structural model parameter estimates and p-values for transformational leadership and its sub-constructs.

Transformational sub-constructs	Estimates	S.E	C.R	*P*
Transfrm<---- Idealised influence (attributes)	0.570	0.055	10.416	***
Transfrm<---- Idealised influence (behaviour)	0.488	0.046	10.628	***
Transfrm<---- Inspirational motivation	0.465	0.046	10.003	***
Transfrm<---- Intellectual stimulation	0.663	0.054	12.179	***
Transfrm<---- Individualised consideration	0.616	0.057	11.858	***

***, $p < 0.001$

TABLE 5: Definition of structural constructs and measurements for the leadership effectiveness model and its sub-constructs.

Model	Construct	Sub-constructs	Measured or observed measuring items
Leadership effectiveness structural model	Leadership effectiveness	Influence, follower commitment, versatility	-
Leadership effectiveness measurement model	-	Influence	Inf1, Inf2, Inf3, Inf4, Inf5
	-	Follower commitment	Fol1, Fol2. Fol3
	-	Versatility	Ver1, Ver2, Ver3, Ver5

TABLE 6: Goodness-of-fit indices for the structural model leadership effectiveness.

Goodness-of-fit measure	Criteria
Sample size	257
Normed Chi-square (χ^2/degree of freedom) (CMIN/DF)	2.671
The root mean square error of approximation (RMSEA)	0.081
Goodness-of-fit index (GFI)	0.924
Comparative fit index (CFI)	0.921

The results demonstrated that *influence, follower commitment* and *versatility* were critical measures of leadership effectiveness.

Transformational leadership and leadership effectiveness

In terms of transformational leadership and leadership effectiveness, the goodness-of-fit indices showed a good fit between the proposed measurement and structural sub-model, therefore representing acceptable approximation of the data (Table 8).

The results of goodness-of-fit shown in Table 8 illustrate a CMIN/DF value of 1.704, signifying a very good fit between data and the sub-model (Politis, 2003; Ullman, 2001). Similarly, the RMSEA value of 0.052 indicates a good fit (Grimm & Yarnold, 2000; Hair et al., 1998; Hu & Bentler, 1999). The GFI value of 0.982 is very good (Ghazali et al., 2013). Finally, the CFI value of 0.922 showed a very good fit (Hair et al., 2006). With four tests (CMIN/DF, RMSEA, GFI

TABLE 7: Structural model parameter estimates and p-values for leadership effectiveness and its sub-constructs.

Leadership effectiveness sub-constructs	Estimates	S.E	C.R	*P*
Leadeff <---- Influence	0.717	0.056	12.747	***
Leadeff <---- Follower commitment	0.664	0.056	11.850	***
Leadeff <---- Versatility	0.483	0.058	8.372	***

***, $p < 0.001$

TABLE 8: Goodness-of-fit indices for transformational leadership and leadership effectiveness.

Goodness-of-fit measure	Criteria
Sample size	257
Normed Chi-square (χ^2/degree of freedom) (CMIN/DF)	1.704
The root mean square error of approximation (RMSEA)	0.052
Goodness-of-fit index (GFI)	0.982
Comparative fit index (CFI)	0.922

TABLE 9: Structural model parameter estimates and p-values for transformational and leadership effectiveness.

Tranformation-leadership constructs	Estimates	S.E	C.R	*P*
Tran_L <---- Lead_compet	0.992	0.065	15.268	***
Inf <-----Lead_compet	0.612	0.051	12.052	***
Fol <-----Lead_compet	1.000	-	-	-
Ver <----Lead_compet	0.660	0.660	9.963	***

***, $p < 0.001$

and CFI) being successful, this indicates a goodness-of-fit between the sub-model and approximation of the data.

The relationship between *transformational leadership* and *leadership effectiveness* constructs was examined as shown in hypothesis H^1:

- **Hypothesis 1 (H^1):** There is a positive correlation between transformational leadership and leadership effectiveness.

Following SEM analysis, the result indicated a strong positive correlation between *transformational leadership* and *leadership effectiveness* constructs. The analysis indicating the parameters and the p-values are shown in Table 9.

Table 9 indicates a strong and positive correlation ($p < 0.001$) between *transformational leadership* construct (estimate = 1.000; $p < 0.001$) and *leadership effectiveness* construct. The findings support hypothesis H^1 and are in agreement with similar studies that advocate the presence of a strong correlation between transformational leadership and leadership effectiveness (Amos, 2012; Avolio & Bass, 2004; Hayward, 2005; Samson & Daft, 2012).

Discussion

Outline of results

The study has found that the *transformational leadership* sub-constructs are an important ingredient for *leadership effectiveness* within the Kenyan indigenous banking industry. The specific transformational leadership sub-constructs were found to be relevant and in order of ranking were *intellectual stimulation, individualised consideration, idealised influence* (*attributes*), *idealised influence* (*behaviour*) and *inspirational motivation*. From the results, it can be concluded that there existed a positive correlation between all transformational sub-constructs and *transformational leadership competency*. This means that effective transformational leaders are able to intellectually stimulate and motivate their followers. The leaders are also able to give individualised consideration to those under their care. Such leaders are also able to apply idealised influence (attributes and behaviour) while at the same time inspiring themselves and their followers. The results of the study are in agreement with similar studies where all the five sub-constructs were found to be significant to *transformational leadership competency* (Avolio & Bass, 2004; Hayward, 2005). The results are significant to the banking leadership and show the need for the leadership to develop their transformational leadership competencies in order to be effective in their performance. The findings are in agreement with similar studies that have demonstrated a strong positive relationship between transformational leadership and leadership effectiveness (Donnelly, 1994; Kubicek, 2011; Northouse, 2013; Weese, 1994; Yukl, 2010). Similarly, the leadership effectiveness construct was found to have three main attributes of effectiveness within indigenous banking in Kenya, namely *follower commitment*, *versatility* and *influence*. From the findings, follower commitment was the most important attributes of leadership effectiveness followed by versatility and then by leader influence. Based on the findings, the bank leadership should ensure that the right transformational leadership competencies are sought from all bank employees in order to ensure effectiveness. With leadership effectiveness, the bank leaders should now be more aware of which attributes are most influential in enhancing the banks' sustainability.

Practical implications

The current study on the relationship between transformational leadership and leadership effectiveness has implications for both theory and practice and organisational leadership in general. First, the study has confirmed the existence of a relationship between transformational leadership and leadership effectiveness in the indigenous banking industry in Kenya. Second, the study has added valuable knowledge to the field of transformational leadership and leadership effectiveness in relation to the banking industry in Kenya. The findings therefore indicate that bank leadership cannot ignore transformational leadership competencies as essential to their success if they have to be effective in their leadership endeavours.

Limitations and recommendations

The study concentration on transformational leadership competency is a limitation because there are other competencies that may affect or influence leadership effectiveness. The study therefore recommends that more studies be conducted on other leadership competencies. This will bring more understanding on the determinants of leadership effectiveness within the banking industry and in other organisations.

Conclusion

The current study found a significant relationship between transformational leadership competencies and leadership effectiveness among the leaders in the Kenyan indigenous banking industry. The study identified required transformational leadership competencies and leadership effectiveness attributes relevant to the Kenyan indigenous banking industry. The findings therefore answered the key questions of this research by indicating that transformational leadership competencies of the leadership in the Kenyan indigenous banks are positively correlated to the leadership effectiveness and could be attributed with the current positive performance of the sector. This study therefore emphasised the need to have banks identify the appropriate competencies for their leaders and employees. It is also necessary to match the appropriate leadership competencies with leadership effectiveness attributes of effectiveness.

Acknowledgements

Competing interests

The authors declare that they have no financial or personal relationships that may have inappropriately influenced them in writing this article.

Authors' contributions

S.M.M. was the principal investigator responsible for the fieldwork and the co-writing of this article. L.L. was the academic supervisor and was responsible for the overall leadership and designing of the study and co-writing, editing, finalisation and submission of this article. S.R. was responsible for the statistical analysis of data, presentation and interpretation using relevant tools and research instrument(s). The writing of the article was a team effort.

References

Adendorff, C.M. (2004). *The development of a cultural family business model of good governance for Greek family businesses in South Africa*. Unpublished doctoral thesis, Rhodes University, Grahamstown.

Al-Zoubi, B.R. (2012). Leadership competencies and competitive advantage: Empirical study on Jordan telecommunications. *European Journal of Business and Management, 4*(7), 234–247.

Ambutsi, P.B. (2005). *A survey of corporate governance practices in selected commercial banks in Kenya*. Unpublished MBA thesis, Daystar University, Nairobi.

Amos, T. (2012). Strategic leadership. In L. Louw & P. Venter (Eds.), *Strategic management: Developing sustainability in Southern Africa* (2nd edn., pp. 439–476). Cape Town: Oxford University Press.

Arnold, J., Cooper, C., & Robertson, I. (1998). *Work psychology. Understanding human behaviour in the workplace*. (3rd edn.). Harlow, England: Pearson Education.

Avolio, B.J., & Bass, B.M. (2004). *Multifactor leadership questionnaire: Third edition manual and sampler set*. Redwood City, CA: Mind Garden.

Avolio, B.J., Howell, J.M., & Sosik, J.J. (1999). A funny thing happened on the way to the bottom line: Humour as a moderator of leadership style effects. *Academy of Management Journal, 42*, 219–227. https://doi.org/10.2307/257094

Barling, J., Slater, F. & Kelloway, E.K. (2000). Transformational leadership and emotional intelligence: An exploratory study. *Leadership and Organizational Development Journal, 21*, 157–161. https://doi.org/10.1108/01437730010325040

Barnes, R. (2013). *Do you know your CEO? The eight essential leadership skills.* Retrieved March 06, 2013, from http://www.marketingmagazine.co.uk/article/1174126/know-ceo-eight-essential-leadership-skills

Bass, B. (1990). *Bass & Stogdill's handbook of leadership: theory research and managerial applications.* (3rd edn.). New York: Free Press.

Bass, B.M. (1981). *Stogdill's handbook of leadership.* New York: Free Press.

Bass, B.M. (1985). *Leadership and performance.* New York: Free Press.

Bass, B.M. (1995). Theory of transformational leadership redux. *Leadership Quarterly, 6*(4), 463–478. https://doi.org/10.1016/1048-9843(95)90021-7

Bass, B.M., & Avolio, B.J. (1990). Developing transformational leadership: 1992 and beyond. *Journal of European Industrial Training, 14*(5), 21–37. https://doi.org/10.1108/03090599010135122

Bass, B.M., & Avolio, B.J. (1994). *Improving organizational effectiveness through transformational leadership.* Thousand Oaks, CA: Sage.

Bass, B.M., & Avolio, B.J. (1995). *Multifactor leadership questionnaire ©.* Randburg: Productivity Development (Pty) Ltd.

Bass, B.M., Waldman, D., & Avolio, B.J. (1978). Transformational leadership and the falling dominoes effect. *Group and Organization Studies, 12*(1), 73–86. https://doi.org/10.1177/105960118701200106

Brunnermerier, M.K. (2009). Deciphering the liquidity and credit crunch 2007–2008. *Journal of Economic Perspectives, 23*(1), 77–100. https://doi.org/10.1257/jep.23.1.77

Burns, J.M. (1978). *Leadership.* New York: Harper Row.

Byrne, B.M. (1998). *Structural equation modeling with LISREL, PRELIS and SIMPLIS: Basic concepts, applications and programming.* Mahwah, NJ: Lawrence Erlbaum Associates.

Cooper, J., Fenimore, J., & Nirenberg, J. (Eds.). (2012). *Leadership effectiveness. Encyclopaedia of leadership.* Thousand Oaks, CA: Sage. Retrieved February 11, 2011, from http://www.sagepub.com/northouse6e/study/materials/reference/reference6.4.pdf

Donnelly, J.H. (1994). Reframing the mind of the banker: The changing skill set and skills mix for effective leadership. *International Journal of Bank Marketing, 12*(8), 12–16. Retrieved February 08, 2010, from http://www.Emeraldinsight.Com/insight/viewpdf.jsp?contenttype=article&filename=html/output/published/emeraldfulltextarticle/pdf/0320120802.pdf

Downton, J.V. (1973). *Rebel leadership: Commitment and charisma in a revolutionary process.* New York: The Free Press.

Earley, P.C. & Ang, S. (2003). *Cultural intelligence. Individual interactions across cultures.* Stanford, CA: Stanford University Press.

Edward, G., & Gill, R. (2012). Transformational leadership across hierarchical levels in UK manufacturing organisations. *Leadership & Organisational Development Journal, 33*(1), 25–50. https://doi.org/10.1108/01437731211193106

Epitropaki, O., & Martin, R. (2005). From ideal to real: A longitudinal study of the role of implicit leadership theories on leader-member exchanges and employee outcomes. *Journal of Applied Psychology, 90*(4), 659–676. https://doi.org/10.1037/0021-9010.90.4.659

Fan, X., Thompson, B. & Wang, L. (1999). Effects of sample size, estimation methods, and model specification on structural equation modeling fix indixes. *Structural Equation Modeling, 6*(1), 56–83. https://doi.org/10.1080/10705519909540119

Farrington, S.M. (2009). *Sibling partnerships in South African small and medium-sized family businesses.* Unpublished MBA thesis, Nelson Mandela Metropolitan University, Port Elizabeth, South Africa.

Ghazali, R., Ahmad, A., Uli, J. Suandi, T., & Hassan, S.A. (2013). Manager commitment to change: Commitment to change among managers in a selected service organization in Malaysia. In J.H. Westover (Ed.), *Leadership and organisational change* (pp. 300–316). Champaign, IL: Common Ground Publication LLC.

Grant Thornton. (2013). *2013 banking outlook: Surviving and thriving in the new normal world of banking regulations.* Chicago, IL: Grant Thornton Ltd.

Green, J.M. (2010). *Factors affecting perceptions of leadership effectiveness in an international organization: A study of middle management in Finnish MNC.* Unpublished PhD dissertation, Aston University, Birmingham, United Kingdom.

Grimm, L.G., & Yarnold, P.R. (2000). *Reading and understanding multivariate statistics.* Washington, DC: American Psychological Association.

Hair, J.F., Anderson, R.E., Tatham, R.L., & Black, W.C. (1998). *Multivariate data analysis.* (5th edn.). Englewood Cliffs, NJ: Prentice hall.

Hair, J.F., Black, W.C., Babin, B.J., Anderson, R.E., & Tatham, R.L. (2006). *Multivariate data analysis.* (6th edn.). Upper Saddle River, NJ: Pearson Prentice Hall.

Hall, J., Johnson, S., Wysocki, A., & Kepner, K. (2012). *Transformational leadership: The transformational of managers and associates.* Gainesville, FL: University of Florida Institute of Food and Agricultural Sciences. Retrieved November 04, 2012, from http://edis.ifas/ufl.edu/DLN

Hayward, B.A. (2005). *Relationship between employee performance, leadership and emotional intelligence in a South African parastatal organisation.* Unpublished master's thesis, Rhodes University, Grahamstown, South Africa.

Hebert, E.B., (2011). *The relationship between emotional intelligence, transformational leadership, effectiveness in school principals.* Unpublished doctoral thesis, Georgia State University, Atlanta, GA.

Hedley, K., White, J., Roche, P.D.D.L., & Banerjea, S. (2006). Banking 2015: A classic strategy battle of scale vs focus. *Strategy & Leadership, 34*(3), 51–58. https://doi.org/10.1108/10878570610700875

Hogan, R., & Warrenfeltz, R. (2003). Educating the modern manager. *Academy of Management Learning and Education, 2*(1), 74–84. https://doi.org/10.5465/AMLE.2003.9324043

Hooper, D., Coughlan, J., & Mullen, M.R. (2008). Structural equation modeling: Guidelines for determining model fit. *The Electronic Journal of Business Research Methods, 6*, 53–60. Retrieved August 30, 2010, from http://www.ejbrm.com

Howell, J. & Hall-Marenda, K. (1999). The ties that bind: The impact of leader-member exchange, transformational and transactional leadership, and distance on predicting follower performance. *Journal of Applied Psychology,* 84(5), 680–694. https://doi.org/10.1037/0021-9010.84.5.680

Hu, L.-T., & Bentler, P.M. (1999). Cut-off criteria for fit indexes in covariance structure analysis: Conventional criteria versus new alternatives. *Structural Equation Modeling, 6*(1), 1–55. https://doi.org/10.1080/10705519909540118

IBM Corporation. (2013). *IBM SPSS Statistics for windows, version 21.0.* Armonk, NY: IBM Corp.

Johnson, J., Lenartowicz, T., & Apud, S. (2006). Cross-cultural competence in international business: Toward a Definition and Model. *Journal of International Business Studies, 37*, 525–543. https://doi.org/10.1057/palgrave.jibs.8400205

Keskin, H.K. (2014). A path analysis of metacognitive strategies in reading, Self-efficacy and task value. *International Journal of Social Science & Education*, 4 (4), 798–808.

Kubicek, J. (2011). *Leadership is dead: How influence is reviving it.* New York: Howard Books.

Li, m. (2007). *modeling the travel motivation of mainland Chinese outbound tourists. Purdue University Graduate School.* Ann Arbor, MI: ProQest Information and Learning Company.

Loehlin, J. C. (1992). *Latent variable models: An introduction to factor, path and structural analysis.* (2nd edn.). Hillsdale: Lawrence Erlbaum.

Maccullum, R.C., Browne, M.W. & Sugawara, H.M. (1996). Power analysis and determination of sample size for covariance structure modelling. In E. Venter (ed.), *The succession process of small and medium-sized family businesses in South Africa.* Unpublished doctoral thesis, Nelson Mandela Metropolitan University, Port Elizabeth.

Mlachila, M., Park, S.G., & Yaraba, M. (2013). *Banking in sub-Sahara Africa: The macroeconomic context.* Washington, DC: International Monetary Fund, Publication Services.

Muriithi, S.M. (2015). *Relationship between leadership and organisational effectiveness among indigenous banks in Kenya.* Unpublished PhD thesis, Rhodes University, Grahamstown, South Africa.

Mwangi, J. (2012). *investors briefing.* Nairobi: Equity Bank.

Nagar, N., Masih, E., & Badugu, D. (2011). Retail banking: The new buzzword of today's world of banking. *Journal of Banking Financial Services and Insurance Research, 1*(8), 1–10.

National Centre for Research in Vocation Education (NCRVE). (1994). *Leadership effectiveness index manual.* Macomb, IL: National Center for Research in Vocational Education.

Njuguna, N. (2013). *The importance of the banking sector in the Kenyan economy.* Nairobi: Speech at the Bank of India, Kenya Branch, Diamond Jubilee Celebrations.

Norma, G.S. (1997). *The role of leadership in business process reengineering: An empirical study of the relationship between leadership behaviour and the reengineering outcome.* Los Angeles, CA: University of California.

Northouse, P.G. (2013). *Leadership: Theory and practice.* (6th edn.). Thousand Oaks, CA: SAGE.

Nunnally, J.C. (1978). *Psychometric theory.* (2nd ed.). New York: McGraw-Hill.

Pagon, M., Banutai, E. & Bizjak, U. (2008). *Leadership competencies for successful change management.* University of Maribor. Retrieved April 10, 2013, from http://www.academia.edu/437506/Leadership_Competencies_for_Successful_Change_Management

Politis, J.D. 2003. The connection between trust and knowledge management: What are its implications for team performance. *Journal of Knowledge Management,* 7(5), 55–66. https://doi.org/10.1108/13673270310505386

Pricewaterhousecoopers (PWC). (2007). *Initial perspectives on strategic and emerging banking issues in key African markets.* Sunninghill: Pricewaterhousecoopers Inc.

Pricewaterhousecoopers (PWC). (2011). *Financial focus 2011.* Retrieved March 15, 2012, from www.pwc.com/ke/FinancialFocus-Jan2011

Samson, D., & Daft, R.L. (2012). *Management: Asia pacific edition.* South Melbourne, Victoria: Cengage Learning Australia.

Shadraconis, S. (2013). Organisational leadership in times of uncertainty: Is transformational leadership the answer? *LUX: A Journal of Transdisciplinary Writing and Research from Clemont Graduate University, 2*(1), 28.

Sokpor, C.K.D. (2006). *The role of CBK in controlling bank failures: an investigative study.* Unpublished MBA thesis, Daystar University, Faculty of Post Graduate Studies, Nairobi, Kenya.

Stogdill, R.M. (1974). *Handbook of leadership.* New York: Free Express.

Tabachnick, B.G., & Fidell, L.S. (2007). *Using multivariate statistics.* (3rd edn.). New York: HarperCollins College Publishers.

Tang, H.V., Yin, M., & Nelson, D.B. (2010). The relationship between emotional intelligence and leadership practices: A cross-cultural study of academic leaders in Taiwan and the USA. *Journal of Managerial Psychology, 25*(8), 899–926. https://doi.org/10.1108/02683941011089143

Tuuk, E. (2012). Transformational leadership in the coming decade: A response to three major workplace trends. *Cornell HR Review*. Retrieved November 15, 2011, from http://digitalcommons.ilr.cornell.edu/chrr/25

Ullman, J.B. (2001). Structural equation modeling. In B.G. Tabachnick & L.S. Fidell (Eds.), *Using Multivariate Statistics* (4th edn.) (pp. 653–771). Needham Heights, MA: Allyn & Bacon.

Walumbwa, F.O., Avolio, B.J., & Zhu, W. (2008). How transformational leadership weaves its influence on individual job performance: The role of identification and efficacy beliefs. *Personnel Psychology, 61*, 793–825. https://doi.org/10.1111/j.1744-6570.2008.00131.x

Waweru, N.M., & Kalani, M.V. (2009). Commercial banking crises in Kenya: Causes and remedies. *African Journal of Accounting, Economics, Finance and Banking Research, 4*, 12–32.

Weese, W.J. (1994). A leadership discussion with Dr. Bernard Bass. *Journal of Sport Management, 8*(3), 176–189.

Yukl, G. (2010). *Leadership in organizations*. (7th edn.). Upper Saddle River, NJ: Pearson Education Inc.

Yukl, G.A. (1994). *Leadership in organizations*. (3rd edn.). Englewood Cliffs: Prentice-Hall.

13

Assessing organisational justice as a predictor of job satisfaction and employee engagement in Windhoek

Author:
Wesley R. Pieters[1]

Affiliation:
[1]Department of Human Sciences, University of Namibia, Namibia

Corresponding author:
Wesley Pieters,
wpieters@unam.na

Orientation: Working in the service industry with similar products and services requires organisations to be proactive and efficient. Enhancing employees' levels of organisational justice is likely to influence job satisfaction and employee engagement.

Research purpose: The purpose of this study was to investigate the dimensions of organisational justice that best predict job satisfaction and employee engagement among employees in Windhoek, Namibia.

Motivation for the study: Poor service delivery is a concern within the service industry and this includes the banks and universities that operate in Windhoek. Having engaged employees is most likely going to improve the quality of service and customer satisfaction.

Research approach/design and method: A cross-sectional survey design was used, employing a questionnaire to collect data on the biographical details, organisational justice, job satisfaction and employee engagement of employees at a bank and university in Windhoek. The sample consisted of employees from a bank, Bank A (n = 106), and administrative staff at a university (n = 97).

Main findings: Significant predictors of employee engagement (work energy) were interpersonal organisational justice and intrinsic job satisfaction. Regarding employee engagement (work focus), intrinsic job satisfaction and extrinsic job satisfaction were the significant predictors.

Practical/managerial implications: Managers and supervisors need to regularly assess, monitor and enhance employees' perception of organisational justice, job satisfaction and employee engagement. Improving organisational justice within the workplace is likely to result in an increase in job satisfaction and employee engagement, resulting in increased productivity and customer satisfaction.

Contribution/value-add: The novelty of this study in Namibia will add to already existing knowledge within industrial and organisational psychology, pave the way for future research and guide the development of interventions aimed at keeping employees satisfied and engaged in their work.

Introduction

Employees working in the service industry may regard their jobs as challenging and exhausting. The manner in which employees or representatives from an organisation interact with clients will have a significant impact on the customers' experience (Bettencourt & Brown, 1997). Furthermore, the nature of the interaction will also impact on customers' decision regarding whether to continue making use of the organisation's service or to look for another service provider. The consequences of poor customer service are related to tertiary institutions and the banking industry.

Ikhide (2000) indicated that banks are critical to a country's financial sector, and in Namibia they account for half of the country's financial assets. Considering that Namibia has five banks that offer similar services, it is important to identify how banks can remain competitive while at the same time remaining productive. Competitiveness and productivity are some of the main reasons why organisations go into business. Apart from the different advertising approaches or reduced banking fees, having the most satisfied and engaged workforce will likely add to that competitive advantage. Soltis, Agneessens, Sasovova and Labianca (2013) indicated that organisations are constantly working hard to retain their top talent, especially considering how much money and time is invested in developing employees to levels of effective functioning. Universities, like many other organisations, are faced with increased challenges without the necessary resources to deal with the challenges (Rothmann & Jordaan, 2006). In order to maintain a competitive advantage and to overcome some of the challenges experienced by employees, apart from other positive experiences, these employees need to experience organisational justice.

Organisational justice can be defined as the perception of employees about fairness within the organisation (Greenberg, 2011). This subjective perception can contradict what the employer believes or does in terms of fairness. Organisational justice has different forms, namely distributive, procedural, informational and interpersonal justice. Organisational justice may also be considered to consist of distributive, procedural and interactional justice. Dajani (2015) found that when employees experience organisational justice they are also more likely to experience job satisfaction at the workplace. When employees perceive interactions to be fair at work they are likely to be more satisfied.

Job satisfaction can be regarded as the overall evaluation of employees regarding their jobs, characterised by gratification and positive feelings about their jobs. Job satisfaction can be determined by different components of the job, namely pay, benefits, collegial relations, advancement opportunities or the meaning they experience from doing their jobs (Judge & Nammeyer-Mueller, 2012). Job satisfaction has been investigated as an antecedent or outcome variable.

Sehunoe, Viviers and Mayer (2015) found that when employees experience job satisfaction, they are also more likely to become more engaged in their work. Employee engagement is defined as a positive, motivational state of work-related well-being that is fulfilling and affective (Bakker, Schaufeli, Leiter, & Taris, 2008). Rothbard and Patil (2012) explained engagement as the psychological presence of an employee in a role. This means that employees who are engaged experience positive emotions and work towards the goals of the organisation, especially if they identify with the specific role. These objectives would include providing quality customer service and ensuring that the objectives of the organisations are met more efficiently.

Rasheed, Khan and Ramzan (2013) indicated that organisational justice is a key factor for enhancing employee engagement within the organisation, and when improving employees' perception of organisational justice, organisations ultimately also increase their competitive position within the job market. Engaged employees also allow an organisation to achieve significant outcomes within their working environment.

Purpose

A number of studies (Alvi & Abbasi, 2012; Biswas, Varma, & Ramaswami, 2013; Dajani, 2015; Rasheed et al., 2013; Saks, 2006; Strom, Sears, & Kelly, 2013; Tessema, 2014) have been conducted on the relationship between organisational justice and employee engagement, but a limited number, if any, has investigated the predictability of employee engagement by organisational justice. The same has been noted in relation to the relationship between job satisfaction and employee engagement. The researcher did not find any research regarding organisational justice, the relation between organisational justice, job satisfaction and employee engagement, nor has any study been found investigating the predictability of employee engagement by organisational justice or job satisfaction in Namibia. This study aims to investigate these relations but also the predictability of organisational justice and job satisfaction on employee engagement. The aim of this study is equally to replicate the study in different industries, trying to influence the perception of employers, importance and understanding of organisational justice within the world of work.

Literature review

Organisational justice and job satisfaction

As noted earlier, organisational justice comprises of three forms of justice, namely, distributive, procedural and interactional justice (interpersonal and informational justice combined). This study will be defining organisational justice based on the three forms of justice. *Distributive justice* refers to the perception of fairness by employees in terms of how the outcomes within the organisation are distributed (rewards, recognition, pay). *Procedural justice* pertains to how fair the procedures are that have been used to determine these outcomes. *Interactional justice* refers to employees' perception of fairness in terms of interpersonal treatment they receive from their authority figures within the organisation (Greenberg, 2011).

In a longitudinal study by Kim, Lin and Leung (2015) conducted in Hong Kong on changes regarding the perception of employees about fairness, it was found that distributive justice at Time 1 had a correlation of 0.29 with job satisfaction and 0.53 at Time 2. Procedural justice had correlations of 0.33 at Time 1 and 0.43 at Time 2 with job satisfaction. Interactional justice also had correlations with job satisfaction, 0.27 at Time 1 and 0.46 at Time 2. This indicates that when employers invest time and effort in clarifying and educating employees on the procedures within organisations, communicating the outcomes of decisions and helping employees understand how decisions were reached, they are likely to increase their levels of perceived distributive, procedural and interactional justice. When these levels of perceived justice increase, they are more likely to experience higher levels of job satisfaction in their respective jobs.

Pinikahana and Happell (2004) referred to job satisfaction as a state that is impacted by the employees' personal characteristics, what they expect from the work and the organisation. In a study on talent management Gelens, Hofmans, Dries and Pepermans (2014) found a positive practical significant relation between job satisfaction and perceived procedural fairness. They also reported a positive practical significant relation between job satisfaction and perceived distributive justice. This means that if employees experience procedural and distributive justice in the organisation, perceiving procedures to be followed fairly and rewards and punishment to be distributed fairly, they are also more likely to experience job satisfaction in the organisation.

Organisational justice was shown to be positively related to job satisfaction in an investigation on employees in Malawi (McAuliffe, Manafa, Maseko, Bowie, & White, 2009). Procedural justice (0.49), distributive justice (0.49), interpersonal justice (0.43) and informational justice (0.51) had a positive relation with job satisfaction (Lawson, Noblet, & Rodwell, 2009). It was further found that distributive and interactional justice significantly influenced job satisfaction (Lopez-Cabarcos, Pinho, & Vazques-Rodriguez, 2014). Al-Tit and Hunitie (2015) conducted research at an academic institution and found that organisational justice was also positively correlated to job satisfaction (0.47). Procedural justice (0.39) and distributive justice (0.51) had significant correlations with job satisfaction among employees working in Canada (Saks, 2006). These findings indicate that when employees perceive organisational justice within the organisation, if rewards and punishment are being distributed fairly, if procedures within the organisation are being followed and if the manner in which supervisors and colleagues interact is collegial, employees are likely to find more pleasure and satisfaction in their jobs. When working for an organisation that is regarded as treating employees fairly, employees are more likely to experience satisfaction in their work.

Considering the literature presenting a link between organisational justice and job satisfaction, the following hypotheses were developed:

> **Hypothesis 1**: Organisational justice has a positive relation with job satisfaction.
>
> **Hypothesis 2**: Organisational justice is a significant predictor of job satisfaction.

Organisational justice and employee engagement

In a study on bank employees conducted in Ethiopia by Tessema (2014), it was found that perceptions of organisational justice positively impacted on employees' level of engagement. It was further stated that when employees perceive fairness within the organisation they are also more likely to feel obliged to be fair in doing their work, resulting in higher levels of employee engagement. Alvi and Abbasi (2012) also undertook a similar study in Pakistan on banking employees and found distributive (0.56), procedural (0.41) and interactional justice (0.43) to be positively correlated to employee engagement. When employees experience interactional justice, they perceive the manner in which supervisors and colleagues interact with them as fair and just. When you have colleagues and supervisors treating you with the necessary respect and dignity, you are also more likely to want to follow the instructions of such a supervisor or work collectively with these colleagues to achieve your organisational goals, becoming more engaged in the work that you are tasked to do.

In an online survey by Strom et al. (2013), distributive justice (0.44) and procedural justice (0.52) had positive correlations with employee engagement. This indicates that when employees perceive the distribution of rewards and punishment to be done fairly and justly, they are more likely to also become engaged in the work that they do in the organisation. Based on the equity theory of 1963 by Stacey Adams (Al-Zawahreh & Al-Madi, 2012), when employees perceive an imbalance between inputs and outcomes, they are likely to find ways to re-establish equity. This means that when employees are treated unfairly (distributive justice, more punishment or fewer rewards), it is expected that these employees might try to find ways to reduce their inputs to justify the outcomes that they receive.

Conducting research on managers in India, Biswas et al. (2013) found that distributive (0.01) and procedural justice (0.39) showed positive correlations with employee engagement. In a study that set out to determine the antecedents and outcomes of employee engagement in Pakistan, Rasheed et al. (2013) reported that procedural justice (0.26) correlated positively with job engagement and organisational engagement (0.47). Distributive justice also had positive correlations with job engagement (0.19) and with organisational engagement (0.27). In an analysis of the antecedents and outcomes of employee engagement Saks (2006) found a positive correlation between procedural justice and job engagement (0.25) and organisational engagement (0.41). Distributive justice was also positively related to job engagement (0.22) and organisational engagement (0.33). In another study on employee engagement, Al-Tit and Hunitie (2015) found that organisational justice was positively related to employee engagement (0.53). Similarly, Dajani (2015) conducted research within the Egyptian banking sector and also found organisational justice to be positively correlated to employee engagement (0.44). When employees perceive the procedures used to determine outcomes as fair, meaning that the way or manner in which decisions within the organisations are made seems to be in line with organisational procedure, employees are more likely to become engaged in the work that they do in the organisation.

Based on the aforementioned literature on the link between organisational justice and employee engagement, the following hypotheses were developed:

> **Hypothesis 3:** Organisational justice has a positive relation with employee engagement.
>
> **Hypothesis 4:** Organisational justice is a significant predictor of employee engagement.

Job satisfaction and employee engagement

Bakker et al. (2008) indicated that employee engagement is characterised by vigour (high levels of energy in executing work tasks), dedication (remaining focused on completing the task even when it becomes challenging) and absorption (being able to work for long periods of time while being actively involved). Harter, Schmidt and Hayes (2002) indicated that job satisfaction and employee engagement are related to meaningful business outcomes, and in order for the business to be successful and productive, it must first impact on individual-level constructs.

Saks (2006) found that job satisfaction is positively related to job engagement (0.52) and organisational engagement (0.57). The same positive correlation was found between job satisfaction and employee engagement (0.43) (Brunetto, Teo, Shacklock, & Farr-Wharton, 2012). Job satisfaction was also proven to have a positive correlation with vigour (0.44), dedication (0.50) and absorption (0.35) (Sehunoe et al., 2015). It was further noted that job satisfaction and employee engagement are strong predictors of organisational commitment (affective commitment). This indicates that when employees are satisfied in their jobs they are more likely to become engaged in their work and are more likely to want to remain with the organisation. Rothmann (2008) found that extrinsic satisfaction had a positive correlation with vigour (0.20) and dedication (0.21); intrinsic satisfaction also correlated positively with vigour (0.16) and dedication (0.23). Al-Tit and Hunitie (2015) have shown that job satisfaction is an outcome of employee engagement.

Based on the aforementioned literature discussing the relation between employee engagement and job satisfaction, the following hypotheses were developed:

> **Hypothesis 5:** Job satisfaction is positively related to employee engagement.
>
> **Hypothesis 6:** Job satisfaction is a significant predictor of employee engagement.

Method

Research approach

Making use of a questionnaire, a cross-sectional research design was used to collect data on the biographical variables of employees, organisational justice, job satisfaction and employee engagement (Creswell, 2003). Research assistants approached institutions that provided a service to customers and these institutions provided approval to conduct the research. These organisations were approached at random and research was only conducted where and when approval was granted.

Participants

Making use of convenience sampling, participants who were fluent in English were included from a bank and a university in Windhoek, Namibia. From Bank A, 106 participants (52.2%) and 97 participants from the university (47.8%) took part in the study. In total, 240 questionnaires were distributed and 203 completed questionnaires were returned. The distribution between males and females was fairly even with 45.3% males ($n = 92$) and 54.7% females ($n = 111$). The larger group in terms of age is of participants between the ages of 24 and 30 years ($n = 85$, 41.9%), with only five participants in the age category of 51 and older (2.5%). The participants had worked for approximately 1–2 years ($n = 56$, 27.6%), and 12 participants (5.9%) had worked for 7–8 years. Looking at marital status, 69.5% ($n = 141$) of the participants were single, 26.6% ($n = 54$) were married and 3.9% ($n = 8$) were divorced. Regarding qualifications, 91 participants (44.8%) had completed Grade 12 and 0.5% ($n = 1$) had obtained post-doctoral qualifications. Regarding the number of dependents, 90 (44.3%) had no dependents and only 1.5% ($n = 3$) had 5–6 dependents. The remainder of the biographical information is presented in Table 1.

Measuring instruments

Biographical information was collected using a questionnaire developed by the researcher to get information regarding the participants' sex, age, marital status, qualifications, tenure and dependents within the two organisations.

Organisational justice was measured using the organisational justice measure developed by Colquitt (2001) measuring procedural, distributive, interpersonal and informational justice. This instrument measures procedural justice by using seven items ('to what extent have those procedures been free from bias?'), four items measuring distributive justice

TABLE 1: Biographical details of sample ($n = 203$).

Item	Category	Frequency	Percentage
Sex	Male	92	45.3
	Female	111	54.7
Age (in years)	18–23	35	17.2
	24–30	85	41.9
	31–35	32	15.8
	36–40	21	10.3
	41–45	17	8.4
	46–50	8	3.9
	51 and older	5	2.5
Marital status	Single	141	69.5
	Married	54	26.6
	Divorced	8	3.9
Qualification	Grade 12	91	44.8
	Honours degree	84	41.4
	MA degree	24	11.8
	PhD	3	1.5
	Post-doctoral	1	0.5
Tenure	Less than 1 year	36	17.7
	1–2 years	56	27.6
	3–4 years	43	21.2
	5–6 years	25	12.3
	7–8 years	12	5.9
	9 years and more	31	15.3
Dependents	None	90	44.3
	1–2	78	38.4
	3–4	32	15.8
	5–6	3	1.5
Organisation	Bank A	106	47.8
	University	97	47.8
Total		**203**	**100.0**

('to what extent is your [outcome] justified, given your performance?'), interpersonal justice being measured by four items ('to what extent has he/she treated you with dignity?'), with informational justice being measured by five items ('to what extent has he/she communicated details in a timely manner?'). This instrument is a self-report questionnaire making use of a Likert-scale response format ranging from 1 (to a very small extent) to 5 (to a very large extent). Cronbach's alphas of 0.86 and 0.90 were also recorded for procedural justice and interpersonal justice, respectively, indicating the reliability of this instrument.

Employee engagement was measured using the Utrecht Work Engagement Scale developed by Schaufeli, Bakker and Salanova (2006), making use of 17 items measuring vigour ('I am bursting with energy in my work'), dedication ('I find the work that I do full of meaning and purpose') and absorption ('time flies when I am working'). This is a self-report questionnaire with responses ranging from 0 (never) to 6 (every day), having reported Cronbach's alphas of 0.70 (Simons & Buitendach, 2013).

Job satisfaction was measured using the Revised Minnesota Job Satisfaction Questionnaire developed by Weiss, Dawis, England and Lofquist (1967). The instrument measures intrinsic and extrinsic job satisfaction ('the working conditions', 'the praise I get for doing a good job'). This is also a self-report questionnaire with response items ranging between 'very dissatisfied' and 'very satisfied'. Pieters (2015) reported Cronbach's alphas ranging between 0.70 and 0.77 for autonomy, social, advancement and intrinsic job satisfaction.

Design

Research assistants were employed to help in conducting the study, and permission to conduct the study was obtained from the participating bank and university. Participants were individually approached for permission to participate in the study. An information sheet and a consent form were distributed, and informed consent was then granted on an individual basis. The data were analysed using SPSS; no participants were harmed during the research; participants' information was anonymised and kept confidential. Furthermore, participants were in no way disadvantaged if deciding not to participate or to withdraw from the study. The questionnaires are kept in a safe place for safety and future consideration.

Analysis

Making use of SPSS version 24.0 (SPSS, 2016) the data were analysed. Cronbach's alpha coefficients (α) were used to determine the internal consistency of the measuring instruments; Pearson correlation coefficients were used to determine the relationship between the variables. Descriptive statistics were also used to describe the means and standard deviations (SDs). Multiple regression analyses were used to investigate whether organisational justice predicted job satisfaction and employee engagement. It was also decided to set the value of significance at 95% confidence interval level ($p < 0.05$). Effect sizes were used to determine the practical significance of the findings (Steyn, 1999), while a cut-off point of 0.30 (medium effect) was set for the practical significance of the correlation coefficient (Cohen, 1988).

Results

Descriptive statistics and correlations

The means, SD, Cronbach's alpha and correlations were analysed and recorded in Table 2.

Cronbach's alphas were obtained on all the measuring instruments and were found to range between 0.68 and 0.86. Resi and Judd (2000) indicated that Cronbach's alphas between 0.80 and 0.60 are acceptable for research.

Means and SDs were analysed to describe the data. A mean score of 18.00 was recorded for procedural justice and 14.85 for interpersonal justice. As part of job satisfaction, a mean score of 23.71 was recorded for intrinsic job satisfaction and a mean score of 25.44 for extrinsic job satisfaction. For employee engagement, a mean score of 13.75 was recorded for employee engagement (work energy) and a mean score of 15.58 for employee engagement (work focus). It terms of the SD, 4.93 was recorded for procedural justice and 3.37 for interpersonal justice. An SD of 4.02 was recorded for intrinsic job satisfaction and 5.26 for extrinsic job satisfaction. For employee

TABLE 2: Descriptive statistics and Pearson correlation coefficient.

Item	Total		α	1	2	3	4	5	6
	Mean	SD							
Organisational justice									
1. PJ	18.00	4.93	0.86	-	-	-	-	-	-
2. INTJ	14.85	3.37	0.90	0.41*†	-	-	-	-	-
Job satisfaction									
3. INTJS	23.71	4.02	0.82	0.35*†	0.41*†	-	-	-	-
4. EXTJS	25.44	5.26	0.85	0.44*†	0.55‡	0.50‡	-	-	-
Employee engagement									
5. EE (energy)	13.75	3.45	0.68	0.22*	0.38*†	0.57‡	0.40*†	-	-
6. EE (focus)	15.58	5.93	0.82	0.37*†	0.36*†	0.50‡	0.51‡	0.50‡	-

SD, standard deviation; PJ, procedural justice; INTJ. interpersonal justice; INTJS, intrinsic job satisfaction; EXTJS, intrinsic job satisfaction; EE (energy), employee engagement (work energy); EE (focus), employee engagement (work focus).

α, alpha coefficients.

*, statistically significant: $p \leq 0.05$.

†, practically significant correlation (medium effect): $0.30 \leq r \leq 0.49$; ‡, practically significant correlation (large effect): $r \geq 0.50$.

engagement (work energy) an SD of 3.45 was reported and 5.93 for employee engagement (work focus).

Making use of Pearson correlation coefficients, it was found that procedural justice had a positive correlation with interpersonal justice ($r = 0.41, p < 0.05$; medium effect); with intrinsic job satisfaction ($r = 0.35, p < 0.05$; medium effect); and with extrinsic job satisfaction ($r = 0.44, p < 0.05$; medium effect). Interpersonal justice was also found to be positively related to intrinsic job satisfaction ($r = 0.41, p < 0.05$; medium effect); with extrinsic job satisfaction ($r = 0.55, p < 0.05$; large effect); supporting Hypothesis 1. Procedural justice had a positive correlation with employee engagement (work energy) ($r = 0.22, p < 0.05$; statistically significant) and with employee engagement (work focus) ($r = 0.37, p < 0.05$; medium effect). Interpersonal justice was also found to be positively related to employee engagement (work energy) ($r = 0.38, p < 0.05$; medium effect) and with employee engagement (work focus) ($r = 0.36, p < 0.05$; medium effect), thereby supporting Hypothesis 3. Intrinsic job satisfaction correlated positively with employee engagement (work energy) ($r = 0.57, p < 0.05$; large effect) and with employee engagement (work focus) ($r = 0.50, p < 0.05$; large effect). Extrinsic job satisfaction also had positive correlation with employee engagement (work energy) ($r = 0.40, p < 0.05$; medium effect) and with employee engagement (work focus) ($r = 0.51, p < 0.05$; large effect), hence supporting Hypothesis 5.

Multiple regression analyses

Multiple regression analyses were carried out to test Hypotheses 2, 4 and 6. In the first model, extrinsic job satisfaction was used as the dependent variable, with procedural justice and interpersonal justice as the independent variables in Step 1. The results are reported in Table 3.

From Table 3 we can see that including procedural justice and interpersonal justice at the first step of the regression analysis produced a statistically significant model ($F_{(2,200)} = 56.82$; $p < 0.00$) and accounted for 36% of the variance. It appears that procedural justice ($\beta = 0.26$; $t = 4.18$; $p < 0.00$) and interpersonal justice ($\beta = 0.45$; $t = 7.22$; $p < 0.00$) are significant predictors of extrinsic job satisfaction.

Multiple regression analyses were performed in order to identify the significant predictors in relation to the hypotheses of this study. The first model analysed used intrinsic job satisfaction as the dependent variable and procedural justice and interpersonal justice as the independent variables (Model 1). The results are reported in Table 4.

As can be seen from Table 4, including procedural justice and interpersonal justice at the first step of the regression analysis produced a statistically significant model ($F_{(2,200)} = 25.83$; $p < 0.00$) and accounted for 20% of the variance. It appears that procedural justice ($\beta = 0.22$; $t = 3.20$; $p < 0.02$) and interpersonal justice ($\beta = 0.32$; $t = 4.55$; $p < 0.00$) are significant predictors of intrinsic job satisfaction.

The first model analysed used employee engagement (work energy) as the dependent variable and procedural justice and interpersonal justice were the independent variables (Model 1). Intrinsic job satisfaction and extrinsic job satisfaction in Model 2. The results are reported in Table 5.

As shown in Table 5, including procedural justice and interpersonal justice at the first step of the regression analysis produced a statistically significant model ($F_{(2,200)} = 17.96$; $p < 0.00$) and accounted for 14% of the variance. It appears that procedural justice ($\beta = 0.08$; $t = 1.11$; $p < 0.27$) is not a significant predictor and that interpersonal justice ($\beta = 0.35$; $t = 4.91$; $p < 0.00$) is a significant predictor of employee engagement (work energy). In the second step of the regression analysis, job satisfaction was entered, and it produced an insignificant model. Job satisfaction being part of the model ($F_{(4,198)} = 27.49$; $p < 0.57$) explained an additional 34% of the total variance. Looking at this together with job satisfaction, interpersonal justice ($\beta = 0.16$; $t = 2.25$; $p < 0.03$)

TABLE 3: Multiple regression analysis with extrinsic job satisfaction being the dependant variable and procedural justice and interpersonal justice the independent variables.

Model	Unstandardised coefficients		Standardised coefficients (β)	t	p	F	R^2	ΔR^2
	B	SE						
(Constant)	10.10	1.47	-	6.88	0.00	56.82	0.36	0.36
Procedural justice	0.28	0.07	0.26	4.18	0.00**	-	-	-
Interpersonal justice	0.70	0.10	0.45	7.22	0.00**	-	-	-

t, test; p, probability value; F, overall significance; R^2, percentage variance explained; ΔR^2, change in percentage variance explained; B, regression coefficient; SE, standard error.
Dependent variable: extrinsic job satisfaction.
*, $p \leq 0.05$; **, $p \leq 0.01$.

TABLE 4: Multiple regression analysis with intrinsic job satisfaction being the dependent variable and procedural justice and interpersonal justice the independent variables.

Model	Unstandardised coefficients		Standardised coefficients (β)	T	p	F	R^2	ΔR^2
	B	SE						
(Constant)	14.90	1.25	-	11.90	0.00	25.83	0.21	0.20
Procedural justice	0.18	0.06	0.22	3.20	0.02*	-	-	-
Interpersonal justice	0.38	0.08	0.32	4.55	0.00**	-	-	-

t, test; p, probability value; F, overall significance; R^2, percentage variance explained; ΔR^2, change in percentage variance explained; B, regression coefficient; SE, standard error.
*, $p \leq 0.05$; **, $p \leq 0.01$.

TABLE 5: Multiple regression analysis with employee engagement (work energy) being the dependent variable and procedural justice, interpersonal justice, intrinsic job satisfaction and extrinsic job satisfaction the independent variables.

Model	Unstandardised coefficients		Standardised coefficients (β)	t	p	F	R^2	ΔR^2
	B	SE						
(Constant)	7.42	1.11	-	6.68	0.00	17.96	0.15	0.14
Procedural justice	0.06	0.05	0.08	1.11	0.27	-	-	-
Interpersonal justice	0.36	0.07	0.35	4.91	0.00**	-	-	-
(Constant)	0.73	1.29	-	0.56	0.57	27.49	0.36	0.34
Procedural justice	-0.35	0.05	-0.05	-0.76	0.45	-	-	-
Interpersonal justice	0.16	0.07	0.16	2.25	0.03*	-	-	-
Intrinsic job satisfaction	0.41	0.06	0.47	7.03	0.00**	-	-	-
Extrinsic job satisfaction	0.06	0.05	0.10	1.26	0.21	-	-	-

t, test; p, probability value; F, overall significance; R^2, percentage variance explained; ΔR^2, change in percentage variance explained; B, regression coefficient; SE, standard error.
Dependent variable: work engagement (work energy).
*, $p \leq 0.05$; **, $p \leq 0.01$.

TABLE 6: Multiple regression analysis with employee engagement (work focus) being the dependent variable and procedural justice, interpersonal justice, intrinsic job satisfaction and extrinsic job satisfaction the independent variables.

Model	Unstandardised coefficients		Standardised coefficients (β)	t	p	F	R^2	ΔR^2
	B	SE						
(Constant)	3.14	1.87	-	1.68	0.94	23.80	0.19	0.18
Procedural justice	0.32	0.08	0.27	3.83	0.00**	-	-	-
Interpersonal justice	0.49	0.12	0.25	3.65	0.00**	-	-	-
(Constant)	-6.79	2.22	-	-3.06	0.03	27.42	0.36	0.34
Procedural justice	0.15	0.08	0.13	1.92	0.56	-	-	-
Interpersonal justice	0.06	0.13	0.03	0.44	0.66	-	-	-
Intrinsic job satisfaction	0.45	0.10	0.30	4.50	0.00**	-	-	-
Extrinsic job satisfaction	0.32	0.09	0.29	3.79	0.00**	-	-	-

t, test; p, probability value; F, overall significance; R^2, percentage variance explained; ΔR^2, change in percentage variance explained; B, regression coefficient; SE, standard error.
Dependent variable: work engagement (work focus).
*, $p \leq 0.05$; **, $p \leq 0.01$.

and intrinsic job satisfaction ($\beta = 0.47$; $t = 7.03$; $p < 0.00$) predicted employee engagement (work energy).

Multiple regression analyses were performed. The first model used employee engagement (work focus) as the dependent variable and procedural justice and interpersonal justice as the independent variables (Model 1). Intrinsic job satisfaction and extrinsic job satisfaction in Model 2. The results are reported in Table 6.

It can be seen from the data in Table 6 that entry of procedural justice and interpersonal justice at the first step of the regression analysis did not produce a statistically significant model ($F_{(2,200)} = 23.80$; $p < 0.09$) and accounted for 18% of the variance. It appears that procedural justice ($\beta = 0.32$; $t = 3.83$; $p < 0.00$) and interpersonal justice ($\beta = 0.49$; $t = 3.65$; $p < 0.00$) are significant predictors of employee engagement (work focus). In the second step of the regression analysis, job satisfaction was entered, and it produced a significant model. Job satisfaction being part of the model ($F_{(4,198)} = 27.42$; $p < 0.00$) explained an additional 34% of the total variance. Looking at this together with job satisfaction, intrinsic job satisfaction ($\beta = 0.30$; $t = 4.50$; $p < 0.00$) and extrinsic job satisfaction ($\beta = 0.29$; $t = 3.79$; $p < 0.00$) predicted employee engagement (work focus). In summary, it has been shown from this discussion that:

- Procedural justice predicted intrinsic job satisfaction ($\beta = 0.22$; $t = 3.20$; $p < 0.02$), intrinsic job satisfaction predicted employee engagement (work energy) ($\beta = 0.47$; $t = 7.03$; $p < 0.00$) and intrinsic job satisfaction predicted employee engagement (work focus) ($\beta = 0.30$; $t = 4.50$; $p < 0.00$).
- Procedural justice ($\beta = 0.26$; $t = 4.18$; $p < 0.00$) predicted extrinsic job satisfaction, and extrinsic job satisfaction predicted employee engagement (work focus) ($\beta = 0.29$; $t = 3.79$; $p < 0.00$).
- Procedural justice predicted employee engagement (work focus) ($\beta = 0.27$; $t = 3.83$; $p < 0.00$).
- Interpersonal justice predicted intrinsic job satisfaction ($\beta = 0.32$; $t = 4.55$; $p < 0.00$), intrinsic job satisfaction predicted employee engagement (work energy) ($\beta = 0.47$; $t = 7.03$; $p < 0.00$) and intrinsic job satisfaction predicted employee engagement (work focus) ($\beta = 0.30$; $t = 4.50$; $p < 0.00$).
- Interpersonal justice predicted extrinsic job satisfaction ($\beta = 0.45$; $t = 7.22$; $p < 0.00$); extrinsic job satisfaction predicted employee engagement (work focus) ($\beta = 0.29$; $t = 3.79$; $p < 0.00$).
- Interpersonal justice predicted employee engagement (work energy) ($\beta = 0.35$; $t = 4.91$; $p < 0.00$).
- Interpersonal justice predicted employee engagement (work focus) ($\beta = 0.25$; $t = 3.65$; $p < 0.00$).

Discussion

Outline of the results

The first hypothesis of this study, *organisational justice has a positive relation with job satisfaction*, was accepted. Procedural justice had a positive correlation with intrinsic job satisfaction and extrinsic job satisfaction. Interpersonal justice also had positive correlations with intrinsic job satisfaction and extrinsic job satisfaction. Interpersonal justice was found to be a stronger predictor of extrinsic job satisfaction and intrinsic job satisfaction over procedural justice, supporting Hypothesis 2. Gelens et al. (2014) also found positive correlations between procedural, distributive justice and job satisfaction. This indicates that when the organisational procedures are followed and applied consistently and fairly, when supervisors and managers treat employees with the necessary respect and dignity, employees are more likely to be satisfied in their jobs.

Several studies, including Al-Tit and Hunitie (2015), Lawson et al. (2009), Lopez-Cabarcos et al. (2014), McAuliffe et al. (2009) and Saks (2006), also found positive correlations between components of organisational justice and job satisfaction. What is interesting to note is that these studies also highlighted the importance of interpersonal justice within the organisation and how it also has a positive correlation with job satisfaction. Once managers or supervisors make a decision, informing employees about how that decision was made and treating them with the necessary respect and dignity enhances interpersonal justice. Another critical component that impacts on job attitudes is the relations supervisors, managers and colleagues have with each other at work. Employees spend 160 hours per month at work, and having negative relations or interactions with colleagues can negatively impact on the levels of job satisfaction.

Procedural justice had a positive correlation with employee engagement (work energy) and with employee engagement (work focus). Interpersonal justice was also found to be positively related to employee engagement (work energy) and with employee engagement (work focus), supporting Hypothesis 3. Tessema (2014) also found similar results and stated that when employees experience fairness and justice within the workplace, they are likely to feel obligated to be fair in doing the work that they are paid for (employee engagement). Interpersonal justice was found to be a significant predictor of work energy (employee engagement), supporting Hypothesis 4 partially. Procedural justice was not found to be a significant predictor of work focus (employee engagement); equally, procedural justice and interpersonal justice were also not found to be significant predictors of work energy (employee engagement). Alvi and Abbasi (2012) found interactional justice to be important in enhancing employees' levels of engagement in their work. When supervisors and managers treat employees with the necessary respect and dignity (interactional justice), they are more likely to follow and execute instructions from these supervisors and managers (employee engagement). It was also found that distributive justice correlated positively to employee engagement. Considering the equity theory by Stacey Adams in 1963 (Al-Zawahreh & Al-Madi, 2012), when rewards and punishment are not distributed fairly, employees will likely try and find ways to re-establish this imbalance between inputs and outcomes. This means that when supervisors favour certain employees, ensuring that these employees get more rewards and less punishment when compared to other employees, the employees who experience lower levels of distributive injustice will likely become disengaged from their work. This positive correlation between organisational justice and employee engagement was also supported by studies conducted in India (Biswas et al., 2013), Pakistan (Rasheed et al., 2013) and Egypt (Dajani, 2015) and by studies conducted by Al-Tit and Hunitie (2015), Saks (2006) and Strom et al. (2013).

Intrinsic job satisfaction correlated positively with employee engagement (work energy) and with employee engagement (work focus). Extrinsic job satisfaction also had positive correlation with employee engagement (work energy) and with employee engagement (work focus), supporting Hypothesis 5. Intrinsic job satisfaction was found to be a significant predictor for employee engagement (work energy). Intrinsic job satisfaction and extrinsic job satisfaction were found to be significant predictors of employee engagement (work focus), thereby supporting Hypothesis 6. These findings are also supported by studies conducted by Al-Tit and Hunitie (2015), Brunetto et al. (2012) and Saks (2006). Rothmann (2008) and Sehunoe et al. (2015) found positive correlations between job satisfaction and vigour, dedication and absorption. This means that when employees are satisfied in their jobs they are more likely to become more engaged in the work that they do. They would experience high levels of energy and mental resilience (vigour); they would be more involved in the work that they do, experience pride, inspiration, enthusiasm and feel like they were making a positive contribution in the work that they do (dedication); they would be fully concentrated on, happy and engrossed (taken in) by their work (absorption) (Bakker et al., 2008).

Kim et al. (2015) found that the perception of justice decreases over time especially for newcomers in an organisation. After the honeymoon phase when joining a new organisation, employees perceive lower levels of organisational justice. Resultantly, employers need to clarify unrealistic expectations, establish fair procedures for allocating rewards and improve communication about procedures and decisions made. When employers improve employees' perception of organisational justice, employees will be more satisfied in their jobs. Overall performance was found to be positively related to distributive justice (0.22) and procedural justice (0.46) (Kassahun, 2005). This supports the importance of organisational justice, indicating how it also impacts on organisational performance.

Brunetto et al. (2012) suggested that possible factors that could influence job satisfaction levels of employees are inadequate supervisory resourcing and support, as well as unrealistic performance targets. This means that when supervisors do not provide the necessary resources and support to employees while having unrealistic work expectations, it could result in employees becoming dissatisfied in their work.

Rothmann and Rothmann (2010) indicated that work role fit was the best predictor of employee engagement. Job resources were also found to be positively related to employee engagement. Organisational support and growth opportunities were the best predictors of vigour, dedication and absorption. It is thus suggested that organisations should put more emphasis on employment practices to ensure that the best-suited candidates are employed in the positions that best fit their abilities and skills. Working in an environment that provides the necessary resources (physical, emotional and cognitive) to execute their duties allows for improved employee engagement. Having policies and work practices in place that support employees, allowing employees to become part of decision-making within the organisation, identifying the needs of the employees and developing career growth paths for advancement (remuneration, promotion and training) also impacts positively on employee engagement.

Practical implications

Managers and organisations need to ensure that when they distribute rewards and punishments, it is done fairly and consistently. It is also important for managers and organisations to apply workplace policies consistently and fairly, giving the same outcomes for the same actions. Gelens et al. (2014), as with this study, found that when employees perceive distributive and procedural justice within the organisation, they are more likely to become more satisfied in their jobs.

Ensuring that employees become more engaged and perceive organisational justice is not a once-off process, but rather one that requires continuous assessment, monitoring and improvement (Kim et al., 2015; Rasheed et al., 2013). It is thus suggested that organisations should monitor employees' engagement levels regularly and improve where needed. The same can be said about employees' levels of perceived organisational justice. When employees do not know or understand how and why certain outcomes were reached, they might perceive these outcomes as being unfair even though the organisation is handling procedures fairly and applying workplace policies consistently.

To keep employees satisfied, conduct regular assessments and identify what would make your employees satisfied. The requirements for job satisfaction are not the same for all employees nor for all organisations. Each organisation and employee will have different aspects that satisfy them in their work. Boonzaier, Ficker and Rust (2001) indicated that in order for employees to be motivated and satisfied in their jobs, the jobs need to have five job characteristics. These job characteristics are *task identity*, the degree to which an employee can identify with a complete or identifiable piece of work, from start to finish; *task significance* has to do with the degree to which the job has an impact on the lives or work of other people, in the organisation or the external environment. *Skill variety* refers to the degree to which the employees can use different skills and talents to execute their duties at work. *Autonomy* can be defined as the degree to which the job allows you to be able to decide, having substantial freedom, independence and discretion in deciding how to execute your duties at work. *Feedback* refers to the extent to which the job requires you to execute your work with direct and clear information about the effectiveness of your work performance. Job resources and support, opportunities for advancement (Marais, de Klerk, Nel, & de Beer, 2014), supportive colleagues and supervisors (Okediji, Etuk, & Anthony, 2011) and total rewards (Smit, Stanz, & Bussin, 2015) may influence job satisfaction of employees.

In order for businesses to become successful and productive, they need to focus on individual-level constructs such as job satisfaction and employee engagement (Harter et al., 2002). One way of enhancing job satisfaction and employee engagement could be to start with organisational justice. Organisational justice can be enhanced by ensuring that rewards and punishment are distributed fairly within the organisation and ensuring that organisational procedures are followed when making decisions that impact on the employees. Managers and supervisors need to communicate these decisions, but they should ensure that the employees have been educated about these policies and procedures. Another measure could be to ensure that managers and supervisors treat employees with the necessary respect and dignity that would not only enhance employees' level of job satisfaction but also make employees more engaged in their work.

Limitations

Some of the limitations experienced when conducting this study include limited access to the bank because of gatekeepers. In addition, some questionnaires were not completed in full and were excluded from this study. Data were collected over a period of a few months because of time constraints.

Recommendations

This research has thrown up many questions in need of further investigation. It is therefore recommended that a similar study should be conducted on a long-term basis (longitudinal study) to solidify the findings in this study. Further research could employ a quasi-experimental approach to explore the impact of educating employees about workplace policies and procedures, being informed about the information used to reach certain outcomes to test how organisational justice can be improved with education, information sharing and transparency.

Conclusion

Rasheed et al. (2013) indicated that because employee engagement is such a critical factor for an organisation to achieve significant outcomes, it should be measured, monitored and improved on a regular basis. When enhancing employees' perception of organisational justice (distributive, procedural and interactional justice), organisations are also enhancing employee engagement within the organisation and improving overall performance (Kassahun, 2005).

Managers need to understand that in order for employees to become more engaged, managers and supervisors need to provide resources and benefits that will motivate employees to want to do more. Some of the factors that might positively influence employees' level of engagement include organisational justice, job satisfaction, social support and job characteristics (Saks, 2006). It is also critical to note that the same motivating factors might not work for all employees, meaning that organisations need to identify what resources and benefits would make employees more likely to become more engaged in their work.

This study found that procedural justice and interpersonal justice are significant predictors of intrinsic job satisfaction, extrinsic job satisfaction and employee engagement (work energy and work focus). If organisations could introduce measures of addressing organisational justice within the workplace, they would be attending to the employees' levels of job satisfaction and enhance their levels of engagement, thus resulting in increased productivity and customer satisfaction.

Acknowledgements

The author would like to thank his research students, A. Norich and N. Neshuku, for assisting with the data collection.

Competing interests

The author declares that he has no financial or personal relationships that may have inappropriately influenced him in writing this article.

References

Al-Tit, A. A., & Hunitie, M. (2015). The mediating effect of employee engagement between its antecedents and consequences. *Journal of Management Research, 7*(5), 47–62. https://doi.org/10.5296/jmr.v7i5.8048

Alvi, A. K., & Abbasi, A. S. (2012). Impact of organisational justice on employee engagement in baking sector of Pakistan. *Middle-East Journal of Scientific Research, 12*(5), 643–649.

Al-Zawahreh, A., & Al-Madi, F. (2012). The utility of Equity Theory in enhancing organizational effectiveness. *European Journal of Economics Finance and Administrative Sciences, 46*, 158–170.

Bakker, A. B., Schaufeli, W. B., Leiter, M. P., & Taris, T. W. (2008). Work engagement: An emerging concept in occupational health psychology. *Journal Work and Stress, 22*(3), 187–200. https://doi.org/10.1080/02678370802393649

Bettencourt, L. A., & Brown, S. W. (1997). Contact employees: Relationships among workplace fairness, job satisfaction and pro-social behavior. *Journal of Retailing, 73*(1), 10–17. https://doi.org/10.1016/S0022-4359(97)90014-2

Biswas, S., Varma, A., & Ramaswami, A. (2013). *Linking distributive and procedural justice to employee engagement through social exchange: A field study in India.* Chicago, IL: Loyola eCommons, School of Business: Faculty Publications and Other works.

Boonzaier, B., Ficker, B., & Rust, B. (2001). A review of research on the job characteristics model and the attendant job diagnostic survey. *South African Journal of Business Management, 32*(1), 11–34.

Brunetto, Y., Teo, S. T. T., Shacklock, K., & Farr-Wharton, R. (2012). Emotional intelligence, job satisfaction, well-being and engagement: Explaining organisational commitment and turnover intentions in policing. *Human Resource Management Journal, 22*(4), 428–441. https://doi.org/10.1111/j.1748-8583.2012.00198.x

Cohen, J. (1988). *Statistical power analysis for the behavioural sciences* (rev. ed.). Orlando, CA: Academic Press.

Colquitt, J. A. (2001). On the dimensionality of organisational justice: A construct validation of a measure. *Journal of Applied Psychology, 86*, 386–400. https://doi.org/10.1037/0021-9010.86.3.386

Creswell, J. W. (2003). *Research design; qualitative, quantitative, and mixed methods approaches* (2nd edn.). London, UK: Sage Publications.

Dajani, M. A. Z. (2015). The impact of employee engagement on job performance and organisational commitment in the Egyptian banking sector. *Journal of Business and Management Sciences, 3*(5), 138–147.

Gelens, J., Hofmans, J., Dries, N., & Pepermans, R. (2014). Talent management and organisational justice: Employee reactions to high potential identification. *Human Resource Management Journal, 24*(2), 159–175. https://doi.org/10.1111/1748-8583.12029

Greenberg, J. (2011). *Behavior in organisations* (10th edn.). Cape Town, South Africa: Pearson.

Harter, J. K., Schmidt, F. L., & Hayes, T. L. (2002). Business-unit level relationship between employee satisfaction, employee engagement, and business outcomes: A meta-analysis. *Journal of Applied Psychology, 87*, 268–279. https://doi.org/10.1037/0021-9010.87.2.268

Ikhide, S. (2000). *Efficiency of commercial banks in Namibia.* Bank of Namibia Occasional Paper, Number 4. Windhoek, Namibia: Bank of Namibia Research Department. Retrieved from https://www.bon.com.na/CMSTemplates/Bon/Files/bon.com.na/b8/b8b60638-88ce-457b-a0c2-554765376e70.pdf

Judge, T. A., & Kammeyer-Mueller, J. D. (2012). Job attitudes. *Annual Review of Psychology, 63*, 341–367. https://doi.org/10.1146/annurev-psych-120710-100511

Kassahun, T. (2005). Level of organisational commitment: Its correlates and predictors. *Indian Journal of Industrial Relations, 41*(1), 29–63.

Kim, T., Lin, X., & Leung, K. (2015). A dynamic approach to fairness: Effects of temporal changes of fairness perceptions on job attitudes. *Journal of Business and Psychology, 30*, 163–175. https://doi.org/10.1007/s10869-013-9341-6

Lawson, K. J., Noblet, A. J., & Rodwell, J. J. (2009). Promoting employee wellbeing: The relevance of work characteristics and organisational justice. *Health Promotion International, 24*(3), 223–233. https://doi.org/10.1093/heapro/dap025

Lopez-Cabarcos, M. A., Pinho, A. I. M., & Vazquez-Rodriguez, P. (2014). The influence of organisational justice and job satisfaction on organisational commitment in Portugal's hotel industry. *Cornell Hospitality Quarterly, 56*(3), 258–272. https://doi.org/10.1177/1938965514545680

Marais, E., De Klerk, M., Nel, J. A., & De Beer, L. (2014). The antecedents and outcomes of work-family enrichment amongst female workers. *South African Journal of Industrial Psychology, 40*(1), 1–14. https://doi.org/10.4102/sajip.v40i1.1186

McAuliffe, E., Manafa, O., Maseko, F., Bowie, C., & White, E. (2009). Understanding job satisfaction amongst mid-level cadres in Malawi: The contribution of organisational justice. *Reproductive Health Matters, 17*(33), 80–90. https://doi.org/10.1016/S0968-8080(09)33443-6

Okediji, A. A., Etuk, A. S., & Anthony, O. U. (2011). Influence of perceived co-worker involvement and supervisory support on job satisfaction. *Ife PsychologyIA, 19*(1), 543–557.

Pieters, W. R. (2015). Psychological empowerment and how it impacts on job satisfaction and organisational commitment of staff members at the University of Namibia (UNAM). *Namibia Journal of Managerial Sciences, 1*(2), 98–120.

Pinikahana, J., & Happell, B. (2004). Stress, burnout and Job satisfaction in Rural Psychiatric nurses: A Victorian study. *Australian Journal of Rural Health, 12*, 120–125. https://doi.org/10.1111/j.1440-1854.2004.00572.x

Rasheed, A., Khan, S., & Ramzan, M. (2013). Antecedents and consequences of employee engagement: The case of Pakistan. *Journal of Business Studies Quarterly, 4*(4), 183–200.

Resi, H. T., & Judd, C. M. (2000). *Handbook of research methods in social and personality psychology.* Cambridge: Cambridge University Press.

Rothbard, N. P., & Patil, S. V. (2012). Being there: Work engagement and positive organizational scholarship. In K. S. Cameron & G. M. Spreitzer (Eds.), *The Oxford handbook of positive organizational scholarship* (pp. 56–68). New York, NY: Oxford University Press.

Rothmann, S. (2008). Job satisfaction, occupational stress, burnout and work engagement as components of work-related wellbeing. *South African Journal of Industrial Psychology, 34*(3), 11–16. https://doi.org/10.4102/sajip.v34i3.424

Rothmann, S. & Jordaan, G. M. E. (2006). Job demands, job resources and work engagement of academic staff in South African higher education institutions. *South African Journal of Industrial Psychology, 32(4)*, 87–96. https://doi.org/10.4102/sajip.v32i4.247

Rothmann, S., & Rothmann, S. (2010). Factors associated with employee engagement in South Africa. *South African Journal of Industrial Psychology, 36*(2), 1–12. https://doi.org/10.4102/sajip.v36i2.925

Saks, A. M. (2006). Antecedents and consequences of employee engagement. *Journal of Managerial Psychology, 21*(7), 600–619. https://doi.org/10.1108/02683940610690169

Schaufeli, W. B., Bakker, A. B., & Salanova, M. (2006). The measurement of work engagement with a short questionnaire: A cross-national study. *Educational and Psychological Measurement, 44*(4), 701–716. https://doi.org/10.1177/0013164405282471

Sehunoe, N., Viviers, R., & Mayer, C. (2015). Job satisfaction, organisational commitment and work engagement in an insurance company. *South African Journal of Labour Relations, 39*(2), 123–144.

Simons, J. C., & Buitendach, J. H. (2013). Psychological capital, work engagement and organisational commitment amongst call centre employees in South Africa. *South African Journal of Industrial Psychology, 39*(2), 1–12. https://doi.org/10.4102/sajip.v39i2.1071

Smit, W., Stanz, K., & Bassin, M. (2015). Retention preferences and the relationship between total rewards, perceived organisational support and perceived supervisory support. *South African Journal of Human Resource Management, 13*(1), 1–13. https://doi.org/10.4102/sajhrm.v13i1.665

Soltis, S. M., Agneessens, F., Sasovova, Z., & Labianca, G. (2013). A social network perspective on turnover intentions: The role of distributive justice and social support. *Human Resource Management, 52(4)*, 561–584. https://doi.org/10.1002/hrm.21542

SPSS (2016). *SPSS 24.0 for Windows*. Chicago, IL: SPSS Incorporated.

Steyn, H. S. (1999). *Praktiese betekenisvolheid: Die gebruik van effekgroottes*. Wetenskaplike bydraes – Reeks B: Natuurwetenskappe Nr. 117. Potchefstroom: PU vir CHO.

Strom, D. L., Sears, K. L., & Kelly, K. M. (2013). Work engagement: The roles of organisational justice and leadership style in predicting engagement among employees. *Journal of Leadership and Organisational Studies*, *20*(5), 1–12.

Tessema, D. (2014). *Determinants of employee engagement in commercial bank of Ethiopia Addis Ababa area*. Unpublished Master's degree in Business administration in management. Addis Ababa University, Ethiopia.

Weiss, D. J., Davis, R. V., England, G. W., & Lofquist, L. M. (1967). *Manual for the Minnesota satisfaction questionnaire*. Minneapolis, MN: University of Minnesota, Industrial Relations Centre.

14

Operationalising performance management in local government: The use of the balanced scorecard

Authors:
Zwelinzima J. Ndevu[1]
Kobus Muller[1]

Affiliations:
[1]School of Public Leadership, Stellenbosch University, South Africa

Corresponding author:
Zwelinzima Ndevu,
ndevuz@yahoo.com

Orientation: Local government forms that part of the public sector closest to citizens and therefore indispensable in its role of providing essential goods and services and developing the local area. Local government has the authority and functions necessary to provide services for the maintenance and promotion of the well-being of all people within their area and should provide access to basic services such as water, electricity and health care.

Research purpose: This study examines performance management as a tool in local government effective provision service delivery. The critical question addressed in this paper was how the balanced scorecard (BSC) can be used to improve performance in the context of local government and assist in eradicating the current challenges of lack of quality services, poverty and infrastructure development.

Motivation for the study: The need for continuous improvement in service delivery at local government compounded by high levels of service delivery protest requires regular review of performance management system.

Research approach: To understand the current context and challenges facing local government, the applicable legislative framework including the Constitution, white paper and the National Development Plans were perused to better understand the legal environment in which local government operates. A literature review was undertaken to evaluate theory on organisational effectiveness. Semi-structured interviews were used to solicit expert opinions.

Main findings/managerial implications: The BSC approach emerged as the preferred tool because the method offered the authors the opportunity to review non-financial and financial factors to arrive at a balanced conclusion. A BSC tool was developed and applied to the Joe Gqabi District Municipality as a case study.

Practical implications: The BSC as a performance management tool enables organisations to clarify their vision and strategy and translate them into goal or actions.

Contribution/value-add: The research findings conclude that there was acknowledgement of the importance of performance measurement instruments in the municipality, yet the municipality still experienced challenges caused by the performance review process not being transparent and not communicated to all stakeholders.

Current context and challenges

Democratic South Africa has introduced two important changes at local government level that have defined the process of service delivery. In the first instance, Section 40 (1) of the Constitution of the Republic of South Africa (RSA, 1996) renders local government as a distinct sphere of government, which in terms of Section 41 (1) is autonomous *vis-à-vis* the national and provincial spheres of government. Secondly, in terms of Section 152 of the Constitution of the Republic of South Africa (RSA, 1996), one of the objects of this system of local government is 'to promote social and economic development'. According to Section 153 (a), municipalities must structure and manage their administration, budgeting and planning processes in such a way that priority is given to the basic needs of the community and to promoting the social and economic development of the community (RSA, 1996).

The White Paper on Local Government discusses the characteristics of developmental local government, identifies a series of development outcomes and proposes several tools to assist municipalities to become developmental (RSA, 1998, p. 17). This makes the importance that national government attaches to service delivery at local government level quite evident. Furthermore, the white paper deals with two interrelated and equally important aspects of developmental local government. The first concept that it deals with is integrated development planning (IDP), which 'provides a powerful tool for municipalities to facilitate integrated and co-ordinated service delivery within their locality' (RSA, 1998, p. 19). Secondly, it also refers to the concept of performance management that ensures that IDP is being implemented and that municipalities are having the desired development impact.

The net effect of these changes has been the establishment of what was generally referred to as 'developmental local government'. The concept of developmental local government was first alluded to in the Constitution of the Republic of South Africa (1996) (see Section 153). According to Section 153 (a), municipalities must structure and manage their administration, budgeting and planning processes in such a way that priority is given to the basic needs of the community and to promoting the social and economic development of the community (RSA, 1996). Local government forms that part of the public sector that was closest to citizens and is therefore indispensable in its role of providing essential goods and services and developing the local area. This paper examines the role of local government in improving service delivery in South Africa with special reference to the Joe Gqabi District Municipality (JGDM) in the Eastern Cape Province. This province, the second biggest in the country, was a predominantly rural province.

Persistent high levels of poverty and food insecurity in rural areas have implications for public policy and the design of a strategy to reduce poverty and improve service delivery. Because of the geographical dispersion of the rural poor, it is more expensive for national government in South Africa to provide provincial government and local government with public infrastructure, social services and a safety environment equivalent to those provided to urban communities. The above background is given to illustrate problems that municipalities in rural areas encounter in their quest to provide basic municipal services to the communities they serve. Despite all the efforts made by the previous governments of South Africa to address poverty in rural areas of the country, local government, for reasons that remain unresolved, still plays a minimal role in addressing these problems. The lack of infrastructure entrenches the problems of poverty and limits the potential of communities to sustain economic growth, rural livelihoods and social development. Efforts to extend the provision of basic services to all people are slow to reach rural areas and farm-dwellers, even while most urban communities have access to free basic services. The National Development Plan (NDP) envisages that by 2030 South Africa will be a state that is capable of playing a developmental and transformative role. In broad terms, such a state intervenes to support and guide development in such a way that the benefits accrue across society, with particular emphasis on the poor.

The South African government has introduced a substantial body of legislation focusing on service delivery in the national, provincial and local spheres of government. Various legislation and policy frameworks significant to local government were briefly explored in the paper and reviewed in terms of their contribution and impact on service delivery. The Constitution (RSA, 1996) gives the following mandate to local government: to provide democratic and accountable government for all communities, to ensure the provision of services to communities in a sustainable manner, to promote social and economic development and to promote a safe and healthy environment. Van der Waldt (2006, p. 142) and Thornhill (2008, p. 492) assert that local government is at the coalface of public service delivery. Mopaki and Mutono (2016, p. 4), who state that local government is often the first point of contact between an individual and a government institution, also articulate this view. The local sphere is often referred to as grassroots government because of its direct association with communities at a local level.

Local government could be described as public organisations authorised to manage and govern the affairs of a given territory or area of jurisdiction. It is also important to note that local government refers to a sphere of government, not an individual municipality. All the individual municipalities in South Africa collectively make up the sphere of local government (Roux, 2005, p. 64). Being the government level closest to the people, it was to be expected that a core function of municipalities was the rendering of a variety of basic but essential services to the community within its jurisdiction (Roux, 2005, p. 69). The provision of services by municipalities was a constitutional obligation. Part B of Schedule 5 of the Constitution (RSA, 1996), concerning functions falling concurrently within the national and provincial competence constituent units, identifies the following services that fall within the ambit of local government and its municipalities. These are water; electricity; town and city planning; road and storm water drainage; waste management; emergency services, for example firefighting; licenses; fresh produce markets; parks and recreation; security; libraries; and economic planning.

The White Paper on Local Government (RSA, 1998) asserts that:

> ... basic services enhance the quality of life of citizens and increase their social and economic opportunities by promoting health and safety, facilitating access to work, to education, to recreation and stimulating new productive activities. (p. 92)

There are nine distinct 'values' in the White Paper on Local Government (RSA, 1998):

- *Accessibility*: The white paper stresses non-discriminatory (race, gender, sexual orientation) access to services, at least at a minimum level. Historical unevenness in service provision was to be addressed by building new infrastructure and rehabilitating/upgrading that which already exists. The mechanism for rolling this out was capital investment in bulk and connector infrastructure via infrastructure grants, at this stage through the Consolidated Municipal Infrastructure Programme. Municipalities were also urged to consider the 'ease of use' of this infrastructure, particularly for the disabled. The question of 'eligibility' was thus firmly established – all citizens were eligible for municipal services irrespective of their social and economic circumstances. Much debate has centred on this principle and the extent to which it has been carried through to implementation programmes and municipal logistics.
- *Affordability*: The White Paper on Local Government (RSA, 1998) notes the importance of considering the affordability of the actual service – even though the service infrastructure may be in place. It urges that tariff levels consider both the economics of providing the service and the potential of the poor to access the services, that is, financial sustainability has to be offset against the needs of the poor and their possible contribution to service costs. Service levels have to reflect local affordability patterns but not in such a way as to perpetuate the existing spatial (and racial) inequality between low, middle or high income users. Cross subsidisation was envisaged within particular service types and across services (e.g. income from electricity can legitimately be used to subsidise water provision). Higher income users may thus subsidise lower income users and commercial users may subsidise residential users.
- *Quality of services*: Quality relates to attributes like relevance to purpose, whether the service was delivered on time, and convenience to users, safety, continuity (minimal breakdown) and responsiveness to the service users.
- *Accountability*: The stress here was on the municipality retaining ultimate responsibility for service provision. Perhaps recognising the overarching international movement to privatisation and 'outsourcing', the white paper emphasises that council remains responsible for delivering appropriate services of the required standard.
- *Services and development*: Integrated development was called for, with consideration of the social and economic impacts of the services provided. Importantly, sustainability was defined as encompassing resource usage that was financially viable, environmentally sound and socially just.
- *Value for money*: It was noted that this attribute compares cost inputs with the quality and value of service outputs and that the aim was the best possible use of public resources to ensure universal access to affordable and sustainable services. It might be argued that this was the most important measure to apply in any assessment of the current service delivery patterns, specifically, useful appraisal was less about the reach and scale of service delivery (where the challenges and achievements were fairly well documented) and more about whether the significant resources allocated to services were optimally deployed.
- *Impact on local commerce and industry*: When considering cross subsidisation between commercial and residential service users and generally when considering tariff levels, municipalities were urged to consider the impact of rates and service charges on commerce and industry in order not to compromise the 'job-creating and competitive nature' of such enterprises. (p. 93)

The key outcomes that the White Paper on Local Government (RSA, 1998) envisages local government to achieve were the provision of household infrastructure and services; creation of liveable, integrated cities, towns and rural areas; local economic development; and community empowerment and redistribution. Drawing from the NDP chapter on a capable and developmental state, by 2030 South Africa will have a developmental state that is accountable, focused on citizens' priorities and capable of delivering high-quality services consistently and sustainably through cooperative governance and participatory democracy.

As depicted in the White Paper on Local Government, developmental local government was (RSA, 1998):

> ... local government committed to working with citizens and groups within the community to find sustainable ways to meet their social, economic and material needs and improve the quality of their lives (p. 27).

In this scenario, local government was at the forefront of participatory democracy, involving citizens in meaningful deliberations regarding governance and development; was responsive to citizens' priorities, enjoying high levels of trust and credibility amongst the public; had employees who were skilled, competent and committed to delivering quality services; was able to cost-effectively increase the quantity and quality of services; and operated within a supportive and empowering intergovernmental system.

The NDP, however, cautions that such a developmental state cannot materialise by decree, nor can it be legislated or waved into existence by declarations. It has to be consciously built and sustained. Local government was at the centre of development, and to achieve the aspiration of a transformed and effective local government system will require strong leadership through a clear and consistent, long-term strategy. Additionally, while the metro municipalities have made significant progress in addressing service delivery backlogs, even these advances are obscured by overwhelming challenges related to the fast pace of urbanisation and in-migration.

The NDP identifies institutional capacity, an enabling environment and the macro context as the main challenges facing local government in South Africa. Table 1 lists the constraints as depicted in the chapter on local government as components of outcome nine in the NDP document. The critical question addressed in the paper was how the balanced scorecard (BSC) tool could be used for improving performance measurement in service delivery in local government and assist in eradicating the current challenges of lack of quality services, poverty and infrastructure development.

TABLE 1: Local government constraints.

Institutional capacity	Enabling environment	Macro context
• Weak political leadership • Technical skills gap and lack of relevant competencies • High staff turnover and vacancy levels • Weak understanding of policies • Political deployments not always competent appointments • Lack of career progression • Poor attitudes and values of staff • Lack of professionalism and regulation thereof by professional bodies and government • Weak strategy – focus on compliance • Weak financial management and low budget spend • Weak council decisions, often contrary to technical advice • Organisational instability, including review of S 57 contracts linked to political term of office • Lack of oversight and accountability • Lack of legal compliance or regulatory support • Weak municipal systems	• Lack of central co-ordination support, information and M&E. • Financial viability of municipalities. • Bulk infrastructure gaps. • Lack of clarity regarding decentralisation of powers and functions and role of the districts. • Role of DCOG unclear. • Lack of planning alignment amongst the three spheres – IDP not taken seriously by other spheres. • Local government financing system, including equitable share, needs to be reviewed. • Unstable political environment. • Inconsistent, incoherent and complex local government legislative environment. • Lack of customised support to municipalities, and support focused on compliance.	• Huge pressures of poverty, unemployment and inequality • Huge service delivery backlogs • Weak public participation • Huge social issues, such as crime, drug abuse, gender-based violence • Weak revenue base of municipalities with low levels of affordability • Political dynamics, including coalitions, resulting in inertia • Pressures of in-migration and urbanisation • Weak education system

Source: National Development Plan (NDP) (2014)

IDP, integrated development planning; M&E, Monitoring & Evaluation; DCOG, Department of Cooperative Governance.

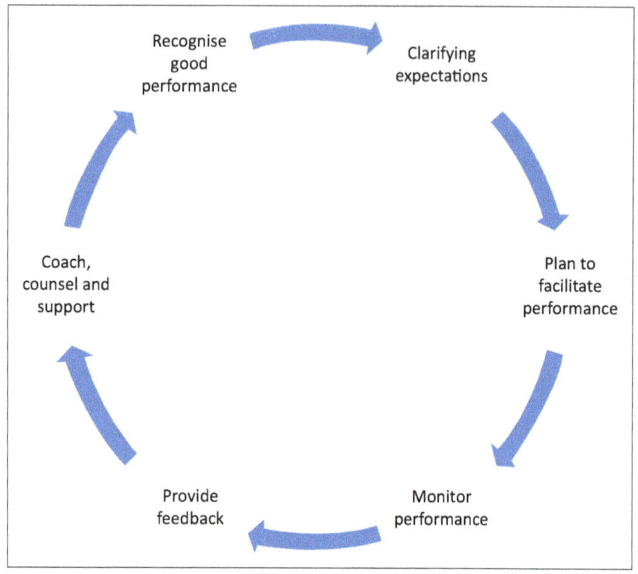

Source: Adapted from Werner, A. (2007). *Organisational behaviour: A contemporary South African perspective*. (p. 109), Pretoria: Van Schaik

FIGURE 1: Individual performance management cycle.

Performance management literature

Armstrong and Baron (1998, p. 7) define 'performance management' as a strategic and integrated approach to delivering sustained success to the organisation by improving the performance of employees and by developing the capabilities of teams and individual contributors. The objective, from this definition, aimed at the improvement of results at the level of the individual, the team and the organisation, as illustrated in Figure 1.

According to Grobler et al. (2011, p. 293), performance management is a process that significantly affects organisational success by having managers and employees work together to set expectations, review results and ultimately reward excellent performance. Hood (1995, p. 98) argues that encouraging a performance management approach in the organisation means managing results, not rules. The interest was more on achieving organisational objectives and goals rather than monitoring how procedures and policies are implemented. Cavalluzzo and Ittner (2004, p. 251) further argue that an organisation that relies on or adopts performance measures should achieve improved decision-making methods.

Clarify expectations

It is important in performance management to first ensure that employees understand what was expected of them in the workplace. They must have a clear understanding not only of what the objectives mean but also of what was necessary to affect the measure associated with the objectives (Grobler et al., 2011; Werner, 2007, p. 110).

Plan to facilitate performance

In this case, a manager asks a subordinate in the initial performance management meeting to identify which areas of work, resources and skills the organisation can assist the employee with in order to achieve the objectives. There are instances in which the organisation has to intervene because the employee has no authority or resources to execute their responsibilities effectively and efficiently (Grobler et al., 2011; Werner, 2007, p. 110).

Monitor performance

At this stage, there is a common understanding of what should be done. It is important to monitor actual performance to check whether the organisation is still on track to achieve the set organisational goals. The frequency of the monitoring process depends on the nature of services provided and the seniority of the employee being monitored. In some environments, monitoring may take place every day; in other cases, especially with middle to senior employees, a performance review session may be held on a monthly or in some cases on a yearly basis (Werner, 2007, p. 110).

Provide feedback

One of the main reasons for monitoring performance is to be able to provide feedback on progress towards achieving organisational goals and on employee performance. According to Werner (2007, p. 111), feedback serves two purposes: it allows the organisation to provide consequences for performance and to redirect employees' efforts if necessary. Feedback allows employees to improve their performance by indicating performance deficits (Grobler et al., 2011).

Coach, counsel and support

If performance monitoring reveals a serious performance deficit, the organisation may have to coach the employee concerned. This consists of discussing the desired performance and if necessary modelling the performance for the employee, requesting the employee to perform and then giving critical feedback until performance is at the required level.

In some instances, employee performance is substandard because of personal or interpersonal problems. In this case, the manager may have to counsel the employee and if possible offer advice on how to overcome the problem. It is also important to support employees and ensure they know that the organisation has confidence in them and will stand by them should the need arise.

Figure 1 demonstrates that far from merely emphasising individual performance and accountability or reporting on compliance with procedures, the performance management process is a useful and essential management process for understanding the performance of programmes, reaching agreement on performance expectations, improving performance and demonstrating to citizens that expectations of performance are successfully met. As part of the overall management strategy, public sector managers need to measure performance to evaluate whether the organisation was performing as expected. According to Niven (2003, p. 56), there is growing recognition that using performance measures to gauge success is vital to any organisation whether in the private or public sector.

Balanced scorecard perspective

The last decade has seen a paradigm shift in the public sector towards more accountability and the adoption of the new style of public management, which is more closely aligned with private sector management systems (Sharma & Gadenne, 2011, p. 167). The above has precipitated the adoption of more sophisticated performance management and control systems such as the BSC. The BSC was originally developed for the private sector by Kaplan and Norton (1992, p. 75). They argued that financial indicators alone were not sufficient to measure performance or manage an organisation. Senior management needs various kinds of information about the goods and services that the organisation is offering (such as quantity, quality, market, consumers, suppliers, competition and technology) as inputs for decision-making and strategic planning (Kaplan & Norton, 1992, p. 75).

It has become apparent that managers need a balanced presentation of both financial and non-financial measures so that they are able to view the organisation's performance simultaneously across several areas or perspectives. Kaplan (2001) is of the view that the BSC has the potential to enable public sector organisations to:

- bridge the gap between vague mission, strategy statement and day-to-day operational actions
- develop a process to achieve strategic focus, avoiding the notion of attempting to be everything to everyone
- shift their focus from programme and initiatives to the outcomes the programs and initiatives are aiming to achieve
- avoid the illusion that they have a strategy because they are managing a diverse set of programs and initiatives
- align initiatives, departments and individuals to work in ways that reinforce each other so that dramatic performance improvements can be achieved (p. 90).

The name BSC comes from the idea that measurable statistics form the basis of the approach and metrics that are applied for different but related elements are important to the organisation's success (Thompson & Mathys, 2008, p. 378). The categories of metrics form a balanced set of measures to assess organisational performance.

In Rampersad's view (2006, pp. 110–113), the alignment of personal ambition informed by a personal BSC with the shared organisational ambition informed by an organisational BSC is central for the purposes of employee commitment, trust, inner involvement, stress and burnout reduction, stimulating enjoyment, active participation, motivation and empowerment of employees. It has to do with reaching a higher degree of compatibility between personal and organisational objectives and mutual value, as illustrated in Figure 2. In a similar manner, recent studies, such as those conducted by Ellangovani and Kamalanabhan (2014, p. 10), the authors have also explored and agreed with the approaches discussed above and argue that the original framework remains the basis for successful implementation of the BSC.

The argument by Rampersad means that employees do not work with devotion or expend energy on something they do not believe in or agree with. As Rampersad (2006, p. 114) puts

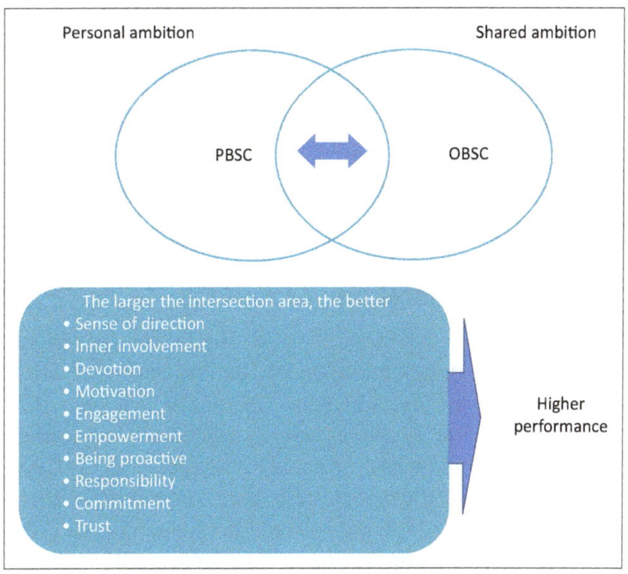

Source: Rampersad, H.K. (2006). *Personal balance scorecard: The way to individual happiness, personal integrity and organisational effectiveness*. (p115), Randburg: Knowres

PBSC, personal balanced scorecard; OBSC, organisational balanced scorecard.

FIGURE 2: Match between personal ambition and shared ambition.

it, clarity and uniformity of personal and organisational values and principles are therefore essential for employees' active involvement and contribution to the achievement of organisational goals. The above demonstrates the importance of understanding that employees join the organisation with personal objectives or have aspirations to achieve at a personal level. Kaplan and Norton (2001, p. 99) cited in Sharma and Gadenne (2011, p. 171) argue that many of the concepts articulated above consist of lists of programmes and initiatives rather than outcomes that the organisation is attempting to achieve. Within this context, Sharma and Gadenne (2011) advocate a modified BSC framework where the organisational mission is featured at the highest level of the scorecard, underpinned by three high level perspectives:

- costs of providing services
- value or benefits of the service
- support of legitimising authorities including the legislature by taxpayers (p. 72).

Introducing a BSC means introducing change in the organisation, which was never an easy process: the organisation can expect to encounter challenges.

Semi-structured interviews – Analysis and interpretation

In this paper, the qualitative method was applied through interviews with a selected number of stakeholder representatives. The participants in the study were officials, the political office bearers, ward committee members, and the business and agriculture forums from JGDM jurisdiction. Welman and Kruger (2002, p. 211) argue that the important factor in collecting data through interviews is to identify themes, as they assist the researcher in analysing interview data.

The researchers used a structured interview questionnaire formulated around themes that were predetermined; JGDM was used as a case study. Examining attitudes to the use of performance measures in a municipality can be particularly interesting because the nature of the community and stakeholders varies considerably. These themes were limited to policy implementation, management commitment, performance measurement and analysis, and performance evaluation approach.

Policy implementation

Participants were asked questions on their awareness of the legislative and policy requirements for the implementation of performance measurement in municipalities. The participants were given a list of legislative and policy requirements that were applicable to the sector, as captured in Appendix 1 for them to indicate their knowledge of these requirements. While ward committee members and the business and agriculture forums were not familiar with or could not remember the policy requirements, the officials and political office bearers explained the policies that oblige the municipality to do performance evaluation.

Management commitment

The need for strong top management commitment to performance measurement is recognised in the government reform literature. Cavalluzzo and Ittner (2004, p. 247) argue that while administrative and technical factors are expected to influence the implementation of performance measurement, their impact is secondary to that of organisational factors. They argue that top management commitment is crucial to implementation success because these managers can focus resources, goals and strategies on initiatives they deem worthwhile and deny resources to initiatives they do not support, as well as provide the political help needed to motivate or push aside individuals who resist the initiative.

The feedback from interviews conducted with all stakeholders reflected different views from participants. The municipality's political office bearers and officials indicated that there was support from council, which is the top management governance structure in the municipality, but the organisation was hampered by a lack of capacity to implement the performance management initiative as well as current budgetary constraints. However, other stakeholders interviewed indicated that top management was not willing to take decisions and commit to support the implementation. They based their argument on the fact that they were not aware of any municipal policy dealing with performance measures.

Performance measurement and analysis

Interviewees were asked to comment on the use of performance measures in the municipality. Categories were given to them to help with the focus of the response. The categories included input, activity/process, output, outcome, benchmarks and customer satisfaction. The interviewees were provided with definitions and explanations for each of these terms to ensure consistent understanding of terminology. All respondents agreed that customer satisfaction was central to the process of implementing performance measures and that community input should be more visible and valued. Participants also indicated that while in practice the programmes that the municipality develops were informed by input from all stakeholders in the area such as the IDP, they were divided on whether performance measurement was focused on shared programme results or rather on the Service Delivery Budget and Implementation Plan, over which they had little input and influence.

Interviewees were questioned about the consequences of performance measures and targets not being met. The interviewees agreed that the current culture at local government did not provide any consequences for measures and targets not being met.

Performance evaluation approach

Judging by responses given to the above theme, it was concluded that while all stakeholders understood and agreed on the importance of a performance measurement review, their opinions about the overall experience with performance measures in the municipality differed fundamentally. More specifically, they all acknowledged the usefulness of performance measures but at the same time indicated problems in their identification and implementation. Some of the points raised by ward committee members and the agriculture and business community were, in no particular order:

- the review process was not transparent
- there was no review system, or if there was it was not communicated to all stakeholders
- lack of commitment by all parties
- reactive approach by management and political office bearers.

While management, on the other hand, identified the following challenges, the list below does not reflect order of importance:

- lack of capacity
- budget and time constraints
- politically driven process
- poor management of the process
- implementation challenges.

Balanced scorecard as a strategic management tool

The scorecard was initially introduced solely as a performance measurement system but the inventors soon realised that a measurement system can help the organisation to navigate the future. Subsequently, the scorecard became the operational framework in which strategy was organised. It can be concluded that a scorecard provides a framework in which strategic objectives are organised within the four perspectives. The strategy's critical elements and the linkage between them is organised top–down on a cause-and-effect relationship basis. According to Kaplan and Norton (2001, p. 91), cause-and-effect relationships should exist between these four perspectives in such a way that learning and growth leads to the improvement of the internal process, which in turn leads to financial improvement, finally bringing about customer satisfaction improvement. Figure 3 shows the design of an ideal scorecard in the context of local government, as supported by the discussion above.

The proposed scorecard framework contains the four standard perspectives, but instead of starting with a learning and growth perspective it starts with a customer perspective. Each perspective represents a strategic goal, objective and Key Performance Indicators (KPI) as depicted in Figure 4.

- Customer perspective: Is the municipality focusing on the needs of its citizens and offering quality services?
- Financial perspective: Is the municipality providing quality service standards at a reasonable and cost-effective rate (value for money)?

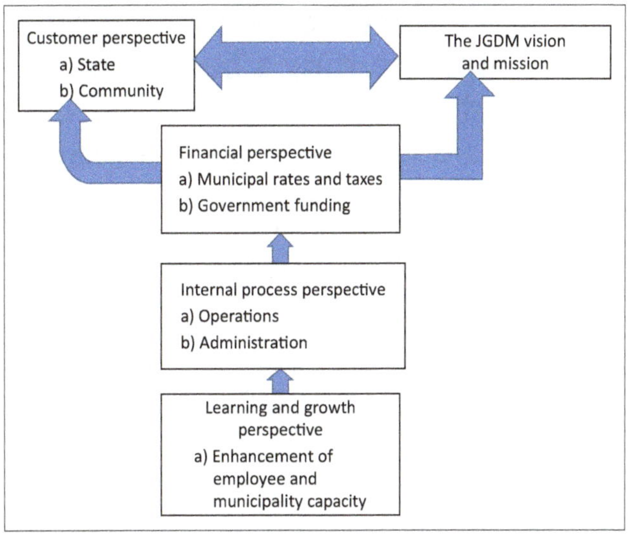

JGDM, Joe Gqabi District Municipality.

FIGURE 3: A design of an ideal scorecard framework.

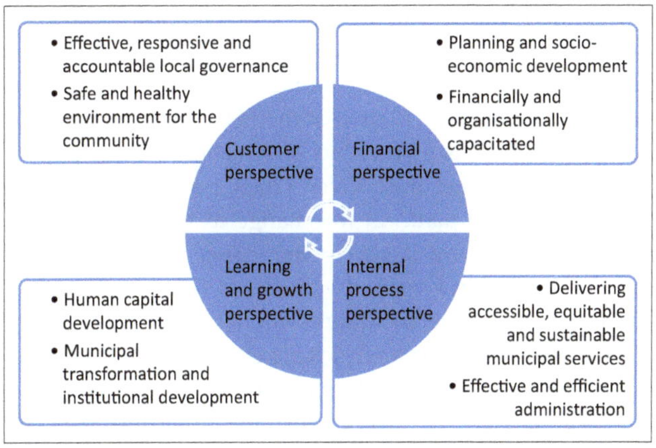

FIGURE 4: The four perspectives of the Joe Gqabi District Municipality scorecard framework.

- Internal process perspective: Is the municipality maintaining its operational systems and striving to improve its method of service provision?
- Learning and growth perspective: Is the municipality able to change or adapt to innovative methods of service provision?

The scorecard design was based on the assumption that the municipality's performance in the achievement of the strategic goal of every perspective was related to its performance in achieving the strategic goal of the lower level perspective. Every subsystem has one strategic goal and contains both outcome measures (objectives) and performance drivers (KPIs). The strategic goal of each perspective takes place on the first level. The second level consists of the outcomes of the measures of the perspective that serve as objectives, while the third level contains the selected KPIs for every objective.

The scorecard provides the municipality with a comprehensive framework that translates vision and strategy into a coherent and linked series of objectives and KPI; it was not just a collection of critical, financial or non-financial indicators of these four perspectives.

Crucial elements to be considered when implementing a balanced scorecard

Leadership and support of senior management

Kaplan and Norton (1996, p. 285) argue that the leadership and support of senior management is crucial for the successful implementation of a BSC. Organisations that complied with the criteria for a fully developed and structurally complete BSC were found to have greater senior management involvement during the BSC implementation process. These organisations also reported fewer BSCs that were cluttered with inappropriate measures or measures not linked to cause-and-effect relationships (Soderberg et al., 2011, p. 704).

Burning platform for change

In addition to senior executive support, Niven (2003, pp. 47–48) was of the opinion that a burning need for change (also referred to as a 'burning platform') has to be determined. A case study article of seven private sector financial companies, which found that the initial reasons given for the implementation of the BSC affect the potential benefits of BSC use (Agostino & Arnaboldi, 2011, pp. 99, 109–111), supported this. Niven (2003, pp. 47–48) explains that the burning platform for change to the BSC includes understanding why it was being done, the need to get involved ('buy-in') and its value to the organisation. Resistance to change is natural (Mooraj, Oyon & Hostettler, 1999, p. 490). Learning anxieties are central to the resistance; consequently, people will only adapt to change when 'survival anxiety … [*is*] greater than learning anxiety' (Niven, 2003, p. 48). The implementation of the BSC helps to encourage change by placing the focus of employees on long-term objectives (Mooraj et al., 1999, p. 490). The objectives that are developed by the BSC team will communicate the survival anxieties of the organisation to the staff and convey why change is required for success. The BSC reduces learning anxiety by providing a safe environment for learning (Niven, 2003, p. 48).

Balanced scorecard team and leader

Kaplan and Norton (1996, p. 64) posit that one person cannot draw up a BSC because no single person has the requisite knowledge to tell the strategic story of the organisation. Kaplan and Norton (1996, p. 64) contend that collective knowledge, experience and input have to be provided by all well-prepared staff members who are part of the BSC team, a position with which Niven (2003, p. 51) concurs. This approach enables the BSC team to own and drive the BSC concept under the guidance of the BSC team leader, driver or architect (Kaplan & Norton, 1996, p. 64, 2001, pp. 362–363). Kaplan and Norton (2001, p. 363) argue that a broader set of people could be involved in smaller subgroups, possibly focusing on one perspective. The work of the subgroups would then be integrated at a bigger meeting.

Why the balanced scorecard may not work?

Balanced scorecards that are not reviewed periodically

A BSC should not be built once and then left unchanged (Niven, 2003, p. 287) but should be maintained (Weinstein & Bukovinsky, 2009, p. 54). In fact, best practice studies have shown that most practitioners do an annual critical evaluation of the BSC to ensure that the strategic story is still being told accurately (Niven, 2003, pp. 287–288).

Balanced scorecard development labelled a short-term project

Niven (2003, p. 289) is of the opinion that the development of a BSC that is seen as a 'project' is doomed to failure. He argues that a project is a short-term endeavour and the BSC should become a fixture in management processes. To reach this level, it should be used continually in every facet of the operation, including decision-making and resource allocation. On the other hand, Nair (2004, p. 157) believes that BSC development should be treated as a project. This reflects a different viewpoint in that Nair (2004, p. 157) does not see a project as short-term but focuses on the strict and controlled sequencing that flows from the planning and implementation of projects. According to Kaplan and Norton (2001, p. 365), the BSC should be seen as a management project and certainly not as a systems project. Kaplan and Norton (2001, p. 365) argue that where consultants are appointed to develop and implement a BSC management system, engagement with managers on strategic dialogue rarely occurs. Consultants are more likely to design a system that gives managers desktop access to masses of data but does not contribute to the organisation's being managed differently and as such is never used.

Lack of disciplined management and leadership

Nair (2004, p. 157) sees disciplined management and leadership as crucial to successful BSC implementation. Nair (2004, p. 157) believes that without disciplined management and leadership, projects tend to be overcommitted, understaffed and miscalculated.

Keeping the balanced scorecard at the top

According to Kaplan and Norton (2001, p. 364), while senior management should support BSC implementation, the mistake of involving them alone should be avoided. In order to be effective, BSC implementation should ultimately involve everyone in the organisation. The aim is for all staff to have an understanding of the strategy and contribute to implementing it, therefore making strategy 'everyone's everyday job'.

Drawn-out development process

Kaplan and Norton (2001, p. 364) caution that the BSC is a building process and that a limited amount of time should be invested in its initial development and implementation.

Even though there may not be data for all measures on the BSC at first, implementation should proceed. Delaying implementation to design the 'perfect' BSC will inevitably lead to it being ineffective or even not being implemented at all. Once the implementation of the initial BSC is embedded in the management system, developments and refinements can be made on a continual basis.

Appointing inexperienced consultants

Kaplan and Norton (2001, p. 366) argue that the appointment of consultants who do not specialise in the BSC and have not implemented multiple successful BSCs will most likely doom it to failure. An inexperienced consultant generally proceeds with the implementation of a measurement or information system that he or she is familiar with, makes minor changes and calls it a BSC, even though it is not.

Only introducing the balanced scorecard for compensation

While BSC implementation can effectively be used as a tool to gain the attention and commitment of individuals, Kaplan and Norton (2001, pp. 366–367) are of the opinion that great care should be taken when a BSC is implemented mainly for compensation, because there is a tendency to skip the conversion of the strategy into measures. When strategy is skipped, a collection of financial and non-financial measures that resemble a stakeholder or strategy scorecard are grouped together and called a BSC.

Concluding remarks

Balanced scorecard is a performance management system that can be used in local government as it allows management to measure financial, internal processes, learning and customer results in operations and organisational potential. However, it is suggested that in local government such a system should start with a definition of community or customer needs and service expectations. Leadership, a transformation orientation and collaborative decision-making are essential to the implementation of a BSC in local government. The implementation of a BSC system should be perceived as a long-term leadership and management project and such a system should be used to develop and implement strategy rather than just as a compensation tool. As such, it should be driven from the top but also cascaded to the individual performance management level.

Research on the BSC has been heavily orientated towards the private sector but as public sector organisations increasingly seek ways to improve their performance management practices, a growing need exists to understand the issues and challenges of BSC implementation in the public sector. An implication of this paper is that where local government is perceived to lack strategic direction, the potential for the BSC to support decision-making and performance improvement may not be recognised. As indicated in other similar studies, the findings of this paper suggest that BSC could be used as an important management tool, as it enables organisations to clarify their vision and strategy and translate them into goal or actions. The reporting based on the BSC can greatly improve accountability.

Acknowledgements

This opinion paper is based on the author's dissertation 'A performance management model for supporting improved local government service delivery: A case study of the Joe Gqabi Disctrict Municipality'. The dissertation can be found at http://scholar.sun.ac.za/handle/10019.1/98102.

We acknowledge the contribution of the participants in the article.

Competing interests

The authors declare that they have no financial or personal relationship(s) that may have inappropriately influenced them in writing this article.

Authors' contributions

Z.J.N. was the principal investigator and K.M. was the co-researcher of this study.

References

Agostino, D., & Arnaboldi, M. (2011). How the BSC implementation process shapes its outcome. *The International Journal of Productivity and Performance Management, 60*(2), 99–114. https://doi.org/10.1108/17410401111101458

Armstrong, M., & Baron, A. (1998). *Performance management*. London: Chartered Institute of Personnel and Development.

Cavalluzzo, K.S., & Ittner, C.D. (2004). Implementing performance measurement innovations: Evidence from government. *Accounting, Organisations and Society, 29*, 243–267. https://doi.org/10.1016/S0361-3682(03)00013-8

Ellangovani, K., & Kamalanabhan, T.J. (2014). Introducing performance management in secondary government hospitals in Kerala and Tamil Nadu using the balanced scorecard framework. *Journal of Multidisciplinary Research in Healthcare, 1*(1), 1–18. https://doi.org/10.15415/jmrh.2014.11001

Grobler, P.A., Warnich, S., Carrell, M.R., Elbert, N.F., & Hatfield, R.D. (2011). *Human resource management in South Africa*. 4th ed. Hampshire: Cengage Learning EMEA.

Hood, C. (1995). The 'New Public Management' in the 1980s: Variations on a theme. *Accounting, Organisations and Society, 20*, 93–109. https://doi.org/10.1016/0361-3682(93)E0001-W

Kaplan, R.S. (2001). Strategic performance measurement and management in non-profit organisations. *Non-Profit Management and Leadership, 11*(3), 353–369. https://doi.org/10.1002/nml.11308

Kaplan, R.S., & Norton, D.P. (1996). *The balanced scorecard: Translating strategy into action*. London: Harvard Business School Press.

Kaplan, R. S., & Norton, D.P. 2001. Transforming the balanced scorecard from performance measurement to strategic management: Part 1. *Accounting Horizons, 15*(1), 87–104.

Mooraj, S., Oyon, D., & Hostettler, D. (1999). The balanced scorecard: A necessary good or an unnecessary evil? *European Management Journal, 17*(5), 481–491. https://doi.org/10.1016/S0263-2373(99)00034-1

Mopaki, O., & Mutono, A. (2016). The balanced scorecard system as a performance measurement tool for public sector organisations: The case of the Media Information Communications Technology Sector Education Training Authority, Republic of South Africa. *British Journal of Applied Science & Technology, 8*(1), 1–9. https://doi.org/10.9734/BJAST/2016/29531

Nair, M. (2004). *Essentials of balanced scorecard*. Hoboken, NJ: Wiley.

Niven, P.R. (2003). *Balance scorecard: Step by step for government and non-profit agencies*. NJ:Johan Wiley and Sons, Inc,Hoboken, New Jersey.

Rampersad, H.K. (2006). *Personal balance scorecard: The way to individual happiness, personal integrity and organisational effectiveness*. Randburg: Knowres.

Republic of South Africa (RSA). (1996). *Constitution of the Republic of South Africa*. Pretoria: Government Printers.

Republic of South Africa (RSA). (1998). *White paper on Local Government, 1998*. Pretoria: Government Printers.

Roux, N.L. (2005). Unrest at the local sphere of government in South Africa: Unrealistic expectations or the inability to implement policies? *Strategic Review for Southern Africa, 27*(2), 55–84.

Sharma, B., & Gadenne, D. (2011). Balanced scorecard implementation in a local government authority: Issues and challenges. *The Australian Journal of Public Administration, 70*(2), 167–184. https://doi.org/10.1111/j.1467-8500.2011.00718.x

Soderberg, M., Kalagnanam, S., Sheehan, N.T., & Vaidyanathan, G. (2011). When is a balanced scorecard a balanced scorecard? *International Journal of Productivity and Performance Management, 60*(7), 688–708. https://doi.org/10.1108/17410401111167780

Thompson, K.R., & Mathys, N.J. (2008). An improved tool for building high performance organisations. *Organisational Dynamics, 37*(4), 378–393. https://doi.org/10.1016/j.orgdyn.2008.07.006

Thornhill, C. (2008). The transformed local government system: Some lessons. *Journal of Public Administration, 32*, 492–511.

Van der Waldt, G. (2006). Managing local government performance: Key considerations and challenges. *Journal of Public Administration, 41*(2), 128–131.

Weinstein, L., & Bukovinsky, D. (2009). Use of the balanced scorecard and performance metrics to achieve operational and strategic alignment in arts and culture not-for-profits. *International Journal of Arts Management, 11*(2), 42–55.

Welman, J., & Kruger, S. (2002). *Research methodology*. 2nd ed. Oxford: Oxford University Press.

Werner, A. (2007). *Organisational behaviour: A contemporary South African perspective*. Pretoria: Van Schaik.

APPENDIX 1

TABLE 1-A1: Policy implementation.

Policy	Explanation
Constitution of the Republic of South Africa, 1996	• provide democratic and accountable government for local communities • ensure the provision of services to communities in a sustainable manner • promote social and economic development • promote a safe and healthy environment • encourage the involvement of communities and community organisations in the matters of local government.
Municipal Systems Act (Act 32 of 2000)	The *Municipal Systems Act* (2000) enforces the idea of a local government performance management system and requires municipalities to: • develop a performance management system • set targets, monitor and review performance based on indicators linked to their IDP • publish an annual report on performance for councillors, staff, the public and other spheres of government • incorporate and report on a set of general indicators prescribed nationally by the minister responsible for local government • conduct an internal audit on performance before tabling the report • have their annual performance report audited by the auditor general • involve the community in setting indicators and targets and reviewing performance.
White Paper on Local Government (1998)	• It states that local government should introduce a performance management system. • It acknowledges, 'involving communities' in developing some municipal performance indicators.
White Paper on Transforming Public Services Delivery (Batho Pele) (1998)	• *Consultation*: Communities should be consulted about the level and quality of public services they receive and, where possible, be given a choice about the services that are provided. • *Service standards*: Communities should know what standard of service to expect. • *Access*: All communities have equal access to the services to which they are entitled. • *Courtesy*: Communities should be treated with courtesy and consideration. • *Information*: Communities should be given full and accurate information about the services they are entitled to receive. • *Openness and transparency*: Communities should know how departments are run, how resources are utilised and who is in charge of particular services. • *Redress*: Should a promised service or a particular standard thereof not be delivered, the community is entitled to full explanation about the service delivery gaps and remedial interventions should be effected. • *Value for money*: Public services should be provided economically and effectively in order to give the communities the best possible value for money.
Municipal Finance Management Act (56 of 2003)	• States the requirement for a municipality to include its annual municipal performance report with its financial statements and other requirements in constituting its annual report. • This must be dealt with by the municipal council within 9 months of the end of the municipal financial year.
Municipal Planning and Performance Management Regulations, 2001	• Sets out how the performance of officials will be uniformly directed, monitored and improved. • The regulations address both the employment contract and performance agreement of municipal managers and managers directly accountable to municipal managers. • Provides a methodology for performance system as well as criteria for performance bonus payments. • Provides an approach for addressing underperformance, should it occur.
Intergovernmental Relations Framework Act (13 of 2005)	• The municipal will establish a Local Intergovernmental Relations forum. The structure will promote cooperation of all local municipalities by bringing together their mayors. • Develops processes in order to align policies and priorities. • Establishes intergovernmental forums to realise these processes. • Implements aligned priorities through joint effort, programmes and projects.

IDP, integrated development planning.

15

Reward preferences in South Africa's media industry

Authors:
Mark H.R. Bussin[1]
Nokwanda N. Thabethe[1]

Affiliations:
[1]Gordon Institute of Business Science, University of Pretoria, South Africa

Corresponding author:
Mark Bussin,
drbussin@mweb.co.za

Orientation: Employee remuneration is a key driver of employee engagement and thus organisational performance. A thorough understanding of employee needs is essential to enable management to develop an equitable mix in reward strategy.

Research purpose: The purpose of this study was to examine context-specific reward preferences in order to determine the overall reward preferences of employees in the media industry with the aim of improving existing reward strategies.

Motivation for the study: The focus on reward preferences has emerged as a critical element in identifying what really motivates productive behaviour within the workplace. A better understanding of reward preferences is required to find ways to improve performance within the world of work.

Research approach/design and method: The research was a quantitative, empirical and descriptive study of reward preferences in an industry-specific context. A self-administered survey was used as a measure and analysed using non-parametric tests to identify variances between dependent and independent groups, testing for internal consistency and non-parametric analysis of variance (ANOVA).

Main findings: The following five reward preferences were rated as most important by participants: base pay or salary, merit increase that is linked to personal performance, incentives and bonus, safety and security at the workplace, and market-related salary. The results indicated that monthly salary (base pay) is the most preferred and/or significant reward category in attracting, retaining and motivating employees.

Practical/managerial implications: Managers in South Africa's media industry should investigate their organisations' rewards through the perspective of the total rewards concept to assess and develop an equitable mix in reward strategy. A comprehensive analysis of reward preferences is required to ensure that all aspects that promote the attraction, retention and motivation of employees are taken into consideration. The importance of base pay should not be under-estimated as it represents the most significant reward preference for employees in the South African media industry.

Contribution/value add: This study adds to the body of social science research, providing a deeper understanding of reward preferences, specifically in the context-specific setting.

Introduction

Problem statement

The 21st century organisations face an economically difficult, highly competitive and ever-changing working environment. The demands on business are therefore to find work structures suitable to a dynamic, diverse and ambiguous workplace. The quality of human resources is of great importance to the success of any organisation, specifically in uncertain working contexts. In terms of employees, organisations require energy, dedication and engagement. Bearing these challenges in mind, organisations need to focus on acquiring and retaining talented employees and keeping them actively engaged in their work (Frank, Finnegan, & Taylor, 2004).

Key focus of the study

An important area in talent management and organisational management is employee engagement. Promoting employee engagement is a key strategy that can be adopted to attract, retain and motivate skilled workers in a complex and dynamic workplace in order to remain competitive (Kerr-Phillips & Thomas, 2009). Understanding reward preferences is one of the key ways in which employee engagement can be realised.

Background to the study

According to Boyd and Salamin (2001), employees offer a significant source of a sustainable competitive advantage for organisations. This was further detailed in a study by Ferreira (2012), which found that the challenges of work in the 21st century have an influence on attracting and retaining employees and that employers need to adopt a vigorous approach when developing employment and retention practices within the organisation. Having the right talent in essential roles is of strategic importance and is linked to the ability to attract, engage and retain talent, leading to competitive advantage.

A report by the South African Board for People Practices (2014) listed the shortage of research on factors influencing employee engagement and the poor alignment or integration of people management as the widest gaps in understanding how South African organisations can best leverage their biggest source of competitive advantage.

Labour market efficiency, which is a key determinant in driving productivity and competitiveness, is a primary indicator of sustainable economic growth. The Global Competitiveness Report 2014–2015 ranks South Africa 136 out of 144 countries in pay and productivity (World Economic Forum, 2015). This rating suggests that the pay scale (remuneration) of organisations within the South African economy is not strongly related to employee productivity. This can potentially hamper the country's competitiveness as it impacts on organisations' ability to deliver on their strategic objectives, can reduce the competitiveness and productivity of organisations and can lower innovation and creativity. This is a worrisome assessment when considering that employees provide an important source of a sustainable competitive advantage for organisations.

As a result, employee remuneration calls for a thorough understanding of employee needs and reward preferences to enable management to develop an equitable mix in reward strategy. A well-designed and relevant reward strategy can enhance the performance of employees and thus positively influence the realisation of the overall organisational objectives. Employee reward is therefore an important topic where innovation is required to optimise people practices, differentiate organisations in the labour market and place organisations in a better position to attract, motivate and retain skilled employees to support sustainable growth.

Armstrong (2012) and Meyer, Mukerjee and Sestero (2001) argue that reward strategies are crucial elements of any human resources (HR) strategy, and they play a strategic role in developing the performance and profitability of an organisation. Furthermore, Armstrong (2012) argues that reward strategy actually delivers performance by helping to foster a high-performance culture; identifying and rewarding key skills, competencies and performance; and making certain that reward systems are market-based, fair and cost-effective.

According to McKinsey (2012), the global shortage of skills has resulted in a 'war for talent' with a progressively competitive backdrop for recruiting and retaining skilled employees. This has resulted in a strategic business challenge where talent serves as a critical driver of organisational performance (Michaels, Handfield-Jones, & Axelrod, 2001).

Organisations can better respond to attraction and retention concerns by understanding the reward preferences that employees have. An early study by Horwitz, Heng and Quazi (2003) identified the need to differentiate HR practices to manage different groups and identified competitive pay packages as the most effectual strategy.

Trends from the research literature

Snelgar, Renard and Venter (2013) argue that a 'one-size-fits-all' reward approach is no longer effective, especially considering that employee retention and motivation are a serious challenge in South Africa. The implications of this are that there is a need for a contemporary understanding of which rewards are preferred by employees to develop strategies for attracting and retaining key staff (Bussin & Toerien, 2015).

Perrow (1986) notes the importance of incentives and self-interest in organisations. In this context, agency theory provides the theoretical foundation for the understanding of reward systems, as the assumption is that employees will not make any more effort than the level that is equal to the value for the pay they are receiving. This leads to the practical interpretation that organisations should tailor their compensation in a way that gets the desired behaviours from employees (Armstrong, 2012). It follows that clear and tailored rewards strategies should then result in reward policies and practices, which provide guidelines and action plans formulated to reward and motivate employees.

Research by Nienaber, Bussin and Henn (2011) in South Africa showed that total rewards models structured according to employee preferences are instrumental in the attraction, motivation and retention of key employees. Furthermore, Schaufeli and Bakker (2004) found that positive attitudes towards work such as organisational commitment, motivation and job involvement are also related to employee engagement.

Research objectives

This research examined context-specific reward preferences to determine the overall reward preferences of employees in the media industry. The implications of the findings can be used to improve existing reward strategies, as opposed to mimicking other organisations' reward practices, which may not be in line with their context-specific culture.

An additional objective was to deepen the understanding of reward preferences in the context-specific setting of the media industry. The PricewaterhouseCoopers (2015) media outlook report argues that South Africa's media market will continue its run of double-digit year-on-year growth, as it had recorded an 11.5% rise to reach R112.7 billion in 2014. The industry forecasts a healthy compound annual growth rate (CAGR) rise of 9.4% by 2019, reaching R176.3 bn. The media sector is set to be a major generator of economic value, and the industry revenue growth is set to outstrip the country's economic growth. Organisations, therefore, need to ensure that they are strategically positioned and leverage this projected growth. As employees have been recognised as the source of competitive advantage, effective rewards should be used to influence the attraction, retention and motivation of key, critical and talented individuals, who must be obtained and kept in order for the industry to be competitive.

Current economic growth in South Africa is slow (World Bank, 2016), and with accompanying economic volatility, employee reward preferences are bound to change. Specifically, money becomes a deficiency need, making it important to look at the impact of rewards on engagement. Organisations need to look at the perspective of total rewards focusing on tangible and intangible reward elements (Royal, 2014).

Research questions

The following research questions were investigated in this study:

- *Research Question 1*: What reward preferences do employees in the media industry have?
- *Research Question 2*: What are the reward preferences that promote attraction in the media industry?
- *Research Question 3*: What are the reward preferences that promote retention in the media industry?
- *Research Question 4*: What are the reward preferences that promote motivation in the media industry?
- *Research Question 5*: Do demographic variables play a significant role in determining the different reward preferences of employees within the media industry?

What will follow?

The article will commence with various theories underlying rewards and reward preferences. Thereafter, the research method used to contest or support the findings of the literature review will be detailed. The research questions will be answered in the results section, and a discussion section, elaborating on the results, will commence thereafter.

Critical evaluation of the literature

In this study, rewards refer to the sum of financial (basic pay, variable pay and employee benefits) and non-financial compensations, such as recognition, learning and development opportunities and increased job responsibility, paid by organisations to employees in exchange for their services (Jiang, Xiao, Qi, & Xiao, 2009). Horwitz et al. (2003) and Kwon and Hein (2013) identified competitive monetary rewards as a basis for attracting and retaining employees. For this reason, compensation formed the base of this research and was considered as one of the key factors influencing employee engagement and achieving organisational success.

According to Bamberger and Levi (2009) and Bussin and Toerien (2015), rewards impact on performance and productivity; so, the alignment of reward strategies with organisational strategies can ensure organisational effectiveness, positive outcomes and increased employee effort, which are important combinations for organisations to ensure competitive advantage. It is therefore important to invest in total rewards programmes (Deloitte Consulting, 2014).

In the ever-changing work environment, Snelgar et al. (2013) conclude that a standard 'one-size-fits-all' reward approach is no longer effective, especially considering that employee retention and motivation are a serious challenge in South Africa. It has been suggested that reward preferences vary based on a number of factors, and preferences may differ across industries and are influenced by various demographic factors.

Theoretical underpinning – Agency theory

According to Perrow (1986), agency theory holds that employees will not make any more effort than the level that is equal to the value for the pay they are receiving. Implications for organisations are that they should tailor their compensation in a way that gets the desired behaviours from employees (Armstrong, 2012).

According to the Human Resource Practice, agency theory draws attention to the different interests and goals of an organisation's stakeholders and the way that employee remuneration can be used to align these interests and goals. In the organisation, employers and employees are the two stakeholders, where the employers assume the role of principals and the employees the role of agents. In this context, the compensation payable to employees is the agency cost. According to the theory, the principal must choose a contracting scheme (reward strategy) that helps align the interests of the agents with the principal's own interests.

A study by Nienaber et al. (2011) and one by Snelgar et al. (2013) found that reward preferences differ in the employee attraction, retention and motivation lifecycle. The study found that base pay (monetary rewards) was the biggest factor in attracting employees, whereas career management (non-monetary rewards) was the biggest factor in motivating employees. Contrary to the above studies, Bhengu and Bussin (2012) showed that monetary rewards were the third-most important influencing factor in attracting, retaining and motivating employees. There is thus conflicting evidence in evaluating the importance of reward in attracting, retaining and motivating employees. According to Stahl et al. (2012), a holistic total reward approach is required for effectiveness across the attraction, retention and motivation life cycle.

Studies by Bloom and Michael (2002), Levine (1991) and Pfeffer and Langton (1993) found that unrestricted compensation practices are related to employee cooperation, involvement, satisfaction and commitment; however, they did not examine specific compensation practices.

In response to the current economic crisis and talent or skills shortages, organisations are concerned with keeping employees engaged and motivating them under such circumstances. As a result, renewed focus on compensation as a catalyst that boosts productivity and having clearly defined reward strategies is essential in improving performance that lends itself to productivity and gives an incentive for employees to perform.

Motivation is defined by Steers and Porter (1991) as a process by which behaviour is energised, directed and sustained to help organisations increase their productivity and is interconnected with engagement. First-hand studies by Alexander (1993), Hall (1986), Strauss and Wohart (2004) and Wakeford (2004) found higher remuneration stimulated employee productivity via the efficiency wage argument. Contrary to the argument that higher remuneration stimulated employee productivity, research by Horwitz et al. (2003) found non-monetary rewards to being the most influential in motivating employees, and consequently, pay and benefits had limited impact on motivating employees. This assertion is supported by the findings of Scott, McMullen, Royal and Stark (2010), who stated that organisations need to look at utilising total rewards strategies (including both monetary and non-monetary rewards) to promote employee engagement.

Theoretical framework surrounding rewards

According to Wilson (2003), the purpose of reward systems is to establish an efficient way to deliver positive outcomes for contribution towards desired performance as it influences the actions of individuals.

Total rewards, according to the WorldatWork Total Rewards Model (the main reward model that forms the basis for this study), describes reward strategies as a combination of five elements of reward in order to create value for the organisation and its employees. It is considered as everything of value that forms part of the relationship between an employer and an employee (Medcof & Rumpel, 2007). According to WorldatWork (2010), the following five elements of reward have a direct relationship on an organisation's ability to attract, motivate and retain employees:

- *Compensation or remuneration*: Any pay provided by an employer to an employee for services rendered.
- *Benefits*: Programmes employers use as an add-on to any cash compensation that employees receive.
- *Work–life*: A set of various organisational practices that support efforts for employees to achieve success both at work and at home.
- *Performance and recognition:* Alignment of employee effort to the achievement of business goals and the acknowledgment of these efforts.
- Development and career opportunities: Learning experiences that enhance employees' skills and competencies and support of individual plans to advance career goals.

The basic premise is that when these elements are properly designed, it results in reward strategies (defined as the direct development and operation of reward practices) that inform reward policies and practices. These practices and policies in turn provide guidelines and action plans formulated to reward and motivate employees (Kwon & Hein, 2013). Research by Nienaber et al. (2011) showed that total rewards models structured according to employee preferences are instrumental in the attraction, motivation and retention of key employees.

According to Schaufeli, Salanova and Gonza´lez-Roma´ (2002), employee engagement is defined as a positive, fulfilling, work-related state of mind that is characterised by energy, commitment and concentration. Employee engagement is a critical driver of success in organisations (Al Mehrzi & Singh, 2016) and is believed to manifest when employees experience an ideal fit and identification of self and their work roles. Employee engagement is linked to higher productivity and lower attrition, and as a result, the concept of engagement has become a fundamental determinant of organisational success.

The drivers of employee engagement are critical factors that lead to employee engagement and create the feeling by employees of being valued and involved. Aon (2015) listed career opportunity, reputation and compensation as the top three engagement drivers across markets and regions from 2013 to 2015 (Rama Devi, 2009). A study by Schaufeli and Bakker (2004) further indicated that positive attitudes towards work, such as organisational commitment, motivation and job involvement, are related to employee engagement. Al Mehrzi and Singh (2016) found that other correlates of employee engagement including perceived organisational support, leadership, teamwork and organisational culture significantly affect employee engagement through employee motivation.

According to Cropanzo and Mitchell (2005), the social exchange theory presumes that when individuals are happy with the rewards provided by the prospective or current organisation, individuals reciprocate with positive attitudes that in turn increase levels of commitment and performance which leads to an increase in productivity (Newman & Sheikh, 2011). A study by Misra, Jain and Sood (2013) agreed with Newman and Sheikh (2011), asserting that when desired rewards are received, individuals respond with greater levels of engagement which is linked to positively influencing motivation, performance and a desire to remain with an organisation.

Coffman and Gonzalez-Molina (2002) found that employee engagement has a statistically significant relationship with productivity, profitability, employee retention and business success. Bakker and Demerouti (2008) concluded that an engaged employee is willing and able to contribute to the success of the organisation, putting discretionary effort into their work, going beyond the required minimum to get the job done as engagement is a predictor of overall job satisfaction, and reducing employee turnover (Kurnia & Welly, 2015).

Reward preferences – Attraction, retention and motivation

Schuler and Rogovsky (1998) and Von Glinow (1985) argue that there is a close interdependence between organisations' rewards, motivation and the culture in which the organisation is embedded. Considering this, it is surprising that the influence of industry-specific culture on reward preferences remains largely unexplored. Lawler (1995), Wilson (1995) and Zingheim and Schuster (1995) found that successful alignment of rewards with business strategy relies very much on understanding employee reward preferences.

A study by Schlechter, Faught and Bussin (2014) provided a generic study in reward preferences of South African employees, and the results of this study showed that base pay was considered to be the most preferred reward component and an important reward component in attracting and retaining employees. This study notably also found differences between reward preferences and demographic variables, including age, gender and job level, providing support for segmentation of rewards based on certain demographic variables.

Considering the needs of different generations, the study by Masibigiri and Nienaber (2011) explored factors that affect the retention of different generations and found specific reward preferences existed among generational groups. However, Moore and Bussin (2012) investigated the reward preferences of veterans, baby boomers, generation X and generation Y and found no preference among generational groups. These research findings provide guidelines to focus on individual and demographic factors to develop reward strategies.

Chiang and Birtch (2005) and Nienaber et al. (2011) found that reward preferences do differ according to various demographic factors. Meyer and Kirsten (2012) also found that many factors such as age, values, gender and culture affect employee reward preferences and therefore are useful to consider in structuring reward packages that suit personal interests.

There is limited research on reward preferences and segmentation of the workforce, and this review of the literature has mostly focused on the financial services industry, knowledge workers of South African information technology companies and artisans, whereas South Africa has a number of industries with diverse characteristics that could benefit from understanding what reward categories employees consider important and how demographic variables influence these reward preferences. There is still much argument over whether reward packages should be tailor-made to suit individual employees as it has been argued that a 'one-size-fits-all' approach to rewards is no longer effective.

Research design

Research approach

The research design is a quantitative, descriptive study entailing the collection of numerical data and describing the characteristics of objects, people or organisations in order to explain a particular phenomenon in answering the research questions (Zikmund, 2003).

Research method

Research participants

The participants in this study consisted of all employees of a large media organisation that has interests in new media, content production, specialised publishing, research, radio broadcasting and television sphere. At the time of the study, the company had 736 permanent employees across its various subsidiaries.

All employees were able to volunteer to complete the survey. One hundred and thirty-one employees completed the survey.

Measuring instrument

The Rewards Preferences Questionnaire (Nienaber & Bussin 2009) was administered online. The questionnaire consisted of a series of questions and prompts to allow participants to answer questions during a single visit and submit their responses (Saunders & Lewis, 2012).

Section A of the questionnaire collected participants' demographic information such as age, gender, race, occupational level, division and department within the organisation. For section B of the questionnaire, the questions were derived from constructs extracted from the WorldatWork Total Rewards Model (WorldatWork, 2010) to measure reward preferences using a 5-point Likert scale on each reward component from the model indicating the level of importance for each component.

Section C of the questionnaire focused on enabling participants to rank which reward component had the greatest impact on attracting, retaining and motivating them. This also functioned as a way to assess the overall reward preferences of participants.

Research procedure

A survey pre-test was conducted with a group of six individuals for input and comments; no revisions were required. All participants completed a self-administered web-based questionnaire hosted by Typeform. With assistance from the different subsidiaries' human resources managers, the questionnaire link was distributed electronically via email to the entire population, with a 6-week response window in order to allow time for targeted individuals to complete the survey. Reminders were sent periodically to encourage participation.

Statistical analysis

The data were analysed quantitatively using a three-stage data analysis process. Stage 1 involved descriptive statistical analysis to describe, show or summarise data in a meaningful way, focusing on measures of centrality and dispersion. Stage 2 pertained to basic inferential statistics used to make generalisations from a sample to a population to help assess the strength of the relationship between the study's independent variables and dependent (effect) variables. Stage 3 inferential and multivariate statistical analysis focused on observations made on many variables (Creswell, 2014). The statistical techniques utilised were means score ranking test and analysis of variance (ANOVA).

Results

The survey was completed by 131 participants. Table 1 shows a summary of the total rewards elements, detailing the reward preference comparisons by demographics. A Kruskal–Wallis ANOVA was completed, comparing two or more independent groups with significant differences shown in shaded areas.

Reward preferences based on demographic variables

Gender

The summary of mean ranks of reward components based on gender showed the extent of rating difference for medical aid, retirement, return to work after maternity and paternity leave, and feedback and performance between the participants. The summary of mean ranks of the reward components

TABLE 1: Total reward preference comparisons by all demographics.

Total rewards element	Reward component	Gender	Age group	Ethnicity	Education level	Number of children	Job role	Job level	Media division
Compensation	Base pay	0.660	**0.053**	0.062	**0.053**	0.508	0.108	0.900	**0.041**
	Incentives & bonuses	0.384	0.287	0.242	0.287	0.362	0.734	0.433	0.250
	Merit	0.197	0.658	0.520	0.343	0.139	0.105	0.879	0.425
	Market-related salary	0.707	0.454	0.331	0.298	0.087	0.714	0.280	0.989
	Remuneration structure	0.802	0.662	0.223	0.535	0.343	0.163	0.090	**0.012**
	Income Inflation	0.556	0.768	0.086	0.221	0.348	0.583	0.718	**0.006**
	Bonus linked to personal performance	0.600	0.781	0.686	0.903	0.852	0.330	0.421	0.182
Benefits	Medical	**0.005**	0.627	0.432	0.627	0.520	0.090	0.296	0.058
	Retirement	**0.007**	0.445	**0.021**	0.445	0.984	0.268	0.748	**0.049**
	Study leave	0.290	**0.040**	**0.000**	**0.040**	0.518	0.071	**0.014**	0.648
	Sabbatical leave	0.090	**0.004**	0.846	**0.004**	0.134	**0.019**	0.109	0.412
	Children's education subsidy	0.248	0.399	**0.019**	0.399	0.081	0.207	0.072	0.359
	Financial assistance for a house	0.176	0.666	**0.002**	0.894	0.321	0.515	0.111	0.249
	Subsidised care for dependents	0.449	0.335	**0.026**	0.628	0.392	0.787	**0.003**	0.531
	Parking bay	0.603	0.563	0.268	0.563	0.862	0.215	0.616	**0.000**
Work–life (environment)	Good working relationship	0.345	0.791	0.446	0.791	0.625	**0.001**	**0.013**	**0.017**
	Office environment	0.372	0.650	0.967	0.650	0.931	**0.010**	**0.015**	0.111
	On-site fitness centre	0.459	0.168	**0.050**	0.168	0.824	0.063	0.222	0.262
	On-site medical centre	0.183	0.627	0.056	0.081	0.434	0.398	**0.034**	0.908
	On-site childcare facilities	0.062	0.498	0.041	0.498	0.125	**0.025**	0.307	0.644
	On-site staff restaurant	0.459	0.384	0.712	0.384	0.701	0.063	0.266	0.665
	On-site convenience store	0.673	0.701	0.410	0.701	0.683	0.092	0.501	0.509
	Working flexible hours	0.067	0.565	0.912	0.565	0.114	**0.018**	0.065	0.995
	Quality of co-workers in the team	0.377	0.604	0.393	0.604	0.964	**0.001**	0.454	0.120
	Safety and security in the workplace	0.406	0.794	0.630	0.794	0.362	0.059	0.058	0.748
	Children holiday programme	0.425	0.358	**0.003**	0.453	**0.001**	0.372	0.080	0.424
	Log into employer's network	0.761	0.542	0.629	0.915	0.368	0.059	0.244	0.229
	Return to work after maternity leave	**0.021**	0.532	0.134	0.885	0.059	0.342	0.646	0.859
Career learning and development	Learning and development	0.131	**0.014**	**0.000**	**0.014**	0.810	0.061	**0.029**	0.072
	Funding for tertiary education	0.686	0.286	**0.000**	0.286	0.740	**0.013**	**0.014**	0.583
	Job rotation	0.161	0.138	**0.003**	0.138	0.868	0.757	0.083	0.239
	Career path planning and interests	0.765	**0.017**	**0.013**	0.324	0.213	0.097	0.190	**0.003**
	International secondment	0.194	**0.001**	0.125	0.236	0.751	0.497	0.732	0.691
Performance and recognition	Feedback and performance	**0.040**	0.217	**0.002**	0.217	0.462	0.099	0.484	0.975
	Balanced scorecard	0.122	0.937	**0.003**	0.937	0.783	0.057	0.929	0.132
	Formal recognition	0.306	0.737	**0.047**	0.737	0.273	0.734	0.691	0.725
	Informal recognition	0.074	0.362	0.324	0.362	**0.050**	**0.001**	**0.040**	0.343
	Monthly communication sessions	0.087	0.380	**0.003**	0.380	0.312	**0.048**	0.661	0.332
	Total control over work	0.796	0.419	0.739	0.802	0.509	0.145	0.111	0.258
	Challenging job	0.853	0.069	**0.006**	0.590	0.362	0.364	0.287	0.184
	Accountable jobs	0.654	0.411	0.123	0.575	0.217	0.753	0.455	**0.032**
	Management and team performance	0.737	0.238	0.598	0.866	0.485	0.132	0.292	0.193

Note: Significant differences in reward preferences is shown in bold.

based on gender showed that female participants have higher mean ranks on all four reward components.

Age

When the data were analysed by age groups, six reward components revealed statistically significant results as presented in Table 1. The mean ranks suggest that study leave, learning and development, career path and international secondment are the most appealing rewards for participants in the age group of 19–29 years.

With a mean rank of 74.41, participants aged between 30 and 39 years consider sabbatical leave as the most important reward. Yet, participants aged between 40 and 49 years recorded the highest mean rank for base pay.

Ethnicity

The summary of mean ranks shows that there was a statistically significant difference among the four racial groups considered for 16 rewards components as presented in Table 1. Notably, mean ranks based on ethnicity showed that participants who indicated that they are African had the highest mean ranks for the majority of significant mean ranks except for retirement, children holiday programme and formal recognition. Further to this, mixed race and white participants did not record any highest mean ranks for reward components which were statistically significant. Indian respondents, on the other hand, had the highest mean ranks for retirement benefits, children holiday programme and formal recognition.

Number of children

The summary of mean ranks of reward components based on the number of children revealed that there was a statistically significant difference among the five groupings of a number of children for children holiday programme and informal recognition. Participants with three or more children stood out for children holiday programme. In particular, participants who indicated that they have four or more children recorded the highest mean rank on children holiday programme. On the contrary, respondents who indicated that they have no children had the highest mean rank for informal recognition.

Education

Participants who indicated that matric is their highest educational qualification had the highest mean rank for base pay. In contrast, participants who stated that in addition to matric, they had also acquired certificates for certain skills stood out for study leave and learning and development. Postgraduate degree holders showed sabbatical leave as their most preferred reward.

Job level

The results show that general staff had the highest mean rank for study level. Specialists recorded the highest mean rank for subsidised care for dependents, office environment, on-site medical facilities, learning development and funding for tertiary education to any other reward benefits. Participants in the other jobs group had the highest mean rank for good working relationship and informal recognition.

Media division

As a group of companies, the Media division comprised different subsidiaries or divisions. A Kruskal–Wallis ANOVA test was conducted to evaluate differences in reward preferences among groups of companies. The summary of mean ranks shows that there was a statistically significant difference among the groups of the Media divisions for seven rewards components.

Participants from radio media had the highest mean rank for good working relationship, whilst participants from the publishing division have parking bay and increases income linked to inflation as their most preferred rewards. Participants working for Media Mark recorded the highest mean rank for retirement. The highest mean rank for participants in other media companies was recorded for career path and accountability for job outputs.

Job role

The results show that participants in from the human resources department have the highest mean rank for sabbatical leave and flexible working hours. Participants from the Internet Technology (IT) department had the highest mean rank for good working relationship and monthly communication sessions. Participants in the marketing department only had the highest mean rank for on-site childcare facilities. Finance department participants had the highest mean rank for funding for tertiary education, whilst participants from the programming department had the highest mean rank for office environment and informal recognition. In addition, the legal department has its participants finding the quality of co-workers in the team of high importance. These results suggest that the reward preferences vary within and across departments.

Overall reward preferences sorted by mean

The most favoured reward component by the participants were salary, merit increase linked to personal performance, and incentives and bonus, and the least preferred reward components were on-site childcare facilities, children holiday programme and subsidised care for dependent. The top and the most preferred category as per the participants in structuring their own rewards package is base pay, and the least preferred is quality work environment category.

Reward preferences in attraction, retention and motivation

To determine the most significant reward factors that drive attraction, retention and motivation, participants were asked to indicate which one of the following six reward categories had the greatest impact on an organisation's ability to attract, retain and motivate them:

- monthly salary or remuneration
- variable pay (bonus or long-term incentive)
- benefits (medical aid or retirement funding)

- performance and career (development opportunities, quality discussions with your manager)
- quality work environment (fitness centre on-site, medical centre on-site, latest technology)
- work or home integration (your ability to balance your work and home commitments, e.g., flexible work schedules and half day leave).

Participants were asked to tick only one block for each category (attraction or retention or motivation). The results are presented in subsequent sections.

Reward preferences in attraction

The majority of participants (68.7%, $n = 90$) indicated that monthly salary was the most significant component of promoting attraction. In contrast, quality work environment stood out as the least significant category in influencing the decision to join an organisation. Figure 1 shows the ranking of factors which promote employee attraction.

Reward preferences for retention

Most participants (46.6%) ranked monthly salary as the most significant way to promote retention. The second-most preferred reward preference category for retention was related to performance and career. In contrast, only 3% ($n = 4$) of the participants indicated that they value the quality of work environment as a driver of retention. Figure 2 shows the ranking of factors which promote employee retention.

Reward preferences for motivation

Most of the participants (46.6%) ranked monthly salary as the most significant means of driving motivation. The second-highest ranked category for motivation was related to performance and career. In contrast, only 3% ($n = 4$) of the participants indicated that they preferred the quality of work environment as a means of motivation. Figure 3 shows the ranking of factors which promote employee motivation.

The results for reward preferences suggest that monthly salary (base pay) is the most highly ranked reward category for promoting employee attraction, retention, and motivation. Quality work environment stood out as the lowest ranked category for attraction, retention and motivation.

Reward category and component internal consistency

Reward components were grouped into the following five categories – compensation; benefits; work–life (work environment); career, learning, and development; and performance and recognition. To ensure consistency, all statements were based on a 5-point Likert scale. The Cronbach Alpha test was used to determine the internal consistency of the reward categories, where scores equal or greater than 0.6 were considered acceptable and scores approaching 1.0 were considered excellent scores. The top and most preferred category as per the participants in structuring their own rewards package is base pay and the least preferred is quality work environment category.

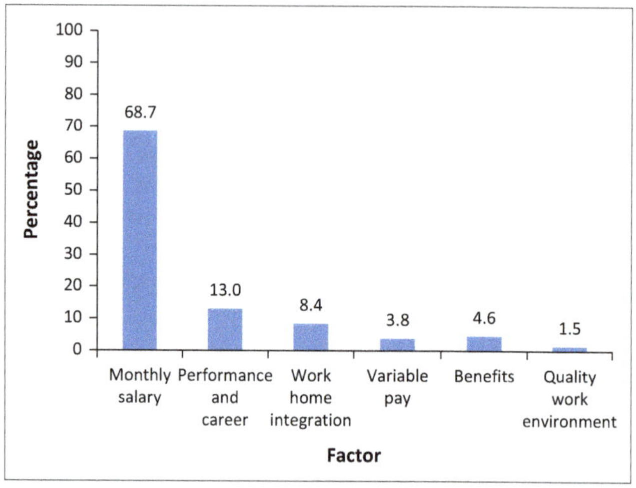

FIGURE 1: Ranking of factors which promote employee attraction.

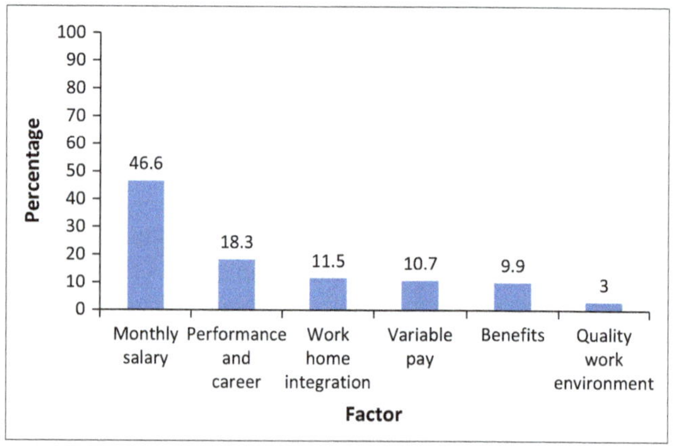

FIGURE 2: Ranking of factors which promote employee retention.

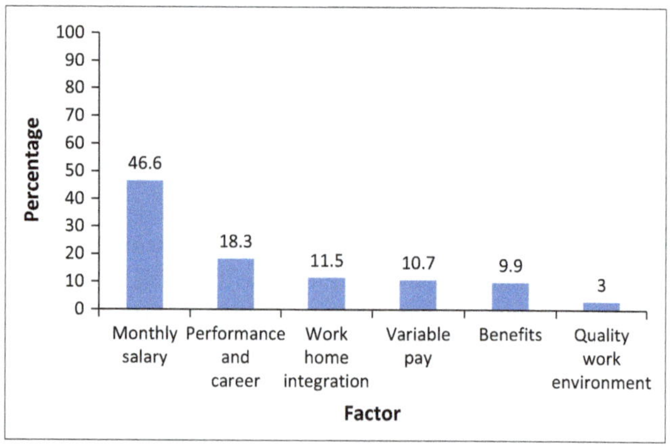

FIGURE 3: Ranking of factors which promote employee motivation.

Discussion

Research question 1: What reward preferences do employees in the media industry have?

Results show that overall participants ranked base pay as the most preferred and/or significant form of reward. This finding differs with the findings of Nienaber et al. (2011) and Snelgar et al. (2013), whose research indicated that career management (a form of non-monetary reward) was the most significant reward preference. The finding supports the conclusion of Schlechter et al. (2014) who also found that base pay was considered to be the most preferred reward component. There remains no clear answer to the question of most significant reward preference, and further research at a larger scale will be required to provide a definitive position.

Research questions 2, 3 and 4: What are the reward preferences that promote attraction, retention and motivation in the media industry?

Reward preferences did not vary across the categories of attraction, retention and motivation. Monthly salary was ranked as the most influential reward preference, followed by performance and career and then work home integration. It is possible that the way the questions were phrased influenced the results, and it is suggested that this potential extraneous variable be considered in how future surveys are designed.

Studies by Nienaber et al. (2011) and Snelgar et al. (2013) indicated that reward preferences differ in the employee attraction, retention and motivation lifecycle. The results for reward preferences for this study indicated that monthly salary (base pay) stood out as the most preferred reward category in attracting, retaining and motivating employees. From an attraction perspective, this correlates positively with the studies of Nienaber et al. (2011) and Snelgar et al. (2013) who also found that base pay (a form of monetary reward) was the most significant factor in attracting employees. From a motivation perspective, the results contradict Nienaber et al. (2011) and Snelgar et al. (2013) who found that career management (a form of non-monetary reward) was the most significant driver of employee motivation.

The results also differ from the study by Bhengu and Bussin. (2012) which showed monetary rewards as the third-most important influencing factor in attracting, retaining and motivating employees. Lazear (1995) concluded that the reward systems of organisations should be tailored to take the characteristics of their workforce into account. Medcof and Rumpel (2007) assert that there is a difference in reward preferences between industries. The results of this study lend support to both Lazear (1995) and Medcof and Rumpel (2007) and support the notion of context-specific reward preferences.

Research question 5: Do demographic variables play a significant role in determining the different reward preferences of employees within the media industry?

Gender: From the study, statistically significant results were indicated for medical aid, retirement, return to work after maternity and paternity leave, and feedback and performance. This indicates that females had a higher preference for medical aid, retirement (benefits component), phased return to work after maternity leave (work–life component), and also feedback and performance (Performance & Recognition component). These results are similar to those of Nienaber et al. (2011) which indicated that women had a higher preference for performance, medical aid and retirement funds as the mean scores for these reward categories were higher than those of men.

Age: Study leave, learning and development, career path, and international secondment are the most appealing rewards for participants in the age group of 19–29 years. Participants aged between 30 and 39 years consider sabbatical leave as the most important reward. Finally, participants aged between 40 and 49 years recorded the highest preference for base pay.

Base pay: This noted a significant relationship between age group, educational level and division. The findings match the study by Nienaber et al. (2011) that observed significant differences between age groups are most notable for base pay preference is in the age group 39–48 years. Benefits also revealed an observed relationship between the following demographic variables – gender, age group, study leave and sabbatical leave. Ethnicity also displayed a relationship for retirement, study leave, child educational subsidy and sabbatical leave, in terms of its influence on reward preferences.

Job level: Reward preferences based on job level results showed a statistically significant difference among the groups of job levels for eight reward components as presented in Table 1. The most noteworthy results were that general staff had the highest preference for study leave; specialists recorded the highest preference for subsidised care for dependents, office environment, on-site medical facilities, learning development and funding for tertiary education to any other reward benefits; participants in the other jobs group had the highest preference for good working relationship and informal recognition.

Overall, the results from the study, and as discussed above, support the findings from the study by Schlechter et al. (2014) that also found differences between reward preferences and demographic variables, including age, gender and job level. This provides support for the segmentation of rewards based on certain demographic variables and contributes to the literature on reward preferences. This is also in line with the research findings of Johns and Gratton (2013) who found that the rewards preference profile of certain workers would be different, supporting the notion that demographic and industry-specific factors influence reward preferences.

Internal consistency of reward elements

The key part of this study was assessing the internal consistency of the different reward categories to determine if the results of these categories were fitting to group in order to assess overall reward preferences. Notably, the compensation category did not score acceptable levels as per the Cronbach Alpha reliability test. As the top-rated category and most preferred reward component, its results showed a poor correlation with the elements in its category.

The compensation category included the following elements:

- base pay
- incentives and bonuses
- merit
- market-related salary
- remuneration structure
- income Inflation
- bonus linked to personal performance.

It is both interesting and surprising that the level of internal consistency within this specific category was low. The individual elements are commonly considered to be associated with compensation and it is not clear what caused the low reliability score. Literature on the subject of reward and common sense suggest that these elements should be reflective of a compensation category. Further research with a larger sample size may be able to shed more light on this irregularity in future.

Principal findings

The study showed similar reward preferences in the scenarios of attraction, retention and motivation in principle supporting the literature that asserts that the main elements of monetary compensation are still crucially important (Bunton & Brewer, 2012; Horwitz et al., 2003; Moore & Bussin, 2012; Nienaber et al., 2011; Schlechter et al., 2014; Snelgar et al., 2013). This is an indication that base pay does not seem to lose its desirability and therefore it is important that employees feel that they are adequately rewarded to contribute towards achieving organisational goals.

In examining the relative influence of total rewards elements on reward preferences by employees in this context, participants ranked base pay or salary, merit increase that is linked to personal performance, incentives & bonus, safety and security at the workplace, and market-related salary as the five most important reward components preferred by them, further indicative of the preference towards the monetary elements in the total rewards model.

This is contrary to some of the findings by Bloom and Michael (2002), Levine (1991) and Pfeffer and Langton (1993) who asserted that competing for talent solely on monetary elements may not prove to be the most effective mechanism in gaining competitive advantage. This can be attributed to the fact that the total rewards model adopts a holistic approach and combines five elements of reward to create value for the organisation and its employees.

In a mix of reward elements, the monetary component still remained the most preferred reward across the attraction, retention and motivation lifecycle. This is supported by findings by Scott et al. (2010) in that organisations need to look at utilising total rewards strategies to build on employee engagement.

Another key finding stems from observed significant differences towards reward preferences as a result of demographic variables, similar to the studies by Bussin and Toerin, (2015), Kowalewski and Phillips (2012) and Snelgar et al. (2013), and the notion that it is best for employers to have an understanding of demographic variables and their impact in order to design appropriate reward strategies.

Implications for management

Considering the insight from this study, the results are an important starting point in assessing and developing methods to attract, retain and motivate employees and key talent in organisations. A holistic total rewards approach is required for effectiveness across the attraction, retention and motivation lifecycle, including both monetary and non-monetary rewards. Despite the requirement and best practice of implementing a holistic reward mix, this study suggests that the importance of base pay cannot be minimised and is the most significant reward preference in the South African media industry.

Managers and leaders in the South African media industry need to investigate their organisations' rewards through the perspective of the total rewards concept used in this study in order to evaluate and ensure that they have considered all of the aspects required to attract, retain and motivate employees.

Limitations of the research

The study is descriptive in nature. Therefore, the results are limited to numerical descriptions, and it was not possible to explore reasons for the participants' selection of reward preferences. Additionally, the sample was not representative of the population being studied; the survey did not test the entire population as the majority of employees chose not to participate. The results were also not without external influences such as economic and political factors. The study had a contracted timeframe, and it was therefore not possible to establish if the reward preferences were stable or as a result of temporal external influences. Most importantly, the low internal reliability score for the compensation category could impact the reliability of the main research findings on reward preferences.

Suggestions for future research

Future research should ideally examine specific compensation practices and extend to exploring causal relationship between rewards and attraction, retention and motivation of employees. Another important element is devising a way to fixing the correlation and reliability of the compensation category.

Conclusion

The purpose of this study was to examine context-specific reward preferences in order to determine overall reward preferences of employees in the media industry with the aim of improving existing reward strategies. The study has meet its purpose by illustrating the total reward components preferred by participants in South Africa's media industry and indicates the importance of the adoption of a total rewards strategy as rewards are a key source to persuade individuals and ensure work productivity.

Rewards are used as a primary tool for organisations to attract competent key employees and improve the productivity of their employees. Compensation is an important element in understanding the drivers of engagement to increase employee engagement and promote the attraction, retention and motivation of employees.

Acknowledgements

Competing interests

The authors declare that they have no financial or personal relationships that may have inappropriately influenced them in writing this article.

Authors' contributions

M.H.R.B. was the principal investigator and was responsible for the design and execution of the project and writing up of the article. N.N.T was responsible for field work and writing up of the article.

References

Alexander, C. O. (1993). The changing relationship between productivity, wages and unemployment in the UK. *Oxford Bulletin of Economics and Statistics, 55*, 87–102. https://doi.org/10.1111/j.1468-0084.1993.mp55001005.x

Al Mehrzi, N., & Singh, S.K. (2016). Competing through employee engagement: A proposed framework. *International Journal of Productivity and Performance Management, 65*(6), 831–843. https://doi.org/10.1108/IJPPM-02-2016-0037

Aon, H. (2015). *2015 Trends in global employee engagement.* Retrieved from http://www.aon.com/: http://www.aon.com/attachments/human-capital-consulting/2015-Trends-in-Global-Employee-Engagement-Report.pdf

Armstrong, M. (2012). *Armstrong's handbook of reward management practice: Improving performance through reward.* London: Kogan Page Publishers.

Bakker, A. B., & Demerouti, E. (2008). Towards a model of work engagement. *Career Development International, 13*, 209–223. https://doi.org/10.1108/13620430810870476

Bamberger, P. A., & Levi, R. (2009). Team-based reward allocation structures and the helping behaviors of outcome-interdependent team members. *Journal of Managerial Psychology, 24*, 300–327. https://doi.org/10.1108/02683940910952705

Bhengu, M. B., & Bussin, M. (2012). The perceived effectiveness of employee share options as a mechanism of talent management in South Africa. *Acta Commercii, 12*(1), 85–93. https://doi.org/10.4102/ac.v12i1.135

Bloom, M. C., & Michael, J. G. (2002). The relationship among organizational context, pay dispersion and managerial turnover. *Academy of Management Journal, 45*(1), 33–42.

Boyd, B. K., & Salamin, A. (2001). Strategic rewards systems: A contingency model of pay system design. *Strategic Management Journal 22*(8), 777–792. https://doi.org/10.1002/smj.170

Bunton, T. E., & Brewer, J. L. (2012). Discovering workplace motivators for the millennial generation of IT employees. In *Proceedings of the 1st Annual conference on Research in information technology (RIIT '12) 13–18 October*, (pp. 13–18). New York: ACM.

Bussin, M., & Toerien, W. C. (2015). Influence of reward preferences in attracting, retaining, and motivating knowledge workers in South African information technology companies. *Acta Commercii, 15*(1), Art. #290, 1–13. https://doi.org/10.4102/ac.v15i1.290

Chiang, F. T., & Birtch, T. A. (2005). A taxonomy of reward preference: Examining country differences. *Journal of International Management, 11*, 357–375. https://doi.org/10.1016/j.intman.2005.06.004

Coffman, C., & Gonzalez-Molina, G. (2002). *Follow this path: How the world's greatest organisations drive growth by unleashing human potential.* New York: Warner Books, Inc.

Creswell, J. W. (2014). *Research design: Qualitative, quantitative, and mixed methods approaches.* Thousand Oaks, CA: Sage Publishing.

Cropanzo, R. & Mitchell, M. (2005). Social exchange theory: An interdisciplinary review. *Journal of Management, 31*(6), 874–900.

Deloitte Consulting. (2014). *Global human capital trends 2014. Engaging the 21st century workforce.* Retrieved from http://www2.deloitte.com: http://www2.deloitte.com/global/en/pages/human-capital/articles/human-capital-trends-2014.html

Ferreira, N. (2012). Hardiness in relation to organisational commitment in the Human Resource Management field. *SA Journal of Human Resource Management, 10*(2), 1–10. https://doi.org/10.4102/sajhrm.v10i2.418

Frank, F. D., Finnegan, R. P., & Taylor, C. R. (2004). The race for talent: Retaining and engaging workers in the 21st century. *HR. Human Resources Planning, 27*(3), 12–27.

Hall, S. G. (1986). An application of the Granger and Engle two-step estimation procedure to United Kingdom aggregate wage data. *Oxford Bulletin of Economics and Statistics, 48*, 229–239. https://doi.org/10.1111/j.1468-0084.1986.mp48003003.x

Horwitz, F. M., Heng, C. T., & Quazi, H. A. (2003). Finders, keepers? Attracting, motivating, and retaining knowledge workers. *Human Resource Management Journal, 13*, 23–44. https://doi.org/10.1111/j.1748-8583.2003.tb00103.x

Jiang, Z., Xiao, Q., Qi, H., & Xiao, L. (2009). Total rewards strategy going with the trend of the times. *International Journal of Business and Management, 4*(11) 177–183.

Johns, T., & Gratton, L. (2013). The third wave of virtual work. *Harvard Business Review, 91*(1), 66–72.

Kerr-Phillips, B., & Thomas, T. (2009). Macro and micro challenges for talent retention in South Africa. *South African Journal of Human Resource Management, 7*(1), 82–91. https://doi.org/10.4102/sajhrm.v7i1.157

Kowalewski, S. J., & Phillips, S. L. (2012). Preferences for performance based employee rewards: Evidence from small business environments. *International Journal of Management and Marketing Research, 5*, 65–76.

Kurnia, R., & Welly, J. (2015). The assessment of employee engagement level in a new institution during transition period. *Journal of Business and Management, 4*(1), 218–228.

Kwon, J., & Hein, P. (2013). Employee benefits in a total rewards framework. *Benefits Quarterly; First Quarter (29,1) ProQuest Business Collection,29*(1), 32–38.

Lawler III, E. (1995). The new pay: A strategic approach. *Compensation and Benefits Review, 27*(4), 14–22. https://doi.org/10.1177/088636879502700404

Lazear, E. (1995). *Personnel economics.* Cambridge, MA: MIT Press.

Levine, D. I. (1991). Cohesiveness, productivity and wage dispersion. *Journal of Economic Behavior and Organization, 15*(2), 237–255. https://doi.org/10.1016/0167-2681(91)90031-R

Masibigiri, V., & Nienaber, H. (2011). Factors affecting the retention of Generation X public servants: An exploratory study. *South African Journal of Human Resource Management, 9*(1), 1–11.

McKinsey Global Institute. (2012, June). *The world at work: Jobs, pay and skills for 3.5 billion people.* Retrieved from http://www.mckinsey.com/: http://www.mckinsey.com/global-themes/employment-and-growth/the-world-at-work

Medcof, J. W., & Rumpel, S. (2007). High technology workers and total rewards. *The Journal of High Technology Management Research, 18*, 59–72. https://doi.org/10.1016/j.hitech.2007.03.004

Meyer, C. S., Mukerjee, S., & Sestero, A. (2001). Work-family benefits: Which ones maximize profits? *Journal of Managerial Issues, 13*(1), 28–44.

Meyer, M., & Kirsten, M. (2012). *Introduction to human resource management.* Pretoria: Van Schaik.

Michaels, E., Handfield-Jones, H., & Axelrod, B. (2001). *The war for talent.* Retrieved from https://books.google.co.za/books?id=simZCd_YUC4C&pg=PA1&source=gbs_toc_r&cad=4#v=onepage&q&f=false

Misra, P., Jain, S., & Sood, A. (2013). Compensation: Impact of rewards and organisational justice on turnover intentions and the role of motivation and job satisfaction: A study of retail store operations in NCR. *International Journal of Human Resources Development and Management, 13*(2), 136–152. https://doi.org/10.1504/IJHRDM.2013.055414

Moore, A., & Bussin, M. (2012). Reward preferences for generations in selected Information and Communication Technology companies. *South African Journal of Human Resource Management, 10*(1), 1–9. https://doi.org/10.4102/sajhrm.v10i1.325

Newman, A., & Sheikh, A. Z. (2011). Organizational commitment in Chinese small- and medium-sized enterprises: The role of extrinsic, intrinsic and social rewards. *The International Journal of Human Resource Management, 23*(2), 349–367.

Nienaber, N., & Bussin, M. (2009). *The relationship between personality types and reward preferences.* Doctoral thesis. Johannesburg, South Africa: University of Johannesburg.

Nienaber, R., Bussin, M., & Henn, C. (2011). The relationship between personality types and reward preferences. *Acta Commercii, 11*(2), 1–21. https://doi.org/10.4102/ac.v11i2.153

Perrow, C. (1986). *Complex organizations.* New York: Random House.

Pfeffer, J., & Langton, N. (1993). The Effect of wage dispersion on satisfaction, productivity, and working collaboratively: Evidence from college and university faculty. *Administrative Science Quarterly, 38*(3), 382–407. https://doi.org/10.2307/2393373

PricewaterhouseCoopers. (2015). *Entertainment and Media Outlook: 2015–2019 South Africa –Nigeria – Kenya* (6th edn.). Johannesburg: Pricewaterhouse Coopers.

Rama Devi, V. (2009). Employee engagement is a two-way street. *Human Resource Management International Digest, 17*(2), 3–4. https://doi.org/10.1108/09670730910940186

Royal, M. (2014, March 20). *The role of rewards in building employee engagement*. Retrieved from https://blog.haygroup.com: https://blog.haygroup.com/the-role-of-rewards-in-building-employee-engagement/

Saunders, M., & Lewis, P. (2012). *Doing research in business management: An essential guide to planning your project.* Essex: Pearson Education Limited.

Schaufeli, W. B., & Bakker, A. B. (2004). Job demands, job resources, and their relationship with burnout and engagement: A multi-sample study. *Journal of Organizational Behavior, 25*, 293–315. https://doi.org/10.1002/job.248

Schaufeli, W. B., Salanova, M., & Gonza´lez-Roma´, V. (2002). The measurement of engagement and burnout and: A confirmative analytic approach. *Journal of Happiness, 3*, 71–92. https://doi.org/10.1023/A:1015630930326

Schlechter, A., Faught, C., & Bussin, M. (2014). Total rewards: A study of artisan attraction and retention within a South African context. *South African Journal of Human Resource Management, 12*(1), 1–15. https://doi.org/10.4102/sajhrm.v12i1.648

Schuler, R., & Rogovsky, N. (1998). Understanding Compensation Practice Variations across Firms: The Impact of National Culture. *Journal of International Business Studies, 29*(1), 159–177. https://doi.org/10.1057/palgrave.jibs.8490030

Scott, D., McMullen, T., Royal, M., & Stark, M. (2010). *The impact of rewards programs on employee engagement.* Retrieved from World At Work: https://www.worldatwork.org/adimLink?id=39032

Snelgar, R. J., Renard, M., & Venter, D. (2013). An empirical study if the reward preferences of South African employees. *South African Journal of Human Resource Management, 11*(1) 1–14. https://doi.org/10.4102/sajhrm.v11i1.351

South African Board for People Practices. (2014, October). Employee Engagement. Retrieved from http://sabpp.co.za/fact-sheet-employee-engagement-october-2014/

Stahl, G., Björkman, I., Morris, S. S., Paauwe, J., Stiles, P., & Wright, P. (2012). Six principles of effective global talent management. *Sloan Management Review, 53*(2), 25–42.

Steers, R., & Porter, L. (1991). *Motivation and work behaviour.* New York: McGraw-Hill.

Strauss, J., & Wohar, M. E. (2004). The linkage between process, wage and labour productivity: A panel study of manufacturing industries. *Southern Economic Journal, 70*, 920–941. https://doi.org/10.2307/4135280

von Glinow, M. A. (1985). Reward strategies for attracting, evaluating, and retaining professionals. *Human Resource Management, 24*, 191–206. https://doi.org/10.1002/hrm.3930240207

Wakeford, J. J. (2004). The productivity-wage relationship in South Africa: An empirical investigation. *Development Southern Africa, 21*(1), 109–132. https://doi.org/10.1080/0376835042000181444

Wilson, B. T. (2003). *Innovative reward systems for the changing work place.* New York: McGraw-Hill.

Wilson, T. B. (1995). *Innovative reward systems for the changing workplace.* New York: McGraw-Hill.

WorldatWork. (2010). Retrieved from https://www.worldatwork.org; WorldatWork – The Total rewards Association: https://www.worldatwork.org/adimLink?id=78737

World Bank. (2016, April 12). *#African Can: Overview*. Retrieved from http://www.worldbank.org/en/country/southafrica/overview

World Economic Forum. (2015). *The global competitiveness report 2015–2016.* Geneva: World Economic Forum.

Zikmund, W. (2003). *Business research methods* (7th edn.). OH: Thomson South-Western.

Zingheim, P. K., & Schuster, J. R. (1995). Moving one notch north: Executing the transition to new pay. *Compensation & Benefits Review, 27*(4), 33–39. https://doi.org/10.1177/088636879502700406

16

Exploring employee retention and intention to leave within a call centre

Authors:
Nelesh Dhanpat[1]
Faith D. Modau[1]
Phokela Lugisani[1]
Rethabile Mabojane[1]
Mbail Phiri[1]

Affiliations:
[1]Department of Industrial Psychology and People Management, University of Johannesburg, South Africa

Corresponding author:
Nelesh Dhanpat,
neleshd@uj.ac.za

Orientation: Call centre organisations are plagued with high levels of employee turnover and are challenged by effectively retaining their staff.

Research purpose: The study sets out to establish factors that affect the retention of call centre agents and to determine call centre agents' intention to leave.

Research design, approach and method: The study is quantitative in nature, which follows a cross-sectional approach. Data were collected using an established questionnaire, the retention factor management scale. Psychometric properties of the questionnaire for validity and reliability were assessed using factor analysis and Cronbach's alpha coefficient, respectively, to ensure internal consistency. Data were collected using a convenience sample, and the participants of the study are call centre agents. The sample yielded a response rate of 282 respondents. Subsequently, data were analysed using descriptive and inferential statistics.

Main findings: The findings reflect that a relationship between the retention factors and intention to leave exists, whereby compensation contributes the most towards intention to leave.

Practical and managerial implications: Recommendations are made for the retention factors of call centre agents, which when implemented have the potential to enhance employee retention.

Contribution: The study provided valuable insights to management within call centre organisation towards employee retention and provided recommendations and strategies aligned to factors that will enhance retention, which human resource practitioners need to be cognisant of.

Introduction

The investment in human capital has profound implications for organisations. It is with this in mind that employees are viewed as an asset in any organisation. It can be said that 'no technology can replace skilled communication, problem solving, and customer focus' (Jacobs & Roodt, 2011, p. 1). Organisations may find it easier to attract people; however, retaining them may be a great challenge as people are motivated by various factors (Grobler, Wärnich, Carrell, Elbert & Hatfield, 2011). Employee retention is considered to be one of the biggest challenges affecting organisations (Das, Nandialath & Mohan, 2013). Turnover is a concern in organisations worldwide (Amah 2009) which reduces the operating costs of organisations, leaving significant implications with regard to the loss of human capital and interruptions in organisational activities (Takawiara, Coetzee & Schreuder, 2014).

Issues affecting employee retention include job satisfaction, organisational commitment, emotional labour, person–organisation fit, sense of coherence, perceived organisational support and leader–member relationship (Das et al., 2013; Goodwin, Groth & Frenkel, 2011; Harry & Coetzee, 2013; João & Coetzee, 2012; Mcculloch & Turban, 2007; Wang, Wang, Xu & Ji, 2014). There are several factors that affect employee retention, which include compensation, career opportunities, material working conditions and training and development (Pierre & Tremblay, 2011). It is essential that organisations retain talent in order to gain a competitive advantage. Essentially, organisations need to focus on retaining skilled employees and keeping them engaged in their jobs.

Background to study

The call centre industry is the world's fastest growing industry from the beginning of the 21st century (Pillay, Buitendach & Kanengoni, 2014). According to Simons and Buitendach (2013), the number of employees within the South African call centre sector increased from 50 000 in 2005 to 180 000 in 2010. Furthermore, it was predicted that by 2015 approximately 100 000 new jobs would be created in South Africa. A call centre is defined as an interactive work environment, whereby call centre agents are the main mediators of business by means of computer-based and telephone-based technologies (Pierre & Tremblay, 2011). The computer-based and telephone-based technologies enable the fast and efficient distribution of incoming calls and/or allocation of outgoing calls to available staff, and allow for interaction between customer and call centre agent to occur simultaneously with the use of display screen equipment and the instant access to, and inputting of information.

The levels of complexity in call centre jobs vary and they comprise unskilled call centre agents and/or highly skilled agents (Jacobs & Roodt, 2011; Pierre & Tremblay, 2011). Call centre organisations are characterised by high technology-based work, high work pressure and work overload, which lead to stress and burnout, absenteeism and performance problems (Simons & Buitendach, 2013). This results in employees seeking alternative employment. Therefore, call centres need to find ways of retaining their staff.

Management within the call centres is seen to have power, which is closely linked with that of Taylorism (Taylor & Bain, 1999). With an increase in managerial power, their work is often fragmented by extensive monitoring and controlling of agents through the use of technology, whilst defining practices that may enhance employee well-being and customer satisfaction (Neely, Bourne & Kennerly, 2003). Effective managerial skills assist in reducing employee turnover (Gayathri, Sivaraman & Kamalambal, 2012). Consequently, ineffective management skills will result in agents becoming frustrated and hence leaving their organisation (Tse, Huang & Lam, 2013).

Focus of the study

The call centre industry is growing enormously. A challenge that exists in most call centre organisations is the extreme employee turnover rates (Van Rensburg, Boonzaier & Boonzaier, 2013). According to Pierre and Tremblay (2011), turnover rates of call centres were 70% and increased by 30% from 2008 to 2011. The work environment is associated with impaired employee well-being, namely, shift work resulting into absenteeism and increased turnover rates. Likewise, Van Rensburg et al. (2013) indicated high stress levels, high employee turnover and emotional burnout as factors associated with call centres. Call centre work places a high burden on employees (Pillay et al., 2014). Previous research identified different factors that contribute to the retention of call centre agents (Das et al., 2013; Goodwin, Groth & Frenkel, 2011; Harry & Coetzee, 2013; João & Coetzee, 2012, p. 69; Mcculloch & Turban, 2007; Wang et al., 2014). The call centre industry is in a poor state regarding people management practices. Managers' unwillingness to compromise efficiency for quality customer service on the expense of call centre representatives affects the well-being of those representatives (Van Rensburg et al., 2013). However, it was not indicated which of those factors contributes to the retention of call centre agents within the South African context. Therefore, this study aims to identify factors that affect the retention of call centre agents, determine their intention to leave and explore the differences among biographical groups.

Literature review

Employee retention

Fluctuations in the economy, changes in demographics and in businesses locally and abroad, have caused organisations to shift their attention towards the retention of staff. The underlying reason for this is that employees carry the skill sets and knowledge required for optimal organisational functioning (Kyndt, Dochy, Michielsen & Moeyaert, 2009). According to Kyndt et al. (2009), employees' knowledge and skills are central to an organisation's ability to remain economically competitive. Jacobs and Roodt (2011) stated that the retention of employees has become a challenge. There is a need for retention strategies to keep employees in the organisation by reducing their intention to leave. Notably, such strategies are used for managing employees who are talented by trying to keep them in the organisation for a longer period compared to competitors by using strategic retention management initiatives (Dhanpat & Parumasur, 2014). For an organisation to thrive in the changing world of work, there is a need to attract, develop and retain talent with the right skills and knowledge that will enhance organisational effectiveness and efficiency. Pierre and Tremblay (2011) argued that call centre managers face the difficulty of retaining their employees, resulting in high turnover rates. In the call centre industry, employee retention still lacks management support and fair labour practices. Hence, turnover rates are increasing because of unsatisfactory psychosocial states of call centre agents and work-related stressors. Notably, in understanding the challenges faced by organisations to retain employees, it is essential to understand turnover.

Turnover

Employee turnover refers to an organisation's inability to retain their employees. A challenge that exists is the high rate of employee turnover (Van Rensburg et al., 2013). Employee turnover is defined as:

> the rate at which employees leave the organisation on an annual basis, and this can be expressed as a percentage, by dividing the number of employees who have left over the year by the total number of employees who were with the organisation at the beginning of the year. (Altarawmneh & Al-Kilani, 2010, p. 47)

Notably, employee turnover stems from employees' intentions to leave the organisation. Intention to leave is defined as 'an employee's decision to leave the current job and look onwards to find another job in the near future' (Rizwan, Arshad, Munir, Iqbal & Hussain, 2014, p. 4). This decision may be initiated by job dissatisfaction that is caused by work conditions such as lack of work–life balance, less money, boring work, poor supervision and lack of advancement opportunities (Smit, Stanz & Bussin, 2015). Call centre work is commonly characterised by such work conditions.

The way employees view work has changed in such a way that it is no longer about working just to get paid. Rather, employees prefer work that is challenging, offers growth opportunities, compensates fairly and enables them to achieve work–life balance (Meier, Austin & Crocker, 2010). Failure for an organisation to meet these needs may lead to an employee's intention to leave. However, call centre organisations may not be able to meet such needs (Simons & Buitendach, 2013). Hence, managers need to understand why employees want to leave the organisation in order to develop programmes to mitigate their intentions (Khan & Du, 2014). By doing so, organisations will avoid potential costs associated with replacing employees (Van Rooyen, Du Toit, Botha & Rothmann, 2010).

For the purpose of this study, the definition is simplified as the process by which employees move out of the organisation. Turnover can be differentiated into voluntary and involuntary, functional and dysfunctional, and avoidable and unavoidable (Fleisher, 2011).

Types of turnover

Voluntary turnover and involuntary turnover refer to whether or not the termination of contract was initiated by the individual or the organisation (Fleisher, 2011; Nagadevara, Srinivasan & Valk, 2008; Takawira, Coetzee & Schreuder, 2014). The process of voluntary turnover begins with the employee, whilst involuntary turnover is initiated by the organisation (Allen, Bryant & Vardaman, 2010).

Functional turnover and dysfunctional turnover refer to turnover that is desirable in contrast to turnover that is not desirable. Functional turnover results when poor performers or employees who do not fit into the culture of the organisation leave the organisation. Functional turnover involves employees who can be easily replaced (Allen et al., 2010).

Avoidable turnover and unavoidable turnover involve the viability of an organisation to avoid or prevent turnover (Fleisher, 2011). Avoidable turnover takes place because of factors that are within the organisation's capability to change, for example, higher rewards. In contrast, unavoidable turnover takes place because of factors the organisation has no control over such as death of an employee (Allen et al. 2010). High turnover rates are a gateway to understaffing resulting in increased workloads to the remaining employees and continuous drain in programme funds, as new employees will need to be recruited, and the entire process of interviews, hiring, placement and induction further strains organisational finances (Marinucci et al., 2013). An investigation into retention factors and intention to leave begins to unpack the causes of voluntary, avoidable and dysfunctional turnover.

Turnover intention

Turnover intention is defined as 'the subjective estimation of an individual regarding the probability of leaving the organisation in the near future' (Kashyap & Rangnekar, 2014, p. 224), and it focuses on an employee's decision to quit their job. The decision may be initiated by job dissatisfaction because of lack of appreciation, less money, boring work, poor supervision or inability to take time off (leave) (Smit et al., 2015). Turnover intention results from a mismatch between the organisation and the individual employee from the concept of person–organisation fit that leads to job dissatisfaction. When an organisation cannot supply what the employee needs, or when the employee cannot supply what the organisation needs, then there is imbalance in the person–organisation relationship (Jacobs & Roodt, 2011).

Turnover intentions are likely to lead to voluntary turnover because the decision is initiated by the employee, as compared to the decision being initiated by the organisation, whereby the employer terminates the contract of the employee (Allen et al., 2010). The root cause of voluntary turnover may be because of organisational practices such as unfair treatment of employees, and involuntary turnover may be because of the employee's own doing such as theft or damage of the employer's property leading the employer to terminate the employment relationship. Employees' general decision to leave the organisation results in them seeking alternative employment or accepting a job offer from another organisation (Kashyap & Rangnekar, 2014). Thus, the retention of employees is necessary as the decision of an employee to stay or leave is potentially costly to the organisation (Van Rooyen et al., 2010).

Retention and turnover in the South African call centre industry

The growth of the South African call centre industry has been exponential and had an estimated growth of 50 000–180 000 from 2005 to 2010. It was estimated that approximately 100 000 new jobs were created in 2015. In other countries, call centre work is characterised by work overload, fast changing technology, change in product and services, and employees working under pressure. Such a working environment is likely to lead to stress, burnout and performance problems (Simons & Buitendach, 2013). Barnes (2013) noted that retaining call centre agents in the industry is challenging because turnover is much higher than in other fields of employment. According to Van Rensburg et al. (2013), negative issues related to call centre work environments impact the well-being of employees in terms of long hours of work. This results in absenteeism, increased turnover and negative health-related issues leading to high stress levels and hence results in burnout. Notably, favourable working conditions create higher job satisfaction and a lower intention to leave. However, the call centre environment is characterised by repetitive and monotonous work, unchallenging work, rigid procedures, use of surveillance, lack of resources, restricted work procedures, unfair labour practices and uninteresting organisation culture. All these correlate with the intention to leave the organisation (Barnes, 2013). This background highlights the necessity to identify the factors that influence the retention of call centre agents so that the costs associated with the exiting of employees in the organisation can be reduced (Barnes, 2013). There is a need to identify factors affecting the retention of employees, and hence it may enhance retention strategies such as compensation, job content, training and development, supervisory support, career advancement and work–life balance.

Compensation is critical in contractual and implied agreements between the employer and the employee (Chew & Chan, 2005). It is largely known to play a vital role in attracting employees; it enhances employee's organisational commitment and ensures employee retention. Armache (2014) stated that compensation includes wages and other forms of payments such as bonuses, profit sharing, overtime pay and sales commission. It may also include non-cash assets such as a car, housing paid by the company, company benefits and stock options. A call centre environment comprises of younger individuals who are at an early stage of their careers. Furthermore, it is characterised by low pay (Harry & Coetzee, 2013). Therefore, salary matters are a primary precursor of employee turnover in most call centres. Research by Pierre and Tremblay (2011) indicated an external and internal salary comparison done by agents in their work environments as a confirmation of their low cash pay levels, results to dissatisfaction, absenteeism and increased turnover.

Job content refers to the nature of the job, and this may have an influence on employee's decision to leave or stay within the organisation. A mismatch between the employee's knowledge and skills and the job demands leads to stress (Jacobs & Roodt, 2011). If an employee does not have the necessary skills, knowledge and attitude to perform his or her job, it may lead to frustration and job dissatisfaction. Call centre jobs are characterised as repetitive in nature, lacking creativity and flexibility which leads to an increase in stress levels and boredom (Harry & Coetzee, 2013). Call centre work is also stressful in nature because it is driven by targets. Notably, call centre agents' work is constantly monitored electronically and agents are often exposed to abusive callers (Filwood, 2014). Such negative characteristics of a call centre work may lead to employees leaving the organisation.

Training and development provide opportunities for employees to develop in their career (Van Dyk & Coetzee, 2012). It has a positive psychological effect to employees because they might perceive that the organisation value them and in turn they will remain committed to the organisation. Döckel, Basson and Coetzee (2006) stated that employees will stay in the organisation that provides an opportunity to grow by training and developing them and thus applying their acquired skills and knowledge. Furthermore, companies that provide training and development opportunities to their employees may have a psychological influence on them. Training equips employees with the skills and knowledge that are required to perform their work effectively, and hence, employees become satisfied with their work because they know what they are doing (Armache, 2014). Call centre work is associated with minor room for progression and individual growth as vocational development is infrequent in such institutions (Coetzee & Harry, 2015). It is likely that a lack of growth and continuous development may result in boredom and in employee intentions to seek alternative employment elsewhere.

Supervisory support refers to behaviour of the supervisor that upholds the continuous high performance of employees, such as reward, recognition and feedback (Döckel et al., 2006). Proper and frequent feedback is important to retain employees because perceived organisational support increases the affective commitment of employees in the long term. Van Dyk and Coetzee (2012) emphasise that supervisory support can be viewed as a source of trust in an employee's willingness or drive to be the best in whatever they do. Support from their supervisors reduces work-related stress levels and may create a sense of belonging which provides employees with enough reasons to stay in the organisation.

Personal outreach of supervisors to employees plays a vital role in employee retention, as focus has shifted from monetary factors (i.e. compensation) to more intrinsic factors (i.e. organisational support) (Cianni & Guddy, 2012). Pierre and Tremblay (2011) also elaborated that extensive authoritative measures used by managers to monitor employees in their organisation, managers of most call centres listen during calls, which generally are recorded. The record keeping of agents' calls results in high levels of uncertainty and discomfort as agents experience feelings of being watched which decreases their levels of job satisfaction. This is indicative of uncomfortable emotional work which is embedded in most call centres.

Career advancement refers to an organisation's adherence to career-oriented practices and job security which leads to employee commitment (Döckel et al., 2006). Shoaib, Noor, Tirmizi and Bashi (2009) described career advancement as an organised and formalised system with planned efforts to the success of both individual career needs and organisational objectives in order for the organisation to gain and maintain a competitive advantage. Van Dyk and Coetzee (2012) emphasised that career advancement may be internal or external career opportunities. Internal career advancement improves the employees affective commitment to the organisation and hence less intention for employees to leave the organisation.

The outcomes of career development are beneficial to both individual employees and the organisation. Employees need new challenges to gain new competencies, and at the same time, promotion comes with extra income; on the contrary, the organisation will have talented and motivated employees who will contribute to organisational sustainability and competitive advantage. If employees perceive that they have a better chance to grow or get promoted within the organisation, then they could perform better and reduce their intention to leave. Not all employees may enjoy performing the same job forever, some employees may want to grow and get promoted to more challenging work with more money.

Lack of opportunities to grow may result in job dissatisfaction and lead to employees seeking for better and more challenging to stimulate their growth. In call centre work, not many skills acquired are relevant for progression into other fields as their type of work is governed by routinised activities (Harry & Coetzee, 2013). With the objective to influence agents to stay longer, some call centres guarantee security at least for a medium term whilst agents with least extensive experience and lack of efficiency are not retained (Pierre & Tremblay, 2011).

Work–life balance refers to a synchronised balance between work life and family life, and hence, there is no conflict between these two dimensions of an employee's life (Mafini & Dlodlo, 2014). Work–life balance is described as the ability of employees to integrate their work and family commitments as well as other non-work responsibilities and activities (Van Dyk & Coetzee, 2012). It has been noted that organisational work–life balance policies positively influence employees' psychological attachment to their organisations as they perceive that the organisation cares for them. Döckel et al. (2006) emphasised the importance of work–life balance policy by indicating that a flexible work scheduling is necessary, with policies allowing periods away from work for employees to take care of their family matters. Coetzee and Harry (2015) noted that high levels of hardiness and career adaptability are significant aspects that call centre agents can use to balance their lives and their demanding work life. Hardiness is regarded as a set of stress-resilient personality characteristics, whilst career adaptability is the ability to adjust to the working prescriptions and demands of call centre environment (Coetzee & Harry, 2015). The call centre environment is characterised by work pressure and high workloads, causing an employee to work longer hours to meet deadlines (Simons & Buitendach, 2013). This may cause conflict in work–life balance, leading to exhaustion and employees exiting the organisation.

Gender differences in call centres and links to retention and turnover intention

Call centre work can be characterised as female dominated. According to Bonds (2006), approximately 70% of the call centre agents are made up of a female staff complement. Notably, female call centre agents display effective interpersonal and communication skills. Although male and female call centre agents perceive the work environments differently, it can be noted that male call centre agents are better at call centre work (Korvajärvi, 2009). Hence, there may be a need that call centre organisations equally retain both male and female call centre agents. There are limited studies on gender and employee retention. For example, Du Plooy and Roodt (2013) indicated that genders differ in how they respond to stimuli which are likely to lead to different withdrawal behaviours. In terms of turnover intentions, gender moderates this relationship intentions (Burke, Koyuncu & Fiksenbaum, 2008; Karatepe & Aleshinloye, 2009). With regard to career advancement, female employees differ from male employees, as their counterparts advance faster in organisations with higher levels of pay (Phillips & Irmhoff, 1997).

Strategies to enhance employee retention

It is important to note that when organisations recruit people with the appropriate skills, they develop and implement retention strategies to prevent them from leaving (Smit et al., 2015). Retention strategies include measures taken by the organisation to keep employees. Organisations can gain a competitive advantage by being proactive in terms of introducing innovative human resource practices that can be used as strategies to retain employees, namely, offering a great work environment that is safe and healthy, competitive compensation and benefit packages, allowing employees freedom to make choices on how they will perform their duties. Furthermore, training opportunities, career development, trust and fairness between employees and the employer, regular and fair performance appraisals, potential development and succession planning (Kashyap & Rangnekar, 2014) assist with better retention. Filwood (2014) emphasised on job security as a strategy to retain employees. Call centre jobs are characterised by short-term contracts, and contracts that are on a permanent basis motivate employees to stay in the organisation (Harry & Coetzee, 2013). Armache (2014) also emphasised that by using retention strategies, employees will be highly satisfied and motivated, leading to higher productivity and decreased employee turnover. Although organisations may try to implement those retention strategies, it does not guarantee that all employees will stay with the organisation because an employee can still choose to leave (Kyndt et al., 2009). The reason behind this may be because the employee dislikes the manager or encounters conflict with other colleagues.

Research objectives

The objective of the study was to look at the relationship between retention factors and intention to leave which were tested empirically.

The following are sub-objectives of the study:

- to determine whether male or female call centre agents experience higher or lower intention to leave
- to explore the link between retention factors and intention to leave
- to understand which factors male and female employees perceive as an important factor of retention.

Value-add of the study

This study contributes to the existing body of knowledge regarding employee retention and human resource practices surrounding this phenomenon. Insights are provided within a South African context of a call centre. The study contributes theoretically and empirically towards research on employee retention and intention to leave, whilst noting relationship between the retention factors and intention to leave. The study further determines the best predictor for the retention of call centre agents.

Research method

Research approach

This study used a quantitative research approach and is cross-sectional in nature which is characterised by studying a particular phenomenon at a particular time. The research investigated the relationship between retention factors and intention to leave.

Participants

The target population of the study were call centre agents. Participants of the study were from a large insurance call centre situated in Johannesburg. The company had approximately 500 call centre agents as employees. A non-probability sampling design was selected and a convenience sample was utilised. Questionnaires were handed out to agents on two consecutive days. Out of 347 questionnaires handed out, 282 (81.27%) completed questionnaires were received. According to Sekaran and Bougie (2013), the acceptable sample size for a population of 500 is 260. The sample of the population was made up of 66% female employees and 34% male employees. In terms of age, 49% were 18–24 years old, 46% were between 25 and 34 years old and 12% were 35–44 years old. The majority of participants (70%) had a length of service of 1 year or less.

Measuring instrument

The retention factor measurement scale (RFMS) was utilised for the study, as it aptly measures the retention factors supported by the literature. This scale was developed by Döckel et al. (2006) and measured retention factors and intention to leave. The scale consisted of 35 items. All items in the scale were presented on a five-point Likert scale ranging from 1 strongly disagree to 5 strongly agree. The instrument measured the participants' satisfaction with six retention factors: compensation, job characteristics, opportunities for training and development, supervisor support, career opportunities and work–life balance. In terms of measuring employee retention, the dimension intention to leave was used. The instrument measured the participants' satisfaction with six retention factors, and an example of the item is included next to each factor in brackets:

- Compensation ('On my present job this is how I feel about my benefits package').
- Job characteristics ('The job gives me considerable opportunity for independence and freedom in how I do the work').
- Opportunities for training and development ('There are enough development opportunities for me in this company').
- Supervisor support ('I feel valued by my supervisor').
- Career opportunities ('My chances of being promoted are good').
- Work–life balance ('My work schedule is often in conflict with my personal life').
- Intention to leave ('Do you intend to leave this company voluntarily in the near future?').

The reliability and validity of the RFMS were acceptable by Döckel et al. (2006, p. 23). The following Cronbach's alpha coefficients were reported: compensation 0.90, job characteristics 0.41, opportunities for training and development 0.83, supervisor support 0.90, career opportunities 0.76, work–life balance 0.87 and commitment to the organisation 0.89. In another study, Van Dyk and Coetzee (2012) reported acceptable Cronbach's alpha, namely compensation 0.95, job characteristics 0.67, opportunities for training and development 0.88, supervisor support 0.83, career opportunities 0.73, work–life balance 0.88 and intention to leave 0.89. In assessing reliability through Cronbach's alpha coefficient, this study utilised 0.70 as the level of acceptance. Nunnally and Bernstein (1994) suggest this as a rule of thumb that a level higher than 0.70 is considered for internal consistency.

Research procedure

Data were collected using a paper and pencil questionnaire over 2 days. The researchers went to the organisation and distributed the questionnaires to the station managers and agents. The respondents completed the questionnaires during their work time. The researchers obtained permission from the organisation to conduct the study. The organisation was provided with complete disclosure of the study and its purpose, objectives and benefits of the research, and guaranteed that the best interests of the organisation are protected. In addition, the researchers ensured that agreed time frame of the study was kept (in terms of data collection). All findings of the research will be shared with the organisation. In terms of participation in the study, respondents completed an informed consent noting that participation in the study was voluntary and anonymity was ensured. Respondents were made aware that they can withdraw from the study at any time. The researchers ensured that the instructions provided were clear and concise. Data were not shared with unauthorised people, thereby ensuring that the identities of respondents are protected.

Statistical analysis

The Statistical Programme for Social Sciences (SPSS, version 22) was used to analyse the data. Descriptive statistics and inferential statistics were calculated. In order to assess internal consistency and reliability, Cronbach's alpha coefficients were measured. Factor analysis was computed to ensure validity. Factor analysis was conducted by using the pattern matrix of the principal axis factor analyses using Varimax rotation with Kaiser normalisation. It identified five retention factors and an intention to leave factor. These factors accounted for 55% of the total variance. The reliability of the questionnaire was statistically assessed using Cronbach's alpha coefficient.

In order to determine the direction and strength of the relationships between the variables, Pearson's product–moment correlations were calculated.

Multiple regression analysis was utilised to assess the way in which a set of variables are able to predict a particular outcome (Pallant, 2007). This study looks at the way in which retention factors (independent variable) predict intention to leave (dependent variable).

Analysis of variance was used to assess whether employees differing in biographical profiles (age, type of work, race, tenure and levels of contract significantly differ in their perceptions of the factors that affect retention).

T-tests were used to determine whether male or female call centre agents experience higher or lower intention to leave and to understand which factors do male and female employees perceive as an important factor of retention.

Results

Descriptive statistics

From Table 1, the study identified that having supervisor support is an important retention factor (mean = 3.69); this is closely followed by training and development (mean = 3.65). However, employees believe that experiencing work–life balance (mean = 3.45) is as important. Furthermore, employees perceived career advancement (mean = 2.94) to be a fair retention factor, closely followed by compensation (mean = 2.85). The low mean value for intention to leave (mean = 2.74) accounts for the aforementioned retention factors; employees are not likely to remain in the organisation. All items received the minimum and maximum responses on the Likert scale. The mean ranged from 2.74 to 3.69 and the standard deviation ranged from 0.71 to 1.06.

Frequency analyses for the possibility of enhancing retention

Based on the frequency analyses, call centre organisations should be cognisant of the following as a possibility of enhancing employee retention:

- In terms of compensation, 56.23% of respondents reflected dissatisfaction with their most recent pay increase. Many respondents remained neutral in terms of compensation, namely, 51.6% of respondents were neutral in terms of supervisors' influence on their pay.
- With regard to training and development, 84.4% of respondents felt that their organisation provides them with training specific to their jobs. However, 36.1% of respondents remained neutral on whether sufficient money is allocated for product and solution training.
- In terms of supervisor support, 67.4% of respondents reflected that their supervisor lets them know how well they are performing on the job, whilst 38.7% of respondents remained neutral on whether their supervisor rewards a good idea by implementing it and giving the responsible employee(s) credit.
- In terms of career advancement, 52.1% of respondents felt that an employee who applies for another job in the organisation has a better chance of getting that job than someone from outside the organisation who applies for the same job; 44.1% of respondents were neutral in terms of whether it would be easy to find a job in another department.
- In terms of work–life balance, 63.9% of respondents indicated that their work schedule is often in conflict with their personal life.
- With regard to intention to leave, 40% of respondents expressed that they are not likely to have plans to stay with the organisation, 31.9% remained neutral on how they would rate their chances of still working in the organisation a year from now and 21.4% indicated that they are likely to leave the organisation voluntarily in the near future.

Based on the frequency analysis, it is suffice to say that call centre agents place emphasis on the retention factors. However, there were instances where a significant amount of call centre agents remained neutral, namely, supervisors' influence on their pay, allocation of money for training and rewarding a good idea by their supervisor. Respectively, this could allude to that employees within the call centre are uncertain in terms of pay practices and the administration of having budgets for training. On the contrary, it should be noted that most call centre agents are satisfied with training and development provided by the organisation. Most call centre organisations provide job-specific training to their employees to equip them with the necessary skills required to perform their jobs. When employees are confident with performing their work, they tend to be motivated to work harder and are

TABLE 1: Descriptive statistics for retention factors and intention to leave dimensions.

Dimension	*N*	Valid missing	Mean	95% Confidence interval for mean		Standard Deviation	Minimun	Maximum
				Lower bound	Upper bound			
Compensation	281	1	2.85	2.76	2.93	0.71	1.00	5.00
Training and development	281	1	3.65	3.56	3.74	0.76	1.00	5.00
Supervisor support	281	1	3.69	3.61	3.78	0.71	1.33	5.00
Career advancement	281	1	2.94	2.85	3.04	0.83	1.00	5.00
Work–life balance	281	1	3.45	3.35	3.56	0.92	1.00	5.00
Intention to leave	277	5	2.74	2.62	2.87	1.06	1.00	5.00

more likely to commit themselves to the organisation (Armache, 2014).

Table 2 indicates that a relationship between the dependent and independent variables exists. According to Pallant (2007), a correlation of 1.0 suggests that there is a perfect relationship between the variables regardless of the direction of the relationship. The closer the *r* value is to 1.0, the more satisfied the employees are with the retention factors and the more likely they are to remain in the organisation. The *r* value ranged from 0.35 to 0.52, representing moderate to strong relationship. Work–life balance had a significant negative relationship with intention to leave, as opposed to other retention factors which had a positive correlation.

A multiple regression analysis was calculated to predict intention to leave based on the retention factors. A significant retention equation was found [F(4.267) = 46.082, $p < 0.000$], with an R^2 of 0.408. Table 3 indicates that the total variance in the dependent variable (intention to leave) explained in the model was 40.8% (R^2), and presents the significant results. In terms of multicollinearity, the current study yielded tolerance values close to 1.0 (between ≥ 0.642 and ≤ 0.841) and Variance inflation factor (VIF) values of ≤ 1.55. They are lower than the cut-off of ≥ 2.5 to ≥ 4.0, suggested for small samples. Therefore, multicollinearity was not a particular concern in the context of the current study, and hence beta (β) values are interpreted with more confidence.

Table 3 also indicates how the variables contributed to the prediction of the dependent variable (intention to leave). Compensation had the largest beta coefficient (0.268), suggesting that compensation contributes towards intention to leave more than the other factors, followed by work–life balance (-0.237) which negatively contributed, then career advancement (0.240) and lastly supervisory support which had the smaller beta coefficient (0.112). Training and development was excluded from the model as it did not contribute to intention to leave as it had a beta coefficient of -0.009. It is evident that the retention factors contribute significantly and positively to the variance of intention to leave.

From Table 4, it is evident that all factors scored relatively high reliability coefficients, ranging from 0.717 (the lowest) to 0.933 (the highest). The current study utilised 0.70 as the level of acceptance. It is evident that retention factors and intention to leave show a high level of internal consistency and stability.

Internal consistency for all factors was also noted and so were the average inter-item correlation coefficients. The values ranged between 0.337 and 0.702. A reasonably high correlation between the factors and their component items was noted. Notably, all items loaded on a factor loading > 0.3. The Kaiser–Meyer–Olkin measures of sampling adequacy ranged from 0.702 to 0.939 for each factor which exceeds the recommended value of 0.6. Barlett's test of sphericity also reached statistical significance ($p < 0.001$) and supports the factorability of the correlation matrix (Pallant, 2007). It is notable that normality and homoscedasticity preconditions for the study are fulfilled. It must be noted that the factor of job content was removed for the following reasons, namely, the Kaiser–Meyer–Olkin measures of sampling adequacy value reported was less than 0.6 and had communalities of less than 0.3.

Inferential statistics

An independent samples *t*-test was conducted to compare the retention factors and intention to leave for male and female employees. From Table 5, it is evident that there was no significant difference in scores for male and female employees with regard to retention factors. Notably, the effect sizes for the

TABLE 2: Pearson correlation.

Variables	Intention to leave	Compensation	Training and development	Supervisor support	Career advancement	Work–life balance
Intention to leave	1.000	0.523**	0.406**	0.347**	0.509**	-0.426**
Compensation	0.523**	1.000	0.569**	0.316**	0.512**	-0.305**
Training and development	0.406**	0.569**	1.000	0.440**	0.538**	-0.257**
Supervisor support	0.347**	0.316**	0.440**	1.000	0.352**	-0.206**
Career advancement	0.509**	0.512**	0.538**	0.352**	1.000	-0.315**
Work–life balance	-0.426**	-0.305**	-0.257**	-0.206**	-0.315**	1.000

**, $p \leq 0.01$

TABLE 3: Multiple regression analysis.

Retention factors	Standardised coefficients: beta	T	Sig.	95% confidence interval for B		R	R square	Adjusted R square	Standard error of the estimate	Collinearity statistics	
				Lower bound	Upper bound					Tolerance	Variance inflation factor
Constant	-	2.190	0.029	0.101	1.895	0.639	0.408	0.400	0.818	-	-
Compensation	0.268	4.735	0.000	0.242	0.586	-	-	-	-	0.692	1.445
Supervisor support	0.112	2.185	0.030	0.017	0.323	-	-	-	-	0.841	1.188
Career advancement	0.240	4.083	0.000	0.161	0.462	-	-	-	-	0.642	1.557
Work–life balance	-0.237	-4.475	0.000	-0.408	-0.159	-	-	-	-	0.790	1.266

T, t statistic; Sig, Significance; R, correlation coefficient; R^2, coefficient of determination.

TABLE 4: Factor analysis for Retention Factor Scale.

Factors	Factor loading	Kaiser-Meyer-Olkin	Reliability coefficient	Mean inter-item correlation	Variance % explained
Compensation	-	0.939	0.933	0.520	51.57
q1_7)	0.808	-	-	-	-
q1_8	0.793	-	-	-	-
q1_4	0.767	-	-	-	-
q1_11	0.755	-	-	-	-
q1_9	0.724	-	-	-	-
q1_5	0.723	-	-	-	-
q1_12	0.717	-	-	-	-
q1_1	0.703	-	-	-	-
q1_3	0.702	-	-	-	-
q1_10	0.699	-	-	-	-
q1_13	0.685	-	-	-	-
q1_2	0.663	-	-	-	-
q1_6	0.562	-	-	-	-
Training and development	-	0.837	0.875	0.547	54.64
q1_20	0.814	-	-	-	-
q1_19	0.809	-	-	-	-
q1_22	0.742	-	-	-	-
q1_21	0.695	-	-	-	-
q1_18	0.693	-	-	-	-
q1_23	0.668	-	-	-	-
Supervisor support	-	0.702	0.717	0.337	50.54
q1_24	0.707	-	-	-	-
q1_29	0.637	-	-	-	-
q1_26	-0.579	-	-	-	-
q1_25	-0.574	-	-	-	-
q1_27	0.569	-	-	-	-
Career advancement	-	0.736	0.788	0.480	49.76
q1_31	0.876	-	-	-	-
q1_30	0.699	-	-	-	-
q1_35	0.650	-	-	-	-
q1_33	0.557	-	-	-	-
Work–life balance	-	0.766	0.814	0.522	54.27
q1_37	0.821	-	-	-	-
q1_38	0.798	-	-	-	-
q1_39	0.767	-	-	-	-
q1_36	0.522	-	-	-	-
Intention to leave	-	0.741	0.875	0.702	70.25
q1_41	0.864	-	-	-	-
q1_42	0.828	-	-	-	-
q1_40	0.822	-	-	-	-

retention factors are small and ranged from 0.00 (smallest) to 0.09 (largest). In terms of intention to leave, male participants experienced higher intention to leave than women participants (mean = 3.077 vs. mean = 2.570). Cohen's *d* refers to an appropriate effect size for the comparison between two means, whereby the standardised difference between two means, and expresses this difference in standard deviation units.

Discussion

The study provided insights on how retention factors relate to intention to leave in the context of a South African call centre. In addition, the study further provided insights into which retention factor best predicts intention to leave. The study examined the retention factors identified by Döckel et al. (2006) and how various biographical factors differed in terms of these factors. In terms of the frequency analysis, the discussion below presents the way in which call centre agents perceived the retention factors. Notably, line managers and human resource practitioners need to be cognisant of such factors as this will enhance the retention of call centre agents.

Supervisor support

With regard to supervisor support, an average mean value of 3.69 (maximum = 5) was obtained. This indicates that most of the respondents agree that they receive support from their supervisors. By contrast, Pierre and Tremblay (2011) found that supervisors in call centre organisations use authoritative measures to monitor and keep records of agents' calls and, as a result, agents experience high levels of uncertainty and discomfort which decrease their levels of job satisfaction. Even though strict measures are used to manage the call centre environment, in most organisations supervisors take it upon themselves to ensure that employees work in an environment where they are supported (Russel, 2008).

Work–life balance

With regard to work–life balance, an average mean value of 3.45 (maximum = 5) was obtained. This indicates that employees agree that they do not have a balance between work and their personal lives. Scott-Ladd, Travaglione, Perryer and Pick (2010) found that employees experienced conflict between their work and personal responsibilities as a

TABLE 5: Independent samples *t*-test – significant mean differences (gender).

Variable	Gender	*N*	Mean	Standard deviation	*p* (two-tailed)	Cohen's *d*	Effect size *r*
Compensation	Male	91	2.916	0.69	0.306	0.13	0.06
	Female	177	2.826	0.68	-	-	-
Training and development	Male	91	3.654	0.72	0.950	-0.01	0.00
	Female	177	3.660	0.75	-	-	-
Supervisor support	Male	91	3.655	0.64	0.445	-0.09	0.05
	Female	177	3.723	0.71	-	-	-
Career advancement	Male	91	3.064	0.86	0.129	0.19	0.09
	Female	178	2.904	0.79	-	-	-
Work–life balance	Male	91	3.450	0.89	0.656	-0.05	0.03
	Female	178	3.501	0.89	-	-	-
Intention to leave	Male	91	3.077	1.05	0.000	0.47	0.23
	Female	177	2.570	1.02	-	-	-

result of working long hours and shifts that limit them from focusing on other life commitments. This may then hinder the organisations' progress in terms of the retention of employees as employees prefer to live a more flexible lifestyle (Snelgar, Renard & Venter, 2013). It is important that organisations implement strategies aimed at enhancing work–life balance to assist employees in the pressures of their family and work areas (Amah, 2010).

Career advancement

In terms of career advancement, an average mean value of 2.94 (maximum = 5) was obtained. This indicates that employees disagree that they receive opportunities to grow within the organisation. A lack of growth opportunities (career advancement) has been found to have a negative influence on an individual's attitude towards the organisation, which in turn influences their intention to leave (Van Dyk, Coetzee & Takawira, 2013). Likewise, Shoaib, Noor, Tirmizi and Bashir (2009) also emphasised the importance of career development as they indicated that the development of the employee plays a crucial part in the development of the organisation and therefore the organisation has to create an environment that enhances this development and growth. Organisations need to attend to employees' career advancement needs as they greatly affect employee's decisions in terms of whether they see a future with the organisation (Das et al., 2013).

Compensation

In terms of compensation, an average mean value of 2.85 (maximum = 5) was obtained. This indicates that employees are not satisfied with the compensation they receive from the organisation. Likewise, Harry and Coetzee (2013) found that call centre organisations are characterised by low pay, and as a result, employees may look for alternative work elsewhere with a better compensation plan, thus increasing employees' intentions to leave the organisation. Employees are motivated by an attractive salary package; it provides a greater reason to perform tasks to the best of their abilities which then also benefits the organisation positively (Nagadevara et al., 2008).

The study provided insights on male or female call centre agents' intention to leave and if there is a difference in views of employees varying biographical data regarding relationship retention factors.

Intention to leave and biographical data

The biographical variables, gender and level of education are strong predictors of employee turnover. In this study, it was found that male participants experience higher intention to leave than women. The study revealed that male call centre agents experienced higher intention to leave than their female counterparts. Scholarios and Taylor (2008) alluded that call centre work is typically seen as female-oriented work. This alludes to the fact that women display higher levels of interpersonal skills than their male counterparts. According to Bonds (2006, p. 31), 'women are more patient, have better telephone conduct, and the ability to communicate well with customers'. It was also added that men tend to distance themselves from this type of work and pursue advancement opportunities (Scholarios & Taylor, 2008). A study by Miller and Hendrickse (2016) revealed that within a call centre environment, men experienced a higher level of exhaustion than women. Exhaustion is a result of being continuously exposed to high work pressures and work overload which are some of the characteristics of call centre work (Simons & Buitendach, 2013). This may lead to men constantly feeling drained after work, thereby increasing their intentions to leave. In terms of intention to leave, those participants who are in possession of a grade 12 or equivalent experience higher intention to leave than those with a higher level of education. This may be because they want to go to further their studies.

Intention to leave

The study emphasised the significance of employee retention, which is explained as a way of keeping employees within the organisation by reducing or terminating their intentions to leave. Pierre and Tremblay (2011) noted the difficulty of managers to retain employees (in this case, call centre agents), resulting in high rates of turnover within the call centre organisation. Intention to leave obtained an average mean value of 2.74 (maximum = 5) was obtained. This indicates that majority of the respondents are not likely to stay with the organisation in the near future owing to dissatisfaction with the retention factors. Likewise, Van Rensburg et al. (2013) found that there was a high rate of employee turnover in call centre organisations. Retention factors such as compensation, career advancement, work–life balance and supervisor support contributed significantly in motivating employees to stay in the organisation and it is advised that management focus on them in order to retain their employees.

Retention factors and intention to leave

The results revealed that there is a significant relationship between the retention factors (compensation, career advancement, work–life balance and supervisor support) and intention to leave in the context of a South African call centre. Work–life balance had a negative significant relationship to intention to leave. As work–life balance decreases call centre agents' intention to leave will increase. In this likelihood, call centre organisations need to provide opportunities for their agents to have a balanced lifestyle.

In terms of the overall fit of the model, as indicated by the R^2, compensation contributed the most towards employee's intentions to leave the organisation and can be regarded as the best predictor of intention to leave. Compensation plays a vital role in attracting employees and influencing individuals to greatly commit to the organisation (Chew & Chan, 2008). It was also emphasised that employees work for the sake of earning a salary or wage. Hence, if they are not paid well, they may seek alternative employment that compensates well. Subsequently, career advancement contributed as a predictor of intention to leave. Meier et al. (2010) emphasised that it is not all employees who do not mind doing the same job forever; most employees, especially younger generation, want to advance in their careers and develop their skills and knowledge. If an organisation does not provide them with such opportunities, they may seek those opportunities in other organisations regardless of whether they are paid well or not.

Work–life balance had a negative contribution towards intention to leave. As work–life balance decreases for call centre agents, their chances of leaving the organisation increase. Employees need enough time to take care of other personal commitments such as spending time with family to ensure that both their work life and personal life is balanced. If there is conflict between their work and personal life, they may experience exhaustion and end up not being able to cope with their work and it may lead to job dissatisfaction and increase employee's intention to leave the organisation (Simons & Buitendach, 2013). Supervisor support was the least important factor. However, this does not mean that it does not contribute to the retention of employees. Van Dyk, Coetzee and Takawira (2013) indicated that supervisor support positively enhanced the participants' feelings of organisational fit. Such feelings include satisfaction with the feedback provided by the supervisor, feeling valued and being rewarded and recognised for ideas and work well done. These feelings motivate employees to stay with the organisation.

Limitations of the study

This study has a few limitations. Firstly, the scope of the study limited the generalisation of the results in that it only focused on one call centre organisation in Gauteng and cannot be generalised to other industries. Hence, future studies should incorporate other call centres in varying industries. Secondly, the use of hard copy questionnaires resulted in participants not answering some of the questions. Quantitative studies are characterised by the potential of common method bias as a result of influences such as social desirability and transient mood states (Podsakoff, MacKenzie, Lee & Podsakoff 2003; Spector 1994). The design of the study looked at one point in time. In addition, using a convenience sample results in possible bias in data gathering and difficulties in generalising the results. Lastly, future studies on this topic should adopt a qualitative stance to gain insights into employee experiences.

Recommendation and managerial implications

Based on the findings of the study, recommendations for the study are diagrammatically represented in Figure 1, which when implemented have the potential to enhance employee retention within call centres.

The study can be utilised by human resource practitioners in call centre organisations to develop and implement strategies to enhance employee retention. This study concentrates on one sector; however, the findings of the study can be applied to other industries, depending on the work environment. Human resource practitioners need to be cognisant of retention factors that enhance employee retention.

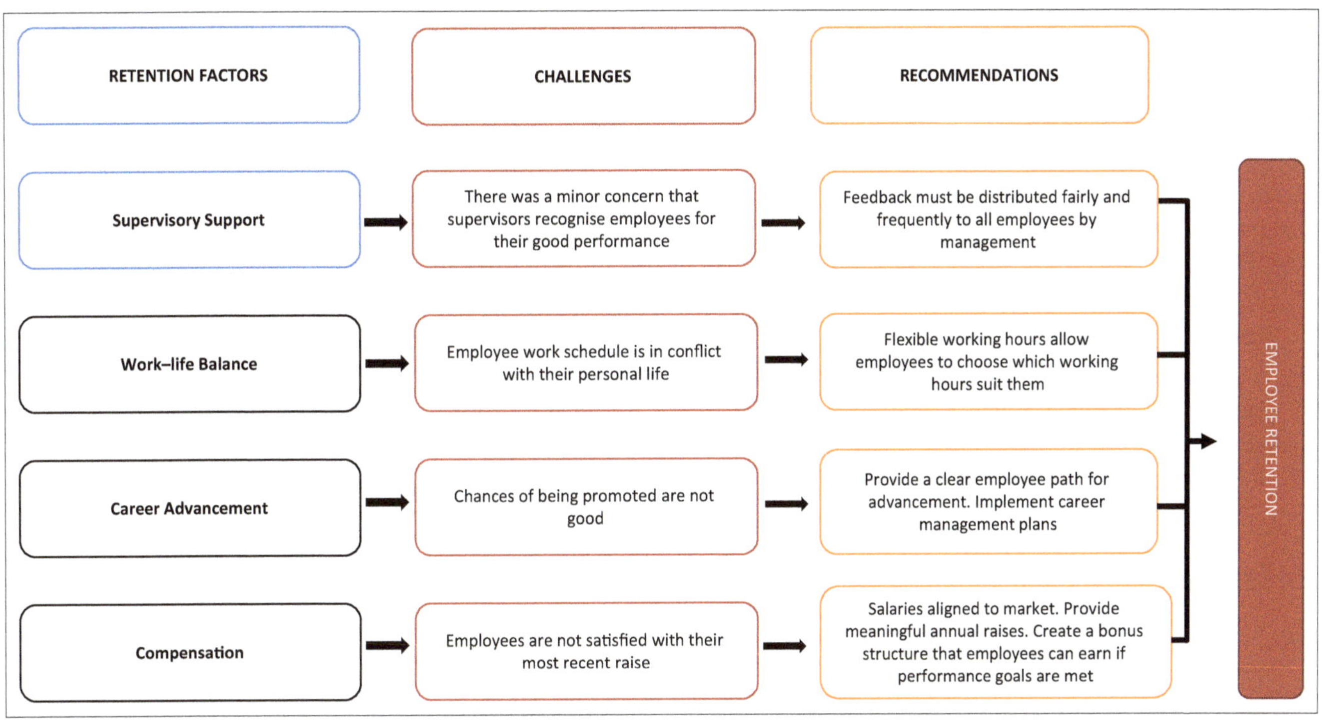

FIGURE 1: Recommendations on how to enhance employee retention.

Recommendations for future research

Future research may focus on more than one organisation in order to enhance the generalisation of results. Factors (training and development and job content) that were excluded from the results may be repeated to determine if they will add value for future study. Future researchers should undertake a qualitative research design which will assist in providing a deeper understanding of retaining call centre agents and provide greater context into reasons they leave.

Conclusion

This study provided insights in terms of factors affecting retention of call centre agents and their levels of intention to leave. The findings of the study suggest that certain retention factors are crucial in influencing employees' intention to leave. Such factors include compensation, career advancement, supervisor support and work–life balance. Nonetheless, the importance of other factors (job content and training and development) should not be taken for granted when developing retention strategies. The study contributed theoretically and empirically towards the literature on employee retention. From this, it is evident that human resource practitioners and management staff of call centre organisations need to be cognisant of such factors and heed the recommendations provided. In order to enhance retention and yield low turnover rates, call centre organisations are encouraged to ensure that agents are remunerated well, and are provided with a work environment where they are able to grow and advance, in addition to a work environment that supports their work and personal life.

Acknowledgements

We thank Ms. Juliana Van Staden (Statistical Consultation Services at the University of Johannesburg) for assisting with the statistical analysis.

Competing interests

The authors declare that they have no financial or personal relationships that may have inappropriately influenced them in writing this article.

Authors' contributions

N.D. was the supervisor of the study and was responsible for consolidating and preparing the manuscript. F.D.M. was responsible for assisting in preparing the manuscript. F.D.M, P.L., R.M. and M.P. were students and contributed to the report for their research project.

References

Allen, D.G., Bryant, P.C., & Vardaman, J.M. (2010). Retaining talent: Replacing misconceptions with evidence-based strategies. *Academy of Management Perspectives, 24*(2), 48–64. https://doi.org/10.5465/AMP.2010.51827775

Altarawmneh, I., & Al-Kilani, M.H. (2010). Human resource management and turnover intentions in the Jordanian hotel sector. *Research and Practice in Human Resource Management, 18*(1), 46–59.

Amah, O.E. (2009). Satisfaction and turnover intention relationship: The moderating effect of job role centrality and life satisfaction. *Research and Practice in Human Resource Management, 17*(1), 24–35. https://doi.org/10.1080/09585192.2012.665067

Amah, O.E. (2010). Family-work conflict and the availability of work-family friendly policy relationships in married employees: The moderating role of work centrality and Career consequence. *Research and Practice in Human Resource Management, 18*(2), 35–46.

Armache, J. (2014). Ways and means to keep employees motivated, productive, and loyal. *Journal of International Diversity, 2014*(2), 87–103.

Barnes, N. (2013). The retention factors of call centre agents at a financial institution in the western cape. *Master administrationis faculty of economic and management sciences department of industrial psychology university of the western cape*, South Africa: University of Western Cape, pp. 1–159.

Bonds, A. (2006). Calling on femininity? Gender, call centers, and restructuring in the rural American West. *ACME: An International Journal for Critical Geographies, 5*(1), 28–49.

Burke, R.J., & Cooper, C.L. (2009). *The peak performing organization*. New York: Routledge.

Chew, J & Chan, C.C.A. (2008). Human resource practices, organizational commitment and intention to stay. *International Journal of Manpower, 29*(6), 503–522. https://doi.org/10.1108/01437720810904194

Cianni, M. & Gundy, P. (2012). Putting performance back into retention. *Financial Executive, 28*(9), 72–77.

Coetzee, M., & Harry, N. (2015). Gender & hardiness as predictors of career adaptability: An exploratory study among black call centre agents. *SA Journal of Psychology, 45*(1), 81–92. https://doi.org/10.1177/0081246314546346

Cohen, J. (1988). *Statistical power analysis for the behavioral sciences* (2nd ed.). New York: Lawrence Earlbaum Associates.

Das, D., Nandialath, A., & Mohan, R. (2013). Feeling unsure: Quit or stay? Uncovering heterogeneity in employees' intention to leave in Indian call centers. *The International Journal of Human Resource Management, 24*(1), 15–34. https://doi.org/10.1080/09585192.2012.665067

Dhanpat, N., & Parumasur, S.B. (2014). Re-establishing the psychological contract as a precursor to employee retention. *Problems and Perspectives in Managemement, 12*(4), 78–90.

Döckel, A., Basson, J.S., & Coetzee, M. (2006). The effect of retention factors on organisational commitment: An investigation of high technology employees. *SA Journal of Human Resource Management, 4*(2), 20–28. https://doi.org/10.4102/sajhrm.v4i2.91

Du Plooy, J., & Roodt, G. (2013). Biographical and demographical variables as moderators in the prediction of turnover intentions. *SA Journal of Industrial Psychology, 39*(1), 12–24. https://doi.org/10.4102/sajip.v39i1.1070

Filwood, D. (2014). Why Do Your Call Center Agents Quit? May 18, Retrieved April 12, 2016, from https://www.linkedin.com/pulse/20140518182546-3995896-why-do-your-call-center-agents-quit/

Fleisher, M.S. (2011). *Temporal patterns of functional and dysfunctional employee turnover*. Doctoral dissertations. University of Tennessee. Retrieved 19 August, 2016, from http://trace.tennessee.edu/utk_graddiss/1181

Gayathri, R., Sivaraman, G.G., & Kamalambal, R.R. (2012). Employee retention strategies in BPO's: An empirical investigation. *Interdisciplinary Journal of Contemporary Research in Business, 3*(12), 572–583.

Goodwin, R.E., Groth, M., & Frenkel, S.J. (2011). Relationships between emotional labor, job performance, and turnover. *Journal of Vocational Behavior, 79*(2), 538–548. http://doi.org/10.1016/j.jvb.2011.03.001

Grobler, A.P., Wärnich, S., Carrell, M.R., Elbert, N.F., & Hatfield, R.D. (2011). *Human resource management in South Africa* (4th ed.). Hampshire: Cengage Learning.

Harry, N., & Coetzee, M. (2013). Sence of coherence, career adaptability and burnout of early-career black staff in call centre environment. *SA Journal of Industrial Psychology, 39*(2), 1–10. https://doi.org/10.4102/sajip.v3912.1138

Jacobs, C., & Roodt, G. (2011). A human capital predictive model for agent performance in contact centres. *SA Journal of Industrial Psychology, 37*(1), 1–19. https://doi.org/10.4102/sajip.v37i1.940

João, T.F., & Coetzee, M. (2012). Job retention factors, perceived career mobility and organisational commitment in the South African financial sector. *Journal of Psychology in Africa, 22*(1), 69–76. https://doi.org/10.1080/14330237.2012.10874523

Karatepe, O. & Aleshinloye, K. (2009). Emotional dissonance and emotional exhaustion among hotel employees in Nigeria. *International Journal of Hospitality Management, 28*, 96–104. https://doi.org/10.1016/j.ijhm.2008.12.002

Kashyap, V., & Rangnekar, S. (2014). A structural equation model for mearsuring the impact of employee retention practices on employee's turnover intentions: An Indian perspective. *South Asian Journal of Human Resources Management, 1*(2), 221–247. https://doi.org/10.1177/2322093714549109

Khan, M.A.S., & Du, J.G. (2014). An empirical study of turnover intentions in call centre industry of Pakistan. *Journal of Human Resource and Sustainability Studies, 2*(4), 206–214. https://doi.org/10.4236/jhrss.2014.24021

Korvajärvi, P. (2009). Attracting customers through practising gender in call-centre work. *Work Organisation, Labour & Globalisation, 3*(1), 131–143. https://doi.org/workorgalaboglob.3.1.0131

Kyndt, E., Dochy, F., Michielsen, M., & Moeyaert, B. (2009). Employee retention: Organisational and personal perspective. *Vocations and Learning, 2*(1), 195–215. https://doi.org/10.1007/s12186-009-9024-7

Mafini, C., & Dlodlo, N. (2014). The linkage between work-related factors, employee satisfaction and organisational commitment. Insights from public health professionals. *SA Journal of Human Resource Management, 12*(1), 1–12. https://doi.org/10.4102/sajhrm.v12i1.616

Marinucci, F., Majigo, M., Wattleworth, M., Paterniti, A.D., Hossain, M.B., & Redfield, R. (2013). Factors affecting job satisfaction and retention of medical laboratory professionals in seven countries of Sub-Saharan Africa. *Human Resources for Health, 11*(1), 38. https://doi.org/10.1186/1478-4491-11-38

Mcculloch, M.C., & Turban, D.B. (2007). Using person – Organization fit to select employees for high- turnover jobs. *International Journal of Selection and Assessment, 15*(1), 63–71. https://doi.org/10.1111/j.1468-2389.2007.00368.x

Miller, N., & Hendrickse, R. (2016). Differences in call centre agents' perception of their job characteristics, physical work environment and wellbeing. *Problems and Perspectives in Management, 14*(1), 51–63. https://doi.org/10.21511/ppm.14(1).2016.06

Meier, J., Austin, S.F., & Crocker, M. (2010). Generation Y in the workforce: Managerial challenges. *The Journal of Human Resource and Adult Learning, 6*(1), 68–78.

Nagadevara, V., Srinivasan, V., & Valk, R. (2008). Estanlishing a link between employee turnover and withdrawal behaviours: Application of data mining techniques. *Research and Practive in Human Resource Management, 16*(2), 81–99.

Neely, A., Bourne, M., & Kennerley, M. (2003). Dysfunctional performance through dysfunctional measures. *Cost Management, 17*(5), 41–45.

Nunnally, J.C., & Bernstein, I.H. (1994). *Psychometric theory* (3rd ed.). New York: McGraw-Hill.

Pallant, J. (2007). *SPSS survival manual, a step by step guide to data analysis using SPSS* (4th ed.). New York: McGraw Hill

Phillips, S., & Irmhoff, A. (1997). Women and career development: A decade of research. *Annual Review of Psychology, 48*(32), 31–59. https://doi.org/10.1146/annurev.psych.48.1.31

Pierre, X., & Tremblay, D.G. (2011). Levels of involvement and retention of agents in call centres: Improving well-being of employees for the better socioeconomic performance. *Journal of Management Policy & Practice, 12*(5), 53–71.

Pillay, K., Buitendach, J.H., & Kanengoni, H. (2014). Psychoplogical capital, job demands and organisational commitment of employees in a call centre in Durban, South Africa. *SA Journal of Human Resource Management, 12*(1). 1–13. https://doi.org/10.4102/sajhrm.v12i1.599

Podsakoff, P.M., MacKenzie, S.B., Lee, J.Y., & Podsakoff, N.P. (2003). Common method biases in behavioral research: A critical review of the literature and recommended remedies. *Journal of applied psychology, 88*(5), 879.

Rizwan, M., Arshad, M.Q., Munir, H.M., Iqbal, F., & Hussain, A. (2014). Determinants of employees intention to leave. *International Journal of Human Resource Studies, 4*(3), 1–18. https://doi.org/10.5296/ijhrs.v4i3.5871

Russel, B. (2008). Call centres: A decade of research. *International Journal of Management Reviews, 10*(3), 195–214. https://doi.org/10.1111/j.1468-2370.2008.00241.x

Scott-Ladd, B., Travaglione, A., Perryer, C., & Pick, D. (2010). Attracting and retaining talent: Social organisational support as an emergent concept. *Research and Practice in Human Resource Management, 18*(2), 1–10.

Scholarios, D., & Taylor, P. (2010). Gender, choice and constraint in call centre employment. *New Technology, Work and Employment, 25*(2), 101–116. https://doi.org/10.1111/j.1468-005X.2010.00242.x

Sekaran, U., & Bougie, R. (2013). *Research methods for business. A skill building approach* (6th ed.). West Sussex: Wiley.

Shoaib, M., Noor, A., Tirmizi, S.R., & Bashi, S. (2009). Determinants of employee retention in telecom. *Proceedings of the 2nd CBRC 14*, 1–18.

Simons, J.C., & Buitendach, J.H. (2013). Psychological capital, work engagement and organisational commitment amongst call centre employees in South Africa. *SA Journal of Industrial Psychology, 39*(2), 1–12. https://doi.org/10.4102/sajip.v39i2.1071

Smit, W., Stanz, K., & Bussin, M. (2015). Retention preferences and the relationship between total rewards, perceived organisational support and perceived supervisor support. *SA Journal of Human Resource Management, 30*(2), 1–13. https://doi.org/doi.org/10.4102/sajhrm.v13i1.665

Snelgar, R.J., Renard, M., & Venter, D. (2013). An empirical study of the reward preferences of South African employees. *SA Journal of Human Resource Management, 11*(1), 1–14. https://doi.org/10.4102/sajhrm.v11i1.351

Spector, P.E. (1994). Using self-report questionnaires in OB research: A comment on the use of a controversial method. *Journal of organizational behavior, 15*(5), 385–392.

Takawiara, N., Coetzee, M., & Schreuder, D. (2014). Job embeddedness, work engagement and turnover intention of staff in a higher education institution: An exploratory study. *SA Journal of Human Resource Management, 12*(1), 1–10. https://doi.org/10.4102/sajhrm.v12i1.524

Taylor, P., & Bain, P. (1999). An assembly line in the head: Work and employee relations in the call centre. *Industrial Relations Journal, 30*(2), 101–117. https://doi.org/10.1111/1468-2338.00113

Tse, H.H., Lam, C.K., Lawrence, S.A., & Huang, X. (2013). When my supervisor dislikes you more than me: The effect of dissimilarity in leader–member exchange on coworkers' interpersonal emotion and perceived help. *Journal of Applied Psychology, 98*(6), 974. https://doi.org/10.1037/a0033862

Van Dyk, J., & Coetzee, M. (2012). Retention factors in relation to organisational commitment in medical and information technology services. *SA Journal of Human Resource Management, 10*(2). 1–11. https://doi.org/10.4102/sajhrm.v10i2.433

Van Dyk, J., Coetzee, M., & Takawira, N. (2013). Satisfaction with retention factors as predictors of the job embeddedness of medical and information technology services staff. *Southern African Business Review, 17*(1), 57–75.

Van Rensburg, Y., Boonzaier, B., & Boonzaier, M. (2013). The job demands-resources model of work engagement in South African call centres. *SA Journal of Human Resource Management, 11*(1), 1–13. https://doi.org/10.4102/sajhrm.v11i1.484

Van Rooyen, L., Du Toit, D. H., Botha, E., & Rothmann, S. (2010). Artisan retention in an organisation in South Africa. *SA Journal of Human Resource Management, 8*(1), 1–8. http://doi.org/10.4102/sajhrm.v8i1.300

Wang, X., Wang, L., Xu, X., & Ji, P. (2014). Identifying employee turnover risks using modified quality function deployment. *Journal of Systems Research and Behavioural Science, 31*(3), 398–404. https://doi.org/10.1002/sres.2282

17

The relationship between demographic variables and well-being of women in South African workplaces

Authors:
Madelyn Geldenhuys[1]
Carolina M. Henn[1]

Affiliations:
[1]Department of Industrial Psychology and People Management, University of Johannesburg, South Africa

Corresponding author:
Madelyn Geldenhuys,
madelyng@uj.ac.za

Orientation: It is important to investigate the determinants of well-being among working women. Given the unique demographic diversity within the South African context, differences in the experience of well-being among women are expected.

Purpose: The study investigated the effects of age, race, marital status and educational status on psychological meaningfulness, life satisfaction, work–family conflict and social support of working women.

Motivation: With the increase of women in the workplace, there is a need for knowledge and understanding of the factors that influence the well-being of women. This study aims to investigate demographic variables as determinants of well-being among working women.

Method: Cross-sectional surveys were used to gather data from a sample (n = 540) of women from various South African companies. The Utrecht Work Engagement Scale (UWES), the Psychological Meaningfulness Scale (PMS), the Satisfaction with Life Scale (SWLS), the Work-Role Conflict Scale and the Job Demands Resources Scale (JDRS) were administered.

Results: Significant relationships were found between life satisfaction, work-to-family conflict and work engagement, respectively, and marital status. Higher levels of education showed significant relationships with life satisfaction and work-to-family conflict. Being white showed significant positive relationships with life satisfaction, work-to-family conflict and work engagement. With regard to social support and psychological meaningfulness, race explained significant amounts of variance in psychological meaningfulness, as did age.

Practical, managerial and methodological implications: The findings indicate that the experiences of well-being among women vary by age, race, marital status and educational status. It is therefore imperative that human resource practitioners appropriately measure these differences, accommodate them in policies through relevant supportive practices and also champion these practices for women.

Introduction

The nature of work and society has changed in such a way that increasing numbers of women enter the workplace. Owing to factors such as organisational and societal architecture, career progression for men and women are different (Fagenson-Eland & Baugh, 2000; O'Neil, Hopkins & Balimoria, 2008). Compared to men, women often fulfil more work roles, which results in them spending time doing both formal and informal work. More specifically, they are employed by organisations on a full-time basis, which constitutes paid work, yet they also do more unpaid work than men do (Organisation for Economic Co-operation and Development [OECD], 2011). *Unpaid work* in the context of this study refers to household – and family tasks such as childrearing and domestic chores. Indeed, although men are assuming greater responsibility for family and household duties, women continue to do most of this work (Douglas & Michaels, 2004; Greenhaus & Parasuraman, 1999). This also holds true in the South African context (Mostert, 2008). Owing to these types of gendered social contexts (O'Neil et al., 2008), it seems prudent to follow women-specific research approaches more often.

It is often the case that women do not properly recover from work stress (cf. Sonnentag, 2003) or struggle to balance multiple roles, resulting in work–family conflict as a negative consequence (Opie & Henn, 2013; Rathi & Barath, 2013). This can, in turn, affect their well-being, which can manifest in different ways. Well-being is described as a reaction to events in life that informs satisfaction, happiness and fulfilment in the personal and work lives of people (Diener, Oishi & Lucas, 2003). Experiencing well-being at work involves work engagement (Rothmann & Rothmann, 2010), meaningfulness at work (Van Zyl, Deacon & Rothmann, 2012) and life satisfaction

(Williamson & Geldenhuys, 2014). Well-being is further affected by the demands and resources placed on people by work (Demerouti, Bakker, Nachreiner & Schaufeli, 2000).

Differences exist in terms of how people experience well-being (Diener, et al., 2003). In this regard, demographic differences can also be expected to affect how women approach work, how they engage at work, how they find meaning, how they use resources, how they respond to work–family conflict and how satisfied they are. As noted by Addai, Opoku-Agyeman and Amanfu (2014) as well as Ngoo, Tey and Tan (2015), more research on how people experience well-being has been conducted in developed countries than in African contexts. Most of the studies in the developed contexts either investigated the main effects of demographic variables such as age, race and educational status, or controlled for them (cf. Addai et al., 2014; Ngoo et al., 2015).

Organisations are giving increasing attention to the fostering of well-being at work (Addai et al., 2014; Van Zyl et al., 2012). However, it becomes more difficult to help employees cope with work as demands at work and home become more complex. The situation is further complicated by personal differences. Specifically, it may benefit organisations, managers and employees if differences based on demographics are acknowledged and understood. This will enhance our understanding of the demographic determinants of work engagement, psychological meaningfulness, life satisfaction, work–family conflict and social support among women in the South African workplace. Holvino (2010) states that:

> … 'women' is not a universal experience or category; we must identify, untangle and suggest interventions to change the differential impact that everyday practices have for different women in different types of organizations. (p. 264)

Organisations, employees and managers can benefit from this knowledge because they would be able to understand that women function, cope and experience work differently and acknowledge that women would be better able to invest themselves in the organisation when receiving appropriate support. Although perhaps it may seem logical that this is understood in organisations, it is in fact not yet fully the case. For example, as pointed out by Bosch (2016), managers often consider female employees to be wonderful, until the moment they fall pregnant. At that point pregnancy in female employees becomes a 'hassle factor' (Bosch, 2016, p. 5). In this example, therefore, it is evident that age (relating to life cycle factors such as childbearing ability and age of children) and income (relating to educational status and ability to afford childcare) become salient demographics that must be considered.

Purpose

Demographic variables are often important determinants of well-being (Addai et al., 2014; Ngoo et al., 2015). There is plentiful literature supporting the notion that demographic variables impact organisations in numerous ways. To name but a few, Mandu, Buitendach, Kanengoni and Bobat (2004) showed that demographics such as age, race and educational status influence turnover intention; Balogun (2014) found that demographic variables impact employees' willingness to share knowledge; and Dwivedi, Kaushik and Luxmi (2015) proved that age, educational status and marital status influenced organisational citizenship behaviour. Therefore, this study aimed to provide information regarding the relationship between race, age, marital status and education on the one hand, and work engagement, psychological meaningfulness, life satisfaction, work–family conflict and social support on the other hand. Not only did the study aim to establish whether there are significant relationships between the demographic variables and well-being constructs, but it also measured the amount of variance in these well-being constructs that are explained by race, age, marital status and education. An understanding of how women appraise their own life circumstances and their subjective well-being will inform workplace policies and managerial principles in such a way that women will benefit from these (cf. Addai et al., 2014). This study provides crucial information regarding the impact of demographic factors on women's well-being in the workplace. A true understanding of women in the workplace is certainly not limited to demographic factors only. Nonetheless, demographic variables are an important piece of the puzzle, so to speak. It can inform policies and managerial principles, for example in the development of wellness programmes suited to female employees, policies relating to maternity leave and other women-related health issues and policies regarding flexitime. As indicated by Nienaber, Bussin and Henn (2011), in terms of reward preferences it is impossible for organisations to take into account all aspects that influence well-being on an individual employee level. Therefore, segmentation of employees into groups with similar characteristics and needs may be an effective strategy (cf. Nienaber et al., 2011). An understanding of demographic factors can enable employers to apply such segmentation to enhance employee well-being and subsequently also overall organisational effectiveness.

Work engagement

The construct of work engagement as a desirable occupational health outcome has received increased research attention in recent years (cf. Bakker, Schaufeli, Leiter & Taris, 2008; Mills, Culbertson & Fullager, 2011). Work engagement is defined as 'a positive, fulfilling, work-related state of mind that is characterized by vigour, dedication and absorption' (Schaufeli, Salanova, González-Romá & Bakker, 2002, p. 74). *Vigour* is described as high energy levels while working, eagerness to devote energy to one's work, resilience and tenacity even when faced with challenges. *Dedication* indicates almost complete involvement in one's work and the experience of meaning, challenge, pride, zeal, motivation and stimulation. And finally, *absorption* refers to being completely submerged in and focused on one's work to such an extent that one loses track of time and finds it difficult to withdraw from work (Bakker et al., 2008). There is international research available regarding the relationship between the demographic variables of interest in this study and work engagement, but little within the South African context (Bezuidenhout & Cilliers, 2011; Durksen & Klassen, 2012; Fong & Ng, 2012; Haley, Mostert & Els, 2013).

With regard to age, Fong and Ng (2012) found significantly higher scores on all three dimensions of work engagement among older Chinese employees. Likewise, Mahboubi et al. (2014) also found higher work engagement levels among older participants. In South African literature, Bezuidenhout and Cilliers (2011) found a significant positive correlation between vigour and absorption on the one hand, and age on the other hand, in a South African sample. Also in a South African sample, older participants reported significantly higher scores on dedication (Haley et al., 2013). It is possible that age acts as a proxy for life stage in terms of its effect on work engagement. More specifically, older employees are more likely to have grown independent children, which enables them to focus more exclusively on their jobs.

Bell and Barkhuizen (2011) reported significant correlations between work engagement and ethnicity in a South African sample. More specifically, white participants scored significantly higher across all three dimensions of work engagement than coloured participants. White participants also scored significantly higher than black participants in terms of absorption. Takawira (2012), however, found no effect for race on work engagement, also in a South African sample.

In terms of education, the literature does not present hard-and-fast findings. Mahboubi et al. (2014) found no significant relationships between work engagement and level of education. In a South African sample, participants with a matric qualification reported significantly higher absorption levels than participants with a doctoral degree (Bell & Barkhuizen, 2011). Barkhuizen and Rothmann (2006) reported almost the exact opposite in a group of South African academics; those with doctoral degrees had significantly higher levels of absorption than those with Honours degrees or equivalent 4-year degrees.

The results relating to work engagement and marital status are indeterminate. Kong (2009) reported significantly higher levels of vigour, absorption and dedication among unmarried employees compared to married ones. Takawira (2012) found higher levels of vigour among married people than among single people. No differences were observed in terms of marital status and either absorption or dedication.

Psychological meaningfulness

In the work context, meaningfulness can manifest in terms of psychological meaningfulness (Geldenhuys, Łaba & Venter, 2014). Meaning is defined as the value of certain work goals in relation to personal views, morals and standards (Geldenhuys et al., 2014; May, Gilson & Harter, 2004; Olivier & Rothmann, 2007). Furthermore, Kahn (1990) defines work-related meaningfulness as '… a feeling that one is receiving a return on investment of one's self in a currency of physical, cognitive and emotional energy' (Kahn, 1990, pp. 703–704).

Meaningfulness in life affects the psychological well-being of people (Frankl, 1997). Meaningful work makes an important contribution to optimal experiences in the workplace (cf. Lips-Wiersma & Wright, 2012). Meaningful work has also been related to work engagement (Van Zyl et al., 2012), life satisfaction (Williamson & Geldenhuys, 2014) and motivation (Chalofsky & Krishna, 2009).

According to Seligman (2002), meaning helps people transcend as well as find a purpose in life (Steger, Oishi & Kashdan, 2009). However, according to Csikszentmihalyi (1990), the construct 'meaning' is difficult to capture and is referred to as the significance something holds for a person. Noting that meaningful work can manifest differently, firstly as a fulfilment – where people pursue their passion – and secondly the view of what people contribute to an aspect that is larger than life (Wolf, 2012).

From a gendered approach, it would appear that there are differences in terms of meaningfulness and work engagement based on gender. Women tend to experience a weaker relationship between these constructs (Williamson & Geldenhuys, 2014). Generally, the demographics of people were found to have a minimal effect on meaning at work (Hodson, 2002). No differences were found based on race and gender respectively and meaningful work (Hodson, 2002). No evidence in the literature could be found to explain any difference based on education. Pertaining to age, no conclusive differences could be found in terms of psychological meaningfulness. However, Chalofsky and Krishna (2009) point out that nearing retirement age, people start questioning the meaning in their work.

Life satisfaction

Life satisfaction is a well-known subjective well-being construct (cf. Henn, 2013). It is defined as a 'cognitive, judgemental process' (Diener, Emmons, Larsen & Griffin, 1985, p. 71). Life satisfaction is seen as the way in which individuals evaluate the quality of their lives from a global and cognitive perspective (McDowell, 2010). It further refers to the judgement of the levels of happiness when a person realises their levels of success (Pavot & Diener, 1993). Thus a person subjectively appraises his or her life by comparing it to an internally derived standard. Literature reveals a number of studies that have found relationships between the selected demographics variables of interest in the current study and life satisfaction.

Fagley (2012), Filiz (2014) and Ngoo et al. (2015) found no significant relationship between age and life satisfaction. Liang and Liu (2014) reported a positive correlation between age and life satisfaction. Schafer, Mustillo and Ferraro (2013) established that as age increased, partner satisfaction became an increasingly important determinant of life satisfaction for females. Botha and Booysen (2012) found a U-shaped relationship between age and life satisfaction. In their overall South African sample, life satisfaction decreased until the age of 36, after which it started to increase again.

Researchers have examined the relationship between ethnicity and life satisfaction. Life satisfaction varied significantly across different Ghanaian ethnic groups (Addai et al., 2014). Davis and Wu (2014) reported that among white Americans, individual life satisfaction decreased when group income increased, whereas among blacks, individual life satisfaction increased with increased group income. This is an interesting finding, indicating that individuals compare themselves with their social group in measuring their life satisfaction. Black people are generally considered to have a collectivistic culture, and an increase in group income is in a sense 'shared' among the group. White people on the other hand are generally considered to have individualistic cultures, and therefore an increase in group income may be perceived as negative by an individual who does not share in that increase (cf. Triandis's 1989 review of the literature in this regard). It should be borne in mind, though, that better education can lead to less collectivism, and one can therefore not merely ascribe these differences to collectivism or individualism. As Oyserman (1993, p. 1006) points out, at university 'an individualistic perspective is likely to be prompted by academic achievement demands that focus on individual striving, competition and actualization of potential'. Furthermore, better education is linked to higher income (i.e. wealth), which is a precursor of individualism (Triandis, 1989).

Davis and Wu (2014, p. 867) state that 'an individual's racial and ethnic identity matters in determining the reference group with which he or she engages in social comparison'. This can, in turn, influence the individual's judgements of subjective well-being. Fagley (2012) did not find any significant relationships between ethnicity and life satisfaction in an American sample. In a South African study, white, coloured and Indian people were significantly more satisfied with life than black people (Botha & Booysen, 2012).

With regard to the impact of education and wealth on life satisfaction, literature reveals varied findings. Daraei and Mohajery (2013) investigated the life satisfaction of female domestic workers in India. Their findings showed that educational level (as well as income and occupation) was positively related to life satisfaction. Addai et al. (2014) also found a higher probability of life satisfaction in upper- and middle-class Ghanaians than in the lower class. In the USA as well as in Great Britain, lower wealth was significantly associated with lower life satisfaction (Jivray & Nazroo, 2014). These findings all seem to point in the direction of a relationship between education and income. Education is indeed a gateway to better job opportunities and higher income occupations (cf. Schimmel, 2009), and therefore it seems likely that it will play a role in the relationships between income and occupation on the one hand, and life satisfaction on the other hand. In the USA, lower levels of education were also associated with lower life satisfaction (Jivray & Nazroo, 2014). In other research, a high school education was associated with higher life satisfaction than those of graduates, and a post-graduate qualification was associated with higher life satisfaction than a lower than high school education (Mahboubi et al., 2014). This shows a curvilinear relationship between education and life satisfaction. Ngoo et al. (2015) reported different findings for different areas in Asia. In South Asia, higher education was significantly related to higher levels of life satisfaction; in Central and West Asia no such relationship was found; and in Southeast Asia the effect was small. However, higher income did have a significant positive impact on life satisfaction in Central and West Asia. This may be because of an indirect influence of education on life satisfaction. Nonetheless, Salinas-Jimenez, Artes and Salinas-Jimenez (2011) found that education had a significant positive correlation with life satisfaction regardless of income. In a South African sample, life satisfaction was significantly positively correlated with income (Botha & Booysen, 2012), which may also be related to educational qualification.

Several studies have investigated the influence of marital status on life satisfaction, and the evidence is overwhelmingly in favour of a positive relationship between being married and higher life satisfaction. Stack and Eshleman (1998) investigated happiness, financial satisfaction and health (all three of which are closely related to life satisfaction) across 17 nations. Their results showed a significant positive relationship between marriage or co-habitation and the three well-being measures. Ngoo et al. (2015), Lee and Lee (2013) and Filiz (2014) likewise found a significant positive relationship between marital status and life satisfaction. Liang and Liu (2014) reported lower levels of life satisfaction among divorced and widowed participants than among married participants. In a similar way, Botha and Booysen (2012) found significantly higher levels of life satisfaction among married women than any other groups (including married men) in their study.

Work–family conflict

A widely used definition of work–family conflict that was developed by Greenhaus and Beutell (1985) is that it is:

> a form of inter-role conflict, in which the demands of work and family roles are incompatible in some respect, so that participation in one role is more difficult because of participation in another role. (p. 77)

With women increasingly joining the formal workforce (Boushey, 2008; Casale, 2004), it stands to reason that they will be faced with the challenge of balancing the demands of work with those of their family life. Work–family conflict is bi-directional, being work-to-family conflict and family-to-work conflict (Greenhaus & Beutell, 1985). In addition, different types of work–family conflict have also been identified, namely time-, behaviour- and strain-based (Voydanoff, 2004). Alternative terms have been utilised to describe the inter-role conflict between work and family responsibilities, of which the most common among these are probably work-interfering-with-family and family-interfering-with-work (WIF and FIW) (Noor, 2003).

In our study, the focus was on work-to-family conflict as research has shown that work-to-family conflict (also called work–family conflict) is of greater concern than family-to-work conflict (cf. Bellavia & Frone, 2005; Greenhaus & Parasuraman, 1999). In this regard, De Klerk, Nel and Koekemoer (2012) have indicated that it is essential that more South African studies be conducted on work–home interaction, a construct similar to work-to-family conflict. However, to provide a clear context with regard to work–family conflict in our study, we have included research findings regarding family-to-work conflict.

Work–family conflict has been linked to age in a number of studies. Older individuals correlated significantly with a decrease in work–family conflict in a sample of Spanish working men and women (Gaspar, 2013). Lambert, Hogan, Kelley, Kim and Garland (2013) reported similar results between age and family-to-work conflict. They also found a negative correlation between behaviour and time-based work-to-family conflict and age. Huffman, Culbertson, Henning and Goh (2013) reported a curvilinear relationship between work–family conflict and age, with young and old participants showing the lowest levels of work–family conflict. This finding suggests that life cycle stages also impact on work–family conflict. Allen and Finkelstein (2014) found a negative correlation between age, and WIF and FIW, respectively. More specifically, they reported a negative relationship between age and WIF only within the empty nest stage of the family life cycle. Erickson, Martinengo, and Hill (2010) reported a similar finding. Although both family life cycle and age had significant relationships with work–family conflict in their study, Allen and Finkelstein (2014) pointed out that the patterns that emerged for family life cycle and work–family conflict were different from those that emerged for age and work–family conflict. It is therefore evident that age and family life cycle relate independently to work–family conflict. Several studies have found no significant relationships between age and work–family conflict, including two South African studies (Gaspar, 2013; Noor, 2003; Pieterse & Mostert, 2005; Steyl & Koekemoer, 2011).

Childers and Sage (2004) found that white women were 2.4 times more likely than Asian-American, black and Hispanic women to experience family-to-work conflict. Conversely, Asian-American, black and Hispanic women were 1.4 times more likely than white women to experience work-to-family conflict. It seems that the context of the women impacted on the findings and should be taken into consideration when observing racial differences in levels of work–family conflict. For example, white women in the Childers and Sage study were mostly in dual-earner families, whereas the majority of Asian-American, black and Hispanic women were the only earners in their families. Also, white women were in positions that indicated higher education and training, whereas Asian-American, black and Hispanic women were much more likely to be employed in lower-paying jobs performing manual work.

Childers and Sage (2004) found education to be the strongest predictor of family-to-work conflict among white women. Gaspar (2013) found that education had a significant impact on work–family conflict in a British sample, with higher education predicting higher levels of work–family conflict. Noor (2003) reported a similar finding, with a significant positive correlation between level of education and FIW, as did Ozutku and Altindis (2013), who found higher behaviour-based work-to-family conflict for health care professionals with doctoral degrees. Schieman and Glavin (2011) reported a curvilinear relationship between education and work–family conflict. Participants with higher (post school) and lower (less than high school) levels of education reported more work–family conflict than those with a high school education. The authors theorised that those with higher levels of education may experience 'stress of higher status' owing to the positions they occupy, with increased difficulty in balancing the demands of work and family (Schieman & Glavin, 2011, p. 1342). Higher work–family conflict levels among participants with lower levels of education may be attributed to factors such as lower incomes and the nature of lower income occupations (e.g. shift work).

With regard to marital status, the literature shows mixed results. Eagle, Icenogle, Maes and Miles (1998) found that divorced women experienced the highest time-based family-to-work conflict. Nomaguchi (2011) reported higher home-to-job conflict (similar to family-to-work conflict) for single mothers than for either single fathers or for married people. Steyl and Koekemoer (2011) similarly reported higher private-work conflict for single participants than for married participants. Ozutku and Altindis (2013), Noor (2003) and Mazerolle, Bruening and Casa (2008) did not find any significant relationships between marital status and work–family conflict.

Supervisor and social support

Organisational support, as an umbrella term for supervisor and social support, is defined as the extent to which an employee's effort is believed to be valued by the organisation and whether the well-being of employees is cared for (Rhoades & Eisenberger, 2002). Support is considered a job resource that can fulfil either an intrinsic or an extrinsic motivational role (De Lange, De Witte & Notelaers, 2008). Intrinsic motivation includes aspects such as personal growth and development, while extrinsic motivation refers to aspects such as the achievement of goals. Social support relates to the individual's belief that he or she is loved, valued and that colleagues are looking out for his or her well-being (Kossek, Pichler, Bodner & Hammer, 2011). Organisational support theory points out the positive effects of support on well-being at work (Aselage & Eisenberger, 2003; Shanock & Eisenberger, 2006). Through social exchange that takes place between people, the perceived organisational support encourages levels of dedication from employees which lead to increased performance. Based on this norm of reciprocity, employees welcome support in the form of tangible rewards (e.g. pay, benefits) and socio-emotional rewards (e.g. esteem, approval, caring) (cf. Rhoades & Eisenberger, 2002; Shanock & Eisengerger, 2006).

In the workplace, support is an important job resource that tends to increase the levels of well-being of employees (Demerouti et al., 2000). Because employees need to be able to actively engage at work, fulfil job expectations and deal with complex careers (Barkhuizen & Rothmann, 2006), support becomes beneficial for subjective well-being (Cusack & Numer, 2012). Social support can enhance positive work outcomes, such as work engagement (De Lange et al., 2008). Supervisor support refers to the extrinsic support offered by a manager to an employee (Shanock & Eisenberger, 2006). It includes the extent to which the manager acknowledges and allows for the demands placed on employees both at work and privately (Thomas & Ganster, 1995). Further, supervisor support also includes emotional and practical support, which contributes to employee well-being and work effectiveness (Kossek et al., 2011).

Few studies report on the relationship between demographic variables and organisational support. In a study on the distribution of social support and social ties among white and black employees in America, it appears that racial diversity at work can impact how social ties are formed (Sloan, Evenson-Newhouse & Thompson, 2013).

In terms of age, Alcover (2012) reported that where older employees experienced breaches in their psychological contract, organisational support mitigated the negative impact thereof. Further, in a sample consisting of married employees, it was found that the interactive term of tenure and organisational support does not reduce work–family conflict (Karatepe, 2009).

It is evident from the literature that results pertaining to demographic differences are not conclusive, yet there is sufficient evidence that demographics do influence well-being. Given the diverse nature of the South African workplace, it is expected that the relationships between demographic variables and well-being variables will differ significantly among women. More specifically, this study therefore hypothesises that women will experience work-related well-being differently based on age, race, marital status, education and language.

Research design

Research approach

To meet the objectives of the study, a cross-sectional survey design was utilised. Data were thus gathered at a particular point in time (Wegner, 2007). The study employed a quantitative approach. Online surveys were utilised to gather the data. Women across various organisations and occupations in Gauteng, South Africa, participated in the study. The online survey was accompanied by a letter explaining the purpose of the study as well as ensuring the participants of both confidentiality and anonymity.

Research method

Research participants

The targeted population consisted of 800 working women. The sample consisted of n = 540 women and resulted in a 67.5% response rate. Non-probability sampling was utilised. Organisations (e.g. media, schools, investment companies) were targeted, based on convenience, in order to obtain a diverse sample of women who have worked for one year or more. The sample was further well represented in terms of language, age, marital status and education. As regards race, 50.2% were white, 25.2% were black, 16.2% were coloured and 7.3% were Indian. Half the women were unmarried (50.9%), while the other half were married (49.1%). Almost 27% (26.9%) of the women spoke Afrikaans, 48.7% of the women were English-speaking and 22.8% spoke an African language. In terms of age groups, 47.9% were between the ages of 18 and 34 years, while 48.1% were between the ages of 35 and 65 years. Pertaining to levels of education, the women were split into two groups: those with a secondary education (54.3%) and those with a university qualification (43.5%).

Research procedure

This study formed part of a larger project. An invitation to participate in the study was sent out by email communication. Participants and organisations voluntarily agreed to complete the survey. An online survey was emailed to participants. A web-link containing the online survey was used, to be accessed via the web, which meant that participants had to have internet access. A cover letter explaining the purpose and significance of the study accompanied the web-link. Further, the confidentiality of the research was explained and guaranteed.

Measuring instruments

The measuring instruments consisted of a biographical questionnaire, the Utrecht Work Engagement Scale (UWES), the Job Demands Resources Scale (JDRS), the Psychological Meaningfulness Scale (PMS), the Satisfaction with Life Scale (SWLS) and the Work-to-Family Conflict Scale. All the questionnaires are in the open domain. Previous research used the UWES (De Bruin & Henn, 2013), the JDRS (Jackson & Rothmann, 2005), the PMS (Geldenhuys et al., 2014), the SWLS (Williamson & Geldenhuys, 2014) and the Work-to-Family Conflict Scale (Opie & Henn, 2013).

The *biographical questionnaire* consisted of questions regarding race, age, language, education and marital status.

The PMS (Spreitzer, 1995), utilised to measure psychological meaningfulness, contains six items that are answered on a 5-point Likert scale ranging from 1 (totally agree) to 5 (totally disagree). The scale measures the degree of meaning that individuals find in work-related activities. A sample item is *My job activities are significant to me*. Satisfactory Cronbach's alpha was reported in previous studies. May et al. (2004) reported a reliability coefficient of 0.90. In a

South African study, Olivier and Rothmann (2007) reported a Cronbach's alpha coefficient of 0.92. The Cronbach's alpha for this study was 0.95.

The JDRS was used to measure social support and supervisor support (Jackson & Rothmann, 2005). The 20 items in this scale are rated on a 4-point scale, ranging from 1 (never) to 4 (always). Social support measures the level of support that is provided by colleagues (*I have support from my colleagues at work*), while supervisor support measured the support provided by the manager to the direct subordinate (*I feel that my manager appreciates my work*). Sufficient reliability scores were found with Cronbach's alpha coefficients of 0.8 for organisational support and 0.76 for social support (Jackson & Rothmann, 2005). This study found a sufficient Cronbach's alpha coefficient of $\alpha = 0.95$ for both organisational and social support.

The SWLS is a widely used measure of life satisfaction (Diener et al. 1985). The five-item scale uses a 7-point Likert rating scale that ranges from 1 = strongly disagree to 7 = strongly agree. Sample items include *I am satisfied with my life* and *If I could live my life over I would change almost nothing*. Braghin (2009) reported a Cronbach's alpha coefficient of 0.91 for this scale. This study found an internal consistency coefficient of 0.88.

The 9-item UWES (UWES-9 item) was utilised to measure work engagement (Schaufeli & Bakker, 2004). The items are scored on a 7-point Likert-type scale ranging from 0 (never) to 6 (always). The scale measures the three factors of work engagement, namely vigour, dedication and absorption. A sample item for vigour is *When I get up in the morning I feel like going to work*. A sample item for dedication is *My job inspires me* and a sample item for absorption is *Time flies when I'm working*. As recommended by De Bruin and Henn (2013), the total score was utilised in the analysis. In a South African study, Opie and Henn (2013) reported an alpha coefficient of 0.93 for the UWES-9. The reliability for the UWES in this study was also $\alpha = 0.93$.

The *Work-to-Family Conflict Scale* (Netemeyer, Boles & McMurrian, 1996) measures work-to-family conflict. It comprises five items that require responses on a 5-point Likert-type scale. Responses range from *strongly agree* to *strongly disagree*. Sample items are *The demands of my work interfere with my home and family life* and *My job produces strain that makes it difficult to fulfil family duties*. A South African study among working women found a Cronbach's alpha coefficient of 0.92 (Braghin, 2009). This study found a Cronbach's alpha of $\alpha = 0.97$.

Statistical analysis

The statistical analysis was carried out by using SPSS (SPSS Inc., 2013). Data were screened for outliers, typing errors and inconsistencies. Descriptive statistics including means, standard deviation, skewness, kurtosis and reliability were analysed.

Product moment correlation coefficients were determined. In terms of effect sizes, Cohen (1992) provides the following guidelines to practical and statistical significance: $r = 0.10$ is indicative of a small effect, $r = 0.30$ is indicative of a medium effect and $r = 0.50$ is indicative of a large effect. This will indicate the practical significance of the correlations between the variables. A correlation is only practically significant if it is statistically significant (Cohen, 1992).

Owing to unequal sample sizes, relationship status was lapsed into two categories, namely married and unmarried. Similarly, age was split into an '18–34 years' group and a '35–65 years' group. Education was split into 'up to secondary education' and 'some form of tertiary education' groups. Independent samples *t*-tests were performed to compare the mean score differences of the well-being factors based on the demographic factors. For the *t*-test for race, the coloured and Indian groups were omitted from the analysis because these two categories were too small for meaningful analysis. The Levene's test for significance was used to determine whether equal variance based on the demographic factors are assumed (Pallant, 2011). Further, Cohen's *d* was also investigated as an addition to the *t*-test result in inferential statistics (Cohen, 1992). Cohen's *d* presents the distance between the two groups being compared based on the standard deviation score. Cohen (1992) suggests that a value of 0.1 is a small effect, 0.3 is a medium effect and 0.5 is large effect. Hierarchical multiple regression analysis was used to determine the amount of variance explained in work engagement, psychological meaningfulness, life satisfaction, work–family conflict and support by age, race, education and marital status. Data were inspected to ensure that the assumptions of normality, linearity and homoscedasticity were met. Multicollinearity values (tolerance and Variance Inflation Factor [VIF]) were within recommended limits (Pallant, 2011).

Results

Descriptive statistics

The descriptive statistics for the well-being constructs are reported in Table 1. The descriptive statistics include mean scores, standard deviations, skewness and kurtosis.

Table 1 shows the mean scores and standard deviations of work engagement, psychological meaningfulness, work–family conflict, life satisfaction social support and supervisor support. In terms of skewness and kurtosis, the results

TABLE 1: Descriptive statistics for work engagement, psychological meaningfulness, work–family conflict, life satisfaction, social support and supervisor support.

Item	Mean	SD	Skewness	Kurtosis
Work engagement	37.44	10.92	-0.76	0.34
Psychological meaningfulness	24.06	4.89	-1.09	1.80
Work–family conflict	13.10	5.35	0.28	0.11
Life satisfaction	23.45	6.65	-0.62	0.25
Social support	40.45	8.48	-0.60	0.41
Supervisor support	33.96	11.43	-0.44	-0.77

SD, standard deviation.

indicate that the data were normally distributed and had a normal peak.

Correlations coefficients

Pearson product moment correlations coefficients for the well-being constructs are reported in Table 2. Effect sizes were determined according to the guideline provided by Cohen (1988). Correlations reflect how the constructs for women relate to each other.

Table 2 shows that work engagement positively relates to psychological meaningfulness (r = 0.74; large effect), life satisfaction (r = 0.43; medium effect), social support (r = 0.48; medium effect) and supervisor support (r = 0.45; medium effect). It negatively relates to work–family conflict (r = -0.15; small effect). Psychological meaningfulness positively relates to life satisfaction (r = 0.41; medium effect), social support (r = 0.48; medium effect) and supervisor support (r = 0.42; medium effect). Work–family conflict negatively relates to supervisor support (r = -0.19; small effect). Life satisfaction positively relates to social support (r = 0.38; medium effect) as well as supervisor support (r = 0.32; medium effect).

TABLE 2: Correlations coefficients for work engagement, psychological meaningfulness, work–family conflict, life satisfaction, social support and supervisor support.

Item	WE	PM	WFC	LS	SS
Work engagement	-	-	-	-	-
Psychological meaningfulness	0.74*	-	-	-	-
Work–family conflict	-0.15*	-0.04	-	-	-
Life satisfaction	0.43*	0.41*	-0.06	-	-
Social support	0.48*	0.48*	-0.05	0.38*	-
Supervisor support	0.45*	0.42*	-0.19*	0.32*	0.54*

WE, work engagement; PM, psychological meaningfulness; WFC, work–family conflict; LS, life satisfaction; SS, social support and supervisor support.

Practical significance: $r < 0.10$ (small effect); $r < 0.30$ (medium effect); $r < 0.50$ (large effect).

*, $p < 0.05$

Supervisor support and social support positively relate to each other (r = 0.54; large effect).

Independent-sample *t*-tests

Independent-sample t-tests are reported for all the demographic variables on well-being of women in Tables 3–6.

Table 3 shows the results of the independent samples t-tests investigating the significance of the relationship between well-being constructs and marital status. It was found that women experience significant differences in levels of work engagement, psychological meaningfulness, work–family conflict and life satisfaction based on marital status. More specifically, married women experienced higher levels of work engagement, psychological meaningfulness, work–family conflict, life satisfaction and social support compared to unmarried women. There is a small effect size for the difference between married and unmarried women for the specified variables.

Table 4 reports the results of the independent samples t-tests investigating the relationship between race and the different well-being variables in our study. Significant differences were found, based on race, in work engagement, work–family conflict and life satisfaction. White women reported higher levels of work engagement, psychological meaningfulness, work–family conflict and life satisfaction than black women. The effect sizes of these differences ranged between 0.19 and 0.35, which indicates a small effect.

Table 5 shows the results of the independent samples t-test examining the relationship between age and the measured well-being constructs. As can be seen, older women reported significantly higher levels of work engagement, psychological

TABLE 3: Independent t-tests of marital status on well-being of women.

Item	Unmarried		Married		t	p	Cohen's d
	Mean	SD	Mean	SD			
Work engagement	36.35	11.66	38.57	9.99	-2.91	0.02*	0.20
Psychological meaningfulness	23.59	5.36	24.55	4.29	-2.24	0.00*	0.20
Work–family conflict	12.39	5.15	13.85	5.45	-4.06	0.00*[a]	0.28
Life satisfaction	22.35	7.11	24.59	5.94	-2.16	0.00*	0.34
Social support	39.99	9.07	40.95	7.78	-1.78	0.02*	0.11
Supervisor support	33.84	11.77	34.08	11.10	-1.48	0.81[a]	0.02

SD, standard deviation.

[a], Equal variance is assumed.

*, $p < 0.05$

TABLE 4: Independent t-tests of race on well-being of women.

Item	Black		White		t	p	d
	Mean	SD	Mean	SD			
Work engagement	35.54	12.26	38.40	9.63	-2.64	0.01*	0.26
Psychological meaningfulness	23.50	5.586	24.54	4.16	-1.83	0.07	0.21
Work–family conflict	11.64	4.99	14.00	5.32	-4.28	0.00**[a]	0.46
Life satisfaction	22.49	6.66	24.07	6.46	-2.25	0.03*[a]	0.24
Social support	40.01	9.11	41.14	7.79	-1.15	0.25	0.13
Supervisor support	32.69	12.09	34.71	11.08	-1.52	0.13	0.17

SD, standard deviation.

[a], Equal variance is assumed.

*, $p < 0.05$; **, $p < 0.01$

TABLE 5: Independent *t*-tests of age on well-being of women.

Item	18–34		35–65		*t*	*p*	*d*
	Mean	SD	Mean	SD			
Work engagement	35.88	10.86	38.94	10.90	-2.57	0.01*	0.28
Psychological meaningfulness	23.40	5.19	24.71	4.46	-3.19	0.00*ª	0.27
Work–family conflict	13.13	5.36	13.25	5.30	-0.31	0.76	0.02
Life satisfaction	23.10	6.96	23.81	6.32	-1.83	0.07	0.11
Social support	39.56	8.88	41.75	7.91	-2.68	0.00*	0.26
Supervisor support	34.35	11.15	33.73	11.73	0.74	0.46	0.05

SD, standard deviation.
ª, Equal variance is assumed.
*, $p < 0.05$

TABLE 6: Independent *t*-tests of education on well-being of women.

Item	Secondary		Tertiary		*t*	*p*	*d*
	Mean	SD	Mean	SD			
Work engagement	36.98	11.64	37.50	9.88	-0.97	0.33	0.05
Psychological meaningfulness	23.85	5.11	24.22	4.65	-0.88	3.84	0.08
Work–family conflict	12.93	5.49	13.68	5.09	-2.04	0.04*ª	0.14
Life satisfaction	22.41	6.84	24.351	6.33	-3.18	0.00*ª	0.29
Social support	40.34	8.97	40.30	7.62	-0.41	0.68	0.00
Supervisor support	33.80	11.66	33.45	10.98	0.08	0.93	0.03

SD, standard deviation.
ª, Equal variance is assumed.
*, $p < 0.05$

meaningfulness and social support than younger women. The effect sizes based on Cohen's *d* indicated small variances.

Table 6 shows the results of the independent samples *t*-tests analysing the relationship between education and the measured well-being constructs. Women with a tertiary qualification experience more work–family conflict and are more satisfied with life compared to women with only a senior certificate (Grade 12). There is a small effect size for the difference in women with and without a tertiary qualification for the specified variables.

Multiple regression analyses

We conducted hierarchical regression analyses to determine the percentage of variance explained by each of the demographic variables. Separate regression analyses were conducted for work engagement, psychological meaningfulness, work–family conflict, life satisfaction social support and supervisor support. In each analysis, the demographic variables were entered step by step (one in each step).

Table 7 shows the results of the regression analysis conducted for work engagement.

Table 7 shows that marital status explained 10% of the variance in work engagement. Further, race explained an additional 14% variance above that of marital status. Age and education did not add significantly to the percentage of variance explained.

Table 8 indicates that marital status explained 10% of the variance in psychological meaningfulness, while race added 8% variance of psychological meaningfulness. An additional variance of 9% in psychological meaningfulness was found

TABLE 7: Variances explained by demographic variables on work engagement.

Model	Variable	*R*	R^2	ΔR^2	*p*
1	Marital status	0.102	0.010	0.01	0.024*
2	Race	0.156	0.024	0.014	0.009*
3	Age	0.167	0.028	0.003	0.188
4	Education	0.176	0.031	0.003	0.199

Dependent: Work engagement.
1, Marital status (β = 2.222); 2, Marital status, race (β = 2.59); 3, Marital status, race, age (β = 1.401); 4, Marital status, race, age, education (β = 1.279).
*, $p < 0.05$

TABLE 8: Variances explained by demographic variable on psychological meaningfulness.

Model	Variable	*R*	R^2	ΔR^2	*p*
1	Marital status	0.098	0.010	0.010	0.03*
2	Race	0.131	0.017	0.008	0.05*
3	Age	0.163	0.027	0.009	0.03*
4	Education	0.173	0.030	0.003	0.19

Dependent: Psychological meaningfulness.
1, Marital status (β = 0.957); 2, Marital status, race (β = 0.859); 3, Marital status, race, age (β = 1.036); 4, Marital status, race, age, education (β = 0.579).
*, $p < 0.05$

because of age. Education did not add significantly to the amount of variance explained.

Table 9 indicates that marital status explained 19% of the variance in work–family conflict. Race added an additional 25% of the variance in work–family conflict, while education added an additional 7% variance therein. Age did not add significant variance to work–family conflict.

Table 10 shows that marital status explains 28% of variance in life satisfaction. Levels of education added a further 23% increase in the variance of life satisfaction.

Table 11 shows that age resulted in an 18% variance in social support. Marital status, race and education did not explain significant variance in social support.

TABLE 9: Variances explained by demographic variable on work–family conflict.

Model	Variable	R	R^2	ΔR^2	p
1	Marital status	0.136	0.019	0.019	0.002*
2	Race	0.210	0.044	0.025	0.000*
3	Age	0.223	0.050	0.006	0.087
4	Education	0.239	0.057	0.007	0.05*

Dependent: Work–family conflict.

1, Marital status (β = 1.458); 2, Marital status, race (β = 1.718); 3, Marital status, race, age (β = -0.869); 4, Marital status, race, age, education (β = 0.931).

*, $p < 0.05$

TABLE 10: Variances explained by demographic variable on life satisfaction.

Model	Variable	R	R^2	ΔR^2	p
1	Marital status	0.169	0.028	0.028	0.000*
2	Race	0.185	0.034	0.006	0.088
3	Age	0.186	0.034	0.000	0.690
4	Education	0.240	0.058	0.023	0.001*

Dependent: Life satisfaction.

1, Marital status (β = 2.241); 2, Marital status, race (β = 1.012); 3, Marital status, race, age (β = 0.255); 4, Marital status, race, age, education (β = 2.062).

*, $p < 0.05$

TABLE 11: Variances explained by demographic variable on social support.

Model	Variable	R	R^2	ΔR^2	p
1	Marital status	0.057	0.003	0.003	0.221
2	Race	0.094	0.009	0.006	0.104
3	Age	0.133	0.018	0.009	0.042*
4	Education	0.138	0.018	0.001	0.443

Dependent: Social support.

1, Marital status (β = 0.961); 2, Marital status, race (β = 1.285); 3, Marital status, race, age (β = 1.733); 4, Marital status, race, age, education (β = 0.611).

*, $p < 0.05$

TABLE 12: Variances explained by demographic variable on supervisor support.

Model	Variable	R	R^2	ΔR^2	p
1	Marital status	0.010	0.000	0.000	0.822
2	Race	0.068	0.005	0.004	0.148
3	Age	0.091	0.008	0.004	0.182
4	Education	0.092	0.009	0.000	0.786

Dependent: Supervisor support.

1, Marital status (β = 0.237); 2, Marital status, race (β = 1.538); 3, Marital status, race, age (β = -1.528); 4, Marital status, race, age, education (β = -0.291).

*, $p < 0.05$

The results reported in Table 12 indicated that none of the measured demographic variables explained significant amounts of variance in supervisor support.

Discussion

Outline of the research

The objective of this study was to examine the demographic differences in the experience of well-being of women in the workplace. Differences in the experiences of work engagement, psychological meaningfulness, life satisfaction, work–family conflict, social support and supervisor support of women were found based on race, age, marital status and education.

Relationships between the well-being variables

The results indicated that most of the well-being constructs were related. Work engagement, psychological meaningfulness, life satisfaction and support are positively related to each other. The findings of this study are in line with previous research on the relationship between work engagement, psychological meaningfulness and life satisfaction (cf. Van Zyl et al., 2012; Williamson & Geldenhuys, 2014) as well as work engagement and support (cf. Barkhuizen & Rothmann, 2006; Schaufeli & Bakker, 2004). Work–family conflict is negatively related to work engagement, as is supervisor support. Previous research attests to the negative effect of work–family conflict on levels of engagement of employees (Opie & Henn, 2013) and organisational support (Karatepe, 2009). The significant correlations found among the well-being constructs demonstrate that they are closely related. Even more significant is that the correlations are among work-related and non-work-related variables. This clearly signifies the importance of work, and experiences at work, in determining overall well-being – and vice versa. Work is an extremely important part of people's lives, and therefore employers cannot merely focus on work-related aspects when dealing with employees. Work cannot be compartmentalised and separated from employees' day-to-day lives, because work and private life are indeed intertwined. This is especially true in a modern work environment where, owing to technology, the boundaries between working time and private time are becoming increasingly blurred. Indeed, Currie and Eveline (2011) refer to 'work extensification and intensification' (Eveline, 2011, p. 539) to describe this blurring of lines between work and private life. In their study among academics with young children, one of the participants described the fact that technology allows him to work from anywhere, including home, as both a 'blessing and a curse' (Eveline, 2011, p. 542).

Marital status

The results indicate that married women experience higher levels of work engagement, psychological meaningfulness and life satisfaction compared to unmarried women. The findings of this study contradict those of Kong (2009), who reported that unmarried employees are more engaged. Takawira (2012) did find higher levels of vigour among married people. In the current study, marital status explained 10% of the variance in work engagement. It should be borne in mind that the current study only investigated women, whereas the other studies involved both genders. It seems plausible that being in a committed relationship enhances the well-being of participants, which spills over into positive appraisals of work. This can include enhanced work engagement and experiencing meaningfulness in work. Hakanen, Peeters and Perhoniemi's longitudinal study (2011) demonstrates the inter-relatedness of work and marriage: they found that job resources predicted work-to-family enrichment and the latter predicted work engagement (both over time). They also found that family-to-work enrichment had a positive influence on marital satisfaction (over time). These findings once again illustrate the enmeshed nature of work and family, and more specifically how work does indeed influence marital satisfaction indirectly. Combining these research findings, one comes to a tenable conclusion, namely that there may exist a reciprocal relationship between marital aspects such as quality of marital life, and work experiences such as work engagement.

In terms of life satisfaction, this study endorses the findings of numerous other studies that have shown that married people experience higher levels of life satisfaction (Botha & Booysen, 2012; Filiz, 2014; Lee & Lee, 2014; Ngoo et al., 2015; Stack & Eshleman, 1998). Indeed, marital status explained a substantial 28% of the variance in life satisfaction. Increased life satisfaction, in turn, can influence work experiences positively. For instance, literature has shown job satisfaction to be an area-specific element of life satisfaction (refer to Bowling, Echlesman & Wang, 2010; Veenhoven, 1991).

Married women also reported more work–family conflict. This study reports a 19% variance in work–family conflict because of marital status. Given that women bear the brunt of the household (taking care of children, husband and so forth), and based on the fact that women do more work in the home environment (OECD, 2011), it is expected that married women, especially those with families, will experience more work–family conflict.

Race

With regard to race, white women experienced significantly higher levels of work engagement, work–family conflict and life satisfaction compared to black women. Additionally, race explained a significant 14% of variance in work engagement, and a significant 25% of variance in work-to-family conflict. This is in line with previous research findings regarding race and work engagement (Bell & Barkhuizen, 2011) as well as with life satisfaction (Addai et al., 2014; Botha & Booysen, 2012). Research by Fagley (2012), however, indicated no significant relationship between race and life satisfaction. It seems likely, as explained by Davis and Wu (2014), that racial identity determines the social group with which an individual compares himself. This, in turn, determines the individual's subjective perceptions of life satisfaction. Race may also act as a proxy for other factors that impact on life satisfaction, such as access to education and higher paying occupations.

There was no significant difference in the mean scores of psychological meaningfulness between black and white women, and this is in line with Hodson's (2002) findings in his study. In terms of work–family conflict, white women in this study experienced more conflict than black women, and this was a medium effect size. Previous research has been inconclusive in this regard. One study was found to be in line with the findings of this study (Childers & Sage, 2004), while another study indicated that black employees experienced more conflict within their home-to-work life (cf. Steyl & Koekemoer, 2011). The differences in findings may be sample-specific, and more research concerning the antecedents of work–family conflict is necessary. The experiences of black and white women with regard to employment, and subsequent work–family conflict, should be interpreted against the backdrop of South Africa's socio-political history. During the era of apartheid, many black women had to leave their children in the care of grandparents while they themselves migrated to the cities where they could find employment. It stands to reason that these working mothers could focus on their work without having to balance it with childcare (of course migratory labour had many disadvantages – among them the emotional impact of being separated from one's children for extended periods of time – but it is not the purpose of this discussion to dwell on these). As Russell (2003) puts it, migrant workers are 'geographically mobile and effectively single' (Russell, 2003, p. 171), and this makes them rather desirable employees. Implicit herein is the understanding that these 'effectively single' employees will not be distracted from their work by family demands. There are currently still many black women who are involved in migratory labour (cf. Phillips & James, 2014). Although the extended family remains the dominant family structure among black South Africans, there is also a shift towards nuclear families (i.e. mother, father and children living together) (cf. Amoateng & Heaton, 2015). Given this mixture of nuclear families, extended families and families affected by migratory labour, it is difficult to obtain a clear answer as to the experiences of work–family conflict among black people, hence the inconclusive research results.

Age

Women between the ages of 35 and 65 experienced higher levels of work engagement and psychological meaningfulness compared to women between the ages of 18 and 34. Research attests to the positive correlation between age and work engagement (Bezuidenhout & Cilliers, 2011; Fong & Ng, 2012; Mahboubi et al., 2014). With age comes greater maturity, and women may be better able to decide what job they should be doing. Older employees are also, by implication, further along in their career paths, so chances are good that they find themselves doing what they really want to do. It is plausible that this combination of factors can result in older women being more likely to find meaning in their work, and consequently also be more engaged in it. Other research found no such relationship (cf. Durksen & Klassen, 2012; Takawira, 2012). It is assumed that older people may experience more meaning in work, as Chalofsky and Krishna (2009) allude to the idea of older people becoming more aware of their purpose in life. One way to interpret research findings is to refer to life stages and life cycle, as these are closely aligned to age. In this regard, Erik Erikson's eight stages of psycho-social development (described in Meyer & Van Ede, 1990) present us with a theoretical context within which to explain our findings. According to this theory, the greatest challenge in early adulthood is to find a relationship to which to commit. In middle adulthood, the main challenge revolves around making a meaningful contribution in life, and in retirement the main challenge is to find satisfaction with life in general and the contributions you have made. The latter two phases of adulthood lend themselves to a greater search for meaning, which would also find expression in a search for meaning in terms of work.

Interestingly, there was a significant difference in the experience of social support between the two age groups, with women aged 18–34 reporting higher levels of social support than women aged 35–65. Unfortunately, owing to unequal group sizes, we had to lapse the age categories into two categories, making it difficult to interpret the results regarding age. Notwithstanding this challenge, Erikson's theory may also contribute towards explaining our findings regarding age and social support. In the earlier phases of adulthood, individuals are more concerned with the establishment of meaningful relationships, whereas in later phases individuals are more concerned with their contributions to the world and having peace with their life. Older individuals may therefore be less concerned with support from others. Older employees may also be more confident and self-reliant, as they have built competency and skill over time. More research with larger samples is required to truly understand the relationship between perceptions of social support and age.

Education

The results showed that participants with some form of tertiary education experienced higher levels of life satisfaction and work-to-family conflict. With regard to life satisfaction, this finding is in line with literature (Daraei & Mohajery, 2013). As indicted earlier, education is a portal to higher paying occupations and subsequent higher standards of living (cf. Schimmel, 2009). Higher incomes and socio-economic class have in fact been positively linked with life satisfaction in previous studies (Addai et al., 2014; Botha & Booysen, 2012; Jivray & Nazroo, 2014). Indeed, education explained a significant 23% of variance in life satisfaction. Educated women are able to attract higher level jobs because of their qualification. This can result in women being more satisfied with their life because they might be able to afford a better lifestyle.

The finding that participants with tertiary education experienced higher levels of work-to-family conflict than those with a high school education is similar to the findings in a number of other studies (Childers & Sage, 2014; Gaspar, 2013; Noor, 2003; Ozutku & Altindis, 2013). As mentioned, Schieman and Glavin (2011) reported a curvilinear relationship between education and work–family conflict, with participants with higher (post school) and lower (less than high school) levels of education reporting higher levels of work–family conflict than those with a high school education. They proposed that participants with higher levels of education may experience 'stress of higher status' (Schieman & Glavin, 2011, p. 1342), in other words, the demands placed on them by senior levels of work may cause increasing strain in terms of balancing work and family.

Limitations and recommendations

As this study worked with an existing database, it is possible that well-being constructs not included in our study may also be affected by demographic variables. Future studies can include variables such as job satisfaction, family-to-work conflict and burnout. The study was cross-sectional, and therefore no conclusions regarding cause and effect could be drawn. Owing to unequal sample sizes in terms of the demographic variables, we had to collapse each demographic variable into two categories. Future studies should aim to increase sample size, with large enough numbers of participants across all categories in a variable in order to maximise generalisability. This will enable the researchers to measure finer distinctions in demographic categories such as race, age, education and marital status.

Practical implications

The study provides ample support for the importance of demographic variables as determinants of well-being. Thus, from an organisational and managerial perspective, performance can be enhanced by acknowledging the different demographics of women that affect their work experiences. In this regard, it can be helpful to segment the workforce (e.g. in terms of relationship status, income, seniority level or education) to manage and support employees (cf. Nienaber et al., 2011). Further, it could be helpful in understanding the context within which women function or go about their work and personal life. In connection with this, employers should be mindful that demographic factors often serve as a proxy for lifecycle stages. For example, age can be an indicator of childbearing or menopause, and age of children can be an indicator of childcare – and flexitime needs.

Human resource (HR) practitioners have a pivotal role in ensuring appropriate and supportive workplace practices for women (Abbott, 2012). More specifically, Abbott mentions aspects such as 'working hours, location of work, remuneration, and benefits' (Abbott, 2012, p. 21). Furthermore she also points out that the HR practitioner should ensure an appropriate fit between the employee and the organisation, and this includes lifestyle factors of the individual. Knowledge of the possible impact of demographic factors on employee well-being and hence organisational performance is therefore indispensable.

Kossek and Ozeki (1999) allude to two important factors that HR managers must pay attention to. Firstly, although many HR policies already allow for employees to utilise supportive practices (such as flexitime), employees often do not avail themselves of these opportunities. In their literature review, they found that a possible cause for this may be an unsupportive organisational culture. Indeed, an employee must 'experience' (Kossek & Ozeki, 1999, p. 25) a policy as conducive before it will actually result in positive returns such as employee well-being and organisational commitment. Regarding work accommodation for pregnant women, Boninelli (2016) states that:

> it is important that work accommodation not be viewed as unfortunate organisational costs needed to placate a special category of employees, but rather as an investment in a changed social climate and in female talent. (p. 10)

This statement is in fact true for all supportive practices that an organisation makes available for women and certainly addresses the aspect of a non-supportive organisational culture.

Secondly, they advise that it is important to pin down the supportive practices considered most helpful and imperative for employees. They further urge researchers to utilise reliable scales to measure these. In the same way, HR practitioners should also utilise reliable scales to obtain this necessary information. More specific to our study, they should obtain data from different demographic groups in the organisation to ensure truly valuable results. Such scientifically valid results, combined with workforce segmentation, can assist employers in ensuring that best practices are applied that meet the needs of their employees while also serving the best interests of the organisation.

The practical implications of our research findings stretch further than merely addressing it through particular supportive practices and allowances in policies. It is essential that HR practitioners and HR managers ensure that policies are made available widely throughout the organisations, and to create awareness and tolerance thereof. Line managers should receive training so as to ensure that they understand the practical implications of the relevant policies (cf. Boninelli, 2016). This will prevent situations where line managers do not sanction, either directly or indirectly, their female employees' utilisation of allowed practices. HR practitioners should in fact champion the cause for the well-being of women (Abbott, 2012).

In line with our particular findings, HR practitioners should note the effect of age on well-being factors and link this to where an employee is in her life cycle. This will help towards establishing family-friendly workplace policies. With regard to relationship status, married women report higher levels of work–family conflict and may have a greater need for flexible work times, to name but one. Higher educational status can increase life satisfaction, and HR practitioners should consider practices such as opportunities for employees to improve their education. Concerning race, employees will benefit from diversity training. These are but a few ways in which HR practitioners can make practical use of our and other similar research findings.

Conclusion

This study demonstrates that demographic factors do influence well-being among working women. Being married correlated significantly with higher levels of life satisfaction, work-to-family conflict and work engagement. Marital status explained significant proportions of variance in work engagement, life satisfaction and work-to-family conflict. Being older correlated significantly with higher levels of work engagement. Age also explained significant percentages of variance in psychological meaningfulness, and social support at work. Higher education correlated positively with higher levels of life satisfaction and work-to-family conflict. Education also explained significant proportions of variance in life satisfaction and work-to-family conflict. In terms of race, white women experienced significantly higher levels of life satisfaction, work-to-family conflict and work engagement than black women. Race explained significant amounts of variance in psychological meaningfulness and work-to-family conflict. Understanding the impact of these factors can assist HR practitioners in effectively supporting and managing employees and designing policies and interventions – such as talent management – and retention strategies.

Acknowledgements

Competing interests

The authors declare that they have no financial or personal relationships that may have inappropriately influenced them in writing this article.

Authors' contributions

M.G. and C.M.H. made an equal contribution on all sections (title, abstract, introduction, literature review, methodology and results, analyses and discussions) of this manuscript.

References

Abbott, P. (2012). Retention of women in the workplace – What HR practitioners can do. In A. Bosch (Ed.), *South African board for people practices women's report 2012* (pp. 21–24). Parktown, South Africa: SABPP.

Addai, I., Opoku-Agyeman, C., & Amanfu, S.K. (2014). Exploring predictors of subjective well-being in Ghana: A micro-level study. *Journal of Happiness Studies, 15*, 869–890. https://doi.org/10.1007/s10902-013-9454-7

Alcover, C.-M. (2012). Ageism in organizations? Perceived organizational support as a mediator of the relations between age and psychological contract breach. *Revista Psicologia Organizacoes e Trabalho, 12*, 299–313.

Allen, T.D., & Finkelstein, L.M. (2014). Work-family conflict among members of full-time dual-earner couples: An examination of family life stage, gender and age. *Journal of Occupational Health Psychology, 19*(3), 376–384. https://doi.org/10.1037/a0036941

Amoateng, A.Y., & Heaton, T.B. (2015). Changing race differences in family structure and household composition in South Africa. *South African Review of Sociology, 46*(4), 59–79. https://doi.org/10.1080/21528586.2015.1109476

Aselage, J., & Eisenberger, R. (2003). Perceived organizational support and psychological contracts: A theoretical integration. *Journal of Organizational Behavior, 24*, 491–509. https://doi.org/10.1002/job.211

Bakker, A.B., Schaufeli, W.B., Leiter, M.P., & Taris, T.W. (2008). Work engagement: An emerging concept in occupational health psychology. *Work and Stress, 22*(3), 187–200. https://doi.org/10.1080/02678370802393649

Balogun, A.G. (2014). Demographic variables predicting employee willingness to share tacit knowledge in service occupations. *IFE PsychologIA, 22*(2), 42–49.

Barkhuizen, E.N., & Rothmann, S. (2006). Work engagement of academic staff in South African higher education institutions. *Management Dynamics, 15*(1), 38–48.

Bell, E., & Barkhuizen, N. (2011). The relationship between barriers to change and the work engagement of employees in a South African property management company. *South African Journal of Industrial Psychology, 37*(1), 1–11. https://doi.org/10.4102/sajip.v37il.935

Bellavia, G.M., & Frone, M.R. (2005). Work-family conflict. In J. Barling, E.K. Kelloway, & M.R. Frone (Eds.), *Handbook of work stress* (pp. 113–147). Thousand Oaks, CA: Sage.

Bezuidenhout, A., & Cilliers, F. (2011). Age, burnout, work engagement and sense of coherence in female academics at two South African universities. *South African Journal of Labour Relations, 35*(1), 61–80.

Boninelli, I. (2016). Career decisions for women considering pregnancy. In A. Bosch (Ed.), *South African board for people practices women's report 2016* (pp. 7–13). Parktown, South Africa: SABPP.

Bosch, A. (2016). Pregnancy is here to stay – Or is it? In A. Bosch (Ed.), *South African board for people practices women's report 2016* (pp. 3–6). Parktown, South Africa: SABPP.

Botha, F., & Booysen, F. (2012). The relationship between marital status and life satisfaction among South African adults. *Acta Academica, 45*(2), 150–178.

Boushey, H. (2008). "Opting out?" The effect of children on women's employment in the United States. *Feminist Economics, 14*(1), 1–36. https://doi.org/10.1080/13545700701716672

Bowling, N.A., Eschleman, K.J., & Wang, Q. (2010). A meta-analytic examination of the relationship between job satisfaction and subjective wellbeing. *The British Psychological Society, 83*, 915–934. https://doi.org/10.1348/096317909X478557

Braghin, C. (2009). *Time-based constraints and work-to-family conflict among working mothers.* Unpublished master's dissertation, University of Johannesburg, Johannesburg.

Casale, D. (2004). *What has the feminisation of the labour market 'bought' women in South Africa? Trends in labour force participation, employment and earnings, 1995–2001.* Working Paper 04/84. Cape Town, South Africa: Development Policy Research Unit.

Chalofsky, N., & Krishna, V. (2009). Meaningfulness, commitment and engagement: The intersection of a deeper level of intrinsic motivation. *Advances in Developing Human Resources, 11*, 189–204.

Childers, C.D., & Sage, J.A. (2004, August). *Working women, work-family and family-work conflicts: A first look at differences in white women and women of colour.* Paper presented at the American Sociological Association Conference, San Francisco, CA.

Cohen, J. (1988). *Statistical power analysis for the behavioral sciences.* (2nd edn.). Hillside, NJ: Erlbaum.

Cohen, J. (1992). A power primer. *Psychological Bulletin, 112*(1), 155–159. https://doi.org/10.1037/0033-2909.112.1.155

Csikszentmihalyi, M. (1990). *Flow: The psychology of optimal experience.* New York: Harper & Row.

Currie, J., & Eveline, J. (2011). E-technology and work/life balance for academics with young children. *Higher Education, 62*, 533–550. https://doi.org/10.1007/s10734-010-9404-9

Cusack, E.E., & Numer, M. (2012). A phenomenological inquiry of social support in relation to health and wellbeing among rural queer female youth. *The International Journal of Interdisciplinary Social Sciences, 6*(4), 36–48. https://doi.org/10.18848/1833-1882/cgp/v06i04/52067

Daraei, M., & Mohajery, A. (2013). The impact of socioeconomic status on life satisfaction. *Social Indicators Research, 112*(1), 69–81. https://doi.org/10.1007/s11205-012-0040-x

Davis, L., & Wu, S. (2014). Social comparisons and life satisfaction across racial and ethnic groups: The effects of status, information and solidarity. *Social Indicators Research, 117*, 849–869. https://doi.org/10.1007/s11205-013-0367-y

De Bruin, G.P., & Henn, C.M. (2013). Uni-dimensionality of the Utrecht Work Engagement Scale 9 (UWES-9). *Psychological Reports, 112*(3), 1–12. https://doi.org/10.2466/01.03.PR0.112.3.788-799

De Klerk, M., Nel, J.A., & Koekemoer, E. (2012). Positive side of the work-family interface: A theoretical review. *Journal of Psychology in Africa, 22*(4), 683–694.

De Lange, A.H., De Witte, H., & Notelaers, G. (2008). Should I stay or should I go? Examining longitudinal relations among job resources and work engagement for stayers versus movers. *Work & Stress, 22*(3), 201–223. https://doi.org/10.1080/02678370802390132

Demerouti, E., Bakker, A.B., Nachreiner, F., & Schaufeli, W.B. (2000). A model of burnout and life satisfaction amongst nurses. *Journal of Advanced Nursing, 32*(2), 454–464. https://doi.org/10.1046/j.1365-2648.2000.01496.x

Diener, E., Emmons, A., Larsen, R.J., & Griffin, S. (1985). The satisfaction with life scale. *Journal of Personality Assessment, 49*(1), 72–75. https://doi.org/10.1207/s15327752jpa4901_13

Diener, E., Oishi, S., & Lucas, R.E. (2003). Personality, culture, and subjective well-being: Emotional and cognitive evaluations of life. *Annual Review of Psychology, 54*, 403–425.

Douglas, S., & Michaels, M. (2004). *The mommy myth: The idealisation of motherhood and how it has undermined women.* New York: Free Press.

Durksen, T.L., & Klassen, R.M. (2012). Pre-service teachers' weekly commitment and engagement during a final training placement: A longitudinal mixed methods study. *Educational & Child Psychology, 29*(4), 32–46.

Dwivedi, S., Kaushik, S., & Luxmi. (2015). Organizational citizenship behaviour and demographic variables of employees in Indian Business Processing Outsourcing (BPO) sector. *IUP Journal of Organizational Behaviour, 14*(1), 39–57. https://doi.org/10.1002/job.2040

Eagle, B.W., Icenogle, M.L., Maes, J.D., & Miles, E. (1998). The importance of employee demographic profiles for understanding experiences of work-family inter-role conflicts. *The Journal of Social Psychology, 138*(6), 690–709. https://doi.org/10.1080/00224549809603255

Erickson, J., Martinengo, G., & Hill, E.J. (2010). Putting work and family experiences in context: Differences by family life stage. *Human Relations, 63*(7), 955–979. https://doi.org/10.1177/0018726709353138

Fagenson-Eland, E., & Baugh, G. (2000). Career paths, networking, and mentoring. In D. Smith (Ed.), *Women at work – Leadership for the next century* (pp. 145–161). NJ: Prentice Hall.

Fagley, N.S. (2012). Appreciation uniquely predicts life satisfaction above demographics, the Big 5 personality factors, and gratitude. *Personality and Individual Differences, 53*, 59–63. https://doi.org/10.1016/j.paid.2012.02.019

Filiz, Z. (2014). An analysis of the levels of job satisfaction and life satisfaction of academic staff. *Social Indicators Research, 116*, 793–808. https://doi.org/10.1007/s11205-013-0319-6

Fong, T.C., & Ng, S. (2012). Measuring engagement at work: Validation of the Chinese version of the Utrecht Work Engagement Scale. *International Journal of Behavioral Medicine, 19*(3), 391–397.

Frankl, V.E. (1997). *Man's search for ultimate meaning.* New York: Plenum Press.

Gaspar, M.O. (2013). The modernisation process through the perceptions of work-family in Spain and Great Britain. *European Societies, 15*(5), 707–728. https://doi.org/10.1080/14616696/2013.829241

Geldenhuys, M., Łaba, K., & Venter, C.M. (2014). Meaningful work, work engagement and organisational commitment. *South African Journal of Industrial Psychology, 40*(1), 1–10. https://doi.org/10.4102/sajip.v40i1.1098

Greenhaus, J.H., & Beutell, N.J. (1985). Sources of conflict between work and family roles. *Academic of Management Review, 10*, 76–88. https://doi.org/10.2307/258214, https://doi.org/10.5465/AMR.1985.4277352

Greenhaus, J.H., & Parasuraman, S. (1999). Research on work, family and gender: Current status and future directions. In G.N. Powell (Ed.), *Handbook of gender & work* (pp. 391–415). Thousand Oaks, CA: Sage.

Hakanen, J.J., Peeters, M.C.W., & Perhoniemi, R. (2011). Enrichment processes and gain spirals at work and at home: A 3-year cross-lagged panel study. *Journal of Occupational and Organizational Psychology, 84*(1), 8–30. https://doi.org/10.1111/j.2044-8325.2010.02014.x

Haley, L., Mostert, K., & Els, C. (2013). Burnout and work engagement for different age groups: Examining group-level differences and predictors. *Journal of Psychology in Africa, 23*(2), 283–296.

Henn, C.M. (2013). Measures of well-being. In C. Foxcroft & G. Roodt (Eds.), *Introduction to psychological assessment in the South African context* (4th edn., pp. 171–184). Cape Town, South Africa: Oxford University Press.

Hodson, R. (2002). Demography or respect? Work group demography versus organizational dynamics as determinants of meaning and satisfaction at work. *British Journal of Sociology,* 53, 291–317. https://doi.org/10.1080/00071310220133359

Holvino, E. (2010). Intersections: The simultaneity of race, gender and class in organization studies. *Gender, Work and Organisation, 17*, 248–277. https://doi.org/10.1111/j.1468-0432.2008.00400.x

Huffman, A., Culbertson, S.S., Henning, J.B., & Goh, A. (2013). Work-family conflict across the lifespan. *Journal of Managerial Psychology, 28*(7/8), 761–780. https://doi.org/10.1108/JMP-07-2013-022

Jackson, L., & Rothmann, S. (2005). Work-related well-being of educators in a district of the North-West Province. *Perspectives in Education, 23*(3), 107–122.

Jivray, S., & Nazroo, J. (2014). Determinants of socioeconomic inequalities in subjective well-being in later life: A cross-country comparison in England and the USA. *Quality of Life Research, 23*, 2545–2558. https://doi.org/10.1007/s11136-014-0694-8

Kahn, W. (1990). Psychological conditions of personal engagement and disengagement at work. *Academy of Management Journal, 33*(4), 692–724. https://doi.org/10.2307/256287

Karatepe, O.M. (2009). An investigation of the joint effects of organisational tenure and supervisor support on work–family conflict and turnover intentions. *Journal of Hospitality and Tourism Management, 16*, 73–81. https://doi.org/10.1375/jhtm.16.1.73

Kong, Y. (2009). A study on the job engagement of company employees. *International Journal of Psychological Services, 1*(2), 65–68. https://doi.org/10.5539/ijps.v1n2p65

Kossek, E.E., & Ozeki, C. (1999). Briding the work-family policy and productivity gap: A literature Review. *Community, Work and Family, 2*(1), 7–32. https://doi.org/10.1080/13668809908414247

Kossek, E.E., Pichler, S., Bodner, T., & Hammer, L.B. (2011). Work place social support and work-family conflict: A meta-analysis clarifying the influence of general and work-family specific supervisor and organisational support. *Personnel Psychology, 64*, 289–313. https://doi.org/10.1111/j.1744-6570.2011.01211.x

Lambert, E.G., Hogan, N.L., Kelly, T.M., Kim, B., & Garland, B. (2013). When domains spill over: The relationships of affective and continuance commitment with work-family conflict among correctional staff. *Criminal Justice Policy Review, 25*(4), 476–502. https://doi.org/10.1177/0887403412474889

Lee, E-K.O., & Lee, J. (2013) Education, functional limitations, and life satisfaction among older adults in South Korea, *Educational Gerontology, 39*(7), 514–526. https://doi.org/10.1080/03601277.2012.701154

Liang, Y., & Lu, P. (2014). Effect of occupational mobility and health status on life satisfaction of Chinese residents of different occupations: Logistic diagonal mobility models analysis of cross-sectional data on eight Chinese provinces. *International Journal for Equity in Health, 13*, 15.

Lips-Wiersma, M., & Wright, S. (2012). Measuring the meaning of meaningful work: Developing and validation of the comprehensive meaningful work scale (CMWS). *Group & Organisation Management 37*, 655–685. https://doi.org/10.1177/1059601112461578

Mahboubi, M., Ghahramani, F., Mohammadi, M., Amanis, N., Mousavi, S.H., Moradi, F., et al. (2014). Evaluation of work engagement and its determinants in Kermanshah hospitals staff in 2013. *Global Journal of Health Sciences, 7*, 170–176. https://doi.org/10.5539/gjhs.v7n2p170

Mandu, S., Buitendach, J., Kanengoni, H., & Bobat, S. (2014). The prediction of turnover intention by means of employee engagement and demographic variables in a telecommunications organisation. *Journal of Psychology in Africa, 24*(2), 131–143.

Martinussen, M., Adolfsen, F., Lauritzen, C., & Richardsen, A.M. (2012). Improving interprofessional collaboration in a community setting: Relationships with burnout, engagement and service quality. *Journal of Interprofessional Care, 26*, 219–225. https://doi.org/10.3109/13561820.2011.647125

May, D., Gilson, R., & Harter, L. (2004). The psychological conditions of meaningfulness, safety and availability and the engagement of the human spirit at work. *Journal of Organisational Psychology, 77*(1), 11–37. https://doi.org/10.1348/096317904322915892

Mazerolle, S.G., Bruening, J.E., & Casa, D.J. (2008). Work-family conflict, Part I: Antecedents of work-family conflict in National Collegiate Athletic Association Division I-A certified athletic trainers. *Journal of Athletic Training, 43*(5), 505–512. https://doi.org/10.4085/1062-6050-43.5.505

McDowell, I. (2010). Measures of self-perceived well-being. *Journal of Psychosomatic Research, 69*, 69–79. https://doi.org/10.1016/j.jpsychores.2009.07.002

Meyer, W.F., & Van Ede, D.M. (1990). Ontwikkelingsteorieë. In D.A. Louw (Ed.), *Menslike Ontwikkeling* (2de uitgawe, pp. 51–99). Pretoria, Suid Afrika: HAUM Tersiêr.

Mills, M.J., Culbertson, S.S., & Fullagar, C.J. (2011). Conceptualizing and measuring engagement: An analysis of the Utrecht Work Engagement Scale. *Journal of Happiness Studies, 13*(3), 519–545. https://doi.org/10.1007/s10902-011-9277-3

Mostert, K. (2008). Time-based and strain-based work-family conflict in the South African police service: Examining the relationship with work characteristics and exhaustion. *Acta Criminologica, 21*(3), 1–18.

Netemeyer, R.G., Boles, J.S., & McMurrian, R. (1996). Development and validation of work-family conflict scales. *Journal of Applied Psychology, 81*, 400–401. https://doi.org/10.1037/0021-9010.81.4.400

Ngoo, Y.T., Tey, N.P., & Tan, E.C. (2015). Determinants of life satisfaction in Asia. *Social Indicators Research, 124*, 141–156. https://doi.org/10.1007/s11205-014-0772-x

Nienaber, R., Bussin, M.H.R., & Henn, C.M. (2011). The relationship between personality types and reward preferences. *Acta Commercii, 1*, 56–79.

Nomaguchi, K.M. (2011). Marital status, gender, and home-to-job conflict among employed parents. *Journal of Family Issues, 33*(3), 271–294. https://doi.org/10.1177/0192513X11415613

Noor, N.M. (2003). Work- and family-related variables, work-family conflict and women's well-being: Some observations. *Community, Work & Family, 6*(3), 297–319. https://doi.org/1080/1366880032000143474

OECD (2011). *Society at a glance 2011: OECD social indicators*. OECD. Retrieved n.d., from https://www.oecd.org

Olivier, A.L., & Rothmann, S. (2007). Antecedents of work engagement in a multinational oil company. *South African Journal of Industrial Psychology, 33*(3), 49–56. https://doi.org/10.4102/sajip.v33i3.396

O'Neil, D.A., Hopkins, M.M., & Bilimoria, D. (2008). Women's career at the start of the 21st century: Patterns and paradoxes. *Journal of Business Ethics, 80*, 727–743. https://doi.org/10.1007/s10551-007-9465-6

Opie, T., & Henn, S.M. (2013). Work-family conflict and work engagement among mothers: Conscientiousness and neuroticism as moderators. *South African Journal of Industrial Psychology, 39*(1), 1–12. https://doi.org/10.4102/sajip.v39i1.1082

Oyserman, D. (1993). The lens of personhood: Viewing the self and others in a multi-cultural society. *Journal of Personality and Social Psychology, 65*(5), 993–1009. https://doi.org/10.1037/0022-3514.65.5.993

Ozutku, H., & Altindis, S. (2013). The relations between work intensity and work-family conflict in collectivist culture: Evidence from Turkish health care professionals. *Journal of Health Management, 15*(3), 361–382. https://doi.org/10.1177/0972063413492049

Pallant, J. (2011). *SPPS survival manual.* (4th edn.). Buckingham: Open University Press.

Pavot, W., & Diener, E. (1993). Review of the satisfaction with life scale. *Psychological Assessment, 5*, 164–172. https://doi.org/10.1037/1040-3590.5.2.164

Phillips, L., & James, D. (2014). Labour, lodging and linkages: Migrant women's experience in South Africa. *African Studies, 73*(3), 410–431. https://doi.org/10.1080/00020184.2014.962875

Pieterse, M., & Mostert, K. (2005). Measuring the work-home interface: Validation of the survey work-home interaction – (SWING) instrument. *Management Dynamics, 14*(2), 2–15.

Rathi, N., & Barath, M. (2013). Work-family conflict and job and family satisfaction: Moderating effect of social support among police personnel. *Equality, Diversity and Inclusion: An International Journal, 32*, 438–454. https://doi.org/10.1108/EDI-10-2012-0092

Rhoades, L., & Eisenberger, R. (2002). Perceived organizational support: A review of the literature. *Journal of Applied Psychology, 87*, 698–714. https://doi.org/10.1037/0021-9010.87.4.698

Rothmann, S., & Rothmann, S. (2010). Factors associated with employee engagement in South Africa. *South Africa Journal of Industrial Psychology, 36*(2), 1–12. https://doi.org/10.4102/sajip.v36i2.925

Russell, M. (2003). Are urban black families nuclear? A comparative study of black and white South African family norms. *Social Dynamics, 29*(2), 153–176. https://doi.org/10.1080/02533950308628679

Salinas-Jiménez, M., Artés, J., & Salinas-Jiménez, J. (2011). Education as a positional good: A life satisfaction approach. *Social Indicators Research, 103*, 409–426. https://doi.org/10.1007/s11205-010-9709-1

Schafer, M.H., Mustillo, S.A., & Ferraro, K.F. (2013). Age and the tenses of life satisfaction. *Journals of Gerontology, Series B: Psychological Sciences and Social Sciences, 68*(4), 571–579. https://doi.org/10.1093/geronb/gbt038

Schaufeli, W.B., & Bakker, A.B. (2004). Job demands and job resources, and their relationship with burnout and engagement: A multi-sample study. *Journal of Organisational Behaviour, 25*(3), 293–315. https://doi.org/10.1002/job.248

Schaufeli, W.B., Salanova, M., González-Romá, V., & Bakker, A.B. (2002). The measurement of engagement and burnout: A two sample confirmatory factor analytic approach. *Journal of Happiness Studies, 3*, 71–92. https://doi.org/10.1023/A:1015630930326

Schieman, S., & Glavin, P. (2011). Education and work-family conflict: Explanations, contingencies and mental health consequences. *Social Forces, 89*(4), 1341–1362. https://doi.org/10.1093/sf/89.4.1341

Schimmel, J. (2009). Development as happiness: The subjective perception of happiness and UNDP's analysis of poverty, wealth and development. *Journal of Happiness Studies, 10*(1), 93–111. https://doi.org/10.1007/s10902-007-9063-4

Seligman, M.E.P. (2002). *Authentic happiness*. New York: Free Press.

Shanock, L.R., & Eisenberger, R. (2006). When supervisors feel supported: The relationship with subordinates' perceived supervisor support, perceived organisational support and performance. *Journal of Applied Psychology, 91*, 689–695. https://doi.org/10.1037/0021-9010.91.3.689

Sloan, M.M., Evenson-Newhouse, R.J., & Thompson, A.B. (2013). Counting on co-workers: Race, social support and emotional experiences on the job. *Social Psychology Quarterly, 76*, 343–372. https://doi.org/10.1177/0190272513504937

Sonnentag, S. (2003). Recovery, work engagement, and proactive behavior: A new look at the interface between non-work and work. *Journal of Applied Psychology, 88(*3), 518–528. https://doi.org/10.1037/0021-9010.88.3.518

Spreitzer, G. (1995). Psychological empowerment in the workplace: Dimensions, measurement and validation. *Academy of Management Journal, 38*(5), 1442–1465. https://doi.org/10.2307/256865

SPSS Inc. (2013). *SPSS statistics for windows, version 22.00*. Chicago, IL: SPSS Inc.

Stack, S., & Eshleman, J.R. (1998). Marital status and happiness: A 17-nation study. *Journal of Marriage and the Family, 60*, 527–536. https://doi.org/10.2307/353867

Steger, M., Oishi, S., & Kashdan, T. (2009). Meaning in life across the life span: Levels and correlates of meaning in life from emerging adulthood to older adulthood. *The Journal of Positive Psychology, 4*(1), 43–52. https://doi.org/10.1080/17439760802303127

Steyl, B., & Koekemoer, E. (2011). Conflict between work and non-work roles of employees in the mining industry: Prevalence and differences between demographic groups. *South African Journal of Human Resource Management, 9*(1), 1–14. https://doi.org/10.4102/sajhrm.v9i1.277

Takawira, N. (2012). *Job embeddedness, work engagement and turnover intention of staff in a higher education institution.* Unpublished master's dissertation, University of South Africa, Pretoria.

Thomas, L., & Ganster, D. (1995). The impact of family supportive work variables on work-family conflict and strain: A control perspective. *Journal of Applied Psychology, 80*, 6–5. https://doi.org/10.1037/0021-9010.80.1.6

Triandis, H.C. (1989). The self and social behaviour in differing cultural contexts. *Psychological Review, 96*, 506–520. https://doi.org/10.1037/0033-295X.96.3.506

Van Zyl, L., Deacon, E., & Rothmann, S. (2010). Towards happiness: Experiences of work-role fit, meaningfulness and work engagement of industrial/organisational psychologists in South Africa. *South African Journal of Industrial Psychology, 36*(1), 10–20. https://doi.org/10.4102/sajip.v36i1.890

Veenhoven, R. (1991). Is happiness relative? *Social Indicators Research, 24*(1), 1–34. https://doi.org/10.1007/BF00292648

Voydanoff, P. (2004). The effects of work demand and resources on work-to-family conflict and facilitation. *Journal of Marriage and Family, 66*(2), 398–412. https://doi.org/10.1111/j.1741-3737.2004.00028.x

Wegner, T. (2007). *Applied business statistics: Method and excel-based applications.* (2nd edn.). Cape Town, South Africa: Juta.

Williamson, J.C., & Geldenhuys, M. (2014). Positive work experiences and life satisfaction: The moderating effect of gender. *Journal of Psychology in Africa, 24*, 315–320.

Wolf, S. (2012). *Meaning in life and why it matters.* Princeton, NJ: Princeton University Press.

18

Total rewards and its effects on organisational commitment in higher education institutions

Authors:
Calvin M. Mabaso[1]
Bongani I. Dlamini[2]

Affiliations:
[1]Department of Industrial Psychology and People Management, University of Johannesburg, South Africa

[2]Faculty of Management Sciences, Durban University of Technology, South Africa

Corresponding author:
Calvin Mabaso,
calvinm@uj.ac.za

Orientation: Retaining staff with special endeavours within higher education institutions has become a top priority and crucial for any organisational productivity and competiveness. Attracting and retaining talent has remained a critical and complex issue for human capital management in organisations.

Research purpose: The purpose of this study was to investigate the impact of total rewards on organisational commitment measured by Total Rewards Scale and Organisational Commitment Questionnaire.

Motivation for the study: There is paucity in research on the impact of total rewards on organisational commitment. Commitment of academic staff is significant as higher education institutions are influential in the development of a country.

Research design, approach and method: This study employed the quantitative research method using a survey design. A semi-structured questionnaire was used to collect survey data. A sample of 279 academic staff, which was the total population of participants, was selected for this study.

Main findings: Results show a positive and significant correlation between elements of total rewards (performance management, 0.387; recognition, 0.335; talent development and career opportunities, 0.328; compensation, 0.231; benefits, 0.213; work–life balance, 0.024) and organisational commitment. A variance of 52.3% of total rewards explained organisational commitment. Performance management, compensation, benefits, recognition, talent development and career opportunities significantly predicted organisational commitment. However, work–life balance indicated a negative effect on organisational commitment.

Practical managerial implications: Findings of the study has implications to managers because they have to encourage and promote total rewards in order to enforce talent retention within higher education institutions for the benefit of both institutions and employees.

Contribution: The results are important to managers with great interest in talent retention and can be used as guideline to develop rewards strategy.

Introduction

Key focus of the study

Talent retention has been reported as a significant challenge for organisations operating in a competitive environment. Competing for employees with the required skillset and attracting and retaining employees with expertise has emerged as the biggest challenge for human capital managers. However, in higher education institutions, retaining of staff has become a priority. In addition, higher education is influential in the development of a country. It not only functions as a provider of knowledge but also as a pertinent sector for the nation's grown and societal well-being. Higher education institutions play a significant role in development of skills, which improves the economy; therefore, a high quality of staff is required. Higher education institutions are also considered as a centre of research, knowledge, change and excellence that is skilled in acquiring, generating and transferring knowledge to society. The study aims to investigate the relationship between total rewards and retention factors in relation to organisational commitment in higher education institutions.

Background to the study

Enhancing organisational commitment among academic staff is an essential element because it will eventually result in higher employee commitment, retention and improved performance. Therefore, identifying total rewards that influence organisational commitment in higher education institutions will aid the sector to foster organisational commitment, while maintaining high satisfaction and improved performance. Ihionkhan and Aigbomian (2014) attest that organisations are effective to the degree which it achieve its objectives through committed employees. In addition, Korir and Kepkebut (2016) state that committed employees have a sense of identification and belonging with an organisation. Dubihlela and Rundora (2014) affirm that an increase in global competition has forced businesses to ensure increased employee commitment in order to enable them to have a high level of excellence and competitiveness. Wasiu and Adelajo (2014) suggest that the importance of total rewards cannot be over emphasised. Well-rewarded employees feel that they are valued by the organisation. Anku-Tsede and Kutin (2013) state that rewarding employees is ideal in today's complex human resources market, which leads to continually changing settings in which organisations compete for survival. Obicci (2015) affirms that as employees are the engines of organisational vehicles, total rewards is the fuel through which organisations' stated objectives can be achieved. Ihionkhan and Aigbomian (2014) state that rewards management strategies can be used to increase employee commitment by creating a sense of belonging in the organisation. Increased levels of employee commitment can be achieved through effective rewards management strategies. Korir and Kipkebut (2016) advised organisations to take actions such that employee commitment can be obtained through total rewards management.

Research purpose and objectives

There is a limited research investigating specifically the relationship between total rewards and organisational commitment both locally and internationally. The main purpose of this study was to investigate the impact of total rewards on organisational commitment. The objectives of the study were to investigate the relationship between total rewards and organisational commitment. In addition, the following research questions were investigated:

- Research question 1: What is the relationship between total rewards and organisational commitment?
- Research question 2: Which total rewards elements influence organisational commitment significantly?

Significance of the study

Highly qualified and experienced employees of the academic institutions are continuously leaving in search of greener pastures and opportunities in other institutions and in the private sector. Those left behind may end up underperforming owing to low motivation because of insufficient reward strategies (Al-Jarradi, 2011). This study aims to assist the management of universities of technology to have the opportunity to be more aware about the influence of total rewards on organisational commitment. The findings of the research should also contribute to broader understanding in both public and private sectors on the significant role of total rewards in organisational commitment among employees. The study will benefit other institutions of higher learning, that is, traditional universities, universities of technology to understand total rewards that best drive organisational commitment.

Literature review

Organisational commitment

Commitment in the workplace is a concept that has attracted a great deal of attention from scholars in many disciplines, including industrial psychology, organisational behaviour, management, business administration and public administration (Cohen, 2007). In addition, high interest in research, which is concerned with organisational commitment of employees, has been observed within the private sector, public sector and higher education sector (Dixit & Bhati, 2012). Khan et al. (2014) state that organisational commitment is a link, association or bond of the employee with the institution, a psychosomatic state that distinguishes the individual association with the proposition for the decision to carry on attachment to the organisation. Lamba and Choudhary (2013) view organisational commitment as the individual psychological attachment to the organisation, and commitment represents something beyond loyalty to an organisation and involves an active relationship with the organisation such that individuals are willing to dedicate their talents in order to contribute to the organisation's well-being.

SamGnanakkan (2010) states that organisational commitment is a bi-dimensional concept that includes an attitudinal and a behavioural aspect. Committed employees have an active curiosity, a passion for learning, a willingness to challenge the status quo and an eagerness to experiment with new methods and strategies (Jafri, 2010). In addition, Cunningham (2012) states that an employee with a high level of organisational commitment wishes to maintain membership of the organisation, and this commitment differs from other types, such as occupational commitment. Welty, Burton and Wells (2014) reveal that employees with higher level of organisational commitment will be less likely to engage in job search behaviours as they would wish to stay and be associated with their organisation. In addition, employees with high level of commitment contributes positively to the organisation. In addition, organisational commitment encompasses an employee's belief in an organisation's goals and values, and reflects a desire by an employee to remain a member of the organisation and be loyal to it. Committed employees have an active curiosity, a passion for learning, a willingness to challenge the status quo and an eagerness to experiment with new methods and strategies (Jafri, 2010). Organisational commitment is a psychological state that impels an individual towards a course of action of relevance to one or more targets (Smith, Mitchell & Mitchell, 2009). Therefore, organisational commitment results in positive attitudes to jobs and affects outcomes like employee's intention to leave, organisational citizenship behaviour, performance and job satisfaction (Neininger, Lehmann-Willenbrock, Kauffeld & Henschel, 2010). However, human resources practices like total rewards influence the commitment of employees in both positive and negative manner (Döckel, 2003; Lumley, 2010). Hence, these practices are significant in retaining talent within organisations.

Total rewards that retain talent

In order to attract, retain and satisfy committed employees to the organisation, employers need appropriate total rewards (Obicci, 2015). Owing to competition for scarce skills, the attraction and retention of quality employees has emerged as the biggest challenge in human capital management (Terera & Ngirande, 2014). Enhancing organisational commitment among employees is an essential element because that will result in higher employee commitment, enhancing retention, increasing their job satisfaction and improving performance (Omotayo, Pavithra, & Adenike, 2014). In addition, bringing out the effects of total rewards will assist organisations foster commitment among employees. Research by Armstrong, Brown and Reilly (2010) reveals that competitive wages and benefits have repeatedly been listed as a means of attracting and retaining employees. Chelangat and Gachunga's (2016) study reveals that total rewards are considered as one of the tools for enhancing organisational commitment. Obicci (2015) attests that total rewards play a vital role in job satisfaction and enhances employee commitment with their respective organisations. Wages, therefore, influence the attraction and retention of the workforce. Organisations need to look for alternative methods of retaining key talent to ensure organisational success (Mabaso, 2016). Hence, total rewards can be used in order to enforce talent retention among academic staff in higher education institutions.

Total rewards

WorldatWork (2015) recommended a total rewards model with six essential elements, which are discussed in detail below. WorldatWork (2015) asserts that these elements of total rewards collectively define an organisation's strategy to attract, motivate, retain and engage employees.

Compensation as element of total rewards

Compensation is the reward that employees receive in exchange for performing organisational tasks (Omotayo, Pavithra & Adenike, 2014). In addition, WorldatWork (2015) postulates that compensation refers to remuneration provided by the employer for services rendered by employees, which include skills, time and their efforts. WorldatWork (2015) affirms that compensation consists of both fixed and variable pay, and it is sometimes tied to performance. Martocchio (2013) states that compensation represents both intrinsic and extrinsic rewards employees receive for performing their jobs. Intrinsic compensation reflects employee's psychological mindsets that result from performing their jobs. Extrinsic compensation includes both monetary and non-monetary rewards (Martocchio, 2013). Total compensation is 'the total of all rewards provided to employees in return for their services' (Phonsanam, 2010:6). Ray and Ray (2011) observed that the main reason people work for is compensation. Rose (2014) confirms that compensation forms part of the elements of total rewards aiming to attract and retain talent in organisations.

Fringe benefits as element of total rewards

WorldatWork (2015) states that benefits comprise non-monetary rewards to supplement financial compensation that employees receive. Martocchio (2013) states that fringe benefits include any variety of programmes that provide time off, employee services and protection programmes. According to Van der Westhuizen (2017), fringe benefits refer to indirect forms of compensation which are intended to attract, retain and motivate employees. Rose (2014) attests that fringe benefits consist of non-cash parts of the reward that are provided by the employer either to all employees or differentiated by level. Employee benefits consist of arrangements made by employers to enhance their employees' well-being. The benefits are provided in addition to pay and form important parts of the total rewards package (Armstrong, 2012). Benefit packages for employees are integral to the financial reward package, and for many organisations, the employer brand determines the type of benefits offered, which turn, support the messages to be delivered via the employer brand.

Work-life balance as element of total rewards

WorldatWork (2015) states that work–life programmes are intended and introduced as policies that enable employers to reach a better work–life balance. This factor includes the extent to which a specific job is interesting and challenging to an individual, the degree to which the job provides the opportunity for an individual to keep abreast of new things (WorldatWork, 2015). According to Mukhtar (2012), integrating and maintaining work–life balance into our lives is the current need. Rumpel and Medcof (2006) attest that usually the balance time spent at work and home is included in the work environment. Flexible working is one of the most important aspects for a balanced life (Hondor, 2014).

Performance as element of total rewards

Aguinis (2013) defines performance management as a continuous process of identifying, measuring and developing the performance of individuals, teams and aligning performance with the strategic goals of the organisation. In addition, Swanepoel et al. (2014) affirm that performance management is an action based on performance measures and reporting, which results in improvement in employee behaviour, motivation and work processes as well as promoting innovation. Performance management is viewed more broadly as a management tool that aims to improve the performance of an organisation (Goh, 2012).

Recognition as element of total rewards

Rose (2014) states that recognition refers to a process of acknowledging or giving special attention to a high level of accomplishment or performance, such as customer care or support to colleagues, which is not dependent on achievement against a given target or objective. Greene (2011) attests that recognition can be used in lieu of financial awards, as particularly it could be argued that people used time that theoretically should have been spent on other organisational businesses and that the salary provided compensation. Abu Bakar, Mohamad and Sharmeela-Banu (2015) posit that recognition is the demonstration of appreciation for a level of performance, an achievement or a contribution to an objective. It can be confidential or public, causal or formal and it is always in addition to pay. The link between recognition, teamwork and job satisfaction is an important occurrence to take note of as it indicates that dimensions, which constitute job satisfaction, do not necessarily act alone in determining the job satisfaction of employees. The lack of recognition would not lead to job dissatisfaction, but employees are unlikely to be unmotivated (Smerek & Peterson, 2007).

Talent development and career opportunities as element of total rewards

It is a set of learning experiences intended to improve employees' functional expertise and capabilities. It motivates employees to complete their tasks quickly which in turn improves their productivity (Hondor, 2014). WorldatWork (2015) states that career opportunities involve a strategy for employees to develop their career goals, which may include advancement into a more responsible position in an organisation. Greene (2011) affirms that the investment in training and development is to increase capacity among employees which will enable career opportunities in the workplace. Martocchio (2013) concurs that talent development will enable employees to maintain their focus and assume greater responsibilities and advance in the organisation hierarchy.

Research hypothesis

Based on the above literature, the following hypothesis was developed:

- **Hypothesis 1 (H_1):** There is a positive relationship between total rewards and organisational commitment.

Research design

Research approach

In the present study, a quantitative research design was employed using the survey questionnaire. The aim of the quantitative research is to describe patterns, trends and relationships in numerical data (Lochmiller & Lester, 2017). The main reason for choosing this method was that variables used in the present study could be easily measured quantitatively. In addition, the quantitative research method is concerned with the facts or responses of participants (Creswell, 2014). The most common characteristic of quantitative studies is generalisability of the results. Generalisability is the assumption that data from a sample represent the larger population from which the sample is drawn. Lochmiller and Lester (2017) affirm that in the quantitative research method, the research assumes that the results represent the broader population on some measures.

Research method

Research participants

This study was conducted in the higher education sector of South Africa. The target population in the present study comprised 279 (University of Technology A = 79; University of Technology B = 200) academic staff from two universities of technology (UOT) in Gauteng and Free State (from level of lecturers, senior lecturers, head of departments and professors). Of the 279 participants, 225 returned the questionnaires to the researcher. However, upon scrutiny it was discovered that 23 respondents did not answer the majority of the questions. These questionnaires were therefore discarded completely. A response rate of 72.4% was achieved. Therefore, questionnaires returned for analysis equated to n = 202 questionnaires which was appropriate to be used on the study. An analysis of the demographic profile of respondents (Table 1) has been distributed to as per response from both universities of technology. In addition, Table 1 reveals that 50.5% (n = 102) of the respondents were female, whereas 49.5% (n = 100) were male. After collapsing the respondents' ages, it emerged that the largest group of respondents (43.6%; n = 88) were aged between 30 and 45 years. In addition, 38.1% (n = 77) of the respondents were in possession of a master's degree. In terms of racial group, Africans (68.8%; n = 139) constituted the highest number. With regard to the position occupied, the largest group of

TABLE 1: Demographic profile of respondents (N = 202).

Variable	Categories	UOT A	UOT B	N	%
Gender	Male	34	66	100	49.5
	Female	45	57	102	50.5
Age	18–29	18	32	49	24.3
	30–45	22	66	88	43.6
	46–64	37	24	61	30.2
	> 65	2	2	4	1.9
Race	African	41	108	139	68.8
	Indian	3	12	14	6.9
	White	29	12	41	20.3
	Mixed race	6	2	8	4.0
Tenure	0–1 year	18	4	22	10.9
	1–4 years	13	37	50	24.8
	5–7 years	13	55	68	33.7
	7–15 years	35	27	62	30.7
Qualification	Honours degree	7	21	33	16.3
	Master's degree	36	33	77	38.1
	PhD	7	10	17	8.4
	B.Tech	17	20	35	17.3
	M.Tech	5	28	33	16.3
	D.Tech	7	0	7	3.5
Rank	Lecturer	70	111	181	89.6
	Senior lecturer	5	9	14	6.9
	Associate professor	0	1	1	0.5
	Professor	2	0	2	1.0
	Head of department	0	4	4	2.0

UOT, universities of technology.

respondents (89.6%; n = 181) were lecturers, followed by senior lecturers (6.9%; n = 14), with associate professors (0.5%; n = 1) being the least in number.

Measuring instrument

A structured questionnaire was designed to gather information from participants. The current study used two measuring instruments; that is, 'Total Rewards Questionnaire' and 'Organisational Commitment Questionnaire'. Total Rewards Questionnaire was adopted from WorldatWork Rewards (2015), while Meyer and Allen (1997) developed Organisational Commitment Questionnaire. These two questionnaires were administered to the selected respondents. Both these instruments are based on the five-point Likert scale. The respondents were asked to indicate the extent of their agreement or disagreement with the statements on a scale of 1–5, where 1 would mean that they strongly disagreed and 5 would mean that they strongly agreed with the statement provided.

Ethical consideration and research procedure

Permission to conduct the research was obtained from the participating universities of technology. Research participants were requested to participate in the study voluntarily by completing questionnaires. A covering letter accompanied each questionnaire stating the purpose of the research and guaranteeing protection of their identity as this was an anonymous survey. A total of 279 questionnaires were distributed to all academic staff using a personal method of data collection. To ensure confidentiality, questionnaires were to be returned in enclosed envelopes provided during distribution.

Reliability

Maree (2017) states that reliability refers to the consistency or dependability of a measuring instrument. A measuring instrument that is reliable will produce the same results if a variable is repeatedly measured under almost identical circumstances. The Cronbach's alpha was calculated for each construct to determine the scale reliability. Thurston and McNall (2010) reported that Cronbach's alpha should range from the lowest of 0.68 and to the highest of 0.93. The Total Rewards Scale results (0.822).

Data analysis

Data were analysed with the aid of the Statistical Package for the Social Sciences (SPSS version 24). Descriptive statistics was used to analyse biographical information. Initially, demographic data of the subjects, frequencies and the scores of the overall work-related factors as well as measures of central tendency were established. Pearson correlation analysis and linear regression were computed on all the variables.

Ethical considerations

The study accompanied a letter explaining the ethical considerations involved, notably that participating in the study was a voluntary exercise and that the respondents could withdraw from the study at any point.

Results

The following results will be presented: correlation and regression analysis.

Research question 1 and hypothesis 1

In order to answer the first research question to determine the relationship between total rewards and organisational commitment and hypothesis 1, correlation analysis was performed to test the strength and directions of the relationship between variables as illustrated in Table 2.

Pearson correlations allowed the researcher to identify the direction and strength of the relationship between each variable. As illustrated in Table 2, significant and positive relationships were observed between variables of total rewards and organisational commitment. The results of the correlation indicate a positive and significant relationship between the elements of total rewards and organisational commitment (performance management, 0.387; recognition, 0.335; talent development and career opportunities, 0.328; compensation, 0.231; benefits, 0.213; work–life balance, 0.024). The results in Table 2 reveal a positive and significant relationship between organisational commitment and four elements of total rewards (performance management, recognition, talent development and career opportunities, compensation and benefits). No significant relationship between work–life balance and organisational commitment was observed. This reveals that academic employees in higher education institutions will be committed if these elements of total rewards are provided by the employer. Based on the results in Table 2, the relationship between total rewards and organisational commitment is positive and the

TABLE 2: Significant Pearson correlations.

Variables	1	2	3	4	5	6	7
Compensation	1.000	-	-	-	-	-	-
Benefits	0.087	1	-	-	-	-	-
Work–life balance	0.045	-0.172*	1.000	-	-	-	-
Performance management	0.285**	-0.011	0.307**	1.000	-	-	-
Recognition	0.184**	0.073	0.067	0.335**	1.000	-	-
Talent development and career opportunities	0.121	0.088	0.077	0.291**	0.335**	1.000	-
Organisational commitment	0.231**	0.213**	0.024	0.387**	0.328**	0.404**	1.000

*, Correlation is significant at the 0.05 level (2-tailed); **, Correlation is significant at the 0.01 level (2-tailed).

TABLE 3: Regression and model summary and analysis of variance results.

Total rewards	R	R^2	Adjusted R^2	F	p
Model 1	0.503ᵃ	0.523	0.516	114.316	0.000

TABLE 4: Contribution of independent variables for predicting organisational commitment.

Independent variables	Standardised beta coefficients	T	I
Compensation	0.103	1.645	0.101
Benefits	0.178	2.926	0.004*
Work–life balance	-0.064	-1.006	0.316
Performance management	0.318	4.709	0.000*
Recognition	0.160	1.440	0.151
Talent development and career opportunities	0.213	3.406	0.001*

*, Statistically significant at $p < 0.05$.

hypothesis is accepted that total rewards is positively related to organisational commitment. Pallant (2010) explains that the strength of the association between variables depends on the size (whether positive or negative) of the correlation value. A value ranging from 0.10 to 0.29 denotes a small relationship, values between 0.30 and 0.49 represent a medium relationship and a value of 0.5–1.0 depicts a strong relationship between the variables.

Multivariate regression analysis was undertaken to determine the effects of total rewards on organisational commitment among academic staff. In Table 3, the regression model summary and ANOVA results are reported. Regression analysis is a statistical technique that focuses on investigating and modelling the relationship between variables (Montgomery, Peck & Vining, 2012). Regression analysis aids to measure the relative strength of an independent variable on a dependent variable.

As illustrated in Table 3, the significant F-ratio infers that the regression model predicts effects of total rewards. The value of R^2 indicates that the model tested is significant, that is, the value of R^2 is 0.523, which means that there is 52.3% relationship between independent variable (total rewards) and dependent variable (organisational commitment). Cohen, Manion and Morrison (2011) suggested that $R^2 > 0.5$ indicates a strong model fit. Therefore, these results confirm that total rewards have a greater impact on organisational commitment.

Additionally, regression was conducted as to evaluate the independent variables prediction of organisational commitment and is delineated in Table 4.

These results outlined in Table 4 suggest that compensation ($\beta = 0.103$), benefits ($\beta = 0.178$), performance management ($\beta = 0.318$), recognition ($\beta = 0.160$), talent development and career opportunities ($\beta = 0.213$) all have a statistically positive effect on organisational commitment. However, work–life balance ($\beta = -0.64$) has a negative effect on organisational commitment. This means that work–life balance does not influence organisational commitment. In terms of the largest beta coefficients recorded, performance management and talent development and career opportunities seem to make the strongest contribution to explaining organisational commitment. The t-values of the independent variables are greater than 0.107. Ndungu (2017) states that values greater than 0.107 indicate a strong impact of the predicting quality of the coefficient.

Discussion

The purpose of this study was to examine the impact of total rewards on organisational commitment among academic staff in higher education institutions. This was important as there is paucity on the studies that deals with impact of total rewards in higher education institutions. The findings in the current study reveal that performance management has a significant and positive relationship with organisational commitment. This finding is in line with the results of Abrokwah and Ge (2017) and Asamany and Shaorong (2018). In addition, the findings of the present study demonstrated the relationship between total rewards and organisational commitment. Moreover, these findings are in line with findings of Obicci (2015); Eslami and Gharakhani (2012) reported strong association between job-related factors, which include compensation and organisational commitment. Work- and job-related features are powerfully related to organisational commitment (Al-Kahtani, 2012). Saeed et al. (2013) reported that compensation and job characteristics have a weak positive and significant impact on organisational commitment, but career development has insignificant impact on organisational commitment. Saqib, Abrar, Sabir, Bashir and Baig's (2015) study indicated that there is a relationship between the tangible, intangible rewards and organisational commitment. The empirical results supported the relationship between the tangible rewards and organisational commitment. These findings showed that rewards had a positive and significant impact on the organisational commitment, which are in line with the literature. The Ndungu (2017) study reported that recognition and career opportunities are associated with increased performance among employees, which will enable them to be committed to their employer. In addition, Ndungu (2017) attests that if employees are not satisfied with salaries and fringe benefits, they will have no choice other than to look for alternative organisations that will be providing better salaries and benefits. Cao, Chen and Song's (2013) study confirms that total rewards elements (compensation, benefits, work–life balance, performance management and recognition, talent development and career opportunities) can be used to reduce turnover intention among employees. If total rewards are implemented fairly, employees can be committed to the organisation. Performance management specialists over the years have learnt that for organisations to achieve outstanding results in the competitive environment, practice of performance management is required. Thus, effective performance management system will aid organisations to improve organisational commitment and talent retention. Greene (2011) concurs that rewarding performance equitably and effectively is critical for organisations that aim to enforce organisational commitment.

Chelangat and Gachunga (2016) affirm that total reward practices play a pivotal role in organisational commitment among employees. Total rewards change the way employees think about work, and attracts and retains high-performing employees. If organisations want to increase organisational commitment, they should review their reward management practices (Chelangat & Gachunga, 2016). The current study is in line with the study of Cheah, Chong, Yeo and Pee (2016) which revealed that talent development and compensation significantly affect organisational commitment. Korir and Kipkebut (2016) reported a positive significant relationship between total rewards and organisational commitment. The study suggested that financial rewards have an effect on organisational commitment and suggested that universities should carry out salary revisions in order to develop a reward management structure that is externally competitive, internally fair and consistent with the current acceptable international rates. Research by Zaitouni, Sawalha and Sharif (2011) suggests that employees who are provided with benefits, such as increased salary, bonuses and promotion, develop strong feelings of loyalty to the organisation. Perceptions of fair rewards and justice lead to higher levels of satisfaction and long-term commitment too.

Implications for managers and recommendations

The findings of this study, which support previous studies in the area, have significant implications as it further confirmed that total rewards impact organisational commitment. These results have implications to managers because they have to encourage and promote total rewards in order to enforce talent retention within higher education institutions for the benefit of both institutions and employees. Moreover, higher education institutions need to create an environment in which employees can work effectively. Recognising and rewarding employees effectively will further increase commitment among academics. Lastly, performance management cannot be overlooked as it has been done previously, this study reveal a great influence in ensuring organisational commitment and talent retention.

Conclusion

For higher education institutions to attract, retain and motivate talent, sound rewards strategy needs to be formulated. Total rewards can be used to retain talent. In addition, performance management should be improved as it influences organisational commitment among academic staff. Results of the present study can be used to craft a rewards strategy aimed at retaining high-performing resources.

Acknowledgements

The authors would like to thank academic staff who took part in the study.

Competing interests

The authors declare that they have no financial or personal relationships that may have inappropriately influenced them in writing this article.

Authors' contributions

The study was conducted by C.M.M. as part of the Doctor of Philosophy in Management Sciences: Human Resources Management research project and was responsible for preparing the manuscript. B.I.D. was the promoter and edited the article for publication.

References

Abu Bakar, J.A., Mohamad, Z.Z., & Sharmeela-Banu, S.A. (2015). Factors affecting female lecturer retention in private higher institution in Perak. *International Journal of Academic Research in Business and Social Sciences, 5*(1), 17–25.

Abrokwah, E., & Ge, Y. (2017). Mediating role of work motivation: Does organizational commitment impact on Non-Governmental Organizations (NGOs) performances? *Transylvanian Review Journal, XXV*(17), 15–38.

Aguinis, H. (2013). *Performance management* (3rd ed.). Upper Saddle River, NJ: Pearson Prentice Hall.

Al-Jarradi, K.S. (2011). *An investigation into the effectiveness of the reward system in the government sector in the Sultanate of Oman and the potential for introducing a total reward strategy*. (Unpublished PhD thesis). University of Manchester, Manchester.

Al-Kahtani, S.N. (2012). An exploratory study of organisational commitment, demographic variables and job & work related variables among employees in Kingdom of Saudi Arabia. *Online International Interdisciplinary Research Journal, 3*, 1–13.

Anku-Tsede, A.O., & Kitui, E. (2013). Total rewards concept: A key motivational tool for corporate Ghana. *Business and Economic Research, 3*(2), 173–182. https://doi.org/10.5296/ber.v3i2.4291

Armstrong, M. (2012). *Armstrong's handbook of reward management practice*. London: Kogan Page.

Armstrong, M., Brown, D., & Reilly, P. (2010). *Evidence-based reward management: Creating measurable business impact from your pay and reward practices*. London: Kogan Page.

Asamany, A., & Shaorong, S. (2018). The ripple effects of performance management on employees' perceptions and affective commitment among small and medium scale enterprises (SMEs). *International Journal of Business Administration, 9*(1), 55–63. https://doi.org/10.5430/ijba.v9n1p55

Cao, Z., Chen, J., & Song, Y. (2013). Does total rewards reduce the core employees' turnover intention? *International Journal of Business and Management, 8*(20), 62–75. https://doi.org/10.5539/ijbm.v8n20p62

Cheah, C.S., Chong, W.V.S., Yeo, S.F., & Pee, K.W. (2016). An empirical study on factors affecting organisational commitment among Generation X. *Procedia – Social and Behavioral Sciences, 219*, 167–174. https://doi.org/10.1016/j.sbspro.2016.05.002

Chelangat, Z., & Gachunga, H. (2016). Effect of reward management practices on organisational commitment in state corporations in Kenya: A case study of Kefr. *The Strategic Journal of Business and Change Management, 3*(3), 325–346.

Cohen, A. (2007). *Dynamics between occupational and organisational commitment in the context of flexible labor markets: A review of literature and suggestions for a future research agenda*. Bremen: Institut Technik und Bildung, UniversitŠt Bremen.

Cohen, L., Manion, L., & Morrison, K. (2011). *Research methods in education*. London: Routledge.

Creswell, J. (2014). *Research design qualitative, quantitative and mixed methods approaches* (4th ed.). Thousand Oaks, CA: Sage.

Cunningham, G.B. (2012). The relationships among commitment to change, coping with change, and turnover intentions. *European Journal of Work and Organisational Psychology, 15*(1), 29–45. https://doi.org/10.1080/13594320500418766

Dixit, V., & Bhati, M. (2012). A study about employee commitment and its impact on sustained productivity in Indian auto-component industry. *European Journal of Business and Social Sciences, 1*(6), 34–51.

Döckel, A. (2003). *The effect of retention factors on organisational commitment: An investigation of high technology employees*. (Unpublished master's thesis). University of Pretoria, South Africa.

Dubihlela, J., & Rundora, R. (2014). Employee training, managerial commitment and the implementation of activity based costing; Impact on performance of SMEs. *The International Business & Economics Research Journal, 13*(1), 27–42.

Eslami, J., & Gharakhani, D. (2012).Organisational commitment and job satisfaction. *ARPN Journal of Science and Technology, 2*(2), 85–91.

Goh, S.C. (2012). Making performance measurement systems more effective in public sector organizations. *Measuring Business Excellence, 16*(1), 31–42. https://doi.org/10.1108/13683041211204653

Greene, R.J. (2011). *Rewarding performance: Guiding principles; custom strategies*. London, United Kingdom: Taylor & Francis Ltd.

Hondor, E.S. (2014). Total rewards model in Romanian companies. *Cross-Cultural Management Journal, 16*(30), 313–319.

Ihionkhan, P.A., & Aigbomian, E.E. (2014). The influence of human resource management practices on organisational commitment: A study of manufacturing organisations in Nigeria. *Indian Journal of Commerce & Management Studies, 5*(1), 18–28.

Jafri, M.H. (2010). Organisational commitment and employee's innovative behaviour. *Journal of Management Research, 10*(1), 62–68.

Khan, M.S., Khan, I., Kundi, G.M., Khan, S., Nawaz, A., Khan, F., & Yar, N.B. (2014). The impact of job satisfaction and organisational commitment on the Intention to leave among the Academicians. *International Journal of Academic Research in Business and Social Sciences, 4*(2), 114–131.

Korir, I., & Kepkebut, D. (2016). The effect of reward management on employees commitment in the Universities of Nakuru Country – Kenya. *Journal of Human Resources Management, 4*(4), 37–48. https://doi.org/10.11648/j.jhrm.20160404.12

Lamba, S., & Choudhary, N. (2013). Impact of HRM practices on organisational commitment of employees. *International Journal of Advancements in Research and Technology, 2*(4), 407–423.

Lochmiller, C.R., & Lester, J.N. (2017). *An introduction to educational research connecting methods to practice* (1st ed.). Los Angeles, CA: Sage.

Lumley, E. (2010). *The relationship between career anchors, job satisfaction and organisational commitment.* (Unpublished master's dissertation). University of South Africa, Pretoria.

Mabaso, C. (2016). *The influence of rewards on talent attraction and retention at a further education and training college in Gauteng.* (Unpublished masters dissertation). Vaal University of Technology, South Africa.

Maree, K. (2017). *First steps in research.* Pretoria, South Africa: Van Schaik Publishers.

Martocchio, J.J. (2013). *Strategic compensation: A human resource management approach* (7th ed.). Upper Saddle River, NJ: Pearson.

Meyer, J., & Allen, N. (1997). *Commitment in the workplace: Theory, research, and application.* Thousand Oaks, CA: Sage.

Montgomery, D.C., Peck, E.A., & Vining, G. (2012). *Introduction to linear regression analysis* (5th ed.). New York: John Wiley & Sons.

Mukhtar, F. (2012). *Work life balance and job satisfaction among faculty at Iowa State University.* (Unpublished doctoral dissertation). Iowa State University, Ames: IA.

Ndungu, D.N. (2017). The effects of rewards and recognition on employee performance in public educational institutions: A case of Kenyatta University, Kenya. *Global Journal of Management and Business Research: Administration and Management, 17*(1), 43–68.

Neininger, A., Lehmann-Willenbrock, N., Kauffeld, S., & Henschel, A. (2010). Effects of team and organisational commitment – A longitudinal study. *Journal of Vocational Behavior, 76*(3), 567–579. https://doi.org/10.1016/j.jvb.2010.01.009

Obicci, P.A. (2015). Influence of total rewards on employee satisfaction and commitment in government organization. *International Journal of Research in Management, Science and Technology, 3*(1), 47–56.

Omotayo, O.A., Pavithra, S., & Adenike, A.A., (2014). Compensation management and organisational commitment in developing economies: Indian perspective. *International Journal of Research in Management, Social Sciences & Technology, 8*(8), 1–15.

Pallant, J. (2010). *SPSS survival manual: A step-by-step guide to data analysis using the SPSS program* (4th ed.). New York: McGraw Hill.

Phonsanam, S.T. (2010). *Total compensation practices and their relationship to hospitality employee retention.* (Unpublished master of science dissertation). University of Nevada, Las Vegas.

Ray, S., & Ray, I.A. (2011). Human resource management practices and its effect on employees' job satisfaction: A study on selected small and medium sized iron and steel firms in India. *Public Policy and Administration Research, 1*(1), 22–31.

Rose, M. (2014). *Reward management.* London: Kogan Page.

Rumpel, S., & Medcof, J.W. (2006). Total rewards: Good fit for tech workers. *Research Technology Management, 49*(5): 27–35.

Saeed, R., Lodhi, R.N., Iqbal, A., Nayyab, H.H., Mussawar, S., & Yaseen, S. (2013). Factors influencing job satisfaction of employees in telecom sector of Pakistan. *Middle-East Journal of Scientific Research, 16*(11), 1476–1482.

SamGnanakkan, S. (2010). Mediating role of organisational commitment on HR practices and turnover intention among ICT professionals. *Journal of Management Research, 10*(1), 39–61.

Saqib, S., Abrar, M., Sabir, H.M., Bashir, M., & Baig, S.A. (2015). Impact of tangible and intangible rewards on organisational commitment: Evidence from the textile sector of Pakistan. *American Journal of Industrial and Business Management, 5*(3), 138–147. https://doi.org/10.4236/ajibm.2015.53015

Smerek, R.E. & Peterson, M. (2007). Examining Herzberg's theory: Improving job satisfaction among non-academic employees at a university. *Research in Higher Education, 48*(2), 229–250.

Smith, J.B., Mitchell, J.R., &Mitchell, R.K. (2009). Entrepreneurial scripts and the new transaction commitment mindset: Extending the expert information processing theory approach to entrepreneurial cognition research. *Entrepreneurship Theory and Practice, 33*(3), 815–844. https://doi.org/10.1111/j.1540-6520.2009.00328.x

Swanepoel, B.J., Erasmus, B.J., Schenk, H.W., & Tshilongamulenzhe, T. (2014). *South African human resource management: Theory and practice* (4th ed.). Cape Town, South Africa: Juta.

Terera, S.R., & Ngirande, H. (2014). The impact of rewards on job satisfaction and employee retention. *Mediterranean Journal of Social Sciences, 5*(1), 481–487. https://doi.org/10.5901/mjss.2014.v5n1p481

Thurston, P.W. Jr., & McNall, L. (2010). Justice perceptions of performance appraisal practices. *Journal of Management Psychology, 25*(3), 201–228. https://doi.org/10.1108/02683941011023712

Van der Westhuizen, E. (2017). *Human Resource Management in Government: A South African perspective of theories, politics and processes* (1st ed.). Cape Town, South Africa: Juta & Co.

Wasiu, D.O., & Adebajo, A.A. (2014). Reward systems and employee performance in Lagos state (a study of selected public secondary schools). *Kuwait Chapter of Arabian Journal of Business and Management Review, 3*(8), 14–23. https://doi.org/10.12816/0018303

Welty, J., Burton, L., & Wells, J.E. (2014). Examining the influence of transformational leadership, leader-member exchange, organisational commitment, job embeddedness and job search on turnover intentions of Division I senior administrators. *Leadership & Organisational Development Journal, 35*(8), 740–755. https://doi.org/10.1108/LODJ-10-2012-0128

WorldatWork. (2015). Total rewards model a framework for strategies to attract, motivate and retain employees. Retrieved from https://www.worldatwork.org/waw/adimLink?id=28330

Zaitouni, M., Sawalha, N.N., & Sharif, A. (2011). The impact of human resource management practices on organisational commitment in the banking sector in Kuwait. *International Journal Business and Management, 6*(6), 108–123. https://doi.org/10.5539/ijbm.v6n6p108

19

Hospital volunteerism as human resource solution: Motivation for both volunteers and the public health sector

Authors:
Guinevere M. Lourens[1,2]
Danielle K. Daniels-Felix[1]

Affiliations:
[1]Ukwanda Centre for Rural Health, Stellenbosch University, South Africa

[2]Department of Nursing and Midwifery, Stellenbosch University, South Africa

Corresponding author:
Guinevere Lourens,
guin@sun.ac.za

Background: A volunteer programme with 50 registered volunteers was established in 2007 at a secondary-level public, semi-rural regional hospital in the Cape Winelands, South Africa. This was a rapid response to the extensive renovations and system changes brought about by the hospital revitalisation initiated in 2006 and the resultant expanded services, which required additional human resources. This study describes the hospital volunteer programme and provides hospital administrators with practical planning guidance for hospital volunteer programme implementation.

Purpose: The purpose of this study is to (1) describe the outcomes of the hospital volunteer programme implementation intervention and (2) to make sound recommendations for volunteer programme implementation.

Methodology and approach: A qualitative case-study methodology was employed using purposive sampling as a technique. Participants were recruited from a public hospital in the Western Cape. A case-study design was applied to explore the hospital volunteer programme implementation. In-depth interviews and a focus group discussion with thematic content analysis of transcripts as well as document reviews were conducted to conclude the study during 2015. The key participants were individually interviewed and included two members of the hospital management, two volunteers and one volunteer coordinator. A focus group discussion consisting of three volunteers was also conducted.

Findings: The findings of this study indicate that a volunteer programme can meet needs and be a motivational force for both the individual volunteer and the organisation. However, it requires co-ordination and some secure funding to remain sustainable. Such a programme holds huge benefits in terms of human resource supplementation, organisational development, as well as the possibility of gainful employment for the previously unemployed.

Practical implications: In practice, a health service contemplating a volunteer programme should develop criteria for recruitment and selection of volunteers, accompanied by the necessary documentation for applications. A coordinator of the volunteer service needs to be identified. Volunteers will need to be orientated, given access to in-service training and supervised. Consideration needs to be given to risk management of vicarious liability by developing a code of conduct, clear roles and responsibilities, managing staff and volunteer relationships and providing emergency care for injuries while on duty as a volunteer.

Introduction

Volunteers play a crucial role within the health care system (Prabhu, Hanley & Kearney, 2008, p. 265). There is scope to further the promise of possibility and opportunity for both the volunteers involved and the hospital in which a volunteer programme is established. Hotchkiss, Fottler and Unruh (2009, p. 127) found a positive relationship between volunteerism and hospital cost saving but suggested a need for further research. The exploration of the sensitive issue of the relationship between volunteer and paid labour is also an area for future research (Handy, Mook & Quarter, 2008, p. 16), which could have implications for volunteerism policy, as well as public leadership.

Penner (2002, p. 448) defined volunteerism as 'long-term, planned prosocial behaviour that benefits strangers and occurs within an organizational setting. Volunteerism has four salient attributes: longevity, planfulness, non-obligatory helping and an organizational context'. Hotchkiss, Unruh and Fottler (2014, p. 15) call for health care executives to share best practices in volunteer recruitment, screening, orientation, training, policies, service guidelines and risk management plans in formalisation of volunteer programmes.

The National Department of Health of South Africa implemented a Hospital Revitalisation Grant to modernise and transform the infrastructure and health technology of public hospitals and improve the access to health care as well as quality of care. A secondary-level, semi-rural, public regional hospital in the Cape Winelands was entered into the Hospital Revitalisation Programme (HRP) in May 2006 and reached practical completion on 23 March 2012.

Hospital revitalisation is an organisational development intervention in its own right as it brings about organisation-wide changes in the physical surroundings, workflow and modernised technology requiring skills training. The expanded services make way for human resource expansion. However, the expanded services were not well aligned to the existing staff establishment, and funding constraints prevented filling of required posts.

The management at this hospital implemented a volunteer programme in 2007 as one of the planned interventions to cope with the rapid change brought about by revitalisation and the expanded services as a result of these renovations. The hospital board initiated a volunteer programme whereby 50 individuals volunteered to assist by working in the pharmacy, linen bank, porter service and cleaning team, or to be part of the Pamper Team, a group of volunteers doing hair and nail care. Although the number of volunteers on any given day may fluctuate, the hospital has subsequently retained this number of a maximum of 50 volunteers, which can be accommodated daily in the volunteer service.

Following this opportunity to volunteer, there have been numerous success stories arising from this programme. The advantage of being volunteers at a hospital when a position becomes vacant is that they have a competitive edge on application and during the interview over other candidates. However, the literature should culminate on success stories of volunteers at hospitals such as the case illustrated of the hospital in this study.

The literature search revealed many hospitals providing case studies on the success of their volunteer programmes, but they have used 'volunteer' as a broader term meaning an individual who provides work for no profit. It should be noted that there are different categories of volunteers: professional volunteers (retired nurses and doctors and allied health professionals) and non-professional volunteers (housekeepers, cleaners, porters, etc.). Most of the literature focuses on professional volunteers. There is a scarcity of literature concentrating on non-professional volunteers in hospitals, who have secured jobs as a result of their non-profit labour experience.

This area of volunteerism has been under-researched because volunteerism in health care organisations in a broader context usually involves patient care and administration. In this particular study, volunteerism involves working in various service support departments such as pharmacy, medical records, kitchen, linen bank, porter service and cleaning and Pamper teams. The volunteers in this study do not assist with caring for the physical health of the patients.

Volunteers assist an organisation to 'increase capacity and resources within the health services' (Jones, 2004, p. 5). Connors (2011, p. 117) concurs that volunteers enable expansion of service despite budgetary limitations. International studies on volunteerism indicate that volunteers perform tasks in different areas such as transporting patients, assisting with clerical duties and providing information. A study conducted by Jones (2004) indicated that 60% of the participants within the health setting found that volunteers improved services by supporting staff and adding value to the services being rendered. According to Handy and Srinivasan (2004), volunteers are assigned to: escort patients on outings, provide companionship and support to patients, assist with recreational and social programmes, help with shopping and doing errands, and accompany patients from one facility to another and administrative work. However, in Japanese hospitals, volunteer activities were related to 'recreation, conversation partners, music and entertainment, wheelchair pushing and helping with administration' (Aragaki, Saito, Takahashi & Kai, 2007). The dynamics of volunteer activities show how volunteer roles are emerging through closer contact with the patients and how volunteer positions have evolved over the years.

According to Connors (2011), all volunteer involvement generates risks. Ellis (2012) suggests that risk assessment is always valid, as an organisation should want to keep all participants safe.

Hotchkiss et al. (2014) indicate a gap within volunteerism theory and mention that the types of positions in which volunteers are used should be measured in future research. Because this area is under-researched, it is advisable that studies are done on non-professional volunteers in hospitals. Studies should evaluate success stories of non-professional volunteer programmes in other hospitals and examine whether there are rewards or benefits that go along with being a volunteer.

Research aim or purpose

This study aimed to provide a description of a hospital volunteer programme, which will contribute to the body of knowledge on hospital volunteer programme implementation. The public health sector and role-players in public health management stand to benefit from this research.

Theoretical framework

The conceptual framework in qualitative research utilises concepts from existing theories and relates the findings to these. Theories help to understand the phenomenon and incorporate our understanding of the setting, people, processes and the interrelationships (Maxwell, 2012, pp. 85–87).

Motivational theories build on the extrinsic conditions which stimulate certain behaviours and the intrinsic responses sustained by sources of energy or motives which drive action (Jooste, 2009, p. 69). The humanistic content theories of motivation focus on inner needs that motivate behaviour and are associated with thinkers such as Maslow, Alderfer, Atkinson, Herzberg, McClelland and McGregor. Maslow's theory of motivation was helpful in understanding the motives served by volunteerism. The Maslow (1954) motivation theory is one of the best known, influential theories on workplace motivation, which suggests that humans have a hierarchy of needs and that when basic psychological and physical needs are met, the focus on safety, a sense of belonging, esteem and self-actualisation follows.

Blanchard (2006, p. 31) found that motivations to volunteer in a hospital are complex. Volunteers can be sustained by non-altruistic motives of the social benefits and upskilling for personal enhancement. Besides personal fulfilment, generosity was also found to be influential in volunteering. Other studies highlight social rewards of volunteering and the draw of personal and indirect economic rewards.

Methods

A case-study design with a qualitative approach was utilised for this study. In case-study research, all evidence is collated in data collection and qualitative methods are regarded as primary. The case-study design involves an intensive exploration of a single unit of study (Bowling, 2009, p. 434) such as the hospital being studied and was therefore selected as most suited to exploring this public secondary regional hospital institution volunteer programme.

The goal of qualitative studies is not to generalise but to understand the processes and meanings for the specific setting. The guiding principle in a qualitative study is selecting the setting and individual or participants who are most accessible and conducive to gaining the understanding on what you want to know (Maxwell, 2012, pp. 94–95).

Qualitative content analysis with thematic coding was applied to the data set.

The interviews took place in private office spaces and the focus group in the boardroom of the hospital, which was most convenient for the participants. Five participants from the hospital were asked to participate in individual interviews and another three in a focus group. The individual interviewees included two members of hospital management, two volunteers and one volunteer coordinator. The focus group consisted of three volunteers. A purposive sampling technique was used and the eight participants joined in the study. The interview schedule and focus group consisted of four questions and provided information regarding the participant's involvement and experience of the volunteer programme, the challenges experienced and their recommendations going forward. With the consent of the participants, the interviews were recorded and transcribed verbatim. The interviews and focus groups were conducted face to face and did not exceed an hour.

The qualitative methodology adopted included the following data collection methods: individual interviews and a focus group with purposively sampled key participants and the analysis of documents pertaining to the volunteer implementation programme. Although the in-depth interviews and the focus group were the primary source of data collection, reviewing documents was also used to build a description of the case. The following documents were reviewed: (1) volunteer recruitment document, (2) application documents developed, (3) the volunteer register, (4) attendance register and (5) statistics on volunteer training and those gainfully employed at the hospital or other placements during the course of revitalisation. The different sources of data enabled multi-method data collection, which serves to triangulate data (Ross, 2012, pp. 134–135).

Ethical considerations

Ethics approval for the study was obtained from the Human Research Ethics Committee of Stellenbosch University.

Findings

In May 2007, a volunteer programme was established by employing a part-time coordinator. She had to coordinate the volunteers who wanted to assist the hospital for 4 h daily, initially on week days only. She was mentored by an experienced manager in the Radiology Department. She initially handled a team of 30 volunteers daily and was assisted by the whole of the Radiology Department, which adopted this campaign and assisted her whenever assistance was needed or when she was on leave or off sick.

The programme was mainly advertised by word of mouth and soon the number of volunteers had to be restricted to 50, which could be handled on a daily basis. The volunteers included semi-skilled and unskilled people. Volunteers worked as cleaners, porters, administrative clerks, medical records clerks, stores assistants and linen assistants. There was also the establishment of the Pampering Team, which renders hair and nail care to clients admitted to hospital in a state of neglect or those far from home with no relatives close by. The necessities such as a trolley with stationery, shampoo, soap, and hair and nail equipment for this programme were funded by the Hospital Facility Board.

With the introduction of Clinicom (a new client record database) to the hospital, new human resource challenges emerged, and dedicated volunteers were trained to assist some of the service departments with this added work load. The programme was extended on request by the emergency centre to include having volunteers on duty over weekends to assist the patients and their family or as escorts in the waiting rooms by handing out beverages for those waiting for long periods of time. Volunteers also assist the patients by asking the nursing staff about waiting times. Later volunteers were utilised as queue marshals in the busy outpatients department.

The one aspect regarded by informants as the main success of the programme was the number of volunteers who were subsequently permanently employed, both at this hospital and at other public health sector institutions or the private sector. By the conclusion of this study, seven people were employed as porters, eight people as general assistants, seven people as clerks, five people in the food service department and one person in the linen bank. Six people were employed as pharmacy assistants, two at this institution and the others at other institutions. There are also many volunteers working as paid locums, 6 in the pharmacy, 20 as general assistants and 1 as a porter.

The five participants were interviewed individually, and three members joined in a focus group discussion on the programme experience, challenges and recommendations. Those involved in the programme at the hospital expressed pride in their contribution, to give the volunteers a chance to gain experience and provide them with testimonials via the coordinator when needed at the end of their volunteer time. Two main themes emerged, namely economic and altruistic drivers. Four sub-themes emerged from the participants' responses and the quotes are presented below. These themes are displayed diagrammatically in Figure 1. Responses given in Afrikaans have been translated into English and are indicated by square brackets. Each theme is explained and participant quotes from the interviews and focus group discussion are added to illuminate the meaning of each theme.

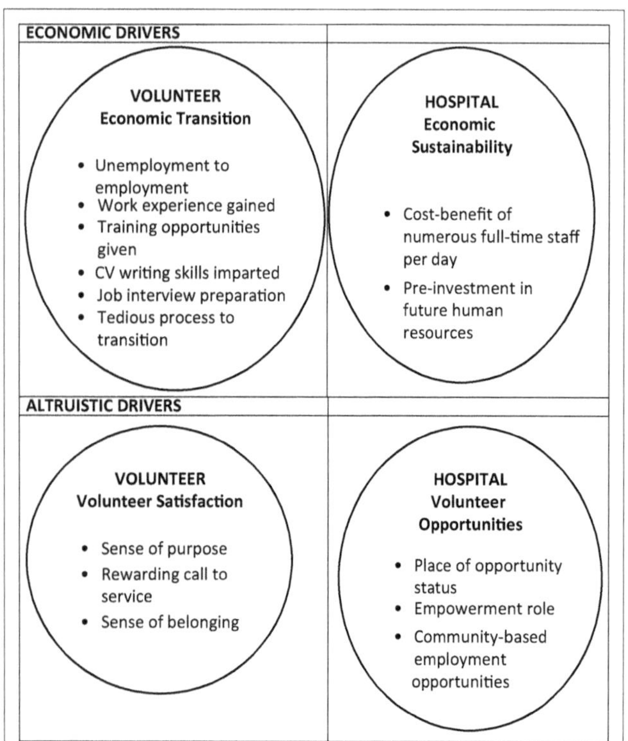

FIGURE 1: Economic and altruistic drivers in volunteer programme.

Economic transition

For the volunteers, the opportunity to be a volunteer in this programme led to some form of economic transition, albeit a tedious process. For some volunteers, it took many years of volunteering before they realised this transition.

The transition was moving from unemployment to gainful employment, either in positions at the hospital, other health facilities or as contract workers for locum agencies. Volunteers were asked to register with locum agencies and were given preference when paid locum jobs became available. Volunteers were assisted with on-the-job training, gaining work experience, CV-writing skills and job interview skills, all of which were seen as contributing factors towards making this transition. Informants said that it was the power of this possibility which kept them in the programme so long.

The comments included:

> Volunteerism ... is a foot in the door and you get experience ... The volunteers got opportunities to earn money in locum positions; based on the experience they gained. (Respondent 2, Female, Volunteer)

> I can only say to those who want to volunteer, only good can come from volunteering. What you sow, you will reap. You need to be prepared to plough and your heart needs to be right. (Respondent 4, Female, Volunteer)

Economic sustainability

For the hospital, the economic driver for the volunteer programme was the economic benefits it held. The cost-benefit of the volunteer programme totalled the equivalent of 14 full-time staff members in the hours volunteered in various departments. The 'pre-investment' in volunteers in terms of on-the-job training paid off when those volunteers successfully applied for vacant posts. The transition into the job was relatively seamless as pre-knowledge existed about the position and the organisational environment.

The following participant had calculated that the hours put in by volunteers equated to 14 full-time staff members:

> Stats show we recruit the equivalent of 14 full-time workers at the hospital through the volunteer programme. (Respondent 5, Male, Hospital Management)

> Prior investment in people took place and the fact that the volunteers had already been trained in their jobs means that the investments pays off when the person starts working and they already have some skills. (Respondent 5, Male, Hospital Management)

Volunteer satisfaction

For the volunteers, satisfaction came from having a sense of purpose on a daily basis. As they become known at the hospital, they developed a sense of belonging. They described the personal satisfaction of being 'seen', and noticed by others. They acknowledged that it was sometimes a difficult environment with so many diverse people, but found it purposeful.

The comments included:

> I got purpose … and I feel that I belong … I was motivated and felt acknowledged which makes you feel that you belong. (Respondent 3, Male, Volunteer)

> We are in a people business. People are the essence. It is give and take. It is not a high profile job, but purposeful. Being out there is difficult. (Respondent 3, Male, Volunteer)

> I want to add that as a volunteer, you introduce yourself to the staff. They get used to you and it is one of the advantages. If you enter the building, the people get used to you; they see you on a daily basis … Daily visibility – you become known and seen. (Respondent 4, Female, Volunteer)

Volunteer opportunities

The hospital being studied took pride in being seen as a place of opportunity. However, a volunteer coordinator was deemed essential as well as the funding for such a post to make the programme viable and sustainable. Management bought into the volunteer programme, which contributed to the success thereof. Experienced volunteers were used to train new recruits.

The comments included:

> I think one of the great successes is that management bought into it. (Respondent 1, Female, Hospital management)

> He is so valuable for me, because now if we want to place volunteers, we place them with him and he trains them because he knows what it was like when he was a volunteer. (Respondent 1, Female, Hospital management)

> The hospital is now a place of opportunity. (Focus group discussion)

> It was pointed out to us that it was a program where no promises are made. It is a voluntary service, but it can lead to a permanent position at the hospital. (Respondent 3, Male, Volunteer)

> People went from volunteering to get jobs in different places … Gainful employment and we are very proud of that. (Respondent 5, Male, Hospital Management)

In some cases, permanent staff took a back seat when volunteers were deployed to a department. Tight control of work allocation and the management of roles, responsibilities and relationships between volunteers and hospital staff were required, as evidenced in the comment below:

> They will stand talking to each other, and the volunteer will do the work and that is a challenge for their manager, because that manager needs to manage their people together with the volunteers, but sometimes is does not work so well. (Respondent 1, Female, Hospital management)

Discussion

Where Blanchard (2006, p. 36) found that reputational gains and experience were not significant factors in volunteer motivation, this study found the contrary. It could be argued that in the South African context, with unemployment rates of around 25% and youth unemployment over 60% (Statistics South Africa, 2015), such motives are more critical. Respondents reported having a sense of belonging and daily importance in their work as volunteers. Connors (2011) acknowledges that volunteer and staff relations remain critical and complex and calls for adequate communication between these parties as well as orientation and training of volunteers. Skill development to gain experience towards paid employment was a significant factor in the motivations of respondents. The hospital management also felt that training and experience had the benefit to the volunteer towards possible employment and to the hospital should they recruit the volunteer, as they were 'pre-trained' for the job.

Motivation is a concept used to describe the intrinsic responses sustained by human needs, which in turn stimulate people to action in order to seek and achieve goals to satisfy those needs. The data that emerged from this study were well aligned to the Maslow's (1954) hierarchy of needs and confirmed that needs are continuous and that volunteers are more enthusiastically motivated by what they are seeking. No matter what they have achieved in terms of volunteerism; lower order needs such as a sustainable income will always be the focus and energy (Jooste, 2009, pp. 69–71).

Maslow's theory of motivation serves the purpose of explaining the volunteerism phenomenon and was used in the inductive process of building from the data to themes. The data collected from the volunteer participants in terms of motive were applied to Maslow's motivational theory and tabulated in Table 1.

From the themes which emerged and the literature (Botma, Greeff, Mulaudzi & Wright, 2010, p. 199), the theory could also be applied to the motivation of the hospital with regard to the volunteer programme and is depicted in Table 2.

TABLE 1: Maslow's motivational theory as applied to the volunteers experiences.

Volunteer needs	Volunteer rewards
Self-actualisation	Maximising potential and growth opportunities are offered in terms of choice of placement, relevant training and assistance with job application processes.
Esteem or status needs	Volunteers are known in the hospital, which makes them feel good about themselves thus boosting self-esteem. They are valued by staff, given responsibility and can achieve certificates for training.
Social or belonging needs	Volunteers work in groups or are placed in teams, included in training and develop relationships with fellow volunteers and staff.
Safety or security needs	An ordered, safe working environment is provided and access to workplace injury services.
Physiological or survival needs	Experience and skill can lead to wage-earning to pay for basic needs.

TABLE 2: Maslow's motivational theory as applied to the hospital's perspective.

Hospital needs	Hospital rewards
Self-actualisation	Self-actualisation is achieved by the hospital by affording growth opportunities to others and empowering the community it serves.
Esteem or status needs	The hospital gains esteem by being seen as a place of opportunity.
Social or belonging needs	The hospital expands its engagement with the community by embracing the volunteers from the community.
Safety or security needs	Patient safety and quality are enhanced by essential support services being supplemented by volunteers.
Survival or survival needs	The cost–benefit analysis indicates that the man-hours gained from volunteers impact well on the bottom line.

From an implementation of a volunteer programme perspective, the interviews with management illuminated the risk management requirements. Wyngaard (2012, p. 31) warns about vicarious liability and volunteers. This means that the organisation could be held liable for unlawful conduct of volunteers. Connors (2011) calls for courses in volunteer resource management at facilities and dedicated attention to volunteerism policy development. In this study, a volunteer policy was drawn up and overseen by the chief executive officer (CEO).

Documentation on application to volunteer initially included declarations on criminal records. A subsequent innovation under consideration is to get police criminal record clearance certificates for volunteers, but had not been implemented until the end of this study. However, a code of conduct for volunteers is a recommendation of this study, as well as a rigorous application process. Hotchkiss et al. (2014, p. 15) concur that health care organisations need to carefully screen volunteers prior to selection to maximise the quality benefits.

Constant redefining of risk management boundaries when it comes to having volunteers in a health setting makes for good governance. Risk assessment leads to appropriate volunteer assignments, identification of the necessary qualifications to fill those roles, targeted recruitment for those skills, proper screening, solid orientation and training and monitoring (Ellis, 2012). In this study setting, the volunteers are managed by a coordinator, who in turn is managed by a senior manager in the hospital. The CEO oversees the programme and reports to the Hospital Facility Board, which would fund the costs of the programme, appoint the coordinator and act on behalf of the public should any complaints or concerns be raised about the volunteer programme.

Volunteerism is important in the management of health care facilities as it allows the organisation to substitute volunteers for paid staff, offers significant cost savings to hospitals and is likely to impact on quality indicators such as patient satisfaction and safety (Hotchkiss et al., 2014, p. 2). More research is required to measure the cost–benefit ratio and impact on organisational performance. This study found a definite benefit in volunteers bolstering human capital and an impact in the health care organisational performance through contributions made by volunteers in many different settings in the hospital. Health care organisations should assess which additional activities, duties and responsibilities could be assumed by volunteers.

Recommendations

The findings of this study could serve to inform health service practice management of recommendations for hospital volunteer programmes. Initially, the hospital needs to secure seed funding to appoint a coordinator and for the start-up equipment. Hospital management needs to develop a risk management strategy. Risk management strategies should include careful selection of volunteers and character interrogation, such as criminal record clearance to prevent vicarious liability.

The volunteers need to be integrated into the orientation and induction processes, as well as staff training opportunities. By the same token, volunteers should take advantage of training opportunities afforded to them. Volunteers should have some choice of the section they want to work in to ensure a good fit.

However, the relationships between hospital staff and volunteers need to be clarified. In most cases, the relationship between hospital staff and volunteers should be actively managed. Exploitation of volunteers by permanent hospital staff must be prevented. Volunteers need some initial guidance on how to engage in various departments and with hospital staff. They need to develop resilience for some of the relationship challenges between volunteers and hospital staff. Although the volunteering holds distinct benefit in terms of self-development, self-esteem and self-actualisation, perseverance is required on the part of the volunteer. Volunteers need to be acknowledged and valued for the contribution they make to the health care environment.

Conclusion

Hospital volunteerism promises to be a quid pro quo, or something for something, intervention which benefits both hospital and volunteer. The hospital benefits in efficiency gains, development of local community members and in recruitment of potential future staff members. Volunteers benefit, by giving of their time, in learning new skills, gaining experience and belonging to a setting where they have a daily purpose and are valued. Provided risk is managed and minimised, the promise of possibility permeates to both volunteer and hospital facility.

Acknowledgements

This study has been supported and is funded by Stellenbosch University, Fund for Innovation and Research in Rural Health (FIRRH).

Competing interests

The authors declare that they have no financial or personal relationships that may have inappropriately influenced them in writing this article.

Authors' contributions

G.M.L. was responsible for the research proposal, ethics applications, data collection and data analysis of this article. D.K.D-F. carried out the literature review and performed the data analysis triangulation.

References

Aragaki, M., Saito, T., Takahashi, M., & Kai, I. (2007). Hospital volunteer's role and accident prevention systems. A nationwide survey of Japanese hospitals. *Health Services Management Research, 20*, 220–226. https://doi.org/10.1258/095148407782219021

Blanchard, J.A. (2006). Hospital volunteers: A qualitative study of motivation. *The International Journal of Volunteers Administration, 14*(2), 31–40.

Botma, Y., Greeff, M., Malaudzi, F., & Wright, S. (2010). *Research in health sciences*. Cape Town: Pearson.

Bowling, A. (2009). *Research methods in health*. Berkshire: Open University Press.

Connors, T. (2011). *The volunteer management handbook: Leadership strategies for success* (2nd ed.). Hoboken, NJ: Wiley.

Ellis, S. (2012). *Common sense and volunteer involvement*. Retrieved May 14, 2017, from https://www.energizeinc.com/hot-topics/2012/april

Handy, F., Mook, L., & Quarter, J. (2008). The inter changeability of paid staff and volunteers in nonprofit organizations. *Nonprofit and Volunteer Sector Quarterly, 37*(1), 76–92. https://doi.org/10.1177/0899764007303528

Handy, F., & Srinivasan, N. (2004). Valuing volunteers: An economic evaluation of the net benefits of hospital volunteers. *Nonprofit and Voluntary Sector Quarterly, 33*, 28–54. https://doi.org/10.1177/0899764003260961

Hotchkiss, R.B., Fottler, M.D., & Unruh, L. (2009). Valuing volunteers: The impact of volunteerism on hospital performance. *Health Care Management Review, 34*(2), 119–128.

Hotchkiss, R.B., Unruh, L., & Fottler, M.D. (2014). The role, measurement, and impact of volunteerism in hospitals. *Nonprofit and Voluntary Sector Quarterly*, 1–18. https://doi.org/10.1097/HMR.0b013e31819e919a

Jones, H. (2004). *Volunteering for health*. Wales Council for Voluntary Action, Welsh Assembly Government. Retrieved May 17, 2017, from http://www.wales.nhs.uk/documents/volunteering-for-health-report-e.pdf

Jooste, K. (Ed.). (2009). *Leadership in health services management* (2nd ed.). Landsdowne: Juta.

Maslow, A.H. (1954). *Motivation and personality*. New York: Harper & Row.

Maxwell, J.A. (2012). *A realist approach for qualitative research*. Thousand Oaks, CA: Sage.

Penner, L.A. (2002). Dispositional and organizational influences on sustained volunteerism: An interactionist perspective. *Journal of Social Issues, 58*, 448. https://doi.org/10.1111/1540-4560.00270

Prabhu, V.R., Hanley, A., & Kearney, S. (2008). Evaluation of a hospital volunteer programme in rural Australia. *Australian Health Review, 32*(2), 265–269. https://doi.org/10.1071/AH080265

Ross, T. (2012). *A survival guide for health research methods*. Berkshire: Open University Press.

Statistics South Africa. (2015). *Quarterly labour force survey: Quarter 2*. Pretoria: South African Government.

Wyngaard, R. (2012). *A practical legal guide to South African volunteers*. Cape Town: Ricardo Wyngaard Attorneys.

Permissions

All chapters in this book were first published in SAJHRM, by AOSIS; hereby published with permission under the Creative Commons Attribution License or equivalent. Every chapter published in this book has been scrutinized by our experts. Their significance has been extensively debated. The topics covered herein carry significant findings which will fuel the growth of the discipline. They may even be implemented as practical applications or may be referred to as a beginning point for another development.

The contributors of this book come from diverse backgrounds, making this book a truly international effort. This book will bring forth new frontiers with its revolutionizing research information and detailed analysis of the nascent developments around the world.

We would like to thank all the contributing authors for lending their expertise to make the book truly unique. They have played a crucial role in the development of this book. Without their invaluable contributions this book wouldn't have been possible. They have made vital efforts to compile up to date information on the varied aspects of this subject to make this book a valuable addition to the collection of many professionals and students.

This book was conceptualized with the vision of imparting up-to-date information and advanced data in this field. To ensure the same, a matchless editorial board was set up. Every individual on the board went through rigorous rounds of assessment to prove their worth. After which they invested a large part of their time researching and compiling the most relevant data for our readers.

The editorial board has been involved in producing this book since its inception. They have spent rigorous hours researching and exploring the diverse topics which have resulted in the successful publishing of this book. They have passed on their knowledge of decades through this book. To expedite this challenging task, the publisher supported the team at every step. A small team of assistant editors was also appointed to further simplify the editing procedure and attain best results for the readers.

Apart from the editorial board, the designing team has also invested a significant amount of their time in understanding the subject and creating the most relevant covers. They scrutinized every image to scout for the most suitable representation of the subject and create an appropriate cover for the book.

The publishing team has been an ardent support to the editorial, designing and production team. Their endless efforts to recruit the best for this project, has resulted in the accomplishment of this book. They are a veteran in the field of academics and their pool of knowledge is as vast as their experience in printing. Their expertise and guidance has proved useful at every step. Their uncompromising quality standards have made this book an exceptional effort. Their encouragement from time to time has been an inspiration for everyone.

The publisher and the editorial board hope that this book will prove to be a valuable piece of knowledge for researchers, students, practitioners and scholars across the globe.

List of Contributors

Massad A. Alatawi
Department of Management, Taibah University, Saudi Arabia

Liezel Cilliers
Department of Information Systems, University of Fort Hare, South Africa

Willie T. Chinyamurindi and Kim Viljoen
Department of Business Management, University of Fort Hare, South Africa

Popi C. Madlala and Cookie M. Govender
Department of Industrial Psychology and People Management, University of Johannesburg, South Africa

Paul Poisat
Graduate School, Nelson Mandela Metropolitan University, South Africa

Michelle R. Mey
School of Industrial Psychology and Human Resources, Nelson Mandela Metropolitan University, South Africa

Marieta du Plessis and Adre B. Boshoff
Department of Industrial Psychology, University of the Western Cape, South Africa

Paul Poisat
Graduate School of Business, Nelson Mandela University, South Africa

Michelle R. Mey
School of Industrial Psychology and Human Resource Management, Nelson Mandela University, South Africa

Gary Sharp
Department of Statistics, Nelson Mandela University, South Africa

Lucky L. Motaung, Mark H.R. Bussin and Renjini M. Joseph
Department of Industrial Psychology and People Management, University of Johannesburg, South Africa

J. Veli Mazibuko
Department of Business Administration and Management, Regenesys Business School, South Africa

Krishna K. Govender
School of Management, IT and Governance, University of KwaZulu-Natal, South Africa

Petronella Jonck
Research and Innovation Unit, National School of Government, South Africa

Freda van der Walt and Nthombi Sobayeni
Faculty of Management Sciences, Central University of Technology, South Africa

Dzivhuluwani Mavhungu and Mark H. R. Bussin
Department of Industrial Psychology and People Management, University of Johannesburg, South Africa

Michael A. W. Seymour and Dirk J. Geldenhuys
Department of Industrial and Organisational Psychology, University of South Africa, South Africa

Lynette Louw and Samuel M. Muriithi
Department of Management, Rhodes University, South Africa

Sarah Radloff
Department of Statistics, Rhodes University, South Africa

Wesley R. Pieters
Department of Human Sciences, University of Namibia, Namibia

Zwelinzima J. Ndevu and Kobus Muller
School of Public Leadership, Stellenbosch University, South Africa

Mark H. R. Bussin and Nokwanda N. Thabethe
Gordon Institute of Business Science, University of Pretoria, South Africa

Nelesh Dhanpat, Faith D. Modau, Phokela Lugisani, Rethabile Mabojane, Mbail Phiri, Madelyn Geldenhuys and Carolina M. Henn
Department of Industrial Psychology and People Management, University of Johannesburg, South Africa

Calvin M. Mabaso
Department of Industrial Psychology and People Management, University of Johannesburg, South Africa

Bongani I. Dlamini
Faculty of Management Sciences, Durban University of Technology, South Africa

Danielle K. Daniels-Felix
Ukwanda Centre for Rural Health, Stellenbosch University, South Africa

Guinevere M. Lourens
Ukwanda Centre for Rural Health, Stellenbosch University, South Africa
Department of Nursing and Midwifery, Stellenbosch University, South Africa

Index

CPSIA information can be obtained
at www.ICGtesting.com
Printed in the USA
LVHW060849030122
707669LV00002B/44

9 781647 260835